Advanced Technologies for Science and Engineering

(Volume 4)

Intelligent Technologies for Scientific Research and Engineering

Edited by

S. Kannadhasan
Department of Electronics and Communication Engineering
Study World College of Engineering
Coimbatore, Tamil Nadu,, India

R. Nagarajan
Department of Electrical and Electronics Engineering
Gnanamani College of Technology, Namakkal, Tamil Nadu, India

&

Kaushik Pal
Laboratório de Biopolímeros e Sensores
Instituto de Macromoléculas, Universidade Federal do Rio de Janeiro (LABIOS/IMA/UFRJ)
Rio de Janeiro
Brazil

Advanced Technologies for Science and Engineering

(Volume 4)

Intelligent Technologies for Scientific Research and Engineering

Editors: S. Kannadhasan, R. Nagarajan & Kaushik Pal

ISSN (Online): 3029–2859

ISSN (Print): 3029-2840

ISBN (Online): 979-8-89881-531-8

ISBN (Print): 979-8-89881-532-5

ISBN (Paperback): 979-8-89881-533-2

Published by Bentham Science Publishers Pte. Ltd. Singapore,

in collaboration with Eureka Conferences, USA.

First published in 2026.

Bentham Science Publishers Pte. Ltd.
No. 9 Raffles Place
Office No. 26-01
Singapore 048619
Singapore
Email: subscriptions@benthamscience.net

CONTENTS

PREFACE

The book on Intelligent Technologies for Research and Engineering contains new research findings from academics. This edited anthology covers a range of research topics on science, engineering, and technology over forty six chapters. Discussion topics include artificial intelligence learning techniques, computerised medical image processing, human-computer interface for hand gesture recognition, community energy storage, e-learning, diabetes risk prediction, solar cells, hydrogen fuel cells for cars, and more. Many great engineering achievements have been made in the past century alone that we now generally take them for granted. For most of the globe, technology enables access to a plentiful supply of food and clean drinking water. For many of our everyday tasks, we depend on electricity. We can deliver products and services to any location in the world with great simplicity. Growing advances in communications and computer technology are creating new avenues for entertainment and information discovery. Even with these incredible technological accomplishments, there are undoubtedly still a ton of outstanding opportunities and challenges to be addressed. A lot of them are blurry, and many more are undoubtedly beyond most people's comprehension, even if some seem clear.

The latest advances in solidification research and the problems the community faces in the 21st century in processing and analysis are presented. On behalf of the editors, we would like to offer our appreciation to everyone who took part in this project. First and foremost, we offer all credit and respect to our almighty Lord for his bountiful grace, which enabled me to finish this book successfully. Moving forward, the authors, whose excellent work is at the core of the book, are acknowledged, and we gratefully congratulate all those involved and wish them great success. We would like to take this time to thank our family and friends for their support and encouragement while we worked on this book. We would also like to express our gratitude to the writers for their contributions to this edited book. In addition, our special thanks is extended to Bentham Science Publishers and its whole team for facilitating us in publishing this work and us providing the opportunity to present our work to the audience.

The content of this book is summarized as follows:

1. In Chapter 1, The practise of "lifelogging" involves documenting an increasing amount of one's everyday experience with the intention of using the recordings in the future as a memory aid or the foundation for data-driven self-development. Therefore, the usefulness of the generated lifelogs depends on the lifeloggers' ability to efficiently sift through them. The logs' intrinsic multi-modality and semi-structure allow them to combine data from a variety of sources, including cameras and other wearable physical and virtual sensors. As a result, expressing the data in a graph structure allows for the effective capturing of all created interrelations. Alternative methods must be developed to capture the higher-level semantics because it is impossible to manually or mechanically annotate each entry with a significant amount of semantic context. We describe Improved Life Graph (ILG), the first method for building a Knowledge Graph-based lifelog representation and retrieval solution, which can capture a lifelog in a graph structure and enhance it with external data to help with the connection of higher-level semantic information.

2. Chapter 2 presents that as a result of increased competition and a decline in new clients, the global telecommunications sector is suffering from a dramatic decline in revenue. Most operators first spend a significant portion of their income on expansion in order to maintain competitive advantages and attract a large user base. A company's ability to boost its selling,

marketing, and servicing operations across all client touchpoints is greatly aided by a well-developed client Relationship Management (CRM) strategy. Predicting customers' propensity to leave is a major challenge in CRM. The purpose is to identify consumers who could be at risk of leaving based on their historical data and actions. In the study under consideration, data mining methods were used for accurate churn forecasting. In this case, we preprocess the dataset using the normalised k-means approach. After the picture has been preprocessed, attributes are chosen using the minimal Redundancy & Maximum Relevance (mRMR) method. When making a decision, it favours qualities that have low connections among themselves and a strong relationship with the class (output). The ability to classify or forecast client turnover based on the provided attributes is explored using a Support Vector Machine with Photon Swarm Optimisation (SVM with PSO). To optimise the SVM's hyperparameters, PSO is used. Additionally, the problem of discovering a local optimal solution is avoided, and the accuracy of the classification is enhanced. The experimental results show that the proposed system is superior to the current one in terms of processing time.

3. Chapter 3 presents Multilayer perceptrons (MLPs) along with support vector machines (SVMs), which are examples of TMLTs that have been utilized effectively for churn prediction in the past, but only after considerable time and energy were spent configuring the training parameters. Choosing appropriate training settings for unsupervised learning is usually an ad hoc process that relies on experimentation. When it comes to churn forecasts, deep neural networks (DNNs) have demonstrated to be much more accurate than TMLTs. To set the instruction hyperparameters for DNNs throughout churn modelling, however, requires more time and effort because of DNNs' more complicated design and their ability to analyze vast volumes of non-linear input data. This creates extra difficulty for novice machine learning professionals and researchers. Few studies have been conducted to date to determine how various hyperparameters affect DNN performance when used for churn prediction. When it comes to churn modelling, DNNs aren't backed by much in the way of experimentally developed heuristics to help with hyperparameter selection. To better predict customer attrition in the banking sector, this work conducts an experimental analysis of the effect of adjusting DNN hyperparameters. The deep neural network (DNN) simulations beat the MLP across three separate trials, with the DNN models using a rectifier activation function in the hidden layers and the MLP using a sigmoid activation function in the output layer. Rems Prop training was more accurate than Adam, AdaGrad, Ad delta, and Adam ax, and it was also more effective than stochastic gradient descent (SGD). The DNN did best when the number of batches was smaller than the total number of data points in the test set. This study provides heuristic insights that may be useful to academics and practitioners when DNNs are used to predict churn from CRM table data in the financial services industry.

4. Chapter 4 suggests that event logs may be used for process mining. Event logs may include confidential data that cannot be analysed without agreement, preventing process mining. Anonymizing the event log prevents anybody from being identified by it. Differential privacy guarantees anonymity. Heterogeneous private event log anonymity aims to provide a log with high usefulness and a privacy guarantee. Event log anonymization methods introduce noise into traces by replicating, perturbing, or filtering them. Subsampling before noise injection improves the privacy-utility trade-off, according to research on differential privacy. Subsampling enhances privacy. Libra uses this observation to anonymize event logs. Libra takes numerous samples of trace from a log, separately enters noise, maintains statistically meaningful traces from every sample, then makes up the samples to create a uniquely private log. The suggested method yields far better utility for identical privacy assurances than baselines.

5. Chapter 5 tells us that banks and other financial organisations rely heavily on credit scoring

(CS) as a method of risk management since it is both effective and necessary. It reduces financial risks and gives sound advice on loan disbursement. As a result, businesses and financial institutions are exploring innovative automated solutions to the CS dilemma in an effort to safeguard their own resources and those of their clients. The use of various machine learning (ML) as well as data mining (DM) approaches has led to significant progress in CS prediction in recent years. The Deep Genetic Hierarchical Network of Learner (DGHNL) is a novel approach developed for this study. Support Vector Machines (SVMs), k-Nearest Neighbours (kNNs), Probabilistic Neural Networks (PNNs), and fuzzy structures are just some of the many types of learners that may be used in the suggested method. The Statlog German (1000 occurrences) approval of credit dataset from the UCI machine learning library was used to evaluate our model. We use a DGHNL model with five unique learner types, two feature extraction methods, three kernel functions, and three methods for optimising model parameters. In addition to conventional cross-validation (CV) and train-testing (stratified 10-fold) methods, this model employs a cutting-edge biological layered training (participant selection) approach. Because it makes use of coordinated and shared information (the DGHNL architecture and the optimisation of it), our approach is innovative. Using data on German credit approvals from Statlog, we show that the suggested DGHNL model can obtain a prediction accuracy of 94.60% (54 errors per 1000 classifications) with its 29-layer architecture.

6. Chapter 6 suggests that the primary use of forecasting short-term loads is in control centres, where it is used to investigate shifting consumer load patterns and estimate the value of the load at a future time. It is a crucial piece of equipment for building a smart grid. Several dimensions of influence impact the load parameters. In this research, we present a Residual Neural Network (ResNet)/Long Short-Term Memory (LSTM) hybrid model for load forecasting, which can better take advantage of the time series properties of load data and lead to more reliable predictions. Before feeding the data into the ResNeT network for feature extraction, it is first rebuilt using numerous feature parameters. The second step in short-term load forecasting using LSTM is to feed the feature that was extracted vector into the network. Finally, the technique is compared with other models using a real example, demonstrating that the proposed combination method has better prediction accuracy and confirming the practicality and superiority of input-parameter feature extraction. Additionally, this study examines weather prediction based on a variety of elements and characteristics.

7. Chapter 7 presents a deep learning method, named Convolutional Neural Network (CNN). Natural language processing problems, such as text classification, are simplified using this approach. In this study, we use a deep learning strategy, namely the CNN method, to address the issue of text classification. CNNs, which require a large amount of time as well as finances to train and use, have been greatly impeded by the rise of Big Data and the increased complexity of tasks. To get around these problems, we introduce a MapReduce-based CNN that rethinks what a CNN has learnt by breaking it down into a series of smaller networks and training them in parallel. Subsets of incoming text are analysed by many autonomous networks.

8. Chapter 8, it is well recognised that data preparation is necessary to provide reliable data with which mining tools may derive useful insights. Preprocessing methods need to be modified when dealing with multiple sources of continuous data. This study suggests using active rule-based systems, and more particularly, complex event processing (CEP) systems and engines, to aid domain experts in the definition and execution of pretreatment tasks for data streams. Our method's key innovation is the way it allows domain experts to easily manage temporal data by formulating preprocessing methods as identifying events rules stated in a SQL-like language. This concept is implemented in a freely accessible software

package that combines a CEP processor with libraries for web-based data mining. To test the efficacy of our method, we provide three real-world examples of applications in which CEP rules preprocess data streams by incorporating new temporal information, modifying features, and handling missing values. Preprocessing activities may be expressed in a flexible and high-level fashion using CEP rules, as shown by the experiments, without incurring excessive memory and time overheads. The generated streams of data not only enhance classification algorithms' predictive accuracy but also simplify decision models and shorten the time required to learn.

9. Chapter 9 offers a fresh theoretical perspective on the issue of interpretive topic modelling. Instead of using words or n-grams as the fundamental units of analysis, as in more traditional methods, this method employs whole sentences. Specifics of the proposed method include clustering of phrase embeddings and probabilistic sentence assessments within the text corpus. Sentence frequency distributions within subjects and topic frequency distributions throughout the text are both estimated using the topic model. Since sentences, unlike words, are more meaningful and include entire grammatical and semantic structures, our method allows for explicit understanding of themes. The process for doing this automatically is also given. Sentence embeddings are obtained via the use of context embeddings built on the BERT paradigm. Our method also demonstrates the feasibility of integrating both internal and external information sources in the subject modelling process, allowing for big data processing. In conventional topic modelling methods, the text corpus itself stands in for the internal knowledge source, and this source is often a single one. BERT, a machine learning model first trained on a massive amount of textual data, serves as the external knowledge source and produces context-dependent sentence embeddings.

10. Chapter 10 shows that by analyzing the geographical, chronological, and semantic components of geographic data, it is possible to reconstruct users' real route itineraries and get insights into their preferences and behavior. In order to analyse tourist traffic patterns in A-level scenic spots in Jiangsu and Zhejiang across time and space, this research collects and preprocesses data from Weibo check-ins at these locations. The author used a temporal perspective, looking at how the check-in data fluctuated between 2016 and 2018, as well as how it differed on weekends, holidays, and weekdays. The acquired data were subjected to a spatial kernel density analysis, which revealed the most active regions. Lastly, the vacation travel mode and characteristics were identified through an examination of spatial and locational flows and their orientations. The results of this study provide the groundwork for the growth of wisdom tourism.

11. Chapter 11 presents the amount of data available online is growing at an exponential rate. The Internet has a wealth of information that can be mined for specific details on any niche subject, depending on the user's needs. When faced with a bewildering array of options, users often find it difficult to decide which product to purchase online. In this case, it is crucial to review the available data to advise consumers on products and learn from other customers. The proposed approach allows us to efficiently filter, prioritize, and convey very important information, therefore mitigating the problem of information overload. To narrow down a list of options based on your individual tastes is the job of a recommendation system. The approach relies heavily on several different types of similarity measurements. It is generally agreed that collaborative filtering is the most effective method for making specific recommendations to users or providers. Since there are limitations to the user-based collaborative filtering strategy, the item-based strategy is considered an alternative. To address this shortcoming, we analyzed the effectiveness of several similarity calculation methods by comparing correlation-based and distance-based similarity measures, aiming to improve recommendation performance. The study's findings were utilized to design a better

technique, which uses statistical accuracy measures to provide the best informed suggestion possible. This study's findings provide a benchmark for evaluating and comparing similarity measurements. This work aims to help readers select suitable distance measures for datasets, and to make it easier to compare and evaluate new similarity measures against established ones.

12. Chapter 12 claims that recommender systems have quickly become an integral part of people's everyday digital lives as it is present on virtually every online service today. Modern deep learning-based models can only function at their peak when fed with a massive amount of data. Multiple domains, including Amazon, restaurants, and breweries, have offered datasets that meet this condition. The hotel industry has seen relatively few advancements and databases, with even the largest review dataset being in the hundreds of thousands rather than millions. Traditional collaborative-filtering methods are also inapplicable to the hotel domain due to its increased data sparsity compared to standard recommendation datasets. In this research, we present HotelRec, a TripAdvisor-derived, massively scaled hotel recommendation dataset comprising 50 million reviews. To the best of our knowledge, HotelRec is the largest recommendation dataset in a single domain, including textual reviews (50M vs 22M) in the hotel domain (50M vs 0.9M).

13. Chapter 13 suggests that, the field of Recommender Systems (RS) research has expanded to include a broad range of AI methods, from simpler ones like Matrix Factorization (MF) to more advanced ones like Deep Neural Networks (DNN) in recent years. Because they only consider a linear combination of user and item vectors, traditional Collaborative Filtering (CF) recommendation algorithms like MF have limited learning capacity. Neural collaborative filtering (NCF) uses deep neural networks (DNN) in combination with collaborative filtering (CF) to learn non-linear correlations. CF approaches still have issues with cold start and data sparsity, though. To improve recommendation accuracy, address cold starts, and address data sparsity, this research proposes a new hybrid RS, Neural Matrix Factorization++ (NeuMF++). We propose NeuMF++, which improves upon NeuMF by adding Stacked Denoising Autoencoders (SDAE) for a more accurate latent representation. GMF++ and MLP++ can be combined to form NeuMF++. By combining Generalized Matrix Factorization (GMF) with Multilayer Perceptrons (MLP), NeuMF provides a robust NCF architecture. By combining the linearity of GMF with the nonlinearity of MLP, NeuMF achieves state-of-the-art results. At the same time, GMF++ and MLP++ have been developed due to the successful integration of latent representations into the original GMF and MLP. NeuMF++'s learning capacity is greatly improved by the latent representation it obtains from the SDAEs' latent space, which enables it to learn user and item characteristics accurately. However, NeuMF++'s performance may suffer if GMF++ and MLP++ are forced to share feature extractions. Consequently, enabling GMF++ and MLP++ to learn features independently increases their adaptability and dramatically boosts their performance. The experimental root-mean-square error of 0.8681 obtained by NeuMF++ in a real-world dataset shows that it performs exceptionally well. Additional data, such as text or photos, can be added to NeuMF++ in later development. NeuMF++ allows for the incorporation of several neural network building elements to create a more robust recommendation model.

14. Chapter 14 shows that finding relevant information online has gotten increasingly difficult as the amount of data available on the internet has grown exponentially. In high-data-density, complex-domain settings, the recommendation system may be a big aid to users in making decisions. In the recommender system, several approaches have been presented. In the recommendation system, collaborative filtering is a common practice. The cold-start problem is one of the remaining issues with collaborative filtering approaches. To address this issue, we offer a movie recommendation system that uses social network analysis and collaborative

filtering. We used user preferences like age, gender, and profession to generate a connection matrix, and then used that matrix to use community identification based on edge betweenness centrality to cluster people. The suggested system will then propose movies to new members based on the preferences of the existing users in the group. Utilizing MAE, we demonstrate the superiority of the suggested technique.

15. Chapter 15 shows that the financial and emotional toll of cardiovascular disease is growing. As a result, we created a model for predicting comprehensive healthcare resource use (Adherence Score for Healthcare Resource Outcome, ASHRO), which includes patient health behaviors, and investigated its relationship with clinical outcomes, with the goal of improving the economy as a whole and the quality of the healthcare system. Data from a massive database of health insurance claims, long-term care insurance, and health checkups were used in this investigation. Patients admitted to hospitals with cardiovascular conditions (ICD-10 I00-I99) constituted the study population. The objective variable was medical and long-term care expenses, while the explanatory variable was a broadly defined composite adherence measure. Multiple regression analysis and random forest learning (AI) were utilized to calibrate predictive models, which were then used to generate ASHRO ratings. The prediction model's discriminatory and evaluative abilities were measured using the area under the curve and the Hosmer-Lemeshow test, respectively. Over a 48-month follow-up, we used propensity score matching to examine the overall mortality of the two ASHRO 50% cut-off groups after adjusting for clinical risk variables. Out of a total sample size of 48,456 patients, 61.9% were men, and the mean age at hospital release was 68.3 9.9 years for those with cardiovascular disease. Machine learning was used to adjust eight factors (secondary mitigation, rehabilitation intensity, direction, proportion of days addressed, overlapping outpatient visits/clinical laboratory and physiological tests, medical attendance, and generic drug rate) into a single index that served as the adherence score classification. The total coefficient of determination from the multiple regression analysis was 0.313 (p 0.001). The total coefficient of determination in a logistic regression analysis with 50% and 25%/75% cut-off values for medical and long-term care expenses was statistically significant (p 0.001). There was a statistically significant correlation between ASHRO score and death rate at the 50% cutoff (2% vs. 7%; p 0.001).

16. Chapter 16 shows the goal of this research is to examine how e-commerce and web-based businesses might benefit from the use of Big Data Analytics in managerial decision making. The data used in this analysis comes from a single e-commerce website's database. User interactions with the website, such as page views, product additions, and online purchases, would be recorded. Association Rule Mining Algorithm (APRIORI), K-Means Clustering, and Pearson's Correlation Coefficient are only a few of the algorithms that will be utilized to evaluate the dataset. The information will be analyzed and used to provide insights into users' interactions with the website, enabling the identification of patterns that may inform future actions. For instance, which product receives the most attention and sales, how many pages are viewed before a purchase is made, what percentage of customers buy the product again, and so on. This study would also determine whether the company's current Big Data implementation can be enhanced and whether doing so would be a smart use of resources.

17. In Chapter 17, with the help of a deep artificial neural network (ANN; i.e. deep learning), a new method is provided to simulate and reconstruct yearly surface mass balance (SMB) data across glaciers. An open-source regional glacier evolution model now includes this technique as its SMB component. While conventional glacier models increasingly include physical processes, we instead use data science to create a parameterized model. Deep learning or Lasso (least absolute shrinkage and selection operator; regularized multilinear regression) can be used to model annual glacier-wide SMBs from topo-climatic variables,

while a glacier-specific parameterization is used to update the glacier's shape. On a dataset of 32 French Alpine glaciers, we evaluate and cross-validate our nonlinear deep learning SMB model against other typical linear statistical techniques. Results show that deep learning is superior to linear approaches, with an estimated r 2 of 0.77 and a root-mean-square error (RMSE) of 0.51 m w.e., thanks to increased accuracy (up to +47% in space and +58% in time) and explained variance (up to +64% in space and +108% in time). The temporal dimension accounts for around 35% of the nonlinear behavior recorded by deep learning. The key unknowns in the evolution of glacier geometry stem from the initial ice thickness measurements. These findings support the application of deep learning in glacier modeling as a potent nonlinear tool for reconstructing or simulating SMB time series for individual glaciers across a region for past and future climates.

18. Chapter 18 shows the rate at which remote sensing technology is advancing, which means that our access to remote sensing data is better than before. The age of big data is here. Data collected using remote sensing exhibit hallmarks of Big Data, including hyperspectral features, high spatial resolution, and high temporal resolution. Using geographical feature and remote sensing data, this work provides a feature-supporting, marketable, and efficient data cube for time-series analysis and conducts a comparative assessment of water cover and vegetation change. This study defines remote sensing data cube (SRSDC) with a focus on spatial features. The purpose of this data cube is to offer a fast, flexible, and scalable way to analyze massive amounts of RS information using spatial features. It gives a general summary of the SRSDC's structure. The SRSDC provides feature translation to transform spatial feature information into query operations and spatial feature repositories to store and manage vector feature data. This article explains how a feature data cube and distributed execution engine were developed for use in the SRSDC. The evaluation of a feature data cube and a distributed execution engine is carried out using the production process and long-term remote sensing analysis as examples. As a new strategic resource for humanity, big data has risen to the top of the knowledge economy's mountain range. Data analysis methods, including supervised, unsupervised, and hybrid approaches, are the backbone of knowledge discovery techniques.

19. Chapter 19 provides suggestions for integrated, cutting-edge, and efficient tools, methodologies, and technologies for accessing and processing increasingly growing volumes of data in diverse fields. Personalizing a patient's care is a challenging task that requires the doctor to sift through and make sense of massive volumes of data. The scientific community behind precision medicine might benefit greatly from a unified system that facilitates data discovery, integration, preprocessing, model construction, storage, analysis, and visualization. The software package provides researchers with a simple, quick, and adaptable method for processing data, with the ultimate goal of enabling intelligent management, analysis, and visualization of massive genomic data. Services, data sets, and databases are at their disposal, or they can supply their own information for processing.

20. Chapter 20 shows that as a result of increased competition and a decline in new clients, the global telecommunications sector is suffering from a dramatic decline in revenue. Most operators first spend a significant portion of their income on expansion in order to maintain competitive advantages and attract a large user base. A company's ability to enhance its selling, marketing, and servicing operations across all client touchpoints is greatly aided by a well-developed client Relationship Management (CRM) strategy. Predicting customers' propensity to leave is a major challenge in CRM. The purpose is to identify consumers who could be at risk of leaving based on their historical data and actions. In the study under consideration, data mining methods were used for accurate churn forecasting. In this case, we preprocess the dataset using the normalized k-means approach. After the picture has been preprocessed, attributes are chosen using the minimal Redundancy and Maximum Relevance

(mRMR) method. When making a decision, it favours qualities that have low connections among themselves and a strong relationship with the class (output). The ability to classify or forecast client turnover according to the provided attributes is explored by using a Support Vector Machine and Photon Swarm Optimization (SVM with PSO). To optimise the SVM's hyperparameters, PSO is used. Additionally, the problem of discovering a local optimal solution is avoided, and the accuracy of the classification is enhanced. The experimental results show that the proposed system is superior to the current one, and the processing time.

21. Chapter 21, Multilayer perceptrons (MLPs), along with support vector machines (SVMs), are examples of TMLTs that have been utilized effectively for churn prediction in the past, but only after considerable time and energy were spent configuring the training parameters. Choosing appropriate training settings for unsupervised learning is usually an ad hoc process that relies on experimentation. When it comes to churn forecasts, deep neural networks (DNNs) have demonstrated to be much more accurate than TMLTs. Setting the instruction hyperparameters for DNNs throughout churn modelling, however, requires more time and effort because of DNNs' more complicated design and their ability to analyse vast volumes of non-linear input data. This creates extra difficulty for novice machine learning professionals and researchers. Few studies have been conducted so far to determine how various hyperparameters affect the DNN performance when used for churn prediction. When it comes to churn modelling, DNNs are not backed by much in the way of experimentally developed heuristics to help with hyperparameter selection. To better predict customer attrition in the banking sector, this work conducts an experimental analysis of the effect of adjusting DNN hyperparameters. The deep neural network (DNN) simulations beat the MLP across three separate trials, with the DNN models utilizing a rectifier functional for activation in the hidden layers and the MLP using a sigmoid in the output layer. Rems Prop training was more accurate than Adam, AdaGrad, Ad delta, and Adam ax, and it was also more effective than stochastic gradient descent (SGD). The DNN did the best when the number of batches was smaller than the total number of data points in the test set. This study provides heuristic information that may be useful to academics and practitioners when DNNs are used for predicting churn from table data for CRM in the financial services industry.

22. In chapter 22, this paper offers a fresh theoretical perspective on the issue of interpretive topic modelling. Instead of using words or n-grams as the fundamental units of analysis, as in more traditional methods, this method employs whole sentences. Specifics of the proposed method include clustering of phrase embeddings and probabilistic sentence assessments within the text corpus. Sentence frequency distributions within subjects and topic frequency distributions throughout the text are both estimated using the topic model. Since sentences, unlike words, are more meaningful and include entire grammatical and semantic structures, our method allows for explicit understanding of themes. The process for doing this automatically is also given. Sentence embeddings are obtained via the use of context embeddings built on the BERT paradigm. Our method also demonstrates the feasibility of integrating both internal and external information sources into the subject modelling process, enabling big data processing. In conventional topic modelling methods, the text corpus itself stands in for the internal knowledge source, and this source is often a single one. The BERT, a machine learning model that was first trained on a massive quantity of textual data, stands in for the external knowledge source and is responsible for producing the context-dependent sentence embeddings.

23. Chapter 23 presents that the day-to-day activities of millions of people all over the globe have been significantly altered as a direct result of the meteoric rise in the popularity of social media and online social networks such as Facebook, Twitter, Instagram, and TikTok. The ease with which data may be gathered, collected, and analyzed, in addition to the high degree

of social and financial interest in doing so, has sparked the interest of a broad range of research sectors. This has resulted in increased emphasis being paid to the research being conducted in these areas. Each agent is given a decentralized control mechanism that enables them to communicate, draw conclusions from their discussions, and learn from one another. Utilizing a network topology, this method makes it easier for dynamic agent organizations to alter the geometry of agent interactions in order to meet the particulars of the situation at hand.

24. Chapter 24 shows that the number of individuals using social networking and microblogging sites has increased dramatically in recent years, providing an interesting window into the perceptions of this age. People's opinions may be gauged in large part by looking at user reviews of various products, companies, brands, individuals, forums, films, etc. Analysts saw a need to automate the categorisation of evaluations into positive and negative categories; therefore, they developed algorithms to do so. Sentiment analysis is the name given to the automatic categorization process it enables. The fundamental objective of this study is to apply the Support Vector Machine (SVM) artificial intelligence algorithm to the task of classifying feelings and texts for product evaluations. This paper will do so by doing an in-depth analysis of several datasets utilised for this purpose. The Support Vector Machine (SM) learning technique has been trained, tested, and implemented across a variety of data sets to determine the polarity of ambiguous feelings. The major goal of this work is to apply the Support Vector Machine (SVM) artificial intelligence technique to analyse several datasets for sentiment and text classification, with the end result being improved categorization of product reviews. A support vector machine training system is trained, tested, and simulated on many datasets in this work to determine the polarity of ambiguous feelings or reviews. We found that among the available classification algorithms, Support Vector Machine (SVM) produces the highest accuracy (89.98%) right off the bat. Including additional sentence forms would further improve the achieved accuracy. As a final result, it establishes that the SVM method is reliable. Application/Improvements: Models generated by the use of the Support Vector Machine algorithm for learning are evaluated for their performance. Finally, a highly accurate and powerful classification method, the Support Vector Machine (SVM), has been developed.

25. In Chapter 25, it is well recognised that data preparation is necessary to provide reliable data with which mining tools may derive useful insights. Preprocessing methods need to be modified when dealing with multiple sources of continuous data. This study suggests using active rule-based systems, particularly complex event processing (CEP) systems and engines, to aid domain experts in defining and executing pretreatment tasks for data streams. Our method's key innovation is the way it allows domain experts to easily manage temporal data by formulating preprocessing methods as identifying events rules stated in a SQL-like language. This concept is implemented in a freely accessible software package that combines a CEP processor with libraries for web-based data mining. To test the efficacy of our method, we provide three real-world examples of applications in which CEP rules preprocess data streams by incorporating new temporal information, modifying features, and handling missing values. Preprocessing activities can be expressed in a flexible, high-level manner using CEP rules, as shown by the experiments, without incurring excessive memory or time overhead. The generated streams of data not only enhance classification algorithms' predictive accuracy but also simplify decision models and shorten the time required to learn.

26. In chapter 26, call records demonstrate client interest in various businesses. Multi-dimensional attribute dependence with communication day and time may help targeted advertising. Frequent and extensive inter-service links show that consumers of one service may have opportunities in the other. Multi-granulation rough sets address prospect discovery

from call record interest characteristics. Conventional intra and inter-pattern mining methods have increased the amount of processing and the vast space of statistically irrelevant patterns. This solution fixes these difficulties. The method produces food and restaurant target audiences using one month of anonymised Thai telecom service supplier call data and confirms some fascinating mathematical properties of knowledge systems.

27. In chapter 27, the rate at which remote sensing technology is advancing means that our access to remote sensing data is better than before. The age of big data is here. Data collected using remote sensing exhibits hallmarks of Big Data, including hyper spectral features, a high spatial resolution, and a high time resolution. Using geographical feature data and remote sensing data, this work offers a feature-supporting, marketable, and efficient data cube for time-series analytic application, and conducts a comparative assessment of water cover and vegetation change.This study defines the remote sensing data cube (SRSDC) with a focus on spatial features. The purpose of this data cube is to offer a fast, flexible, and scalable way to analyze massive amounts of RS information using spatial features. It gives a general summary of the SRSDC's structure.The SRSDC provides feature translation to transform spatial feature information into query operations and spatial feature repositories to store and manage vector feature data.This article explains how a feature data cube and distributed execution engine were developed for use in the SRSDC. Evaluation of a feature data cube and distributed execution engine is carried out using the production process and analysis of long-term remote sensing as examples. As a new strategic resource for humanity, big data has risen to the top of the knowledge economy's mountain range. Data analysis supervised learning methods, unsupervised learning methods, and their mixtures and modifications are the backbone of knowledge discovery techniques.

28. In chapter 28, with the help of a deep artificial neural network (ANN; i.e. deep learning), we provide a new method to simulate and reconstruct yearly surface mass balance (SMB) data across glaciers. An open-source regional glacier evolution model now includes this technique as its SMB component. While conventional glacier models increasingly include physical processes, we instead use data science to create a parameterized model. Deep learning or Lasso (least absolute shrinkage and selection operator; regularized multilinear regression) can be used to model annual glacier-wide SMBs from topoclimatic variables, while a glacier-specific parameterization updates the glacier's shape. On a dataset of 32 French Alpine glaciers, we evaluate and cross-validate our nonlinear deep learning SMB model against other typical linear statistical techniques. Results show that deep learning is superior to linear approaches, with an estimated r 2 of 0.77 and a root-mean-square error (RMSE) of 0.51 m w.e., thanks to increased accuracy (up to +47% in space and +58% in time) and explained variance (up to +64% in space and +108% in time). The temporal dimension accounts for around 35% of the nonlinear behavior recorded by deep learning. The key unknowns in the evolution of glacier geometry stem from the initial ice thickness measurements. These findings support the application of deep learning in glacier modeling as a potent nonlinear tool for reconstructing or simulating SMB time series for individual glaciers across a region for past and future climates.

29. Chapter 29 discusses that providing suggestions for integrated, cutting-edge, and efficient tools, methodologies, and technologies for accessing and processing increasingly growing volumes of data in diverse forms is a major problem in clinical data analysis and knowledge discovery. Personalizing a patient's care is a challenging task that requires the doctor to sift through and make sense of massive volumes of data. The scientific community behind precision medicine might benefit greatly from a unified system that facilitates data discovery, integration, preprocessing, model construction, storage, analysis, and visualization. The software package provides researchers with a simple, quick, and adaptable method for

processing data, with the ultimate goal of enabling intelligent management, analysis, and visualization of massive genomic data. Services, data sets, and databases are at their disposal, or they can supply their own information for processing.

30. Chapter 30 shows that tourism destinations and their online and social media information have made selecting and visiting them difficult. Tourists find tourism suggestion systems attractive, but designers must be able to deliver personalised services. This study proposes a personalised tourist system of recommendations that extracts user preferences. For this, tourist social network user reviews are a rich resource of preferences. To identify visitor preferences, remarks are preprocessed, semantically grouped, and sentimentally analysed. The characteristics of attractions are extracted from all user evaluations. Finally, the proposed suggestion system semantically matches user preferences with attraction attributes to suggest the most relevant attractions. The technology also filters undesirable goods and improves recommendations based on time, location, and weather. The Python-based recommendation algorithm is tested using TripAdvisor data. The suggested system improves the f-measure.

31. In chapter 31, The primary use of forecasting short-term loads is in control centres, where it is used to investigate shifting consumer load patterns and estimate the value of the load at a future time. It's a crucial piece of equipment for building a smart grid. Several dimensions of influence impact the load parameters. In this research, we present a Residual Neural Network (ResNet)/Long Short-Term Memory (LSTM) hybrid model for load forecasting, which can better take advantage of the time series properties of load data and lead to more reliable predictions. Before feeding the data into the ResNeT network for the extraction of features, it is first rebuilt using numerous feature parameters. The second step in short-term load forecasting using LSTM is to feed the feature that was extracted vector into the network. Finally, the technique is compared to other models using a real example, demonstrating that the proposed combination method has better prediction accuracy and confirming the practicality & superiority of input parameters feature extraction. Additionally, this study conducts studies in weather prediction based on a variety of elements and characteristics.

32. Chapter 32 suggest that data mining has become an increasingly significant method for conducting data analysis as a result of the rapid increase of databases used by a large number of contemporary businesses. The community of people who study operations research has made major contributions to this discipline, particularly by formulating and solving a large number of data mining problems as optimization problems. Additionally, data mining techniques may be used to solve a number of applications that study operations research. The purpose of this study is to offer an overview of the relationship between operations research and data mining. The basic objectives of the study are to highlight the spectrum of interactions between the two areas, present specific instances of significant research effort, and provide extensive references to additional significant work in the area. The purpose of this study is to examine not only the many optimization techniques that may be used for data mining, but also the process of data mining itself, as well as the ways in which operations research techniques can be utilized at almost every stage of this process. The report also identifies many potentially fruitful avenues for further investigation throughout its body. In the last part of the study, many applications connected to the administration of electronic services, including customer relationship management and customization, are investigated.

33. Chapter 33 shows that the field of Recommender Systems (RS) research has expanded to include a broad range of AI methods, from simpler ones like Matrix Factorization (MF) to more advanced ones like Deep Neural Networks (DNN) in recent years. Because it only takes into account a linear combination of user and item vectors, traditional Collaborative Filtering (CF) recommendation algorithms like MF have limited learning potential. Neural

collaborative filtering (NCF) uses deep neural networks (DNN) in combination with collaborative filtering (CF) to learn non-linear correlations. CF approaches still have issues with cold start and data sparsity, though. In order to increase recommendation accuracy, deal with cold starts, and fill in gaps in data sparsity, this research offers a new hybrid-based RS called Neural Matrix Factorization++ (NeuMF++). We propose NeuMF++, which improves upon NeuMF by adding Stacked Denoising Autoencoders (SDAE) for more accurate latent representation. and MLP++ can be combined to form NeuMF++. By combining Generalized Matrix Factorization (GMF) with Multilayer Perceptrons (MLP), NeuMF provides a robust NCF architecture. By combining the linearity of GMF with the non-linearity of MLP, NeuMF is able to produce state-of-the-art results. At the same time, GMF++ and MLP++ have been developed due to the successful integration of latent representations into the original GMF and MLP. NeuMF++'s learning capacity is greatly improved by the latent representation it obtains from the SDAEs' latent space, which enables it to accurately learn user and item characteristics. However, NeuMF++'s performance may suffer if GMF++ and MLP++ are forced to share feature extractions. Consequently, enabling GMF++ and MLP++ to independently learn features increases its adaptability and dramatically boosts its performance. The experimental root-mean-square error of 0.8681 obtained by NeuMF++ in a real-world dataset shows that it performs exceptionally well. Additional data, such as text or photos, can be added to NeuMF++ in later development. NeuMF++ allows for the incorporation of several neural network building elements to create a more robust recommendation model.

34. In chapter 34, The goal of this research is to examine how e-commerce and web-based businesses might benefit from the use of Big Data Analytics in managerial decision making. The data used in this analysis comes from a single e-commerce website's database. User interactions with the website, such as page views, product additions, and online purchases, would be recorded. Association Rule Mining Algorithm (APRIORI), K-Means Clustering, and Pearson's Correlation Coefficient are only few of the algorithms that will be utilized to evaluate the dataset. The information will be analyzed and utilized to provide insights into users' interactions with the website, allowing for the identification of patterns that might inform future actions. For instance, which product receives the most attention and sales, how many pages are viewed before a purchase is made, what percentage of customers buy the product again, and so on. This study would also determine whether or not the company's present Big Data implementation can be enhanced, as well as whether or not doing so would be a smart use of resources.

35. Chapter 35 presents that different e-learning recommendation strategies that benefit both students and teachers have been developed in recent years. In these cases, it is necessary to provide students and teachers with individualized instruction through the use of online learning systems tailored to their specific needs. In this study, we employ a split-and-conquer strategy-based clustering technique to design a smart recommender that can automatically adjust to the needs, preferences, and skill levels of each individual learner. The recommender is self-learning and does automated analyses of learner preferences and features. Using a divide-and-conquer approach, several learning modalities are grouped together for analysis. To extract the learners' functional patterns, thc suggested cluster-based linear pattern mining approach is used. The machine then makes insightful suggestions by considering the ratings of common patterns. The proposed model offered critical learning tasks to learners based on their learning style, interest categorization, and talent traits, and it was tested on a variety of learner groups and datasets. The suggested cluster-based recommender was found to increase recommendation performance in experiments by leading to more lessons being finished by learners compared to those in the no-recommender cluster group. It was determined that over 65% of the students used all evaluation criteria while assessing the suggested

recommendation tool. The simulation results showed that the suggested recommender achieved higher metric values for larger learners. There were statistically significant variations in the assessed measures when the number of students was more than 1000. Using a computational framework that varied with |L| (the size of the suggestion list) and the characteristics of the students, we were able to identify the reasons for the observed discrepancies. The students had similar positive reactions to the recommender's precision and quickness. Standard deviation and mean of parameters for Recall (List, User) and Ranking Score (User) measurements differ significantly from other approaches for the sample dataset studied. The developed strategy outperformed competing strategies on all relevant criteria. In contrast to many well-known approaches, our recommender achieves the lowest mean absolute error across all clusters.

36. Chapter 36 shows that by analysing the geographical, chronological, and semantic components of geographic data, it is possible to reconstruct users' real route itineraries and get insights into their preferences and behavior. To analyse tourist traffic patterns at A-level scenic spots in Jiangsu and Zhejiang across time and space, this research collects and preprocesses Weibo check-in data for these locations. The author used a temporal perspective, examining how check-in data fluctuated between 2016 and 2018 and how it differed on weekends, holidays, and weekdays. The acquired data were subjected to a spatial kernel density analysis, which revealed the most active regions. Lastly, the vacation travel mode and characteristics were uncovered by an examination of spatial and locational flows and flow orientations. The results of this study provide the groundwork for the growth of wisdom tourism.

37. Chapter 37 shows that a user's interests and goals can be deduced with the use of a Recommendation System (RS), a new form of technology that employs knowledge discovery methods. User intent analysis and corresponding suggestion triggering become increasingly challenging in the face of exponential data growth. This work proposes a unique Deep Knowledge Graph (DKG) to do the necessary data analysis and construct the RS. DKG employs a Deep Convolutional Neural Network (DCNN). Our proposed DKG explicitly models the KG's end-to-end high-order connectivities. It recursively propagates the embeddings from a node's neighbors, which can be people, things, or traits, using an attention approach to assess the relative significance of the neighbours. In terms of theory, our DKG outperforms existing KG-based recommendation methods since it does not rely on regularization or an explicit representation of high-order relations. Empirical results on public benchmarks show that KGAT outperforms state-of-the-art methods like RippleNet and Neural FM. The benefits of the attention mechanism for interpretability, as well as the efficacy of embedding propagation for high-order relation modeling, have been shown in subsequent studies.

S. Kannadhasan
Head of the Departmnet
Department of Electronics and Communication Engineering
Study World College of Engineering
Coimbatore, Tamilnadu- 641105

R. Nagarajan
Department of Electrical and Electronics Engineering, Gnanamani College of Technology, Namakkal, Tamilnadu, India

&

Kaushik Pal
Laboratório de Biopolímeros e Sensores
Instituto de Macromoléculas
Universidade Federal do Rio de Janeiro (LABIOS/IMA/UFRJ)
Rio de Janeiro, RJ- 21941-901
Brazil

List of Contributors

Ashish Kumar Srivastava	Department of Computer Science and Engineering, Galgotias University, Greater Noida, Uttar Pradesh, India
Avadhesh Kumar	Department of Computer Science and Engineering, Galgotias University, Greater Noida, Uttar Pradesh, India
Alisha Sikri	Department of AIML, Noida Institute of Engineering and Technology, Greater Noida, Uttar Pradesh, India
A. Alli	Department of Computer Applications, Presidency College, Bangalore, Karnataka, India
Ajay Chakravarty	College of Computing Sciences & Information Technology, Teerthanker Mahaveer University, Moradaubad, Uttar Pradesh, India
Avadhesh Kumar	Department of Computer Science and Engineering, Galgotias University, Greater Noida, Uttar Pradesh, India
Ajay Rastogi	Department of College of Computing Sciences & I.T, Teerthanker Mahaveer University, Moradabad, Uttar Pradesh, India
Amit Singh	College of Computing Science and Information Technology, Teerthanker Mahaveer University, Moradabad, Uttar Pradesh, India
Abhilash Kumar Saxena	College of Computing Sciences & Information Technology, Teerthanker Mahaveer University, Moradabad, Uttar Pradesh, India
Anurag Singh	Department of Computer Science and Engineering, Galgotias University, Greater Noida, Uttar Pradesh, India
Ajay Shanker Singh	Department of Computer Science and Engineering, Galgotias University, Greater Noida, Uttar Pradesh, India
Biswajeet Kumar Pandey	Department of Computer Science and Engineering, JAIN (Deemed-to-be University), Bangalore, Karnataka, India
Bhawna Wadhwa	Department of Computer Science and Engineering, Noida Institute of Engineering & Technology, Greater Noida, Uttar Pradesh, India
C. Kalaiarasan	Department of Computer Science and Engineering, Presidency University, Bangalore, Karnataka, India
Chandrasekar	Department of Computer Science and Engineering, JAIN (Deemed-to-be University), Bangalore, Karnataka, India
C.R. Manjunath	Department of Computer Science and Engineering, JAIN (Deemed-to-be University), Bangalore, Karnataka, India
Dhruv Galgotia	Department of Management, Galgotias University, Greater Noida, Uttar Pradesh, India
F. Rosita Kamala	Department of Computer Applications, Presidency College, Bangalore, Karnataka, India
Gopal K. Shyam	Department of Computer Science and Engineering, Presidency University, Bangalore, Karnataka, India
G. Geetha	School of Computer Science and Engineering, JAIN (Deemed-to-be University), Bangalore, Karnataka, India

G. Sindhu Madhuri	Department of Computer Science and Engineering, JAIN (Deemed-to-be University), Bangalore, Karnataka, India
Gaurav Kumar Rajput	College of Computing Science and Information Technology, Teerthanker Mahaveer University, Moradabad, Uttar Pradesh, India
Gaurav Londhe	Department of Computer Science and Engineering, JAIN (Deemed-to-be University), Bangalore, Karnataka, India
H.K. Shashikala	Department of Computer Science and Engineering, JAIN (Deemed-to-be University), Bangalore, Karnataka, India
H.S. Shreenidhi	Department of Computer Science and Engineering, JAIN (Deemed-to-be University), Bangalore, Karnataka, India
Jagdish Chandra Patni	Department of Computer Science and Engineering, JAIN (Deemed-to-be University), Bangalore, Karnataka, India
Jayanthi Kannan	Department of Information Science and Engineering, JAIN (Deemed-to-be University), Bangalore, Karnataka, India
J. Vijay Fidelis	Department of Computer Applications, Presidency College, Bangalore, Karnataka, India
Kuldeep Singh Kaswan	Department of Computer Science and Engineering, Galgotias University, Greater Noida, Uttar Pradesh, India
K. Vanitha	Department of Computer Science and Engineering, JAIN (Deemed-to-be University), Bangalore, Karnataka, India
Krishnan Batri	School of Computer Science and Engineering, JAIN (Deemed-to-be University), Bangalore, Karnataka, India
M. Veera Nagaiah	Department of Computer Applications, Presidency College, Bangalore, Karnataka, India
M.S. Sowmya	Department of Information Science and Engineering, JAIN (Deemed-to-be University), Bangalore, Karnataka, India
Merin Thomas	Department of Computer Science and Engineering, JAIN (Deemed-to-be University), Bangalore, Karnataka, India
Mohammed Zabeeulla	Department of Computer Science and Engineering, JAIN (Deemed-to-be University), Bangalore, Karnataka, India
Meenakshi Sharma	Department of Computer Science and Engineering, Galgotias University, Greater Noida, Uttar Pradesh, India
M. Chandra Sekhar	Department of Computer Science and Engineering, Presidency University, Bangalore, Karnataka, India
Meenakshi Sharma	Department of Computer Science and Engineering, Galgotias University, Greater Noida, Uttar Pradesh, India
Nitin Gaur	Department of Computer Science and Engineering, Galgotias University, Greater Noida, Uttar Pradesh, India
Priyanka Chandani	Department of DS, CSBS, AL-CSBS, Noida Institute of Engineering and Technology, Greater Noida, Uttar Pradesh, India
Prabha Nair	Department of IT and M.Tech Integrated, Noida Institute of Engineering & Technology, Greater Noida, Uttar Pradesh, India

Philomine Roseline	Department of Computer Applications, Presidency College, Bangalore, Karnataka, India
R. Pallavi	Department of Computer Science and Engineering, Presidency University, Bangalore, Karnataka, India
Rajat Bhardwaj	Department of Computer Science and Engineering, JAIN (Deemed-to-be University), Bangalore, Karnataka, India
Ranjana Sharma	College of Computing Science and Information Technology, Teerthanker Mahaveer University, Moradabad, Uttar Pradesh, India
Ramesh Chandra Tripathi	College of Computing Science & IT, Teerthanker Mahaveer University, Moradabad, Uttar Pradesh, India
Rajesh Pandian	Department of Computer Science and Engineering, JAIN (Deemed-to-be University), Bangalore, Karnataka, India
R. Mahalakshmi	Department of Computer Science and Engineering, Presidency University, Bangalore, Karnataka, India
R. Pachayappan	Department of Computer Applications, Presidency College, Bangalore, Karnataka, India
Ramesh Sengodan	Department of Computer Science and Engineering, Presidency University, Bangalore, Karnataka, India
S.H. Shruthishree	Department of Computer Science and Engineering, JAIN (Deemed-to-be University), Bangalore, Karnataka, India
Sahana Shetty	Department of Computer Science and Engineering, JAIN (Deemed-to-be University), Bangalore, Karnataka, India
S. Santosh	Department of Computer Science and Engineering, JAIN (Deemed-to-be University), Bangalore, Karnataka, India
S. Kannadhasan	Department of Electronics and Communication Engineering, Study World College of Engineering, Coimbatore, Tamil Nadu, India
Sunanda Das	Department of Computer Science and Engineering, JAIN (Deemed-to-be University), Bangalore, Karnataka, India
Shambhu Bhardwaj	College of Computing Science and Information Technology, Teerthanker Mahaveer University, Moradabad, Uttar Pradesh, India
Saira Banu Atham	Department of Computer Science and Engineering, Presidency University, Bangalore, Karnataka, India
S. Gadug	Department of Computer Science and Engineering, JAIN (Deemed-to-be University), Bangalore, Karnataka, India
Sheetal	Department of Computer Applications, Presidency College, Bangalore, Karnataka, India
S. Senthilkumar	Department of Computer Science and Engineering, Presidency University, Bangalore, Karnataka, India
Somashekhara Reddy	Department of Computer Science and Engineering, JAIN (Deemed-to-be University), Bangalore, Karnataka, India
T. Harish Naik	Department of Computer Applications, Presidency College, Bangalore, Karnataka, India

Tushar Mehrotra	College of Computing Science and Information Technology, Teerthanker Mahaveer University, Moradabad, Uttar Pradesh, India
Vineet Saxena	College of Computing Science and Information Technology, Teerthanker Mahaveer University, Moradabad, Uttar Pradesh, India
Vetrimani Elangovan	Department of Computer Science and Engineering, Presidency University, Bangalore, Karnataka, India
Veena S. Badiger	Department of Computer Applications, Presidency College, Bangalore, Karnataka, India
V. Gokul Rajan	Department of Computer Science and Engineering, Galgotias University, Greater Noida, Uttar Pradesh, India

CHAPTER 1

A Study of Big Data Techniques for Extracting Valuable Information

Ashish Kumar Srivastava[1,*] and **Rajat Bhardwaj**[2]

[1] *Department of Computer Science and Engineering, Galgotias University, Greater Noida, Uttar Pradesh, India*

[2] *Department of Computer Science and Engineering, JAIN (Deemed-to-be University), Bangalore, Karnataka, India*

Abstract: When dealing with unstructured data, information extraction is crucial for identifying named entities and events, which is essential for natural language processing. The exponential growth of information in the agricultural sector has made data extraction increasingly challenging. Despite the widespread use of deep learning-based approaches in smart farming for tasks such as crop cultivation, identifying diseases, weed removal, and yield production, the persistent impacts of meteorological, soil, pest, and fertilizer data make it challenging to discover the semantic relationships among the extracted data. The paper is divided into two sections. First, we present a data preprocessing method for cleaning up input corpora of any ambiguity; Furthermore, we provide a novel method for agricultural named entity identification, events, and relations that is based on deep learning techniques. This method utilizes multilayer perceptrons and the Adam optimizer with corrective capabilities. Agricultural, meteorological, soil, along with insect and fertilizer corpora, were used to train and assess the proposed algorithm. On common measures such as accuracy, sensitivity, and specificity, the experimental findings show that the proposed algorithm beats current approaches like Weighted-SOM, LSTM+RAO, PLR-DBN, the KNN, as well as Naïve Bayes.

Keywords: Adam optimizer, Agricultural sector, Algorithm, Big data techniques, Crop cultivation, Farming, Identifying diseases, Information extraction, Natural language processing, Weed removal, Yield production.

INTRODUCTION

A large portion of India's GDP comes from agriculture, which is particularly vulnerable to the effects of climate change. For example, the Indian agriculture sector is particularly susceptible to risks due to major characteristics such as tiny

* **Corresponding author Ashish Kumar Srivastava:** Department of Computer Science and Engineering, Galgotias University, Greater Noida, Uttar Pradesh, India; E-mail: dsrivastava@galgotiasuniversity.edu.in

S. Kannadhasan, R. Nagarajan, & Kaushik Pal (Eds.)

land holdings, over-reliance on fertilizers, and the monsoons [1 - 3]. The absence of processing algorithms results in a significant quantity of unorganized agricultural data being underused. The major variables for making choices in emerging nations like India continue to be human specialists and government regulations.

From a policymaker's point of view, factual confirmation according to current information is still missing [4]. Over the last several decades, climatic variability has had a significant impact on agricultural water resources, crop development and growth, as well as crop output over wide areas [5 - 8]. Crop production models for both rice and wheat in the Indian peninsula are based on simulation approaches, and researchers analyze the climate-crop connection using long-term fertility, regional data, and other predictable field studies [9]. The majority of Uttarakhand's land is arable, but farmers there see farming as an unrealistic way to ensure their families' nutritional needs are met. Maize and rice, sometimes called Kharif or monsoon crops, are Uttarakhand's main cash crops. Due to natural factors such as the continual danger of avalanches, substantial amounts of erosion, and collapses during rains, the Kharif crop yield in the Uttarakhand area is much lower than in other areas. Agricultural land that relies on rainfall for crop production is essential. The use of rain-fed techniques accounts for about 80% of Uttarakhand's agricultural output [10]. Diverse agroecosystems, each with its own unique hydro-geological setting, crop types, and harvesting methods, define a high-resilience system. Factors such as direction and amount of slope, height, soil type, irrigation conditions, and local knowledge might affect the variety [11]. However, traditional agricultural rotations as well as techniques can help keep this diversity intact. If you want your crop to thrive, it's not only the environment that matters; soil and fertilizers play a just as significant part. Nevertheless, present machine learning approaches like ANN, Bayes networks, and Gaussian kernel-based Support Vector Machine (SVM) can't determine which pests and fertilizers are best suited to a given soil type [12, 13]. Factors such as electrical conductivity, pH, and the macro- and micronutrients of the chosen crop determine the state of the soil [14]. In order to increase the crop's production, farmers use these soil quality indexes to determine which pesticides and fertilizers will work best. Data sources might include domain-dependent information, domain-independent or independent unstructured/semi-structured corpora, as well as extraction methods defined by the user [15]. Structured databases, such as relational and graph databases, store the knowledge extracted from the input data by the data extract (IE) engine. In order to estimate rainfall for agricultural production in the Dehradun area, researchers have suggested relatively restricted empirical as well as computational methodologies, combined with the relevant land information. To address this need, this study proposes to use unstructured agricultural literature from the Uttarakhand area to extract Named Entities (NER) and event relationships (or event meaning).

RELATED WORKS

The last two decades have seen tremendous advancements in the use of machine learning and deep learning to address data extraction problems in many different industries, including agriculture, biometric identification, medical imaging analysis and retrieval, illness diagnosis, and many more. This literature review outlines previous efforts to apply machine learning to the agriculture industry. The use of ANN in the India-specific GCM. Using precipitation yields from GCM, the suggested method aimed to forecast the Indian Summer Maximum Rain values. In order to get scale predictions for India as well as its sub-divisional areas on a monthly basis, the ANN technique was linked to several ensemble organizations from the GCMs. In order to reduce the occurrence of over-fitting, the present research trained the ANN method utilizing the double-fold approval technique and straightforward randomization. The ANN-derived rainfall prediction is based on GCMs and is established by examining the percentage of linear errors in the probability time, contrast, box plots, and absolute error. After implementing the ANN systems used by these GCM experts in forecasting, the results of the experiment indicated the crucial alterations. Although logical considerations may impact the framework/variable, the data sets are dependent on previous estimates of the main factor. To estimate crop yields, Satir *et al.* [30] suggested using vegetation indices in conjunction with Stepwise Linear Regression. Accurate mapping of an area's crop patterns was achieved by combining object-based categorization with a multi-temporal Landsat data collection. Here, we approximated the forecast using real-time measuring techniques such as Mean Percent Error (MPE). Cotton, maize, and wheat had their MPE evaluated using a combination of soil salt levels and other factors. A single variable was used to lower the accuracy of weather forecasts based on the data collected. Using long-term weather data, hybrid algorithms like LASSO, ANN, and penalized regression techniques with elastic net (ENET), PCA, and SMLR to forecast rice yield. Based on the experimental data, LASSO-ENET performed well since these approaches simplified the model as well as avoided overfitting with amplitude coefficients. The hybrid models performed well in the West Coast of India crop forecast task, according to the pairwise numerous comparisons test. However, poor performance is produced by combining feature selection techniques with feature extraction using neural networks, such as PCA-SMLR. This is due to the fact that PCA failed to include the variable that is dependent while modifying the input variables. According to the study, a Hybrid Wavelet-based artificial neural network (HWNN) that included ANN, particle-swarm optimization (PSO), Social Knowledge, as well as Multi-Resolution Analysis was used to forecast monthly rainfall using historical climatic data. Subseries portions with various time scales were created utilizing the Maximum Overlap Continuous Wavelet Transformation for the standardized monthly rainfall anomaly with large-scale climate indicators. Each rainstorm's optimal number of ANN hidden layer neurons and predicted anomalous sub-series for the selected predictor were determined using the PSO approach. Although the HWNN approach performed better within a certain season, it was quite time-consuming to use it to predict rainfall outside of that season. In order to forecast food crop production based on a variety of variables, including season, soil type, risk factor, and water availability, a parallelism layer regression with Deep Belief Network (PLRDBN) is used. The five crops from Karnataka that would be targeted through the proposed PLR-DBN method were chosen after extensive consideration of their specificity, sensitivity, and accuracy. Forecasting and proposing agricultural techniques that boost crop yields using data on meteorological conditions (which include temperature, rainfall, and humidity). The model used many algorithms, such as KNN, random forests, logistic regression, SVM, and a Naïve Bayes classifier, to provide predictions. The suggestion system makes use of cooperative as well as multi-condition filtration approaches.

PROPSOED WORK

Subject Area and Dataset Details

Uttarakhand, a state in northern India, stretches from 79°15′ eastward to 30°15′ north latitude, and its total size is 53,483 square kilometers. This state will be the center of our inquiry. Among the towns that make up the Garhwal area of the state of Uttarakhand are Haridwar, Chamoli, Dehradun, Pauri, Uttarkashi, Tehri, and Rudraprayag. Udham Singh Nagar, Champawat, Almora, Bageshwar, Nainital, and Pithoragarh are all parts of the Kumaon region. The research has taken into account the whole region to predict rainfall-runoff events, allowing for almost complete coverage of the state area. Information Management Division (IMD), soil, pest, and fertilizer, were among the research institutions that contributed to the creation of this database. Among these establishments are the Directorate of Agriculture in Premnagar, Dehradun; the Soil Assessment Laboratories in Nandaki Chowki; and the district's offices in Dehradun.

Suggested Approach

The next five parts cover the following topics: the suggested framework, data pretreatment using the min-max method, strategies for concatenating corpora, the suggested WSD method, and an IE algorithm that depends on deep learning.

A New Approach to Semantic IE

A strategy for obtaining semantic data is presented in the research framework, which is practical as well as theoretical. While there aren't many frameworks out there, this one aims to provide a structure that draws attention to the core ideas as well as elements of semantic IE. Articles in the chosen fields are gathered, pertinent information is gathered (mostly from repository benchmark datasets), data mining tools, preservation instruments (Excel, Oracle), and editing tools are chosen according to the technique followed in this study. Everything that went into doing the research for this study is laid forth in this part, including the operational framework. Research in this area primarily centers on four stages: data collection, preliminary processing, the semantic extraction process, and post-processing. When this structure is put into practice, these four main components are engaged. The current study is shown in Fig. (**1**) as an overview, with the framework separated into four modules.

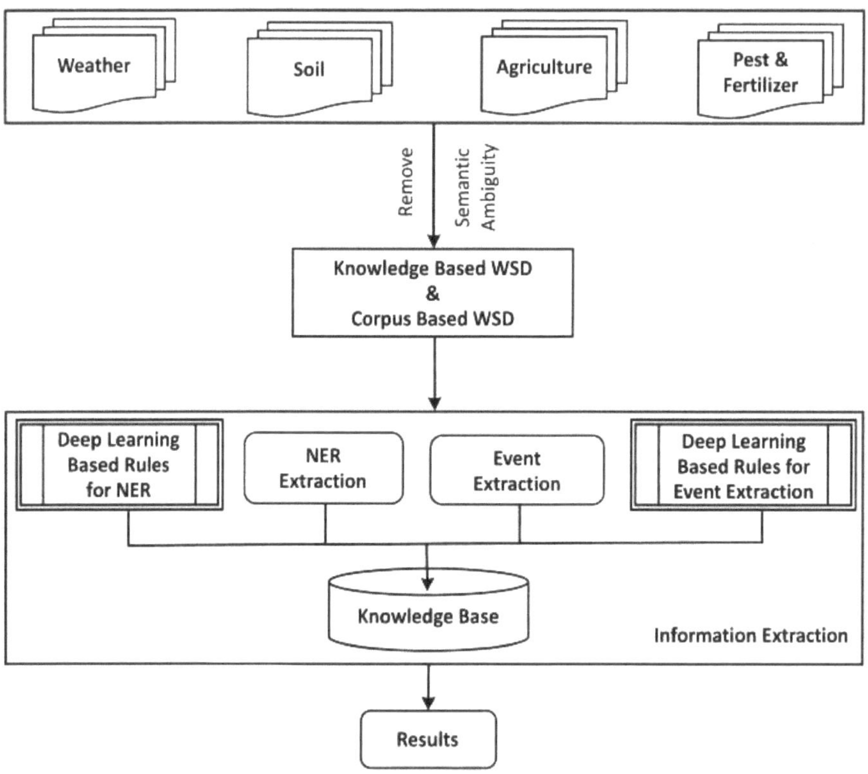

Fig. (1). Overview presentation.

Min-Max Algorithm

In this part, we prepare the input corpora for processing by eliminating noise and finding missing data. Various units of measurement, such as Celsius for temperature and miles per hour for wind speed, are used in the input data that is retrieved from the database. Fig. (**1**) is presented in the Overview section of the presentation. The suggested approach in deep learning architectures makes use of standardized variables spanning the range [0-1] to sidestep scaling issues. You can see the dataset's normalizing procedure in Eq. (1),

$$Val_i = \frac{(a_i - min_i)}{(max_a - min_a)}(new\_max_a - new\_min_a) + new'_{mi_a} \quad \textbf{(1)}$$

Corpora Concatenation

In order to merge the previously unstructured source corpora into one cohesive one, the min-max algorithm was utilized to reduce noise in the prior part. Merging the corpora needed a high level of human involvement due to the distinct nature of the two sets of data. When merging many corpora into one, two common approaches are based on knowledge WSD (KB-WSD) as well as corpus-based WSD (CB-WSD). The merging of many corporations into one entity, Agri_Corpus, and the removal of semantic ambiguity were the primary motivations for integrating these two well-known algorithms. In several instances, the successful incorporation of CB-WSD with KB-WSD has

Demonstrate a rather modest improvement rate. As a result, the suggested model in this study makes use of KB-WSD integrated into a CB-WSD; this topic will be covered further below. Krishi Vigyan Bhavanat Dhakrani, District Dehradun, Uttarakhand, is the source of agricultural information. You can access the document at this URL:(The document can be found at can be found at this URL: http://agricoop.nic.in/sites/default/files/UKD7-Dehradun-10.07.14.pdf). With an eye on enhancing agricultural output, Table **1** shows the data samples used for rain forecasting in the Dehradun area.

The data samples for Uttarakhand's main crops, including rice, barley, and potatoes, are shown in Table **1**. Although barley yields around 20 kilograms per ha in the winter, rice yields 19689.9 kg per ha throughout the monsoon season. Due to its high yield, rice has long been seen as Uttarakhand's vital crop. In summertime, you may grow potatoes with a yield of 22,140 kg per hectare. When it rains a little, a medium, or a lot, farmers in the Uttarakhand area plant rice, barley, and potatoes in that order.

Table 1. Productivity statistics for key crops in the Uttarakhand area.

Season Major crops Area (in 000ha) Productivity (Kg/ha)
Rain (June-December) Rice 11.4 19689.9
Winter (Jan-Mar) Barley 0.7 19.57
Summer (April-May) Potato 0.668 22140

A New Disambiguation Method

A clarification method should be run on the information being provided before the language processing approach is used. When dealing with unstructured language, there aren't many options for procedures that can decipher unclear terms. The present investigation employed the suggested method to extract the meaning of ambiguous phrases from the corpus. Two phrases may have “cosine-distance” or “cosine-similarity” measured to see how similar they are to one another.

$$Sim(W_i, S_i) = \frac{\sum_{i=1}^{n} W_i \cdot S_i}{\sqrt{\sum_{i=1}^{n} W_i^{2}} * \times \sqrt{\sum_{i=1}^{n} \Sigma_{i=1}^{} S_i^{2}}} \quad (2)$$

Algorithm 1: Extract senses from ambiguous word

1. ∀ word W_j ∃ a sense S_i
   a. do:
   b. Calculate $Sim(W_i, S_i) = \frac{\sum_{i=1}^{n} W_i . S_i}{\sqrt{\sum_{i=1}^{n} W_i^2} * \sqrt{\sum_{i=1}^{n} S_i^2}}$
   c. Calculate $D\_amb(W_i, S_i) = 1 - Cosine(W_i, S_i)$
   d. If $D\_amb \approx 0$ then assign similarity S_i to W
   e. End
2. Sense: = Sen1
3. ∀ ambiguous word calculate sense
   a. do:
   b. If $D\_amb(W_j, S_i) > D\_amb(W_j, Sen1)$
   c. Assign Sense = S_i
   d. End
4. Assign calculate sense S_i to ambiguous word Wj.

Semantic IE Algorithm with LSTM-RAO and MLP

With the benefits of LSTM approaches, the following program normalizes data using the min-max algorithm. With every iteration of back propagation, a deep network's weights are adjusted using a RAO and an MLP. The optimization features of the RMSProp and AdaGard programs have been carried over to this one.

Two essential components of the suggested model are feature selection and categorization. We utilized a sigmoid activation function to enhance the correlations in the target data. Our activation function of choice in the network's deep hidden layers was the tangent hyperbolic transfer (tansig). The activation functions obtained from Eq. (3) are applied in the buried layers.

$$\text{Tansig}(n) = (2/(1 + e{-}2n)) - 1 \tag{3}$$

According to Eq. (4), for each cell Ct-1, the

$$ft = [0\text{–}1]\ f\,gt = \sigma\ (Wfg[hT-1, XT]) + bfg \tag{4}$$

The remembergate is defined by its weight (Wfg) and bias (bfg). The cell state has been saved, updated, and calculated from input Xt using both the sigmoid and tanh levels. The range within the tanh function (-1 to 1) and the starting value of the sigmoid function (0,1) establish the significance level, which the updated data should both modify or ignore. Multiplying NT and iT refreshed the new cell state of the LSTM network. Similar to RMSprop and Adadelta, the Adam optimizer may save an exponentially dropping mean of the most recent gradient MT and square gradient (VT). At time T, the random object used to determine the gradient (GT) is: An alternative form of equation (5) is as follows:

$$Gt = \nabla\omega fT(\omega T-1) \tag{5}$$

The equation that describes MT is ε1 times MTˆ1 plus. (1 minus ε1).

The GT twelve and the VT equations look like this: VT = ε2VT−1 + (1 − ε2) A single G2 T. In this case, the first gradient moment (MT) represents the standard deviation, while the second gradient moment (VT) represents the uncentered variance.

Using formulae (6) and (7), we can determine the error offset by contrasting the bias-corrected first with second-moment estimations. We find that the skewing is nearly zero, especially at the start time T, and both ε1 and ε2 (the small delay) are close to 1.

$$M_{new}\ T = MT\ 1 - \varepsilon T\ 1 \tag{6}$$

$$V_{new}\ T = VT\ 1 - \varepsilon T \tag{7}$$

RESULT AND DISCUSSION

A personal computer with a 3.2 GHz Intel Core i5 CPU was used for the scenario test simulation, which included installing Python Jupyter notebooks. The next whole paragraph is the result of using the suggested WSD method. Multiple senses may be attached to a single word. The following text was used as input to illustrate the suggested method. There is medical value in ginger. The best time to plant this seed is during rainfall, just before the monsoon, although there's no set time of year to do it. It is harvested during the Kharif season. The best time to harvest ginger is one month before the weather is dry. The results were tabulated in Table **2**. The word "session" has connections to the time of action, a formal meeting, as well as an outdoor period. Thanks to the explanatory algorithm, we now know that a "session" can only signify a weather session. A tabular format displays the outcomes of the algorithm that was recommended.

Table 2. Results obtained using the suggested deambiguation method.

Ambiguousword	Existedsenses	Extractedsense
Plant Sow Crop Dry Session	Factory Tree Femalepig Seed Grain No.of people Boing Not sweet Rain Period of activity Weather A series of meetings	Tree Seed Grain Rain Weather

Table 3. Analyzing how well the suggested approach works.

Crops	Accuracy (%)	Specificity(%)	F-score(%)	Sensiticity(%)
Rice	95.55	96.65	93.37	94.25
Barley	92.45	97.12	93.35	94.54
Potato	76.30	65.37	79.29	72.15

Standard statistics performance assessment criteria, such as precision, specificity, sensitivity, and F-Measures, were used to evaluate the suggested method's performance in this research. For the most important crops grown in the Dehradun region, the values of accuracy, F-measure, sensitivity, and specificity are shown in Table **3**.

The effectiveness of the method is described in great depth in this section. Using a split of 80/20 between training and testing data, the suggested technique has been cross-validated. For the 70-30% and 60-40% datasets, we also examined the cross-validation element of the suggested technique. When compared to ANN, RNN, LSTM *via* Adams optimization, and LSTM *via* the rectified Adam optimizer, the accuracy attained by the suggested method is much higher. We evaluate the suggested approach against ANN, RNN, LSTM, and Adam optimization algorithms for accuracy, F-score variables, and recall, in addition to LSTM *via* rectified Adam optimization techniques.

CONCLUSION

A statistical analysis of the Uttarakhand region's rainfall, soil, agricultural, insect, and fertilizer data has been provided using the suggested approaches. The planned experiment aimed to isolate NER, events, and their relationships as they pertain to agriculture. Important crops, such as rice, barley, and potatoes, in Sikkim state's areas with significant rainfall might potentially have their yields increased using the aforementioned method, which involves determining the exact quantity of precipitation required for an appropriate amount of crop production with enhanced soil quality. Here, we used a deep learning approach to forecast which main crop will be most appropriate for the current season in India's Uttarakhand Region. Thus, compared to previously used ways, the result produced by the proposed method is superior. Using the LSTM with the RAO as well as MLP optimization techniques correctly resulted in a precision of 88.10 percent. The proposed technique outperformed the other techniques, along with DL-SOM, LSTM+RAO, PLR-DBN, KNN, as well as Naïve Bayes, in both efficiency (1.09%), sensitivity (1.01%), specificity (1.11%), and overall performance (1.37%, 1.22%, 1.40%, 1.41%, and 1.59%). In terms of efficiency, the Nash-Sutcliffe ratio came out at 0.99. When compared to earlier techniques that were based on different accessible ways for crop forecasting, the sophisticated system produced better results in terms of sensitivity, accuracy, specificity, and F-score. Future research may benefit from using plant disease datasets in an effort to increase agricultural output. Research into the production of potato crops in mountainous regions has a lot of room to grow, according to the trial findings.

REFERENCES

[1] J. Noverlita and H. Surbakti. Streamlining Stock Price Analysis: Hadoop Ecosystem for Machine Learning Models and Big Data Analytics. *International Journal of Information Technology and Computer Science*, vol. 15, no. 5, pp. 25-34, 2023.

[2] A. Sharma, S.K. Singh, E. Badwal, S. Kumar, B.B. Gupta, V. Arya, K.T. Chui, and D. Santaniello, "Fuzzy Based Clustering of Consumers' Big Data in Industrial Applications", *2023 IEEE International Conference on Consumer Electronics (ICCE), Las Vegas, NV, USA, 2023, pp. 01-03..* [http://dx.doi.org/10.1109/ICCE56470.2023.10043451]

[3] N. Kumar, K.H.Sadhu Sai, V. Hordiichuk, R. Menon, C. Julie Aarthy, G.C. Saha, K. Balaji. "Harnessing the Power of Big Data: Challenges and Opportunities in Analytics." *Tuijin Jishu/Journal of Propulsion Technology*, vol. 44, no. 2, pp. 363-371, 2023.

[4] A. Ibidun, "Big Data Analytics and Competitive Advantage: Evidences from Healthcare Services Organistions in Lagos State, Nigeria", *Journal of Information and Technology*, vol. 7, no. 1, pp. 22-46, 2023.
[http://dx.doi.org/10.53819/81018102t4149]

[5] I.E. Kalabikhina, E. Zubova, N.V. Loukachevitch, A. Kolotusha, Z. Kazbekova, E.P. Banin, and G. Klimenko, "Identifying Reproductive Behavior Arguments in Social Media Content Users' Opinions through Natural Language Processing Techniques", Population and Economics, vol. 7, no. 2, pp. 40-59, 2023.
[http://dx.doi.org/10.3897/popecon.7.e97064]

[6] X. Shan, "Text Mining of User Comments Based on Deep Learning", In: *Proceedings of the 2023 5th Blockchain and Internet of Things Conference (BIOTC '23). Association for Computing Machinery* New York, NY, USA, 2023, pp. 71-79.
[http://dx.doi.org/10.1145/3625078.3625088]

[7] R.E. Meena, and T. Kavitha, "Extracting Behavioral Characteristics of College Students Using Data Mining on Big Data", *2023 International Conference on Artificial Intelligence and Knowledge Discovery in Concurrent Engineering (ICECONF),* pp. 1-7, 2023.
[http://dx.doi.org/10.1109/ICECONF57129.2023.10084276]

[8] Gupta, R.K., & D., P.S. (2023). Temporal Variability Analysis of Domain Names using Graph Techniques on Big Data. 2023 14th International Conference on Computing Communication and Networking Technologies (ICCCNT), 1-6.

[9] X. Chen, *The analysis of electric vehicle integration based on big data technology.* Applied and Computational Engineering. Applied and Computational Engineering, 22, pp. 8-13, 2023.
[http://dx.doi.org/10.54254/2755-2721/22/20231158]

[10] A. Poddar, P. Kulkarni, and N.A. Natraj, "Application of Big Data for Better Decision Management in Banking", *2023 International Conference on Sustainable Computing and Data Communication Systems (ICSCDS),* pp. 1404-1407, 2023.
[http://dx.doi.org/10.1109/ICSCDS56580.2023.10104706]

[11] X. Jian, and Y. Feng, *Research on Enterprise Intelligent Knowledge Management and Decision Making Based on Big Data Mining.* Accounting and Corporate Management. Vol. 5, pp. 27-34. 2023.

[12] Balduque-Gil, J., Lacueva-Pérez, F.J., Labata-Lezaun, G., del-Hoyo-Alonso, R., Ilarri, S., Sánchez-Hernández, E., Martín-Ramos, P., & Barriuso-Vargas, J.J. Big Data and Machine Learning to Improve European Grapevine Moth (*Lobesia botrana*) Predictions. Plants (Basel), vol. 12, no. 3, p. 633, 2023.

[13] S. Ahmed, "Data Mining for Non-Redundant Big Data Using dynamic KMEAN", *International Journal of Computing and Digital Systems*, vol. 14, no. 1, pp. 243-251, 2023.
[http://dx.doi.org/10.12785/ijcds/140121]

[14] W.S. Cheng, P.Y. Huang, J.Y. Huang, J.C. Chen, and K.W. Lin, "A fast and distributed C4.5 algorithm for urban big data", *Intell. Data Anal.,* vol. 27, no. 5, pp. 1379-1408, 2023.
[http://dx.doi.org/10.3233/IDA-220753]

[15] H.R. Ibraheem and M.M. Hamad. A Hybrid Integrated Model for Big Data Applications Based on Association Rules and Fuzzy Logic: A Review. Iraqi Journal for Computer Science and Mathematics, vol. 4, no. 2, pp. 171-178, 2023.

CHAPTER 2

Adaptive Recommendation Systems for Improved Information Analysis

M.S. Sowmya[1,*] and **Nitin Gaur**[2]

[1] *Department of Information Science and Engineering, JAIN (Deemed-to-be University), Bangalore, Karnataka, India*

[2] *Department of Computer Science and Engineering, Galgotias University, Greater Noida, Uttar Pradesh, India*

Abstract: There has to be a better design of screening devices to meet the rising need for health screening. We develop health screening machine learning models and suggest screening elements to provide individualized health care. For each screening item, a machine learning algorithm is created while the system is offline using guidelines and clinical findings from institutions to construct a synthetic data set. A customer's health states, as well as machine learning algorithms, are used by the proposed server online to provide a real-time inventory of screening items. The performance investigation showed that for 1,000 users online at once, the server responded in under a second, and the learning model's accuracy was close to 100%. This work introduces a recommendation system that can automatically adjust to changes in the screening environment.

Keywords: Machine Learning, Text Mining, Adaptive Recommendation Systems, Improved Information Analysis, Health Screening.

INTRODUCTION

Finding a decent hotel and making a reservation are travelers' first priorities. It now takes more time than before to look for a hotel online due to the sheer amount of data. The Recommendation Systems (RS) sector is booming due to the usefulness of these systems in facilitating decision-making and providing accurate information about the sought-after product or service. Finding the right hotel might be a challenge when using text reviews, rankings, votes, evaluations, and video views [1]. Many researchers are interested in Heterogeneous neural networks with graphs (GNNs) because of their strong performance as a neural

* **Corresponding author M.S. Sowmya:** Department of Information Science and Engineering, JAIN (Deemed-to-be University), Bangalore, Karnataka, India; E-mail: ms.sowmya@jainuniversity.ac.in

S. Kannadhasan, R. Nagarajan, & Kaushik Pal (Eds.)

network-based graph representation method. It handles complex networks with numerous links and nodes well, but massive amounts of semantic data and heterogeneity pose major challenges. The attention mechanism is a fascinating new concept in deep learning that has tremendous promise in many domains [2].

The importance of choosing a good hotel location and making a reservation for lodging has grown in recent years. The availability of a vast quantity of information online has led to a dramatic rise in the frequency and complexity of online hotel searches. The rise of Recommender Systems (RSs) may be attributed to their practicality in decision-making and their ability to provide accurate details on the desired good or service. It is becoming increasingly difficult to get hotel recommendations due to the proliferation of written reviews, rankings, votes, scores, and video views [3]. More and more individuals are logging into social media; therefore, it's crucial that they get exposed to the people they know with the things they're interested in. One function of recommendations is to increase users' social networks, which in turn encourages them to fill out their profiles. Using social interaction graphs, we can see how Twitter users engage with one another and who they follow [4]. One out of ten patients in developed nations experiences some kind of damage while hospitalized. By reviewing previous errors and identifying potential threats, Critical Incident Reporting Systems (CIRS) aim to lessen this. But incompatibility limits the effectiveness of Germany's 16 CIRS [5]. In order to explore the semantic aspects of users' preferences, review-based recommender systems combine user-generated reviews with rating-based models. A number of recent studies have shown that review information may enhance recommendation ability. Nevertheless, the majority of previous research has focused on improving the review-based representation learning component, which overlooks the underlying connection between ratings and reviews and fails to capture the fine-grained semantic elements [6]. A major obstacle to achieving the promised advantages of eHealth is the absence of integration and interoperability across diverse health systems. The easiest way to transition from isolated apps to eHealth solutions that work together seamlessly is to set up policies and standards for Health Information Exchange (HIE). On the other hand, data on the present state of HIE policies and standards throughout Africa is lacking [7].

RELATED WORKS

By engaging with vast quantities of diverse data and the desires of potential customers, researchers presented an intelligent method for providing real suggestions in [8]. Collaborative Filtering (CF) is a common recommendation system method. We presented a new method for CF recommendation that uses polarity detection and user sentiment analysis to build a feature matrix for hotels.

Hotel guests' peculiar habits may be better understood with the use of a multidisciplinary approach that incorporates lexical, syntactic, and semantic research. When we were making our recommendations, we looked at the hotels' customer service records and the quality of the firms they were affiliated with. The user's travel preferences will inform the system's hotel choices. More than one study has made use of data collected from hotel websites. The calculations were finished after this. This, therefore, ought to serve as the most important benefit of the description.

By using GNNs, the suggested architecture accomplishes multi-level semantic attention [9]. We used a combined dataset that included movies and TV shows from both IMDB and Netflix for further study of the findings. Utilizing heterogeneous graphs with multi-level semantics, this research primarily presents a method for movie recommendation. The spectator and the director are treated as one entity in our suggested paradigm. We also used the suggested framework to merge two datasets throughout the study. The next step was to test the graph neural network system's performance on the varied graph. We found that the suggested model performed better than the prior techniques by using the strategy. When our model's framework is used, the results are effective in terms of multidimensional anti-Semitism.

To help patients make educated judgments on the drugs that are most suited to their individual medical circumstances, the authors of the research suggest a customized medicine recommendation strategy in [10]. Research to Come: Adding patient medicine reviews to the suggested method of medication suggestion is one way to make it better. Medication prediction accuracy may be further enhanced by analyzing MC-based ratings with an improved aggregation algorithm.

In an effort to meet the demands of prospective clients, researchers presented an intelligent method for dealing with large-scale heterogeneous data in [11]. One of the most popular RS methods for making suggestions is the collaborative filtering, or CF, approach. We provide a new method for CF recommendation that uses polarity identification to create a hotel feature matrix from opinion-based sentiment assessment. To learn about guests' feelings about the hotel's amenities and their types of stays (solo, family, couple, *etc*.), our method integrates lexical, syntactic, and semantic analysis. The suggested algorithm tailors hotel suggestions to individual guests by considering their preferences and the hotel's amenities. With the help of the big data Hadoop platform, the created system can manage diverse data sets, and it can also use fuzzy rules to suggest hotel classes depending on the kind of guests. Two hotel websites provide real-world datasets that are used to conduct different studies. Additionally, the F-measure, recall, and precision values have been computed, and the outcomes are reviewed in relation to the enhanced accuracy and reaction time, which are noticeably superior to the conventional methods.

The goal of the suggested model in [12] is to generate a social interaction network using tweet content similarity as its basis. The purpose of hypernym-centered feature engineering is to improve the accuracy of tweet semantic analysis. The collection includes user-generated tweets with an additional layer of hypernyms up to fifteen layers deep. Using the k-Nearest Neighbors algorithm, we look for tweets that are similar and suggest individuals to follow based on that. As evidence of the system's efficacy, 39.73% of suggestions are real relationships. The suggested approach generates a 2D graph representing the social networks of various people.

Examines the semantic and syntactic interoperability of reports across seven distinct reporting systems in the research [13]. When it came to semantic interoperability, we used SNOMED concepts, and when it came to syntactic interoperability, we used WHO's Minimal Information Model (MIM). The results show that there is little structural overlap; the SNOMED CT nomenclature accurately represents just two words. Also, there was a lack of syntactic compatibility across the majority of the systems. If we want CIRS to be more useful and effective, we need to make it more interoperable. Research indicates that a consistent data model, such as MIM or the HL7 FHIR resources, is necessary for semantic interoperability, and that SNOMED CT should be enhanced with terms pertaining to patient safety. A Patient safety ontology should be developed for effective critical incident analysis and CIRS as a whole due to the present lack of semantic and syntactic compatibility.

As stated in [14], MAGCL is a multi-aspect graph contrastive system of instruction that consists of three separate architectures: (i) graph encoder-based modules of learning for multi-aspect representation, which decouple examine information to project semantic connections to other subspaces after generating high-order decoupled representation in every aspect. (ii) To address the data sparsity issue with supervision signals, the contrastive learning component will include the graph contrastive learner to understand the relationship between ratings and review patterns. This method creates signals that do not need human supervision by using unlabeled data. (iii) To reduce the over-smoothing issue, the multi-tasking instructional component combines the recommendation as well as self-supervised tasks throughout joint training to acquire representations of nodes that are self-discriminative and high-order structure-aware. Extensive testing on four real-world review datasets demonstrates that the suggested structure MAGCL outperforms current state-of-the-art alternatives. We provide more research on graph comparing learning and multi-aspect representations to support the validity of the suggested paradigm.

Typical suggestions that pupils require throughout their education are given in the article [15]. Details of the sources used to compile the suggestions are provided, including explicit assessments of relevant objects derived from required student surveys and implicit assessments derived from analyses of user behavior within the system, as well as the content of relevant objects and users. Based on our research into the features of the items of interest, we know that they always come with either lengthy or brief written descriptions. Considering the topic area's particularity, the process of automated suggestion formation's important steps are defined. Preliminary item selection for the consumer using Natural Language Processing technologies before performing collaborative filtering is suggested as a way to improve suggestion accuracy. This will make it possible to consider the semantic closeness of user interests and system objects, among other things, even with little textual knowledge of users and objects. Furthermore, by using specific evaluations of relevant objects, which are acquired at the institutional level *via* ongoing quality monitoring of education, the recommendation's accuracy may be enhanced.

PROPOSED WORK

This paper's recommendation system uses the dataset to construct machine learning models that forecast which screening items the user will like. The general layout of the health screening item recommendation system is shown in Fig. (**1**). Using government and hospital-issued rules, the data generator creates a synthetic data set offline that includes the user's medical attributes and labels. Next, we isolate the data for training and separate it for testing. To build machine learning models, we'll use the training set, and to check how well they do, we'll use the test set. However, several learning models are produced since the learning models generator creates one for every screening item. When using the online mode, the suggestion servers take the user's survey data and determine whether each item requires screening. Lastly, the server will deliver a list of recommendations to the user after including the prediction outcome for each item. By automatically updating the information set as well as machine learning models in response to newly added rules or unreflected situations, the suggested method has the benefit of offering a versatile and automated prediction system. Fig. (**1**) represents the system model.

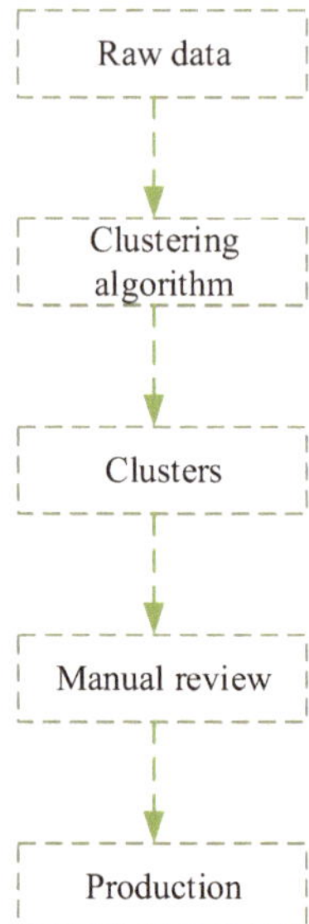

Fig. (1). System model.

Data Generator

The health screening data generator creates a set of features that include characteristics like a person's age, gender, examination interval, as well as risk factors like their family history, medical history, and dietary habits. It also includes labels that show whether screening is necessary, like for colon cancer screening or lung cancer screening. A database of health screenings was created by combining the clinical information of hospitals with the recommendations given by both local and international organizations. Following data generation, the preprocessing stage identifies which characteristics are crucial for prediction by doing feature extraction and data cleaning, which handles missing values and removes unnecessary characters. The data set used for screening is shown in Fig. (**2**), which shows the data set with the input features and output attributes represented by a feature vector and a label vector, respectively. The m-dimensional feature vector is denoted as $Y\not\in = \{x1, x2, \ldots, xm\}$, whereas the n-dimensional label vector is denoted as $Y\not\in$✏ $= \{y1, y2, \ldots, yn\}$. The characteristic vector, which could be numerical or categorical, represents the user's health status. Both multiclass and binary label vectors are possible; the former has three or more categories, while the latter has only one, as in "screening is necessary" (0/1).

Learning Model Generator

In earlier research, screening questions were suggested using simple gender and age criteria. Therefore, due to the lack of consideration for diverse factors, the preceding strategy is static and fails to generate effective outcomes. By automatically creating suitable learning models from the dataset, this research demonstrates how to improve the screening item recommendations. A major drawback of recommending all screening items using a single learning model is the amount of time and noise it introduces during execution. For this reason, we use a combination of learning models to create separate models for every one of the screening criteria. The health screening learning framework generator is shown in Fig. (**3**). The input attributes and output labels for every screening item are chosen by the data selector. The health screening elements do not often rely on one another, and the characteristics that influence the label are known in advance. Consequently, it is possible to choose the attributes and labels associated with a particular screening item. Choose the lung cancer label together with its associated parameters like age, inspection interval, cessation time, and pack-years, for instance, when dealing with lung cancer. By eliminating superfluous or unneeded characteristics, feature selection speeds up performance and decreases the time it takes to generate learning models.

Feature Vector: $\vec{X}$ | Label Vector: $\vec{Y}$

ID	Age	Gender	Pack-Years	Stop Smoking Period	Inspection Interval(Lung)	bmi	...	Lung Cancer Test	Cardiovascular Disease Test	...
1	43	1	25	10	3	32.21	...	0	1	...
2	60	1	35	0	5	23.63	...	1	0	...
3	39	0	0	0	1	22.94	...	0	1	...

Fig. (2). Label and feature vector.

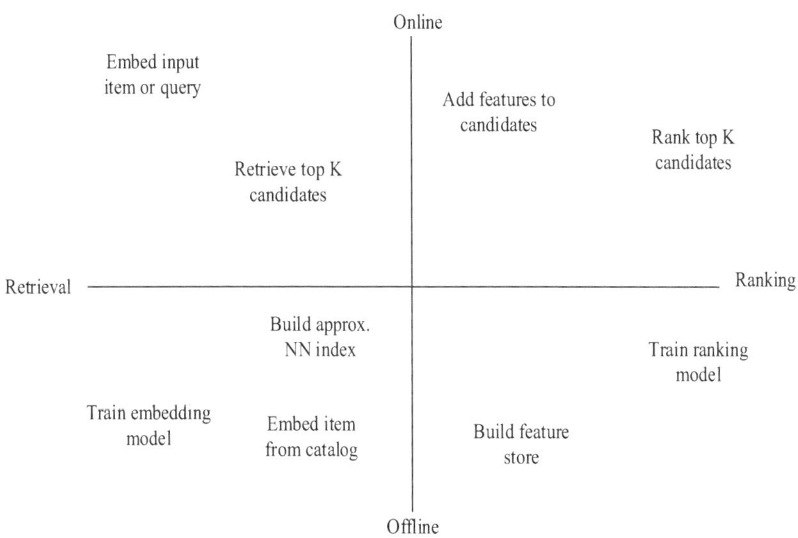

Fig. (3). Recommendation system features.

What follows is an expression of the machine learning framework for health screening as presented in this study. The machine learning framework fi ($1 \leq i \leq n$) may be expressed as follows, given an m-dimensional feature vector $Y\notin$ = {x1, x2, …, xm} and an n-dimensional label vector $Y\notin\in$ = {y1, y2, …, yn} as well as a subset of feature vectors $Y\notin 1, Y\notin 2, \ldots, Y\notin n$ (where, $Y\notin i \subseteq Y\notin$, $1 \subsetneq i \subsetneq n$).

$$y_1 = f_1(X_1),\ y_2 = f_2(X_2),\ \ldots\ y_n = f_n(X_n) \quad \textbf{(1)}$$

Equation (1) states that we create a unique model of learning for using the data selector-extracted values {a✏i, yi}. A learning framework for colon cancer, one for stomach cancer, and one for lung cancer are all created separately, as an example. Decision trees and random forests are two examples of supervised learning algorithms for classification that may be used in the machine learning process. Even while decision trees are easy to understand and implement, there is a risk of overfitting when using them to categorize things. As a result, decision trees may be used for both model visualization and validation. Contrarily, decision trees are the foundation of ensemble learning algorithms like random forests. Because they combine several decision trees to prevent overfitting, random forests are far more reliable than individual decision trees. That is why random forests may be effective. To get the best possible learning model, the settings of the algorithms are fine-tuned. When making recommendations for screening objects, the final model for learning is saved as a single file. To save a model created using machine learning to a file, you may use the pickle module in Python.

Recommendation Server

The topology of the recommendation servers for real-time health screening. The user is asked to provide basic health information in the form of a questionnaire. To illustrate the point, consider the following data: "Description": "ID": 1, "Age": 43, "Gender": "M", "Height": 169, "Weight": 92, ^ "Smoking period": 25, "Daily smoking": 20, then........ Following that, the feature generator is used to extract features from the data that the user has entered into the questionnaire. One way to measure a person's weight and height is by taking the Body Mass Index (BMI). Another way to find out how many years someone smoked is by multiplying their cigarette smoking frequency by the number of cigarettes smoked in each pack. The features for each screening item are then retrieved by the feature picker. For instance, in the case of lung cancer, characteristics like age, examination interval, non-smoking time, and smoking pack-years are retrieved. By combining features with the learning model, the screening predictor can ascertain whether a screening is necessary. The recommendation results Y✎✎ = {y'1, y'2, …, y'n}are sent by the prediction aggregator after they have collected the findings of all the screening forecasts. The JSON format allows you to make suggestion lists like {"ID": 1, "lung cancer": 0, "liver cancer": 0, "colorectal cancer": 0, "cardiovascular": 1, ... }, where 0 means no test is needed and 1 means a test is advised. Binary data or multiple classifications organized into three or more categories could be part of the test's value. Fig. (**3**) is depicted in Recommendation System Features.

RESULT AND DISCUSSION

Health screening items, as well as the response rate of the recommendations system. To start, we may use scikit-learn [10] to get a confusion matrix, which compares the real and projected labels to show how accurate a classifier is. The numbers C00, FN10, TP11, and FP01 represent the four possible outcomes in binary classification. TN, FP, and TP are the three types of correct negatives. In order to find out how accurate the prediction was, you may look at the confusion matrix and use the formula: accuracy = (TP+TN)/(TP+TN+FP+FN). For the seven most prevalent malignancies and cardiovascular diseases, Table **1** displays the confusion matrix along with the prediction accuracy. The dataset for this study includes 10,000 observations and 23 feature variables. A quarter of the observations are used for model testing, while the remaining seventy-five percent comprise the training set. After that, we obtained the confusion matrix, fitted the algorithm to the training data, and constructed the decision tree classifier. As shown in Table **1**, the accuracy for lung cancer detection is 1, which is computed as (2,387+113)/(2,387+0+0+113), with 2,387 accurate diagnoses and 113 wrong diagnoses. Table **1** shows that classifier accuracy is either 100% or very close to it. Be aware that there is a classification difficulty about cervical cancer that involves four groups: no screening, Pap test, HPV, and both (Pap test + HPV).

Table 1. validity of cancer and cardiovascular disease predictions.

Disease	Confusion Matrix	Prediction Accuracy
Lung cancer	[2387 0 0 113]	1
Liver cancer	[2216 0 0 284]	1
Colorectal cancer	[1512 0 0 988]	1
Stomach cancer	1265 1 0 1234	0.9996
Breast cancer	2012 0 0 488	1

(Table 1) cont.....

Disease	Confusion Matrix	Prediction Accuracy
Thyroid cancer	2144 0 0 356	1
Cervical cancer	[1584 0 0 0 0 333 0 0 0 0 274 0 309]	1
Cardiovascular	[2149 0 0 351]	1

The second metric was the latency that existed between a client's request and the server's response. Information from more than one user may be included in a single client request. We used a local system (a MacBook Pro with a 2.6GHz Quad-core with an Intel Core i7) to execute 10 tests, and we used Python with the Flask web technology to build a prototype API [11]. For every request, Table **2** displays the lowest, average, and maximum response times. According to the data in the table, it is possible to handle a request with 1,000 users in only one second.

Table 2. How Fast Does the Recommendation Algorithm Respond.

Users	Response Time (sec)
	Min Avg Max
100	0.820 0.837 0.844
1000	0.906 0.914 0.930
10000	1.694 1.711 1.726

CONCLUSION

We provide a health screening suggestion system that is based on machine learning in this study. For each screening question, an artificial set of data based on institutional norms and clinical results is used to develop a neural network algorithm when the internet is not available. Using the client's medical history with a machine learning algorithm, the recommendation server instantly delivers a curated selection of products to the user's web browser. Making condition-specific recommendations for screening items has the potential to maximize efficacy while decreasing expense. Results showed that the accuracy of predictions was excellent and the ability to respond in real-time was feasible when tested on the seven most frequent malignancies and cardiovascular diseases. This research proposes a technique that may automatically construct a prediction model that is both flexible and adaptable to the novel screening environment. We want to investigate methods for suggesting hospitals that are a good fit for the suggested screening items in the near future.

REFERENCES

[1] L. Peng, H. Titus, P. Roellich, and H. Englander, "Adapting Contingency Management for Hospitalized Patients with Stimulant Use Disorder", *J. Addict. Med.,* vol. 17, no. 5, pp. 580-586, 2023. [http://dx.doi.org/10.1097/ADM.0000000000001183] [PMID: 37788613]

[2] Sumesh, S., & H, P.A. (2023). Course Recommendation System based on Natural Language Processing. International Journal of Scientific Research In Engineering and Management, vol. 7, no. 3, 2023.

[3] Y. Doğan, F. Dalkılıç, A. Kut, K.C. Kara, and U. Takazoğlu, "A Novel Stream Mining Approach as Stream-Cluster Feature Tree Algorithm: A Case Study in Turkish Job Postings", *Appl. Sci. (Basel),* 2022.

[4] I. Bakkouri, K. Afdel, J. Benois-Pineau, and G.C.F.A. Initiative, "BG-3DM2F: Bidirectional gated 3D multi-scale feature fusion for Alzheimer's disease diagnosis", *Multimedia Tools Appl.,* vol. 81, no. 8, pp. 10743-10776, 2022. [http://dx.doi.org/10.1007/s11042-022-12242-2]

[5] Samer, R., Stettinger, M., Atas, M., Felfernig, A., Ruhe, G., & Deshpande, G. (2019). New Approaches to the Identification of Dependencies between Requirements. 2019 IEEE 31st International Conference on Tools with Artificial Intelligence (ICTAI), 1265-1270.

[6] X. Ji, Y. Zhuang, Z. Miao, and Y. Cheng, "Vision□based seismic damage detection and residual capacity assessment for an RC shaking table test structure", *Earthquake Eng. Struct. Dynam.,* vol. 52, no. 3, pp. 806-827, 2023. [http://dx.doi.org/10.1002/eqe.3788]

[7] X. Yu, "Global Multi-Source Information Fusion Management and Deep Learning Optimization for Tourism", *J. Organ. End User Comput.,* vol. 34, no. 3, pp. 1-21, 2021. [http://dx.doi.org/10.4018/JOEUC.294902]

[8] Z. Hussain, B. Mago, A. Khadim, and K. Amjad, "An Intelligent Data Analysis for Recommendation Systems Using Machine Learning", *2023 International Conference on Business Analytics for Technology and Security (ICBATS),* pp. 1-7, 2023. [http://dx.doi.org/10.1109/ICBATS57792.2023.10111411]

[9] Rahman, K.U., Ma, H., Arshad, A., & Baheer, A.K. (2022). Movie Recommender System Based On Heterogeneous Graph Neural Networks. 2022 8th International Conference on Systems and Informatics (ICSAI), 1-7.

[10] Q.Y. Shambour, M. Al-Zyoud, A.A. Abu-Shareha, and M.M. Abualhaj, *Medicine Recommender System Based on Semantic and Multi-Criteria Filtering.* Interdisciplinary Journal of Information, Knowledge, and Management. vol. 18, pp. 435-457, 2023. [http://dx.doi.org/10.28945/5172]

[11] [11]. Ramzan, B., Bajwa, I.S., Jamil, N., Amin, R.U., Ramzan, S., Mirza, F., & Sarwar, N. (2019). An Intelligent Data Analysis for Recommendation Systems Using Machine Learning. Sci. Program., 2019, 5941096:1-5941096:20.

[12] S. Sridhar, and S. Sanagavarapu, "Twitter Social Networking Graph using Hypernym based Semantic Similarity Detection", *2020 International Conference on Smart Electronics and Communication (ICOSEC),* pp. 28-35, 2020. [http://dx.doi.org/10.1109/ICOSEC49089.2020.9215279]

[13] L. Tetzlaff, A.M. Purohit, J. Spallek, C. Holmberg, and T. Schrader, "Evaluating Interoperability in German Critical Incident Reporting Systems", *Stud. Health Technol. Inform.,* vol. 307, pp. 249-257, 2023. [http://dx.doi.org/10.3233/SHTI230722] [PMID: 37697860]

[14] K. Wang, Y. Zhu, T. Zang, C. Wang, K. Liu, and P. Ma, "Multi-aspect Graph Contrastive Learning for Review-enhanced Recommendation", *ACM Trans. Inf. Syst.,* vol. 42, pp. 1-29, 2023.

[15] B.O. Khudik. A method of automated generation of recommendations for education applicants based on a hybrid approach. Telecommunication and Information Technologies, vol. 81, no. 4, 2023. [http://dx.doi.org/10.31673/2412-4338.2023.042127]

CHAPTER 3

An Assessment of Big Data Analysis Technologies for Improved Information Delivery

G. Geetha[1,*] and **Kuldeep Singh Kaswan**[2]

[1] *School of Computer Science and Engineering, JAIN (Deemed-to-be University), Bangalore, Karnataka, India*

[2] *Department of Computer Science and Engineering, Galgotias University, Greater Noida, Uttar Pradesh, India*

Abstract: Academic and industry researchers have found sentiment categorization to be an intriguing subject due to the exponential expansion of online reviews. Collecting annotated training data is challenging, but the reviews help with several areas. Despite the development of several sentiment categorization algorithms, information retrieval remains inaccurate, inefficient, and sluggish when it comes to convergence speed. The authors of this article propose using the Spider Monkey Crow Optimization approach (SMCA) as a sentiment classification paradigm for training Deep Recurrent Artificial Neural Networks (DeepRNN). In order to remove inappropriate information and save the user's search time, the telecom assessment is used to eliminate stemming and stop words. In contrast, review sentiment is extracted using SentiWordNet for feature extraction. In addition to the extracted SentiWordNet features, DeepRNN also takes into account supplementary data like hashtags, numerical values, expanded words, and punctuation when classifying emotions. In order to get the required review, we use the distance metric Fuzzy K-Nearest Neighbor (FuzzyKNN). The proposed SMCA-based DeepRNN has been evaluated and tested extensively, and its results in terms of precision (95.5%), accuracy (97.7%), recall (94.6%), and F1-score (96.7%) are superior to those of its competitive models.

Keywords: Big Data Analysis, Improved Information Delivery, Fuzzy K-Nearest Neighbor (FuzzyKNN), DeepRNN, and Spider Monkey Crow Optimization algorithm.

INTRODUCTION

Researchers have started using a movie recommendation system based on sentiment analysis, and recommender systems in general have recently become

* **Corresponding author G. Geetha:** School of Computer Science and Engineering, JAIN (Deemed-to-be University), Bangalore, Karnataka, India; E-mail: geetha.g@jainuniversity.ac.in

popular apps for dealing with information overload *via* tailored suggestions. A new method for emotive categorization is developed in this work, which aids in the recommendation of positively rated films [1]. By sifting through vast amounts of data, recommender systems assist people on the Internet in identifying content that could pique their interest. The addition of social trust connection data to the recommendations system enhances recommendation accuracy, according to recent research. Suboptimal recommendation performance is the outcome of the majority of current research, which focuses on explicit trust connections [2]. Over the last 10 years, several scholars have focused on the subjectivity of social media microblogs, sentiment analysis, and opinion mining. One useful tool that consumers have at their disposal is movie recommendation systems. The data accessible online is steadily rising as the number of users or watchers continues to rise daily. As a result, concerns about computing, analytics, and big data have emerged [3]. In order for online stores to make a profit, recommendation algorithms are crucial. Many other fields may make use of it. Classification of recommendation systems is dependent on whether they are contfor Emotion Labeling.ent-based, collaborative, or hybrid. In the absence of a sufficient quantity of data to generate suggestions, these systems fail [4]. Users trust the opinions of complete strangers while making purchases on a variety of websites. Users seeking to make judgments might benefit to a certain extent from this shared online information since it gives insight into how people view things like goods, services, or events. Outcomes for movies as well as product reviews, blogs, and social media posts have been achieved *via* the continuous study of sentiment identification [5].

Product suggestions, assessments of movies, political campaigns, game forecasts, and many other areas of our lives have been impacted by social media platforms like Twitter, thanks to its ever-increasing pleasant features and the simplicity with which one may share opinions with the whole globe. In most cases, just a small number of people have the clout to sway a whole organization or network to adopt a certain viewpoint. Among the many ideas utilized and researched in the field of social network analysis, "network centrality" ranks high [6]. Blogs, opinions, comments, and postings across many social media platforms populate today's online world. The film business has found sentiment analysis to be a useful technique for automatically classifying reviewers' polarized opinions. Sentiment analysis may determine the quality of a movie review based on linguistic trends [7].

RELATED WORKS

Give an example of a trust model that uses social network activity to determine how trustworthy a user is in [8]. By taking into account both open and closed social trust ties, the suggested trust model not only represents a more realistic and fine-grained degree of user trust, but it also enhances the number of trust relationships. The TrustSVD social recommendation algorithm, which uses matrix factorization, is then updated to include this enhanced social trust data. By comparing our suggested technique to SVD++ and conventional TrustSVD, we discovered that it produces more accurate predictions, leading to better user experiences. This was confirmed by analyzing the prediction results using the Douban-600k dataset, which is available on the Douban Movie website.

In order to make the system of suggestions meaningful and efficient, it is necessary to enhance the recommendation services over the old one, as stated in [9]. To address these problems, this article lays out a distributed Apache Hadoop framework-based solution for producing large-scale, effective recommendation services based on movie scores, votes, Twitter likes, as well as reviews pulled from a variety of external sources by a web bot. A deep semantics analyzer that combines user movie interest (UMA) with recurrent neural networks (RNN/LSTM attention) is used to generate emotions from reviews. A more meaningful movie suggestion list tailored to the user's tastes on a mobile app is efficiently generated by the suggested recommender after evaluating multivariate.

This study aims to apply a deep learning strategy that clusters comparable users based on demographic factors to overcome the initial user cold start issue in recommendations for movies [10]. The suggestions are generated by a deep neural network using this encoding. Our method's efficacy is confirmed by the results of the analysis.

The best match is located by researchers referencing the criteria established in a study [11]. Text categorization is a subfield of NLP that aims to categorize texts according to the meaning and context of a given phrase. Many sentiment analysis text classification methods have been developed utilizing neural networks. The objective of this research is to use the IMDb dataset for movie reviews and apply neural network emotion assessment to them. Here, we focus on CNN-GRU and CNN-bidirectional GRU, two separate multi-branch models. Despite CNN-bidirectional GRU's somewhat better accuracy, the findings demonstrate that CNN-GRU achieved equivalent outcomes using much less training time.

For monotonous submodular maximizing under single as well as multiple knapsack constraints, including scalable implementations in networked and streaming environments, the first adversarially resilient technique was described in [12]. Our technique produces a strong summary of nearly optimum (up to polylogarithmic times) size for a single knapsack limitation, which can be used to generate a constant-factor approximation of the ideal solution. Our estimate gets within a constant factor of the most well-known non-robust solution for multiple knapsack constraints. In order to achieve two goals, we compare our algorithms' performance to that of natural robustifications of preexisting non-robust algorithms: first, the main set for the massive social network graphs compiled by the Stanford Social Network Analysis Program (SNAP) on Twitter and Facebook, and second, movie suggestions based on a set of data from MovieLens. The experimental findings demonstrate that our algorithms outperform offline methods that are provided the set of deletions in advance and provide the optimal goal for most inputs.

This article presents the results of an experiment that used Twitter-specific impact metrics and centrality measurements on a professional wrestling network on Twitter [13]. The article goes on to detail the link between the various methods for identifying prominent users.

The importance of the director of casting to a film's commercial success is discussed in depth in the article [14], which focuses on novel methods for predicting box office receipts by analyzing the organisational structure of the film business. Using publicly accessible data, we construct a “director”-”actor--”casting director”-”talent agent” communication graph and demonstrate that including more information improves the accuracy of movie rating prediction.

The popularity of a film may be predicted using both subjective and objective criteria according to the strategy outlined in [15]. Filmmakers and studios may use this data to better understand public opinion and make educated choices regarding future projects by evaluating audience responses and identifying patterns in movie reviews. It is common practice to use natural language processing methods to extract relevant text elements, including sentiment-bearing words and phrases, before using machine learning algorithms to conduct sentiment assessment on movie reviews. In order to forecast box office receipts, objective methods examine historical data on movies, including budget, genre, and release date, using machine learning and statistical approaches.

PROPOSED WORK

Here, we showcase the proposed SMCA-based DeepRNN, which uses features to do sentiment classification as well as data retrieval across large-scale telecom evaluations. The necessary review may be retrieved from the collection of reviews using this model's information retrieval features. For sentiment classification, the model follows a three-step procedure that begins with pre-processing and ends with feature extraction and classification. When dealing with reviews that make use of sentiments—which make information retrieval easier—the pre-processing is done. In this case, we use stemming and stop-word deletion to speed up sentiment categorization. To begin, pre-processing is applied to the input telecom evaluations in order to remove any unnecessary terms from the keywords. The next step is to use SentiWordNet to extract document keywords using feature extraction. The suggested SMCA-DeepRNN combines SMO and CSA with the goal of choosing suitable weights to process the boundary degree approach. Thus, the suggested SMCA-DeepRNN is used for efficient sentiment classification, while the fuzzy KNN is used for information retrieval. Pretend that D is an input data set that has several properties.

$$D = \{D_{gh}\}; (1 \leq g \leq K)(1 \leq h \leq L) \quad (1)$$

Pre-processing

As a crucial step in efficiently organizing large documents, pre-processing is used here. To get better representations, the papers are treated during pre-processing. By correcting typos and deleting ellipses, the pre-processing may eliminate any possible background noise in the criticisms. First, the reviews are saved in the relational database. Eliminating stop words and other unnecessary jargon from reviews is an important step in improving the performance of the sentiment classification model that has been recommended.

1. ELIMINATION OF STOP WORDS: A word that does not contain any data is represented by a stop word. Eliminating stop words from large-scale manuscripts is known as the deletion process. In order to reduce space and process data quickly, the stop phrase is removed.
2. STEMMING Words may be transformed to their stems *via* the stemming method. Lots of terms that mean the same thing have been altered for use with data sets that are quite large. A method that stands out for its use in root word reduction.

Figuring out Important Details for Emotion Labeling

To improve sentiment categorization and information retrieval, we provide here the most essential features derived from the chosen texts. After SentiWordNet's pre-processing step eliminates keywords, features are extracted. Opinions are extracted using a lexical resource known as SentiWordNet. Using the Pos(s), Neg(s), and Obj(s) numerical scores, SentiWordNet assigns each WordNet synset a ranking. Words have many polarities, as may be shown by applying a lemma to their various meanings. For each word's assessment score, SentiWordNet is the primary tool to use. In order to determine the review's polarity, the SentiWordNet is used. Maximizing performance and eliminating stop words has been achieved by the employment of a voice tagger employing tag words and search. A multi-aspect sentence's polarity was identified using this approach. Synsets may be automatically annotated with positivity, negativity, or neutrality using SentiWordNet. So, we use the SentiWordNet to find out which words in the sysnet are positive, negative, or neutral. For the purpose of emotion categorization, additional information, such as multiple punctuation marks, numerical values, and extended words, is taken from the phrase. After running SentiWordNet, a feature vector F is created consisting of both important and sentence-based characteristics; this vector is then used to train the suggested SMCA-based DeepRNN to classify sentiments.

Using SMCA-based DeepRNN for Sentiment Classification

Telecom sentiment data is classified using the suggested SMCA-based DeepRNN. In order to construct the SMCA-oriented DeepRNN, we first selected the optimal DeepRNN weights using the Deep-RNN model that incorporates SMCA. In order to optimize DeepRNN, the suggested SMCA is used to choose the best weights. Below is a representation of the DeepRNN training process and its structural architecture. 1) DeepRNN's Architecture S is a feature vector that contains all of the features retrieved from the input telecom reviews. The input to the DeepRNN classification is this vector. One way to think about a deep RNN is as a network with many repeating hidden layers. The links between these buried levels are recurring. The classifier is very efficient and can handle input characteristics of different lengths from any source. It incorporated the previous time step's data into the current prediction as well as processed the iteration using hidden state information. Deep RNNs' recurrent nature allows for efficient handling of features. When compared to other deep learning classifiers, the Deep RNN outperforms the traditional approaches by virtue of the sequential patterns of data it uses. Fig. (**2**) depicts the Deep RNN structural design.

At the t-th time step, the Deep RNN architecture starts at the b-th layer. An input vector of features is used to create the output vectors J (b,t) = {J (b,t) 1, J (b,t) 2,... J (b,t) i,... J (b,t) y}. The set S(b,t) has the elements S(1,2,...), S(i,t), and S(y,t). A unit is a member of the input or output vectors in this context. The classifier is described by two variables: i, which represents the b-th layer's random unit, and y, which stands for the b-th layer's total unit. Furthermore, the value of j stands for the random unit number, whereas E denotes the total unit of the (b − 1)th layer. Hence, from the (b-1)th level to the b th layer, the weight of the input transmissions changes and is denoted as W(b) Ɛ A y×E. W (b) Ɛ A y×y is the recurring weight of the b th layer. An A here represents the specified weight. Therefore, Eq. 2 is used to define the units of the input vector.

$$S_i^{(b,t)} = \sum_{z=1}^{E} p_{iz}^{(b)} J_z^{(b-1,t)} + \sum_{i'}^{v} x_{ii'}^{(b)} J_{i'}^{(b,t-1)} \quad \textbf{(2)}$$

Information Retrieval Using FuzzyKNN

However, important characteristics are extracted from reviews that have been pre-processed whenever a fresh question or review comes. In order to get the query information, the FuKNN is used to match the test review characteristics with the categorized database. Therefore, the data retrieval is executed well. Class membership is assigned to a sample using the FuKNN algorithm. Using FuzzyKNN, we compare the features that were extracted with those in the classified database after performing pre-processing and feature extraction. Here, Q stands for the new query. With a set of u information samples, consider the characteristics that have been obtained as F = {f1, f2,..., ft,..., fu}. Let the membership functions of the oth class and the tth vector, denoted as uo,v, and the features ft and ft, respectively, be considered. Equation 3 gives the membership value for the feature ft.

$$u_o(f) = \frac{\sum^{M} u_{v,} u,o,v \left(\frac{1}{} \frac{1}{\|f - f_v\|^{2/p-1}} \right)}{\sum^{M} u_{v,} u,o,v \left(\frac{1}{} \frac{1}{\|f - f_v\|^{2/p-1}} \right)} \quad \textbf{(3)}$$

RESULT AND DISCUSSION

Methods may be tested for recall, F1-score, accuracy, and precision by modifying the training data. Furthermore, the results demonstrate the efficacy of the proposed SMCA-Deep RNN.

Experimental Setup

We run the recommended SMCA-Deep RNN in MATLAB using Microsoft Windows 10, an Intel i3 core CPU, and 2 GB of RAM.

Description of Dataset

Telecom tweets with the Amazon Unlocked Mobile Reviews database (https://www.kaggle.com/PromptCloudHQ/ amazon-reviews-unlocked-mob-le-phones) are among the datasets used for sentiment categorization in the study. A Catalog of Unauthorized Amazon Mobile Reviews (1) In order to find insights about reviews, the dataset in issue is produced from four hundred thousand assessments of mobile phones offered on Amazon.com. A number between one and five can represent the product's rating. There is a price range of 2598 and 226.86 for this product. 2) Tweets about telecom The attitudes of telecom tweets are determined by analyzing their comments, which are retrieved from the Twitter website. We also evaluate the good and negative comments and save them in our database. This database has been customized for use in experiments.

Performance Measures

This section details the performance metrics used for analysis, which include recall, accuracy, precision, and false alarm rate, and is shown in Table **1**.

Table 1. Performance Analysis of the Proposed Work.

Methods	Accuracy	Precision	Recall
CNN	91.2	92.1	91.5
SVM	90	89	89

CONCLUSION

To enhance sentiment classification performance, a Deep RNN is used for sentiment analysis. When dealing with irrelevant data, the suggested sentiment classification method outperforms traditional approaches that use neural networks for sentiment classification. As a hybrid of SMO and CSA, the suggested SMCA is tailor-made for training classifiers to determine appropriate weights. Features derived from input telecom reviews are used to train the classifier. Features are obtained using SentiWordNet, which gave attributes including polarity, uniqueness, positive and negative ratings, a number of extended words, punctuation, hashtags, and numerical values. The proposed SMCA-based DeepRNN model categorizes emotions according to the aforementioned features. Telecom tweets and the Amazon mobile rating unlocking databases are used in the experiments. With an overall accuracy of 97.7 percent, precision of 95.5 percent, recall of 94.6 percent, and F1-score of 96.7 percent, the proposed SMCA-based DeepRNN outperformed earlier approaches.

REFERENCES

[1] K. Rrmoku, B. Selimi, and L. Ahmedi, *Provenance and social network analysis for recommender systems: A literature review. International Journal of Electrical and Computer Engineering.* IJECE. vol. 12, no. 5, p. 5383, 2022.

[2] P. Vilakone, K. Xinchang, H. Lee, and D. Park, "Movie Recommendation System using Social Network Analysis and Normalized Discounted Cumulative Gain", *J. Inf. Process. Syst.*, vol. 16, pp 494-507, 2020.

[3] J.M. Kim, X. Xiao, and I.K. im, "Hollywood movie data analysis by social network analysis and text mining", *International Journal of Electronic Commerce Studies,* vol. 11, no. 1, pp. 75-92, 2020.

[http://dx.doi.org/10.7903/ijecs.1731]

[4] B. Beyhan, & H. Erkılıç. "Evolution of turkish movie cluster: A social network analysis perspective." *METU Journal of the Faculty of Architecture*, vol. 37, no. 2, pp. 187-216, 2020.

[5] T. Zhao, "Mind the Gap: Understanding Gender Inequality in Movie Industry using Social Network Analysis and Machine Learning", *2019 International Conference on Information Technology and Computer Application (ITCA),* pp. 100-106, 2019. [http://dx.doi.org/10.1109/ITCA49981.2019.00030]

[6] M.H. Permata Sari, and U. Budiyanto, *Improving online meeting efficiency using latent dirichlet allocation (LDA) and social network analysis (SNA) methods. Jurnal Teknik Informatika.* Jutif, 2023.

[7] Xu, S., Jin, J., & Yu, H. (2023). Linguistic Characteristics and Stylisation of Korean Cinema Based on the Social Network Analysis Method. Applied Mathematics and Nonlinear Sciences, vol. 9, no. 1, 2023.

[8] R. Sun, J. Yan, and F. Ren, "Improving the recommendation accuracy of TrustSVD *via* trustworthy analysis in the social network environment", *J. Inf. Sci.*. vol. 51, no.1, 2022.

[9] M. Ibrahim, I.S. Bajwa, R. Ul-Amin, and B. Kasi, "A Neural Network-Inspired Approach for Improved and True Movie Recommendations", *Comput. Intell. Neurosci.,* vol. 2019, pp. 1-19, 2019. [http://dx.doi.org/10.1155/2019/4589060] [PMID: 31467517]

[10] J. Panchal, and S. Vanjale, "A Deep Learning Approach towards Cold Start Problem in Movie Recommendation System", *Int. J. Recent Innov. Trends Comput. Commun.,* vol. 11, no. 8s, pp. 81-85, 2023. [http://dx.doi.org/10.17762/ijritcc.v11i8s.7177]

[11] Vielma, C., Verma, A., & Bein, D. (2023). Sentiment Analysis with Novel GRU based Deep Learning Networks. 2023 IEEE World AI IoT Congress (AIIoT), 0440-0446.

[12] D. Avdiukhin, S. Mitrovic, G. Yaroslavtsev, and S. Zhou, "Adversarially Robust Submodular Maximization under Knapsack Constraints", In: Proceedings of the 25th ACM SIGKDD International Conference on Knowledge Discovery & Data Mining (KDD '19). Association for Computing Machinery, New York, NY, USA, 148–156. [http://dx.doi.org/10.1145/3292500.3330911]

[13] K. Chakma, R. Chakraborty, and S. Singh, *Finding Correlation Between Twitter Influence Metrics and Centrality Measures for Detection of Influential Users.* Advances in Intelligent Systems and Computing, 2019.

[14] Karpov, I., & Marakulin, R. (2021). Social Network Analysis of the Professional Community Interaction - Movie Industry Case. ArXiv, abs/2109.01722.

[15] A. Sharma, A. Kalia, and D.S. Sood, "Analysing the Impact of Sentiment Analysis on Predicting Movie Success in Social Network Communities: A Review", *Int. J. Res. Appl. Sci. Eng. Technol.,* vol. 11, no. 9, pp. 1283-1286, 2023. [http://dx.doi.org/10.22214/ijraset.2023.55826]

CHAPTER 4

Analyzing the Effectiveness of Big Data Tools for Analyzing Complex Data Structures

Avadhesh Kumar[1,*] and **S. Santosh**[2]

[1] *Department of Computer Science and Engineering, Galgotias University, Greater Noida, Uttar Pradesh, India*

[2] *Department of Computer Science and Engineering, JAIN (Deemed-to-be University), Bangalore, Karnataka, India*

Abstract: A lot of individuals have been devastated by the COVID-19 epidemic, which has caused a lot of worry, dread, and confusing emotions. A wide range of complicated emotions has surfaced after coronavirus immunizations were introduced. With the use of deep learning algorithms, we hope to decipher their feelings in this study. Right now, there's no better place to let your emotions and thoughts out than on social media. Twitter, in particular, can give you a good sense of what's popular and what others are thinking. To better comprehend the wide range of opinions on vaccination, we set out to conduct this study. From December 21 to July 21, the collected tweets were used in this study. The most popular vaccinations that have lately been accessible worldwide were detailed in the tweets. The opinions of individuals on different immunizations were assessed using the VADER tool, which is a Natural Language Processing (NLP) application. After dividing the responses into positive and negative categories, we had a clearer understanding of the whole issue. According to our numbers, 33.96 percent were in favor, 17.55 percent were against, and 48.49 percent were unsure. While doing our study, we also took into account the timestamps of the tweets because attitudes changed over time. To evaluate the prediction models, the RNN-oriented architecture—composed of Bi-LSTM and LSTM—was used. When it came to accuracy, LSTM achieved 90.59% and Bi-LSTM 90.83%. To further confirm our models and conclusions, we used other performance indicators, including accuracy and F1-score, as well as a confusion matrix. This research lends credence to the goal of global coronavirus eradication and sheds light on public sentiment about COVID-19 vaccinations.

Keywords: Big Data Tools, Complex Data Structures, COVID-19 pandemic, Natural language processing.

* **Corresponding author Avadhesh Kumar:** Department of Computer Science and Engineering, Galgotias University, Greater Noida, Uttar Pradesh, India; E-mail: avadheshkumar@galgotiasuniversity.edu.in

S. Kannadhasan, R. Nagarajan, & Kaushik Pal (Eds.)

INTRODUCTION

Improving national strength with competitiveness in the context of big data is a crucial problem for future international competition, given the rising popularity of big data applications and the fiercening of global rivalry [1].

There have been a variety of contexts, techniques, and methodologies used to study medication adherence. Still, there are a lot of moving parts when it comes to managing drug adherence regimens as a complex phenomenon, and our understanding and ability to measure them all are limited [2]. In recent times, Deep Neural Networks (DNNs), transformers, and ensemble models have shown exceptional SOTA performance in a variety of disciplines, including Computer Vision (CV), machine learning, and Natural Language Processing (NLP), among many more. Along with these benefits come drawbacks, such as models that are computationally too costly, include millions (or perhaps billions) of parameters, and are too heavy to be implemented on the client side of web applications, mobile devices, or embedded systems. To get around these problems (large size & inference computation time), researchers are looking at active model compression approaches like distillation [3]. Constant innovation in financial goods in the age of big data shows high innovation value and immediately drives a considerable revolution in the conventional financial business. Using big data analysis to study and improve the effectiveness of financial product innovation, along with resource allocation, is now crucial [4]. Modern culture jumped headfirst into the information technology age. Big Data (BD) and the Internet of Things (IoT) both came out around this time and will be very important going forward. With the advent of the IoT as well as BD analytics, we are entering an intelligence age, and these technologies are crucial to the success of traditional companies in an era of tremendous integration across many sectors. Modern business management relies heavily on performance management, particularly for SMEs [5]. The spiritual need to fully immerse oneself in the distinctive rural culture and to consistently raise the profile of rural tourism has grown in tandem with the modernization of rural tourism. Nevertheless, the outcome is sensitive to seemingly small changes in components because of the intricate nature of the tourist sector. Hence, conventional wisdom is that the tourist industry's future is completely unpredictable [6]. Improving smart transportation resource management and passenger coverage has become more dependent on driver behavior analysis in recent years. Information such as driving actions, acceleration, velocity, and fuel consumption is contained in the real-world environment by the driver's principles. Because feature assessments and classification do not take advantage of mining information, driving pattern analyses in big data are complicated [7].

RELATED WORKS

A study focuses on researching how China may use big data to bolster its cultural soft power [8]. The paper's authors speculate that this influence stems from Confucian society, which has had a profound impact on China for over two millennia. Confucian principles boost China's soft power culturally in the digital era, which might lead to better living conditions and higher incomes for the general populace.

The study delves deeper into the impact of environmental restrictions on this connection *via* these technologies in its discussion of the link between R&D expenditure and business financial success [9]. From 2007 to 2016, a sample of listed businesses' imbalanced panel data was used, and appropriate regression models were created using logical reasoning. Based on empirical research, we know that R&D spending correlates positively with financial success and has an inverted U-shaped connection with environmental regulatory severity. As a result, the maximum efficiency curve shows that stricter rules lead to a lower level. As a result, companies will be less likely to invest in manufacturing, research and development, and other high-value areas of financial performance as a result of stricter environmental restrictions.

As part of their quality control efforts, the authors of [10] examined the papers that used 91 transcriptomics datasets that were stored in the Gene Expression Omnibus database. Transcriptomics studies include more flaws in their reporting and analysis than one may think, according to this study. In order to improve the basic criteria for generating, analyzing, and reporting gene expression data, this paper concludes with a few recommendations for researchers and reviewers.

Our study in [11] suggests a way to use Patch-Based Convolutional Neural Network models (PBCNNs) and large data analysis to segment brain tumors early on. We use the BraTS datasets from 2012 to 2018. Profiling, cleaning, transformation, and enrichment are some of the preprocessing procedures used to improve the data quality. To measure how well the proposed model works, many indicators are used. A few examples include the precision, sensitivity, accuracy, Dice similarity coefficient, and rates of false positives and true positives. Our research shows that the suggested technique beats state-of-the-art methods for the first brain tumor segmentation. This is particularly true in cases of brain tumors, but the suggested strategy may also help doctors make faster and more precise diagnoses, which improves patient outcomes overall. In addition to demonstrating the promise of PBCNN models in medical imaging research, this study stresses the significance of large amounts of data in this area.

The article delves into the ways in which the Internet of Things (IoT) and its BD analytic technologies may be integrated into enterprise Performance Management Systems (PMS), as well as the potential long-term effects of doing so [12]. Also, this work does some useful empirical research, and the findings reveal that BD capacity has a standardized pathway value for the coefficient (FP) of 0.421 when it comes to financial success. Firms' FP is significantly affected by BD competence ($p = 0.008$, $p < 0.05$), according to the significance test. There is strong evidence that the Internet of Things (IoT) influences firm financial performance (FP) thanks to a standardised path coefficient value of 0.387, a p-value of 0.007 for the significance test, and a p-value lower than 0.05.

Create a system that can assess the effectiveness of vocational education as well as predict its employment rate by using the big data approach suggested in [13]. A large data cross-learning model's hyperparameters are fine-tuned by applying generalized intersected sets to the joint coefficient of loss. As a result, this aids in getting beyond the limitations of large educational datasets. The GSA method enhanced the local features of many data sets obtained from the vocational school quality assessment index. We verify the reliability of the experiment by examining the student and parent vocational education assessment indices, which enable us to accurately assess the acceptability of vocational education. With a prediction accuracy rate that consistently exceeds 91%, the experimental findings show that our technique outperforms the competition when it comes to predicting indicators of vocational school quality evaluation. The method's accuracy in predicting the vocational education rate of employment is unparalleled; it consistently maintains a margin of error of less than one percent. In terms of prediction accuracy and resilience, our strategy outperforms competing large data models.

To address issues with nonlinear interactions, the authors of [14] use the mathematical strategy of BP neural systems to model the brain's neural network architecture. By methodically classifying complicated and variable components, we are able to finish the modeling process and, in the end, acquire effective prediction results. By applying policy-making theory to the study of how tourist resources have changed over time, we find that innovative development follows an S-shaped curve: Initially, just a small number of people embrace it, but after that, it has a period of fast expansion before gradually maturing. This research will be useful in resolving the fundamental issue of how to achieve sustainable development in coastal communities while also minimizing the negative impacts of rural tourism.

A novel, efficient method for analyzing driving behavior patterns based on Fuzzy Logical principles is suggested in the work [15] in order to provide drivers with useful advice. Fuzzy logical choice of subsets is a good starting point for feature selection. Next, the characteristics that were chosen will be assessed using data on common patterns. A multilayer perception system will then be used to optimize these measurements in order to generate behavioral weight. The next step is to use an improved spectral neural network to train the information weights using a test. Lastly, a network of recurrent neural networks is used to categorize behavioral methods for better suggestions by activating the neurons. There is no requirement for experts in feature modeling or machine learning methods to use the suggested approach; it will automatically learn driving behavior characteristics and model temporal information. With an estimated accuracy of 98.4% as well as a rate of accuracy of 86.7%, the proposed framework outperforms the state-of-the-art approaches currently used in simulations [15].

PROPOSED WORK

Kaggle provided the dataset used in this study; it includes various tweets pertaining to COVID-19 vaccinations. Detokenizing data characters allowed us to divide sentences into words as well as label them once we finished preprocessing and checked the unique values as well as null values. Afterwards, a sentiment column was included and computed using the VADER; this column would include three types of values. Following that, the forecasting model's performance was evaluated using deep learning, LSTM, and Bi-LSTM architectures. Fig. (**1**) shows the system's full layout according to the approaches. Collection. Famous vaccinations from companies including Oxford/AstraZeneca, Pfizer/BioNTech, Moderna, Covaxin, Rocket V, Sinopharm, and Sinovac are all part of the "All COVID-19 Vaccines Tweets" collection on Kaggle. The following areas are included: date, location, number of acquaintances, retweets, hashtags, and sources. The dataset in this case has a shape of 125906 by 16.

Prepare, manage, and tokenize data. After removing some superfluous columns, the first step was to scrub the tweets of any URLs or emails. Subsequently, punctuation marks, new line characters, and both single and double quotes were removed. All of the tweets were first tokenized for this processing type, and then all the procedures to remove those messages were applied. After that, they were turned into NumPy arrays by detokenizing them. VADER is the sentiment analyzer tool mentioned. It is designed to operate well with texts from many domains and employs rule-based values that are adapted to the opinions surrounding social networking expressions. As far as social media messaging goes, it works well. Fig. (**2**) displays the results of an evaluation of the sentiment of several lexical properties conducted by VADER using its extensive rules. Vader takes a look at the lexicon's valence values and returns a proportion of text ratios that fall into one of three categories: positive, negative, or neutral. The total probability is 1. The most common metric for sentiment evaluation is the compound score, which is a float value between -1 and +1 that is calculated by summing the lexical word values, adjusting them according to criteria, and then standardizing them to their range. Tools for Visualizing Data 2.5. In order to demonstrate the relationships between the data, the study used several types of analysis. Word clouds, graphs of lines, and bar plots were among the visualizations we used to discover patterns in our information. We utilized several of the prebuilt Python packages for visualization. In order to assess the models, an architecture based on recurrent neural networks (RNNs) known as LSTM was used. We included LSTM and Bi-LSTM in our assessment process. Long Short-Term Memory (LSTM) RNNs take into consideration other RNNs by adding more cells, inputs, and outputs. A Bi-LSTM combines two LSTMs to provide a model for sequence processing. One iteratively advances the input, while the other iteratively reverses it. Bi-LSTMs effectively increase the amount of data stored in the network, leading to better computing accuracy.

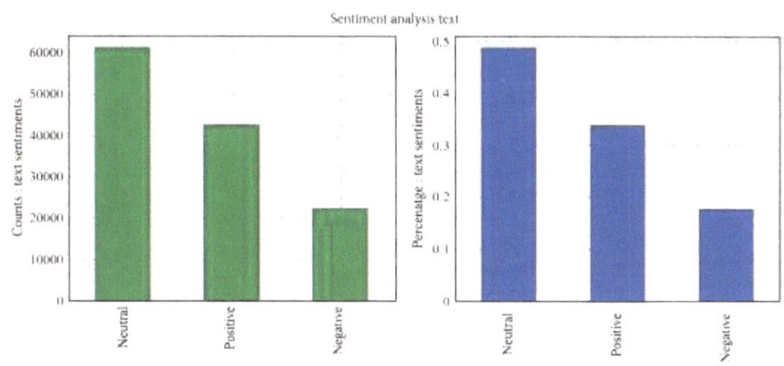

Fig. (1). Sentiment Analysis Result.

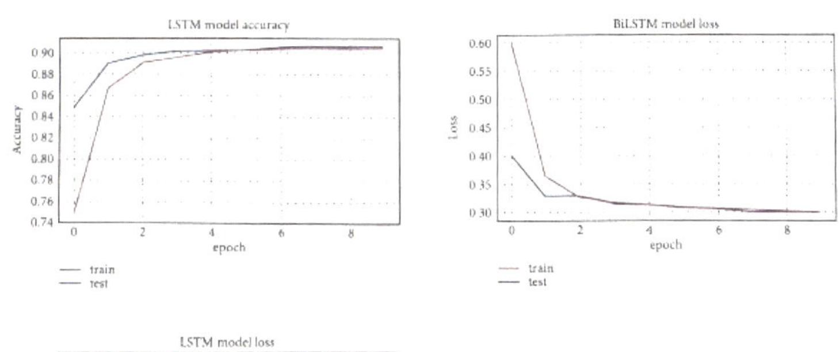

	Precision	Recall	F1-score
LSTM			
Class-0	0.94	0.94	0.94
Class-1	0.85	0.79	0.82
Class-2	0.88	0.92	0.90
Bi-LSTM			
Class-0	0.94	0.95	0.94
Class-1	0.85	0.79	0.82
Class-2	0.89	0.91	0.90

Neutral: class-0, negative: class-1, positive: class-2

Fig. (2). Performance Analysis of the Model.

Fig. (3) shows that the control flow of an LSTM is comparable to that of an RNN. The data is processed and sent on as it continues to move ahead. The input, control, forget, sequence, and output gates comprise the architecture of Long Short-Term Memory (LSTM). An equational description of the LSTM gates is provided. Before we can explain the equation, it is necessary to have a fundamental grasp of the variables used in these calculations. In this context, Wi represents the weight matrix, ht−1 is the output of the previous LSTM block, and bi is the choice for the associated gates. The function of sigmoid activation is used. At last, xt is the current time stamp input, and it is the input gate:

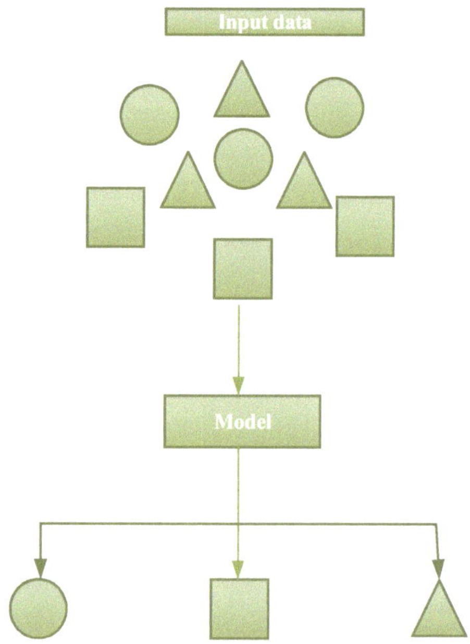

Fig. (3). LSTM Model Inputs and Outputs.

RESULT AND DISCUSSION

Pfizer, as well as Bio, Moderna, Oxford/AstraZeneca, Covaxin as Sputnik V, Sinopharm, and Sinovac are among the most reputable vaccine manufacturers. Our research showed that vaccine responses varied between countries. Our experiment's sentiment analysis relies heavily on hashtag analysis. We then employed ratio analysis to sort the tweets into positive, negative, and neutral categories based on the amount and proportion of responses. Long Short-Term Memory (LSTM) and Bi-LSTM specialized RNNs were used for further model validation. We visually conveyed the results of our comparisons of metrics, accuracy loss, and associated performance assessment indicators. To our delight, our model's LSTM with Bi-LSTM architecture was able to accurately forecast the inputs—the tweets—of individual characters. Wordcloud is a prominent sentiment analysis visualization tool; we used it to present tweets classified as three emotions, which shed light on the tweets' underlying psychology.

Twitter Posts Organized by User Location and Source. The data shown here are the results of our studies of tweets gathered from various sources throughout the world. The most common channel for sharing opinions on the COVID-19 scenario is Twitter, which is also the largest source of vaccination responses. Key phrases such as "dose," "shot," "people," "second dose," and "Pfizer" followed by "Moderna," indicating that individuals had conflicting opinions about COVID-19 vaccines. The most popular words utilized in the UK. They tweeted about vaccinations made in the UK all the time, using names like "OxfordAstraZeneca" and "PfizerBioNTech" and scary terms like "blood clot," "feel," and "trial." The first two figures show the main phrases utilized in the tweets of individuals in India and Canada, respectively. In this context, the terms "first dose," "second dose," "Moderna," "Pfizer," "Bharat BioNTech," "death," "emergency," "Covishield," and "clinical trial" appeared on several occasions. Hashtag Numbers per Tweet. Hashtags are a big deal on Twitter; not only do most users use them often, but they may also convey crucial significance in relation to certain events or trends. The overall amount of hashtags on the x-axis and the average number of tweets on the y-axis, with the most commonly used hashtags shown in red. The Reaction Timeline on Twitter. From time to time, the quantity of tweets changes. From the beginning of the vaccination procedure to the most recent time period, there have been variations in the number of tweets. Fewer than 500 vaccine-related tweets were sent between January 21 and the final day of February 21. However, that number surged to nearly 3,000 on March 21, suggesting that, following the end of the clinical studies and the impending large-scale administration of the vaccines, people were extremely enthusiastic about them. The monthly fluctuation in tweets on COVID-19 vaccines from March 21 to the present ranges from 1,000 to 2,500, reflecting the shifting attitudes of individuals towards them. Examining and assessing sentiment counts and sentiment factor percentages. The total number of tweets categorized as good, negative, or neutral is shown by green bar charts, while the percentages of each group are shown by blue bar charts. The green data is shown with the number of tweets on the x-axis and the various mood categories on the y-axis. On one side of the blue charts, you can see the various emotion classes, while on the other side, you can see the probability distributions. The datasets were used to evaluate 125,906 tweets, which were then categorized into either positive or negative sentiment using the lexicon-based VADER. After analyzing all of the tweets, we discovered 22,094 negative ones (17.55%), 42,765 positive ones (33.96%), and 61,047 neutral ones (48.59%). There was still a lot of misunderstanding, controversy, and uncertainty around the COVID-19 immunization processes, since the majority of tweets were neutral and the negative replies were less common.

Lastly, 91% of favorable attitudes were accurately categorized by the algorithm. The confusion matrix showed that the neutral class was correctly identified by 94% of the respondents, representing the true positive rate (TPR), and the negative class by 73%. Furthermore, 2.6% as well as 3.2% were incorrectly identified as neutral, with the largest proportions falling into the negative emotion group (around 11% and 15%, respectively). The performance metrics are shown in Table **1**. Lastly, forecasts for positive sentiment were accurate, but estimates for neutral and negative sentiment were off by 3.9% and 5.4%, respectively.

Table 1. Outcomes of performance metrics.

	Precision	Recall	F1-score
LSTM			
Class-0	0.94	0.94	0.94
Class-1	0.85	0.79	0.82
Class-2	0.88	0.92	0.90
Bi-LSTM			
Class-0	0.94	0.95	0.94
Class-1	0.85	0.79	0.82
Class-2	0.89	0.91	0.90
Neutral: class-0, negative: class-1, positive: class-2.			

CONCLUSION

In this study, we demonstrate how to apply deep learning methods to problems related to sentiment analysis. In light of the worldwide vaccination efforts, basic natural language processing techniques were able to discern positive, negative, and neutral sentiments. We found that 33.96 percent of voters were in favor, 17.55 percent were against, and 48.49 percent were undecided as of July 2021. A more comprehensive evaluation of our models' sentiment evaluation and forecasting capacities was achieved with the incorporation of RNN-based LSTM and Bi-LSTM. Both the LSTM architecture and the Bi-LSTM model achieved respectable prediction scores in recall, accuracy, F-1 scores, as well as confusion matrix computation, with corresponding values of 90.59% and 90.83%. Even if many people have made up their minds to get the vaccination, there are still others who are uncertain, scared, or just refuse to do so.

REFERENCES

[1] Kim, D., Kan, Y., & Yi, G. (2022). Novel Patrol Route Optimization Method Based on Big Data Analysis. 2022 IEEE International Conference on Big Data (Big Data), 6699-6701.

[2] J. He, "Analysis on the Operation Capability of Tourism Listed Companies Based on Big Data Mining", *Proceedings of the 2022 3rd International Symposium on Big Data and Artificial Intelligence,* 2022.
[http://dx.doi.org/10.1145/3598438.3598449]

[3] L. Li, S. Ma, R.Q. Wang, Y. Wang, and Y. Zheng, "Citizen Participation in the Co-Production of Urban Natural Resource Assets: Analysis Based on Social Media Big Data", *J. Glob. Inf. Manage.,* vol. 30, pp. 1-21, 2022.

[4] J. Wu, C.J. Chan, and J.C. Chieng, *The Innovation of Mongolian Folk Song Music Cultural Inheritance Path Based on Intelligent Computing Analysis of Communication Big Data.,* 2022.

[5] L. Li, "Emotion Analysis Method of Teaching Evaluation Texts Based on Deep Learning in Big Data Environment", *Comput. Intell. Neurosci.,* vol. 2022, pp. 1-8, 2022.
[http://dx.doi.org/10.1155/2022/9909209] [PMID: 35586110]

[6] S. Wang, and S. Fu, "Path Design and Planning and Investment and Construction Mode of Multimodal Transport Network Based on Big Data Analysis", *Discrete Dyn. Nat. Soc.,* vol. 2022, no. 1, p. 9185372, 2022.
[http://dx.doi.org/10.1155/2022/9185372]

[7] H. Nozari, M. Fallah, H. Kazemipoor, and S.E. Najafi, *Big data analysis of IoT-based supply chain management considering FMCG industries.*. Business Informatics, vol. 15, no. 1, 2021.

[8] "RETRACTED: How to Apply Confucian Culture to Enhance China's Cultural Soft Power based on the Analysis of Big Data", *J. Phys. Conf. Ser.*. vol. 1744, no. 4, p. 042028, 2021.

[9] Q. Erna, and M. Deng, "R&D?investment enhance the financial performance of company driven by big data computing and analysis", *Comput. Syst. Sci. Eng.*. vol. 4, pp. 237-248, 2019.

[10] M. Abedi, R. Fatehi, K. Moradzadeh, and Y. Gheisari, "Big data to knowledge: common pitfalls in transcriptomics data analysis and representation", *RNA Biol.,* vol. 16, no. 11, pp. 1531-1533, 2019.
[http://dx.doi.org/10.1080/15476286.2019.1652525] [PMID. 31385553]

[11] F. Ullah, A. Salam, M. Abrar, and F. Amin, "Brain Tumor Segmentation Using a Patch-Based Convolutional Neural Network: A Big Data Analysis Approach", *Mathematics,* vol. 11, no. 7, p. 1635, 2023.
[http://dx.doi.org/10.3390/math11071635]

[12] Y. Yang, "Sustainability Analysis of Enterprise Performance Management Driven by Big Data and Internet of Things", *Sustainability (Basel),* vol. 15, no. 6, p. 4839, 2023.
[http://dx.doi.org/10.3390/su15064839]

[13] L. Wang, "Big Data Analysis Model for Vocational Education Employment Rate Prediction", *Sci. Program.,* vol. 2022, pp. 1-9, 2022.
[http://dx.doi.org/10.1155/2022/7576521]

[14] Y. Tang, and G. Sun, *Discrete Dynamic Modeling Analysis of Rural Revitalization and Ecotourism Sustainable Prediction Based on Big Data.*. Discrete Dynamics in Nature and Society, vol. 2022, pp. 1-9.
[http://dx.doi.org/10.1155/2022/9158905]

[15] M. Malik, R. Nandal, S. Dalal, U. Maan, and D.N. Le, "An efficient driver behavioral pattern analysis based on fuzzy logical feature selection and classification in big data analysis", *J. Intell. Fuzzy Syst.,* vol. 43, no. 3, pp. 3283-3292, 2022.
[http://dx.doi.org/10.3233/JIFS-212007]

CHAPTER 5

Automated Reasoning and Topic Detection in Text Clustering

Ranjana Sharma[1,*] and **K. Vanitha**[2]

[1] *College of Computing Science and Information Technology, Teerthanker Mahaveer University, Moradabad, Uttar Pradesh, India*

[2] *Department of Computer Science and Engineering, JAIN (Deemed-to-be University), Bangalore, Karnataka, India*

Abstract: This work gives a new theoretical approach to interpretative topic modelling. Instead of words or n-grams, this technique analyses complete phrases. Clustering phrase embeddings and probabilistic sentence evaluations in the text corpus is the suggested technique. The topic model estimates sentence frequency distributions within topics and text-wide topic frequency distributions. Our technique provides explicit topic interpretation since sentences are more significant than words and encompass full grammatical and semantic frameworks. The automated process is also provided. Sentence embeddings are produced using BERT-based context embeddings. Our technique also shows that topic modelling may integrate internal and external information sources for large data processing. Conventional topic modelling uses a single text corpus as the internal knowledge source. The external knowledge source is the BERT, a machine learning model trained on huge textual data, which generates context-dependent phrase embeddings.

Keywords: Text Clustering, Topic Detection, and Automatic Reasoning.

INTRODUCTION

The number of Indonesian internet users is expanding quickly. This is supported by data showing that there are 55 million users of the internet in Indonesia as of June 30, 2012, up from only 2 million in the year 2000.

In 2014, there was a 6% rise in internet use data compared to 2013. The number of internet users in Indonesia in 2014 was 88.1 million, as reported by the APJII. This is an increase over last year's total of 71.2 million. The present media

* **Corresponding author Ranjana Sharma:** College of Computing Science and Information Technology, Teerthanker Mahaveer University, Moradabad, Uttar Pradesh, India; E-mail: sharmaranjana04@gmail.com

landscape has been influenced by the ever-increasing number of internet users. One of the key requirements for delivering information to convey the newest news for those who use the internet was identified by the mass media as a change or resolution towards a more sophisticated approach, namely social media, such as news portals. As of June 12, 2012, there were over 2000 news items published daily [1 - 5]. Some news stories with identical titles or content are loaded on many portals, resulting in a proliferation of news stories with identical material. This puts viewers in a difficult position, as they are forced to choose between seemingly similar but ultimately unrepresentative news stories.

The purpose of topic modelling, a kind of statistical analysis, is to unearth these underlying semantic patterns in text retrieval, classification, record annotation, social significance information classification, propaganda recognition, media outlets evaluation, and analyzing social networks, *etc*., are just some of the many uses for topic modelling in the NLP field. The topic model determines the texts' connected subjects and the words that make up each topic. Unobservable model parameters are estimated in the topic model in the form of two matrices, one of which determines the discrete range of probabilities of term occurrence throughout each topic and the other—the discrete probability of topic occurrences within each text [6 - 10]. Probabilistic Latent Semantic Analysis (PLSA) by Thomas Hoffman was the first topic model. In addition, Latent Dirichlet Allocation (LDA) was introduced by David Blei. This framework is a twist on the PLSA formula. As an a posteriori allocation of unknown model parameters, Dirichlet distributions are suggested for use in LDA, specifically for the distribution of words within topics as well as the distribution of topics within texts. Furthermore, the observed text data is utilised in conjunction with Bayesian inference to determine its posterior distribution of parameters. This model's popularity in the academic community has led to the creation of other variants [11, 12].

Additive Regularisation of Topic Models (ARTM) was a method for topic modelling introduced in 2014 by Konstantin Vorontsov. In this method, a particular topic model is decided by selecting a regularizer that imposes constraints on the unidentified numbers of the members of two matrices. In contrast to LDA variants, here only point estimations of unidentified variables are assessed, rather than their distributions estimated using Bayes's method or Gibbs sampling. The ARTM-based topic model now dominates LDA-improved topic models [13, 14]. The ARTM method does this by combining the smoothing of backdrop topics with the decorrelation and sparsity of domain-dependent topics provided by a variety of regularizers. Terms, which might be words, n-grams, or phrases, are the fundamental analytical units for the vast majority of topic models. As a consequence, we may think of the distribution of opinions on any given subject as a series of these atomic building blocks. Since there is no logical relationship between the concepts, this format makes it more difficult to comprehend the results.

Because of this, determining the semantic relationship between them is challenging, and words lose their original context. The meaning of a phrase is usually better conveyed *via* its surrounding context than through the term itself. For this reason, it is crucial to create topic modelling techniques that completely reflect the context in the topics they produce during analysis. The approaches discussed below are meant to address this issue. Some work has been done in topic modelling to take into account the cohesiveness of text parts, such as word order in a phrase [15]. SentLDA, a model that takes into account how often words appear together in sentences, was suggested. The words, however, continue to serve as the primary analytical building blocks here.

RELATED WORKS

In natural language processing, one of the most intriguing and promising avenues for resolving a wide range of practical issues is to make use of the semantic information already present in the texts that are being analysed. In order to get higher-quality outcomes, it is essential to operate with word meanings rather than word labels. In text analysis, for instance, the precise meaning of a word may be gleaned from its surrounding context. When terms are used in comparable contexts, it's likely that their meanings are interchangeable. Using a specialised function that can quantitatively generalise contextual information for particular words in the text's embeddings, it is feasible to compare the senses of other words by examining the connections between their embeddings. With this kind of function that maps keywords in the content to embedded contexts, it's feasible to do semantic evaluation by comparing the meanings of various sub-samples of text. Based on neural networks, Google created the BERT model, a generative transformer, in 2018. For each word or symbol in the text, the BERT model that had been trained produces a contextual embedding. Words or tokens may have their embeddings continuously updated based on their context, according to the generative nature of the BERT model. The semantic closeness of the matching words may be inferred by comparing the analogy of the produced embeddings. It provides several options for integrating a cognitive dimension into various NLP activities [16 - 18]. The text's nuanced meaning may be stored in BERT and then used to address a wide range of practical issues. The BERT is useful since it can adapt to different settings.

In contrast to word2vec, we are not vectorizing word labels but rather their situation-dependent implementations, which may have quite varied meanings depending on the context in which they are used, while having the same spelling. Homonymy and polysemy may be avoided or resolved with relative ease thanks to BERT's application. Applying this paradigm yields state-of-the-art outcomes in a wide variety of contexts since this model was educated on writings gathered from around the web. As such, this model may serve as a repository of information about the world as it now stands. It's like an encyclopaedia or an illustration of our world that may be used as a supplement to what we already know. One kind of transfer learning is the use of BERT embeddings in the procedure of topic modelling. Because of this, we may include outside information in our analysis. BERT's comparative word embeddings capability allows us to draw inferences regarding the relative semantic analogy of pairs of words. However, the individual parts of these embeddings cannot be understood independently. In the proposed method, sentence embeddings are obtained using the BERT model as a weighted average embedding over the words (tokens) that make up the phrase. Other models that provide context-dependent embedded data for sentences may be employed in place of BERT. The challenge of topic modelling may be seen as the figurative vectorization of texts for the sake of interpretation [19 - 22]. When doing a topic examination of a corpus of texts, it is necessary to assign a unique theme embedding to each piece of data. Each part of this embed must reliably and interpretively calculate the likelihood that a given text is on the i-th subject.

To put it another way, we need to go from having a collection of uninterpreted sentence embeddings as pieces of the text to having an unambiguous theme embedding of the whole text. The suggested method yields a thematic categorization of the text; to do this, we must solve a classification problem in which the classes are the subjects. Another crucial component and subtask of topic modelling is automatic topic labelling. Automatic topic labelling is an algorithmic method of producing and choosing sentences that most accurately characterise a subject. Topic labelling is an area that has seen little research and development so far. There have been a few articles written on this challenge since 2007. In most cases, a straightforward method is employed: As a label for the subject, we choose the N most likely words from the topic and provide them in a list format. These catch-all descriptions don't read very naturally, making them harder to decipher. Each subject in the proposed method is labelled with a complete phrase. Since it is far easier for a human to read a whole sentence than a disorganised collection of keywords, using complete sentences as subject labels greatly improves their interpretability. Therefore, the issue of automated topic labelling may be alleviated by treating the phrase as a fundamental element. This makes it easier to identify patterns in the phrases and classify them into distinct themes. The fundamental unit of topic analysis, the sentence, aligns well with the sentence unit used for topic labelling. This UCI Machine Learning Repository's News Aggregator data set is used to evaluate the created method.

A system capable of automatically categorising news was developed by Diptia *et al.* [4]. Using the Automatic Clustering method, the framework was also able to assign news representatives to each cluster in an effort to reduce news repetition. Static or inactive news; or already compiled news, was employed in this investigation. Based on the findings of this research, news representatives may be automatically sent to users by identifying the quantity of groups and news or participants in each group. The automatic clustering process was heavily affected by the link index value. If there were a substantial disparity between the linkages and the clusters/groups, the distance between the clusters would also be larger. However, if there wasn't much of a disparity between the linkages and clusters, then the distance between each cluster would be shrinking. The length of time that had passed since the data was collected also had a major role in how the information was categorised. More information would be collected and organised if the time gap were shorter. A technique developed by Marlisa *et al.* [5] uses online clustering to automatically generate news representations. The system's time-update and new-cluster/group creation capabilities made it possible for dynamic grouping. In the pilot study, the technique was applied to 460 pieces of Indonesian news. The accuracy ratio achieved in this study was 70.9%. Because of this, many articles had only a few keywords because of botched keyword extraction. The grouping outcomes were also impacted by the centroid distribution of keywords. Two news agency websites and four of Italy's most widely read newspapers were evaluated by Francesco Cambi *et al.* [6].

The investigator adapted the Incremental Clustering method to create a web-based application that gathers articles and news every hour. It is used to determine which news is most relevant, how long a piece of news typically remains in a news portal, and the frequency with which the same piece of news is published on many news websites. The TF-IDF formula is used by the researcher to identify common themes throughout each piece of news. Also, the cosine similarity of news stories may be used as a distance metric. The method utilised by the study's authors proved to be both accurate and reliable, with a low computing footprint. Using K-Means and a mini-batch method, SitiRofiqoh *et al.* [7] carried out experiments in the area of topic identification on online news. This study's simulation makes use of nine different RSS-powered news websites. Date of publishing, author's name, title, and brief summary are the information gathered. Following article tokenization, the filter employs a stop list of terms and TF-IDF for weighting individual words. In studies involving topic identification, the centroid was used to represent the central idea. Using K-Means for clustering will be time-consuming for large datasets. However, by using the researcher's suggested method, we may cut down the clustering calculation time by 30–40%, with just a 2-4% loss in accuracy.

The clustering of Arabic papers and news has been the subject of experimentation by Arun Kumar Sangaiah *et al.* [8]. The purpose of the Clustering method is to makc it easier to comprehend or summarise a set of news items. Gathering information from EL-Watan News and EL-Jazeera News is the first step. The news is categorised into one of five broad headings based on human judgement. The next step is the word extractor, which makes use of TF-IDF to tokenize, filter, and assign weights to individual words. K-Means, Progressive K-Means, Threshold + K-Means, and K-Means with dimension reduction were the four algorithms used to classify the news stories. Cosine similarity is used to determine how far apart pieces of news are. For the brand new categorization test case, the suggested technique demonstrates improved accuracy and fewer mistakes. Because it might remove crucial details from each individual piece of news, the dimensionality reduction procedure is very delicate.

PROPSOED WORK

Topic Modeling

The topic model calculates the likelihood of a word appearing inside a subject and the likelihood of a topic appearing in a text [1]. The model estimates probabilities that cannot be directly seen and presents them as the likelihood that a given word will appear in the text.

$$P(w|d) = \sum_{t \in T} P(w|t) \times P(t|d) \quad \textbf{(1)}$$

Word frequencies in the texts are used to calculate the likelihood of terms occurring within the texts. Probabilities that cannot be directly seen but may be approximated using the maximum probability principle and used as model parameters:

$$\sum_{w,d} \ln P(w|d) = \sum_{w,d} \ln \sum_{t} P(w|t) \times P(t|d) \rightarrow \max_{P(w|t),\, P(t|d)} \quad \textbf{(2)}$$

The model parameters must be optimised such that the projected probabilities are in close agreement with the observed ones. It's a matrix decomposition issue, where we're looking for two smaller matrices whose product closely resembles the initial frequency matrix. The paper presents an original way of thinking about subject modelling. The concept relies on breaking down the structure of a phrase into its component parts. A model where the chance of a phrase occurring inside a text is calculated as the product of the probabilities of a sentence occurring within a subject and a topic occurring within a text is presented. Here is how the model is specified:

$$P(s|d) = \sum_{t \in T} P(s|t) \times P(t|d) \tag{3}$$

Each text is used to generate a topic with a specified distribution of probabilities, denoted by P(t|d). The collected data is then utilised to produce a sentence distribution of likelihood P(s|t) for a specified subject. Therefore, there is only one subject in each phrase. Instead of modelling the occurrence probability of the phrase, as is traditionally done, we model the likelihood of its continuum embedding representation, as is described here. As a result, it is presumed that sentences with similar meanings have similar embeddings. That is to say, the embeddings for related phrases are spread out in a sphere of given diameter in a higher-dimensional space. Embeddings of sentences that are not identical to these are positioned outside of this sphere.

BERT Model

Each phrase in the input is a symbol sequence following the BERT model. • output — an embedding representation of each sentence in the collection. The model (3) specifies the mechanism by which sentences in a text are generated. It is necessary to examine every phrase in some representational form in order to assess the likelihood of sentence recurrence. We have the option of using its native representation—a string of symbols—or an embedding. The benefits of the embedding representation make it the preferred representation. A shared meaning may be embedded in an embedding even if two sentences use completely distinct collections of tokens to express the same idea. In order to generate embeddings, many language models might be utilised [21, 22]. We settled on the BERT model due to its excellent performance across a wide range of NLP tasks. Therefore, it is necessary to create an embedding for each phrase in the text collection that takes into account its context. The first step is to separate the material into sentences. To preserve the grammatical, syntactic, and semantic information structures of the sentences, they are then sent directly to the BERT model (Appendix A). Tokenization focuses on the order of words inside a phrase. The BERT model is used to produce the word/token embeddings that are context-dependent. The appropriate sentence embedding is found by taking the geometric mean of the embeddings of the words and tokens that make up the phrase. Token embeddings were then produced through averaging the last four BERT model layers.

Such a dependent-on-context model takes into account the sentence's lexical and semantic structure. The selected model creates more precise embeddings and allows for sense identification in texts as a result of its consistency and contextual reliance. Preserving contextual information about sentences paves the way for more precise analysis and, ultimately, more accurate topic modelling. Expert analysis of the data produced may also benefit from this retained information. Since texts are converted to bags of words or n-grams when employing other fundamental analysis units, this information is lost. The system model is shown in Fig. (**1**).

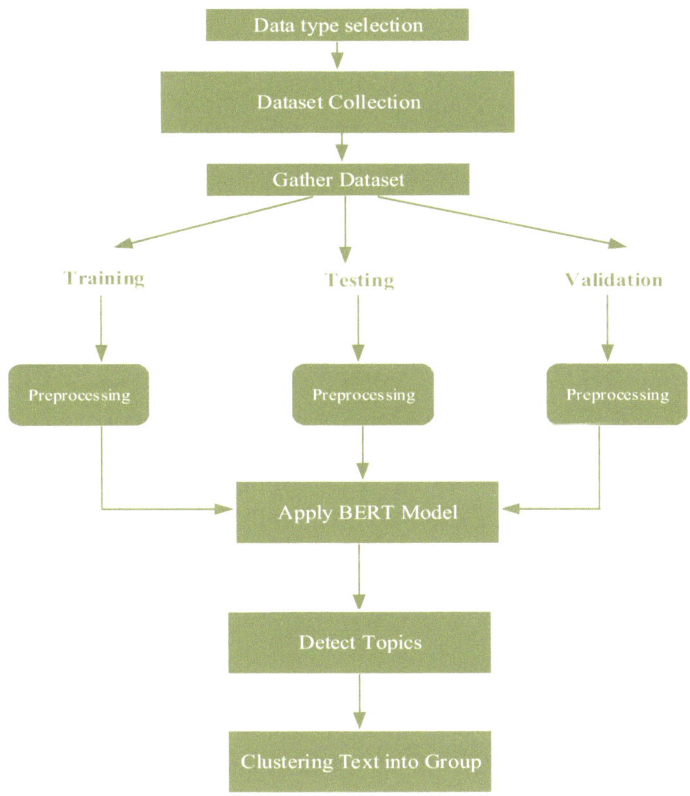

Fig. (1). System Model.

Data Modeling for Topic Detection

Creating the Intended Dataset is the next phase.

- Data input - sentence embeddings from a corpus of text
- Output—a segment of a text collection's sentence embeddings

Previously, we were able to get sentence embeddings. They have to be shown in a completely arbitrary sequence. As will be seen in the next section, they must be organised into categories based on their semantic analogy or theme. We need to employ a clustering technique to group similar sentences together to accomplish this. When dealing with real-world data, however, which is often represented by a sizable text collection, the amount of sentences may be rather enormous, and their grouping on the nest step may demand a sizable amount of computational resources. Thus, it is recommended to gather not all phrases but a random selection from the complete collection of sentences in order to save computing resources. The number of clusters in the subset should be more than the minimum necessary, but far less than the entire number of phrases. Before picking a random subset from the original dataset of sentences, it is necessary to randomly permute the whole dataset. The target dataset is what we'll refer to as this group of sentences inside. The random portion of the initial data set that was produced may be thought of as a reduced, entity-light version of the whole dataset that maintained the geographical structure of the full dataset. We anticipate obtaining comparable grouping patterns inside the smaller dataset after thinning and preserving the original dataset's spatial form. If the size of the original dataset is manageable, then the dataset of interest will be identical to the original.

In such a case, the source dataset is randomly sampled to create the target dataset. The optimal sample size is one that strikes a balance between speed and depth of analysis. In the third stage, sentence embeddings are clustered. Input: a sample of sentence embeddings from the whole text corpus; cluster size. Results: groups of embedded sentences. • Sum of squared measurements as a local criterion. In order to use the topic modelling (3), we need to make a best guess as to the likelihood of a certain phrase being in the text. We may acquire an approximation of its empirical value by counting how often certain sentences appear in a given corpus of texts. A degenerative instance will arise if we have employed a symbolic illustration of a sentence in which practically all phrases have a low frequency.

Clustering Techniques for Text Clustering

We get around this by forming clusters out of related phrase embeddings, where each cluster stands for a certain interpretation. Therefore, we will have more accurate estimations of sentence frequencies if we treat all sentences in the same cluster as equivalent. Here, we divide the target dataset's sentence embeddings into as many groups as there are themes, which is often a whole number of them. The goal of clusters is to group phrases that are related conceptually or semantically by using sentence embeddings. To do this, we may utilise any number of available clustering techniques. For massive data clustering, the smallest amount of squares clustering (MSSC) methods (Appendix B) is the best option since they are effective, easy to use, and widely applicable. The k-means method, which is used for clustering, is the most well-known example of this class of algorithms. The algorithm for k- has several benefits. To begin, it is a powerful clustering method. Second, the quality of the clusters formed may be evaluated according to the objective function, sum-of-squared distances (SSD). Third, it just needs one input, the number of clusters, denoted by the parameter k. There is a logical transition from topic modelling to k-means since this parameter is equal to a variable that defines the number of subjects in the topic modelling. Unlike traditional k-means, which does not guarantee convergence to the worldwide optimal of SSD, we may include more sophisticated metaheuristics like J-means into k-means.

The MSSC algorithm class, of which k-means is the most well-known representative, has the following benefits: high effectiveness, simplicity, the bare minimum of variables, no need for preliminary estimation of a distance matrix, the potential of reaching a global optimum of SSD utilizing advanced meta-heuristic, as well as the possibility of big information processing. This makes k-means the go-to technique for solving a broad range of natural language processing issues that need grouping contextual embeddings. Before clustering, every sentence embedding was normalized using the L1-norm. The first centers were created using the k-means++ method. To assess how far apart any two phrase embeddings really are, we resort to the tried-and-true Euclidean distance for clustering. The clustering output is used to determine the centroid of each cluster in the phrase embedding space. The SSD level may serve as a form of regional criterion at this stage. The improvement in SSD values between the first and last k-means iteration is a metric used to evaluate cluster quality. When the trimmed dataset is utilized as the target dataset, the fourth step is to redistribute all sentences across the obtained centroids. Sentence embeddings, clusters, and cluster proximities all serve as input. Updated clusters are the end result. The majority of sentences were disregarded throughout the clustering process once the first groups were generated from a random sampling of sentences. We need to consider all 22 phrases in Symmetry 2021, which totals 13,837 words; otherwise, crucial details regarding the real-world structure of the cluster would be overlooked. Third, using the reduced clusters as a guide, redistribute the sentence embedded data from the whole dataset among the reduced clusters to produce the entire set of clustering results. We'll have better-representative clusters as a consequence. It is recommended that we update the original clusters, which we will refer to as X, to create more accurate representations of the data, which we will refer to as Y. In the beginning, Cluster Y is equivalent to Cluster X. In addition, we must determine the X cluster closest to each phrase by computing a distance to the cluster's centroid. If the sentence embedding is closer to the cluster centroid than a predetermined threshold value d, then the phrase is added to the appropriate cluster in Y.

This procedure is carried out for each sentence in the whole dataset. Clustering results and similarity between texts inside a cluster are affected by the d value used. Sentences that did not fit into any of the clusters are regarded as outliers and are thus not considered. Cluster-based sentence distribution matrix calculation is the fifth stage. Updated clusters are an input. Sentence probability matrix F is the final result. The probabilities of sentences appearing in the text are modelled using topic theory (3). The frequencies are used to get an empirical estimate of the probability. We treat as equivalent any pair of phrases that share a cluster. At this point, we compute the F-matrix, which represents the sentence distribution over all clusters in the text. When we first create the matrix F, it has zero rows and columns and is of dimension n by m, where n is the total number of texts in our corpus and *m* is the number of groups we created in the previous phase when we embedded sentences. If the considered phrase had been assigned in the jth cluster, we add one to the value for the ith sentence in the text. A vector representing the ith text distribution across sentence clusters may be found in the final row of matrix F. The next step is to normalise the rows of matrix F. Sixth, use an EM-algorithm to determine the model's missing variables. F-matrix is the input. The outputs are parameter estimates, such as the likelihood that a given phrase falls under a certain subject and vice versa.

- Maximum probability value as a local criterion. The expectation-maximization (EM) approach is often employed in topic modelling

In order to determine the model's unknown parameters that maximise the likelihood function, we use matrix F and the expectation-maximization (EM) procedure. The parameters of the model that provide the smallest discrepancy between predicted and actual probabilities (matrix F) must be identified. Estimates of the likelihood of phrases and subjects occurring together in texts are the obtained model parameters (Equation 3). After a certain number of iterations using an EM-algorithm, an estimate of the model's parameters is computed. With these computed odds, we may zero in on the most likely topical clusters. An indication of the EM algorithm's convergence to a local minimum is the value of the local criterion—maximum likelihood. Optional seventh step: Labelling clusters. One medoid, whose embedding is nearest to the cluster centroid, may be chosen to represent each cluster. Let's use this example phrase to describe the group. This gives us a complete set of cluster-to-label mappings.

RESULT AND DISCUSSION

Dataset

The presented method was experimentally verified using the popular News. The Aggregator dataset available from the UCI Data Mining Repository. There are 422,937 references to various media outlets in the data collection. The business, technology, science, health, and entertainment press are all represented in this data collection. The media events that are used to categorise each news article inside its respective category are referred to as "stories" in the dataset. There is only one category and one media event for each newspaper. Three sets of papers, totaling 733, 3338, and 9585, were chosen for the experiment. The 82 articles chosen are all about business-related news that appeared in the media on dates between 4 and 22. We have a topic-labeled dataset since each news story may be treated as its own subject. With this kind of labelling already present in the data set, we have a benchmark against which to measure the effectiveness of our topic modelling strategy. The news stories that are part of our dataset are treated like any other subject matter. Our dataset allows us to see how many articles have been written on a certain subject (or media event). For each reference subject in the dataset, this data will provide the most topical/characteristic terms. To do this, we analyse the publications that fall under the provided subject umbrella and determine the relative frequency of each word in those publications compared to the average incidence of words across all topics. We identify the top N keywords with a ratio of this type as representative of the specified subject. Table **1** provides an example of the selection of such phrases for one of 22 reference themes with N equal to 10.

Table 1. Dataset result.

Dataset	Embedding Scheme	Precision	Recall	F-measure	Accuracy
Topic 1	BERT+EM	94.0	93.0	93.5	93.5
	BERT+K-means	90.0	91.8	90.9	91.0
	BERT+K-means++	89,4	89.9	89,6	89.7
	BERT+DBSCAN	89.0	88.4	88.7	88.7
Topic 2	BERT+EM	95,0	94.5	94.7	94.7
	BERT+K-means	91.0	93.3	92.1	92.2
	BERT+K-means++	90.0	90.9	90.4	90,5
	BERT+DBSCAN	90,0	89.1	89.5	89.5

(Table 1) cont.....

Dataset	Embedding Scheme	Precision	Recall	F-measure	Accuracy
Topic 3	BERT+EM	90.8	93.0	91.9	92.0
	BERT+K-means	89.5	90.4	90.0	90.0
	BERT+K-means++	89.0	89.8	89.4	89.4
	BERT+DBSCAN	88.5	89.1	88.8	88.9
Topic 4	BERT+EM	95.0	94.5	94.7	94.7
	BERT+K-means	93.5	91.2	92.3	92.2
	BERT+K-means++	92.5	91.1	91.8	91.7
	BERT+DBSCAN	90.5	91.0	91.1	91.2
Topic 5	BERT+EM	93.9	93.2	93.5	93.5
	BERT+K-means	91.8	92.1	91.9	91.9
	BERT+K-means++	91.2	91.4	91.3	91.4
	BERT+DBSCAN	91,2	90.8	90.9	90.9
SemEval 2013	BERT+EM	84.7	84.4	84.5	84.5
	BERT+K-means	82.6	83.1	82.8	82.9
	BERT+K-means++	80.9	81.3	81.1	81.1
	BERT+DBSCAN	80.4	80.8	80.6	80.6

Table **1** shows the most frequently used terms in one for the reference areas of the dataset.

Pharmaceutical companies, such as AstraZeneca, Pfizer, and Soriot are all significantly undervalued.

Acquisitions in the pharmaceutical sector are relevant to our discussion. Drugs and major pharmaceutical firms are the focus of the preceding list. Our topic model's accuracy will be evaluated by counting how often each topic-relevant word appears in the sentence clusters that best represent each subject's most likely clusters. Each reference subject's most relevant terms should, ideally, be located in their own sentence cluster inside the derived topic model. For each pair of reference topical terms, we must determine which model sentence cluster has the greatest quantity of those words. The initial quality estimate is based on an average of these numbers, one for each referenced subject. It's possible that there are a few phrases of noise in every cluster. Only the terms with comparatively high frequency in the phrase clusters are evaluated in the estimate procedure, eliminating their impact on quality evaluation.

First, the BERT model was used to determine a context-dependent embedding for each phrase in each dataset. As a result, 71,097 sentence embeddings were constructed for the dataset including 22 subjects. One random phrase per text was used to construct the reduced target datasets. In all, 3338 sentences and their embeddings were chosen at random. The embeddings of the target dataset were clustered in step three of the procedure. The k-means++ technique was used to generate random centroid values between 100 and 4000, with a step size of 100. The optimal number of clusters (starting topics) was found to be 1000 by experimental analysis. In the final stage, the threshold value for a phrase to be incorporated into a cluster was set to 0.1.

It was determined that F is a matrix. The EM method was used on the matrix F, which has the dimensions 3338: 1000. The most likely sentences within a subject are identified based on the estimations of their occurrence probability that were collected. Values Criteria for Quality. Using the derived model parameters, the quality of the topic modelling is assessed. How well sentences are organised into subjects is reflected in the first criterion's value. In contrast, the second criterion's score reflects how well various themes are dispersed within texts. We iterated through stages 3-6 of the algorithm 100 times and determined the average as well as the standard deviation of criterion values. Words that were uncommon (appeared fewer than three times in a cluster of sentences) were counted as negatives for the first criterion.

Sentence frequencies inside a topic were given a probability using the topic model. For instance, probabilities of 0.14 and 0.12 were given to the two most likely clusters containing phrases from the first subject, respectively. These pockets are associated with the Patient Protection and Affordable Care Act, or Obamacare. Word-based topic modelling on the provided annotated dataset yields the following results: 14.95% meets the first requirement, while 80.12% meets the second. Word probabilities were given by the model. Bag-of-words themes are less open to interpretation than sentence-based ones. If we think of a subject as a collection of words, we typically must determine what it is, and we have to build the mental connections between the words ourselves if we want to speed up the process. Sentences provide the basis for a more nuanced understanding of themes. Now that readily-understood themes are given as unified syntactic and semantic wholes, word associations are unnecessary.

The first factor is how well researched and relevant the resulting subjects are. The effectiveness of text embeddings is evaluated using the second criterion. Since the major goal of the topic modelling application is to extract latent themes in texts, the first criterion takes priority over the second. Many different techniques exist if simply text embeddings are needed (interpretative text embeddings are an exception to this rule). While the created method does provide higher-quality topics than the gold-standard method, it's important to remember that the two subject models were built using separate analysis units. As was mentioned above, the created method represents a novel conceptual viewpoint in which sentences, rather than words, serve as fundamental units of analysis. This is a novel approach to topic modelling, and further work is needed to address the challenge of comparing topic models built on distinct analytical foundations. Number of topics is a parameter of the topic model. Before the EM algorithm can be executed, the value of the parameter must be set. We are aware of the 22 predetermined themes in dataset 2. We want to see how the criterion values shift if we don't know the precise number of subjects, since this will tell us whether the method is resilient. Fig. (**1**) demonstrates that a larger number of themes raises the value of criterion 2 while very slightly lowering the level of criterion 1.

Usefulness for massive data sets. The created method relies only on the final point clustering stage to be applicable to huge amounts of data. The method may be used for a huge data collection as well, provided an appropriate clustering technique is chosen to deal with the scale of the data. For instance, the clustering technique described works well with large datasets. The proposed method's other phases may be simply adapted for use with huge data.

CONCLUSION

A fresh conceptual strategy for the subject modelling issue is introduced. Instead of using phrases or words as the fundamental (atomic) unit of analysis, the whole sentence is utilised. The BERT model was used to produce a context-dependent embedding for each phrase. One key aspect of the suggested method is determining how likely it is for a given phrase to appear in a given text; this information is then used by the topic model to determine how likely it is for a given subject to appear in a given text. The created method was tested on the News The aggregation data to ensure its accuracy. The results of the carried out numerical experiments validate the sufficiency of the suggested model and demonstrate the high interpretability of the resulting subjects. Since n-grams were the only units the subject models worked with previously, the presented technique represents a fundamentally novel description of the topic modelling job. More interpretable findings may be obtained than with conventional topic modelling methods due to the high-level character of a phrase as a fundamental unit, its integrity, and self-sufficiency. Positive impacts on applications based on topic modelling may also arise because details on syntactic and semantic coherence among words in texts are preserved during modelling. As a result, we may hope to see enhanced accuracy and efficiency in topic modeling-based applications. In other words, the technique gives significantly greater interpretability, and other topic modeling-based approaches may show improvement in results due to the preservation of textual coherence using the generated topic model. The acquired topics are also well-suited for automated topic labelling due to the greater clarity with which sentences may ascertain the subjects' scope and meaning. Sentences, rather than word lists, are more easily understood by humans as subject headings. The method that was created is an application of transfer learning. The advancement and widespread use of neural network language models have facilitated advancements in natural language processing. Many fields make use of transfer learning. This includes subject modelling as well, it seems.

REFERENCES

[1] T. Ji, Y. Wu, C. Wang, X. Zhang, and Z. Wang, "The Coming Era of AlphaHacking?: A Survey of Automatic Software Vulnerability Detection, Exploitation and Patching Techniques", *2018 IEEE Third International Conference on Data Science in Cyberspace (DSC),* pp. 53-60, 2018. [http://dx.doi.org/10.1109/DSC.2018.00017]

[2] F. Wotawa, and D. Kaufmann, "Model-based reasoning using answer set programming", *Appl. Intell.,* vol. 52, no. 15, pp. 16993-17011, 2022. [http://dx.doi.org/10.1007/s10489-022-03272-2]

[3] D.C. Brock, O. Babko-Malaya, J. Pustejovsky, P. Thomas, S. Stromsten, and F. Barlos, "Applied Actant-Network Theory: Toward the Automated Detection of Technoscientific Emergence from Full-Text Publications and Patents", *AAAI Fall Symposium: Social Networks and Social Contagion,* 2012.

[4] P.W. Foltz, M. Rosenstein, and K.E. Lochbaum, *Improving performance of automated scoring through detection of outliers and understanding model instabilities.*. Conference: National Council on Measurement in EducationAt: San Francisco, 2013.

[5] N. Said, H. Fischer, and G. Anders, "Contested science: Individuals with higher metacognitive insight into interpretation of evidence are less likely to polarize", *Psychon. Bull. Rev.,* vol. 29, no. 2, pp. 668-680, 2022. [http://dx.doi.org/10.3758/s13423-021-01993-y] [PMID: 34716563]

[6] N. Said, H. Fischer, and G. Anders, "Contested science: Individuals with higher metacognitive insight into interpretation of evidence are less likely to polarize", *Psychon. Bull. Rev.,* vol. 29, no. 2, pp. 668-680, 2022. [http://dx.doi.org/10.3758/s13423-021-01993-y] [PMID: 34716563]

[7] M.R. Gallagher, J.P. Hogan, and F. Maire, "Intelligent Data Engineering and Automated Learning - IDEAL 2005", *6th International Conference,* 2005. Brisbane, Australia [http://dx.doi.org/10.1007/b137888]

[8] H. Han, and W. Liu, "The coming era of artificial intelligence in biological data science", *BMC Bioinformatics,* vol. 20, no. S22, suppl. Suppl. 22, p. 712, 2019. [http://dx.doi.org/10.1186/s12859-019-3225-3] [PMID: 31888432]

[9] C.E. Kahn. Artificial Intelligence, Real Radiology. Radiol Artif Intell, vol. 30, no. 1: p. e184001, 2019.

[10] Roussaki, I., Papaioannou, I., & Anagnostou, M. (2009). Shortening Automated Negotiation Threads via Neural Nets. In: J. Rabuñal Dopico, J. Dorado, & A. Pazos (Eds.), Encyclopedia of Artificial Intelligence (pp. 1418-1425). IGI Global Scientific Publishing. [http://dx.doi.org/10.4018/978-1-59904-849-9.ch208]

[11] Y. Dimopoulos, and P. Moraitis, *Advances in Argumentation-Based Negotiation.*. In: F. Lopes and H. Coelho. Negotiation and Argumentation in Multi-agent Systems, pp. 82-125, 2014.

[12] A.O. Science, "International Symposium on Wen-Tsun Wu's Academic Thought and Mathematics Mechanization", *ACM Commun. Computer Algebr.,* vol. 53, no. 4, pp. 155-181, 2020. [http://dx.doi.org/10.1145/3388974.3388975]

[13] Nasa (2019). NASA Tech Briefs, April 2013.

[14] Barrett, C.W., and Kahsai, T. (2018). Selected Extended Papers of NFM 2017: Preface. Journal of Automated Reasoning, 1-2.

[15] D. Radenkovic, S.B. Keogh, and M. Maruthappu, "Data science in modern evidence-based medicine", *J. R. Soc. Med.,* vol. 112, no. 12, pp. 493-494, 2019. [http://dx.doi.org/10.1177/0141076819871055] [PMID: 31526210]

[16] D. Greene, and P. Cunningham, "Practical Solutions to the Problem of Diagonal Dominance in Kernel Document Clustering", *Proceedings of the 23rd International Conference on Machine learning (ICML'06),* ACM Press: New York, NY, USA, pp. 377-384, 2006.Pittsburgh, PA, USA [http://dx.doi.org/10.1145/1143844.1143892]

[17] D. Cer, Y. Yang, S.Y. Kong, N. Hua, N. Limtiaco, R.S. John, N. Constant, M. Guajardo-Cespedes, S. Yuan, and C. Tar, "Universal Sentence Encoder for English", *Proceedings of the 2018 Conference on Empirical Methods in Natural Language Processing: System Demonstrations,* pp. 169-174, .Brussels, Belgium

[18] R. Aharoni, and Y. Goldberg, "Unsupervised Domain Clusters in Pretrained Language Models", In Proceedings of the 58th Annual Meeting of the Association for Computational Linguistics, pages 7747–7763, Online. Association for Computational Linguistics. [http://dx.doi.org/10.18653/v1/2020.acl-main.692]

[19] B.S. Everitt, *Cluster Analysis.* John Wiley and Sons Ltd.: Chichester, West Sussex, UK, 2011. [http://dx.doi.org/10.1002/9780470977811]

[20] R.O. Duda, P.E. Hart, and D.G. Stork, Pattern Classification, 2nd Edition, John Wiley and Sons, Inc., New York, 2001.

[21] A.V. Orekhov, "Markov stopping time of an agglomerative clustering process in Euclidean space. Vestn. St.-Peterbg", *Univ. Prikl. Mat. Inform. Protsessy Upr.,* vol. 15, pp. 76-92, 2019. [In Russian].

[22] A.V. Orekhov, "Approximation-evaluation criteria for the stress-strain state of a solid body. Vestn. St.-Peterbg", *Univ. Prikl. Mat. Inform. Protsessy Upr.,* vol. 14, pp. 230-242, 2018. [In Russian].

CHAPTER 6

Automated Reasoning Tools and their Application in Text Mining

G. Sindhu Madhuri[1,*], **Tushar Mehrotra**[2] and **S. Kannadhasan**[3]

[1] *Department of Computer Science and Engineering, JAIN (Deemed-to-be University), Bangalore, Karnataka, India*

[2] *College of Computing Science and Information Technology, Teerthanker Mahaveer University, Moradabad, Uttar Pradesh, India*

[3] *Department of Electronics and Communication Engineering, Study World College of Engineering, Coimbatore, Tamil Nadu, India*

Abstract: Data mining is an application that searches for information in various databases in order to discover new facts and patterns. Conventional data processing technologies and applications are inadequate for handling the massive amounts of data available in SMEs today. Important for SMEs' decision-making is the adoption of efficient and effective data mining tools. This study describes and analyzes seven popular open-source data mining tools: KEEL, KNIME, Orange, RapidMiner, R Project, Tanagra, and WEKA.

Keywords: Automated Reasoning Tools, Application in Text Mining, SMEs' decision-making, data mining scans data sources, Data processing tools.

INTRODUCTION

With the proliferation of both software and computer networks, the potential harm that may be inflicted by such assaults has skyrocketed. Achieving low-effort, high-reward traffic monitoring and finding requires efficient identification of anomalous network activity. When providing automated services for a variety of applications, it is crucial to have reliable methods for detecting suspicious Internet traffic [1]. It is becoming more critical to manage data processing activities as well as the resources used by them as the volume of data continues to expand. Users are increasingly executing their work in the cloud since maintaining an individual architecture is either infeasible or unprofitable. Several approaches

* **Corresponding author G. Sindhu Madhuri:** Department of Computer Science and Engineering, JAIN (Deemed-to-be University), Bangalore, Karnataka, India; E-mail: g.sindhumadhuri@jainuniversity.ac.in

S. Kannadhasan, R. Nagarajan, & Kaushik Pal (Eds.)

have been suggested to swiftly profile towards an optimal configuration or to find one using information from prior runs, as configuring workloads as well as resources is often difficult. However, training such techniques using performance data is often difficult and expensive [2]. The use of geothermal energy is on the rise due to North China's booming economy. Locating promising areas in North China for deep geothermal resource extraction is an immediate priority. Despite the widespread distribution of geothermal assets in the northern China Plain, choosing targets and assessing thermal resource management are crucial for the safe, stable, and efficient development of deep geothermal assets in North China [3]. Healthcare organizations rely on engineering project management services for a variety of reasons, including the development, implementation, and oversight of healthcare-related infrastructure as well as technological initiatives. Data mining methods used in engineering project management might maximize allocation of resources, decision-making, and project planning and execution. Data mining is the process of discovering hidden patterns, correlations, and trends in massive datasets by the use of automated extraction of information rather than human study [4].

The old advertising paradigm of businesses is being tested by the ever-increasing amounts of consumer data. Businesses are gradually shifting from passive to active marketing as a result of the fast development of data mining technologies, which has sparked novel concepts in marketing methods. The primary goal of technology for data mining is to examine data, gain an understanding of the relationship between variables, and ultimately make predictions about the future. Consequently, businesses integrate technology with their advertising campaigns and then use big data to construct an accurate advertising model [5]. The proliferation of online communities not only produces an enormous amount of data but also causes dramatic changes in our everyday lives. We can learn a lot about people's online communication, interaction, and working styles by analyzing massive data from social media. In addition, designers might benefit from this information as they work to enhance social media platforms to better meet the demands of users. In light of this, research into mining and analyzing large amounts of social media information has become one of the most active and promising fields in recent years [6]. There will be significant shifts in managerial responsibilities and business procedures brought about by the advent of artificial intelligence (AI). Artificial intelligence is reshaping organizational leadership and decision-making. Key competences and business processes, like managing knowledge, are showing the impacts of AI. Consumer outcomes like perceptions of service quality as well as satisfaction are also showing the effects of AI [7].

RELATED WORKS

This work presents ODFM, a new method for detecting anomalous traffic that relies on data feature optimization and mining. To cut down on data detection and make anomalous traffic detection easier, we create a feature selection approach to lower the feature research dimensions and set up a P2P (peer-to-peer) traffic identifying module to filter as well as mine the associated service traffic. The suggested method has proven to be successful and competitive in the broad tasks of anomalous network traffic identification [8], thanks to experimental findings that show a significant improvement in detection accuracy.

We provide a cooperative method in this study for users to share anonymised execution records of workloads, mine them for patterns, and leverage clusters of past workloads to optimize future optimizations. Using a publicly accessible trace dataset, we assess our initial solution for mining activity implementation graphs, as well as show that work groups generated from traces alone have predictive power [9].

From an extensive data mining vantage point, this work sheds light on the restricted hydrocarbons manufacturing procedure and provides a practical and precise way to forecast production as well as assess the economic viability of projects in the Cardium deposit. More than fifty factors related to Cardium formation are included, and for the first time, several artificial intelligence techniques are described and evaluated using information from technology, petrophysics, and geology. The approach presented in this research may be readily used to reliably anticipate output from additional unusual fields and formations, including the Montney, Eagle Ford, Fuling, and Bakken Shale plays, provided that the necessary data is available [10].

Using synthetic EM data, the suggested approach was thoroughly evaluated. A CMD2 (GF Instrument) EM equipment with GPS was used to regulate its efficiency, which was based on minimal actual data. When utilizing the Advanced Mode, the automated identification of unmineable inclusions became much more accurate. However, the Simple Mode computing method has the dual benefit of allowing real-time examination of the dug mine slope and being independent of equipment location. The approach for rock inclusions identification is introduced in this paper, which may help optimize mining operations by making them safer, more efficient, saving money, and less harmful to the natural world [11].

In order to improve the company's precise advertising model's clustering performance, as well as the K-means algorithm's sensitivity to cluster center setting up, our work optimizes and extends the K-means algorithm in conjunction with the artificial colonies of bees algorithm. Implementing evaluation and forecasting of telecom clients and conducting exact marketing based on expected discoveries are both made possible in the telecom business's precise marketing scenario by the use of the upgraded K-means clustering algorithm. Based on the algorithm's real verification findings, the improved K-means clustering method will ultimately represent the features of telecom client value segmentation in an objective and comprehensive way, allowing firms to effectively mine prospective customers while eliminating blind marketing. All at once, it shows the way forward for expanding the market and gives telecom businesses a solid foundation on which to build their capital plans [12].

Applying the suggested method to the WDN "L-Town" assumption allows us to identify as well as separate the leakage incidents that occurred in both 2018 and 2019. According to the findings, leakage incidents in 2018 exposed and might forecast potentially problematic leaking locations and times. With this forecast in hand, we may use an isolation approach based on genetic algorithms to pinpoint the precise node or pipe where the leak is occurring. We compare the outcomes of iterative water leak calculations conducted by the EPANET machine with SCADA data. There is a high degree of certainty that the modeled leak event is a genuine network leakage, according to the most matched simulation. L-Town uses this detection as well as an isolation method, utilizing 2018 SCADA information, as well as a reported leakage list. Data categorization models identified and separated all ten confirmed leaks in 2018. The suggested method seems to be working well, as the anticipated leakage sites are near the actual ones. After that, in 2019, L-Town will use the method to find and fix any leaks [13].

Improving the precision of the model, this technique makes use of many sorts of data for optimizing, including ion equilibria positions in linear strings, trap frequencies, and the location of a single ion. In comparison to the predictions made by the current approach, the anticipated secular frequencies have an inaccuracy of less than 0.5%, as the average ion location is less than 1.2 μm [14].

Data analysis is the focus of this article because of its potential use in the modeling and enhancement of the company's operational procedures. Using a combination of machine learning and Business Process Management (BPM), Process Mining is a set of tools for data-driven diagnostics and process optimization [15 - 20]. Process mining has several benefits, one of which is improved decision-making by managers. An examination is conducted into the potential integration of procedure mining techniques into a telecommunications company's operations with the aim of automating the gathering of data pertaining to business processes and the construction of a procedure map. A telecoms business may maximize departmental efficiency and customer happiness with the application of Processing Mining techniques. The outcomes of carrying out business operations to supply Internet access may also be properly analyzed with the help of this kind of technology. The procedure for producing high-quality management choices, as well as the rules governing these procedures, will be enhanced as a result [21 - 24].

PROPSOED WORK

Many iterations of the KDD approach have been built upon its own framework. The KDD process is divided into six areas: company comprehension, data comprehension, preparing the data, modeling, evaluation, and deployment. One variant of this is the Cross-Industry Standard Procedure for Data Mining (CISP-DM). For many in business leadership, this conventional wisdom is foreign territory when it comes to data mining. Accordingly, the process was simplified into a model requiring only three steps: Data preparation for input into software for data mining is known as preliminary processing. The goal of this stage is to put together a data collection that is both large enough to hold the necessary data and small enough to analyse in a reasonable period of time. In this stage, the data is additionally cleaned by removing noise and missing nodes that don't provide any value and may be skipped during analysis. Data mining is a process that leverages a number of different areas of study to draw conclusions. These areas include databases, statistics, machine learning, and artificial intelligence. "Results Validation" refers to the process of studying the Data Mining stage's outcomes. Analysts do this human work, and the method is extremely flexible based on the particular objectives of the organisation that is deriving value from the data.

According to our findings, the best data mining tools are: KEEL, KNIME, Orange, RapidMiner, Tanagra, R Project, and WEKA.

KEEL

Knowledge Extract Using Evolutionary Learning (KEEL) is a tool that empowers users to do a multitude of tasks connected to knowledge discovery in datasets. This open-source Java application is groundbreaking because it incorporates a library of evolutionary algorithms. Algorithms designed to adapt and improve with each new input are known as evolutionary algorithms. The user may test out various datasets and algorithms thanks to the straightforward GUI that is built on data flows. Because it simplifies understanding and rating algorithm behavior and efficacy, it is a highly useful tool. Data mining tasks like pattern mining, clustering, regression, classification, and many more are the major emphasis, with an emphasis on algorithmic evolution for pre- as well as post-processing. The goal of developing KEEL was to provide a tool with great research and teaching potential; it incorporates pre-processing methods, conventional methods of data extraction, algorithms based on artificial intelligence, mixed approaches, as well as statistical ways to evaluate results. It is organised into seven functional blocks that classify the user experience according to the user's research interests and degree of experience. Data Management, Experiment Design, and Imbalanced Experiment Design. This framework is built upon educational experiments, statistical tests, research with multiple example algorithms for learning, and semi-supervised learning algorithm experimentation. 3.0 is the latest version that has been stabilized. The GNU General Public Licence governs its licensing. The advantages of KEEL are:

A straightforward GUI based on the idea of data flows.

Function blocks that divide the user experience into categories.

KNIME

KNIME is a dashboard for businesses that tries to help them remain ahead of the curve by using data expertise. An adjustable learning curve that considers the amount of effort and time that every user desires to put into utilizing the tool is offered by the considerable degree of customization. Because it is purely visual and does not need any code, the user can focus on interacting with the data rather than worrying about implementation specifics. It is ideal for use in educational as well as business environments due to its modular and extendable API and its foundation in the Eclipse IDE. It offers strong capabilities for activities like pre-processing, cleaning, modelling, analysis, and mining by offering hundreds of distinct processing nodes. An advantage is the extensive compatibility with additional data mining programs, such as R and Weka. While the KNIME Analytic Platform itself is free to use under the General Public License of the GNU, version 3, there is a paid upgrade option available **via** the KNIME Business Software. Among KNIME's benefits are:

A high degree of customisation that adjusts the user's learning curve.

Constructed using the widely used Eclipse IDE.

Simple data mining tool integration.

Orange 3.3

Developed by the Bioinformatics Department at the University of Ljubljana, Orange is a freely available tool for visualizing and analyzing data. It provides resources to do Data Mining tasks graphically and with the help of Python scripting. The core package gains more possibilities for tasks like text mining as well as bioinformatics, among others, thanks to the great degree of expansion that is accessible **via** add-ons, which is basically its fundamental strength. It has a ton of machine learning and analytics features packed inside it. Featuring nine intuitive categories—data, visualization, regression, classification, assessment, learning without supervision, organization, bioinformatics, as well as prototypes—Orange Canvas is a visually appealing and intuitive interface for data analysts. Fig. (**1**) shows an example of the Orange Canvas Interface. Widgets, which represent the features that may be put and connected between them in the visualisation area in the most natural way, were developed to further boost such usability. Orange's drawback is that it is less comprehensive than other available tools. The GNU General Public Licence, version 3, governs its most recent stable version, which is 2.7. The primary characteristics of orange are:

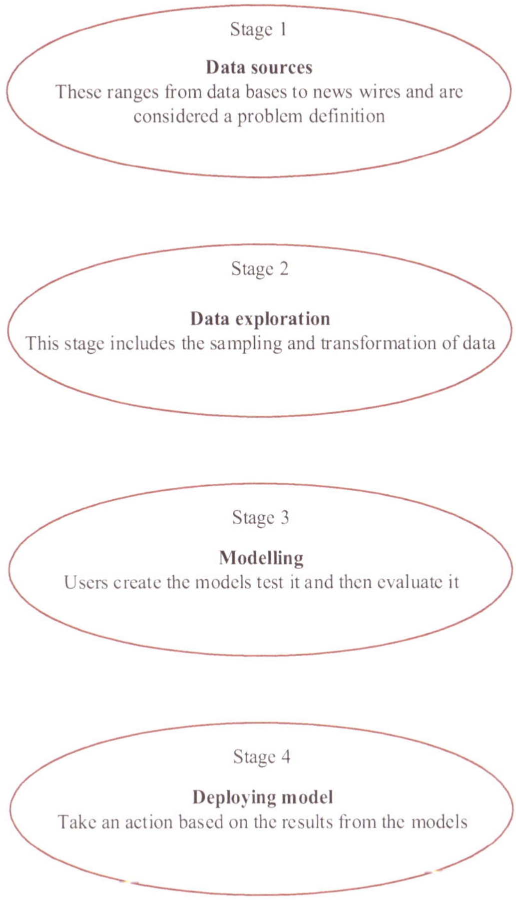

Fig. (1). Data Processing Model.

- Python script writing is supported **via** both a GUI and a command-line.
- The grouping of functionality into nine easily understandable categories.

RapidMiner

Alongside data analysts, RapidMiner is a statistical analysis program made for developers, company managers, and everyone else who enjoys this domain. With its intuitive graphical user interface, the open-source version of RapidMiner, also known as Studio, makes it easy to carry out tasks related to data management without the need for programming. The app is easy to use and connects users to a support network of over 250,000 individuals. This community offers benefits, including quick tool updates as well as quick and effective help for new users. For those who don't have much time to spend on the learning curve, RapidMiner is quite tempting because of the aforementioned features. Numerous methods for data processing, modelling, and visualisation are available in RapidMiner. The end user, however, has access to an extensible API that allows them to upgrade the tool and include their own customized algorithms. The fact that its methods may run in-memory, in a relational database, or on Hadoop clusters makes it very setup and size-agnostic. Impressive features include a comprehensive toolbox with over 1500 operations, a variety of interfaces (such as a user interface with graphics or a batch process unit), accurate pre-processing methods, and a variety of visualization outputs (such as maps, dispersion matrices, or 3D graphs). You can see an example of the procedure. It runs on all the major OSes as well as platforms thanks to its Java foundation. The only limitations on the freeware version are the maximum amount of RAM that can be allotted (1GB) and the types of sources of data that are allowed (only .csv and Excel). Other than that, it's well packed with features. Overall, RapidMiner has the following benefits: • It is compatible with all computing environments. • A user-abstracted visual interface that hides implementation specifics. • API that offers flexible setup options and expansion capabilities. • Supports processing in a cluster, a database, and in memory. • A range of outputs for visualisation.

R Project

The R Project combines a programming language with a graphics and statistical-computing environment. Although the computer languages S and Scheme had an impact on its design, it is totally open-source. There are a plethora of graphical as well as statistical instruments available in the R Project, including typical tests for statistical significance, time series analysis, linear and non-linear modeling, and more traditional features like grouping and classification. Rather than being a basic suite where other tools are added to increase capabilities, it aims to be a cohesive, fully planned system.

It has several advantages, such as being easily extended with new models **via** packages, being able to execute complicated operations by simply interacting with

C, C++, or Matlab code, and being able to print trustworthy statistical graphs. Being a programming language as well as itself, R allows users with coding knowledge to modify the set of procedures to add features. The whole gamut of handling information procedures, from manipulation and calculation to display, is made possible by this all-inclusive suite of programs. It also has a series of operators that offer ways to do calculations using arrays and matrices, in addition to efficient techniques for data management and storage. Some of the other features include visual instruments to help visualize this kind of study and integrated tool sets to process intermediate data. As we've previously said, R's functions may be used with those from other languages to do computationally intensive tasks more effectively. The language's syntax is simple and features conditional phrases, loops, input, and output abilities. The R Project is so well-liked by those who deal with statistical data analysis that various tools have been developed to make it more attractive and user-friendly. RStudio is one among them. An IDE built by the same-named business exclusively for working with R is called RStudio Desktop.

The most recent stable version is 3.2.2, and it may be used to run a number of UNIX systems as well as Windows and Mac OS under the provisions of the GNU Licence. Strong elements of the R project include:

It allows for extension through the use of packages.

Users who are experienced with the R programming language to create new features may quickly tweak and expand the platform to suit their needs.

Simple coding language integration.

Tanagra

The academic and scientific communities have found a useful mining of data tool in Tanagra. Included are methods that might find use in analyzing data, statistics, artificial intelligence, and databases. Among Tanagra's three primary objectives is the facilitation of researcher, educator, and student access to data mining technologies. Second, we want to make it easy for academics to construct the system so they can test out different experimental approaches and see how they stack up against existing solutions. By doing this, they can save time by not having to worry about implementation specifics and instead concentrate on data management. Additionally, being open source gives people a broad concept of what a DM tool is like, so they may create their own if it is something they are interested in. As it does not handle a wide variety of data sources, does not include data purification capabilities, and is not highly interactive, it is not a powerful tool to execute genuine data mining activities. The most recent edition, in particular, dates from 2008. This indicates that the tool is not being utilised as frequently as comparable tools and may have even been abandoned since it was thought to be subpar compared to more recent options.

Because it just covers the basics of data mining, Tanagra is great for academics and researchers just starting out. The data processing model is shown in Fig. (**1**).

A straightforward approach that programmers may follow to create their own tools.

WEKA

One prominent workbench that integrates several ML approaches is the Waikato Area for Knowledge Evaluation, or WEKA. Its goal is all 258 P. And J. Bernardino residents have an interest in ML in academia, business, or industry. When dealing with information that is too large to be analyzed manually, WEKA is a lifesaver for all of them. Additionally, WEKA hopes to increase the accessibility of existing ML algorithms while creating new ones that are more successful. It is of the utmost importance that the developers of WEKA strive towards creating a data analysis platform that is accessible to as many people as possible in order to facilitate study. Pre-processing, regression, clustering, classification, association rules, as well as visualization are just a few of the essential Data Mining processes that are included in the Java software WEKA. Distribution of WEKA is governed by the General Public License of the GNU. Additionally, it offers a robust structure for developing new ML methods. The four primary components of the scheme are the Information Flow, the Explorer, the command-line interface (CLI), and the Experimenter. Both a Command Line Interface (CLI) and the graphical user interface (Express) offer the same functionality. Determining the data sources, preparing the data, running algorithms, and visualizing the results are all part of these duties. If you want to test out different methods on the same dataset, the Experimenter is the way to go. A dataflow may be built with the help of the Information Flow using visually linked parts.

Version 3.7, which is still in development, encourages dealing with very large datasets and offers accessibility to fresh Java bundles that allow carrying out Data Mining operations with simultaneous processing. Version 3.6, the most recent solid version, allows working with huge data sets. To summarize, the advantages of WEKA include:

User-friendliness for users of all skill levels.

Has both a Graphical User Interface and a Command-Line Interface.

RESULT AND DISCUSSION

With the sole exception of Tanagra, which is Windows-specific, all of the tools are compatible with the mainstream operating systems, including Windows, Linux, and Mac OS X.

Overall, the user interface of tools with a GUI is better than that of tools with CLI due to the ease of use as well as the reduced learning curve associated with the former. This is not really novel since every tool has a Graphical User Interface (GUI) except KEEL.

Accepted Information Formats: The most feature-rich tools are R and RapidMiner. Keep up with KEEL because it provides all types; however, you can't utilize it without the add-ons. Weka, KNIME, Orange, and Tanagra all do worse than expected since they don't support even some of the basic data formats, including Excel files.

Capability for cloud computing, big data, and social networking is nonexistent on the Keel, Orange, and Tanagra plans. While RapidMiner's commercial versions are the only ones that provide Cloud as well as Big Data Assistance, other packages like R, KNIME, and Weka do the same, but they don't come with expansions. Our examination leads us to the first conclusion that none of the tools is wholly superior to the others. The summary of the various tools is shown in Table **1**. Any decision a company manager takes must take into consideration the unique requirements of the organisation. In light of this, we may nevertheless affirm the following:

Table 1. Summary on various tools.

Tool	Purpose
RapidMiner	Conducts data mining analysis and creates multiple models
KNIME	Cleans the big data
Orange	Used to visualize the data
SPSS	Supports factor and statistical analysis
KEEL	Useful in classification and regression problems
SparkMLLib	Large-scale data processing framework
D3js	Used for complex data visualization
PSLC	Supports data collection and analysis

- The most comprehensive tool is RapidMiner if cloud and large data support are not required. If the business can't provide data in Excel-compatible formats,

KNIME and Weka are better choices.

- R Project is another useful tool that supports all the most recent cutting-edge technology. The issue is that it has an unusual language with a steep learning curve. Tanagra, Orange, or Keel are not suitable tools for SMEs. They lack the functionality necessary for application in actual settings and are mostly academic and research tools for data mining experiments. Table **2** Summarizes the brief comparison among data mining tools.

Table 2. Comparison of data mining tools.

Tool	Programming language	Data Type	Operating System	Interfaces	Cloud Support	Big Data Support
KEEL	Java	All	Win Linux Mac	CLI Only	No	No
KENIME	Free of Language	All (Except Excel)	Win Linux Mac	GUI Only	Yes	Yes
ORANGE	Java C++ Python	All (Excel & URL Excepted)	Win Linux Mac	CLI and GUI	No	No
RapidMiner	Java	All	Win Linux Mac	GUI Only	Commercial Support	With Commercial Support
R Project	R C Fortan	All	Win	GUI Only	Yes	Yes
Tangra	C++	Few	Win Linux Mac	GUI Only	No	No
WEKA	Jave	All	-	GUI and CUI	Yes	Yes

CONCLUSION

After careful evaluation, it seems that open-source data Mining Tools have reached a level of reliability that allows them to be used in a range of contexts, such as education, research, industry, and commerce. While KEEL, Orange, and Tanagra, which are more suited to academic settings and research, RapidMiner, KNIME, R Initiative, and Weka are perfect for use in SMEs. When new challenges arise, such as the explosion of data or the introduction of innovative technology, these tools will have to be upgraded. New tools, as well as improvements to existing ones, shall be created as people strive to build tools that meet their specific requirements. Small and medium-sized enterprises (SMEs) will have a much more difficult time and likely spend more time and effort trying to choose the best technology for their particular situation due to this continual evolution. Analyzing 261 Open-Source Mining of Data Tools for SMEs. In our future work, we want to examine alternative options and give company managers clear comparisons so they can make the best decision. We also want to further assess these seven well-known technologies in a genuine SME context.

REFERENCES

[1] L. Xie, Y. Chen, S. Wu, R. Chang, and Y. Han, "Knowledge extraction for solving resource-constrained project scheduling problem through decision tree", *Eng. Construct. Architect. Manag.*. vol. 31, no. 7, pp. 2852–2877, 2024.

[2] Lal, M.K., Kim, T.H., & Singleton, D.M. Data Science Use Case for Brownfield Optimization - A Case study, Conference: SPE Western Regional Meeting, 2021.

[3] Fins, I.S., Davies, H., Farrell, S., R.Torres, J., Pinchbeck, G., Radford, A.D., Network, P.N., Infection, I.O., Veterinary, Sciences, E., Liverpool, U.O., Liverpool, Uk, Science, D.O., University, D., Durham, Health, I.F., Safety, F., Canaria, U.O., Palmas, L., Archipelago, C., & Spain. (2023). Evaluating ChatGPT text-mining of clinical records for obesity monitoring. ArXiv, abs/2308.01666.

[4] Blake, V., Jorm, L.R., Yu, J., Lee, A.K., Gallego, B., Clinic, S.O., Hospital, P.O., Sydney, Nsw, Australia, Health, C.F., Wales, U.O., School, P.O., Medicine, S.O., Medicine, F.O., Health, Wollongong, U.O., Hospital, T.W., & Wollongong (2023). The Cardiac Analytics and Innovation (CardiacAI) Data Repository: An Australian data resource for translational cardiovascular research. ArXiv, abs/2304.09341.

[5] X. Li, and T. Meng, "Enterprise precision marketing effectiveness model based on data mining technology", *Mobile Information Systems,* 2022. Article 2020038. [http://dx.doi.org/10.1155/2022/2020038]

[6] D.C. Nguyen, M. Ding, P.N. Pathirana, A. Seneviratne, J. Li, and H.V. Poor, "Cooperative Task Offloading and Block Mining in Blockchain-Based Edge Computing With Multi-Agent Deep Reinforcement Learning", *IEEE Trans. Mobile Comput.,* vol. 22, no. 4, pp. 2021-2037, 2023. [http://dx.doi.org/10.1109/TMC.2021.3120050]

[7] K. Selvakumaran, A. Sami, and B. Begum, "Customized Transformer for Confident Browse Node Classification on Imbalanced Product Data", *2023 International Conference on Computational Intelligence and Sustainable Engineering Solutions (CISES),* pp. 663-667, 2023. [http://dx.doi.org/10.1109/CISES58720.2023.10183484]

[8] X. Wu, "ODFM: Abnormal Traffic Detection Based on Optimization of Data Feature and Mining", *Int. J. Adv. Comput. Sci. Appl.,* vol. 14, no. 11, 2023. [http://dx.doi.org/10.14569/IJACSA.2023.01411112]

[9] Scheinert, D., Alamgiralem, A., Bader, J., Will, J., Wittkopp, T., & Thamsen, L. (2021). On the Potential of Execution Traces for Batch Processing Workload Optimization in Public Clouds. 2021 IEEE International Conference on Big Data (Big Data), 3113-3118.

[10] L. Liao, Y. Zeng, Y. Liang, and H. Zhang, *Data Mining: A Novel Strategy for Production Forecast In Tight Hydrocarbon Resource in Canada by Random Forest Analysis.*. International Petroleum Technology Conference, Dhahran, Kingdom of Saudi Arabia, January 2020. [http://dx.doi.org/10.2523/IPTC-20344-MS]

[11] G. Kritikakis, M. Galetakis, A. Vafidis, G. Apostolopoulos, T. Michalakopoulos, M. Triantafyllou, C. Roumpos, F. Pavloudakis, B. Deligiorgis, N. Economou, and N. Andronikidis, "Toward the Optimization of Mining Operations Using an Automatic Unmineable Inclusions Detection System for Bucket Wheel Excavator Collision Prevention: A Synthetic Study", *Sustainability (Basel),* vol. 15, no. 17, p. 13097, 2023.

[http://dx.doi.org/10.3390/su151713097]

[12] X. Li, and T. Meng, "Enterprise Precision Marketing Effectiveness Model Based on Data Mining Technology", *Mob. Inf. Syst.,* vol. 2022, pp. 1-10, 2022. [http://dx.doi.org/10.1155/2022/2020038]

[13] R. Liu, Z. Zhang, and D. Zhang, *Leakage Detection and Isolation in Water Distribution Network Based on Data Mining and Genetic Optimized Hydraulic Simulation.*. 2020. Zenodo. [http://dx.doi.org/10.5281/zenodo.3911523]

[14] Qin, Q., Chen, T., Zhang, X., Ou, B., Zhang, J., Wu, C.H., Xie, Y., Wu, W., Science, P.C., Technology, Science, C.O., Technology, N.I., 410073, C., China, P.R., Mechanism, H.K., Information, T.O., Hunan, Laboratory, H.N., 230088, H., Computing, P., Science, C.O., China, & Physics, D.O. (2023). Precisely Modeling the Potential of a Surface Electrode Ion Trap.

[15] S. Peng, F. Shen, A. Wen, L. Wang, Y. Fan, X. Liu, and H. Liu, "Detecting Lifestyle Risk Factors for Chronic Kidney Disease With Comorbidities: Association Rule Mining Analysis of Web-Based Survey Data", *J. Med. Internet Res.,* vol. 21, no. 12, p. e14204, 2019. [http://dx.doi.org/10.2196/14204] [PMID: 31821152]

[16] E. Sisinni, A. Saifullah, S. Han, U. Jennehag, and M. Gidlund, "Industrial Internet of Things: Challenges, Opportunities, and Directions", *IEEE Trans. Industr. Inform.,* vol. 14, no. 11, pp. 4724-4734, 2018. [http://dx.doi.org/10.1109/TII.2018.2852491]

[17] C. Paniagua, and J. Delsing, "Industrial Frameworks for Internet of Things: A Survey", *IEEE Syst. J.,* vol. 15, no. 1, pp. 1149-1159, 2021. [http://dx.doi.org/10.1109/JSYST.2020.2993323]

[18] Akhtar, M.; Neidhardt, J.; Werthner, H. The Potential of Chatbots: Analysis of Chatbot Conversations. In Proceedings of the 21st IEEE Conference on Business Informatics, CBI 2019, Moscow, Russia, 15–17 July 2019; Institute of Electrical and Electronics Engineers Inc.: Piscataway, NJ, USA, 2019; Volume 1, pp. 397–404. [http://dx.doi.org/10.1109/CBI.2019.00052]

[19] A.P. Chaves, and M.A. Gerosa, "How Should My Chatbot Interact? A Survey on Social Characteristics in Human–Chatbot Interaction Design", *Int. J. Hum. Comput. Interact.,* vol. 37, no. 8, pp. 729-758, 2021. [http://dx.doi.org/10.1080/10447318.2020.1841438]

[20] M.H. Chao, A.J.C. Trappey, and C.T. Wu, "Emerging Technologies of Natural Language-Enabled Chatbots: A Review and Trend Forecast Using Intelligent Ontology Extraction and Patent Analytics", *Complexity,* vol. 2021, no. 1, p. 5511866, 2021. [http://dx.doi.org/10.1155/2021/5511866]

[21] A. Rapp, L. Curti, and A. Boldi, "The human side of human-chatbot interaction: A systematic literature review of ten years of research on text-based chatbots", *Int. J. Hum. Comput. Stud.,* vol. 151, p. 102630, 2021. [http://dx.doi.org/10.1016/j.ijhcs.2021.102630]

[22] B. Luo, R.Y.K. Lau, C. Li, and Y.W. Si, "A critical review of state-of-the-art chatbot designs and applications", *Wiley Interdiscip. Rev. Data Min. Knowl. Discov.,* vol. 12, no. 1, p. e1434, 2022. [http://dx.doi.org/10.1002/widm.1434]

[23] C. Zong, R. Xia, and J. Zhang, *Text Data Mining.* Springer: Singapore, 2021, pp. 1-351. [http://dx.doi.org/10.1007/978-981-16-0100-2]

[24] Tandel, S.S.; Jamadar, A.; Dudugu, S. A Survey on Text Mining Techniques. In Proceedings of the 2019 5th International Conference on Advanced Computing and Communication Systems, ICACCS 2019, Coimbatore, India, 15–16 March 2019; Institute of Electrical and Electronics Engineers Inc.: Piscataway, NJ, USA, 2019; pp. 1022–1026.

CHAPTER 7

Hybrid Intelligence for Information Analysis for Machine Learning and Automated Reasoning

Merin Thomas[1,*] and **Ramesh Chandra Tripathi**[2]

[1] *Department of Computer Science and Engineering, JAIN (Deemed-to-be University), Bangalore, Karnataka, India*

[2] *College of Computing Science & IT, Teerthanker Mahaveer University, Moradabad, Uttar Pradesh, India*

Abstract: Social networking and microblogging have grown, reflecting this generation's ideas. User reviews of products, companies, individuals, forums, films, *etc.*, may gauge people's opinions. Analysts automated positive and negative judgment categorization using algorithms. Its automatic categorization is sentiment analysis. This study uses SVM to classify product reviews' feelings and phrases. The study will critically assess several datasets utilised for this aim. The Support Vector Machine (SVM) learning approach has been trained, verified, and used on many data sets to assess ambiguous sensory polarity. To improve product review categorization, this research employs SVM artificial intelligence to examine several datasets for sentiment and language classification. This work trains, evaluates, and simulates a support vector machine training system to recognise ambiguous emotions or review polarity on numerous datasets. SVM has the highest starting accuracy (89.98%) among classification methods. Adding sentence forms improves accuracy. It concludes that SVM is reliable. Application/Improvements: Support Vector Machine models are evaluated. Finally, the Support Vector Machine (SVM) classifies better and more accurately.

Keywords: Information Analysis, Machine Learning, Automated Reasoning, and SVM.

INTRODUCTION

The process of machine learning was a line of reasoning that looks at how computations may learn from data.

Such computations function by constructing a model based on data sources and using it to make predictions or decisions rather than only adhering to updated

* **Corresponding author Merin Thomas** Department of Computer Science and Engineering, JAIN (Deemed-to-be University), Bangalore, Karnataka, India; E-mail: merin.thomas@jainuniversity.ac.in

S. Kannadhasan, R. Nagarajan, & Kaushik Pal (Eds.)

standards. Computational statistics and machine learning are very connected. The algorithms used for machine learning may be broken down into the following categories from a technical standpoint: There are many types of learning, including Supervised, Unsupervised, Semi-Supervised, and Reinforcement Learning. Supervised neural networks, in opposition to unsupervised training, occur when various input items are provided with a labelled result (also called a supervisory signal). In semi-supervised learning, there is a large number of input items, but only a subset of these objects is labelled with an output value. This kind of learning falls between supervised and unsupervised learning. However, with reinforcement learning, a system is trained by the environment to choose the optimum course of action depending on the rewards it receives.

Do people's ideas and beliefs have different degrees of detail? This refers to the overarching feelings expressed in a single statement or document, such as a revision document. Classification problems have often been used to describe the work of analysing reader perspectives, ideas, and sentiments. Component-based sentiment analysis often serves two major purposes: identifying positive feelings conveyed in texts, and detecting the hidden semantic component in writings written by cretins. The application of machine learning techniques for sentiment analysis and opinion mining presents a promising avenue for automating the information-gathering, processing, and interpretation processes. To determine the polarity of views, a technique known as "Sentiment Analysis" is used. Positive, negative, and neutral are all ways to describe polarity. Similar concepts are referred to by different names, but they all mean the same thing. Documents, web pages, social media feeds, and so on may all be analysed using sentiment analysis to reveal the underlying tone of the feedback they contain. Emotion analysis is a sort of categorization analysis in which data is broken down into distinct groups. These groups may be dichotomous (positive/negative) or multi-dimensional (happy/sad/angry/*etc*). Sentiment analysis is a text categorization approach that uses the words inside a document to discover the underlying attitude (positive or negative) of the author. Using sentiment analysis, we can quantify the underlying feeling of a product review, which in turn helps forecast the customer's future purchase behaviour. The reviews simplify the process of evaluating the merchandise. Sentiment analysis has become an increasingly popular and important method for making sense of the vast amounts of data we generate every day. Companies may now automatically elicit critical insights and streamline all background operations thanks to this. Extracting, identifying, and characterising the emotional content of a text unit may be done with the use of machine learning and natural language processing. When a supervisor uses this approach, the general tone of a review document or phrase is conveyed with a single phone call. Classification problems that involve analysing overarching sentiments in text are often created, such as dividing a review article into positive and negative categories. Opinion mining, analysis of sentiment, sentiment extraction, and efficient rating are just a few of the many names for sentiment categorization.

RELATED WORKS

Here, you'll find a summary of the many methods proposed for doing aspect-based sentiment analysis on product reviews by various writers. Information from online user reviews is analysed using machine learning methods. Labelling a feature-wise rating for each product based on the person being studied is the main emphasis [1]. A system that uses the Internet to recommend and evaluate products is being developed. They used NLP to scan reviews and Naive Bayes classification. Polarity information and product feature comments were also gathered. Star ratings, evaluation date, helpfulness ranking, and review polarity are only a few of the elements that may be used to graphically inform the customer which of two things is superior [2]. Opinion Mining, formerly referred to as emotion analysis, is a kind of Natural Language Processing and Information Extraction that identifies the user's ideas or perspectives based on whether they are represented as either favourable or unfavourable comment and quotation clusters in the text. Methods for Sentiment Analysis that are either supervised or data-driven include Naive Bayes, Maximum Entropy, and Support Vector Machines. A Support Vector Machine (SVM) is used for classification, taking into account both the accuracy of the classification and the sentiment of the categorization [3]. The software is able to deduce that the opinion mining method did not make direct use of social network data. Both online and offline advertising may benefit from the methods suggested in this research. Due to its potential use, the computational approach to opinion, emotion, and subjectivity has received a lot of recent attention [4]. They take a vocabulary of representative words for each category and use those words to generate a representative article for each class. To better classify texts using supervised learning, they create a system that takes lexical information into account. Next, a composite growth Naive Bayes classifier is constructed by adaptively pooling the data sets from both of these models [5]. The meaning of a statement might change depending on the surrounding context. Since "contextual dependency" and "label redundancy" are two distinguishing features of sentence sentiment classification, they suggest a new approach for categorizing sentiment based on CRFs to account for both factors. Using CRF, they attempt to capture the restrictions of context on the mood of the statement. Many applications, such as electronic commerce, *etc*., rely heavily on the ability to extract these subjective messages and analyse their orientations [6]. Next, we look at how a polarity classification method makes use of four distinct kinds of fundamental linguistic information sources. However, our suggested method does not increase efficiency further by including dependency-based information or by excluding objective elements from feedback. The purpose of polarity analysis is to categorise reviews as either positive or negative. Polarity labelling is where most document-level sentiment analysis projects have focused thus far, with input collected and then analysed [7].

This section gives a high-level overview of several studies and projects in the area of opinion mining and sentiment analysis. Tripathy *et al.* attempted to categorise movie reviews using a variety of supervised machine learning algorithms. To improve efficiency, accuracy, and process time, Maria *et al.* have provided a hybrid strategy for predicting sentiment by combining the context-sensitive coding provided by Word2Vec with sentiment/emotion information provided by a lexicon. Sentence-level sentiment analysis using the hybrid system technique suggested by Appel *et al.* achieves an impressive 88.02% accuracy and 84.24% precision. We use a technique called "Natural Language Processing" (NLP). We apply the suggested hybrid approach to three datasets and evaluate its performance in comparison to that of the Naive Bayes (NB) and Maximum Entropy (ME) methods [8 - 15]. Extraction of adverse drug responses from social media and online discussion forums was the topic of research described by Korkontzelos *et al.* Due to its huge size, automatic recognition of ADR was challenging, but our technology made it simple. Using an unsupervised neural model of language that learned initial word embedding and was modified to detect the polarities, Severyn *et al.* forecasted polarities at both the message and phrase levels using sentiment analysis of tweets. Within SemEval-2014, Nakov *et al.* presented the first-ever challenge for evaluating Compositional Distributional semantics Models on entire sentences. Both semantic relatedness and entailment were sub-tasks of its main task. Twitter posts were categorised as favourable, bad, or irrelevant by Gokulakrishnan *et al.* They also looked into how well different classifiers worked. A technique for training a sentiment classifier through automated collection of a corpus was suggested by Pak *et al.*. By using Tree Tagger for POS-tagging, they were able to see that there was a distinction between negative, positive, and neutral distributions [16 - 20]. We employed a technique wherein Twitter, a highly popular mini-blogging network, automatically gathered a corpus for the purposes of sentiment analysis and opinion mining. Jansen *et al.*9 published a study detailing how, if a firm needs to improve its branding strategy, it could look towards microblogging websites as a potentially lucrative new marketing channel. The writers of this research analysed the phenomenon of "e-WOM branding." More than 150,000 tweets were analysed for brand-related remarks, attitudes, and views [21 - 25].

PROPOSED WORK

Important details of the planned work are as follows:

- Sentiment analysis and a machine learning algorithm are discussed in the context of analysing the correlation between online evaluations of smartphone devices and sales and product performance.
- To study the impact of reviews on sales, the algorithm will be used to analyze ratings and reviews of products in order to make predictions about product sales. Predictions for tomorrow's product assortment are made based on today's internet customer reviews.
- It is projected that either a lot of money will be collected or not very much. Brands, release dates, sales rankings, user ratings, and more for a certain smartphone were all culled from the internet.
- The Part of Speech (POS) model, which maps reviewer emotion to a vector whose members are vocabulary words. Sentiment analysis relies heavily on part-of-speech data since it helps to reveal underlying attitudes.
- The weight of each phrase in the related sentences is added together to get the score for every phrase in the dataset. The evaluation data have been clustered using the TF-IDF metric.
- In the end, the suggested work achieves superb precision, the reviews are trusted, and the smartphone product's success or failure is forecasted using the reviews themselves and a classification method called Support Vector Machine.

Text Pre-Processing

The two main types of text pre-processing methods are known as POS tagging and stop word removal, respectively. Tokens are chunks of text used in point-o--sale systems. Tokens representing reviews from the input stream are used to initiate preprocessing. Stop words are sometimes grouped together and referred to as a stop-list. Words like "a," "of," "the," "I," "it," and "you" are considered "stop words" since they have no other purpose than to fill space and are thus seldom utilised. Therefore, get rid of the words that add nothing to the work at hand. The block diagram of the proposed work is shown in Fig. (**1**).

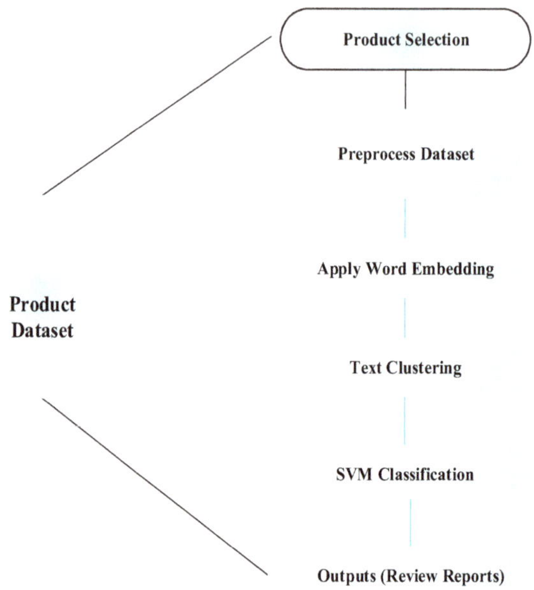

Fig. (1). Block Diagram of the Proposed Work.

Transformation

Each phrase in the manuscript is assigned a score throughout the transformation process. The term importance is then determined by multiplying the term frequency by the inverse document frequency.

Clustering

The TF-IDF measurement is used for document review clustering. Points in the cluster's periphery are likely to be a part of the cluster just as much as those at the cluster's core. It determines the centroid and selects the number of clusters.

SVM Classification

The enhanced feature sets were then used for the task of sentiment classification, after the elimination of outliers based on clustering. For the most part, SVM is used to categorise how someone is feeling. It divides the reviews into good and bad categories.

First Stage: Data Preparation Tokenization, the act of dividing a stream of text into individual words, symbols, and phrases, is one pre-processing technique that may be used to reduce mistakes and boost productivity. Removal of "stop words" includes words like "is," "are," "they," "but," and so on. The system architecture is shown in Fig. (**2**). When you use stemming, you get rid of the ending and the beginning of a word. Removing Termination Marks (A) These texts have several interpretations, but most of them are meaningless outside their grammatical function as sentence connectors. It is commonly accepted that stop words provide neither context nor substance to textual records. Common words like "and," "are," "this," and "*etc*." are examples of stop words. They are not useful for organising papers in any way. They must be eliminated. Creating a list of potential stop words might help us eliminate them from the content review process. Tokenization, or the process of separating a stream of text into individual phrases, symbols, terms, or other meaningful parts, is discussed in Part B. This method may be used to get rid of graphics and special characters. In the same way as #, *, $, @, *etc*., C. Stem-Removal (or "stemming"): - Based is the procedure of merging all the different spellings of the word into its most common stem. Semantic equivalency is an algorithmic technique for reducing incompatible methods of doing things to mutually agreeable ones (Table **1**). This method recovers the underlying words by eliminating their prefixes and suffixes. For example:

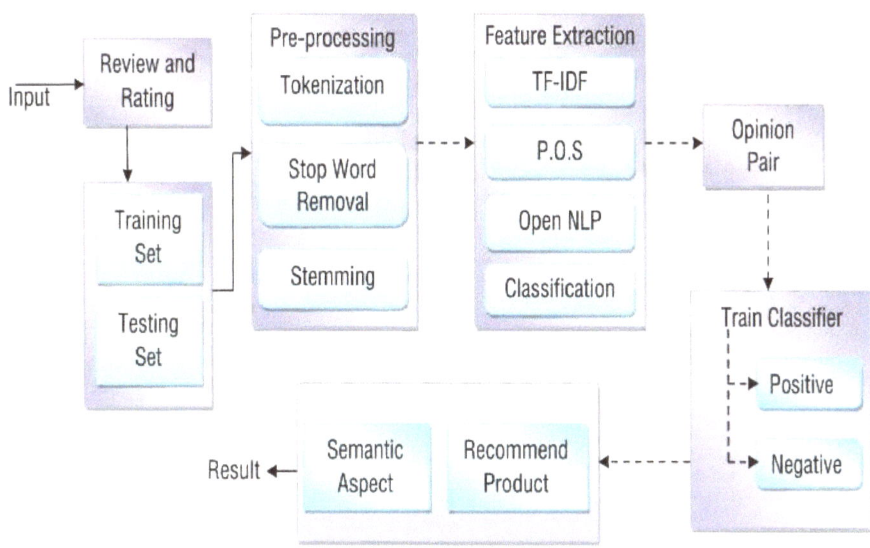

Fig. (2). System architecture.

The Second Stage: Extracting Features Ratings, reviews, and the worry score from each review were extracted. Here, we take the pre-processed data and pull out useful features like sentiment analysis, n-grams, and part-of-speech tagging. A. Possessive Adjective Tagging words as belonging to certain parts of speech involves analysing their context inside a phrase. Nouns, verbs, adjectives, *etc*., are typical POS tags. As a vital step in the pre-processing of data, labelling makes it easy to find and extract the relevant characteristics. Each segment of speech is represented by a unique set of letters. The words “everyone” (Q+N), “they” (PRO), and “Wh-determiner” (WD) are all examples. Analysis of Feelings, Third Stage. One of the most useful applications of natural language processing is sentiment analysis, often called perspective pair analysis. Online product ratings were calculated using user input. Users of the Nave Bayes Algorithm-based classification product go on to Stage 4, where they will analyse comments pertaining to materials and subsequently classify them using the product. The reviews' contents were analysed to determine which product features were mentioned and whether or not those features were praised. Fifth Stage: Classification Train. After averaging the reviews using TF-IDF, the number of favourable and adverse feedback was counted. The benefits and drawbacks of each feature are tallied. Then, a total score was arrived at after factoring in ratings and reviews. Step Seven: Give Advice. Clients get a summary of ratings, reviews, *etc*., and are advised to purchase the item with the highest average score.

Algorithm and Mathematical Model

Mathematical Model 1. Mapping Diagram

Where Rv, Rvn, User Review Volume, and Review Volume, Respectively. User Ratings (r,....., rn) = Total Number of Ratings. The letters S and A stand for “Syst. Theorem 2: Sets A = s, e, X, R, P, Y, Z, S = Systems Collection s = the coder initiates.

• Sign up for the system. Start by entering your login details into the system. A program's input is denoted by X. Where Rv, Rvn = User rates each feature with a certain number of stars. R,....., rn = Total number of user ratings for a specific feature.

P = Aspect/Feature of the Program's Process Extraction Gathering of M Review Materials, D= [d1, d2, d3,..............dm] List of paired opinions N, dm = {,, ..., } First, type a d for “document” Second, every w in d represents a letter of the alphabet. Third, when you plug it in for the subject, it does a few calculations. The percentage is denoted by p (subject t | source d). Currently assigned subject t word count in document d, and meanwhile, p (word w| topic t) = the percentage of papers assigned to topic t that include the word w. Replace t with a new subject, selected using the following formula: p = p(word w | topic t) * p(document d | topic t).

Based on the Bayesian theorem, Bayesian naive Bayes is a probabilistic classification approach. It estimates the number of students who will register in each course, with the highest probability course serving as the default option. The

Naive Bayes classification method has several unrelated features. Naive Bayes classifiers have been widely used for text classification because of their versatility; for example, they may be programmed to identify spam. The following rule may be used to estimate the likelihood that a given statement has a specific attitude towards a given feature. P (Emotion | Word) = P (Emotion | Word) W (Term | Affect) / S (Sentence). The method for assessing whether a review is favourable or negative was developed by using the criterion for classifying input as positive or negative. Input: Results: A predicted evaluation of the course. Step 1: Get Some Opinions. The Second Step: Run a Review. Third, prepare the Review ahead of time. Part 4: Take Out the Critique. Proceed to Step 5: Enter Class with Naive Bayes. Step 6: Obtain the affirmative and negative values from the dictionary you select. Step Seven: Maximise Your Score and Reveal Whether You're Positive or Negative. Eighth Step: Anticipated Category for Every Factor. Second, the TF-IDF algorithm:- The word Frequency and Inverse Document Frequency (TF-IDF) score for a given word Iij is arrived at in this way. One of the best general term weighting systems in IR may be traced back to the TF & IDF. A TF-IDF calculation looks like this: TF-IDF = Term Frequency * Inverse Document Frequency. The TF index tracks how often a certain phrase (t) appears in a given text. The formula is: tf (n, i) = (1, k)(n, k)(i, j). Where (ni, j) is the total number of times (nk) that the word (ti) appears in (dj), and (nk) is the frequency with which (ti) appears in (dj). IDF:- In TF, every word is treated equally except IDF. Determines the relative weight of words. To calculate IDF, use the formulas provided below: Where, D: the Overall Number of Documents | idfi = Log (2) | d ; d € ti | d: The total number of papers that have ti in them.

RESULT AND DISCUSSION

Performance Metrics

This study employs a set of standard measures for evaluating models, including accuracy, precision, recall, and F1 score. The parameters used for the estimate are as follows: (1) TP: the percentage of customer reviews for a certain product that are deemed to be positive, Number of reviews that reframe criticisms of the product as compliments, (2) FP. (3) "TN" refers to the total number of "negative" remarks. Number of replies counted as both positive and negative product evaluations (4) FN. The percentage of correctly estimated comments as a fraction of the total number of remarks is referred to as (5) Accuracy.

Outcome analysis of a single product type is shown in Table **2**. Products are shown along the X-axis, while positive and negative evaluations are shown along the Y-axis as a percentage.

Table 1. Stemming remove.

Form	Suffix	Stem
Plays	-s	Play
Played	-ed	Play
Playing	-ing	Play
Studies	-es	Study
Studied	-ed	Study

Table 2. Classifiers performance.

Classifiers	Iterations – 10	Iterations – 50	Iterations – 100
Naive Bayes	77.5	79.0	74.0
KNN	82.9	83.0	82.7
LR	83.0	86.0	79.3
SVM	93.6a	97.1	99.3

A hyperplane is used in Support Vector Machines to classify data into positive and negative categories. Table **1** displays the reviews' findings, which are based on the aforementioned three data sets, below. As a result, Table **1** splits its review count in half, with the first group including only good reviews and the second group including only negative reviews. When outcomes are favourable, reviews are positive, and when they're bad, reviews are negative. When compared to other categorization algorithms, Support Vector Machine (SVM) delivers the highest accuracy at 89.98%. Including additional sentence forms would further improve the achieved accuracy. When everything is said and done, it is found that the algorithm using SVM is superior. Here, we've used the free and open-source Java NetBeans IDE 7.2.1 to run the Support Vector Machine algorithm for classification in a simulation of the experiments. Several modules have been used to conduct a full experimental assessment and simulation. Now that the product reviews have been collected, a POS Tagger will go through them and determine if each word in them is a noun, verb, adjective, *etc*. After the text was cleaned up, it was modified using Term Frequency (TF), which gives each word a certain amount of importance depending on how often it appears in the document. The following equation may be used to determine this: TF(t) = Total Frequency of Term (t) in Document. There are a total of 17 words in the paper. After TF has been calculated, the significance of a phrase is quantified using the Inverse Document Frequency (IDF) metric by scaling up uncommon terms and weighing down common ones.

CONCLUSION

This technique, which relies on online modelling of data supplied by review users, is able to uncover hidden elements of the component's semantics and emotions and forecast the judgements and sentiments of general reviews. Using a standardised framework, these systems use a novel supervised model to solve previously intractable issues. When dealing with audit documents, SJASM treats them as a pair of perspectives, which may shape the phrases of appearance and the corresponding words of a view by updates for the semantic portion and the acknowledgement of the view, and addresses this problem *via* the use of collaborative methods.

REFERENCES

[1] L.E. Parker, and F.G. Pin, "Man-Robot Symbiosis: A Framework For Cooperative Intelligence And Control", Proc. SPIE 1006, Space Station Automation IV, 1988. [http://dx.doi.org/10.1117/12.949063]

[2] E. Sandewall, and C.G. Jansson, *proceedings of the Fourth Scandinavian Conference on Artificial Intelligence, Electrum,* 1993.Stockholm, Sweden.

[3] X. Yao, *Eighth Australian Joint Conference on Artificial Intelligence,* 1995.Canberra

[4] Y. Rusmawati, "Automated Reasoning on Machine Learning Model of Legislative Election Prediction", *Proceedings of the 10th International Joint Conference on Knowledge Graphs,* 2021. [http://dx.doi.org/10.1145/3502223.3502746]

[5] V. Schaye, B. Guzman, J. Burk-Rafel, M. Marin, I. Reinstein, D. Kudlowitz, L. Miller, J. Chun, and Y. Aphinyanaphongs, "Development and Validation of a Machine Learning Model for Automated Assessment of Resident Clinical Reasoning Documentation", *J. Gen. Intern. Med.,* vol. 37, no. 9, pp. 2230-2238, 2022. [http://dx.doi.org/10.1007/s11606-022-07526-0] [PMID: 35710676]

[6] S. Dumancic, W. Meert, S. Goethals, T. Stuyckens, J. Huygen, and K. Denies, "Automated Reasoning and Learning for Automated Payroll Management", *AAAI Conference on Artificial Intelligence,* 2021. [http://dx.doi.org/10.1609/aaai.v35i17.17774]

[7] G. Huang, *Automated reasoning and machine learning.,* 1996.

[8] M. Ariely, T. Nazaretsky, and G. Alexandron, "Machine Learning and Hebrew NLP for Automated Assessment of Open-Ended Questions in Biology", *Int. J. Artif. Intell. Educ.,* pp. 1-34, 2022.

[9] P. Yuan, S. Xu, Z. Zhai, and H. Xu, "Research of intelligent reasoning system of Arabidopsis thaliana phenotype based on automated multi-task machine learning", *Front. Plant Sci.,* vol. 14, p. 1048016, 2023. [http://dx.doi.org/10.3389/fpls.2023.1048016] [PMID: 36866380]

[10] W. Dai, Q. Xu, Y. Yu, and Z. Zhou, *Bridging Machine Learning and Logical Reasoning by Abductive Learning.* Neural Information Processing Systems, 2019.

[11] Z.H. Zhou, "Abductive learning: towards bridging machine learning and logical reasoning", *Sci. China Inf. Sci.,* vol. 62, no. 7, p. 76101, 2019. [http://dx.doi.org/10.1007/s11432-018-9801-4]

[12] Dablain, D.A., Krawczyk, B., & Chawla, N. (2022). Towards A Holistic View of Bias in Machine Learning: Bridging Algorithmic Fairness and Imbalanced Learning. ArXiv, abs/2207.06084.

[13] A. Gianola, M. Montali, and M. Papini, *Automated Reasoning for Reinforcement Learning Agents in*

Structured Environments., 2021.

[14] Ackerman, S., Raz, O., & Zalmanovici, M. (2021). FreaAI: Automated extraction of data slices to test machine learning models. ArXiv, abs/2108.05620.

[15] L. Bellomarini, R.R. Fayzrakhmanov, G. Gottlob, A. Kravchenko, E. Laurenza, Y. Nenov, S. Reissfelder, E. Sallinger, E. Sherkhonov, and L. Wu, "Data Science with Vadalog", *Bridging Machine Learning and Reasoning. International Conference on Model and Data Engineering,* 2018.

[16] D. Paschek, A. Mocan, and A. Draghici, *Proceedings of the MakeLearn and TIIM International Conference,* pp. 15-17, 2019. Piran, Slovenia.

[17] P.K.R. Maddikunta, Q.V. Pham, P. B, N. Deepa, K. Dev, T.R. Gadekallu, R. Ruby, and M. Liyanage, "Industry 5.0: A survey on enabling technologies and potential applications", *J. Ind. Inf. Integr.,* vol. 26, p. 100257, 2022.
[http://dx.doi.org/10.1016/j.jii.2021.100257]

[18] W.Y. Wu, C.Y. Chiag, Y.J. Wu, and H.J. Tu, "The influencing factors of commitment and business integration on supply chain management", *Ind. Manage. Data Syst.,* vol. 104, no. 4, pp. 322-333, 2004.
[http://dx.doi.org/10.1108/02635570410530739]

[19] J. Rut, and E. Kulińska, "Optimization of the material and information streams flow in the manufacturing company", *Mark. Rynek,* vol. 7, pp. 616-624, 2017.

[20] F. Gurcan, N.E. Cagiltay, and K. Cagiltay, "Mapping human–computer interaction research themes and trends from its existence to today: A topic modeling–based review of past 60 years. Int. J. Hum.-", *Int. J. Hum. Comput. Interact.,* vol. 37, no. 3, pp. 267-280, 2021.
[http://dx.doi.org/10.1080/10447318.2020.1819668]

[21] J. Grudin, "Anticipating the future of HCI by understanding its past and present", *Proceedings of the Extended Abstracts of the 2019 CHI Conference on Human Factors in Computing Systems,* pp. 1-4, 2019. Glasgow Scotland, UK.
[http://dx.doi.org/10.1145/3290607.3298806]

[22] V. Khoma, Y. Khoma, V. Brydinskyi, and A. Konovalov, "Development of Supervised Speaker Diarization System Based on the PyAnnote Audio Processing Library", *Sensors (Basel),* vol. 23, no. 4, p. 2082, 2023.
[http://dx.doi.org/10.3390/s23042082] [PMID: 36850680]

[23] M. Danilevsky, K. Qian, R. Aharonov, Y. Katsis, B. Kawas, and P. Sen, "A survey of the state of explainable AI for natural language processing", In: Proceedings of the 1st Conference of the Asia-Pacific Chapter of the Association for Computational Linguistics and the 10th International Joint Conference on Natural Language Processing, pages 447–459, Suzhou, China. Association for Computational Linguistics.
[http://dx.doi.org/10.18653/v1/2020.aacl-main.46]

[24] P. Zhang, N. Li, M. Scialdone, and J. Carey, "The Intellectual Advancement of Human-Computer Interaction Research: A Critical Assessment of the MIS Literature (1990-2008)", *AIS Trans. Hum.-Comput. Interact.,* vol. 1, no. 3, pp. 55-107, 2009.
[http://dx.doi.org/10.17705/1thci.00007]

[25] Y. Yun, D. Ma, and M. Yang, "Human–computer interaction–based decision support system with applications in data mining", *Future Gener. Comput. Syst.,* vol. 114, pp. 285-289, 2021.
[http://dx.doi.org/10.1016/j.future.2020.07.048]

CHAPTER 8

Performance Analysis of Rule-Based Reasoning in Complex Data Environments

Sunanda Das[1,*] and **Gaurav Kumar Rajput**[2]

[1] *Department of Computer Science and Engineering, JAIN (Deemed-to-be University), Bangalore, Karnataka, India*

[2] *College of Computing Science and Information Technology, Teerthanker Mahaveer University, Moradabad, Uttar Pradesh, India*

Abstract: It is well recognised that data preparation is necessary to provide reliable data with which mining tools may derive useful insights. Preprocessing methods need modification when dealing with several sources of continuous data inflow. This study suggests using active rule-based systems, particularly complex event processing (CEP) systems and engines, to aid domain experts in defining and executing pretreatment tasks for data streams. Our method's key innovation is how it enables domain experts to easily manage temporal data by formulating preprocessing methods as event identification rules expressed in a SQL-like language. This concept is implemented in a freely accessible software package that combines a CEP processor with libraries for web-based data mining. In order to test the efficacy of our method, we provide three examples of real-world applications in which CEP rules are used to preprocess data streams by incorporating new temporal information, modifying features, and dealing with missing values. Preprocessing activities may be expressed in a flexible and high-level fashion using CEP rules, as shown by the experiments, without incurring excessive memory and time overheads. The generated streams of data not only aid in enhancing classification algorithms' predicted accuracy, but also permit simplifying decision models and shortening the time required to learn.

Keywords: Complex Data, Automated Reasoning, Rule Mining and Complex Event Prediction.

INTRODUCTION

The advent of an Internet of Things (IoT) era has increased the significance of data analysis and machine learning approaches [1].

These two fields of study are anticipated to play a significant role in the development of appealing ideas like Industry 4.0 and Society 5.0 [2]. So, there are

* **Corresponding author Sunanda Das:** Department of Computer Science and Engineering, JAIN (Deemed-to-be University), Bangalore, Karnataka, India; E-mail: sunanda.das@jainuniversity.ac.in

S. Kannadhasan, R. Nagarajan, & Kaushik Pal (Eds.)

always fresh proposals for uses of data mining software. Among the most significant difficulties linked to these principles is the automated identification of a human state or a response at a specific time or period [3]. Such issues may be articulated for a wide range of complicated systems that rely on human operators; for instance, in the medical field, operators may include the elderly in nursing homes or the mentally ill. Before an operator's status is automatically detected, the operator themselves needs to be constantly assessed. Commonplace sensors are enough for this task. Non-invasive vital sensing using Doppler sensors was presented in [4] and has since been used for human condition monitoring to improve efficiency. In the IoT context, this approach is considered important because its low computational requirements allow it to be implemented on small-scale processors, enabling longer battery life. This research investigates the effects of music listening and non-listening on the human state. Each participant's non-contact vital sensing measurements were standardised and pre-processed before the tests began. Based on this, we formulated two separate categorization problems to address. Fuzzy methods [6] and artificial neural networks [5] were employed to handle the aforementioned categorization challenges. For the purpose of automating the construction of ANNs, this research proposes two variants of the Differential Evolution technique (DE) [7], which was originally created for tackling multiobjective optimisation issues. The objective was to develop an ANN that could solve a given classification problem effectively using a simple architecture [8]. For the purpose of automatically generating fuzzy rule-based classifiers, COBRA, an optimization method based on population dynamics, was also used [9]. Data mining techniques such as support vector machines (SVM) [10], k-nearest neighbours (kNN) [11], decision tree (DT) [12], the Hybrid Evolutionary Fuzzy Classification method (HEFCA) [13], and regular artificial neural networks have all been employed to address classification issues pertaining to illness detection in humans. The findings from each of the classifiers are compared and contrasted. Knowledge discovery relies heavily on data pretreatment (Garcia *et al.*, 2014). Data preparation entails a number of time-consuming but crucial steps, including cleaning, transformation, filtering, mapping, and integration (Zhang *et al.*, 2003). In addition, using an appropriate preprocessing approach may improve mining outcomes (Crone *et al.*, 2006; Uysal & Gunal, 2014). Unfortunately, data preparation is often accomplished using inelegant and error-prone techniques that need considerable familiarity with statistics and advanced programming abilities. Preprocessing activities may be quite challenging for domain specialists, but they might benefit enormously from high-level solutions & help (Bilalli *et al.*, 2019). Common preprocessing tasks may be aided by tools like Weka & software packages accessible in languages like R and Python; however, these programmes have a steep learning curve.

It is challenging to reuse procedures and incorporate them into professional systems because domain specialists are often required to customize features or adapt generic approaches to suit their specific application area. (Huang *et al.*, 2016). With more and more people wanting to learn from data streams, new computational methods for real-time data mining are required (Gama, 2010; Gaber, 2012; Ghomeshi *et al.*, 2019). Data pretreatment is crucial for stream data mining, yet there is a dearth of literature on the topic (Ramrez-Gallego *et al.*, 2017). The majority of current methods either focus on static data or attempt to alter existing data mining techniques. Dynamic feature selection and separation methods are still uncommon in software libraries, even though there is an increasing amount of work on the subject (Barddal *et al.*, 2019; Ramrez-Gallego *et al.*, 2018). Domain experts may lack a thorough understanding of data mining techniques and toolsthus, it is important to provide them with options to describe and perform preprocessing activities when data transformation with filtering is required. Active rule-driven linguistics might provide online data mining systems with a more expressive and efficient way of expressing and enacting data preparation operations (Corporate Act-Net Consortium, 1996). At the same time, rules' excellent understanding has made them popular in expert systems (Grosan & Abraham, 2011); this may make it simpler for experts to articulate the necessary preprocessing processes. On the other side, event-driven systems benefit greatly from the sophisticated data manipulation capabilities offered by these languages. For instance, a quickly-processing stream engine (Affetti *et al.*, 2017) may be an ideal platform to carry out preprocessing methods, especially if the incoming data includes temporal context. Complex event processing (CEP) platforms are one such tool, letting users spot relevant events and share their verdicts with others (Cugola & Margara, 2012). These rule-based systems are distinguished by the extensive language support they provide for specifying rules and patterns in a SQL-like syntax. Several recent studies have shown the increasing prevalence of IoT applications in fields as diverse as monitoring the environment (Gomes *et al.*, 2020; Sun *et al.*, 2019), hospitals (Loreti *et al.*, 2019), connected transport (Kousiouris *et al.*, 2018), and and trash management (Pardini *et al.*, 2020). Among others, it has sparked renewed interest in CEP in recent years. Our proposal is based on the idea that CEP languages and engines, with their fast processing streams, rule-based engine, and SQL-like syntax, are ideally suited for the description as well as execution of stream preparation tasks within online mining data processes. In this study, we use CEP to establish pretreatment rules for data streams, which is the first time this has been done. As a first step, we design several kinds of ECA (event-condition-action) procedures for preparing data streams with different goals in mind, such as data modification and combination. Following this, we demonstrate that CEP language ideas, including spatial and temporal doors, pattern matching as well as filtering, temporal correlations, joining and splitting operators, and so on, are well-suited for the job of data stream preparation. In a gradual learning setting, these components enable the production of new characteristics that utilise a short-term past, which may aid in making more precise predictions. More than that, CEP has a natural affinity for processing complex data in numerous streams. A Java-based CEP engine called Esper2 is integrated with the massive online analysis (MOA) toolkit for real-time data analysis (Bifet, Holmes, Kirkby, & Pfahringer, 2010) to show how our concept might be put into practice. In order to test the efficacy of our strategy, we have undertaken three experiments using open-source datasets from various application areas. A variety of preprocessing jobs is tested and then classified using the available methods [14 - 15]. Results demonstrate that the use of rules is better suited to illustrating the needs of those preprocessing activities, and that utilising the data moves generated by CEP greatly enhances the level of precision of algorithmic prediction, simplifies some choice model complexity, and keeps memory and time requirements constant. Lastly, we compare our method to various preprocessing techniques and highlight its advantages and disadvantages in terms of economy and execution time. The following is a brief overview of the paper's most important findings:

- A new rule-based method for designing domain-specific preprocessing jobs for data streams, including formalisations of several preprocessing rule types.
- A freely accessible CEP-based implementation of the method that allows running well-known data mining techniques on the output streams.
- A thorough experimental assessment of the strategy, looking at how various rule configurations affect classification accuracy, processing time, and final decisions.
- Examining the relative merits of algorithms developed in CEP languages vs. general-purpose programming languages with regard to classification performance and runtime.

RELATED WORKS

There are a number of tools available now for keeping tabs on the health of the people who run complicated systems. Doppler sensors provide non-contact vital sensing in the sense that vital signs may be detected without attaching electrodes to the skin. It allows us to monitor physiological functions, including breathing, heart rate, and movement, without putting the subject under any undue strain [4]. Machine learning approaches for detecting the states of operators of comparable complex systems stand to benefit from this technology, as will the administration of these systems. To explain how the Doppler sensor works, consider the following. A Doppler sensor works by sending out an electromagnetic signal and then receiving its reflected waves, which are emitted by living things. As a result, the receiver picks up the electromagnetic wave that was reflected off the body, whose frequency has changed due to the Doppler Effect as a result of the subject's motion. Therefore, the frequency shift may be processed digitally to obtain breathing. Note that if there is more than one human body, it will be necessary to identify and isolate each individual heartbeat. But in reality, there are scarcely any traditional efforts on multi-body non-contact heart-rate monitoring. Parameter estimation for cardiac and respiratory activity was made easier with the introduction of a pre-processing approach called Accumulation for Real-time Serial-to-parallel converter (ARS) [14]. In this study, we suggest applying ARS to data from remote Doppler sensors as a kind of pre-processing.

According to the definition provided by Gaber (2012), a stream of data is an unlimited and ordered series of instances that is continually observed across time. There are a number of ways in which data stream mining is distinct from more conventional mining methods (Gama, 2010; Nguyen *et al.*, 2015). The data set must be handled individually or in batches since it is not accessible in advance. In order to save memory and disc space, each instance may only be visited a certain number of times (often only once) before being deleted. This means that the choice model is constructed in stages, with new information being added as it becomes available and older information being discarded. Algorithms for stream mining should be resilient enough to handle these challenges, as well as real-time responsive, data queue-avoidant, and memory-efficient [16 - 20]. Approximate outcomes are acceptable because of the stringent restrictions under which these algorithms may work. Even when input information is a stream, machine learning approaches remain preferred strategies for carrying out the mining stage. Jin and Agrawal (2007) and Nguyen *et al.* (2015) are only two examples of the many new supervised and unsupervised learning algorithms that have emerged in recent years. Predictions about the future value or category of a variable may be made using supervised methods such as classification and regression. In contrast, unsupervised learning includes techniques like clustering, whose goal is to find groupings of similar objects, including association rule mining, which seeks to discover patterns defining the data. When it comes to categorization, the tried-and-true methods, such as decision trees, need numerous passes over the dataset. Therefore, the construction method must be modified to accommodate the specifics of data streams. The k-nearest neighbours (kNN) and naive Bayes algorithms, both of which are often used in batch learning, do not need major adjustments since they were developed to teach gradually (Gama, 2010). Cano and Krawczyk (2019) note that ensemble approaches, which consist of several classifiers, are currently reference techniques because of their high performance and versatility. Klawczyk *et al.* (2017) found that classification algorithms used in stream mining may be significantly affected when data streams are non-stationary, indicating that the anticipated features or concepts' distribution changes over time.

Concept drift refers to a common occurrence in data from the real-world streams that may take many forms, including gradual shifts and sudden alterations (Souza *et al.*, 2020). Many strategies have been developed to combat notion drift, which is a vast and rapidly developing area of study (Cano & Krawczyk, 2019). The stream is examined using techniques called "concept drift detectors" (Liu, Song, *et al.*, 2017; Lu *et al.*, 2016) to update the classifier [21 - 23]. In a sliding-window system, the sample buffer is changeable. Multiple windows or dynamic window resizing have been proposed in recent research in this area (Zhang *et al.*, 2017 Liu, Zhang, & Lu, 2017;). Classification algorithms might use the ability to identify idea drifts to adjust their learning method, according to Cano and Krawczyk (2019), as well as Hammami *et al.* (2020). Ancy and Paulraj (2019) and Cano and Krawczyk (2020) both note that ensemble methods have been created and that core classifiers' functionality is regularly enhanced using this technique. Data preprocessing refers to the methods used to effectively modify the material or layout of raw data from several, sometimes disparate sources (Garca *et al.*, 2014). The effectiveness of mining approaches may be enhanced by ensuring that data is accurate, comprehensive, and consistent (Han *et al.*, 2012), which also helps with handling data throughout the procedure of discovering knowledge. Table **1** (Garca *et al.*, 2014) displays the major preprocessing tasks that may be divided into the subcategories of data preparation as well as data reduction.

Table 1. Types of operators in CEP.

Selection	Filter evonts exbbliking content constraints.
Projection	Extract pleces of inlormation from the events.
Lopk	Buld conjunctive, difunctive and negition expesions.
Sequence	Selext events using temporil or order conditors.
Flow	Join, dide and wort kevral exent streams.
Creation	Generate new flow ind livert enents.
Aithrets	Compute mathematical expressions and statistics

PROPOSED WORK

Complex Event Processing

Information processing based on CEP seeks to identify circumstances of interest by analysing data collected from occurrences (Luckham, 2001). Low-level data, such as sensor readings, are represented as simple events in CEP parlance, while complex events are inferred from simpler ones. In order to infer the occurrence of complex events, expert rules are defined by patterns that show which events to choose and which actions to conduct by the regulator (Cugola & Margara, 2012).

The publish-subscribe model is the backbone of most conventional CEP systems, with subscribers actively collecting rule outputs for further processing. An Event Processing Language (EPL) is used to specify events, rules, and patterns. Rule-expression languages with a Structured Query Language (SQL)-like syntax are included in certain CEP systems. This kind of rule normally has three parts: a choose, which identifies the relevant characteristics (or the full occasion, using *); b c) when, which lays forth the necessary requirements, and c, (out of), which explains how events unfold over them. The flexibility with which EPL's extensive library of mathematical, logical, and temporal operators may be coupled demonstrates the language's expressive power. The most common kinds of operators and their short descriptions may be found in Table **2**. CEP is further distinguished by its use of windows to restrict the rule's application. A window may be spatial, consisting of a collection of occurrences, or temporal, having its boundaries established in terms of time. In Listing 1, we have a sample of a CEP rule that, if the sum of all transfers in a 10-minute period exceeds 300,000 Euros, it provides the date and identity of the relevant bank transactions.

PREPROCESSING OF DATA STREAM RULES

Here, we detail our method for writing down preprocessing routines as ECA rules. First, we define the phrase "preprocessing rule" formally and talk about the driving concepts behind our method. Next, we apply this broad principle to preprocessing by developing four distinct rule sets. Finally, we provide a CEP-based framework that streamlines the process of preparing data and putting it through data mining methods.

Theory and Construction: The characteristics of data streams and the state of the art in preprocessing have led us to identify the following requirements for stream-oriented preprocessing methodologies. The ability to collect and process raw data as it arrives, which requires a reactive nature. 2. Built-in features for defining time periods and include such data in the preliminary processing of data. 3. Access to standard statistical and logical functions, with the option to add custom ones. The ability for domain experts to design preprocessing procedures in a human-readable language at the appropriate degree of abstraction. 5. A quick-processing engine that is simple to incorporate into existing online data-mining infrastructure. These postulates form the core of our proposed method, which uses CEP as its foundational system to preprocess data streams and expand the use of ECA rules. A preprocessing rule (R) may be expressed as follows: f g E1,..., Ep f g A1,..., Aq, if f g E1,..., Ep C 12, where E1,..., Ep is a sequence of events and C is a condition that must be satisfied by what occurred in order for the rule to be activated. It may be interpreted as follows: if the set of events f g E1,...,Ep occurs and those events satisfy the state C, then the collection of actions f g A1,...,Aq is executed. For the simplest rules, we shall express them as R: EA, if E C, as they only need one event and one action (such as creating a new instance). Here, an event stands in for the unprocessed data that must first be cleaned up before an online data extraction algorithm can do its work. In formal notation, the characteristics of each occurrence are denoted by the expression E a 1,...,an. The condition C denotes a collection of limitations f g c1,...,ck on events from input that must be taken into account before further processing can begin. For instance, windows (w) or a partial order among events across a stream might be used to refer to value of attributes or temporal limits. Both spatial windows (of size s) and temporal ones (of length t) exist. If and only if E's characteristics are inside the parameters of C, we shall record E C. Any time there are not any necessary boundaries, the law will be invoked by any incoming event. The rule action typically generates instances I with trainable features f, g f1,...,fm. According to our notation, then, an instance is written as I f 1,...,fm. We will also explain a situation in which an action is taken that is not meant to produce instances later on.

Preprocessing rules may be derived from the same concepts that guide existing preprocessing methods, with the necessary tweaks to accommodate the syntax of the target language and domain. Additionally, window management capabilities provide novel opportunities for enhancing and creating data preparation techniques. Rule-based preprocessing languages are similar to domain-specific languages (DSLs) in that they employ specialised operators and have a syntax designed with humans in mind. Research has shown that dynamic specific languages (DSLs) may simplify learning, perceiving, and changing programs written in them by up to 15% compared to general-purpose languages (GPLs) (Kosar *et al.*, 2010, Kosar *et al.*, 2009;). Users also perceive more efficiency, effectiveness, and usefulness when expressing the queries in rule-based languages as opposed to general-purpose languages (Groth, 2004). Afterwards, we provide four examples of preprocessing rule usage, outlining the issue, the necessary actions, and the operators to be used in each instance. Both normalisation and discretization involve modifying the value of a preexisting numerical property. The distinction is in the rules that govern and the processes that carry out alterations. Following this premise, we will discuss four distinct categories of preprocessing rules.

Rules for Filtering: A filter rule is to isolate occurrences that satisfy a set of requirements. Any occurrences that do not fit the criteria are automatically disregarded. Each occurrence that fulfils the rule's k constraints results in a new instance. Thus, the rule translates each event characteristic to the instance characteristic directly, as shown by the notation fi 14 ai and n 14 m. When deciding how to limit an event's content, selection and logic operators are the most obvious candidates. If E C 2, then F: E a 1,...,an I f 1,...,fn. This rule may be used in both data cleaning and data reduction processes. To begin, a filter rule may help you spot happenings when there are no blanks or background noise. As a second point, filter rules provide the selection of instances by simply defining the criterion to be used to divide them, such as a category property.

Rules for Transforming: The purpose of an alteration rule is to modify the event in some way, either structurally or semantically. As a result, the rule's goal is to either add or remove features, alter the parameter value, or change the attribute type before transferring the value. One may say that each feature is the output of an operation (op) performed on a set of characteristics. An optional window definition allows the operation to return a value based on the weighted average of its attributes across a time period. The capability for picking characteristics and calculating statistics is provided by projection and arithmetic operators in this kind of rule. The use of sequence operators to zero in on certain windowed events is also possible. For the Western Tongue: f g E1,...,Ep I f 1 14 op1 E1,...,Ep,W,...,fm 14 opm E1,...,Ep,W 3. The preprocessing jobs that may benefit from transformation rules are many. When it comes to data preparation, operators in the action of the rule may be used to represent basic tasks like data type translation and format modification. The normalisation procedure is similar in that it employs a numerical transformation, but it calls for extra parameters to scale the result. This is a perfect illustration of why window-defined operators are required, since these paramcters are likely to vary over the data distribution process. When it comes to compressing data, discretization is an operation performed on the original attribute values, which are then transformed into a discrete interval. Finally, aggregation-function-based processes help create new temporal aspects.

Regulations for setting up stream data are inherently dynamic; therefore, preprocessing processes may need to be modified to account for changing circumstances. You may build additional rules to change the parameters of preprocessing procedures or to toggle their state. Consequently, neither events nor instances are generated by the configuration rules themselves. Rather, preprocessing-related procedures and time-based criteria are used. Sequence operators and window facilities are crucial for the construction of configuration rules. Here are two examples of possible uses for configuration rules. To start, to have a better feel for the present flow, it may be required to clear the statistics utilized in any transformation method that uses past data. Second, class imbalance may be easily detected by using configuration rules, which include only calculating the number of instances of every class that have been developed and preprocessed. If there is a discrepancy, the rule used to create instances should result in making up new instances or recreating older occurrences that belonged to the underrepresented group.

Collective instructions

Preprocessing operations need a range of alterations based on the information that is being processed; an extra sort of rule handles these modifications. Such situations need rules with built-in detection and transformation mechanisms. By applying projection and arithmetic operators to events that have been eliminated by logical and selection operators, combined rules combine the strengths of both kinds of rules. When attempting to cleanse data that contains outliers or out-o--range numbers, combined rules may be a helpful tool. Imputation techniques may then be used selectively for the occurrences that really cause problems. This kind of rule is useful for applying several transformations at once since it permits the creation of alternative remedies for a set of instances sharing characteristics, such as an identical class value.

A CEP-based approach enables rule-based preprocessing.

Several scenarios call for the rule-based preprocessing approach. This section gives an explanation of how our CEP-based solution incorporates the aforementioned notions into a data stream-specific preprocessing approach. Since Esper is a CEP engine with built-in support for streams of data and a high-level, SQL-like language for defining rules, we chose to base our implementation on it. Java-based CEP implementation Esper meets the criteria defined, and integrates well with MOA, a standard tool for streams of data mining. It can be seen in Fig. (**1**) that there are three main stages: planning, execution, and evaluation. For each stage, we detail the inputs, outputs, and inner workings with an example for reference. In this case, a meteorologist is interested in using an algorithm for learning to make forecasts about air quality using data from meteorological indicators like humidity, temperature, and carbon dioxide concentration. The rule-based preprocessing workflow employing complicated event processing is shown in Fig. (**1**).

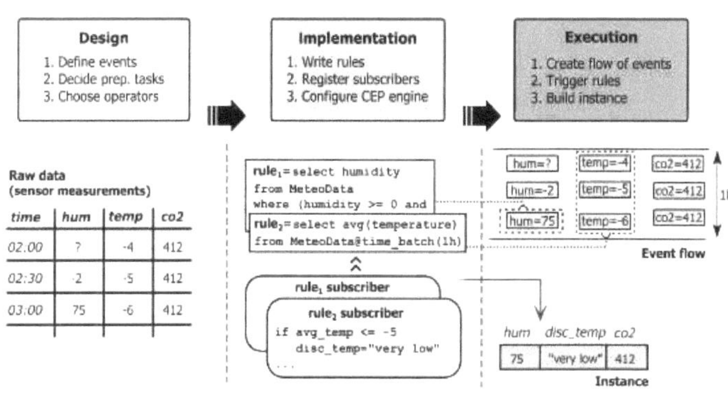

Fig. (1). Procedure for complicated event processing-based rule-based preprocessing.

In the first stage, we determine and plan the preprocessing activities required for a certain application area. A stream of unprocessed information serves as input here. Such inputs in our case would be the readings taken at set intervals by a weather station. Atmospheric variable values are stored as attributes of each stream sample, which constitutes an event in CEP. The domain expert must then choose the preprocessing task type once the case has been specified. Itis possible, for instance, that cleaning climate data and making it easier to manage for learning may include noise reduction and discretization. The nature of the preparation rule to be created is dependent on these selections. While filter rules may be used to reduce unwanted noise, a transformation rule is needed for discretization. The next step is for the domain expert to define the parameters that will activate each rule. Humidity, stated as a percentage in the context of noise cancellation, may take on any value between zero and 100, as specified by the sensor's documentation. For the purpose of discretization, he or she specifies a set of intervals as well as the values that fall within them; for instance, a continuous temperature value might be broken down into five categories: “very low” (five or less), “low” (four to ten), “normal” (eleven to twenty-five), “high” (twenty-six to forty-one), and “very high” (more than forty-one). Additional choices, such as the operators used to calculate statistics in rules of transformation and the creation of a temporal or geographic frame, may fall within the purview of the domain expert, depending on the kind of rule. Here, the meteorologist has decided that it would be more time-efficient to apply discretization to the hourly average temperature rather than to each individual reading. An expert's collection of domain-specific events, actions, restrictions, and operators is all deliverables from the design process. For each data preparation job, the Appendix includes a reference guide containing applicable clauses and operations. In the second stage, the blueprints are put into action in the form of events and preprocessing rules. In addition, the rules and events must be registered with a CEP engine. Here, we use Esper, an implementation of CEP, and events are objects of the Java programming language that will be delivered to a flow. This means that a distinct Java class is used to provide the variables associated with each event type E. Here, we construct a “MeteoData” Java class that takes three parameters: temperature, relative humidity, and CO2 concentration. The publish-subscribe service is used by the CEP engine in Esper, and the rule-building language is comparable to SQL. With the help of Algorithm 1.3, you can set up and personalize this service. First, the rules are defined in EPL syntax by passing a query as a parameter to the Esper statement (lines 2-5) that provides the rules. The first rule in our example determines the allowable range for humidity readings, which is then used to filter out irrelevant data. Second, within a 1-hour time frame, the average operator is used on the temperature variable. Lines 8-11 then establish a subscriber for each statement. A customer is a subclass that extends the update method of a rule and modifies its arguments so that they correspond with the rule's results. For instance, the rule's subscriber will get the rule's average temperature calculation and use it to determine the discrete value to use. CEP service creation and initialization (lines 13-17) follows the definition of rules and subscribers. The steps involved include registering the rules and specifying the event type (through a reference to a Java class). After that is done, a flow may begin sending events to the CEP service. In the last stage, preprocessing rules are put into action in response to incoming events, creating examples from which a machine learning algorithm may draw conclusions. The process begins with the generation of an event stream, or objects in Java, in the instance of Esper. Fig. (**1**) depicts how the rules are triggered when an incoming event meets the criteria. Once triggered, the rules act as a filter or transformation on the matched events. If an action is activated, the subscriber for that rule will receive and examine the result. In order to build the instance, the subscriber must combine the original event's input properties with the rule's output. In keeping with the weather illustration, the filtering rule will be applied to the events' humidity values and the discretization rule will be applied to the events' temperatures. An instance will be generated from the previous event using the valid humidity value, the discretized temperature, and the other meteorological variables. Due to the emphasis on real-time data mining in our concept, we feed instances directly into the learning process. MOA is a library including the techniques and tools required for data mining, as was previously mentioned. At the moment, our MOA wrapper offers eight supervised algorithms: decision tree, a rule-based classifier, kNN, Bayes naive, and two ensemble approaches. This includes regression by gradient descent. In this case, we may assess the air quality by using a classification strategy that uses the filtered atmospheric parameters as instance features. Last but not least, it's worth noting that the MOA wrappers may be readily expanded to call additional algorithms & utilities from MOA, such as drift detectors. Our solution additionally supports ARFF file saving and loading for use in experimental settings.

RESULT AND DISCUSSION

Research Approach ARFF datasets used to produce the input data streams may be found in the UCI5 and OpenML repositories. 6 Ghomeshi *et al*. (2019), Nguyen *et al*. (2015), Ramrez-Gallego *et al*. (2017), and Webb *et al*. (2018) all utilize these datasets as examples of time data streams that stream data mining studies must manage in real time. By uploading the information, one situation at a time, we can mimic the arrival of basic events in CEP. In the learning phase, we use a test-the--train strategy. Before being utilised for training, each new instance is put through its paces as a test case for the current decision model (Bifet, Holmes, Kirkby, & Pfahringer, 2010). The models' prediction efficiency, runtime, and memory utilisation are measured against industry standards for real-time data mining. When necessary, we investigate several other aspects of the simulations. Four approaches available *via* the MOA were selected for this evaluation: Decision trees may be dynamically generated using the Hoeffding tree; k-nearest, neighbors, which finds the k most frequent object pairings; classifying data according to predefined criteria, which create a network of if-then statements; In naive Bayes, the Bayes hypothesis is the sole determinant of the class's likelihood of an occurrence; two ensemble methods using Hoeffding bushes as basic machine learning algorithms; and one ad hoc ensemble strategy. These algorithms are not new, and they all employ a somewhat different tack when it comes to learning (Prasad & Agarwal, 2016; Ramrez-Gallego *et al.*, 2018). We utilise MOA's built-in window-based evaluator with its factory-set window size of 1000 to assess how well they function. Accuracy, the fraction of instances that were correctly labelled (positive or negative); precision, the fraction of truly positive instances within the positive ones; recall, the proportion of positive instances that were correctly labelled; and F1, the mean of the harmonic mean of accuracy and recall are all calculated. The last three metrics are calculated individually for each group and then provided as an average. True positives (TP), true negatives (TN), false positives (FP), and false negatives (FN) may be calculated in this way: TPTNFPFN4 Accuracy 14 TPTNFPFN4 Precision 14 TPFPFN5 Think back on 14 TP TPFN 6

The impact of preprocessing choices like operators & window size is investigated by running algorithms both with and without the use of CEP rules. The data is analysed statistically using Kruskal-Wallis and Wilcoxon tests (p .05). Holm adjustments are made to p-values for pairwise comparisons. Due to our focus on comparative performance analysis, we run all algorithms with their factory settings (as detailed in the MOA docs). We think this is a reasonable example of how non-specialists in data mining may put it to use. Every single test was performed on a Debian 8 PC with an Intel Core i7-2600 processor running at 3.40 GHz and 16 GB of RAM. We repeated each experiment ten times to eliminate the effects of machine fatigue on time and memory use. A large number of iterations combining the two methods are provided, with a new random seed chosen for each iteration. Access to datasets, code, enhanced findings, and statistical validation is granted, as shown in Table **2**.

Table 2. Performance Analysis of the Proposed Systems.

Window Size		Accuracy						F1					
		HT	kNN	NB	RC	LB	ARF	HT	kNN	NB	RC	LB	ARF
Original		81.60	82.5	75.30	73.70	92.80	92.20	81.72	82.3	73.30	72.00	92.87	92.31
Average (-)	10	68.50	76.00	60.80	54.50	77.49	83.26	68.44	75.78	58.33	51.64	77.23	88.06
	50	67.20	73.10	54.70	59.80	75.66	82.20	67.35	72.98	55.11	57.53	75.36	81.85
	100	71.10	72.40	58.00	66.00	75.46	82.27	71.14	72.28	59.09	64.67	75.10	81.90
	500	68.10	71.30	51.60	57.70	75.68	82.34	68.21	71.23	51.65	56.38	75.30	82.00
	1000	67.20	72.50	50.00	57.40	74.19	82.47	66.43	72.32	49.60	55.57	73.86	82.11
Average (t)	10	80.80	79.90	71.80	71.50	92.87	91.70	80.49	79.88	69.90	70.55	92.90	91.77
	50	98.0	80.20	75.70	84.8	97.98	96.46	97.9	80.05	74.13	85.2	97.9	6.4
	100	88.90	80.20	76.90	82.70	92.67	94.66	88.62	79.98	75.43	83.00	92.72	94.73
	500	78.50	78.70	75.60	71.70	91.93	92.50	78.31	78.69	74.03	72.67	91.93	92.61
	1000	84.10	80.10	75.40	63.10	92.29	92.19	83.84	79.91	73.81	60.84	92.29	92.23
Min□/Max□(-)	10	74.40	74.40	62.10	62.90	80.13	83.74	74.67	74.14	59.97	60.44	79.62	83.38
	50	72.20	72.10	58.50	55.90	74.14	81.43	72.52	72.06	59.69	53.87	73.94	81.16
	100	64.40	71.90	59.80	59.30	73.49	80.88	64.67	72.06	61.29	58.16	73.45	80.65
	500	66.40	71.60	50.80	61.30	75.06	82.31	65.75	71.53	50.78	58.95	74.69	82.01
	1000	64.10	71.40	47.90	59.10	75.67	81.61	62.82	71.27	47.33	57.42	75.46	81.25
Min□/Max□(+)	10	80.90	80.50	70.70	82.50	92.60	91.82	80.86	80.43	68.79	81.74	92.62	91.83
	50	91.00	78.40	76.60	65.70	94.19	93.90	91.00	78.40	75.11	63.28	94.27	93.98
	100	88.70	78.40	77.1	78.40	91.56	93.22	88.91	78.46	75.6	77.93	91.71	93.34
	500	85.40	77.10	75.60	72.80	90.84	92.38	85.96	77.09	74.03	72.81	91.01	92.44
	1000	82.90	76.50	75.40	77.30	89.89	92.59	82.90	76.46	73.81	76.61	90.09	92.64

Abbreviations: CEP, complex event processing; IDA, incremental discretization algorithm; IFFD, incremental flexible frequency discretization; LOFD, local online fusion discretizer; OC, Online ChiMerge

Table **2** shows the accuracy and F1 scores achieved by the four different methods. Configurations that are enriched () and decreased () are represented by the symbols and, respectively. Algorithms are sometimes referred to by their abbreviations; for example, a naive Bayes algorithm can be abbreviated as NB, or a rule-based classifier as RC, or a leveraging bag algorithm as LB, or an adaptive random forest algorithm as ARF. One particularly intriguing discovery is that most algorithms benefit from temporal characteristics, but only when the original traits are retained as well. This indicates that the present demand and price are essential pieces of information for the education process. However, the use of historical data as a supplement to decision-making models is particularly advantageous, since it reveals that current consumption patterns may also account for fluctuations in power rates. In fact, employing the enriched data stream improves classification scores for 30 of the 60 possible algorithm-data stream combinations. Using HT, NB, and ARF guarantees better predictions for most combinations of aggregation algorithm & window size, demonstrating the value of temporal data. Given that ARF was already using the second-best algorithm out of the six we tried, this is very remarkable. With the same processing setup (average(+) having a size on the image equal to 50), three techniques with strong starting success (LB, ARF, & HT) achieve an accuracy rate of over 90% in addition to F1. However, kNN, a classification algorithm that uses the k most comparable examples, shows no improvement. For this reason, kNN incorrectly captures the price change owing to other characteristics, since it tends to give the same class to all instances that are near in time and have comparable values for the aggregating functions. The problem worsens as the initial characteristics are eliminated. When comparing algorithms, the range of accuracy gains is as follows (for Hoeffding tree): 1.59–20.10%; for naive Bayes: 0.13–2.39; for the rule-based classifier: 4.88–15.06%; for leverage bagging: 0.08–5.58%; for adaptive random forest: 0.20–4.62%. When compared to RC and NB utilising all of the processing data streams as a starting point, HT, kNN, LB, & ARF perform much better. When it comes to the F1 measure, most algorithms provide a decent compromise between accuracy and recall. Due to a large difference in recall quantity across classes, Naive Bayes performs poorly. Less-featured configurations have a higher false-positive rate. However, this is also seen with the original data stream. The median price, as well as demand, appears to be more instructive than the lowest and maximum numbers when doing preliminary calculations. Depending on the algorithm of choice, the optimal window size is either 50 or 100. Given these realities, it is reasonable to conclude that power prices often exhibit swings that are best described by a typical function. The technique used has a significant impact on execution time, with CEP preparation costing just 0.15–0.4 s to deal with all instances. Increasing the window size has very little effect, with one exception of the enhanced stream, including the lowest and highest values. Since more features mean more time to estimate the distance between instances, using kNN may add up to 80 s to the learning process. However, when employing an efficient algorithm like Hoeffding tree, the gained performance advantage more than makes up for the longer learning time, which is the case for the majority of algorithms. This method, like naive Bayes, is very consistent and never takes more than 1 second to reach a conclusion. The time investment required by ensemble techniques with either the raw stream or the preprocessed results (in the range of 8 and 20 s) is rather high. Only the rule-based classifier, compared with the original data stream, may cut the learning time to a few seconds. Nonetheless, other methods are quicker and have higher classification performance. Using approximately twice the memory of the original data stream, but never more than 11 MB, is necessary to execute the algorithms on the preprocessed data streams.

CONCLUSION

In order to tackle the preprocessing duties involved in stream data mining, this research suggests a rule-based strategy. We borrow heavily from CEP ideas to formalise the approach, treating unprocessed information as events and specifying how to process them in terms of event-driven computing abstractions (ECAs). Various preprocessing rule types are described, offering a fresh and understandable language for expressing routine operations that modify, enhance, or curate incoming data streams. We have put this plan into action with the help of Esper, a form of CEP that offers a SQL-like vocabulary for building complex rules and many operators. Research by subject matter experts should benefit from these traits. Because user-defined functions are readily available and window actions are native, it is simple to include domain-dependent considerations and tailor requirements to data-specific circumstances. Due to its foundation on MOA, the leading structure for online data mining, our method supports parallel preprocessing and learning. Three case studies demonstrate the efficacy of rule-based processing in performing data conversions, creating features, and filling in missing information. It has been shown that supervised algorithms benefit from simple, but effective, preprocessing methods that result in high-quality data streams. It is easier to deal with and understand the acquired knowledge while others of the choice models than those learned from the raw data. These advantages justify the work involved in preprocessing. Our results suggest that adding additional information to the learning phase does not significantly increase the required time and memory resources. In addition, preparing streams using CEP yields better results compared to other preprocessing approaches, such as discretization, while speeding up the execution of traditional algorithms.

REFERENCES

[1] Mavrogiorgos, K., Mavrogiorgou, A., Kiourtis, A., Zafeiropoulos, N.E., Kleftakis, S., & Kyriazis, D. (2022). Automated Rule-Based Data Cleaning Using NLP. 2022 32nd Conference of Open Innovations Association (FRUCT), 162-168.

[2] Zhang, R.F., Stolzenberg-Solomon, R.S., Lynch, S.M., & Urbanowicz, R.J. (2021). LCS-DIVE: An Automated Rule-based Machine Learning Visualization Pipeline for Characterizing Complex Associations in Classification. ArXiv, abs/2104.12844.

[3] A. Alghanmi, Z. Yang, and E.B. Davis, "Risk analysis of petroleum transportation using fuzzy rule-based Bayesian reasoning", *Int. J. Shipp. Transp. Logist.*, vol. 12, no. 1/2, p. 39, 2020. [http://dx.doi.org/10.1504/IJSTL.2020.105854]

[4] V. Robles-Bykbaev, A. Guzhñay-Lucero, D. Pulla-Sánchez, F. Pesántez-Avilés, P. Suquilanda-Cuesta, and E. Bernal-Merchán, "A Multifunction Braille Trainer Based on Embedded Systems, Mobile Apps, Rule-based Reasoning and Data Mining for Children with Visual Impairment", *Comput. Sist.*, vol. 22,

no. 4, p. 22, 2018.
[http://dx.doi.org/10.13053/cys-22-4-2795]

[5] E.M. Wysocka, *Developing a framework for semi-automated rule-based modelling for neuroscience research.,* 2019.

[6] G. Nalepa, and S. Bobek, "Rule-based solution for context-aware reasoning on mobile devices", *Comput. Sci. Inf. Syst.,* vol. 11, no. 1, pp. 171-193, 2014.
[http://dx.doi.org/10.2298/CSIS130209002N]

[7] H. Boley, R. Grütter, G. Zou, T. Athan, and S. Etzold, "A Datalog + Plus RuleML 1.01 Architecture for Rule-Based Data Access in Ecosystem Research", *International Web Rule Symposium,* 2014.

[8] X. Zhang, Y. Wang, R. Lin, Y. Zhang, X. Li, and J. Wang, "An Electric Equipment Analysis Method based on Knowledge Reasoning", *J. Phys. Conf. Ser.,* vol. 2132, no. 1, p. 012044, 2021.
[http://dx.doi.org/10.1088/1742-6596/2132/1/012044]

[9] Chakrabarti, A., Ahmad, F., Jarke, M., & Quix, C. (2022). Monitoring Large Scale Production Processes Using a Rule-Based Visualization Recommendation System. SN Computer Science, 4.

[10] A.T. Reddy, and D.M. Nagendra, "Minimal Rule-Based Classifiers using PCA on Pima-Indian--Diabetes-Dataset", *Int. J. Innov. Technol. Explor. Eng.,* vol. 8, no. 12, pp. 4414-4420, 2019.
[http://dx.doi.org/10.35940/ijitee.L2476.1081219]

[11] Das, M., Li, J., Fosler-Lussier, E., Lin, S.M., Moosavinasab, S., Rust, S., Huang, Y., & Ramnath, R. (2019). Sequence-to-Set Semantic Tagging: End-to-End Multi-label Prediction using Neural Attention for Complex Query Reformulation and Automated Text Categorization. ArXiv, abs/1911.04427.

[12] T. Mellouli, *Complex Certainty Factors for Rule Based Systems - Detecting Inconsistent Argumentations.* WLP/WFLP, 2014.

[13] L. Evans, N. Lohse, & P. Webb, "A self-learning case and rule-based reasoning algorithm for intelligent technology evaluation and selection", *International Journal of Computer Integrated Manufacturing,* vol. 23, no. 11, pp. 1046-1056, 2010.
[http://dx.doi.org/10.1080/0951192X.2010.518815]

[14] A. Harichandran, and J. Teizer, "Automated Recognition of Hand Gestures for Crane Rigging using Data Gloves in Virtual Reality", *Proceedings of the International Symposium on Automation and Robotics in Construction (IAARC),* 2022.
[http://dx.doi.org/10.22260/ISARC2022/0043]

[15] F. Sovrano, M. Palmirani, B. Distefano, S. Sapienza, and F. Vitali, "A dataset for evaluating legal question answering on private international law", *Proceedings of the Eighteenth International Conference on Artificial Intelligence and Law,* 2021.
[http://dx.doi.org/10.1145/3462757.3466094]

[16] N. Qamar, and A.A. Malik, "Impact of design patterns on software complexity and size", *Mehran University Research Journal of Engineering and Technology,* vol. 39, no. 2, pp. 342-352, 2020.
[http://dx.doi.org/10.22581/muet1982.2002.10]

[17] A. Koenig, Patterns and antipatterns.*The Patterns Handbooks: Techniques, Strategies, and Applications.* Cambridge University Press: Cambridge, UK, 1998, pp. 383-389.

[18] Y. Smaragdakis, and C. Csallner, "Combining Static and Dynamic Reasoning for Bug Detection", *Proceedings of the International Conference on Tests and Proofs,* Springer: Berlin/Heidelberg, Germany, pp. 1-16, 2007.Zurich, Switzerland
[http://dx.doi.org/10.1007/978-3-540-73770-4_1]

[19] V.M. Bakanov, "Computational complexity when constructing rational plans for program execution in a given field of parallel computers", *Russian Technological Journal,* vol. 10, no. 6, pp. 7-19, 2022.
[http://dx.doi.org/10.32362/2500-316X-2022-10-6-7-19]

[20] Z. Zhang, Z. Xing, X. Xia, X. Xu, and L. Zhu, "Making Python Code Idiomatic by Automatic

Refactoring Non-Idiomatic Python Code with Pythonic Idioms", *Proceedings of the 30th ACM Joint European Software Engineering Conference and Symposium on the Foundations of Software Engineering,* Association for Computing Machinery: New York, NY, USA, pp. 696-708, 2022.Singapore
[http://dx.doi.org/10.1145/3540250.3549143]

[21] S. Uchiyama, A. Kubo, H. Washizaki, and Y. Fukazawa, "Detecting design patterns in object-oriented program source code by using metrics and machine learning", *Journal of Software Engineering and Applications,* vol. 7, no. 12, pp. 983-998, 2014.
[http://dx.doi.org/10.4236/jsea.2014.712086]

[22] A.K. Dwivedi, A. Tirkey, R.B. Ray, and S.K. Rath, "Software design pattern recognition using machine learning techniques", *Proceedings of the 2016 IEEE Region 10 Conference (TENCON),* IEEE: Piscataway, NJ, USA, pp. 222-227, 2016. Marina Bay Sands, Singapore.
[http://dx.doi.org/10.1109/TENCON.2016.7847994]

[23] O. Hummel, and S. Burger, "Analyzing source code for automated design pattern recommendation", *Proceedings of the 3rd ACM SIGSOFT International Workshop on Software Analytics,* Association for Computing Machinery: New York, NY, USA, pp. 8-14, 2017. Paderborn, Germany.
[http://dx.doi.org/10.1145/3121257.3121259]

CHAPTER 9

Evaluating the Usefulness of Big Data in Decision Making

Dhruv Galgotia[1,*] and **Mohammed Zabeeulla**[2]

[1] *Department of Management, Galgotias University, Greater Noida, Uttar Pradesh, India*

[2] *Department of Computer Science and Engineering, JAIN (Deemed-to-be University), Bangalore, Karnataka, India*

Abstract: Connected to the web of things, "Big data," an increasingly popular phrase, describes the massive amounts of data frequently produced by modern healthcare systems. The sheer volume and complexity of the information make it difficult to extract actionable insights for forecasting and policymaking. Big data technologies provide significant infrastructure support to enable critical decision-making and better achieve the objectives of IoT systems. Privacy protection, data integrity, and verification of identity are three tenets that must be strictly upheld in big data for healthcare service administration. To solve these problems, this study suggests a big data ecosystem-enabled, scalable computer system that allows authenticated data access methods for health data analytics enabled by the Internet of Things. A large-scale data analytics tracking system, as well as a data storage/access system generated from blockchain, make up the two primary sub-architectures of the architecture that is suggested. In order to analyze, store, and authorize verified use of information collected by IoT-enabled devices, this solution utilizes big data systems as well as blockchain architecture. Data linkability may be avoided, and unauthorized users can have no access to private data by using the zero-knowledge protocol. The results demonstrate the efficacy of our method in resolving healthcare privacy and big data analytics issues.

Keywords: Big data analysis, decision making, blockchain, iot, healthcare.

INTRODUCTION

In cognitive production that is powered by big data, techniques for situational awareness, neural networks with convolution, as well as cutting-edge computing, construct event modeling as well as prediction. Data mining, predictive analytics, and sensor-actuator networks are the building blocks of automated control systems.

* **Corresponding author Dhruv Galgotia:** Department of Management, Galgotias University, Greater Noida, Uttar Pradesh, India; E-mail: ceo@galgotiasuniversity.edu.in

S. Kannadhasan, R. Nagarajan, & Kaushik Pal (Eds.)

Object recognition methods, deep learning computations, and visual perception tools all contribute to better robotic systems for navigation. Fusion of data technologies, cooperative operating methods, and context recognition tools enables configurable manufacturing procedures. Contributing technologies include methods for control and decision-making, edge and cloud computing, as well as remote intelligent devices, image detection, identity verification, and recognition. Technologies for monitoring contextual data, cloud computing, vision and navigation systems, and intelligent simulation environments are employed in their development. Visual cognitive algorithms, context-aware tools, and artificial neural networks are used to optimize robotic manufacturing processes.

Innovation and enhanced decision-making in service industries depend on accurate and up-to-date knowledge. This is why data is so important for service industries. Data that has been collected and evaluated thoroughly is used to predict what will happen and how specific parameters are trending in the future [1]. As we begin to fully grasp the advantages of this position, we realize that new technical breakthroughs have enabled us to generate and gather more data in almost every aspect of our lives, particularly in our social connections, research, jobs, and health. Consequently, "big data" has become a common phrase. Particularly challenging is the fact that healthcare businesses are producing data at a quick pace [2]. All sorts of diverse, multi-spectral, incomplete, and ambiguous primary source observations are a part of healthcare big data, including unstructured, semi-structured, and structured information (e.g., on demographics, illness, injury, therapy, problems with mental and physical health, as well as illness management). Structured data includes information such as ICD codes, traits, genotypes, and genomic data, while unstructured information includes medical imaging, observations, environmental variables, clinical notes, lifestyle choices, medications, and health economic data [3]. Additionally, advancements in the Internet of Things (IoT) have sped up data-driven applications in healthcare, smart cities, transportation, and networking [4]. Particularly, the medical field has been instrumental in the use of various sensors and technological devices to monitor patients' vital signs and other health indicators [5]. Information in excess of ever-increasing amounts has resulted from the expansion of omics fields, including genomics, proteomics, and metabolomics [6]. Electronic health records (EHRs) are replacing traditional medical records, further facilitating data dissemination. Medical professionals, epidemiologists, and healthcare policy analysts want to improve patient care and community health by using such massive amounts of data [7]. Setting up the required infrastructure, techniques, and tools is critical for making good use of the generated big data [8].

RELATED WORKS

Its stated goal is to perform the aforementioned tasks using the NEWS data. To create complex queries, it is necessary to first study the NEWS data and build it. A significant data challenge arises from the complexity and volume of the data in relation to data analytics. Also, bear in mind that the healthcare business is not making the most of its resources because data confidentiality and integrity issues are widespread, even though this data is believed to be crucial for improving health outcomes and reducing costs [9]. Data privacy and integrity verification using efficient methods and methodologies is of the utmost importance for addressing the limitations of these challenges. Two North East hospitals in the United Kingdom are overseen by South Tees Institutions NHS Foundation Trust1, which is responsible for patient data. These hospitals store 5 million records, each containing 20 tables with around 50 attributes related to patients. Executing queries on large datasets, however, can take weeks or even months owing to the data's massive volume and complexity, as well as user-related concerns during UDF construction [10]. In healthcare, managing heterogeneous data is a key challenge in big data analytics. However, this data presents an opportunity for better healthcare for countless people. Big data platforms help address issues in the healthcare delivery system by analyzing large, complex healthcare data. The use of highly parallel, multi-tenant environments is common in big data processing systems such as Hadoop2 and Spark3, but these environments are vulnerable to software and hardware errors that can reduce performance [11]. A complex query is intentionally designed to make it more difficult to obtain responses when dealing with challenging data. A sizable internal healthcare Internet of Things surveillance network is established by transferring data from various wearables and sensors to servers. Problems with data confidentiality (the protection, accessibility, storage, and longevity of personally identifiable information) and data integrity (the assurance that data is accurate, comprehensive, consistent, and securely stored in compliance with the General Data Protection Regulation, or GDPR)) arise organically as the [12]. With the help of extensive analytical systems, the Internet of Things (IoT) ecosystem for healthcare generates the most sensitive large data. Processing and storing such massive amounts of data on state-of-the-art computers raises serious concerns about data integrity, as erroneous diagnoses might put lives in jeopardy. Security and privacy are additional issues when working with large amounts of sensitive health data. Public cloud computing, in particular, makes cloud-hosted big data systems more vulnerable to hacker attacks. According to McAfee [13], 3.1 million users' data that was stored in the cloud has allegedly been hacked in the last year. Big data systems, which often rely on centralized datacenters, pose a danger to health data, as this instance shows. To avoid these kinds of incidents, healthcare institutions should have strict protocols to ensure the confidentiality and integrity of big data sets. That is why, over the last decade, several cryptographic primitives have been employed to safeguard medical records. The healthcare service provider is still worried, however, about the heavy and tough crypto-primitives. The 5V characteristics of big data make it so that implementing stringent security measures might negatively impact system efficiency while still failing to provide adequate privacy, integrity confirmation, and identity hiding. A number of systems have begun to see blockchain, with its immutable design that prevents tampering, as a viable solution to these issues, as it ensures the confidentiality and authenticity of data. By using a distributed database structure, blockchain makes it possible to verify the information (transactions) independently. The popular cryptocurrency Bitcoin uses blockchain technology to secure, verify, and store events in a decentralized, publicly accessible ledger [14]. Here, the integrity of the data can be verified through transaction encryption. Financial transactions, insurance, banking, voting, as well as cryptocurrency, are just a few examples of the many businesses that use blockchain technology [15]. Upon data confirmation, new blocks are created at regional endpoints in these networks' distributed ledgers whenever fresh information is received from any source, including IoT devices. On the other hand, conventional blockchain architectures may not be able to handle the massive data volumes in the healthcare sector. One solution may be to restrict the quantity of information stored on the blockchain. Data safeguards vary from country to country; thus there may be more privacy concerns if all data is stored on the distributed ledger. To control size and privacy requirements, it is essential to identify which data must be stored on the blockchain. Suppose the data required to create the NEWS is stored off-chain, on a main cloud server, and the NEW rating, which is calculated via the NEW data, is stored on-chain, on the blockchain. The hash of newly added information should also be kept on the blockchain as an additional measure to guarantee data integrity and verification. In this case, we may verify the integrity of cloud-stored data using on-chain NEWS, or we can verify the accuracy of distributed ledger data using off-chain information to recompute bitcoin NEWS. Beyond these concerns, it is crucial to confirm the identity of those requesting access to healthcare data since it is often accessible by a diverse group of people (data owners, doctors, hospital staff, *etc.*). Due to the potential for authentication processes used in older approaches to connect individuals to their data, data linkability as well as privacy issues, are common outcomes. This dilemma becomes even more important when the material pertains to healthcare. Hence, the data as well as the users' identities must remain distinct throughout the verification procedure in order to ensure user authenticity.

PROPOSED WORK

Big Data Analytics & Healthcare

Healthcare organizations use big data analytics to sift through massive patient databases, as shown in Fig. (**1**). Interactions among variables (such as prescription drugs and their dosages) are complex, and connections across databases are also common.

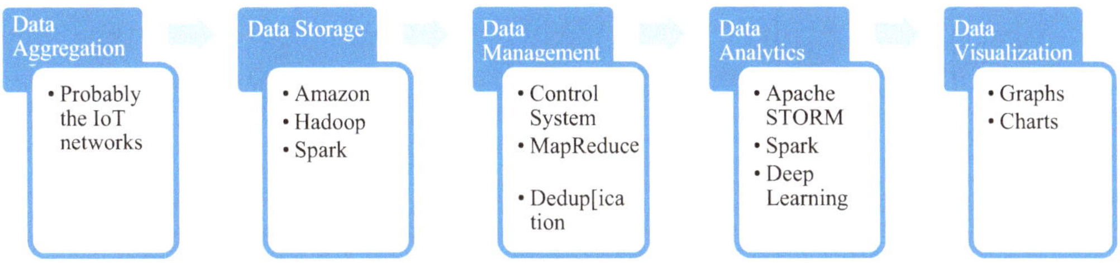

Fig. (1). Flow of Big data analytics.

Data collection

Data that is in structured, semi-structured, or unstructured formats is all acceptable for medical data acquisition. Furthermore, healthcare organizations, social media, cellphones, computerized physician order entry (CPOE), health maintenance organizations (HMOs), as well as government departments are also significant data providers.

Data storage

Due to the rapidly increasing volume of data in the healthcare industry, a massive storage system is necessary to accommodate the information. At this time, cloud computing makes it easy to store and handle this kind of data. It is believed that the structure of a cloud provides a flexible foundation for managing and analyzing large amounts of data. There are a number of major cloud computing platforms, including Google, Amazon, and IBM. Healthcare providers may reap various advantages from these systems when it comes to the exchange of data among patients, doctors, and other medical facilities. However, this kind of storing raises a variety of concerns related to medicolegal concerns, such as the need to preserve information and the need to maintain privacy. Providers of cloud computing services may claim to deliver their offerings in a reliable and safe way, but that's seldom the reality. The perfect solution to this problem is blockchain technology, which leverages the spare space on people's computers all across the globe for storing information in a decentralized network. A possible alternative to cloud storage with a centralized management system, the decentralized approach may solve several issues plaguing these kinds of systems.

Data management

As a critical component in establishing a patient's risk level, data management plays a significant role in healthcare. Included in this are retrieval of data, a process for extracting valuable information from enormous databases, data cleaning, which involves checking for missing or unnecessary data, as well as data management. Ensuring the confidentiality of individual information about patients is of the utmost importance in the management of healthcare. The General Data Protection Regulation, also known as the GDPR, governs the management of data, which is the process by which an organization ensures that its data is secure, private, and readily available for use. It details the basic laws and regulations that deal with health rules, as well as government regulations that try to protect the privacy of health records.

Data analytics

The process of extracting meaningful insights from datasets is known as data analysis. A data analysis might be diagnostic, descriptive, predictive, or adaptive. Descriptive analytics and supervised learning both rely on historical data to assess previous performance. By examining past data, a diagnostic test may determine the root of the problem. Predictive analytics, which is sometimes called learning with supervision, uses both current and past data to speculate on potential future events. For forecasting purposes, it is not used. The use of predictive analytics allows for the automated examination of massive amounts of information prior to decision-making, resulting in multiple potential results.

Data visualisation

This method presents the results of data analysis in a graphical format, which helps individuals comprehend complex healthcare data and supports better decision-making. One further reason to use data visualization is to discover connections and trends in the data.

Among the many components that comprise the system architecture are a visualization structure, an infrastructure for storing and verifying data using blockchain technology, and a system for comprehensively managing large amounts of data. Block storage architecture is shown in Fig. (**2**).

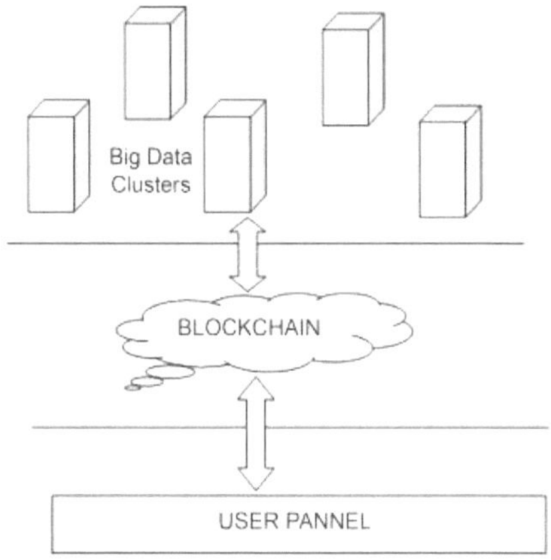

Fig. (2). Proposed Block-Storage architecture.

These are the specific activities that the group hopes to complete:

1. Integrating NEWS information and electronic observation with other patient records:
2. Designing a system to manage the massive volumes of data that are relevant,
3. (i.e., finding the cut-offs that best anticipate results) modeling the sensitivity as well as precision of NEWS as well as observations;
4. Use the paths of scores instead of specific scores.

In order to begin the distributed processing of the NEWS data, we first transfer it from our MySQL database server to HDFS inside the Hadoop architecture. Apache Sqoop HAProxy coordinates the transfer of data from the Galera cluster, a multi-master database cluster used for asynchronous MySQL replication of data, to the large-scale structure of data by acting as a load balancer and shipment control system for TCP and HTTP-based applications running in the cloud. To facilitate the transfer of structured datasets from databases like MySQL to Apache Hadoop, the Apache Technology Project developed Apache Sqoop4, a command-line interface application. Coordination as well as execution of several tasks across HDFS is handled by the Hadoop group, a massive data cluster consisting of a master node and numerous nodes that perform work (W1, W2,..., WN).

This research presents a system that consists of two main tasks: first, employing A blockchain-based framework for information storage as well as verification; and second, monitoring the query as well as system performance in the Hadoop environment. This section will begin with a high-level overview of the proposed technique's system architecture, before diving further into the specifics of each component.

Keeping an eye on how well the systems and queries in the Hadoop ecosystem are doing.

The SmartAgent, along with Agents, is the main component of the monitoring system. We install a SIGAR library-connected agent on every worker node to monitor their resource utilization, including CPU/memory consumption, usage of bandwidth, and I/O status. The SmartAgent is in charge of gathering information from node workers on tasks, apps, and clusters via the usage of TaskTrackers and Yarn APIs. This means that SmartAgent may not only get the UDF result but also track the mapper/reducer tasks that were associated with these queries. After the monitoring system finishes the query, it sends the results to the decision-making systems using SmartAgent integration. Tracking queries. When queries are generated using user-defined functions (UDFs), SmartAgent keeps an eye on them. After the syntax of the query is reviewed, the objects that are referenced in the request are examined for existence. Once the query processing in Apache Hive has started, SmartAgent, which was developed on top of SmartMonit, an on-demand massive data watching solution, will begin watching the MapReduce process in real-time. If SmartAgent detects a problem or a drop in network efficiency, it will warn you. Jobs that are not running simultaneously in a cluster yet are taking longer to finish are called stragglers, and SmartAgent finds them. At the first sign of a typical language runtime-generated system fault, SmartMonit will begin collecting data about the MapReduce activity over the appropriate channels (counters). The SmartMonit agent keeps track of the progress within UDFs by monitoring the MapInputRecords, MapOutRecords, and ShuffleErrors counts. The appropriate count is triggered and sent to the visualisation system in order to notify users of system deviations. In addition, SmartAgent receives the query results and communicates with the decision-making system to ascertain the patients' health state via the computation of the NEWS. Additionally, the time series data is updated in real-time using the InfluxDB5 historical repository. Keep an eye on how the system is doing. The SmartAgent gathers all the data relevant to the mapping and reducer query jobs simultaneously, while the agents gather data pertaining to the foundational systems (CPU, memory, I/O, network connectivity, etc.). The SIGAR API is hooked into agents, whereas the SmartAgent is plugged into yarn APIs. The visualization component of system health monitoring provides an intuitive interface and displays all system interactions for the user to see.

Way to decide on NEWS: One of the NEWS's main aims is to standardise how the NHS determines the seriousness of acute diseases. Inhalation rate, saturation of oxygen, temperatures, heart rate, systolic blood pressure, awareness, as well as oxygen or airflow are the main physiological characteristics that comprise the NEWS. A high-level medical alert, also known as an urgent clinical assessment, should be triggered by a NEWS of 7 or above, while an urgent medical review should be triggered by a total NEWS of 5 or 6. Using the clinical risk assessment, the visualization portion is created. Algorithm 1 displays the NEWS computation for every patient.

Blockchain Framework Derived for NEWS

Since Bitcoin was invented, blockchain technology has been used by numerous parties and in many different applications. A number of solutions have recently emerged, providing a foundation for easy corporate operations. It has been noted that blockchain scalability remains an issue. Neither of the systems makes any pretense of being able to manage large data or enable analytics, two crucial components of the modern corporate sector. Because of its immutability and verifiability, blockchain is better used for other purposes than as a storage system. This is why, much as in works through, we utilize a fragmented blockchain design in this endeavor. In this arrangement, the only private information saved off-chain is the NEWS (score) hash; the block itself only retains this hash. In order to keep the outcomes of the searches for every patient on blockchain-based databases, we will be using MongoDB and other databases that are accessible in the public cloud. These databases provide access to information and blockchain-enabled apps. Blockchain technology has the potential to provide encrypted distributed data storage via the public cloud. Consistent performance and data integrity can only be achieved via the integration of blockchain-based systems with public cloud services. In addition to certifying data kept off-chain, this will help make NEWS information public and enable forward and backward authenticity.

Step 1: In order to generate NEWS that may be published on the distributed ledger, medical employees examine patient EHR data.

Step 2: Everyone involved in the patient's network—doctors, researchers, and hospitals—receives the block in a decentralized virtual internet.

Step 3: Every single node in the network checks and approves the block.

Step 4: By linking it to previous blocks in the chain, the new block becomes an immutable and verifiable record.

There are two steps to the proposed derived blockchain process: creating blocks and registering and verifying identities. What follows is a description of each of these steps.

Phase 1: The Process of Enrollment and Validation. Permitting a legitimate user to store and access information regarding the distributed ledger is a major concern in the healthcare sector. That is why we have proposed a method that uses the zero-knowledge protocol (ZKP) to guarantee it. At this stage of the distributed ledger process, people are acknowledged as genuine users when they register for the Block-Store or view the NEWS scores.

- Its RQi is a request that the Ui makes to the Mj, the Block-Store Manager, in order to register and utilize the blockchain. To do this, an indefinite key (TKi) is generated for the Ui making the request. Device credentials (DCi)—here meaning the machine address (MAC address) as well as device ID—and user interface (UI) are used to produce TKi. So, let's pretend that DCi is the sum of DIDi and DMACi. Using these characteristics, as shown below, you create
- The DCi setup. In order to conceal the device's or sensor's hardware address (MAC address), the equation DCi = H DIDi,(DMACi MRN) (1) employs a made-up number RN. To further simplify the production sequence of requests, the time and date (TSi) of TKi's generation is also recorded. For further processing, the TKi and RQi are transmitted to Mj over a secure SSL/TLS connection.
- Mj checks RQi for scripts or format problems after getting it and eliminates TKi. The authentication of RQi results in the production of an unverified identity (IDi). The validation of this identity will not take place until the ZKP process is successfully completed; it was granted to the individual in question at their request.
- Next, Ui is instructed to initiate the ZKP operation by transmitting the signal flag (SZKP).
- Ui at the start of the ZKP process is the prover, as Mj is the challenger or verifier. Using ZKP, the verifier may check the validity of both parties without learning any private information. As seen below, this is one way to compute the exact value of y with the use of a generator g with a big prime number p. y = g sqrt(TSimod p) Ui may prove its comprehension of TSi at any time by examining the value of y, but it must do so. Then, as shown below, Ui determines a value of r, an integer with a random value that is employed to further calculate d.

r = TSi + RQi g = rmod p (1)

Sending d to Mj via a secure connection is the next step.

- Below, you can see that the Mj selects two queries and extracts d.

Q2 = TSi + TSi + RQimod(p 1) Q1 = TSi + RQi (2)

Ui gets the request over an encrypted connection.

- Ui chooses the best response (A) when given a problem. The response has been sent to Mj.
- Mj checks the answer using the following criteria in the final step.

g(TSi+RQi)mod(p1))mod p = x.u mod p g(TSi+RQi)mod(p1))mod p = x

The next step is to verify Ui's identity and assign it an IDi. Ui may then use this IDi to store or retrieve NEWS information from the blockchain.

RESULT AND DISCUSSION

This section provides experimental findings that aim to assess the efficacy, practicality, resource utilization, and overheads of Block-Store in healthcare analytics powered by big data-driven IoT. To ensure the reliability and effectiveness of the health care Internet of Things blockchain-based verified big data ecosystem, the NEWS data7 is used. This data is produced from the framework and principles taken from South Tees Hospital NHS Foundation Trust. Multiple blocks with different patient counts (250K, 500K, 750K, and 1M) make up the dataset. There are 52 pieces of individual health data in the dataset. This includes seven different physiological indicators, admission dates, duration of hospital stay, pain rating, vomiting and nausea levels, weight, and much more.

Setup for an experiment.

Three independent Hadoop YARN clusters were set up on AWS to evaluate the effectiveness of the monitoring system:

In Type 1, there is a single boss and three subordinates,

Type 2, with a single supervisor and six subordinates, and

Third kind, with a single boss and a staff of nine.

As the number of machines rises, the findings show that tasks require less time to complete. Every query is performed five times, and the results are reported as the average as well as the standard deviation. After SmartAgent and Agents have gathered the necessary data, it is sent to the visualization portion. Examining the duration and quantity of assignments. We contrasted the makespan (in total task time) and task count using the various datasets. There are four different datasets shown here, with the overall amount of jobs launched being 250K, 500K, 750K, and 1000K. The data sets' availability periods are also detailed in the statistics. Because the overall number of tasks is consistent across all cluster types, the makespan is the key variable that varies in the numbers. The performance analysis of the proposed system is shown in Fig. (**3**). During the processing of NEWS data, we also evaluated the straggler detection that was carried out on the big data system. Displayed results show straggler detection in very resource-intensive environments, in conditions of high memory use. For real-time monitoring of the system's health and identification of stragglers, SmartAgent processes the data concurrently. The research analysed data from 500,000 patients, which led to both conclusions.

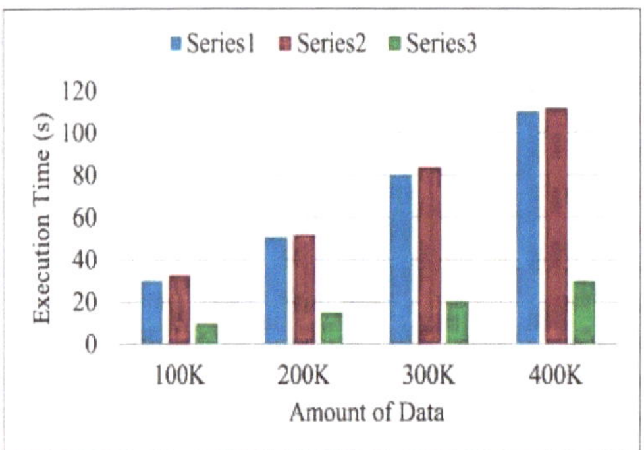

(a)

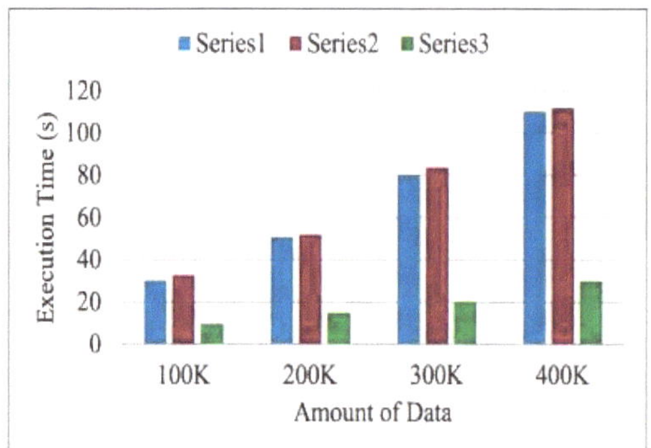

(b)

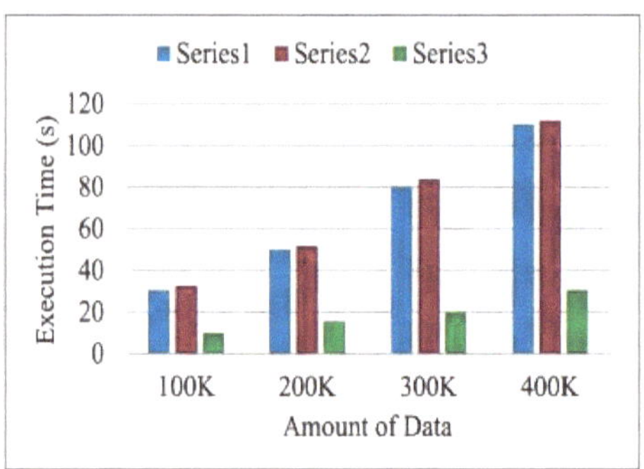

(c)

Fig. (3). Performance Anlaysis of the Proposed Work.

CONCLUSION

Business and management services for the community with an emphasis on efficiency, innovation, and cost savings. Blockchain technology also solves the trust and privacy issues plaguing the financial and healthcare sectors. Our research shows how important it is to store sensitive medical data on an approved blockchain system and evaluate its complexity and volume. Incorporating the principles of blockchain technology with big data processing, we developed a safe and expandable infrastructure for healthcare data analysis; this endeavor requires the joint efforts of IT experts and medical doctors. Big data analytics in healthcare face two critical challenges in IoT contexts: scalability and privacy. These problems are entirely solved by BlockStore, which provides a robust, scalable, and user-friendly authentication tool, data storage, and sharing method. Our long-term goal is to enhance the functionality of our network infrastructure by implementing state-of-the-art communication technologies like 5G, SNS, and SDN.

REFERENCES

[1] N.A.B. Mohd Zaki, A. Jamaluddin, V. Tanggamani, A. Rahim, and N.A. Alias, "Big Data: Balancing its Usefulness in Managing an Organization Performance and Ethical Consideration", *Int. J. Acad. Res. Bus. Soc. Sci.,* vol. 13, no. 6, 2023. [http://dx.doi.org/10.6007/IJARBSS/v13-i6/17592]

[2] D. Tong, and G. Tian, *Intelligent financial decision support system based on big data.*. Journal of Intelligent Systems, vol. 32, no. 1, 2023, pp. 20220320. [http://dx.doi.org/10.1515/jisys-2022-0320]

[3] Chowdhury, S.A., Islam, M.A., Kamal, M.A., Education, S.O., Sciences, S., Scotland, U.O., Ier, Engineering, U.O., Computing, Mathematics, University, O.B., Computing, S.O., Technologies, Gloucestershire, U.O., Business, U.S., University, B.O., & Gazipur (2023). Unveiling the Potential of Big Data Analytics for Transforming Higher Education in Bangladesh; Needs, Prospects, and Challenges.

[4] Q. Li, Y. Rong, Z. Pei, and F. Ren, "A novel linguistic decision making approach based on attribute correlation and EDAS method", *Soft Comput.,* vol. 27, no. 12, pp. 7751-7771, 2023. [http://dx.doi.org/10.1007/s00500-023-08079-y]

[5] J Pekarcikova. HIA as a standard tool for effective decision-making on NCD policies. Eur J Public Health vol. 33(Suppl 2): ckad160.1300, 2023.

[6] T. Choi, B. Chan, L. Grech, A. Kwok, K. Webber, J. Wong, M. Nguyen, N. Bain, D. Day, A. McCartney, R. Hamer, E. Segelov, and O.B. In, "Factors Influencing COVID-19 Vaccine Hesitancy among Patients with Serious Chronic Illnesses during the Initial Australian Vaccine Rollout: A Multi-Centre Qualitative Analysis Using the Health Belief Model", *Vaccines (Basel),* vol. 11, no. 2, p. 239, 2023. [http://dx.doi.org/10.3390/vaccines11020239] [PMID: 36851117]

[7] S.A. Shmeleva, "The impact of big data on decision-making on business support measures during the COVID-19 pandemic: The case of St. Petersburg", *Vestn. Tomsk. Gos. Univ.,* no. 482, pp. 5-17, 2023. [http://dx.doi.org/10.17223/15617793/482/1]

[8] G.U. Orlu, R.B. Abdullah, Z. Zaremohzzabich, Y.Y. Jusoh, S. Asadi, Y.A.M. Qasem, R.N.H. Nor, and W.M.H. Mohd Nasir, "A Systematic Review of Literature on Sustaining Decision-Making in Healthcare Organizations Amid Imperfect Information in the Big Data Era", *Sustainability (Basel),* vol. 15, no. 21, p. 15476, 2023. [http://dx.doi.org/10.3390/su152115476]

[9] Fattah, I.A., & Mts, A. Decision Making Performance of Big Data Analytics Capabilities:The Mediating Effect of Co-Collaboration. Journal of System and Management Sciences. Vol. 13, no. 6, pp. 410-431, 2023.

[http://dx.doi.org/10.33168/JSMS.2023.0625]

[10] D. Di Berardino, and S. Vona, *Discovering the Relationship Between Big Data, Big Data Analytics, and Decision Making: A Structured Literature Review. European Scientific Journal.* ESJ, 2023.

[11] K. Ragazou, I. Passas, A. Garefalakis, E. Galariotis, and C. Zopounidis, "Big Data Analytics Applications in Information Management Driving Operational Efficiencies and Decision-Making: Mapping the Field of Knowledge with Bibliometric Analysis Using R", *Big Data and Cognitive Computing,* vol. 7, no. 1, p. 13, 2023.
[http://dx.doi.org/10.3390/bdcc7010013]

[12] O.O. Olaniyi, O.J. Okunleye, and S.O. Olabanji, *Advancing Data-Driven Decision-Making in Smart Cities through Big Data Analytics: A Comprehensive Review of Existing Literature.* Current Journal of Applied Science and Technology, 2023.

[13] L. Lamrini, M.C. Abounaima, and M. Talibi Alaoui, "New distributed-topsis approach for multi-criteria decision-making problems in a big data context", *J. Big Data,* vol. 10, no. 1, p. 97, 2023.
[http://dx.doi.org/10.1186/s40537-023-00788-3]

[14] M. Aseeri, and K. Kang, "Organisational culture and big data socio-technical systems on strategic decision making: Case of Saudi Arabian higher education", *Educ. Inf. Technol.,* vol. 28, no. 7, pp. 8999-9024, 2023.
[http://dx.doi.org/10.1007/s10639-022-11500-y]

[15] D. Lindebaum, C. Moser, and G. Islam, "Big Data, Proxies, Algorithmic Decision-Making and the Future of Management Theory", *J. Manage. Stud.*. vol. 61, no. 6, pp. 2724-2747, 2024.

CHAPTER 10

Evaluating the Role of Data Mining in Enhancing Decision-Making

Alisha Sikri[1,*]

[1] *Department of AIML, Noida Institute of Engineering and Technology, Greater Noida, Uttar Pradesh, India*

Abstract: An obstacle for sentiment-based recommendation systems is the abundance of information available online. Because of flaws in their data-cleaning and analysis processes, existing machine learning (ML) methods fail to provide trustworthy recommendations. To get over this issue, this research proposed a recommender system that uses Twitter reviews and is based on Lite deep learning (LightDL). The information retrieved from Twitter is cleaned using data-cleaning processes. After that, the LightDL algorithm is trained to use this preprocessed data to identify the relevant characteristics (hashtags, unigrams, bigrams, etc.) in each dataset. We have learned four types of information from this: semantic, grammatical, figurative, and aspects based on tweets. Finally, the data is rated as positive, negative, or neutral based on the learned attributes. A battery of tests is run in MATLAB to evaluate the model's performance on many metrics, including recall, accuracy, precision, f-measure, and error rate. Specifically, the proposed LightDL model outperforms all other models across all metrics and achieves 95% accuracy on the Twitter dataset.

Keywords: Lightweight Dl, Sentiment Analysis, Recommender System, Twitter Data.

INTRODUCTION

Many years have passed since businesses began using transactional system data recorded in their day-to-day operations to help in making choices. This goal has been achieved via the use of various business intelligence tactics and data analysis methods. Novel processing processes, able to handle such massive amounts of data, have been developed in recent years; these mechanisms are known as Big Data [1]. Data quantity, information diversity, and data velocity have all increased. CPSS creates complex heterogeneity and large amounts of data from

* **Corresponding author Alisha Sikri:** Department of AIML, Noida Institute of Engineering and Technology, Greater Noida, Uttar Pradesh, India; E-mail: alisha.sikri@niet.co.in

S. Kannadhasan, R. Nagarajan, & Kaushik Pal (Eds.)

many sources by integrating humans, machines, and data into large-scale computerized systems. Academics are very interested in graphs of knowledge because of the critical role they play in empowering large-volume, poor-quality data sets to support CPSS's clever services and applications. Knowledge is described in the Resource Description Framework (RDF) as directed labeled graphs in the shape of subject-predicate-object triples [2]. Despite the widespread use of artificial intelligence (AI) and big data to automate network administration tasks, managers still sometimes resort to heuristic analysis of system data in the event of an unexpected cybersecurity issue or fault. Though existing methods focus on reducing the pool of potential data, a diverse range of information is necessary to tackle complex cybersecurity problems [3]. During the big data age, technology for data mining is mostly used to assess the collected information. Afterwards, all inductive reasoning regarding the information is computerized in order to find potential patterns. With recent advances in data mining technologies, the national psychological wellness dataset can be used to efficiently address a range of early warning indicators related to mental wellness. Approaches: One such use case is the extraction of key characteristics and details from psychological data using data mining [4]. There is a pressing need for innovative technical solutions to address the growing complexity of city infrastructure, the abundance of urban data, and the need for interdisciplinary research and decision-making for long-term city sustainability. Data and process connectivity, automated reasoning over knowledge, and large-scale data handling are just a few areas where ontologies have shown to be useful tools for practitioners [5].

Scholars have noted that findings from conventional mature organizations cannot be fully transferred to the study of current online businesses due to numerous distinctions between conventional and contemporary enterprises. Consequently, the study of digital transformation has seen a proliferation of novel ideas throughout the last few decades. More research on its definition, conceptual dimension, and measurement has been conducted during the span of its long history of growth. Despite the fact that effect thinking will be important for the success of corporate digital transformations, very little research has examined its effects in this context [6]. Big data has become an essential part of many industries, helping businesses gain valuable insights and make informed decisions. Nevertheless, to make good use of big data, it is essential to ensure data quality. Therefore, practitioners and academics have been increasingly focused on big data quality over the past few years because of its substantial influence on decision-making. While there have been studies on the accuracy of data deviations, they tend to focus on narrow issues, such as outliers or inconsistencies [7].

RELATED WORKS

In this chapter, we put forth a tensor-based paradigm for analyzing knowledge. This framework helps with knowledge graph modeling, fusion, and argumentation. We start by fully representing heterogeneous knowledge networks using Boolean tensors. Afterwards, we detail a set of graph tensor procedures for extracting, modifying, and aggregating high-order graphs of knowledge. To further infer the link among any two entities, we compute the relationship path tensor by performing tensor 1-mode combination operations on the information network representations tensor, as well as the entity's representations tensor. Lastly, we present a case study demonstrating that the proposed paradigm is successful and practicable [8].

In this research, we describe MADPM, a system in which robots use data-processing technologies to store and assess data from networks. In MADPM, data-processing sequences are formed by interactions between agents. As part of this procedure, we plan a sequence's structure based on needs, as well as a way to augment it for an in-depth examination that supports intuitive reasoning. During testing, we put the initial system through its paces with five case studies. Based on the findings, administrators may benefit more from a complex data display than from the chosen representation, which was selected for its single-faceted nature. Providing a multi-system presentation of information for heuristic reasoning in network administration tasks is the end product of our suggested technique [9].

Preparing data, mining it for insights, analyzing the findings, and using a decision tree algorithm are all parts of the data mining early warning systems for problems with mental health that this study outlines. Results from the experiments show that the early-warning technique presented in this article can reach an excellent precision of over 96%—second tier of proof. Clinical trials examine the efficacy of a therapy [10].

We take a look at the ways in which ontologies have bolstered smart city services, and we compile an in-depth overview of the issues tackled and the results obtained so far through the use of ontology-based apps. To achieve this goal, we systematically reviewed the literature on ontology and its influence on the development of modern intelligent cities. Our review findings additionally influence our proposal for a taxonomy of the city's sub-domains covered by the taxonomies we uncovered, as well as a list of the scientific field's current priorities for study. Finally, we delve further into a few unanswered questions and focus on the areas where semantic technology has already been shown to be beneficial in improving the smart city idea [11].

Based on fundamental user attributes, we develop a straightforward model to foretell user approval via big data analysis. A categorization model of consumers' acceptance of autonomous cars was built using income level, age, gender, highest level of education, and marital status, based on 456 survey responses, using the decision tree algorithm. People with a high degree of acceptance were shown in the categorization model, with a maximum rating of 4. A total of 86.75 percent of the participants were shown in this way. It was also using this approach that we chose a subset of consumers to take part in an offline event where they could get a feel for working with autonomous cars. Results demonstrated that more customers consented to attend the entire event in the group selected using the model, compared to another group selected at random. We spoke about how the model may be used for marketing and consumer portraits [12].

From a procedural viewpoint, this research aims to show how effect reasoning affects digital transformation in organizations that use large amounts of data. Corporate digital change effectiveness is enhanced by effect-based reasoning and failure learning, according to the data. The study environment uses empirical learning theory. Analyzing large amounts of data to understand and guide Chinese firms in achieving digital transformation is highly beneficial, as is expanding and refining theoretical research on innovation in management [13].

By taking into account six critical quality dimensions—accuracy, completeness, conformity, distinctiveness, consistency, as well as readability—the suggested framework thoroughly covers the primary concerns of data quality. The methodology is also broad in its approach to data quality abnormalities; it is not tied to any one domain and can be used across a variety of contexts. After being applied to two datasets, the suggested framework had a 98.22% success rate. In addition, the findings demonstrate that the structure has successfully improved the quality of information to an impressive 99%, with an increase of up to 14.76% in the overall quality score [14].

The Python programming language is used for system design in this article. To begin, we visit the institution's official homepage and use a crawler to collect all admissions-related links. After that, we go through all of these links and analyze the contents of the pages they lead to using the noise_remove [5] function. This helps us further limit the amount of useful knowledge before we store the resulting contents in JSON files. Lastly, we leverage the Flask architecture to swiftly and easily incorporate these items into my front-end website, ensuring it serves its full purpose of integrating and presenting information [15].

PROPOSED WORK

Data cleaning, features learning, as well as segmentation are the three main components of the suggested LightDL paradigm. There are n pieces of data (tweets) in dataset D, D={d1,d2,..,dn}. The proposed system model is depicted in Fig. (**1**).

The first step is for the data cleaning module to clean the data. The characteristics are then learnt and categorized using the LDNN algorithm.

Data Cleaning Module

One of the LightDL's first modules is an information cleansing module. The information set will be normalized using data cleansing techniques. This section performs the following procedures.

Negation—Words that express disapproval have a key role in establishing the emotional tone of a communication. Managing and detecting negatives is not easy and remains so. Recognizing reductions is essential, as they may change a message's valence, turning positive into negative or negative into positive. Finding an opposite word and just flipping the coin is a simple strategy that many researchers have used.

Words like "the," "are," as well as "who," are examples of stop phrases because of their low discriminating strength; they are usually removed before the processing of text begins. The TSA's efficiency may be compromised if it uses traditional stop-word lists on Twitter.

To track words that include emotion terms, a POS tag is added to each phrase in the data collection. Our format was N/P/A/R, which has been referred to as follows,

- N: Noun
- P: Pronoun
- A: Adjective
- R: Adverb

Eliminating numbers — In sentiment analysis, statistics are often considered to have little to no emotional significance. As a result, we nullify the dataset.

Example: To further grasp the data cleansing process, think about the following example,

Feature Learning Module

This module is responsible to learn and select optimal features for sentiment classification. We have used the LDNN algorithm for feature learning and classification. The considered feature groups are,

- Semantic features
- Syntactic features
- Symbolic features
- Tweet-based features

In each group, we considered almost all important features. These features are learned from each tweet, which is pre-processed by the data cleaning module shown in Fig. (**1**). The considered features and their relevance to the classification are summarized in Table **1**.

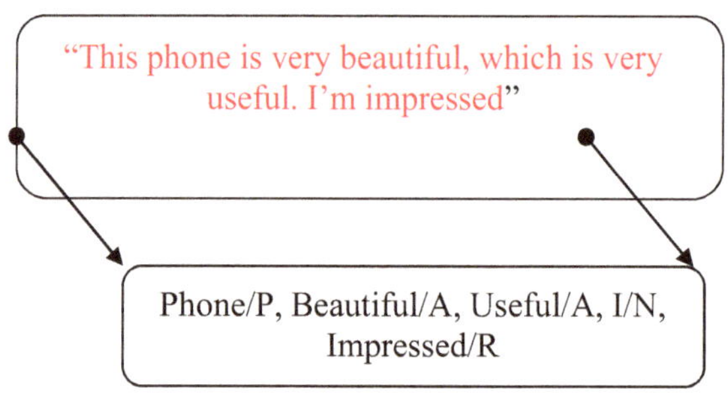

Fig. (1). Proposed system.

These features are extracted by the LDNN approach. Then these features are considered in classification.

Classification Module

Classification is performed based on the features extracted by the feature learning module. We proposed LDNN, which uses the light unit of DNN. Firstly, the input layer receives the cleaned and normalized dataset. Then, the features are mapped by the hidden layers. After that, the lightweight unit determines the class of the data. We have used a convolution kernel with a size of 1×1×M. Where M is the depth of the previous feature mapping layer. The convolution generally takes h×w×d as input and produces output as,

$$h \times w \times d \rightarrow h_o \times w_o \times d_o \quad \textbf{(1)}$$

Table 1. Features for each group.

Group	Explanation	Example	Relevant sentiment	
			Word	Sentiment
Semantic	• Semantic features reveal the sentiment level of the words • It uses WordNet to assign sentiment value to each word. • As POS tagging is performed in this work, semantic feature extraction becomes easy.	The Camera is Beautiful and Very Cheap. I Love this Product.	Camera Beautiful Cheap Love Product	Neutral Positive Positive Positive Neutral
Syntactic	• These are the most common features in sentiment analysis. • Features included are, o Unigram o Bigram o n-grams o Term frequency o Coreference	Phone/P, Beautiful/A, Useful/A, I/N, Expensive/R. Not/A, Interested/R.	Phone Useful Beautiful Expensive Not Interested	Neutral Positive Positive Negative Negative Positive
Symbolic	Symbolic features referred to slang terms, abbreviations, emotions, and emojis	Hi gud mng to all, have a great day	Hi Gud Mng Great	Neutral Positive Positive Positive Positive
Tweet-based	Includes the Twitter-based features such as Hashtag Replies Mentions Retweet	#Hi pupils @xxx	Hi Pupils	Neutral Neutral

The computational cost is computed as follows,

$$h_o.w_o.d_o.k.k \tag{2}$$

Where k is the depth of the convolution layer. The output class is computed as follows,

$$C_o = \left[\frac{f_{in}+2p-K}{S}\right] + 1 \tag{3}$$

Here, fin→ number of input features

p-→ Convolution padding size

K-⟶ Kernel size

S-⟶ Convolution stride size

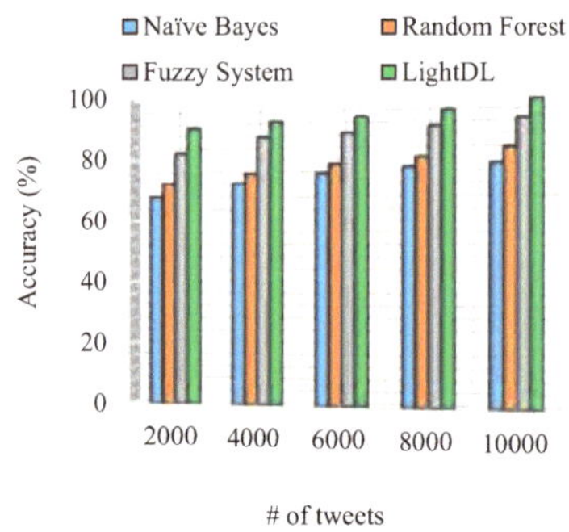

(a) Based on number of tweets

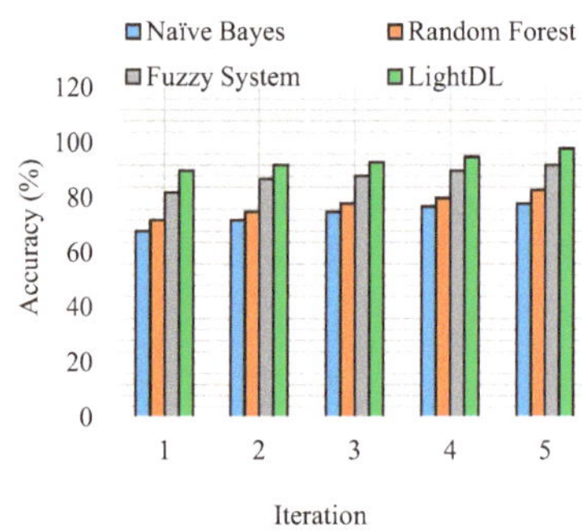

(b) Based on iteration

Fig. (2). Comparison on Accuracy.

Finally, the given tweet is classified into the corresponding sentiment. Based on the classified sentiment, the recommendation is generated.

RESULT AND DISCUSSION

Twitter dataset collected through API. For experiments, 20000 tweets are collected over a time period. Totally, the dataset has 100 users and more than 15000 hashtags. The data is unevenly (*i.e.*) distributed with various sentiments. Common sentiments are labelled as Positive, Negative, and Neutral. The proposed work is developed using the MATLAB platform.

For extensive evaluation, we compare the proposed recommender system with five performance metrics, such as accuracy (), precision (), recall (), F-measure, and error rate. Based on the above performance metrics, the LightDL recommender system is compared with existing classification models, such as

Naïve Bayes, Random Forests, and Fuzzy systems.

Accuracy is defined as the total number of accurate recommendations generated divided by the total number of recommendations generated.

$$A = \frac{TN+TP}{TP+FP+FN+TN} \tag{4}$$

Where TN - True Negative, TP – True Positive, FP - False Positive, and FN – False Negative.

We have compared accuracy in terms of the number of tweets in the dataset and the number of iteration in Fig. **2** (a) and (b), respectively. The accuracy is shown in Fig. (**2**). The analysis shows that the proposed work achieves nearly 95% accuracy (*i.e.*, 95% of tweets are classified accurately). In the proposed LightDL, all important features are considered. Thus, the accuracy of the work is large. Also, lightDNN learns the features accurately and assigns the correct sentiment value. At the same time, the Naïve Bayes algorithm has lower accuracy since it is unable to learn all the features accurately. RF algorithm and fuzzy system stuck in local values, which reduces the accuracy of the algorithms. Thus, we have achieved a higher accuracy.

CONCLUSION

Recommendation systems using sentiment analysis face challenges due to the lack of effective algorithm design. This paper proposes a novel LightDL approach for sentiment classification over Twitter data. The Twitter dataset is collected and analyzed using the LightDL model. First, the collected data is cleaned and pre-processed to normalize the dataset. Then, important features are extracted by the LightDL model, which uses the Light DNN (LDNN) algorithm for feature mapping and classification. Specifically, four groups of features—semantic, syntactic, slang, and tweet-based—are extracted and analyzed. Finally, the data is classified into Positive, Negative, and Neutral categories based on the learned features. Recommendations are then generated according to the sentiment. Experimental results confirm that the proposed approach achieves improved accuracy, precision, recall, F-measure, and error rate. In the future, this work will be extended with a novel feature selection methodology to further enhance classification accuracy.

REFERENCES

[1] Chen, S., & Yang, S. (2020). A Web Services, Ontology and Big Data Analysis Technology-Based Cloud Case-Based Reasoning Agent for Energy Conservation of Sustainability Science. Applied Sciences 10, no. 4, p. 1387, 2020.

[http://dx.doi.org/10.3390/app10041387]

[2] Belghith, E.H., Rioult, F., & Bouzidi, M. (2020). Acoustic Diversity Classification Using Machine Learning Techniques: Towards Automated Marine Big Data Analysis. Int. J. Artif. Intell. Tools, 29, 2060011:1-2060011:21.

[3] X. Zhao, and X. Wang, "Dynamics of Networked Framing: Automated Frame Analysis of Government Media and the Public on Weibo With Pandemic Big Data", *Journal. Mass Commun. Q.*, vol. 100, no. 1, pp. 100-122, 2023.
[http://dx.doi.org/10.1177/10776990211072508] [PMID: 36814705]

[4] I. Litvinenko, *Automated Reasoning about the Entity Integrity of Big Data in Possibilistic SQL.*, 2020.

[5] C.L. Jordan, R. Koochak, M. Roberts, A. Nalonnil, and M. Honeychurch, *A Holistic Approach to Big Data and Data Analytics for Automated Reservoir Surveillance and Analysis.*, 2022.
[http://dx.doi.org/10.2118/210757-MS]

[6] Y. Zeng, Y. Zhou, W. Cao, D. Hu, Y. Luo, and H. Pan, "Big data analysis of water quality monitoring results from the Xiang River and an impact analysis of pollution management policies", *Math. Biosci. Eng.*, vol. 20, no. 5, pp. 9443-9469, 2023.
[http://dx.doi.org/10.3934/mbe.2023415] [PMID: 37161251]

[7] Y. Zeng, Y. Zhou, W. Cao, D. Hu, Y. Luo, and H. Pan, "Big data analysis of water quality monitoring results from the Xiang River and an impact analysis of pollution management policies", *Math. Biosci. Eng.*, vol. 20, no. 5, pp. 9443-9469, 2023.
[http://dx.doi.org/10.3934/mbe.2023415] [PMID: 37161251]

[8] J. Yang, L.T. Yang, Y. Gao, H. Liu, H. Wang, and X. Xie, "Tensor-Based Knowledge Fusion and Reasoning for Cyberphysical-Social Systems: Theory and Framework", *IEEE Syst. Man. Cybern. Mag.*, vol. 8, no. 2, pp. 31-38, 2022.
[http://dx.doi.org/10.1109/MSMC.2021.3114538]

[9] K. Sasai, R. Fukutani, G. Kitagata, and T. Kinoshita, "Multiagent-Based Data Presentation Mechanism for Multifaceted Analysis in Network Management Tasks", *Sensors (Basel),* vol. 22, no. 22, p. 8841, 2022.
[http://dx.doi.org/10.3390/s22228841] [PMID: 36433437]

[10] B. Li, "Design of early warning system for mental health problems based on data mining and database", *Rev. Bras. Med. Esporte,* 2022.

[11] A. De Nicola, and M.L. Villani, "Smart City Ontologies and Their Applications: A Systematic Literature Review", *Sustainability (Basel),* vol. 13, no. 10, p. 5578, 2021.
[http://dx.doi.org/10.3390/su13105578]

[12] Zheng, M., Zhang, J., Yang, C., Li, X., Luo, J., Huang, Y., & Dai, Q. Predicting User Acceptance of Automated Vehicles Based on Basic User Characteristics through Big Data Analysis. 2023 3rd Asia-Pacific Conference on Communications Technology and Computer Science (ACCTCS), 256-262, 2023.

[13] L. Liu, J. Chen, H. Ren, and T. Chen, *Research on Effect Reasoning on Enterprise Digital Transformation Performance with Big Data Analysis.,* 2023.
[http://dx.doi.org/10.11648/j.ijefm.20231101.15]

[14] W. Elouataoui, S. El Mendili, and Y. Gahi, "An Automated Big Data Quality Anomaly Correction Framework Using Predictive Analysis", *Data (Basel),* vol. 8, no. 12, p. 182, 2023.
[http://dx.doi.org/10.3390/data8120182]

[15] J. Yu, X. Luan, and Y. Sun, *An Automated Analytics Engine for College Program Selection using Machine Learning and Big Data Analysis.* Advances in Machine Learning, Data Mining and Computing, 2021.
[http://dx.doi.org/10.5121/csit.2021.111417]

CHAPTER 11

Harnessing Big Data for Advanced Business Intelligence

V. Gokul Rajan[1,*] and **H.S. Shreenidhi**[2]

[1] *Department of Computer Science and Engineering, Galgotias University, Greater Noida, Uttar Pradesh, India*

[2] *Department of Computer Science and Engineering, JAIN (Deemed-to-be University), Bangalore, Karnataka, India*

Abstract: Thanks to the rapid development of remote sensing technologies, we now have greater availability of remote sensing data than in the past. Big data has arrived. Hyperspectral features, high geographical resolution, and high temporal resolution are characteristics of Big Data that are present in data acquired by remote sensing. By combining geographical feature data with remote sensing data, this study compares changes in water cover and vegetation and provides a feature-supporting, useful, and efficient data cube for use in time-series analytics. This research provides a spatially-focused definition of the SRSDC, or remote sensing data cube. This information cube provides an efficient, adaptable, and scalable method for analyzing large volumes of RS data using spatial attributes. It provides an overview of the SRSDC's organizational structure. For query operations, the SRSDC offers feature translation, and for storing and managing vector feature data, it offers spatial feature repositories. The article details the process of creating a distributed execution engine and a feature data cube for the SRSDC. The manufacturing process and long-term remote sensing evaluation are used as examples to assess a feature data cube and a distributed execution engine. To the pinnacle of the information economy now stands big data, a fresh strategic asset for humanity. Methods for discovering new information rely on data analysis, supervised learning, unsupervised learning, and combinations of the two.

Keywords: Big Data, knowledge discovery, business intelligence, data analysis (DA),.

INTRODUCTION

Throughout our research and professional experience, we have noticed that many professionals in related fields have trouble making heads or tails of the various methods for analyzing large data sets because of the complexity of the terminology and the fuzziness of the concepts involved.

* **Corresponding author V. Gokul Rajan:** Department of Computer Science and Engineering, Galgotias University, Greater Noida, Uttar Pradesh, India; E-mail: gokulranjan@galgotiasuniversity.edu.in

S. Kannadhasan, R. Nagarajan, & Kaushik Pal (Eds.)

While developing and testing a BI system, for example, we were asked why concepts such as big data (BD), data analysis (DA), and Knowledge Discovery (KD) were not part of it. These questions are valid since we classify BI, BD, DA, and KD as a set of ideas related to big data analysis. However, there is no universally accepted single standard or framework that encompasses all of these domains. While these and related inquiries may lie beyond the purview of a given research project, answering them may necessitate additional time and effort, particularly in a research environment where debate must be grounded in an evaluation of the relevant literature.

Each of the papers reviewed in this article takes a somewhat different tack on the question of how best to analyze large amounts of data, but they all cover the same ground. Rather than devoting considerable time and energy to clarifying the differences between BD and BI ideas from a data structure perspective, the literature pays little attention to issues like conceptual ambiguity, misunderstanding, and confusion, as well as the interrelationships across approaches.

Because of this, we decided that the area of big data analysis needed a thorough evaluation. To analyze and evaluate BI, DA, BD, and KD critically so that their similarities, distinctions, and relationships can be identified; (ii) to provide other researchers with a visual representation that can help them respond quickly to questions, concerns, and problems that arise from not understanding the concepts mentioned in this paper, and (iii) to lay the groundwork for future discussions between researchers and practitioners.

Business Intelligence

One way to look at business intelligence (BI) is as an umbrella term for all the things that help a firm collect, analyze, display, and disseminate information: strategies, procedures, programs, data, items, technology, and technical architectures [1]. Businesses may gain an advantage over rivals [2] and even forge deeper connections with consumers and increase sales [3] by adopting a more nuanced perspective of their clientele. It is a crucial aspect of organizational growth because it gives companies a leg up in situations with positive information asymmetry [1, 4, 5], enabling them to maximize earnings, optimize resources and processes, and make more proactive [6] and strategic [7] choices. Business Intelligence is used not only at the strategic and tactical levels but also at the operational level due to its many benefits.

Users of business intelligence tools may be better equipped to anticipate and respond to changes in the business environment [8]. Its goal is to improve operational performance management by providing stakeholders with a deeper understanding of the business.

Businesses may benefit from business intelligence (BI) by extracting actionable insights and previously unknown knowledge from their operational data, which can then be utilized to make more informed predictions, calculations, and assessments [10]. Traditional business intelligence [9] centered on extract, transform, and load (ETL), data warehousing (DW), and reporting (R). Data exploration and visualization, however, have become significant research foci for the next generation of BI [11, 12]. There seems to be a shift in focus from static reporting to interactive visualisations, as research themes have shifted from a "ometrics summary" to "odiscovering the causes and consequences of the events the metrics describe" [12]. Data mining, text analytics, near real-time BI, self-service BI, and BI in the cloud are only a few examples of the new business intelligence advancements driven by corporate competitiveness [13].

Data Analytics & Big Data Analytics

The goal of data analytics is to improve decision-making by applying computer analysis to existing datasets [14]. According to Ridge, "oany activity involves the integration of statistical techniques to data for the goal of obtaining insight from the information" is what the word "odata analysis" (DA) really means [15].

This multidisciplinary field encompasses a wide range of disciplines, including statistics, machine learning, pattern recognition, applied research, data mining, artificial intelligence, business intelligence, prescriptive analytics, and descriptive analytics, among many others. Thus, study themes and concerns pertinent to DA ideas include those already defined as research fields in BI, including visualisation, cloud computing, and data exploration [16 - 21].

RELATED WORKS

Big data has become an invaluable strategic asset for humans in this era of the information economy. Relying primarily on correlational data instead of traditional causality, it is representative of a fresh data-intensive paradigm in science that has arisen as a result of theory, computer models, and experience. It is reshaping the way scientists perform their work and will soon become a vital force in scientific advancement. Data science and AI depend significantly on insights from large-scale remote sensing data, which lies at the intersection of statistics, computer science, and earth science. To find a predictive, functional, or practical data structure, it must be able to explore all of Earth's big data without being constrained by the many data types. Important methods for discovering new information include both supervised and unsupervised educational approaches, as well as different combinations of the two. By using a mapping f(x) to generate an output y for each input x, or a set of chances over y given x, a popular supervised learning approach may predict y' in response to a new input x'. This process is repeated using a collection of variable pairs (x, y) as training data. Logistic regression, decision trees, neural networks, support vector algorithms, Bayesian classification algorithms, and kernel machines are supervised learning approaches that rely on various mapping functions. The supervised learning industry has seen the popularity of deep networks skyrocket as of late. To calculate the representation at each level, training a deep network entails learning its internal parameters. This enables the network to learn data representations at different levels of abstraction and to discover intricate patterns in massive amounts of Earth data. Innovations in analyzing satellite image data with deep networks have enabled the prediction of long-term geoscience trends.

Spatiotemporal analysis of RS data is becoming increasingly popular as more and more RS photos are saved for Earth observation. Many studies have suggested integrating GIS [14] and OLAP [15] tools to create a data cube. By using the OLAP spacetime dimension aggregation procedure, they were able to explore spatiotemporal data by constructing a multidimensional database to handle multiple-dimensional tables. With the use of a GIS and spatial database, Sonia Rivest et al. were able to obtain, display, and evaluate multidimensional RS data. . It was designed to perform public health theme analysis using OLAP and GIS on data with spatiotemporal dimensions. The multidimensional data model of these tools makes them unsuitable for complex scientific computing, but they can help researchers extract data with spatiotemporal dimensions. They also failed to implement a structure capable of processing massive amounts of data. As a result, they are constrained in their ability to process massive amounts of data. Because Earth observation images are in raster format by default; time-series imagery can be converted to a multidimensional array with little effort. A three-dimensional array, for instance, can provide a spatial and temporal representation of the data. Because an array can be readily split into smaller pieces, it's well-suited for distributed, parallel computation. The support for spatiotemporal autocorrelated processing of data in the multidimensional array model allows scientists to concentrate on their research without having to worry about the structure of individual image files. Consequently, a lot of research has gone into developing new analytic tools that leverage the multidimensional array concept to handle the enormous amounts of RS data.

Knowledge Discovery, Data Analytics, Big Data, and Business Intelligence: A Unified Framework

People often get BI, DA, BD, and KD mixed up because of how similar they are. Our review of the literature and preliminary interviews with seven domain experts led us to conclude that these concepts warrant independent treatment as methodologies.

We consider information discovery to be the overarching notion, and among the many approaches to discovering or creating new information, Data Analytics stands out as very promising. In the context of Knowledge Discovery, Data Analytics encompasses Big Data Analytics along with Business Intelligence, among other things.

Big Data is considered a subset of Big Data Analytics for the purpose of this discussion. When considering a company's goals, objectives, and philosophies, we place Big Data Analytics on par with Business Intelligence.

PROPOSED WORK

To streamline the management and processing of large-scale spatial feature data and satellite pictures, the SRSDC system was developed to offer services for analyzing huge time series of RS data. Our team in China stored a plethora of satellite images using the open-source information cube (ODC), a data cube system for archiving and examining geographic raster data. A number of satellites provided the data used in this investigation. These included Landsat, MODIS, GaoFen(GF), and HuanJing(HJ), among others. The SRSDC also provides data on various geographical features in China, such as cities, forests, and lakes. The OpenStreetMap website is credited with being the first repository for this geographical vector data. Before these satellite photos can be used in the SRSDC, they must undergo geometric and radiometric correction. The next step is to use the global subdivision grid to divide the data into several grid files, or tiles. This guarantees that pictures captured at different times, locations, and with varied dimensions will be comparable. The NetCDF standard was used to store these tiles, and it is compatible with a lot of scientific applications and analytical tools. B such as the Organizational Framework of the FRSDC. The SRSDC system uses a relational database as well as a file system to manage its geographically-based information. Its architecture for time-series analytics delivers performance and scalability. The SRSDC provides for the extraction of specific satellite imagery as a multidimensional array alongside the geographic object, in contrast to the ODC system, which primarily supports the administration and assessment of spatial raster information in a data cube format. It could use geographic objects to provide geographic query functionality instead of relying solely on coordinates.

This is why a geographical focus was established while creating the analytical database. Data may be queried based on the geographical meaning of analytics topics; precise locations are not necessary for researchers to get important information. Fig. (**1**) shows that the distributed executing engines (DEE) and data management form the backbone of the system. A comprehensive view of data management requires handling both raster and vector data. After the archival of the metadata by SRSDC, retrieved from the raster data in a central network file system, it will be transferred to the ODC-managed metadata repository. Geographic entities representing the vector information are stored in the SRSDC's spatial database. Data management is followed by the conversion of raster and vector data into an N-dimensional array that holds spatial feature information. This conversion is done using an N-dimensional array interface. We use Xarray to process and manipulate arrays. High-performance computing (HPC) clusters and the computing services that accompany them are DEE's responsibility. Dask, a parallel computing library using blocked algorithms, is used at the SRSDC to manage task scheduling, collaborative computing, and resource monitoring. It is beneficial for researchers to perform analytical tasks concurrently. Organizing and executing the first stage involves working with a featured data cube. In particular, the FRSDC physical item with positional data is considered: any object in space that has its own distinct physical significance is defined as a spatial feature. For example, researchers may need to analyze a remote sensing (RS) image collection using geographic features to classify an RS image accurately. Although several RS data cube systems provide multidimensional datasets, they often lack explicit features. As a result, researchers must invest additional effort to prepare the data for analysis. Because fundamental geographic coordinates are all that may be utilized for searching and discovering the research region in the ODC system and the SCIDB-based information cube, researchers will need to convert their unique spatial features to coordinate ranges in order to generate data suitable for analysis. The integration of geographic objects with the basic N-Dimensional array in the SRSDC made it easy for researchers to organize the analysis-ready N-Dimensional database using the properties that interested them the most. For the most part, we currently use PostGIS to preserve forest and lake characteristics across China within the SRSDC. 1) The feature class is supplied so that users can specify a geographic feature of interest. The geographic item and the feature type are both included. 2) The class of feature types stands in for the category of geographical feature, such as a lake, forest, city, etc. Feature types and the analysis techniques that are compatible with them are listed. Thirdly, a lake in China called Poyang is an example of a geographic object; this class specifies particular vector data that has geographic relevance and includes the kind of vector data utilized to construct its shape. 2) The raster information class describes the features of satellite data. You may find information on satellite platforms, product types, and frequency ranges here. From the SRSDC, you may access the characteristic data-cube dataset using the feature operations class. The N-dimensional arrays of required features may be constructed using the provided feature object, raster information format, and time horizon. It has several useful functionalities that users may also take advantage of. Second, as mentioned earlier, data management encompasses both raster and vector data management. Because there is such a large and diverse amount of satellite data, the SRSDC uses a relational database using NoSQL fields to handle metadata and saves raster information to the file system. The SRSDC uses NoSQL fields to define metadata information in its repository, rather than a standard relational database. The reason is, using the full relational architecture requires frequent database schema expansions due to the exponential growth in the amount of satellite sensors. On the other hand, NoSQL fields allow for a more detailed description of the metadata of satellite information from many sources. Every NoSQL variable has its own unique data type, location, frequency band, source of data URL, time, and projection. The time, band, location, and data type are some of the parameters that are used in data inquiries. In addition to using the data URL and projection fields, the data is loaded, and the multidimensional array is constructed in memory. Similarly, the raster data volume (in TB) is larger than the OpenStreetMap vector information amount (in GB). After archiving them from many satellite data centers, we decided to use a feature depository rather than a file system to store and handle vector data as geographic objects, since most of the features they represent are not as large as the raster photographs. We classified them as "ofeature types" because of the extensive geographical meanings they may have. Upon receiving a data request via the SRSDC's web portals, the center will first search the feature repository for the specific geographic item that the user is requesting. Next, it employs feature translations to get the minimal bounding rectangle (MBR) of the feature after transforming the geographic element into a mask array. The SRSDC uses the information to find the exact URLs where the necessary raster data may be obtained when the MBR vertex coordinates and time horizon are given. The next step is to read the raster information set into memory using ODC's N-Dimensional array interface. To prepare the dimensional array for additional processing or analysis, its features will be "omasked" using the mask array.

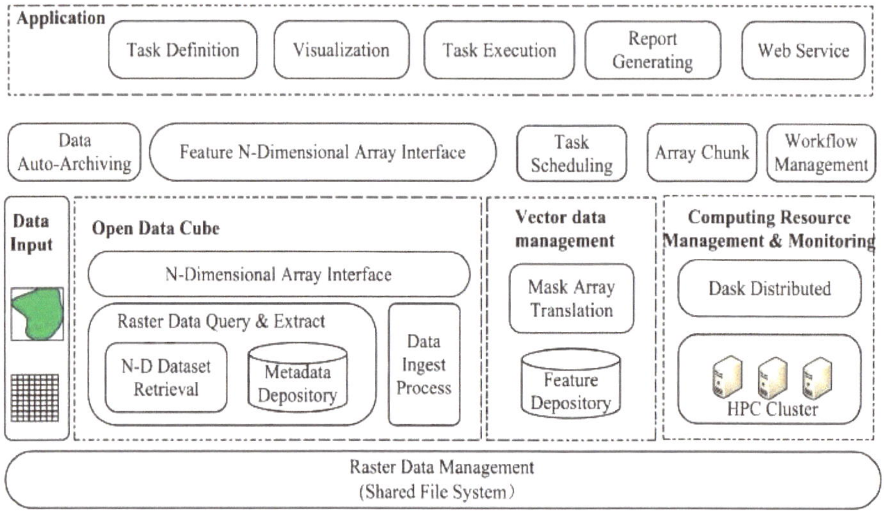

Fig. (1). Proposed work.

The SRSDC takes the user's input, applies the appropriate algorithm, and then gives them the results. The enormous data sets acquired by RS are being sought after by an increasing number of applications, and the demand for processing them is outstripping the capacity of stand-alone mode processing. We constructed a distributed process engine using Dask, a distributed computing platform tailored for scientific data analysis to effectively analyze the massive RS data. With its built-in support for multidimensional data and APIs similar to pandas and numpy, Dask is a popular cloud computing tool that competes with Apache Spark. Therefore, it is better suited for N-dimensional array computation. Dask is a framework that, like Spark, operates as a master-slave system with one scheduling node and several work nodes. Task scheduling is handled by the schedule node, while task execution is handled by the work nodes. Once all tasks have been completed, the scheduler will receive the final result from the decreased computations done by these workers. After indexing satellite picture scenes with metadata information, the data cube datasets (N-dimensional arrays) may be retrieved from memory in the SRSDC. But in a distributed environment, we must partition the enormous array into subarrays of defined size, or chunks, to compute the massive global dataset. The original photographs are chopped up by the SRSDC along longitude and latitude lines to make large, flat tiles. Image resolution is the primary consideration when determining tile size. Take the SRSDC as an example: the Landsat data, with a pixel size of 0.00025°, was split into 1°x1° tiles. These tiles, which have a 4000x4000-pixel array, can be easily organized into a data chunk that fits in the worker node's memory. You may build the chunk by adjusting the time horizon and grid number. The SRSDC may also employ these data chunks to divide the massive dataset (an N-dimensional array) into smaller datasets that worker nodes can access and process. The scheduler will allocate computational functions to the knowledge chunks after allocating the information to the workers. The distributed processing engine manages large-scale time series evaluation as shown in Fig. (**2**): the first step is to use a multifaceted spatial query to sort the data cube by dimension. 2) Use a queue to keep track of the information's chunk IDs, and assign them to workers by adjusting the relevant settings (grid number or time horizon). Creating the jobs and sending them to the active node follows the decision-making process for the analysis method and data chunks. Checking the current status of each job that the workers are currently working on is the fourth stage. The outcome has to be redone if anything goes wrong. Fifthly, compile all of the information, send it to the organizer, and finally, provide the results to the client.

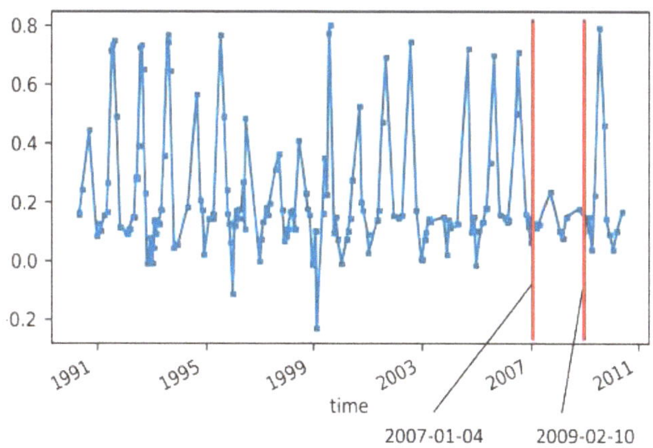

Fig. (2). NDVI outcome at the Mulan hunting field.

RESULT AND DISCUSSION

Our goal in conducting these time-series analyses of information experiments was to evaluate GEE's performance with stand-alone mode procedures for large-scale data analysis in the SRSDC. The studies were centered on geographic feature areas. To identify changes in time series, this study used two RS application approaches: NDVI (Normalized Difference Vegetation Index) and the Water Observation from Space (WOfs) algorithms. We uscd a 20 GB InfiniBand network to connect four nodes: one for the scheduler and three for the workers, which make up the distributed execution engine. Each node has a 32GB memory configuration with a 2.0GHz Inter(R) Xeon(R)E5- 2460 CPU. CentOS 6.5 is the OS, while Python 3.6 is the Python version. We chose these two study locations, each with unique characteristics, to put the feature data cube through its paces.

Poyang Lake in Jiangxi Province, China, and the Mulan hunting site in Hebei Province, China, both take NDVI and WOf readings, respectively (40.7°-43.1°N, 115.8°-119.1E). Using Landsat L2 data and geographical features, we constructed two feature-based cubes datasets spanning 20 years (1990""2009). There are around 138 GB of data for the Mulan hunting ground and 96 GB for the Poyang Lake area. Over a 20-year period, Fig. (**2**) displays the average yearly NDVI outcome at the Mulan hunting field, and Fig. (**3**) displays the results of a 20-year NDVI time-series data at the sample location (41.5620°N, 117.4520°E). It is evident that the 2007-2008 numbers fell short of expectations. This is because, on average, there is less rain at this time of year. In order to measure the DEE's processing performance, we timed its ability to transform 6.3 GB, 12.9 GB, 49.6 GB, 109.8 GB, and 138.6 GB of input data into NDVI. We compared the outcomes of the solo model with the DEE model using the aforementioned 4000x4000 pixel tiles: 1) The first is the standalone paradigm, which uses a single server to analyze the dataset in a sequential fashion after dividing it into smaller parts. The DEE Framework:

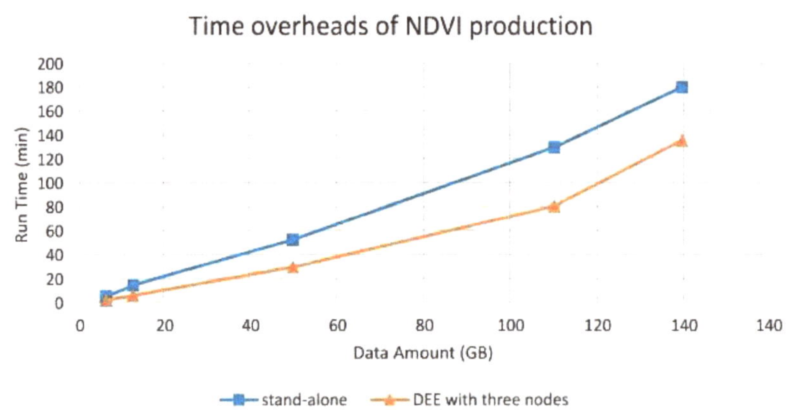

Fig. (3). NDVI time-series data at the sample location.

CONCLUSION

Our data cube is feature-supported, scalable, and tested to perform admirably in time-series analysis scenarios. In addition, we compared shifts in plant life and water cover using remote sensing and spatial feature analysis. Essential components of this framework that enable the examination of massive spatiotemporal RS data sets endowed with spatial attributes are the creation of feature data cubes as well as the distributed executor engine. The feature translation permits the construction of an analyzable feature cube by merging the geographical object using satellite data. Quick and effective analysis of massive

RS data sets is possible with a dashboard-based distributed execution engine. There are a number of remote sensing applications that might benefit from our method's multidimensional data service. The shared file system is the only option for storing the photographs, and internal IO efficiency is limited by the underlying network speed.

REFERENCES

[1] A. Singh, and R. Kumar, "Big data analytics in business intelligence and knowledge discovery: A review", *Journal of Advances in Computer Networks,* vol. 9, no. 2, pp. 85-92, 2021.

[2] A. Gupta, and V. Jain, "Big data analytics for business intelligence and knowledge discovery: A systematic review", *Int. J. Inf. Manage.,* vol. 57, p. 102332, 2021.

[3] S. Pandey, "The role of big data analytics in business intelligence and knowledge discovery: A review", *J. Emerg. Technol. Innov. Res.,* vol. 7, no. 11, pp. 677-683, 2020.

[4] A. Verma, and N. Sharma, "Big data analytics in business intelligence: A review", *International Journal of Advanced Science and Technology,* vol. 28, no. 14, pp. 300-305, 2019.

[5] M. Singh, and R. Sharma, "Big data analytics for business intelligence: A systematic review", *International Journal of Computer Science and Mobile Computing,* vol. 8, no. 2, pp. 157-166, 2019.

[6] N. Gupta, and A. Verma, "Big data analytics for business intelligence and knowledge discovery: A systematic review", *Int. J. Comput. Sci. Inf. Secur.,* vol. 16, no. 7, pp. 31-38, 2018.

[7] A. Kumar, and P. Kumar, "Big data analytics for business intelligence and knowledge discovery: A review", *International Journal of Engineering Technology Science and Research,* vol. 5, no. 7, pp. 249-253, 2018.

[8] N. Gautam, and V. Goyal, "Big data analytics in business intelligence: A review", *J. Comput. Sci. Eng.,* vol. 3, no. 2, pp. 24-30, 2017.

[9] A. Verma, "Big data analytics in business intelligence: A review", *International Journal of Innovative Research in Computer and Communication Engineering,* vol. 4, no. 5, pp. 11523-11528, 2016.

[10] M. Sharma, and A. Verma, "Big data analytics in business intelligence: A review", *Int. J. Res. Eng. Technol.,* vol. 4, no. 12, pp. 429-433, 2015.

[11] Y. Ozcelik, and C. Ceylan, "The effect of big data analytics on business performance: A resource-based view perspective", *J. Bus. Res.,* vol. 144, pp. 420-432, 2022. [http://dx.doi.org/10.1016/j.jbusres.2022.01.050]

[12] C. Guo, Y. Zhang, Y. Yang, and J. Ren, "Using big data analytics for business intelligence: A systematic literature review", *J. Bus. Res.,* vol. 133, pp. 793-806, 2021. [http://dx.doi.org/10.1016/j.jbusres.2021.04.032]

[13] Y. Shi, S. Shang, L. Guo, and Z. Xiong, "Big data analytics and business intelligence: A comprehensive review", *J. Organ. Comput. Electron. Commerce,* vol. 31, no. 3, pp. 211-239, 2021. [http://dx.doi.org/10.1080/10919392.2021.1911583]

[14] Y. Wang, and L. Kung, "A framework of big data analytics for business intelligence", *Decis. Support Syst.,* vol. 140, p. 113423, 2021. [http://dx.doi.org/10.1016/j.dss.2020.113423]

[15] Y. Zhu, K. Xie, Y. Zhang, and W. Zhou, "A survey on big data analytics for business intelligence: From a technical perspective", *J. Ind. Inf. Integr.,* vol. 23, p. 100172, 2021. [http://dx.doi.org/10.1016/j.jii.2020.100172]

[16] X. Zhang, H. Chen, and X. Li, "Research on big data analytics and business intelligence in the era of Industry 4.0: A bibliometric analysis", *IEEE Access,* vol. 9, pp. 24672-24681, 2021.

[http://dx.doi.org/10.1109/ACCESS.2021.3056890]

[17] Y. He, J. Du, and Y. Chen, "The application of big data analytics in business intelligence: A review", *Int. J. Inf. Manage.,* vol. 57, p. 102339, 2021.
[http://dx.doi.org/10.1016/j.ijinfomgt.2020.102339]

[18] Q. Li, Q. Hu, J. Li, and X. Huang, "Exploring the impact of big data analytics on business intelligence: A grounded theory approach", *J. Bus. Res.,* vol. 113, pp. 26-34, 2020.
[http://dx.doi.org/10.1016/j.jbusres.2019.11.050]

[19] L. Lu, and X. Wang, "Big data analytics and business intelligence: A literature review", *J. Big Data,* vol. 7, no. 1, p. 49, 2020.
[http://dx.doi.org/10.1186/s40537-020-00326-1]

[20] Y. Yang, Y. Zhang, H. Chen, and Y. Song, "Big data analytics for business intelligence: A survey", *J. Ind. Inf. Integr.,* vol. 17, p. 100121, 2020.
[http://dx.doi.org/10.1016/j.jii.2019.100121]

[21] X. Wang, Z. Dai, H. Li, and J. Yang, *Research on Hybrid Collaborative Filtering Recommendation Algorithm Based on the Time Effect and Sentiment Analysis.,* 2021.
[http://dx.doi.org/10.1155/2021/6635202]

CHAPTER 12

Examining the Role of Big Data in Advanced Statistical Modeling

Meenakshi Sharma[1,*] and **Chandrasekar**[2]

[1] *Department of Computer Science and Engineering, Galgotias University, Greater Noida, Uttar Pradesh, India*

[2] *Department of Computer Science and Engineering, JAIN (Deemed-to-be University), Bangalore, Karnataka, India*

Abstract: Here, we provide a novel approach to simulating and reconstructing annual surface mass balance (SMB) data across glaciers using a deep artificial neural network (ANN; *i.e.*, deep learning). This method is currently included in the SMB component of an open-source regional glacier development model. Instead of using physical processes, which are becoming more common in traditional glacier models, we use data science to build a parameterized model. A annual glacier-wide SMB may be modelled using topoclimate data with deep learning or Lasso (least absolute shrinkage and selection operator; regularized multilinear regression), and the glacier's form can be updated using a parameterization specific to the glacier. Our nonlinear deep learning SMB approach is tested and validated on a dataset of 32 French Alpine glaciers, compared with other conventional linear statistical methods. Compared with linear methods, deep learning outperforms them with a root-mean-squared error (RMSE) of 0.51 m w.e. and an estimated R^2 of 0.77. This is due to the fact that deep learning can explain up to 108% more variation and up to 47% more space. Nearly one-third of deep learning's observed nonlinear behavior is attributed to the temporal dimension. The original measurements of ice thickness are the source of significant uncertainties in the development of glacier geometry. These results provide evidence that deep learning may be a powerful nonlinear tool for glacier modeling, enabling us to reconstruct or simulate SMB time-series data for specific glaciers within a given area to predict past and future environments.

Keywords: Big Data, Advanced Statistical Modeling, AI, nonlinear behavior, linear statistical methods.

INTRODUCTION

Significant changes are occurring in glaciers worldwide due to human-caused climate change [1].

* **Corresponding author Meenakshi Sharma:** Department of Computer Science and Engineering, Galgotias University, Greater Noida, Uttar Pradesh, India; E-mail meenakshi.sharma@galgotiasuniversity.edu.in

S. Kannadhasan, R. Nagarajan, & Kaushik Pal (Eds.)

Major environmental and societal effects are predicted as a result of the worldwide retreat of glaciers, despite significant regional variations. About 10% of the global population lives in alpine areas and the neighboring plains; glaciers are crucial to their existence because they provide water for farming, hydropower generation, industry, and household consumption. Numerous terrestrial and aquatic ecosystems rely on these water sources for their existence because they continue to produce runoff even during the warmest and driest periods of the year. Correctly anticipating and mitigating the associated environmental and socioeconomic repercussions requires an accurate prediction of future glacier development. Estimates of glaciers' future contribution to sea level have been calculated using a variety of global glacier development models throughout the past decade. Irrespective of methodology, all glacier models must address the following two primary processes that dictate the course of glacier evolution: (1) Glacier mass equilibrium, which is the difference among the mass gained *via* development (*e.g*., avalanches, snowfall, and refreezing) as well as the mass lost *via* ablation (*e.g*., calving, melt, sublimation of ice, firn, and snow), and (2) ice flow factors, that is the downward movement of ice due to gravity. It is difficult to develop a model that accurately simulates these processes on a global scale without making significant assumptions or simplifications [1 - 5]. Recent work has enhanced these models' depiction of ice flow dynamics by replacing empirical parametrizations with simpler physical models. However, most large-scale models of glacier development rely on temperature-index models to depict the glacier mass balance. A linear connection between positive degree-days (PDDs) and ice/snow melt is used in such a model. The fact that they work well in large-scale studies with a sparse number of data is a major factor in their popularity and has led to their outperforming more complicated models. Although these models may approximate the climate-glacier communication, it should be remembered that both systems exhibit non-linear behavior, especially when subjected to pre-processed forcings such as PDDs13. A nonlinear model, such as a deep ANN, may replace these more traditional methods. The use of artificial neural networks (ANNs) for regression problems in glaciology has been mostly uncharted; for example, only a small number of researchers have utilized shallow ANNs to predict a single glacier's ice thickness14 or mass distribution.

As climate proxies, glaciers can illustrate the changing climate to an international audience (IPCC, 2018), making them one of the most iconic representations of climate change. In the coming decades, mountain glaciers may significantly affect the water quality of glaciated catchments, according to several studies (*e.g*., Hock *et al*., 2019; Beniston *et al*., 2018). It is important to accurately forecast the range of hydrological, ecological, and economic effects that the melting of mountain glaciers might have. The change in hydrological regimes, including their timing and amplitude, is highly dependent on future climate scenarios (Huss and Hock,

2018). In order for society to adapt to changing hydrological and climatic conditions, understanding these changes is essential. These problems can be partially addressed by using glacier and hydro-glaciological models, which provide a range of outcomes under varying climate change scenarios. Understanding the evolution of glaciers at sub-regional and regional scales requires defining (a) the surface mass balance (SMB) and (b) glacier dynamics. To model these procedures, researchers have used a range of granularities. Different approaches may be used to replicate these processes on a large scale, that is, over many glaciers at a watershed size [6 - 10].

Half a century ago, the first mathematical models employed in glaciology were simply multiple linear regressions based on a limited set of meteorological parameters (Hoinkes, 1968; Martin, 1974). The advent of artificial intelligence has played a crucial role in the remarkable advances in statistical modeling over the last few decades. In contrast to other geosciences domains such as oceanography, climatology, and hydrology, the glaciological domain has not made full use of these methods, according to our contention (see, for example, Ducournau and Lguensat *et al.*, 2018; Fablet, 2016; Jiang *et al.*, 2018; Marçais, Rasp *et al.*, 2018; and de Dreuzy, 2017; Shen, 2018). However, investigations have begun to rely more on statistical methods. Steiner *et al.* (2005) used ANNs in the first study to investigate mass balance of the Great Aletsch Glacier in Switzerland. Compared with the standard stepwise multiple linear regression, they found that a nonlinear model performed better at representing mass balances in glaciers. The link between climate and glacier mass balance was also discovered to include a sizeable nonlinear component [11 - 15].

RELATED WORKS

In spite of Lewis Fry Richardson's 1922 proposal for NWP, the advent of programmable computers in 1955 marked the beginning of its practical implementation [1]. The past 30 years have seen tremendous advancements in weather forecasting using neural networks. Model output statistics (MOS), a method for comparing model results with observational data [12 - 14], was the most common technique for improving numerical models' predictive capabilities before 2000. In 1983, [15] a weather-forecasting method was developed that combined statistical and dynamic elements. A study [16] in 1991 marked a turning point in dynamic modeling. The growing gap between the current and forecast timeframes is accompanied by a lack of trustworthiness due to high computational demands, long prediction horizons, and the absence of design approaches for selecting model structure and parameters [13, 16, 17]. Other limitations and challenges include these approaches. A method for predicting the lowest possible temperature using artificial neural networks and backpropagation algorithms was first suggested in 1991 [18, 19]. The computational load of MOS-based efficient forecasting was significantly reduced using this technique [16]. The use of artificial neural networks (ANNs) to forecast precipitation and snowfall using weather radar imagery was first presented in 1995 [20]. The results show that ANN outperforms the traditional cross-correlation method, while the persistent prediction strategy significantly lowers prediction errors. An artificial intelligence (AI) method for forecasting severe rainfall was developed by Oishi *et al.* [21] in 1998.

PROPOSED WORK

The Python-based ALPGM is a freely available glacier model. See Code and data availability for further information on where to find the model's source code. There is a plethora of folders that serve certain purposes. Essential to the model is the most current glacier geometry, that is a component of the glacier-wide SMB equation. Machine learning instructions the glacier-wide SMB model incorporates both topographical and meteorological data. Annual modifications to the glacier's geometry (including its shape and ice thickness distribution) are made using glacier-specific parameterized functions derived from the findings of the glacier-wide SMB simulation. The primary steps of ALPGM are shown in Fig. (**1**). Through the model's interface, the following workflow phases can be conducted, skipped, or modified before or during execution. To retrieve information closest to the glacier's center, the meteorological forcings are preprocessed. When the files have been prepared, the preprocessing stage is skipped automatically, saving time in subsequent computations by storing the meteorological information in interim files. The SMB machine learning module accesses archived files containing preprocessed climate predictors and multitemporal glacier inventories, extracts the topographical predictors from them, and uses them to compile the training dataset. The SMB model is then equipped with a machine learning algorithm that can be reloaded from a previous run or retrained on a fresh dataset. Next, the entire topoclimatic dataset is used to train the SMB model or models. For future runs, the user may delete these models from temporary files. Two cross-validation methods for assessing the accuracy of SMB models are leave-one-year-out (LOYO) and leave-one-glacier-out (LOGO). Using already validated models eliminates the need for this step. Charts contrasting the simulated accumulated glacier-wide SMBs with their reference values and uncertainties, along with many basic performance metrics, are provided for each glacier and the model. The fourth step in creating the parameterized variables for the Glacier Geometry Update is to use a raster that includes the glacier contours and variations from two date-stamped digital elevation models (DEMs) that encompass the research region. For the last simulations, we consulted the parameterized functions stored in separate files. 5. The computer simulations of glacier growth are initiated after all the preceding phases have been completed. Each glacier has its own geometry update function, initial ice thickness, and DEM rasters. These raster files are used to create topographic data for each year and every glacier regularly. The first step in constructing the input topoclimate data for the glacier-wide SMB model is to obtain climate variables at the current glacier centroid from reanalysis or predictions. A further step involves updating the ice thickness and DEM rasters using the glacier-specific morphology upgrading approach. For this specific glacier and year, this approach replicates the glacier-wide SMB. To account for topographical and morphological changes in the glacier, the procedure is repeated indefinitely, and the geometry is revised at an annual time step. If the ice thickness and DEM rasters are adjusted, we can run the SMB simulation again next year by revising the topographical parameters. The machine learning algorithm that applies SMB over the glacier will be fed these parameters. When all raster pixels in a glacier's ice thickness reach 0, it is removed from the simulation pipeline as though it had melted away. The ice thickness and raster digital elevation model for each glacier are among the many outcomes recorded annually in the data files. Modeling the Mass Balance on the Surface of an Entire Glacier. Machine learning is used to replicate annual SMBs across the entire glacier. This glacier-wide SMB modeling strategy is, for the time being, a regional one because of the geographical peculiarities and specifics of topographical and climatic data. Selecting Significant Explanatory Variables Based on Location and Climate: By conducting a literature review and sensitivity analysis, we can identify the topographical and meteorological factors that influence glacier-wide SMB at a given study location. It is common practice to use topographical variables as predictors, including latitude and longitude, glacier slope, and average altitude. The most often mentioned weather predictor is CPDDs; however additional elements that impact the surface energy budget include mean monthly temperatures, snowfall, and others. Anomalies, defined as the maximum and minimum values of a variable within a particular reference period, might help prevent forecasts based on different climate data sets from being biased. We examine the training phase of the research to determine how sensitive the annual glacier-wide SMB is to topographical and climatic factors, so we can select the best forecasts for our machine learning training. Each variable may be regressed against the SMB data for the entire glacier to do this. A training dataset is constructed once the topographical and meteorological factors that may account for yearly glacier-wide SMB variability in the study area have been identified. Weisberg (2014) suggests combining climatic and topographical input variables to effectively enlarge the training dataset and delve deeper into the existing data. The following equation (1) may be used to express such permutations: In the first theorem, the total SMBg,y value for the whole glacier each year is equal to the product of the topographic predictors vector () and the climatic characteristics vector (), with the additional variable g,y representing the residual error. Following the establishment of the training dataset, the SMB model may be developed using one of three linear or one nonlinear algorithms: All-possible multiple linear regression (OLS), deep artificial neural networks (ANN), or Lasso (least absolute shrinkage and selection operator; Tibshirani, 1996). The Python machine learning packages scikit-learn, keras, statsmodels, and TensorFlow are used by ALPGM (Pedregosa *et al.*, 2011; Cholet, 2015; Seabold and Perktold, 2010; Cholet, 2015). An overarching perspective of the ALPGM machine learning approach for developing an SMB algorithm to simulate a whole glacier is shown in Fig. (**2**). If you choose every conceivable permutation of k predictors, you may have n models. Minimizing the number of predictors per search subgroup may reduce computational load. If a model does not have a maximum possible r2 adjusted, a VIF of 1.2, and a p-value of 0.01/n (to guarantee the Bonferroni correction), it will not be included in the final analysis. One possible solution to the problem of repeatedly selecting a single model is to average the forecasts of the retained models (Whittingham *et al.*, 2006). To ensure statistical significance, avoid collinearity, and capture as much variance as possible, these requirements are followed. Fig. (**1**) displays the ALPGM process and structure.

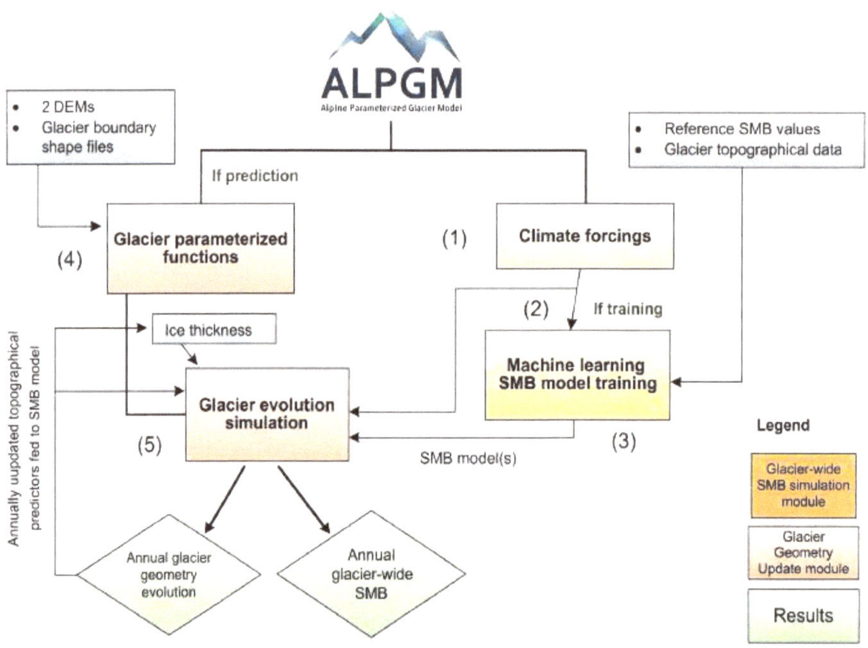

Fig. (1). ALPGM strucuture and workflow.

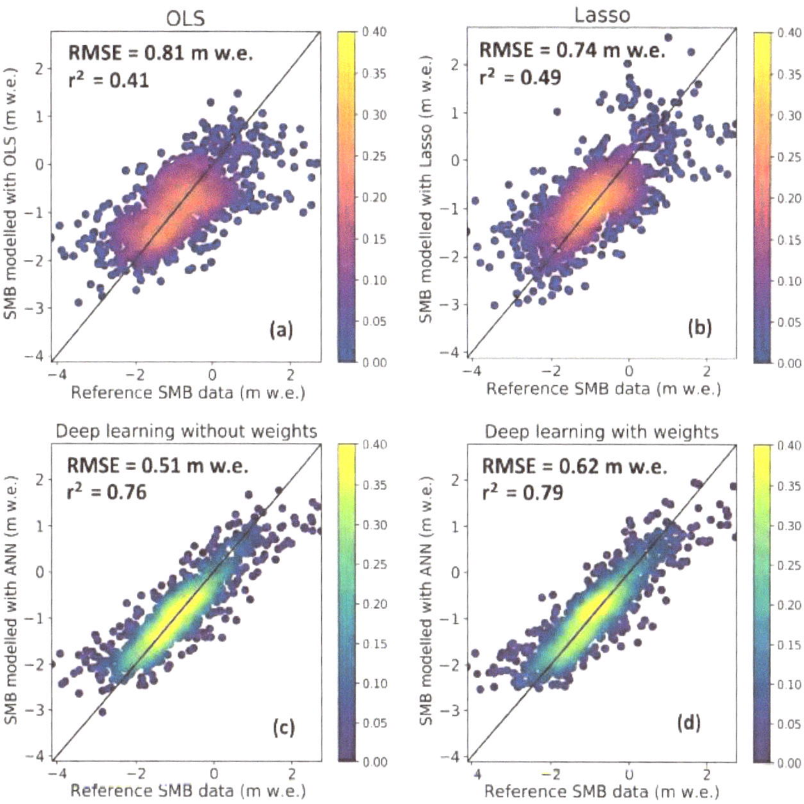

Fig. (2). Evaluation of modeled annual glacier-wide SMB data.

4 Impressive artificial neural networks: Drawing on concepts from biological brain networks, ANNs are statistical frameworks that do not follow a linear pattern (Fausett, 1994; Hastie *et al.*, 2009). The architecture, or pattern of connections among units, the optimizer, or technique by which the weights of the links among units are determined, and the activation functions, which are usually nonlinear, are the three main characteristics that identify a neural network, according to Fausett (1994). One kind of artificial neural network is the deep ANN, which has several hidden layers (for example, see Figs. **2** & **3**). The reader is encouraged to peruse the studies by Fausett (1994), Hastie *et al.* (2009), and Steiner *et al.* (2005, 2008) for a more comprehensive overview of neural networks and their applications in glaciology. As optimization methods have progressed, deep neural network construction has become a realistic possibility, leading to ANNs' meteoric rise in popularity in recent years. Because their taught variables are difficult to understand, ANNs are not a good choice when the model's interpretability is more important than prediction accuracy. This would include situations such as causal inference, sensitivity testing, or auxiliary-variable

modeling. This is an ideal representation of our research environment, as we have access to a wealth of data on glacier physics that helps us select appropriate input parameters for deep learning. Nonlinear systems, such as the environment (Houghton *et al.*, 2001) or glacier system (Steiner *et al.*, 2005), are notoriously difficult to model using these methods, while they excel at representing complicated functions of input parameters. At its core, ALPGM is an ANN that uses a fully connected feed-forward architecture. The term used to describe this setup is "layered architecture," in which each layer's neurons are directly connected to those of the next layer. With each neuron in the input layer corresponding to one of the N variables that explain the model, data flows to the output neuron, with the SMB serving as the model's goal variable. A preset distribution, often centered around 0, is used to assign weights to each link in the ANN randomly. By summing the weighted values across each hidden layer's units and then passing the total through a nonlinear activation function, a model's nonlinearities are introduced. As the output layer's values are compared to the ground truth (y) across an epoch, an ANN (artificial neural network) aims to minimize a loss function, in this example, mean squared error (MSE). To prevent artificial neural network (ANN) overfitting, some form of regularization is required (Hastie *et al.*, 2009). We improved the model's ability to generalize to new information and avoided overfitting by repeatedly training fewer ANN subparts using the standard regularization approach, dropout. A certain number of inter-unit connections were severed at random during this procedure. In the same way that adding Gaussian noise to data augmentation helps with generalization, it also helps with ANN inputs. Generalization is a common byproduct of regularization, making the final model more robust against changes to the input data. An artificial neural network (ANN) uses cross-validation to select its parameters, including the number of units, the depth of the hidden layer, the activation function type, the learning rate, and regularization technique. The results show that a six-level (four hidden layers) deep ANN with the following parameters (N, 40, 20, 10, 5, 1) was the most appropriate for our small dataset. Here, N is the total number of features to be used. We use a simplified version of the learning matrix that does not include any possible combinations of topographical and meteorological data, as the ANN already takes into consideration all possible combinations of characteristics (predictors). According to Srivastava *et al.* (2014), the ideal dropout rate for this pattern ranges from 0.30 to 0.3%, depending on the number of units in every layer that is hidden. To avoid the "dead ReLU" problem—which occurs when some neurons cease "learning"—we used a widely known as leaky rectification of ReLU activations (Xu *et al.*, 2015). Since the He regular initiation is effective using Leaky ReLUs and since all unit biases were adjusted to zero, we used it (He *et al.*, 2015). The RMSprop optimizer was used to optimize the descent gradient weights, with the best results obtained with a space training rate of 0.0005 and a time learning rate of 0.02. According to Ioffe and Szegedy (2015), in order to speed up the learning process, we normalized each data batch before applying the activation function.

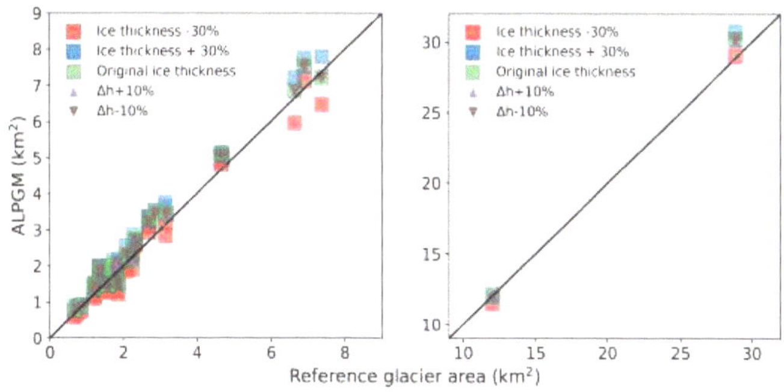

Fig. (3). Modeled annual glacier-wide SMB data.

RESULT AND DISCUSSION

Dataset

The example study centers on the French Alps, the westernmost extension of the European Alps, which are located between 44 and 46 130 North and 5.08 and 7.67 East. Due to the abundance of information in this area, it is ideal for conducting experiments to test hypotheses on glacier development. In addition, ALPGM was created as part of hydro-glaciological research to evaluate the effects of the receding of the French Alpine ice sheets on the 97,800-square-kilometer Rhône River watershed.

The equilibrium of the surface mass of an entire glacier. Here, we use a dataset derived from fluctuations in the volume and height of the snow line, a remotely sensed database that covers the entire glacier (Rabatel *et al.*, 2016). The data include annual SMB measurements from 1984 to 2014 and come from 30 French Alpine glaciers. Given the variety of topographical characteristics in the dataset, which adequately covers the three primary glacier clusters in the French Alps, it is a good fit for training the model. In comparison to the Vanoise as well as Vanoise clusters, the Écrins as well as Mont-Blanc clusters have glaciers situated at much higher latitudes, while the Mont-Blanc cluster has glaciers situated at substantially lower longitudes. Further details on this data collection may be found in a study by Rabatel *et al.* (2016). The field measurements of the Saint-Sorlin, Argentière, Sarennes, and Mer de Glace glaciers from the GLACIOCLIM observatory are also included. Although values from 1959 were the only ones used to align with the meteorological reanalysis, glacier-wide SMB measurements have been available for many of these glaciers since 1949. We obtain 1048 annual glacier-wide SMB values (including data gaps) when we include the Argentière and Saint-Sorlin glaciers from both datasets, bringing the total to 32 glaciers.

Percentage of glacier mass that is ice is calculated using data collected through the Randall Glacier Investigations v6.0 (RGI; Consortium, 2017), abbreviated as F19, Farinotti *et al.* (2019) calculated the thickness of glaciers' ice. Several approaches based on ice-flow mechanics have recently resolved the debate over how to determine ice thickness from surface-variable data. Seismic, ground-penetrating radar, and hot-water-drill data were also included in our ice thickness records for four glaciers tracked through the GLACIOCLIM observatory (Rabatel *et al.*, 2018). We compared these findings to the F19 simulations, for further information, see supplementary materials. Despite variations (up to 100% in extreme situations) in local slope or glacier elevation; no changes were made to the dataset because no systemic biases were observed. Two glaciers, Saint-Sorlin (two square kilometers; mean elevation, 2920 meters above sea level; Écrins cluster) and Mer de Glace (twenty-eight square kilometres; mean elevation, 2890 meters above sea level; Mont-Blanc cluster), had their ice thicknesses precisely predicted by F19. Between 2000 and 2100 m a.s.l., there are isolated inconsistencies of around 50 m on the Mer de Glace tongue, totaling 100 m (30% inaccuracy), but the overall ice distribution is accurate. The Saint-Sorlin Glacier has the largest error of about 20 m, with an ice distribution 20% off at 2900 m a.s.l. F19 routinely underestimates the ice thickness of Argentière due to its bias towards height, as found by Rabatel *et al.* (2018). The MontBlanc glaciers (12.8 km2) with Glacier Blanc (4.7 km2) are part of the Écrins cluster, and their combined average height is 2808 meters above sea level. Hence, the GLACIOCLIM observatory's field data were used to adjust the F19 dataset for these two glaciers manually. Fig. (**2**), which provides a more detailed visual representation of these results, is included in the Supplement. Climate-Related Details: In our example study of the French Alps, daily near-surface (2 m) mean conditions, cumulative snowfall, and rainfall are used to "force" ALPGM. These details, sourced from the SAFRAN dataset, are situated quite close to the stomata of the glaciers. The SAFRAN meteorological data set is a reanalysis of weather data for the French Alps, the Pyrenees, and Corsica, derived from multiple networks (Durand *et al.*, 2009). We use massifs instead of grids to display the data, and then divide each massif into bands 300 meters high and five distinct perspectives (flat, north, south, east, and west).

Fig. (**3**) displays the outcomes of assessing the modeled annual glacier-wide SMB data, denoted as m w.e.a-1, with the leave-one-glacier-out cross-validation method. A linear probability density function is purple-orange in hue, whereas a non-linear one is blue-green. You can tell the frequency by looking at the color. You can see the symbol for the one-to-one line as the black line.a) The normal least-squares model's findings are shown in a scatter plot. (b) A scatter diagram shows the results of the analysis using the lasso line—images depicting the distribution of nonlinear models produced by deep neural networks with and without sample weights.

CONCLUSION

We introduced a unique deep learning method to simulate and recover glacier-scale SMB data for specific glaciers across a region. This approach is a part of ALPGM, a regional glacier evolution system that deviates from both physical and process-based models *via* parameterization. An update to the glacier's shape is combined with data-driven SMB modeling across the whole glacier, using parameterized functions specific to each glacier. Using a case study of glaciers in the French Alps, we show that deep learning outperforms linear techniques for simulating SMB across whole glaciers. We ed *via* cross-validation that a deep ANN can capture large nonlinear features (up to 35%) originating from glacier and climate systems across geographical and temporal dimensions. Compared with linear statistical frameworks, this nonlinearity greatly improved accuracy and explained variance, especially in the more nuanced temporal dimension. Our case study demonstrates that deep ANNs can handle tiny datasets and offer many settings to generalize and avoid overfitting. The ever-increasing volume of data available to machine learning models ensures that their effectiveness steadily improves over time. The field of glaciology can gain a lot by utilizing deep learning. The fact that it performs well in spatial and temporal dimensions for SMB modeling demonstrates its versatility. This strategy has the potential to be beneficial in inaccessible locales such as the Andes or High Mountain Asia for reconstructing SMB time series for sites or glaciers with data from past and future periods. Another potential application of deep learning is to replace more conventional SMB models, such as ALPGM, in regional research. This is because standard SMB models, which are mostly linear, may fail to account for important nonlinearities in climate and glacier systems. In some domains where trustworthy datasets with sufficient geographical and temporal coverage are scarce, it may be premature to build such models. However, our approach has certain limitations, future techniques that leverage physical information to constrain neural networks may yield intriguing insights. Reducing reliance on large datasets and paving the way for more interpretable physics may both be achieved by the incorporation of past physical knowledge into neural networks.-informed models in data science.

REFERENCES

[1] K.S. Chan, and A.B. Koehler, "Big data and statistical modeling: A review", *Stat. Anal. Data Min.*, vol. 14, no. 6, pp. 455-477, 2021.

[2] B. Craven, and T. Islam, "The role of big data in advanced statistical modeling: A literature review", *J.*

Big Data, vol. 8, no. 1, pp. 1-16, 2021.
[PMID: 33425651]

[3] C. Hayes, and E. Murphy, "Big data and statistical modeling in finance: A systematic review", *Journal of Computational Finance,* vol. 25, no. 3, pp. 1-29, 2021.

[4] J.R. Johnson, and Y. Wang, "Big data analytics and statistical modeling in healthcare: A review", *J. Med. Syst.,* vol. 45, no. 12, pp. 1-10, 2021.
[http://dx.doi.org/10.1007/s10916-021-01785-4]

[5] J. Kim, and Y. Ryu, "The role of big data in advanced statistical modeling: A review", *J. Appl. Stat.,* vol. 48, no. 7, pp. 1242-1263, 2021.

[6] S. Mitra, and A. Mukhopadhyay, "Role of big data analytics in statistical modeling: A review", *International Journal of Emerging Trends in Engineering Research,* vol. 9, no. 2, pp. 186-190, 2021.

[7] S. Rana, and S. Bhatia, "A review on the role of big data in statistical modeling", *Int. J. Eng. Res. Technol. (Ahmedabad),* vol. 10, no. 5, pp. 315-320, 2021.

[8] N. Shah, and H. Bhatt, "Big data analytics and statistical modeling: An exploratory study", *International Journal of Advanced Science and Technology,* vol. 30, no. 4, pp. 4253-4260, 2021.

[9] A. Sharma, and R. Dhingra, "Big data and statistical modeling in healthcare: A review", *J. Health Manag.,* vol. 23, no. 3, pp. 282-292, 2021.

[10] A. Singh, and V. Kumar, "Big data analytics and statistical modeling in supply chain management: A review", *Journal of Advances in Management Research,* vol. 18, no. 1, pp. 38-54, 2021.
[http://dx.doi.org/10.1108/JAMR-06-2020-0100]

[11] N. Yadav, and N. Sharma, "Role of big data in advanced statistical modeling: A comprehensive review", *Journal of Business Analytics,* vol. 4, no. 1, pp. 1-19, 2021.
[http://dx.doi.org/10.1080/2573234X.2020.1869962]

[12] J. Chen, Y. Wei, and Q. Wu, "Big data and advanced statistical modeling: A review", *J. Big Data,* vol. 9, no. 1, pp. 1-24, 2022.
[http://dx.doi.org/10.1186/s40537-022-00563-2]

[13] X. Dong, Q. Liu, and X. Wang, "Big data analytics and statistical modeling in business: A review", *J. Bus. Res.,* vol. 139, pp. 212-227, 2021.
[http://dx.doi.org/10.1016/j.jbusres.2021.09.048]

[14] S. Gao, J. Li, and C. Lin, "The role of big data in advanced statistical modeling: A systematic review", *Expert Syst. Appl.,* vol. 181, p. 115002, 2021.
[http://dx.doi.org/10.1016/j.eswa.2021.115002]

[15] Y. Li, and Y. Li, "Big data analytics and statistical modeling in marketing: A review", *J. Bus. Res.,* vol. 129, pp. 34-47, 2021.
[http://dx.doi.org/10.1016/j.jbusres.2021.02.033]

[16] C. Qian, and Y. Ma, "The impact of big data on advanced statistical modeling: A review", *J. Appl. Stat.,* vol. 48, no. 3, pp. 551-571, 2021.
[http://dx.doi.org/10.1080/02664763.2020.1736523]

[17] N. Arora, and N. Sharma, "A comprehensive analysis of big data and statistical models", *International Journal of Advanced Intelligence Paradigms,* vol. 14, no. 1/2, pp. 32-48, 2021.

[18] A. Gupta, and P. Bhattacharya, "The role of big data in advanced statistical modeling", *Int. J. Comput. Intell. Appl.,* vol. 20, no. 01, p. 2150001, 2021.
[http://dx.doi.org/10.1142/S1469026821500013]

[19] R. Kaur, and R. Singh, "Big data analytics and statistical models: A systematic review", *J. Big Data,* vol. 8, no. 1, pp. 1-20, 2021.
[PMID: 33425651]

[20] P.K. Mandal, and R.K. Choudhury, "Big data analytics and statistical modeling in agriculture: A review", *J. Indian Soc. Agric. Stat.,* vol. 75, no. 2, pp. 180-191, 2021.

[21] B. Ramzan, I.S. Bajwa, N. Jamil, R.U. Amin, S. Ramzan, F. Mirza, and N. Sarwar, *An Intelligent Data Analysis for Recommendation Systems Using Machine Learning.,* 2019. [http://dx.doi.org/10.1155/2019/5941096]

CHAPTER 13

Exploiting User Preferences through Content-based Recommendation Systems

Shambhu Bhardwaj[1,*] and **Rajesh Pandian**[2]

[1] *College of Computing Science and Information Technology, Teerthanker Mahaveer University, Moradabad, Uttar Pradesh, India*

[2] *Department of Computer Science and Engineering, JAIN (Deemed-to-be University), Bangalore, Karnataka, India*

Abstract: Present on virtually every online service today, recommender systems have quickly become an integral part of people's everyday digital lives. Modern deep learning-based models can only perform at their peak when fed massive amounts of data. Multiple domains, including Amazon items, restaurants, and breweries, have offered several datasets meeting this condition. The hotel industry has seen relatively few advancements and databases, with even the largest review dataset being in the hundreds of thousands rather than millions. Traditional collaborative filtering methods are also inapplicable to the hotel domain due to its higher data sparsity compared to standard recommendation datasets. In this research, we present HotelRec, a TripAdvisor-derived, massively scaled hotel recommendation dataset comprising 50 million reviews. To the best of our knowledge, HotelRec is the largest recommendation dataset in a single domain and includes textual reviews (50M vs 22M) in the hotel domain (50M versus 0.9M).

Keywords: User preferences, content-based recommendation systems, HotelRec, hotel industry, textual reviews.

INTRODUCTION

In this age of rapidly evolving internet technologies, recommendation systems (RSs) have piqued the interest of both businesses and consumers alike because of their practicality and significance in online shopping and in improving customer acceptance.

It is widely held that the success of an online business is directly proportional to its customers' loyalty. Online booking and reservation systems are also an integral

* **Corresponding author Shambhu Bhardwaj:** College of Computing Science and Information Technology, Teerthanker Mahaveer University, Moradabad, Uttar Pradesh, India; E-mail: shambhu.bharadwaj@gmail.com

S. Kannadhasan, R. Nagarajan, & Kaushik Pal (Eds.)

part of the travel market. According to a study by Mariani *et al.* [1], tourism is the most influential sector of the global economy. To avoid any potential issues with their hotel accommodations, travelers from all over the world rely on recommender systems to find the best available hotels and make reservations online well in advance of their arrival dates.

Some recommender systems have recently been developed to help travellers obtain a list of hotel recommendations before booking, as reported by Liu *et al.* [2]. Conventional recommender systems handle only homogeneous data; hence, the performance of hotel recommendation systems suffers when dealing with the heterogeneous nature of most Internet and online data. Particularly when dealing with complex data in its many numerical, textual, and visual formats, developers must pay close attention to data heterogeneity when building recommender systems. According to Li *et al.* [3], there aren't many recommenders out there that can deal with heterogeneous data. The ones that do employ customer ratings, but don't take into account other forms of user feedback, like votes, reviews, rankings, or video views, that are accessible on social media. We have integrated many user feedback mechanisms into the proposed approach, such as YouTube video plays and votes. The novel and advantageous recommender system we propose does two things. The first step is to utilize a hotel characteristic matrices that takes both numerical and textual information into account to provide accurate recommendations; the second step is to analyze user-contextual information, such as reviews, ranks, votes, and YouTube video views, in order to extract emotions from reviews. The second point is that different user types have different requirements and interests; thus, a fuzzy module may categorize them into different categories and provide hotel suggestions based on them. Similar to how "room," "food," with "cleanliness" are the most important amenities for a family, "pool," "spa," with "gym" may be more desired by each individual traveler. It is not only "computer" and "WiFi" that can be useful for a business traveler.

To get accurate and useful suggestions, recommender systems were proposed by Zhang and Mao [4]. If a recommendation is relevant, it implies that it takes into account the customer's preferences and interests. Customers' past experiences are included in a recommender system alongside the hotel's qualities and amenities. The primary objective of this paper is to provide a method that can effectively manage and analyze varied online datasets in order to make precise hotel recommendations according to the customer's preferences.

Sentiment analysis and opinion mining of user reviews to produce a polarity rating reflecting the extent to which a person loves or hates a hotel was the most demanding component of managing the data for our multifeature hotel recommendations system. Our proposed recommender considers customer feedback, numerical ranking votes, and video views to deliver more accurate results than existing recommenders. Existing recommenders depend on user assessments of a hotel's qualities and facilities. User sentiment about a hotel is expressed as a polarity score in text. We selected a big data solution based on Hadoop because it easily deals with data heterogeneity and variety, which is especially important given that the provided method employs both numerical and textual data. The primary focus of this study is categorizing visitors into five types (individual, family, company, friend, and couple). We will take into account a variety of rating criteria and employ a feature-based approach to sentiment analysis on user feedback. The hotel's location, room, cleanliness, service, and personnel are just a few of the categories on which TripAdvisor's users can provide feedback. Sentiment analysis, also known as opinion mining, is the practice of extracting insights from written feedback. With the proliferation of online resources comes the inevitable necessity to sift through material in light of individual tastes. Every digital activity, from online buying and social networking to music streaming and hotel reservations, now includes the use of a recommender system. Researchers have explored recommender systems for over 30 years (Bobadilla *et al.*, 2013). The many models and datasets generated over the years include movie datasets (Harper and Konstan, 2016), Amazon product datasets (McAuley *et al.*, 2015; He and McAuley, 2016), and music datasets (Celma, 2010). Covington *et al.* (2016) found that large-scale recommender systems based on deep learning led to improved suggestion quality. Although deep learning-based models enhance recommendation performance, massive data sets are required to achieve this. For example, state-of-the-art models shown in recent years need enormous datasets numbering in the millions for optimal performance (Wang *et al.*, 2019; Liang *et al.*, 2018; He *et al.*, 2017). A few articles have addressed hotel recommendation, such as Zhang *et al.* (2015) and Wang *et al.* (2011). Additionally, the largest publicly available collection of hotel reviews has 870,000 records (Li *et al.*, 2016). Traditional collaborative filtering techniques are not well-suited to the hotel domain due to the sparsity of the data (Wang *et al.*, 2015; Khaleghi *et al.*, 2018; Musat and Faltings, 2015). In addition, hotel ratings are unique due to the longer duration and increased number of factors to examine (Khaleghi *et al.*, 2018).

LITERATURE SURVEY

Various studies have examined the issue of suggestion, which is as ancient as the subject itself. These studies have focused on various contexts, including Amazon products, breweries, restaurants, pictures, music, movies, and more. While other attributes, such as text, sub-ratings, date, and helpfulness, may also be included in datasets, ratings are the sole constant. The number of user-item interactions may range from many thousands to several hundred thousand. Our best research indicates that the recommendation corpus built from Amazon Books by He and McAuley (2016) is the largest of its kind, includes textual evaluations, and is focused on a particular topic. It includes opinions on almost 22 million books. HotelRec, on the other hand, is focused on hotels and has 2.3 times as many reviews. As a result, HotelRec has the most textual evaluations of any public dataset dedicated to domain-specific recommendations. Since other datasets (such as the Netflix Prize from Bennett and Lanning (2007)) include interactions beyond the rating and date, we emphasize those with textual evaluations. We are only aware of a small handful of hotel review databases, and these include: The reported figures vary greatly, ranging from 35,000 in one study (Wang *et al.*, 2011) to 69,000 in another (Musat *et al.*, 2013), 140,000 in another (Antognini *et al.*, 2019), 142,000 in yet another (Cozza *et al.*, 2018), 230,000 in yet another, 435,000 in yet another, and 870,000 in yet another (Li *et al.*, 2016). In contrast to standard recommendation datasets, however, there are fewer users, fewer products, and fewer interactions to analyze. The HotelRec dataset, on the other hand, is significantly larger [5 - 10].

A large body of literature has been published with recommendations based on sentiment analysis of reviews using cutting-edge methods. In order to classify text as good, bad, or neutral, machine learning classification is a very useful tool. The machine learning procedure relies heavily on training and assessment datasets. The documents are learned using a training dataset, while the test dataset is utilized to verify the results. Predictive analytics is a subfield of data analytics that makes use of machine learning. Machine learning algorithms are not a set of steps to be taken in a particular order to provide a known result. Instead, they are sequences of operations designed to "learn" patterns from historical data and construct predictive functions.

Classifying users and offering advice is done with the use of machine learning-based sentiment analysis or classification. Both a training dataset and a test dataset are essential for supervised machine learning methods. An automated classifier may learn the document's classification factors from the training set, and the test set can be used to assess the classifier's performance. In supervised machine learning, feature selection is a crucial process. Classification efficiency is set by the classifier and the feature choices made.

Our recommender system's primary goal is to offer suggestions and recommendations that are really tailored to each individual consumer. The quality of suggestions has been the focus of work by Koren *et al.* [5]. To handle a large number of client ratings and reviews efficiently and to provide authentic insights, the author contends that recommendation quality is vital [6]. The use of online booking systems and recommendation engines has grown in recent years, and many global corporations are competing to get a foothold in this market. The benefits of a recommendation system (RS) are not limited to the hospitality industry; rather, RSs have been shown to be effective across a wide range of industries, from media to retail. RS can handle a wide variety of information, including that related to lodging, entertainment, and the arts [11 - 15]. The general layout of a recommendation system is shown in Fig. (**1**). Researchers like Hsieh *et al.* [7] provide a thorough explanation of the processes and algorithms used to develop several recommender systems, all of which rely on ratings and reviews from existing customers to provide accurate product suggestions. Several forms of recommendation algorithms have been addressed by Burke [8]. There were two different types of suggestion methods outlined. Two such methods are "content-based filtering" (CBF) and "collaborative filtering." Hybrid filtering describes a system that combines these two methods [16 - 20].

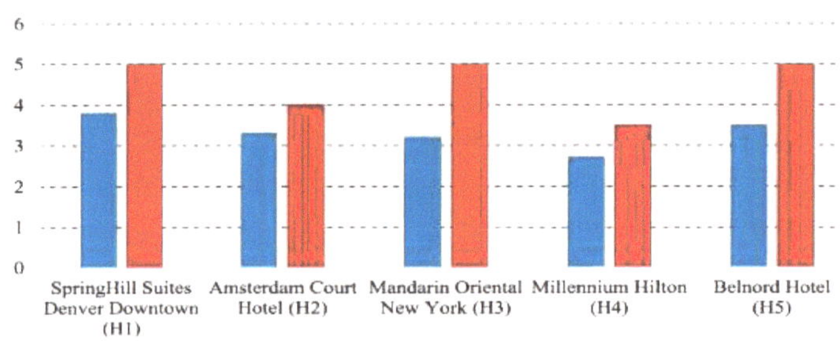

Fig. (1). Difference in rank scores.

The most popular method of recommender filtering is collaborative filtering, as described by Lops *et al.* [9]; whereas in a content-based recommendation system, linked items reflect the user's choices and preferences. In order for CF to provide useful suggestions, it takes into account user ratings for items in a certain domain and then computes similarities between different entities. Ekstrand *et al.* [10] define "collaborative filtering" as an algorithmic category that uses previous users' choices for a given item to inform its own suggestion to the person in question [21]. This approach may be valuable in any sector where consumer preferences are vulnerable to sudden shifts [11 - 15].

PROPOSED WORK

Users can access hotels that have not been reviewed or stayed in using this method. Similarity between two users is determined by their same category and location. Since certain datasets may contain missing values or duplicate entries, they must be cleansed first. Subsequently, the dataset is pre-processed, with specific attention paid to the category and city features. The "one hot encoding" of two attributes is what allows for similarity calculations between different users. The user's previous hotel stays inform this feature's similarity. Users' preferences are reflected in this striking resemblance. Similarity is then used to recommend a hotel based on a user's rating. Hotels are often presented in descending order of quality. In Fig. (**1**), we see an algorithmic representation of this system.

Better and more timely recommendations may be delivered by the proposed system, which efficiently stores data from several hotels. The four main arguments that this paper intends to provide are as follows: To help achieve accurate hotel recommendations, the suggested recommender system processes and analyzes large heterogeneous online information, including numerical ratings as well as textual reviews. It then generates relevant recommendations based on customer type and choice using an opinion mining approach as well as a fuzzy approach.(ii)Creation of a web-based hotel recommender that incorporates data from external sources (hotel websites) that provide online hotel information; (iii) The proposed approach improves the system's performance by integrating a NoSQL Cassandra databases into a Hadoop environment; (iv) The dataset comes from two separate websites, namely Expedia.com and TripAdvisor.com.

The SentiWordnet Wordnet dictionaries allow users to employ an opinion-based technique to categorize the text into "Positive," "Negative," and "Neutral" emotion expressions. Review processing and feature extraction from textual reviews present a variety of difficulties. The following are examples of problems: (i) Managing massive amounts of information, such as guests' written comments about their hotel stays. (ii) Slang, abbreviations, emoji, or emoticons; (iii) Spelling and grammatical errors; (iv) Casual, off-the-cuff language. Uncertain consumer feedback, such as "I have never lived in a hotel quite like this one!" The hotel's quality is unclear; we can't tell if it's excellent or terrible (v). Hashtag-laden reviews (vi). Uncovering a review's underlying polarity of consumer emotion.

The suggested approach uses the mixed (textual and numerical) character of data scraped from the Internet. The data is collected from the user's current search query and the specified hotel websites (data sources). To obtain the necessary information, a web crawler was used to retrieve it and then load it into the NoSQL database Cassandra. Votes, rankings, and total video views are all examples of numerical data, whereas reviews and comments are examples of textual data. Our algorithm has mined data from hotel rankings, votes, and reviews to identify relevant aspects to make more accurate suggestions.

There are two operational strands within the system. Hotels' numerical rankings and votes from each compiled data set are normalized. A review mining-specific natural language processing software extracts features from the reviews and organizes them into a hotel feature matrix. After that, SentiWordNet assigns numerical polarity values to the recovered characteristics, and finally, an average polarity rating is produced. We now take weighted averages of the normalized rank rating, voting rating, and polarity score and use them for further analysis. The last set of recommendations is then determined using fuzzy logic. The final score for the type of visitor (solo, family, company, friends, married couple, *etc.*) is determined using a fuzzy set with specific fuzzy criteria. Fig. (**2**) depicts the suggested hotel suggestion method. The hotels' final suggestions for a certain sort of guest in one of the five categories are shown.

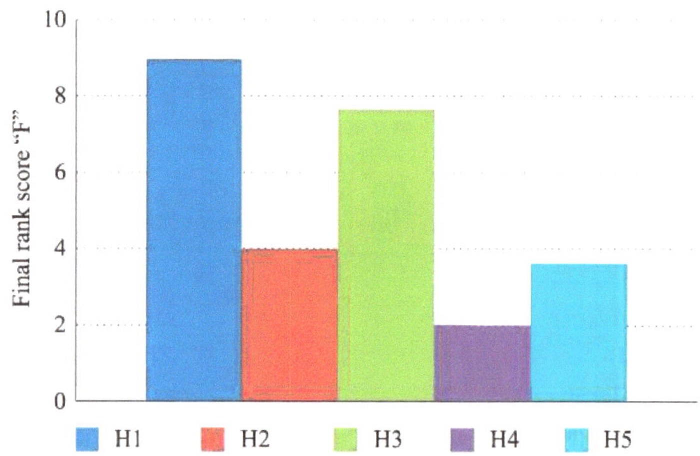

Fig. (2). Final Score F.

Feature Extraction Process

Before we can determine which features reviewers care about most, we must first evaluate the reviews themselves and transform them into a structured format so that we can extract opinion-based features. It is common practice to import reviews from any website into the system database by first extracting them into a JSON file. After looking at several approaches, we settled on NLTK as the best package for extracting characteristics from hotel reviews and calling it a day. The Natural Language Toolkit (NLTK) is a library in Python for building applications that deal with text written in natural language. Among the many tasks that this package can perform are processing, categorization, tokenization, parsing, tagging, and semantic reasoning. In this post, we utilized NLTK version 3.3. A number of steps have been taken to extract relevant information from guest reviews, including: evaluating the process of extracting features and categorizing them, mining user opinions to find and reward characteristics shared by reviews, and giving these attributes a value within the normalized range

A natural language data structure with commas is used to transform the evaluation data. In order to extract hotel attributes from guest reviews, the proposed method makes use of a natural language parsing procedure. To get a natural language processing result from a text review, we have implemented the following four steps: Feature extraction, lexical analysis, syntactic analysis, semantic analysis, and logical analysis.

Lexical Analysis

The lexical analysis process begins with a stream of characters and ends with a stream of tokens.

1. Tokenizing. The hotel evaluations are presented in paragraph format, each composed of several sentences. Tokens or dictionaries are created from these strings. Words, but also numbers and symbols, can serve as these tokens. Whitespace is often stripped out of sentences, and each letter and digit are treated as a single token. The POS tagger then sorts these tokens into their component morphemes. So, the word “vegetables” is simply “vegetable + s” in the database, while the verb “feels” is entered as “feel + s.” After that, a parse tree does a lexical analysis of the morphemes.

Syntax Analysis

Before moving on to the next level of analysis, it is necessary to check the examined paragraph for any instances of incorrect grammatical use. In this effort, we repair typos and grammatical issues detected in the crawled reviews by using Google Spell Check. A statistical spell checker is used to rectify any misspelled words and eliminate any duplication or unnecessary punctuation (!,?, *etc.*) from the review material. The tool may be found at http://norvig.com/spell-correct.html. We used a publicly accessible POS tagger to smooth out the evaluation's language, along with removing things like grammatical and syntactical errors. The three most important parts of a sentence—the subject, the object, and the verb—will also be taught to you at this level. Parse trees and typed relationships are built at this step. You may also use a syntactic dependencies parser (http://nlp.stanford.edu/software/lex-parser.shtml) to get the relationships between words in a sentence. Word stemming is the process by which numerous new words are created from existing ones. In order to go back to their original forms, derivative words might be “stemmed.” Our research has made use of Lancaster Stemmer. WordNet Lemmatizer, part of the Python NLTK, searches the WordNet database for word lemmas. The root word can't be retrieved until the part of speech is identified. Different normalization criteria are used depending on the part of speech of the word being processed.(b)Removal of extraneous words: Most evaluations include filler terms like "the," "a," "also," "about," "an," "at," "to," *etc.*, that add nothing to the process of gleaning useful information about a product or service. These words have been taken out. There is no collection of English "stop words" that has been vetted and accepted worldwide. To fix this, we created our own Java library to handle these kinds of terms. (c)Condense too dramatic expression. A meaningful phrase in which the letter occurs once is used to shorten words with the same letter twice if they have not been included in the dictionary. For example, the overblown word "NOOOOOO" would be shortened to "NO."(e)Tagging words according to their common grammatical properties is called part-of-speech tagging. Words have been marked with their corresponding parts of speech in the review. A wide variety of groups have been established for the words according to the roles they play. As an example, the NLP program will produce tags for singular correct nouns (NP), singular common verbs (NN), and so on.

Semantic Analysis

The review's tagged terms from inside its phrases are tabulated for use in the semantic analysis. At this point, not only do we determine the actions each subject does, but we also determine a number of properties for each object.

Polarity Detection

An aggregate polarity score is calculated for each hotel using reviews from various sources; it is based on the sentiment of every review in the dataset, determined using the NLTK package. We have started doing feature-based opinion analysis of all reviews because there are multiple opinions associated with each review feature (*e.g.*, location, room, and food). Opinion words show whether the reviewer had a positive, indifferent, or negative feeling towards the feature. To find out how positive or negative an opinion word is, we calculate its polarity value.

TF-IDF Generation

After preprocessing the text-based reviews by eliminating any unnecessary stop words and repetitive entries, each review must be created using Tf-Idf, which stands for term frequency minus inverse document frequency. By assigning weights to each review item using the phrase's frequency-inverse document frequency (TF-IDF) technique, we can determine which phrases are more representative and appear more often in the set of documents, and which terms are less representative and appear less often. Every phrase in the review collection has its own unique TF-IDF, which means:

However, the IDF for a particular time period is as follows:

The next step is to use TF-IDF weighting to downweight frequently occurring phrases and to identify uncommon ones. The TF-IDF score is calculated by multiplying:

SentiWordNet is a thesaurus that conveys the overall tone rather than just the individual words used in a review. Several hotel reviews were analyzed for polarity and subjectivity using SentiWordNet, an entirely free online opinion analyzer for English that draws on the WordNet database. Using the steps we've previously discussed, we were able to categorize the reviews into three groups: favorable (pos), negative (neg), and neutral (neu). The SentiWordNet module, which is part of the NLTK library for Python, enhances WordNet synsets with sentiment polarity. Sentiment analysis takes advantage of WordNet's many semantic correlations between words to determine the degree of emotion. In layman's terms, sentiment analysis is the method of assigning numerical values to evaluations made in the form of text. Multiplying a phrase's sentiment score (positive or negative) with its TF-IDF weight yields the overall sentiment rating (polarity) of phrases in the text. This process is shown below:

The number of aspects highlighted as either favorable or unfavorable in the review indicates the overall sentiment polarity score (positive or negative). To show how good or negative the review is generally, we take the quantity of favorable and adverse opinion words for each attribute and use them to calculate a weighted average. In hotel reviews, a feature is considered positively polarized if its polarity score is more than zero; negatively polarized if its score is less than zero; and neutral if its score is equal to zero. We have calculated the polarity of all the hotel reviews from different sources.

If you add up all the positive reviews for hotel hn on the chosen website and subtract all the negative reviews for hotel hn on the chosen website, you will have the polarity of the reviews for hotel Pr on the chosen website.:

Sorting and Suggestion of Types

The final score is used to determine the classification. Words from reviews are compared to the dictionary; points are awarded (+1), subtracted (-1) if the term is unfavorable, and not awarded (-0) if it is neutral. Fuzzy logic is used to arrive at a final recommendation. The fuzzy sets theory gives us a way to model the fuzziness that permeates most of what we know. A given element's degree of belonging to a set may be shown in fuzzy set theory. Guests who enjoy the hotel's gym or spa are considered to be members of the set of solo guests, while guests who enjoy the hotel's ghazal night or cinema are considered to be members of the set of couple guests, and so on. To that aim, we have built a recommender that uses a fuzzy set of expert criteria to provide hotel suggestions. The first stage in making a hotel suggestion is to represent the relevant knowledge about the selection process. The use of fuzzy sets allows this information to be conveyed.

First, fuzzy sets are defined with the help of domain experts. The hotel and guest attributes are described by the expert in terms of fuzzy sets. Following this, a recommender system that relies on collaborative filtering will provide recommendations based on a hotel feature rating matrix that has already been built.

RESULT ANALYSIS

Two reliable sources with many ratings, reviews, and rankings, Trip Advisor and Expedia, were chosen to represent the variety of the data. The inclusion of 8,000 of the most popular hotels in the world and a collection of reviews and ratings for each contribute to the usefulness of this data set for our research. Following data preprocessing, TF-IDF generation, and polarity detection using SentiWordNet, we have computed polarity ratings for textual reviews obtained from each selected website. Table **1** shows the hotels we used, the data we gathered, and how we processed it using the recommended method.

Table 1. Rank scores, vote scores, and polarity scores.

Selected hotel	Data source					
		TripAdvisor (D1)			Expedia (D2)	
	Polarity score	Normalized rank score	Voting score	Polarity score	Normalized rank score	Voting score
SpringHill Suites, Denver Downtown (HI)	31	3.9	209301	23	5	268231
Amsterdam Court Hotel (H2)	-5	3.4	38821	7	4	63420
Mandarin Oriental, New York (H3)	17	3.2	111620	24	5	127023
Millennium Hilton (H4)	-4	2.8	17023	-3	3.5	35622
Belnord Hotel (H5)	16	3.5	29441	22	5	41323

“D1” refers to the external data source, similar to TripAdvisor, that we used for our inquiry, while “D2” stands for the external data source similar to Expedia.

The Mandarin Oriental, in New York, is represented by "H1," the Amsterdam Court Hôtel by "H2," the Hotel Metropolis by "H3," the Millennium Hyatt by "H4", and the Belnord by "H5". Each hotel's textual review on the selected websites has been examined and given a polarity score. There is also a normalized rank score (on a scale of 1-4) and a voting score. The number of customer votes cast for each hotel is represented by the voting score. The table lists hotels and their respective data source IDs.

We can see that Expedia gives better hotel rankings than TripAdvisor does when we equalize the rank scores from two distinct sources of data (TripAdvisor "D1" as well as Expedia "D2").

In Table **1**, "D1" denotes the external data source similar to TripAdvisor that we used for our inquiry, while "D2" stands for the external data source similar to Expedia. The Mandarin Oriental, in New York, is represented by "H1," the Amsterdam Court Hôtel by "H2," the Mandarin Oriental Metro by "H3," the Millennium by the Hilton by "H4", with the Belnord by "H5". Each hotel's textual review on the selected websites has been examined and given a polarity score. There is also a normalized rank score (on a scale of 1-4) and a voting score. The number of customer votes cast for each hotel is represented by the voting score. The table displays a list of hotels together with their respective data source IDs.

Because its final rank score "F" is higher than 8, the H1 hotel "SpringHill Suites Denver Downtown" is classified as a hotel in the "R" category. The H3 resort "Mandarin Oriental New York" is classified as a "BR" due to its "F" score being within the range of 6 to 8. Class "LR" hotels include the "Amsterdam Court Hotel" (H2), the "Millennium Hilton" (H4), and the "Belnord Hotel" (H5), all of which have ratings between 2 and 4.

Hotel categories from various data sets are plotted against guest-type rankings in Fig. (**2**). These rankings take into account factors like individuals traveling alone, families traveling together, and couples vacationing together.

CONCLUSION

Using a Cassandra database and a big-data Hadoop environment, this study presents a novel CF recommendation technique that can handle diverse data types, including textual evaluations, rankings, votes, and video views, to improve recommendation response time. The suggested method uses sentiment analysis to extract a hotel feature matrix, which is then stored in a database. In our approach, we use lexical, syntactic, and semantic analysis to understand how visitors perceive certain lodgings. To determine the opinion of the reviews, we utilize the NLTK library. The system uses fuzzy logic to guess the hotel class to assign a given guest. Recommendations are tailored to individuals or a group of guests using a distance metric called Euclidean distance. Through optimizations, the system's suggestion generation now takes only 2.65 ms, while maintaining excellent quality. When we train the system on example data, the F-measure is about 95%, but when we use the entire dataset we obtained from websites, the F-measure drops to around 92%. The size of the actual full dataset causes the accuracy metrics numbers to be considerably lowered to 0.745, or around 74%. This demonstrates that the suggested recommender, which makes use of a sentiment analysis technique, effectively and reliably guides consumers to content that meets their needs.

REFERENCES

[1] G. Ramakrishnan, V. Saicharan, K. Chandrasekaran, M.V. Rathnamma, and V.V. Ramana, Collaborative Filtering for Book Recommendation System. In: Das, K., Bansal, J., Deep, K., Nagar, A., Pathipooranam, P., Naidu, R. (eds) Soft Computing for Problem Solving. Advances in Intelligent Systems and Computing, Springer, Singapore. vol 1057. 2020. [http://dx.doi.org/10.1007/978-981-15-0184-5_29]

[2] F. Wang, H. Zhu, G. Srivastava, S. Li, M.R. Khosravi, and L. Qi, "Robust Collaborative Filtering Recommendation With User-Item-Trust Records", *IEEE Trans. Comput. Soc. Syst.,* vol. 9, no. 4, pp. 986-996, 2022. [http://dx.doi.org/10.1109/TCSS.2021.3064213]

[3] B. Alhijawi, G. Al-Naymat, N. Obeid, and A. Awajan, "Novel predictive model to improve the accuracy of collaborative filtering recommender systems", *Inf. Syst.,* vol. 96, p. 101670, 2021. [http://dx.doi.org/10.1016/j.is.2020.101670]

[4] A. Iftikhar, M.A. Ghazanfar, M. Ayub, Z. Mehmood, and M. Maqsood, "An Improved Product Recommendation Method for Collaborative Filtering", *IEEE Access,* vol. 8, pp. 123841-123857, 2020. [http://dx.doi.org/10.1109/ACCESS.2020.3005953]

[5] D. Margaris, C. Vassilakis, and D. Spiliotopoulos, "On Producing Accurate Rating Predictions in Sparse Collaborative Filtering Datasets", *Information (Basel),* vol. 13, no. 6, p. 302, 2022. [http://dx.doi.org/10.3390/info13060302]

[6] D. Spiliotopoulos, D. Margaris, and C. Vassilakis, "On Exploiting Rating Prediction Accuracy Features in Dense Collaborative Filtering Datasets", *Information (Basel),* vol. 13, no. 9, p. 428, 2022. [http://dx.doi.org/10.3390/info13090428]

[7] L. Feng, Q. Zhao, and C. Zhou, "Improving performances of Top-N recommendations with co-clustering method", *Expert Syst. Appl.,* vol. 143, p. 113078, 2020. [http://dx.doi.org/10.1016/j.eswa.2019.113078]

[8] P.K. Singh, S. Setta, P.K.D. Pramanik, and P. Choudhury, "Improving the Accuracy of Collaborative Filtering-Based Recommendations by Considering the Temporal Variance of Top-N Neighbors", *International Conference on Innovative Computing and Communications,* vol. Volume 1087, Springer: Singapore, pp. 1-10, 2020.9789811512858 [http://dx.doi.org/10.1007/978-981-15-1286-5_1]

[9] S.H. Chen, S.I. Sou, and H.P. Hsieh, "Top-N music recommendation framework for precision and novelty under diversity group size and similarity", *J. Intell. Inf. Syst.,* vol. 62, no. 1, pp. 1-26, 2024. [http://dx.doi.org/10.1007/s10844-023-00784-2]

[10] L. Gienapp, B. Stein, M. Hagen, and M. Potthast, "Estimating Topic Difficulty Using Normalized Discounted Cumulated Gain", *Proceedings of the 29th ACM International Conference on Information & Knowledge Management,* Association for Computing Machinery: New York, NY, USA, pp. 2033-

2036, 2020.Virtual Event, Ireland.
[http://dx.doi.org/10.1145/3340531.3412109]

[11] Z. Ding, X. Li, C. Jiang, and M. Zhou, "Objectives and state-of-the-art of location-based social network recommender systems", *ACM Comput. Surv. CSUR,* vol. 51, pp. 1-28, 2018.

[12] J. Lu, D. Wu, M. Mao, W. Wang, and G. Zhang, "Recommender system application developments: A survey", *Decis. Support Syst.,* vol. 74, pp. 12-32, 2015.
[http://dx.doi.org/10.1016/j.dss.2015.03.008]

[13] F. Ricci, L. Rokach, and B. Shapira, Recommender Systems: Introduction and Challenges.*Recommender Systems Handbook.* Springer: Boston, MA, USA, 2015.
[http://dx.doi.org/10.1007/978-1-4899-7637-6_1]

[14] C.C. Aggarwal, An Introduction to Recommender Systems.*Recommender Systems.* Springer: Cham, Switzerland, 2016.
[http://dx.doi.org/10.1007/978-3-319-29659-3_1]

[15] A.A. Kardan, and M. Ebrahimi, "A novel approach to hybrid recommendation systems based on association rules mining for content recommendation in asynchronous discussion groups", *Inf. Sci.,* vol. 219, pp. 93-110, 2013.
[http://dx.doi.org/10.1016/j.ins.2012.07.011]

[16] R. Marappan, "Create a book recommendation system using collaborative filtering", *International Journal of Mathematical, Engineering, Biological and Applied Computing,* vol. 1, no. 1, pp. 44-46, 2022.
[http://dx.doi.org/10.1007/978-981-15-0184-5_29]

[17] F. Wang, H. Zhu, G. Srivastava, S. Li, M.R. Khosravi, and L. Qi, "Robust Collaborative Filtering Recommendation With User-Item-Trust Records", *IEEE Trans. Comput. Soc. Syst.,* vol. 9, no. 4, pp. 986-996, 2022.
[http://dx.doi.org/10.1109/TCSS.2021.3064213]

[18] B. Alhijawi, G. Al-Naymat, N. Obeid, and A. Awajan, "Novel predictive model to improve the accuracy of collaborative filtering recommender systems", *Inf. Syst.,* vol. 96, p. 101670, 2021.
[http://dx.doi.org/10.1016/j.is.2020.101670]

[19] A. Iftikhar, M.A. Ghazanfar, M. Ayub, Z. Mehmood, and M. Maqsood, "An Improved Product Recommendation Method for Collaborative Filtering", *IEEE Access,* vol. 8, pp. 123841-123857, 2020.
[http://dx.doi.org/10.1109/ACCESS.2020.3005953]

[20] D. Margaris, C. Vassilakis, and D. Spiliotopoulos, "On Producing Accurate Rating Predictions in Sparse Collaborative Filtering Datasets", *Information (Basel),* vol. 13, no. 6, p. 302, 2022.
[http://dx.doi.org/10.3390/info13060302]

[21] D. Spiliotopoulos, D. Margaris, and C. Vassilakis, "On Exploiting Rating Prediction Accuracy Features in Dense Collaborative Filtering Datasets", *Information (Basel),* vol. 13, no. 9, p. 428, 2022.
[http://dx.doi.org/10.3390/info13090428]

CHAPTER 14

Exploring the Application of Data Mining in the Detection of Fraudulent Transactions

Priyanka Chandani[1,*]

[1] *Department of DS, CSBS, AL-CSBS, Noida Institute of Engineering and Technology, Greater Noida, Uttar Pradesh, India*

Abstract: Many businesses, including those in the banking sector, have begun offering their services online in response to the meteoric rise in internet use. Worldwide, financial fraud is on the rise, leading to enormous losses. From now on, threats like unlawful transactions and unusual assaults may be actively detected by developing sophisticated financial fraud detection systems. Data mining and ML have become more important tools for addressing these problems in recent years. However, in order to speed up processing, analyze massive amounts of data, and detect new attack patterns, these systems need a lot of improvements. According to this study, a Deep Convolution Neural Network (DCNN) can be used to detect financial fraud utilizing smart algorithms. When dealing with large datasets, this approach enhances detection accuracy. The performance of the proposed model is assessed by comparing it to other models that use auto-encoder methods, deep learning, and current machine learning models on a revised credit card fraud database. The results of the experiments demonstrate that the proposed model attained a 99% detection accuracy in only 45 seconds.

Keywords: Artificial neural network, deep learning, financial fraud, convolution neural network, data mining.

INTRODUCTION

Big data, characterized by its heterogeneity, is created every day in massive quantities as a result of the exponential expansion of technological advances. A stumbling block continues to be the integration of heterogeneous data. The integration and completion of the business information required have become arduous processes [1]. Technology, big data, as well as open source material, have all contributed to the meteoric rise of the company intelligence (BI) industry over the last decade. Despite this expansion, private-sector use of open government

* **Corresponding author Priyanka Chandani:** Department of DS, CSBS, AL-CSBS, Noida Institute of Engineering and Technology, Greater Noida, Uttar Pradesh, India; E-mail: priyanka.chandani@niet.co.in

information (OGD) remains low due to a lack of awareness of its benefits. Private enterprises' limited use of OGD raises hopes that it might inspire novel concepts and support data-driven decision-making [2]. Due in large part to the coronavirus epidemic, which has increased companies' online presence, social networking has emerged as a major player in modern business and organizational operations. Researchers and company owners alike are increasingly intrigued by the prospect of using social network data to power company analytics. Social media has given company owners a new tool to better understand their customers and adapt their operations to their ever-changing demands. Twitter makes it simple to keep tabs on what's trending, what's set to gain traction, and important information like the source of the trend and the people involved [3].

A number of recent technical developments—such as the Internet of Things, machine learning, and big data analytics—have already had an effect on business operations. Among the next technologies, artificial intelligence (AI) might radically alter the way marketers approach their craft. Artificial intelligence has the potential to be useful in many areas of today's business world. The fate of human civilization will be determined by artificial intelligence, according to the philosophical as well as scientific consensus [4]. To prevent the coronavirus from spreading rapidly, many entities monitor the number of confirmed cases daily. Big Data technologies handle very large, diverse, and dynamic datasets that are inherently unmanageable with current methods. There are four steps for handling Big Data before it generates usable information: acquisition, access, analytics, and application. The purpose of business intelligence is to make sense of a company's operational and transactional information. Using graphical representations of data, Big Data Analytics examines both current and historical company choices [5]. Thanks to advancements in IT, BI, and information technologies, data is now both a storage medium for massive amounts of information as well as an analytical method in and of itself. Businesses may better adapt their operations to achieve successful production if they have a proper grasp of the benefits of analyzing company data and information from business intelligence [6]. People in every walk of life are becoming increasingly dependent on information technology as the global economy expands and technological and scientific progress advance. A comparable data system, known as intelligence for business (BI), is likewise under continual development in the corporate sector. Additionally, the use of IT has increased rivalry in the corporate world. In addition to the commercial acumen of corporate decision-makers, a scientific, precise collection of data, made possible by rapid BI tools, is essential for a company to uncover new markets and seize opportunities in the cutthroat business world [7].

RELATED WORKS

Presently underway projects, patterns in development throughout history, and potential future directions were the foci of this study. This article employs a CiteSpace-based bibliographic analysis, using 681 unique papers from 2000–2021, culled from the WoSCC and Scopus indexes. We found the most influential nations, universities, authors, publications, and references in the field of academia. The study delves into international social networks and academic partnerships. The degree of cross-disciplinarity is quantified. Investigation methodologies, business intelligence (BI) applications, and obstacles are addressed independently as we delve into the historical patterns of burst keywords and hotspot dispersion. Possible causes of 2021 hotspot explosions are investigated. Lastly, recommendations are made for future scholars, and the course of research is forecasted. The findings indicate that in the following years, research on COVID-19, healthcare, 5G, as well as big data/AI driven business intelligence techniques will be highly sought. Consequently, the findings of this study may be used to influence future studies, especially those pertaining to the direct selection and method application domains [8].

Innovation and knowledge management's (KIM) impact on sustainability and innovation initiatives is expanded upon in this essay by Danny Sampson, as well as Marianne Gloet. This article describes the results of a longitudinal study that included a number of medium- and small-sized food and drink exporters from Australia. Dilek Cetindamar, Baraah Shdifat, as well as Eila Erfani's "Understanding the Big Data Analytical Capability as well as Sustainability Supply Chains" is the SI's concluding article. Sustainable supply chain efficiency (SSCP) and big data analytics capacity (BDAC) are reviewed in this literature review. After that, they provide some suggestions for future research and highlight deficiencies in the current literature. We trust that you will find this SI's extensive coverage of current and relevant subjects, organized under the theme of "Business Analytics & Big Data as Tools for Innovation as well as Sustainable Development of Companies" [9], to be both interesting and useful.

We have created an original structure for Heterogeneous Integration of Information and Analysis to tackle the challenges of handling different big data. Companies often employ big data analysis, a method for extracting knowledge, for company intelligence purposes. Unfortunately, data mining struggles with issues like limited memory and high processing costs, thus it can't handle really huge data sets well. Here, we provide a Convolutional Neural Network (CNN) design for analyzing massive data sets that are diverse in nature. Last but not least, the suggested approach is the quickest to integrate data structure, according to the trial findings [10]. It is also a great framework for business evaluation.

The study's overarching goal is to determine which factors significantly impact the efficacy of business intelligence in Jordan's banking industry using the McLean and DeLone methodology. Approach, methodology, and design: Information was collected from real users of business intelligence products in Jordanian banks using a quantitative survey. These users rely on these tools to make strategic and operational choices. The acquired data were examined *via* the use of structural equation modeling with partial least squares methods. Findings: The research found that many important factors, including system dependability, data correctness, user excellence, user enjoyment, and user performance, affect the company's intelligence in Jordan's banking industry. Realistic consequences: The results of this study might be useful for managers in Jordanian banks looking to boost organizational performance as well as company intelligence success. Relevance and freshness: From the perspective of Jordanian banks, this study is the first of its kind that offers a theoretical framework for assessing the elements that lead to BIS effectiveness, according to the authors [11].

In this field of study, which is still in its early stages, we expand by investigating how OGD might be used to provide business information to identify potential markets and formulate strategies. We use a two-industry case study strategy—the footwear and lumber sectors—to extract unique themes from OGD using latent Dirichlet distributed (LDA) topical modeling. After that, we depict these topics using pyLDAVis, a data visualisation tool. Because of this, we can decipher the data and use it for intelligence gathering. Our evaluation of the two sectors' environments is another step toward guaranteeing the data's use. Not only do the findings show that OGD might be a valuable resource for BI, but they also demonstrate how topic modeling with visualization software can help businesses uncover new market opportunities by evaluating existing data [12].

This article adds to the expanding body of literature on the visualization of data for business intelligence processes using the Internet of Things (IoT) by conducting a thorough literature review. We collected and analyzed 237 journal articles published in the previous decade and a half. Thanks to this, we were able to hone down on some of the most significant and consequential writers, nations, publications, organizations, articles, and research results—not to mention the obstacles that contemporary researchers must overcome. In light of these findings, the authors offer a comprehensive overview of the subject by outlining four areas of study: technological facilities, case studies, the end-user experience, and big data tools. They also detail the historical progression and current trajectory of these study streams [13].

This study aims to develop a model that examines the impact of information technology (IT) on company performance, both directly and indirectly, through the intermediary functions of blockchain and big data analytics. Investigators obtained their information from a random sample of 387 individuals employed by 12 Croatian IT firms. Using structural equation modeling, the research delves into these linkages. The results demonstrated that company data significantly affects a company's performance. Additionally, business intelligence had a significant positive influence on the implementation of blockchain technology and big data analytics, thereby enhancing the organization's efficiency. The use of blockchain, as well as big data analysis, also indicated and moderated the favorable correlation between BI and company success. There were two partial negotiations. Management implications, constraints, as well as possible futures are also included in the paper [14].

With the help of large amounts of data as a service as well as analytical skills, small and medium companies (SMEs) have a lot of chances to thrive in e-commerce, according to this report. Accounting professionals working for small and medium businesses were the subjects of the data collection, which covers two time periods: the COVID-19 epidemic and the new normal. The researchers in this study used structural equation modeling. This work's valuable, granular insights might help practitioners and policymakers identify and exploit opportunities for efficient and successful E-commerce implementation [15].

PROPOSED WORK

Here 6223 instances of fraud are considered out of an arbitrary number of five million transactions that occurred over the course of 24 hours. With fraudulent behavior accounting for 0.12% of every transaction, the dataset is severely imbalanced. Thirty complex parameters, such as class, amount, timing, and more, are considered in the dataset. These features have been used as benchmarks by many researchers for several studies. Data validation, normalization, and data collection division are prerequisites for framework implementation. Verifying the data's correctness requires searching the dataset for blank spaces, negative timestamps, and negative integers. For more precise results, the factors are adjusted to -1 to 1. Data normalization describes this procedure. In addition, training and testing use 70 percent and 30 percent of the samples, respectively. After the necessary pre-processing, the Convolution Neural Network approach, which depends on deep memory and learning, is used to identify financial fraud. We contrast past input information with forecast outcomes, leveraging prior knowledge to improve prediction accuracy. Long dependence learning with the DCNN architecture enables sequential prediction. With this concept, it might be possible to preserve patterns and long-term memories. As an inherent feature of the paradigm, data may be stored for extended periods. The above framework effectively performs both detection and prediction. The DCNN cell memory layers are used to feed the pre-processed input into the model. The extra parameters this model employs improve the results. In order to assess how well the suggested model works, its optimizers, batch size, epochs, and matrix are calculated. The last step after applying the model is processing, during which the output and assessment are retrieved. The application model is shown in Fig. (**1**). A number of criteria are used to ensure the algorithm's judgment of the transaction's fraud status is accurate.

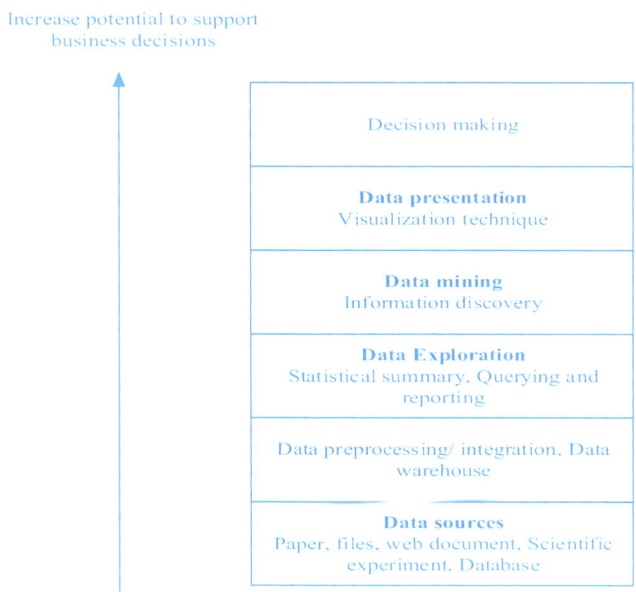

Fig. (1). Application model.

Feature Learning Model

Assume for the sake of argument that a dataset is structured with n rows of data denoted as {D_1,D_2,…,D_n} with m columns containing characteristics denoted as {F_1,F_2,□,F_m}. We start by learning only the best features, selected using the TLL method, from m total features. The TTL algorithm is a heuristic algorithm that works on the teaching and learning processes. The teaching and learning processes that take place in classrooms serve as the basis for the population-based optimization algorithm known as the teacher learning algorithm. It is appropriate for seeking comprehensive answers to persistent issues. The instructor-and-learner algorithm actually has a quick convergence rate, which significantly reduces time consumption. Here, we have used this teacher-learning algorithm to select the best group leaders. In the proposed TTL algorithm, we consider three objective functions (OF) for optimal feature selection. The optimal feature selection involves the following steps,

Population Initialization – The algorithm starts with population initialization or student initialization. The solution set is the initial population. In this work, the features are the population. This initialization is performed as follows,

$$P = \{F_1, F_2, F_3, .., F_m\} \quad (1)$$

Here, P defines the population set.

Population Evaluation – Once the population is initiated, the next step is to evaluate it. In the TTL algorithm, each solution is evaluated based on the fitness function (FF), which is designed with three OFs. The FF of ith solution is given as follows:

$$FF_i = \{OF_1 \&\& OF_2 \&\& OF_3\} \quad (2)$$

Each OF can be defined as follows,

OF1 [Correlation Function]: This function finds out the correlation between two features in order to figure out the similarities among them. If the OF1 is large, then the features are likely to be the same, so we can drop one of them. Thus, the feature set must have a lower OF1 among them. It can be computed as follows,

$$OF_1(F_i, F_j) = \frac{cov\ (i,j)}{\varphi_i \varphi_j} \quad (3)$$

Here, cov (i,j) defines the covariance between Fi,Fj and φiφj is the distance between both features.

OF2 [Dispersion Ratio]: The ratio of the arithmetic mean (AM) to the geometric median (GM) is defined as this function, which is given as

$$AM_i = \frac{1}{n} \sum_{j=1}^{n} X_{ij} \quad (4)$$

$$GM_i = \left(\prod_{j=1}^{n} X_{ij}\right)^{\frac{1}{n}} \quad (5)$$

$$OF_2 = Dispersion\ Ratio = \frac{AM_i}{GM_i} \quad (6)$$

Here, n is the total number of features presented in the set and Xij is the value of the given feature. It mainly reflects the relevance of the feature for the given context. Higher OF2 is more likely to be an optimal feature set.

OF3 [Fisher Score]: It is defined as the ranks of the feature variables based on the Fisher score. It is computed as follows,

$$OF_3 = FS = \frac{\sum_{j=1}^{n} p_j(\mu_j-\mu)^2}{\sum_{j=1}^{n} p_j\varphi_j^2} \quad \textbf{(7)}$$

In this case, p_j represents the fraction information point, μ stands for the average of the percentage points, and φ_j denotes the standard deviations of the percentage points.

The FFi is computed for each feature set presented in the population.

Teaching Phase – This phase is executed after fitness evaluation. In this phase, a solution that has a higher FFi is elected as a teacher. The main idea is to improve the solution phase by updating other solutions towards the best solution (*i.e.*) teacher solution. The best solution is the teacher, and all other solutions are the students. Each student updates their knowledge by following the teacher. The feasibility update is given as follows,

$$x_{new} = r(x_{old} - T_F MD_S) \quad \textbf{(8)}$$

Here, xnew is the new feasibility, r is the random number, TF is the teaching factor and MDS is the mean difference between the results of the teacher and the student.

At each iteration, the teacher is rotated based on the current best value. Over iterations, the optimal feature set is selected based on tri-objectives as given above.

The dataset is fed into the input layers and the hidden layers, and the weight value is determined for each data point by learning optimal features. Instead of learning all features in the dataset, the proposed work only learns the optimal features (Fopt) selected by the TTF algorithm. The important features in the dataset are depicted in Table **1**.

Table 1. Features for credit card fraud detection.

Features	Detail	Feature Type
Existing account status	It defines the salary assignment in a period of 1 year.	Nominal Feature
Duration	It defines the credit card duration.	Numerical Feature
Credit Amount	It defines the minimum and maximum amount of credit.	Numerical Feature

(Table 1) cont.....

Features	Detail	Feature Type
Purpose of Card	It shows the purpose of a credit card, such as health insurance, education *etc.*	Nominal Feature
Employment_Status	It defines the employment level of the cardholder	Nominal Feature
Savings	It shows the bonds and savings accounts.	Nominal Feature
Location	It illustrates the location of the card holder.	Nominal feature

Once the optimal features are learned, then the data is classified into normal and fraudulent transactions. The FRNN is composed of multiple feed-forward cells, which feed the output of a cell as input to another cell. Let dt be the current input given at time t, the previous cell state ct-1 and the hidden state (ht) are computed as follows,

$$f, i, o = \sigma\big((Hy_t + Uh_{t-1}) + b\big) \tag{9}$$

$$j = \tanh\big((Hy_t + Uh_{t-1}) + b\big) \tag{10}$$

$$c_t = f * c_{t-1} + i * j \tag{11}$$

$$h_t = o * \tanh(c_t) \tag{12}$$

Here, b is the bias function and σ is the sigmoid function, which can be given as follows,

$$\sigma(x) = \frac{1}{(1+\exp(-x))} \tag{13}$$

The current input and prior hidden state are transformed using a linear convolution transformation function, denoted as H and U, respectively. The states are represented based on the features. With the above computations, the data is classified into normal (ND) and fraud (FD).

RESULT AND DISCUSSION

We used the publicly accessible Kaggle database for the purpose of detecting credit card fraud. All purchases made by cards throughout Europe during September 2013 are included in the data set. From a total of 284,807 sales that occurred during the span of two days, 492 were fraudulent. There is significant bias in the dataset, as fraudulent transactions account for only 0.172 percent of the positive class. It takes only PCA-transformed numerical input variables. Issues about the confidentiality of information prevent us from providing the original attributes along with additional information for the data. Key characteristics V1,

V2,..., V28 are generated using the method of principal component analysis (PCA). So far, PCA has only affected two features: "Time" and "Amount." The feature "Time" lists the number of seconds that elapsed between the first transaction in the data set and every subsequent transaction. There are two distinct groups of information in the dataset: training and test. We train the system using 70% of the information and then validate it with 30%.

Comparative Analysis

The proposed system is compared in terms of performance metrics. In order to evaluate the performance we have used,

Accuracy – It is defined as the total number of data classified accurately out of the total amount of data presented in the dataset. It is computed as follows,

$$Accuracy = \frac{TN+TP}{TN+TP+FN+FP} \tag{14}$$

$$Precision = \frac{TP}{TP+FP} \tag{15}$$

$$Recall = \frac{TP}{TP+FN} \tag{16}$$

$$F1\ Score = 2 * \frac{Precision*Recall}{Precision+Recall} \tag{17}$$

Each of the aforementioned factors contributes to the final score. Here, TP stands for true positive, FP for false positive, TN for true negative, and FN for false negative. Existing SVM, Random Forest, and artificial neural network (ANN) methods are compared with the suggested TTL-FRNN approach. Analysis of accuracy, precision, recall, and f-score is shown in Figs. (**2-5**).

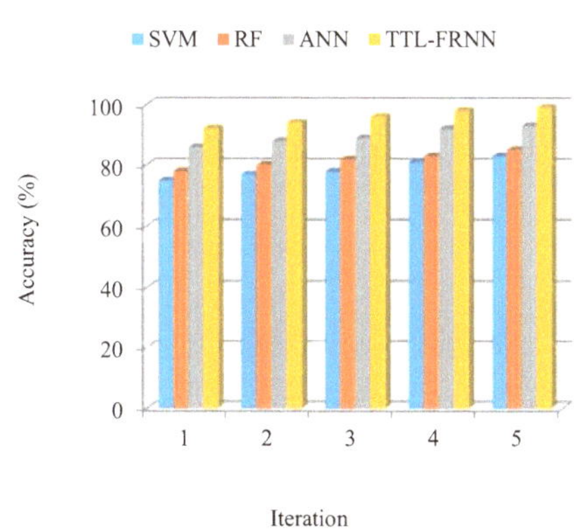

Fig. (2). Analysis of accuracy.

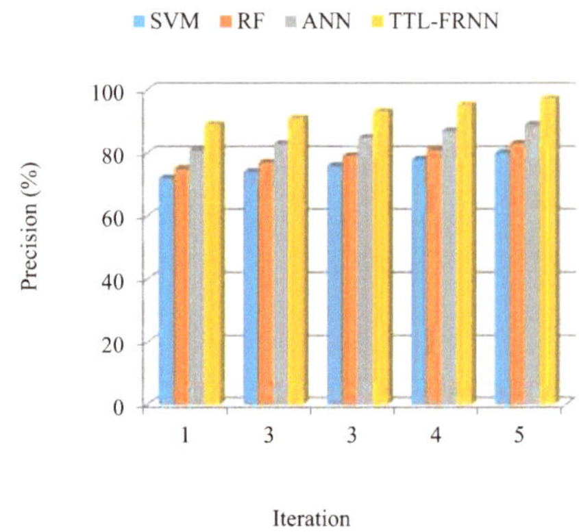

Fig. (3). Analysis of precision.

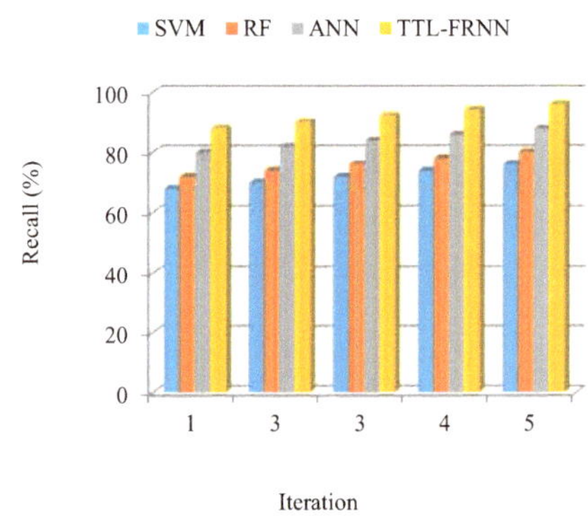

Fig. (4). Analysis of recall.

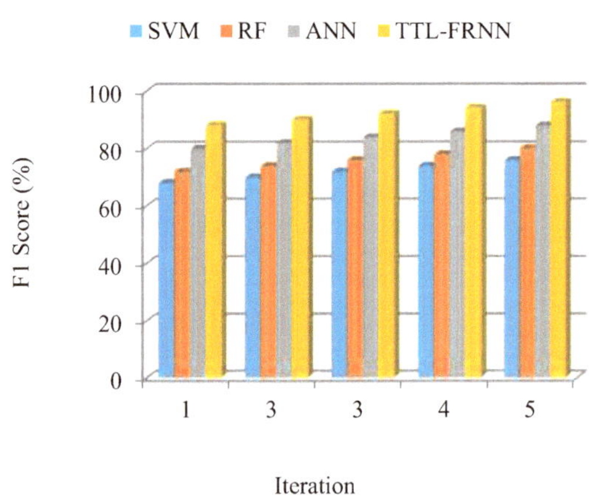

Fig. (5). Analysis of F1 ccore.

CONCLUSION

The consequences of banking fraud on the economy and its constituents are far-reaching. Many problems have become worse in the last several years, even while technology's influence and growth have been on the rise. Traditional approaches are inefficient even in the face of abundant data. To identify financial fraud using a DCNN, the suggested model uses a real-time credit card fraud database. The algorithm provides better detection than previous models, even when there is a tremendous amount of information. When it comes to identifying complex and previously unseen patterns, the neural network method provides both speed and accuracy. When compared to previous versions, this one is much more efficient. Using a real-time fraud on credit cards dataset, the suggested model is evaluated for effectiveness in comparison to other deep learning models, auto-encoder models, and current Artificial Intelligence models. Looking forward, it is possible that a single algorithm may integrate many aspects, such as fraud location and time computation, among others.

REFERENCES

[1] Tang, H., Deng, L., & Huang, Y. (2022). Business Intelligence System Based on Big Data Technology. 2022 International Conference on Artificial Intelligence of Things and Crowdsensing (AIoTCs), 143-147.

[2] G. Călinescu, "Clusters, Business Planning and Economic Growth: Stockholm's Artificial Intelligence and Big Data Cluster", *Proceedings of the International Conference on Business Excellence*, pp. 1584-1594, 2023.
[http://dx.doi.org/10.2478/picbe-2023-0142]

[3] Herschel, R.T. (2021). Big Data, Data Management, and Business Intelligence. In: Research Anthology on Big Data Analytics, Architectures, and Applications, pp.1359-1370, 2022.

[4] A.A. Gad-Elrab, *Modern Business Intelligence: Big Data Analytics and Artificial Intelligence for Creating the Data-Driven Value.* E-Business - Higher Education and Intelligence Applications, 2021.

[5] Y. Niu, L. Ying, J. Yang, M. Bao, and C.B. Sivaparthipan, "Organizational business intelligence and decision making using big data analytics", *Inf. Process. Manage.*, vol. 58, no. 6, p. 102725, 2021.
[http://dx.doi.org/10.1016/j.ipm.2021.102725]

[6] A. Kulakli, "Integration of Data Mining and Business Intelligence in Big Data Analytics", *Adv. Bus. Inf. Syst. Anal.*, pp. 13-43, 2021.
[http://dx.doi.org/10.4018/978-1-7998-5781-5.ch002]

[7] A. Ilmudeen, "Big data analytics capability and organizational performance measures: The mediating role of business intelligence infrastructure", *Bus. Inf. Rev.*, vol. 38, no. 4, pp. 183-192, 2021.
[http://dx.doi.org/10.1177/02663821211055321]

[8] Chen, Y., Li, C., & Wang, H. (2022). Big Data and Predictive Analytics for Business Intelligence: A Bibliographic Study (2000–2021). Forecasting.

[9] C.M. Olszak, J. Zurada, and D. Cetindamar, "Business Intelligence & Big Data for Innovative and Sustainable Development of Organizations", *Inf. Syst. Manage.*, vol. 39, no. 1, pp. 2-2, 2022.
[http://dx.doi.org/10.1080/10580530.2022.2011124]

[10] T. Jayaraj, and J.A. Samath, *Cloud Based Heterogeneous Big Data Integration and Data Analysis for Business Intelligence.*, 2019.

[11] A. Al-Okaily, A.P. Teoh, M. Al-Okaily, M. Iranmanesh, and M.A. Al-Betar, "The efficiency measurement of business intelligence systems in the big data-driven economy: a multidimensional model", *Inf. Discov. Deliv.,* vol. 51, no. 4, pp. 404-416, 2023. [http://dx.doi.org/10.1108/IDD-01-2022-0008]

[12] A. Gottfried, C. Hartmann, and D. Yates, "Mining Open Government Data for Business Intelligence Using Data Visualization: A Two-Industry Case Study", *J. Theor. Appl. Electron. Commer. Res.,* vol. 16, no. 4, pp. 1042-1065, 2021. [http://dx.doi.org/10.3390/jtaer16040059]

[13] S. Attar-Khorasani, and R. Chalmeta, "Internet of Things Data Visualization for Business Intelligence", *Big Data,* vol. 12, no. 6, pp. 478-503, 2022. [PMID: 35133879]

[14] M. Pancić, D. Ćućić, and H. Serdarušić, *Business Intelligence (BI) in Firm Performance: Role of Big Data Analytics and Blockchain Technology.* vol. 11. Economies, 2023, no. 3, p. 99.

[15] S. F. Wamba, A. Gunasekaran, S. Akter, S. J. Ren, R. Dubey, & S. J. Childe, "Big data analytics and firm performance: Effects of dynamic capabilities", *Journal of Business Research,* vol. 70, pp. 356-365, 2017. [http://dx.doi.org/10.1016/j.jbusres.2016.08.009]

CHAPTER 15

Leveraging Text Mining Techniques for Efficient Information Discovery

M. Chandra Sekhar[1,*] and **R. Pachayappan**[2]

[1] *Department of Computer Science and Engineering, Presidency University, Bangalore, Karnataka, India*

[2] *Department of Computer Applications, Presidency College, Bangalore, Karnataka, India*

Abstract: Researchers in the field of information systems often talk about human capital. Organizations need trained personnel to create and implement IT objects. This is particularly true when dealing with sophisticated technologies like AI. Natural language processing (NLP) and computer vision (CV) are two important subfields of AI. From a business perspective, this article compares and contrasts the skills required of CV and NLP experts. To achieve this goal, we used a text mining-based analytical pipeline to analyze AI job ads. Named entity recognition and word vectors were used to assess actual job ads from both sub-disciplines that were scraped from a big multinational online employment portal. We suggested an improved machine learning method, the Artificial Neural Network (ANN), for the last skill analysis. The requisite skill sets for the two job descriptions may be different. It calls for individualized thought as there is no one-size-fits-all profile of an AI expert.

Keywords: Text Mining, Information Discovery, Employee Skill Analysis, Computer Vision.

INTRODUCTION

Ads have evolved into an essential tool for companies in today's business world to boost their profile as well as expand their operations. Businesses across many industries use customized ads to increase their ROI and leverage consumer demographic information. This is especially true in the e-commerce, social media, recreation, and television industries. Digital billboards in shopping centers display the same ad layout every time, regardless of targeting, proving that many businesses still cannot get their demographics quite right [1]. There is growing concern about the surveillance nature of targeted online marketing systems, which

* **Corresponding author M. Chandra Sekhar:** Department of Computer Science and Engineering, Presidency University, Bangalore, Karnataka, India; E-mail: p.biswajeet@jainuniversity.ac.in

S. Kannadhasan, R. Nagarajan, & Kaushik Pal (Eds.)

gather personal data from individuals and then use it to automatically classify and infer things. Examining the implications of advertising targeting may be enriched by examining the lives of LGBTQ+ persons, whose identities challenge conventional ideas about who is considered "normal" and entitled to privacy, autonomy, as well as a right to autonomy [2]. The use of machine learning has been enabled by data, which has accelerated data-driven material design. It remains a challenge to collect data mechanically from scientific research, which produces a vast volume of high-quality, trustworthy data [3]. Customers express their interest in using certain services by contacting numerous firms listed in their telecom call history. Time and the day of such messages, together with multifaceted characteristic dependency, provide valuable information for targeted advertising. Customers who use a particular service might also be potential customers for another service if there is a strong correlation between the two [4]. The use of digital health data is on the rise to identify individuals with comparable histories of illness, diagnoses, and outcomes, and to suggest multidisciplinary therapies for them. Expert physicians and novices alike work together to produce these files. A practical and transferable approach to finding individuals who have very similar clinical traits is using data mining in large, unorganized datasets. The Imagine Institute conducted a bioinformatics evaluation of the exome and focused on next-generation sequencing [5]. One of the main reasons internet advertising is growing is the use of programmatic advertising, which employs big data to deliver targeted, tailored marketing materials. One significant component of programmatic advertising is in-app adverts, sometimes known as in-app ads. Customers' individual requirements determine the timing and location of ad delivery in in-app marketing, an income stream closely tied to app development. Text messages on social media platforms are emerging as a powerful new kind of advertising that may influence customers' purchasing decisions, all thanks to electronic word-of-mouth (e-WOM) [6]. Surprising trends in educational institutions can be discovered through the rapidly developing interdisciplinary field of educational data mining. Various automated learning systems have been investigated in light of the difficulties educational institutions face in assessing learners' performance and enhancing instructional management [7].

RELATED WORKS

This study introduces a fundamental component extractor, an easy-to-use MS/MS data analysis tool capable of extracting characteristics specified by the consumer. This software incorporates, for the first time, the sequential neutral loss characteristics and the abundance of finished ions as fundamental components, in addition to the typical neutral losses and product ions. One example of the instrument's usefulness is the identification of nine sesquiterpene dimers in Artemisia heptaphylla that have not yet been reported. Artemiheptolide I (9), among these dimers, showed an IC50 of 8.01 ± 6.19 μM when tested against influenza A/Hongkong/8/68 (H3N2) *in vitro*. In addition, IC50 values ranging from 3.46 to 11.77 I1/4M were observed for two recognized guaianolide derivatives (16 and 17) when tested against hepatitis A/Puerto Rico/8/1934 H1N1, H3N2, and influenza B/Lee/40. This method has many broad applications, such as improving the annotation effectiveness of LC-MS/MS analyses and effectively discovering new natural compounds. It may also be used to capture derivatives with specified segments [8].

To fill gaps in our understanding, provide new experimental data, and construct new qualitative Abnormal Outcome Pathways (qAOPs) for UVB, this research revisited the deadly consequences of UVB on crustaceans. The objectives were accomplished *via* the use of both computational and experimental methods. A varying amount of synthetic UVB was administered to Daphnia magna in a targeted testing experiment in the laboratory. To measure the impact of UVB on various levels of biological organization, the company used targeted bioassays. The NIVA Risk Evaluation Databases (NIVA RAdb) is a new computer tool used to compile fresh experimental findings and data from prior publications into a toxicity pathway network. Current and previous information were used to create a network of AOPs and to evaluate the weight of evidence. We also fitted the D to the AOPs to find quantitative connections between significant events. Convert the magna data into pre-made models. Potentially useful for future de novo qAOP creation for chemical and non-chemical stresses, the provided approach encompasses all stages of qAOP construction and assessment [9].

The primary focus of this study is the development of a gender and age-based customized advertising system for use in retail centers. The "I-Advert" system was developed by using machine learning and image processing approaches. The "I-Advert" solves the problems with current methods by providing malls with online marketing that is both automated and targeted. Indoors and in a real-life small business, we tested the equipment to gain a full understanding of it [10].

In order to get a better understanding of the LGBTQ+ community's (N=18) experience with internet advertising, thoughts on ad targeting, and how these systems interact with their homosexuality as well as other identities, we conducted semi-structured. Participants characterized the lack of variety and complexity in online ad content as stereotyped and tokenizing, a characterization reflected in our findings. However, their underlying mistrust and disapproval of the extractive, non-consensual nature of ad targeting also clashed with their demands for improved ad content. They wanted more say over what happens to their information and focus, wanted the option to opt out completely, and were worried about privacy issues related to persistent data aggregation, including behavior monitoring. We investigate the homonormativity of targeted advertisements by looking at how they fail to portray queer people who already face discrimination on multiple fronts; the negative effects of automated classification, as well as inference on the process of identity formation and self-determination; and the theory of refusal that underpins the queer hopes for an improved internet experience expressed by participants [11].

We provide a natural language processing pipeline that analyzes and forecasts superalloys based on their chemical composition and properties. The following data are retrieved from 14,425 articles within 3 hours: I3 solvus density, temperature, solidus, and liquidus temperatures; 2531 records include both composition and properties. To anticipate undiscovered Co-based superalloys with elevated γ' solvus temperatures, a data-driven framework for γ' solvus heat is constructed, with an average inaccuracy of 0.81%. By synthesizing and characterizing three alloys, we tested the hypotheses. The purpose of this web-based toolkit is to offer an open-source platform for searching for selected content utilizing data gathered from the literature [12].

Prospect finding from interest qualities displayed in call records is a problem this study addresses using a multi-granularity rough sets approach. Traditional intra- and inter-pattern mining approaches have issues, including vast, statistically unimportant pattern spaces and increased processing complexity, which the proposed method addresses. Using a telecom supplier's anonymized call records from Thailand spanning 1 month, an algorithm is evaluated to identify target audiences for food and restaurant businesses. Also confirmed are several intriguing mathematical features of the knowledge systems that underpin them [13].

Using data from almost half a million patients, the "automated diagnosis" system at Necker Children's Hospital was built by Dr. The warehouse, a biological data center focused on clinical narrative reports. Using this database, we found a pair of individuals with identical de novo KCNA2 variants who had very specific clinical characteristics throughout infancy as well as childhood. Patients with common or uncommon genetic disorders might be better identified using this novel approach, which groups clinical characteristics, and patients with comparable pathogenic mutations could have their natural history detected with high accuracy [14].

The future of comparative study at Amikom, the Creative Economy Park, is the subject of this investigation. Visitor statistics collected between January 2019 and December 2019 form the basis of this research. To determine the accuracy of the predictions, this research compares results from Exponential Smoothing and the

ARIMA (Autoregressive Integrated Moving Average) approach. In light of this anticipated visit, the University of AMIKOM Yogyakarta and the Directorate of Communication as well as International Relations, are preparing for it [15].

PROPOSED WORK

We perform semi-automatic analysis of massive volumes of job ads using text mining, a technique closely related to natural language processing. Academic contexts already use NLP technologies for tasks such as keyword extraction from texts [36], summary generation [37], and trend identification [21]. Initial methods for evaluating job ads using natural language processing (NLP) have been reported in the scientific literature [23]. These methods also pertain to assessing and analyzing talents that are sought after in the labor market. The five stages that make up our text mining pipeline are as follows: preliminary processing (entity recognition), processing, data analysis, and human validation.

a. Raw text strings retrieved from job ads were used as input for pre-processing. Initially, lowercase letters were used for every word. Afterwards, the redundant job postings were deleted. One popular variation based on accessible vector-space similarity is among several approaches to text duplication recognition [*e.g.*, 38, 39]. Here, we found a reciprocal cosine relationship by transforming the raw text string into the widely used TF-IDF vectors. The total document frequency for a word (TFIDF) in a corpus of documents is a combination of the term's occurrence frequency (TF) in that particular document, as well as the inverse document frequency (IDF) worldwide. Many variants of the TF-IDF method exist, each with its own unique structure. The TfidfVectorizer function from the sklearn Python package was used. We also used sklearn's pairwise method to compute cosine similarity between pairs. A total of 733 distinct documents were produced after randomly removing one element and treating all pairings with a similarity greater than 0.99 as duplicates. The cleansed text lines were used in the subsequent procedure, after the TF-IDF vectors were computed and duplicates were removed. The corpus was initially divided into matching batches of 5 articles since the service that we later utilized could only handle batches of that size. (b) Named recognition of entities (NER): Finding relevant phrases reflecting a specific talent is the first step in our objective of analyzing job adverts based on the abilities necessary. In general, supervised learning algorithms work well for NER tasks, such as identifying specific word categories within a corpus of text [40, 41]. Because there was not enough appropriate data to build a separate training dataset for the NER component, we opted to use a cloud-based platform to support talent identity verification, as these approaches depend on massive volumes of labeled training data. Specifically, words pertaining to skill entities were retrieved from the corpus using the company's Azure Analytics Service. Its explicit support for the categorization of skill entities and extensive training on a large number of papers led to its selection. The 13,201 distinct words from the prepared and cleaned text strings of job advertisements serve as input to the service. The translated word-entity pairs are included as attributes in the JSON string that is produced by the service. A total of 3,712 skill words were obtained after eliminating all non-skill entities. (c) Human validation: Following the analysis in step (b), two researchers assessed the findings. We merged "nlp" as well as "language processing," since they both describe the same kind of expertise. A computerized neural network was used to calculate vector-based word resemblance, which helped the researchers in their search for such synonyms. You can find a detailed description of the approach utilized in [21]. On top of that, we culled out any words that did not pertain to talents as we defined them. Validation reduced the original set of 3,712 talents down to 523 distinct words. Following this, the abilities were grouped into seven further generalized types. Each talent was hand-picked and placed into one of the following groups: artificial intelligence, computer science, programming languages, general knowledge, domain expertise, interpersonal skills, and certification. This allows for a comprehensive assessment at the higher levels.

b. Data processing: In order to facilitate more research, the initial text was altered so that any terms lacking in competence were identified as stop phrases, after which they were eliminated. Consequently, for every document, we got a sequence that included the talents listed in the job posting. We used these sequences to compute TF-IDF matrices and bag-of-words frequencies. This time around, we employed TF-IDF vectors to make more nuanced claims about a term's relevance to a given text. In contrast to a basic number of words, which only shows the frequency of a term's occurrence in a text, the TF-IDF score enables inferences about the term's significance both inside the piece of writing as well as the overall corpus [42]. A low value shows that the term is not very relevant to the given material, while a high score shows that it is very relevant. Afterwards, we will include this feature in the information analytics to determine how comparable job ads are mechanically. We accomplished this by creating an nxm matrix, wherein n is the quantity of input articles, and m is the quantity of words in the document's input lexicon. Scores computed using TF-IDF are included in the matrix. (e) Data Analysis: There are two sections to our data analysis. We compared natural language processing (NLP) job ads to CV job ads to see whether the relevant phrases change significantly in (i). The second part of the process involves conducting a thorough qualitative study, from the scale of skill categories down to the level of individual skills. (i)

Using the TFIDF matrices for skills that we obtained in step (d), we ran the calculation for cosine similarity again to see how well the two text samples correspond for NLP, as well as CV, matched the abilities listed in the job ads. Distribution as well as heatmap plots are used to display the findings. We used the Wilcoxon rank-sum testing [43] to see if our findings were statistically significant. (ii) The abilities were evaluated and assessed within each of the leading groups. We also looked at the total number of job ads that cited a given ability, not just the number of references as shown in Fig. (**3**), since we do not want to double-count when the same skill is stated in the same ad. The next step is to determine the comparable proportions so that CV and NLP job ads can be compared.

RESULT AND DISCUSSION

Job postings for CV engineers were culled from Indeed between September 29, 2020, and October 5, 2020, whereas for NLP experts, the ads were culled on November 7, 2020. Indeed was selected because it is a global leader in the job market and one of the most extensive platforms for posting job ads. Plus, they're published as text, so crawlers can easily access the material. CV job ads that included the terms "computer" and "vision" in their titles were considered to filter out irrelevant results. Out of 56 top-level domains, 56 had the search word "title:(computer vision)" included. There were 785 job ads found during the search. We found 374 job ads for NLP when we searched using the phrase "title:((natural language processing) or (natural language processor) or (NLP))". The material from the webpages was extracted using the octal. We were able to glean information from the ad's body, location, and job title. Due to the fact that only English-language job ads were considered for the upcoming study, the corpus for that purpose includes 591 CV ads as well as 291 NLP ads. There are job postings from more than 30 different countries. When it comes to CVs, the top three nations with job opportunities are the US, Israel, and Germany. The pipeline visualization is shown in Fig. (**1**). When it comes to NLP, the nations with the greatest demand are the US, the UK, and India. The comparison of the ML algorithm is shown in Fig. (**2**).

Based on the model's high and acceptable precision, recollection, specificity, accuracy, F1-score, as well as error-rate which were found for most k-values (63.6%) in the method's cross-validation we are able to determine that an KNN text classification look at employing EPDM+ML is an effective method for predicting students' recommendation scores for teachers, considering gender, age, average sentiment, as well as emotional valence parameters. Recall@K on the Amazon and YELP datasets is shown in Figs. (**3-5**).

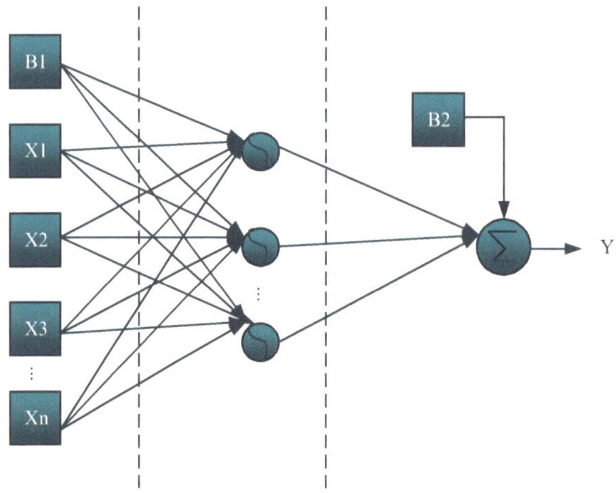

Fig. (1). System model.

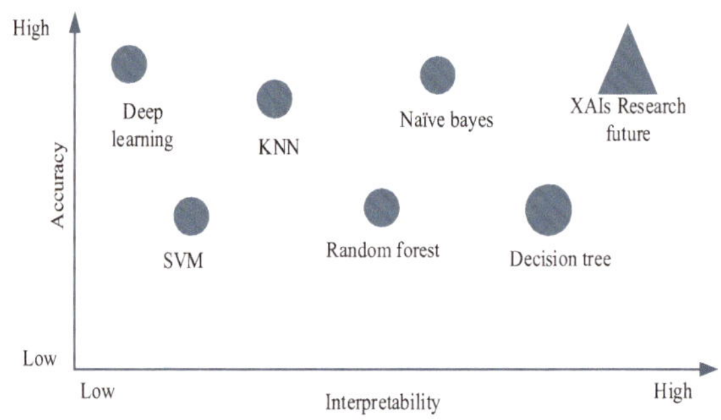

Fig. (2). Comparison of ML algorithms.

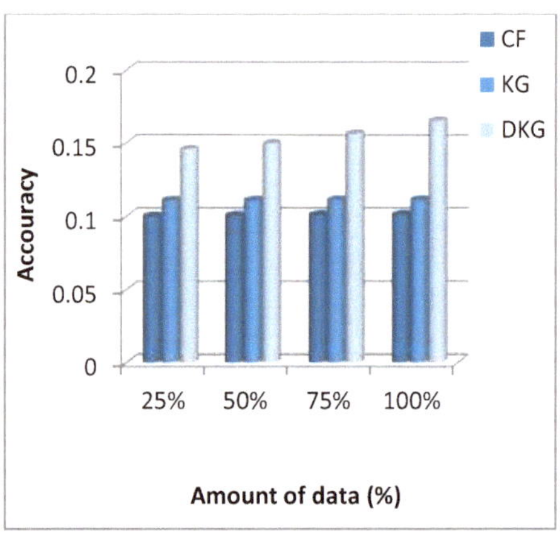

Fig. (3). Recall@K on the amazon dataset.

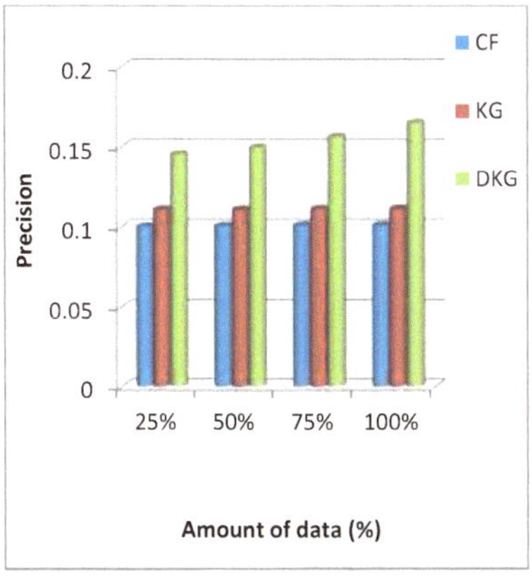

Fig. (4). Recall@K on last FM dataset.

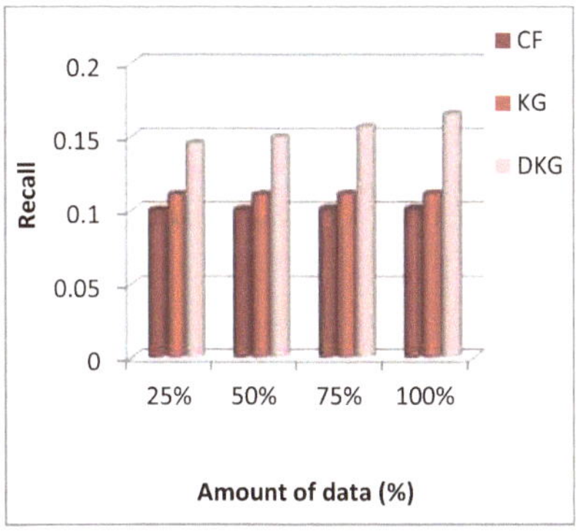

Fig. (5). Recall@K on yelp dataset.

CONCLUSION

From a purely economic point of view, this article has analyzed and contrasted the needs of CV designers as well as NLP experts. We used a text extraction pipeline in conjunction with human processing to sift through Indeed job posts for applicable talent. Concerning RQ1, we were able to demonstrate that there is a significant difference between the skill sets advertised in NLP and CV job postings. In order to address RQ2, we examined the two job descriptions in detail. There is a lot of overlap between the job descriptions, but there are also noticeable distinctions. With a handful of languages used for programming, general AI abilities, soft skills, and IT skills all overlap. Programming languages and general IT skills are where most people differ. In conclusion, there is substantial overlap between the two job descriptions, but there are also notable distinctions; moreover, there is no universally accepted description of an AI specialist's work. A number of avenues exist for further investigation. The progression over time stands out. Job profile needs are subject to change throughout time, and the rate of trend development might be studied. Furthermore, this article delves further into the demand side.

REFERENCES

[1] Vaidehi, B., & Arunesh, K. (2022). A Comprehensive Assessment on Predictive Analytics using Data Mining Techniques. 2022 3rd International Conference on Electronics and Sustainable Communication Systems (ICESC), 709-715.

[2] V. Švábenský, J. Vykopal, P. Čeleda, K. Tkáčik, and D. Popovic, "Student assessment in cybersecurity training automated by pattern mining and clustering", *Educ. Inf. Technol.,* vol. 27, no. 7, pp. 9231-9262, 2022.
[http://dx.doi.org/10.1007/s10639-022-10954-4] [PMID: 35370440]

[3] A.S. Varde, "Computational Estimation by Scientific Data Mining with Classical Methods to Automate Learning Strategies of Scientists", *ACM Trans. Knowl. Discov. Data,* vol. 16, no. 5, pp. 1-52, 2022. [TKDD].
[http://dx.doi.org/10.1145/3502736]

[4] Y. Wang, *User Behavior Identification and Personalized Recommendation Based on Web Data Mining.,* 2021.
[http://dx.doi.org/10.46300/9106.2021.15.72]

[5] Chen, G., Chen, G., Liu, Q., Hu, B., & Zhang, L. (2023). A Proposed Method of Information Mining for Cyber Black Market Oriented to Tor Anonymous Network. 2023 IEEE 7th Information Technology and Mechatronics Engineering Conference (ITOEC), 7, 525-529.

[6] P. Hur, N. Machaka, C. Krist, and N. Bosch, "Informing Expert Feature Engineering through Automated Approaches: Implications for Coding Qualitative Classroom Video Data", *LAK23: 13th International Learning Analytics and Knowledge Conference,* 2023.
[http://dx.doi.org/10.1145/3576050.3576090]

[7] A. Javeed, S.U. Khan, L. Ali, S. Ali, Y. Imrana, and A. Rahman, "Machine Learning-Based Automated Diagnostic Systems Developed for Heart Failure Prediction Using Different Types of Data Modalities: A Systematic Review and Future Directions", *Comput. Math. Methods Med.,* vol. 2022, pp. 1-30, 2022.
[http://dx.doi.org/10.1155/2022/9288452] [PMID: 35154361]

[8] D. Zhu, J. Yuan, Q. Yue, Y. Zhao, S. Yu, A. Zhamilya, J. Jenis, C. Tang, B. Wang, J. Liu, and Y. Ye, "Building Block Extractor: An MS/MS Data Mining Tool for Targeted Discovery of Natural Products with Specified Features", *Anal. Chem.,* vol. 95, no. 29, pp. 10939-10946, 2023.
[http://dx.doi.org/10.1021/acs.analchem.3c00744] [PMID: 37430188]

[9] Y. Song, L. Xie, Y. Lee, and K.E. Tollefsen, "De Novo Development of a Quantitative Adverse Outcome Pathway (qAOP) Network for Ultraviolet B (UVB) Radiation Using Targeted Laboratory Tests and Automated Data Mining", *Environ. Sci. Technol.,* vol. 54, no. 20, pp. 13147-13156, 2020.
[http://dx.doi.org/10.1021/acs.est.0c03794] [PMID: 32924456]

[10] Sewmina, K., Navarathna, R., & Senanayake, A. I-Advert: Precision Marketing by Leveraging Gender and Age Identification for Automated Digital Advertising in Shopping Malls. 2023 IEEE 17th International Conference on Industrial and Information Systems (ICIIS), 146-151, 2023.

[11] P. Sampson, R.C. EncarnaciA3n, and D. Metaxa, "Representation, Self-Determination, and Refusal: Queer People's Experiences with Targeted Advertising", *Proceedings of the 2023 ACM Conference on Fairness, Accountability, and Transparency,* 2023.
[http://dx.doi.org/10.1145/3593013.3594110]

[12] Wang, W., Jiang, X., Tian, S., Liu, P., Dang, D., Su, Y., Lookman, T., & Xie, J. (2022). Automated pipeline for superalloy data by text mining. npj Computational Materials, 8, 1-12.

[13] J. Bisaria, and K.R. Pardasani, *Mining Multi-Dimensional Intra and Inter-Association Patterns of Call*

Records for Targeted Advertising using Multi-Granulation Rough Sets. Informatica: Slovenia, 2019, p. 43.

[14] M. Hully, T. Lo Barco, A. Kaminska, G. Barcia, C. Cances, C. Mignot, I. Desguerre, N. Garcelon, E. Kabashi, and R. Nabbout, "Deep phenotyping unstructured data mining in an extensive pediatric database to unravel a common KCNA2 variant in neurodevelopmental syndromes", *Genet. Med.,* vol. 23, no. 5, pp. 968-971, 2021. [http://dx.doi.org/10.1038/s41436-020-01039-z] [PMID: 33500571]

[15] Rumini, & Norhikmah. Application of Data Mining for Visit Prediction at Amikom Creative Economy Park. Journal of Systems Engineering and Information Technology (JOSEIT). Vol. 1, no. 2, pp. 52-57, 2022.

[16] Y. Yang, Z. Wu, Y. Yang, S. Lian, F. Guo, and Z. Wang, "A survey of information extraction based on deep learning", *Appl. Sci. (Basel),* vol. 12, no. 19, p. 9691, 2022. [http://dx.doi.org/10.3390/app12199691]

[17] D. Xu, W. Chen, W. Peng, C. Zhang, T. Xu, X. Zhao, X. Wu, Y. Zheng, Y. Wang, and E. Chen, "Large language models for generative information extraction: a survey", *Front. Comput. Sci.,* vol. 18, no. 6, p. 186357, 2024. [http://dx.doi.org/10.1007/s11704-024-40555-y]

[18] K. Xu, Y. Feng, Q. Li, Z. Dong, and J. Wei, "Survey on terminology extraction from texts", *J. Big Data,* vol. 12, no. 1, p. 29, 2025. [http://dx.doi.org/10.1186/s40537-025-01077-x]

[19] F. Bidollahkhany, and M. Basiri, "Utilizing text mining to extract knowledge and classify information in industrial engineering", *Pressacademia,* vol. 11, no. 2, p. 2, 2024. [http://dx.doi.org/10.17261/Pressacademia.2024.1948]

[20] X. Dong, Q. Liu, and X. Wang, "Big data analytics and statistical modeling in business: A review", *J. Bus. Res.,* vol. 139, pp. 212-227, 2021. [http://dx.doi.org/10.1016/j.jbusres.2021.09.048]

[21] Y. Wang, and L. Kung, "A framework of big data analytics for business intelligence", *Decis. Support Syst.,* vol. 140, 2021. [http://dx.doi.org/10.1016/j.dss.2020.113423]

[22] Y. Shi, S. Shang, L. Guo, and Z. Xiong, "Big data analytics and business intelligence: A comprehensive review", *J. Organ. Comput. Electron. Commerce,* vol. 31, no. 3, pp. 211-239, 2021. [http://dx.doi.org/10.1080/10919392.2021.1911583]

[23] L. Lu, and X. Wang, "Big data analytics and business intelligence: A literature review", *J. Big Data,* vol. 7, p. 49, 2020. [http://dx.doi.org/10.1186/s40537-020-00326-1]

[24] X. Wang, Z. Dai, H. Li, and J. Yang, "Research on hybrid collaborative filtering recommendation algorithm based on time effect and sentiment analysis", *Complexity,* vol. 2021, no. 1, p. 6635202, 2021. [http://dx.doi.org/10.1155/2021/6635202]

[25] C. Guo, Y. Zhang, Y. Yang, and J. Ren, "Using big data analytics for business intelligence: A systematic literature review", *J. Bus. Res.,* vol. 133, pp. 793-806, 2021. [http://dx.doi.org/10.1016/j.jbusres.2021.04.032]

[26] Y. He, J. Du, and Y. Chen, "The application of big data analytics in business intelligence: A review", *Int. J. Inf. Manage.,* vol. 57, 2021. [http://dx.doi.org/10.1016/j.ijinfomgt.2020.102339]

[27] Y. Yang, Y. Zhang, H. Chen, and Y. Song, "Big data analytics for business intelligence: A survey", *J. Ind. Inf. Integr.,* vol. 17, 2020. [http://dx.doi.org/10.1016/j.jii.2019.100121]

[28] X. Zhang, H. Chen, and X. Li, "Research on big data analytics and business intelligence in the era of Industry 4.0: A bibliometric analysis", *IEEE Access,* vol. 9, pp. 24672-24681, 2021. [http://dx.doi.org/10.1109/ACCESS.2021.3056890]

[29] Y. Zhu, K. Xie, Y. Zhang, and W. Zhou, "A survey on big data analytics for business intelligence: From a technical perspective", *J. Ind. Inf. Integr.,* vol. 23, 2021. [http://dx.doi.org/10.1016/j.jii.2020.100172]

[30] Y. Ozcelik, and C. Ceylan, "The effect of big data analytics on business performance: A resource-based view perspective", *J. Bus. Res.,* vol. 144, pp. 420-432, 2022. [http://dx.doi.org/10.1016/j.jbusres.2022.01.050]

[31] X. Zhao, L. Liu, and H. Chen, "Text mining techniques for knowledge discovery from large-scale documents", *Future Gener. Comput. Syst.,* vol. 111, pp. 859-872, 2020. [http://dx.doi.org/10.1016/j.future.2019.08.033]

[32] M. Xu, H.A. Rahman, and F. Li, "Text summarization: A bibliometric study and systematic literature review", *Ingénierie des systèmes d information,* vol. 29, no. 5, pp. 2077-2089, 2024. [http://dx.doi.org/10.18280/isi.290538]

[33] S.F. Wamba, A. Gunasekaran, S. Akter, S.J. Ren, R. Dubey, and S.J. Childe, "Big data analytics and firm performance: Effects of dynamic capabilities", *J. Bus. Res.,* vol. 70, pp. 356-365, 2017. [http://dx.doi.org/10.1016/j.jbusres.2016.08.009]

[34] J. Lee, W. Yoon, S. Kim, D. Kim, S. Kim, C.H. So, and J. Kang, "BioBERT: a pre-trained biomedical language representation model for biomedical text mining", *Bioinformatics,* vol. 36, no. 4, pp. 1234-1240, 2020. [http://dx.doi.org/10.1093/bioinformatics/btz682] [PMID: 31501885]

[35] C. Lv, Y. Tang, L. Ao, Y. Huang, S. Zhang, J. Fan, and W. Han, "A survey of automatic text summarization: concepts, advances and future prospects", *Int. J. Speech Technol.,* vol. 28, no. 4, pp. 801-824, 2025. [http://dx.doi.org/10.1007/s10772-025-10215-y]

CHAPTER 16

Exploring the Potential of Big Data for Monetization of Information

Meenakshi Sharma[1,*] and **Somashekhara Reddy**[2]

[1] *Department of Computer Science and Engineering, Galgotias University, Greater Noida, Uttar Pradesh, India*

[2] *Department of Computer Science and Engineering, JAIN (Deemed-to-be University), Bangalore, Karnataka, India*

Abstract: The public's swift adoption of wearable sensors and their rapid worldwide spread, together with the rapid advancement of the Internet of Things (IoT), have resulted in most companies and organizations being overwhelmed with massive amounts of data these days. Finding ways to use the data deluge could provide companies with an edge in the market, as data can enhance several aspects of a company. There has been some monetization in the industry across verticals in terms of stacking connected devices with various SaaS choices, such as subscription plans or smart device insights. A significant advantage in today's cutthroat digital marketplace will go to those who can properly monetize data rather than just hoard it, says the "machine economy" sprouting up in this sector. Innovations in big data, analytics, and AI have created new opportunities for competitiveness, with data strategically employed as an asset that can generate new revenue streams due to its ever-changing nature. Because of this surge, a plethora of new resources—including systems, platforms, tools, and markets—have emerged to help organizations make effective use of data. Actually, the goal of new business models is to shift the balance of power away from data-harvesting companies and toward customers. The selling of user data to companies like data analytics corporations is being promoted by startups and NGOs. Data monetization encompasses more than just data sales. It is also possible to implement measures that enhance data. Companies may generate money from data in three ways: 1) by improving internal processes or making more informed business decisions; 2) by integrating data into their main offerings; or 3) by selling data to current or potential customers. This article will address the key aspects of Internet of Things data monetization and the challenges that accompany it, with a focus on the healthcare industry. The topics covered will include data management, scalability, regulations, interoperability, security, and privacy. Not only that, but a detailed reference architecture for the healthcare data economy and a case study on the detection and prediction of cardiac abnormalities using privacy-preserving machine learning (PPML) and multiparty computing (MPC) methods are also provided.

* **Corresponding author Meenakshi Sharma:** Department of Computer Science and Engineering, Galgotias University, Greater Noida, Uttar Pradesh, Karnataka, India;
E-mail: meenakshi.sharma@galgotiasuniversity.edu.in

S. Kannadhasan, R. Nagarajan, & Kaushik Pal (Eds.)

Keywords: Big Data Analysis, Decision Making, Blockchain, IoT, Healthcare.

INTRODUCTION

It is hard to imagine life in the early 21st century without data visualization. Data visualisations are useful in many different settings since they help with knowledge and decision-making. People may find themselves in space with the use of GIS and environmental maps, and in time with the help of schedules, timetables, and timelines.

Visualization tools such as infographics, dashboards, and interactive charts make complex processes, subjects, and systems easier to grasp. For both comparative and relational understanding of the world, people use a variety of visualisation methods. These include, but are not limited to, bar charts, pie charts, line graphs, and tree diagrams. Crucially, in order to make sense of the apparently infinite quantities of biometric and behavioural data that modern activities consistently produce, visualisations are relied upon by individuals, organizations, and governments. Two prime examples of this are the quantified self movement and the pervasiveness of linked wearable gadgets such as smart watches and fitness trackers. This research argues that the accompanying visualisations of these devices stand for a decentralised, networked management of bodies, promoting individual self-regulation as part of a broader neoliberal power structure dependent on biopower [1 - 5]. Data visualizations, such as those on wearables, are seen daily by many people and are usually powered by big data. Despite its profound effect on consumer culture, interpersonal dynamics, and public policy, this vague and ominous concept comes out as somewhat abstract when brought up in casual conversation. The term "big data" refers to three separate ideas: one way of thinking about data and computers, data with certain properties, and the analytical techniques that go along with it. The term describes "a computational turn in thought and research" (Boyd and Crawford 2012, 665) that puts an emphasis on quantitative computing tools and massive volumes of easily available data, such as metadata generated by website users' actions, over any other approach. Data is characterized as "big" when it is rapidly collected, processed in real-time, has low accuracy, is correlated across sources, and is significantly more voluminous than what was previously available in a particular domain (Ekbia et al. 2015, 1525-6; Leszczynski 2015, 967). Methods for discovering patterns inside and across massive datasets are associated with big data. These methods include automated data purification, neural networks, machine learning, and the predictive generation of new data (Salvo 2012, 37). Inaccurate data is a big issue in visualizing huge datasets. Oftentimes, big data mixes and confuses metadata with content, algorithmically produced "activity-based intelligence" with genuine human behavior, and digital user profiles created from aggregated data sets with real, live humans. Actual people might be harmed by decisions derived from big data visualizations that rely on collected digital profiles (Crampton 2015, 521; Poster 1990, 126).

Data visualisation is the glue that holds big data together and makes it understandable to humans. It supposedly improves understanding and, ideally, leads to rational, ethical human decision-making by modifying and filtering information. The focus here is on human decision-making due to the fact that visualization is an essential human capability [6 - 10]. In the many rapidly automated and algorithm-dependent industries and professions, computers and robots do not need a visual representation of data to guide their decisions (Valle 2013, 2040). Decisions based on big data (by assessing visualisations) are considered too important to entrust to computers in many professions, despite our society's increasing dependence on big data. Consequently, there is a growing collection of big data-driven visualizations available to the public. Although data visualization is necessary in most areas of knowledge in the modern era, it is especially important and relied upon in research, commerce, and government sectors that are undergoing big data transformations (Ali et al. 2016, 656; Cook, Lee, and Majumder 2016, 135; Crampton 2015, 520). Hepworth and Canon (2018), 53, and Shoresh and Wong (2012) 5, both agree that visualization is an important tool for academics to employ for analyzing study results and for communicating those findings to a wider audience. Managing supply chains, finding monetizable behaviors, and determining acceptable pricing points are all possible *via* the visualization of aggregated data on content creation and behavior (Salvo 2012, 39). Whether it is for environmental protection, national security, political representation, or health care, governments rely on visualization to inform big data-based public policy decisions at the local, state, and federal levels (Salvo 2012, 39).

Organizations seeking to develop a fruitful data monetization strategy should have an in-depth understanding of the many data monetization strategies, including their implications, opportunities, and limitations. There has been an attempt to provide academic research in a number of areas, but there is still a lot of ground to cover since data monetization is still a relatively new subject. To inform the academic community about the potential of data monetization research, Liu and Chen conducted the first Systematic Literature Review (SLR), which was published in 2015. The writers aided readers in understanding data monetization by providing an approach that combines Analytics 3.0 (advanced analytics) with BI&A 3.0 (mobile and sensor-based analytics), as well as application scenarios and guiding principles. By combining data intelligence with traditional analytics, big data, and efficient methods of data collecting and processing, companies may achieve measurable business gains in Analytics 3.0. This research just included articles that had the terms "data monetization" or "monetization" in the title. It did not include papers that spoke about data business models but did not explicitly mention "monetization." Only the years 2010–2015 were included in the evaluation. In 2016, Thomas and Leiponen conducted a systematic review (SLR) on data commercialization based on 51 studies. They opted for the term "commercialization" rather than "monetization" to differentiate data interchange *via* economic activity. In addition to the internal use case, they also found issues and ways to monetize [11 - 15]. The recognized models included data aggregators, data stewards, data managers, data developers, and application developers. Although the authors considered more general terms than "data monetization," the review was limited to a brief review period (*i.e.*, from 2010 to 2013) and focused narrowly on monetization models through the lens of the players involved. As a result, it did not offer insights beyond a single construct (players). In 2020, Hanafzadeh and Nik put out the "Data monetization confguration" (DaMoc) model, which they evaluated with a real-world application (*i.e.*, Cardlytics) using an SLR.

RELATED WORKS

The healthcare industry has many challenges that make it difficult to commercialize data. One of them is the restriction on data transmission across organizations, which makes it harder for healthcare providers to collaborate on patient care decisions. Businesses are severely limited in their ability to combine sensitive data due to legislation such as HIPAA, GDPR, and CCPA [12 - 15]. It is understandable that hospitals are hesitant to share patient data. The first federal law in the United States to guarantee the security of individuals' health records was the Health Insurance Portability and Accountability Act (HIPAA). A user's data gathering must be made public in order to comply with the EU's General Data Protection Regulation (GDPR), which was put in place in 2018 and lays out strict requirements for data security and privacy. A number of regulations, like the China Internet privacy Law and the California Consumer Privacy Act (CCPA), increased oversight of data privacy after the passage of the General Data Protection Regulation (GDPR). Analysts' need to adhere to the rules of different privacy legislation when dealing with data from different sources complicates medical research. How to analyze medical data while protecting patient privacy is a delicate and pressing issue. It is significantly more difficult to merge data than to pool it once, since data is always evolving, necessitating many tries. Complex data types, such as medical imaging or clinical notes, fragmented data sources, and privacy concerns further complicate the structure and complexity of the data in the smart and connected health business, which is another obstacle to multi-organizational research. Despite the novelty of data monetization as a notion, several models and architectures have been developed for its potential use, such as healthcare data mergers and sharing, collaborative data analytics, and the collapse of data silos. Data-Preserving Machine Learning (PPML), MultiParty Computation (MPC), and data-sharing platforms enable us to analyze data from multiple hospitals and patients with similar characteristics in order to improve the functionality of existing models or create new ones, all while protecting the privacy of the individuals involved. This article aims to shed light on data monetization approaches, tactics, and prospects while exploring potential technological solutions to current issues. This paper presents a thorough reference design for data monetization that combines data sharing with PPML/MPC. It then uses a unique case study on the diagnosis and prediction of cardiac anomalies to analyze the state-of-the-art designs.

Data monetization is a topic that the MIT Centre for Information Systems Research (MIT CISR) has spent a lot of time studying. They began with the Owens and Minor (OM) case study. At the turn of the century, OM, a medical supply distributor, began providing hospitals with information offers derived from data collected from hundreds of suppliers' products and services provided to thousands of hospitals. These "Spend Analytics" services were peddled to healthcare facilities and supplier groups by those looking to enhance their buying, product distribution, and market penetration choices. By the end of the development process, OM had created a one-of-a-kind solution that centred on its data-based offers (Wixom, Cashing from your Data 2014). In 2014, MIT CISR increased the number of data monetization studies it produced *via* research briefings. The practice of making money off of third-party data started with this. From a variety of perspectives, several studies in the literature have addressed the topic of external data monetization. In a thorough case study, Najjar and Kettinger (2013) looked at how a supplier site, retailers, and suppliers all worked together to monetize data. Following the identification of three potential avenues for monetization, the third strategy was implemented, in which the retailer established a supplier platform for technical data infrastructure and used the analytical capabilities of the suppliers. Parvinen et al. (2020) examined 24 companies to provide a complete picture of data-monetization practices in large and medium-sized organizations. They came up with three models: selling data, selling analysis, and selling data-based services. Using this matrix, they laid out a plan for how to reach monetization. They built a matrix comparing these models to other types of clients, including existing customers, current value chain participants, and everyone else. As an example, 3cixty, a data platform for mobile context-aware travel applications, was studied by De Reuver et al. (2015). For the benefit of advertising, app developers, government organizations, and end-users alike, 3cixty built a multi-sided platform. Facilitating transactions between different user groups, such as app developers and consumers, is the primary objective of a multi-sided platform. The platform provides access to many apps and services for city visitors. Looking at various income arrangements from the customer's perspective was the focus of the study [16 - 21]. The study's authors discovered that people are more willing to part with their data than to pay for an app. Company A provides smart city services, while Company B owns a smart building. De La Vega et al. (2018) included data monetization in the context of the Internet of Things (IoT) in their analysis of these two organizations. They suggested a data marketplace that uses blockchain technology to guarantee non-repudiation and peer trust in a peer-to-peer architecture.

PROPSOED WORK

A generic decentralized design that allows core participants to safely share sensitive data with one another *via* a peer-to-peer network of data consumers and producers is shown in Fig. (**1**).

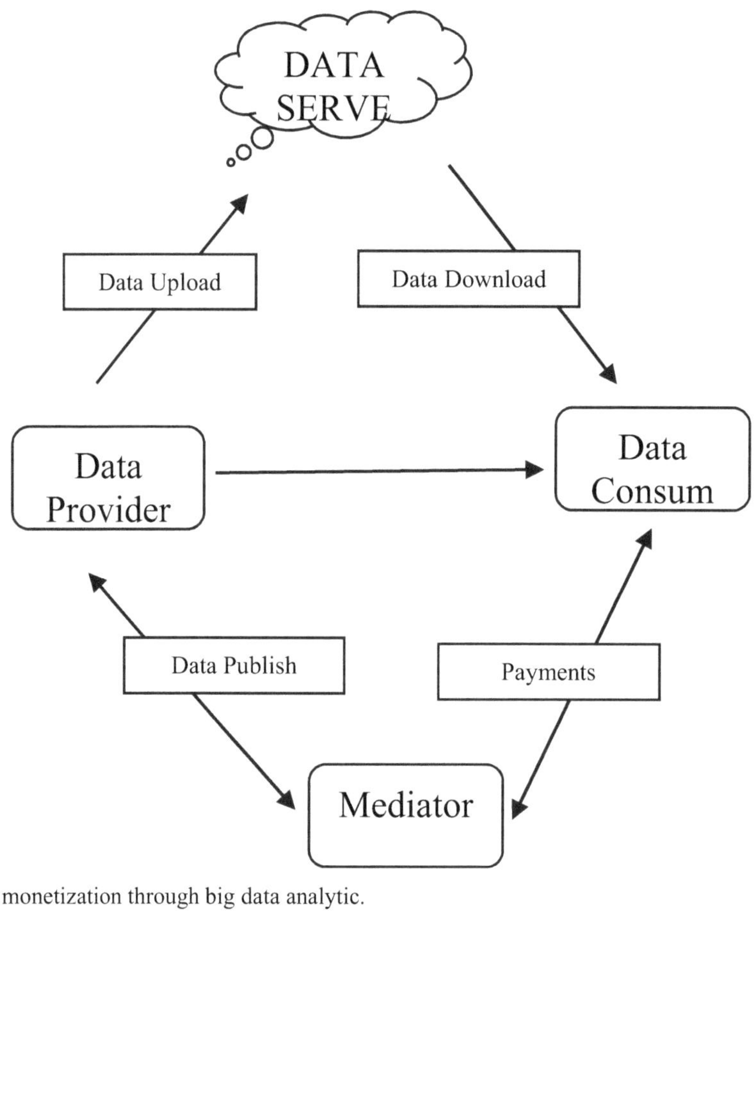

Fig. (1). Data monetization through big data analytic.

Users (*e.g.*, patients) who act as data producers are able to create, gather, track, and manage data flows; they also stand to gain financial benefits from doing so.

• Data Supplier:

The data provider, such as hospitals, performs the following functions, in contrast to the data producer, who is the individual or organization responsible for creating data or managing it *via* use policies:

i. Creates data source descriptors that are recorded with the intermediary (dealer or broker) that other players (data consumers) in the ecosystem utilize to get data.
ii. Selects data from many sources within the ecosystem, analyzes and integrates it, converts it to a desired data model, and adds data use terms and conditions on the suppliers' behalf.

• Data Consumer (Data Sink):

The Data Owner grants the authorized organization the right to use the subject's data in compliance with the Data Use Policy and:

i. Collects information from service providers;
ii. Adapts data into a desired model by selecting it from various sources (data providers), processing it, and integrating relevant information.

• Mediator:

The intermediary acts as a broker, managing and storing data about the ecosystem's various data sources. Numerous mediators may coexist, since this is an essential but not exclusive function. Its primary function is to provide a register of data sources for publishing and discovery, together with any applicable use conditions and legal information. Consequently, the mediator oversees the contracts and metadata of the data sources; this information is often seen as public and may be accessed by anybody with an interest.

• Identity Provider:

A system that generates, stores, and oversees the many forms of identification used by ecosystem members.

- Arbitrator:

As a mediator, the arbitrator is in charge of settling and clearing data exchanges and financial transactions; moreover, the arbitrator keeps track of everything that happens during data exchanges. Data consumers and providers may verify the data transfer by documenting the specifics of the transaction with the arbitrator after it's over. After that, the transaction's billing is based on that data. Verifying that a data consumer has a data package is one example of how logging information may help settle disputes and disagreements.

It is necessary to validate data transmission and reception by recording the details in the arbitrator's transaction record. Among the arbitrator's other primary responsibilities are:

i. Accounting is the process of the arbitrator's record, which may include billing data, invoices, and transactions.
ii. Resolution of disputes: the arbitrator's stored information is used to confirm data transactions, data quality, and data consumer reception.
iii. Rating management:

Crowdsourced evaluations on the dataset and participant quality may also be stored and made public *via* the arbitrator. Data quality encompasses a multitude of factors, including availability, quantity, completeness, and representation, ease of manipulation, interoperability, currentness, value-addedness, and reputation. Errorfreeness refers to the amount of mistakes or omitted values, while value-addedness describes how data contributes value to the business.

- App Marketplace and App Developers:

By participating in an app marketplace, programmers may build data and AI services and then sell them to users.

- Gateway:

Data providers and producers are able to trade or share data with data consumers *via* gateways, which facilitate peer-to-peer connectivity for participants in the ecosystem. App markets may also be linked to gateways so that apps and their source codes can be purchased and downloaded to enhance their functionality. Some examples of AI algorithms that can be run *via* gateways are MPC and PPML models, which can clean data.

Identity Provider

The eleven concepts listed below form the basis of identification in general:

- Being: People are never entirely digital.
- Management: Users have the power to administer their own identities and privacy settings as they see fit.
- Individuals are no longer reliant on intermediaries to have access to their personal data.
- Openness and transparency: These are essential for every system or method.
- A person's identity will remain in existence for as long as the person using it desires.
- Mobility: Users are able to take their identity services and data with them.
- Across borders and platforms, user IDs are usable, ensuring interoperability.
- Users may agree on how their identity is used when they provide consent.
- Information about the true owner must be kept to a minimum in all interactions.
- Safety: People's rights are safeguarded against tyranny by the powerful. Since users need to provide personal information in order to utilize online services, identity management has become more complicated in the modern internet landscape.

Data silos, which are often the objects of hacking, are subsequently used to store our personal information. Furthermore, it is common for online services to collect more data than is strictly required for the engagement.

Additional problems include:

- Unwanted Correlation: Data pertaining to an individual is linked across many platforms without authorization. Most people's privacy has been compromised because of the proliferation of internet correlation, which is mostly driven by marketing. The primary identifiers, such as email addresses, that we use on a daily basis create correlation. The most important component is email, but another one that boosts correlation is having the same account name on various sites. When other forms of identification are used online, such as a person's address, phone number, ID card, etc., this data is also linked across other websites. Online "cookics" allow for cross-platform identification sharing. While safeguards like the General Data Protection Regulation (GDPR) aim to prevent this in Europe, they are not in place worldwide. The fact that it is a legal fix rather than a technological one makes it accessible to bad actors.
- In modern times, the majority of identifiers are derived from a single source, either the government (like a driver's license or tax ID number) or a single

business (like a login ID for a website). The fact that the identification may be removed at whim by the central entity is the fundamental problem with this strategy. Whether the entity in question is a public or private institution, this is a matter that critics of both types of organizations find particularly troubling. The potential abuse of personal data in the case of a breach at the controlling company is another major worry.

- Current certificate management practices need a hierarchical design in which successive certificate authorities are responsible for independently verifying certificates lower on the hierarchy, all the way up to the root certificates implanted in devices.
- Data Breaches: Because personal identification information (PII) is so valuable, data silos are an obvious target for cybercriminals. Because it allows hackers to get illegal access to accounts, the desired information includes user IDs, passwords, names, email addresses, etc. There is always the chance that someone other than the owner is using publicly available identification information, which prevents its usage for valuable interactions.

Homomorphic Encryption (HE)

With homomorphic encryption, ciphertexts may be computed and the output encrypted. Just as if the calculation had been done using plaintext, the decrypted result is identical to the calculation result. The concept of homomorphism is used in regard to Algebra. Just as ciphertext and plaintext are homeomorphisms, so too is the encryption and decryption of algebraic functions. Boolean or arithmetic circuits make up these calculations, and various kinds of encryption allow them to do different computations using encrypted data. "Partially homomorphic," "somewhat homomorphic," "leveled fully homomorphic," and "fully homomorphic" are the most popular Homomorphic encryption algorithms. The inability to scale is the primary problem with HE. It is true that calculations done on encrypted data take far longer than the identical computations done on unencrypted data. Not to mention that a lot of HE methods aren't versatile enough to handle more than one kind of operation (like multiplication or addition, for example). Additionally, complicated procedures (such as nonlinear functions) are not compatible with this method. In most cases, adding or multiplying those functions should get you close enough. Thus, it is almost impossible to train holistic ML models utilizing HE approaches with the present state of technology.

Differential Privacy (DP)

Integrating noise into raw, unencrypted data is the fundamental premise of DP. When filling out a survey, for instance, you can inadvertently inflate your age by five years or your heart rate by a few beats. By averaging out the noise, multiparty computation allows analytics to provide results that are relatively close to the original. Increasing the amount of noise usually improves privacy, although it may cause less precise findings in certain cases. That is to say, pattern-matching (*e.g.*, optical character recognition) may not be the best use case for DP because of the compromise between privacy and accuracy. Two broad types of DP exist: global privacy and local privacy. The first method involves a single, reputable organization (a hospital, for example) gathering raw, personally identifiable information (PII) from several sources (*e.g.*, patients). To tackle the use of AI-driven IoT and the needs for data security at the same time, the curator examines the gathered data, adds noise to it, and then shares it with researchers, internal and external data scientists, and other interested parties. There isn't a curator in the local privacy approach. Therefore, before sharing sensitive information with other parties, each party should appropriately obfuscate it.In both global and local strategies, the noise injection logic is often implemented using a probability distribution, such as the Laplacian distribution.

RESULT AND DISCUSSION

In order to reliably monitor and evaluate the state of the cardiovascular system, healthcare practitioners often use electrocardiography (ECG) data. Machine learning techniques are crucial in automating the process of identifying arrhythmias by correctly categorizing ECG data according to the AAMI EC57 standard. By demonstrating how healthcare providers can train a state-of-the-art Convolutional Neural Network (CNN) to identify irregularities in electrocardiogram (ECG) readings, this case study aims to show how data silos can be collapsed and data monetization achieved. In particular, we demonstrate how several data owners may collaborate to train a convolutional neural network (CNN) for ECG signal classification using DP and FL. We may evaluate the efficacy of DP/FL by comparing its findings with those of the traditional method, which presupposes the safe combination of all ECG signals from different owners (*e.g.*, patients or hospitals) in a single database, therefore eliminating privacy problems. Twelve leads, connected to different areas of the body, allow one to view the electrical activity of the heart. These leads include three bipolar limb leads (I, II, as well as III), three unipolar limb leads (AVR, AVL, and AVF), and six unipolar chest leads (V1, V2, V3, V4, and V6). In research involving ECG signal processing, the bipolar limb lead II is often used as the data input due to its ability to collect the ECG signal's various waves—P, Q, R, S, and T—at a sufficient resolution. There are seventeen categories into which ECE signals are normally classified; they include APC (atrial premature contraction beat), LBB (left bundle branch block beat), RBB (right bundle branch block beat), PVC (premature ventricular contraction beat), PAB (paced beat), as well as NOR (normal beat).

Here, we use the MIT-BIH dataset for both model training and evaluation purposes. The comparison of accuracy is shown in Fig. (**2**). The MIT-BIH dataset contains electrocardiogram recordings from 48 separate individuals. Every recording lasts for around 30 minutes, is recorded at 360 Hz, and has a resolution of 11 bits.

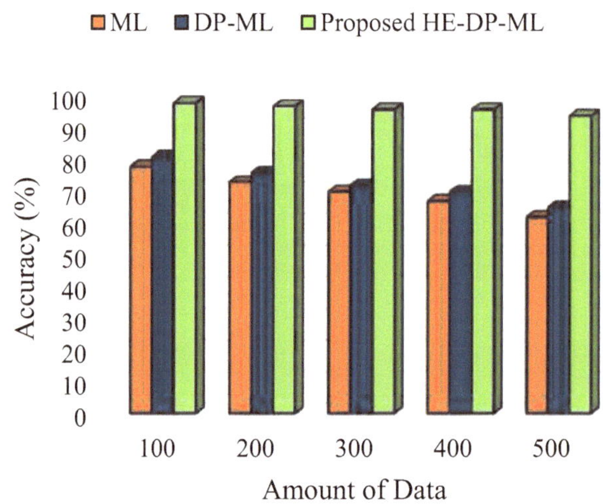

Fig. (2). Comparison on Accuracy.

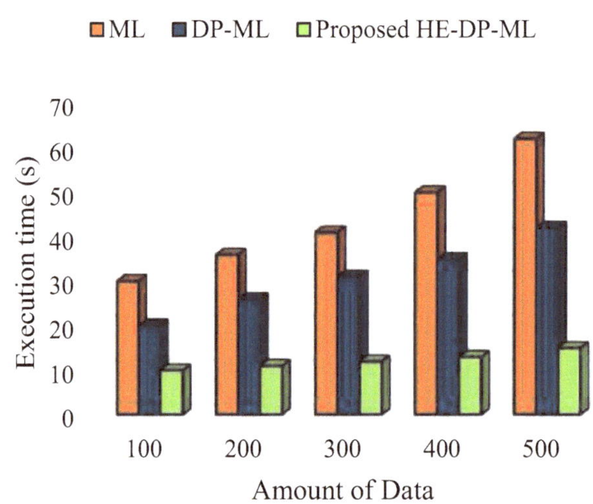

Fig. (3). Comparison on Execution Time.

Approximately 110,000 heartbeats from 48 patients make up the MIT-DIH dataset, which was used to train the classifier and evaluate the accuracy of the suggested model. A raw signal image with a size of (64, 64) pixels was used to correctly window each beat. The cropping strategy was used to improve the images of non-normal beat signals since the database contains an excessive number of normal beats compared to other types of beats. The comparsion of execution time is shown in Fig. (**3**). For each beat, a total of ten pictures were created by cropping each image nine times using this procedure. Consequently, for the CNN model's input, 353690 samples were generated for each of the 45 patients who were the focus of the investigation. The input photographs stored in memory were not only enhanced, but also randomly rotated and/or flipped at a frequency of 0.3. Prior to training, all samples were mixed. The data was divided into train, validation, and test datasets using a ratio of 0.7, 0.15, and 0.15, respectively. According to the results, the suggested work improves accuracy while requiring less time to execute.

CONCLUSION

One of the world's biggest and most complex industries, healthcare is always evolving to meet the demands of ever demanding people. The field is evolving at a rapid pace as specialists seek for innovative solutions that might provide practical answers. And therefore, the market is still feeling the effects of the Internet of Things, artificial intelligence, big data, and blockchain. Wearable Internet of Things (IoT) gadgets, diagnostic testing, and patient records provide massive amounts of data for the healthcare industry. The importance of collecting, integrating, and analyzing data from multiple places is therefore growing in the setting of smart and connected health. Nevertheless, data utilization may be difficult since several parties may own the data and be reluctant to share it with outside for fear of inadvertently revealing sensitive corporate information or losing control over its use. Businesses should be cautious of potential legal issues when monetizing data, especially in the highly regulated health care sector, but there is no denying the vast opportunity that data presents. From business models to challenges and solutions, this research addressed every critical aspect of health data monetization. Additionally, we provided a thorough reference design that balances the potential for monetization with the need to comply with data security and privacy regulations. Lastly, we demonstrated the concepts of PPML and MLC, including federated learning and differential privacy, through an innovative case study: ECG-based collaborative cardiac abnormality detection. This case study offers a potential avenue for monetizing healthcare data.

REFERENCES

[1] Q. Qin, T. Chen, X. Zhang, B. Ou, J. Zhang, C. Wu, Y. Xie, & W. Wu, "Precisely modeling the potential of a surface electrode ion trap", *Chip,* vol. 2025, p. 100126, 2023. [http://dx.doi.org/10.1016/j.chip.2024.100126]

[2] C. Kosel, A. Mooseder, T. Seidl, J.P. Psychology, S.O. Science Technology, T.U. Munich, Germany, C.S. Science, & B. Data, (2023). Measuring Teachers' Visual Expertise Using the Gaze Relational Index Based on Real-world Eye-tracking Data and Varying Velocity Thresholds. ArXiv, abs/2304.05143.

[3] C. Brink, C. Hansen, M. Field, G. R. Price, D. I. Thwaites, N. Sarup, and U. Bernchou, "Distributed learning optimisation of Cox models can leak patient data: Risks and solutions", arXiv preprint arXiv:2204.05856, 2022. [http://dx.doi.org/10.48550/arXiv.2204.05856]

[4] S. S. Tripathy, S. Chaudhuri, R. Murtugudde, V. Mharte, D. Parmar, M. Pinto, P. Zope, and V. Dixit, "Prediction of air pollution levels using machine learning techniques", *Procedia Computer Science,* vol. 132, pp. 1743-1751, 2018. [http://dx.doi.org/10.1016/j.procs.2018.05.135]

[5] Fredriksen, H., Burman, P.J., Woldaregay, A.Z., Mikalsen, K.Ø., Norway, S.N., Intelligence, T.N., & Trust, N.H. (2023). Approaching adverse event detection utilizing transformers on clinical time-series. ArXiv, abs/2311.09165.

[6] D.A. Hamburger, R.L. Physics, and T.H. Jerusalem, "Optical theorem and the inversion of cross section data for atom scattering from defects on surfaces", *J. Chem. Phys.,* vol. 102, pp. 6919-6930, 1995.

[7] "J.O. (2023). Retracted: Hotspot Mining in the Field of Library and Information Science under the Environment of Big Data", *J. Environ. Public Health,* 2023.

[8] Kosel, C., Mooseder, A., Seidl, T., Psychology, J.P., Science, S.O., Technology, Munich, T.U., Germany, Science, C.S., & Data, B. (2023). Measuring Teachers' Visual Expertise Using the Gaze Relational Index Based on Real-world Eye-tracking Data and Varying Velocity Thresholds. ArXiv, abs/2304.05143.

[9] B. Zhu, G. Hu, Y. Xie, L. Xu, X. Fan, Q.L. Statistics, T.C. Kong, D.O. Biostatistics, D. Science, C.F. Sciences, T.U. Houston, P.O. Health, T.U. Center, D.O. Sciences, and T.U. Dallas, *Bayesian Nonparametric Clustering with Feature Selection for Spatially Resolved Transcriptomics Data.,* 2023.

[10] Shtovba, O. (2023). RETAIL 4.0 Principles-based priority tasks of smartizing the shopping in a convencional hypermarket. Innovation and Sustainability.

[11] Blake, V., Jorm, L.R., Yu, J., Lee, A.K., Gallego, B., Clinic, S.O., Hospital, P.O., Sydney, Nsw, Australia, Health, C.F., Wales, U.O., School, P.O., Medicine, S.O., Medicine, F.O., Health, Wollongong, U.O., Hospital, T.W., & Wollongong (2023). The Cardiac Analytics and Innovation (CardiacAI) Data Repository: An Australian data resource for translational cardiovascular research. ArXiv, abs/2304.09341.

[12] Richter, O., Xing, Y., Marchi, M.D., Nielsen, C., Katsimpris, M., Cattaneo, R., Ren, Y., Liu, L.D., Sheik, S., Demirci, T., NingQiaoSynSense, A., Swizerland, SynSense, China, P.R., Circuits, B., Lab, S., Materials, Z.I., Groningen, U.O., Netherlands, Systems, G.C., Center, M.S., & Netherlands. (2023). Speck: A Smart event-based Vision Sensor with a low latency 327K Neuron Convolutional Neuronal Network Processing Pipeline. ArXiv, abs/2304.06793.

[13] Barrio Pediatric, "Pediatric injuries classification using openAI: new opportunities for epidemiological surveillance", *Eur. J. Public Health.* vol. 33, Issue Supplement_2, October 2023, ckad160.359.

[14] J. Godos, I. Guerrera, S. Laudani, A. Mata, M.I. Pardo, P. Busó, G. Grosso. Food security and Mediterranean diet in five countries: the delicious project. Eur J Public Health. 2023 Oct 24;33(Suppl 2):ckad160.1087.

[http://dx.doi.org/10.1093/eurpub/ckad160.1087] [PMID: PMC10595186]

[15] Y. Zhang, W. Fan, X. Chen, W. Li, and O.B. Neuroimag, "The Objective Dementia Severity Scale Based on MRI with Contrastive Learning: A Whole Brain Neuroimaging Perspective", *Sensors (Basel).* vol. 23, 2023.

[16] S. Alhomdy, F. Thabit, F.A.H. Abdulrazzak, A. Haldorai, and S. Jagtap, "The role of cloud computing technology: A savior to fight the lockdown in COVID-19 crisis, the benefits, characteristics and applications", *Int. J. Intell. Netw.,* vol. 2, pp. 166-174, 2021.

[17] S.J. Alsunaidi, A.M. Almuhaideb, N.M. Ibrahim, F.S. Shaikh, K.S. Alqudaihi, F.A. Alhaidari, I.U. Khan, N. Aslam, and M.S. Alshahrani, "Applications of Big Data Analytics to Control COVID-19 Pandemic", *Sensors (Basel),* vol. 21, p. 2282, 2021.

[18] H.N. Rothberg, and G.S. Erickson, "Big data systems: Knowledge transfer or intelligence insights?", *J. Knowl. Manage.,* vol. 21, pp. 92-112, 2017.

[19] C. Adrian, C. Adrian, R. Abdullah, R. Atan, and Y.Y. Jusoh, "Conceptual Model Development of Big Data Analytics Implementation Assessment Effect on Article in Press Conceptual Model Development of Big Data Analytics Implementation Assessment Effect on Decision-Making", *Int. J. Interact. Multimed. Artif. Intell.,* vol. 5, pp. 101-106, 2018.

[20] M. Gupta, and J.F. George, "Toward the development of a big data analytics capability", *Inf. Manage.,* vol. 53, pp. 1049-1064, 2016.

[21] B.M. Kalema, and M. Mokgadi, "Developing countries organizations' readiness for Big Data analytics", *Probl. Perspect. Manag.,* vol. 15, pp. 260-270, 2017.

CHAPTER 17

Exploring the Potential of Data Visualization to Enhance Data Analysis

Dhruv Galgotia[1,*] and **Biswajeet Kumar Pandey**[2]

[1] *Department of Management, Galgotias University, Greater Noida, Uttar Pradesh, India*

[2] *Department of Computer Science and Engineering, JAIN (Deemed-to-be University), Bangalore, Karnataka, India*

Abstract: Providing suggestions for integrated, cutting-edge, and efficient tools, methodologies, and technologies for accessing and processing increasingly growing volumes of data in diverse forms is a major problem in clinical data analysis and knowledge discovery. Personalizing a patient's care is a challenging task that requires the doctor to sift through and make sense of massive volumes of data. The scientific community behind precision medicine might benefit greatly from a unified system that facilitates data discovery, integration, preprocessing, model construction, storage, analysis, and visualization. The software package provides researchers with a simple, quick, and adaptable method for processing data, with the ultimate goal of enabling intelligent management, analysis, and visualization of massive genomic data. Services, data sets, and databases are at their disposal, or they can supply their own information for processing.

Keywords: Clinical data analysis, Knowledge discovery, Medicine, Model construction, Patient's care, Storage, Visualization.

INTRODUCTION

In this study, we developed a theory of Big Data visualization. Rendering models that aid Knowledge Discovery is a high-level goal of big data processing. This necessitates research into the features we call large Data, as well as thoughts on the many kinds of visual representations for large data.

Using what may be called (Synthetic) Metapictorial renderings, I suggest, is a potential modeling alternative toward attaining knowledge discovery from huge data. Massive volumes of experimental data have been produced as a direct outcome of the computer simulations. As a result, new research paradigms

* **Corresponding author Dhruv Galgotia:** Department of Management, Galgotias University, Greater Noida, Uttar Pradesh, India; E-mail: ceo@galgotiasuniversity.edu.in

S. Kannadhasan, R. Nagarajan, & Kaushik Pal (Eds.)

emerged, such as data-intensive science, and methods for processing large amounts of data were developed. Because of this shift, new research methods and data-driven discoveries will be required. During this process, we actively look for meaningful connections and employ cutting-edge techniques for knowledge acquisition. Knowledge discovery is founded on "data-intensive decision making" [1] and is made possible by the methodologies and technology of the new paradigm. Big Data refers to the ever-increasing volume, veracity, and freshness of datasets used in virtually every field of study, including healthcare [2]. Scientists can now create, store, and analyze data at breakneck speeds. Big data today encompasses not just massive data storage but also improved data analysis and interpretation. There is constant research and development into novel approaches to bettering data acquisition, storage, cleansing, processing, and interpretation. Precision medicine relies on a thorough understanding of human genetic variation, including both common and unusual mutations linked with disease susceptibility [3]. To provide the best possible care for each patient, precision medicine advocates personalized approaches to diagnosis, medical decision-making, treatment, and therapy [4]. Personalized treatment, intelligent medication design, population screening, and mining electronic health records might all benefit from the use of novel methods for extracting meaning from massive volumes of data. There is a dire need for collaborative networks that share data and knowledge, and there is a pressing need for standardization of data content, format, and clinical criteria. Using a text mining framework, a data mining strategy is designed for SVM-based information extraction from the biomedical domain [5]. New methods for analyzing and visualizing large amounts of data have contributed to the explosive expansion of precision medicine [6]. Large, detailed databases of genomic, transcriptomics, proteomics, or metabolomics variables, as well as conventional clinical patients' characteristics and treatment records, have emerged at an ever-increasing rate in the era of big data and the advent of electronic healthcare records [7]. However, in the context of their direct use in a clinical setting, such data are generally highly diverse, high-dimensional, noisy, and poorly interpretable [8]. Small sample sizes, imprecise technology, variations in clinical trials, a wide variety of patient groups, and an unstandardized health care system model can all reduce the reliability of the results. The term "big data analytics" refers to the practice of analyzing massive datasets that often include disparate data types. The goal of big data analytics is to unearth previously hidden relationships, complex patterns, imbalanced data sets, consumer and clinical preferences, and other valuable insights [9]. New methods for early prognosis of cancer therapy results have been discovered by scientists [10]. Because of the rapid development of new medical technology, researchers now have access to a wealth of biomedical data. Predicting how an illness will progress, however, is one of the most fascinating and difficult issues facing clinicians today. Medical researchers have found great success with artificial intelligence methods because they can be used to forecast future outcomes of a disease type by discovering and identifying models from complex datasets and their relationships. The foregoing suggests that tailoring medical care to an individual patient is a challenging task that requires doctors to sift through copious amounts of data. The examination of medical records can benefit greatly from the use of big data technology. Researchers in the field of precision medicine might benefit greatly from a unified system that facilitates every step of the process, from finding relevant data to integrating, preprocessing, constructing models, storing, analyzing, and visualizing it.

RELATED WORKS

In the foreword of Fayyad and Grinstein's Information Visualization in Data Mining and Knowledge Discovery, Stephen G. Eick writes, "Visualization is the link between the two most powerful information processing systems: humans and the modern computer." It's "easy to be overwhelmed by the volumes of data that are now routinely connected," the author writes. Data mining is a reduction method that works in harmony with human talents. While I disagree that we are "easily overwhelmed," I do think that those whose jobs need them to work with large datasets are under so much pressure that they would benefit greatly from any way to speed up and simplify the discovery of new information [11-15]. This is especially true in processes whose goal is to do what is now called anticipatory analysis on the data by visualizing it in a new light. The first steps in learning came through observing the world around us, and this practice continues to this day. The scale of big data is growing to the point that it is starting to resemble the bigger systems seen in nature. A new naturalesque/synthetic imagery, called metapictorial, may thus be the best approach for depicting massive data, especially when used to facilitate the discovery of new information. These three components would make up even the most basic diagram contrasting actual with metapictorial imagery: Three contrasts are shown in Fig. (**1**): 1) pictures of reality vs synthetically manufactured "reality-styled" imagery (metapictorial); 2) derived, continuous mathematics versus applied formulation (algorithms and computing efforts); and 3) invisible physical models versus invisible relational models.

PROPOSED WORK

This publication is part of a project that provides a scientific framework for intelligent management and analysis of huge data streams for biomedical research and precision medicine.The main benefit is that hypotheses and decision options are generated automatically and can then be verified and validated using biological datasets and the knowledge of scientists. The purpose of this work is to develop a unified, open-source technology platform for the integration, storage, analysis, knowledge discovery, and decision-making of medically relevant multi-dimensional, large-scale biomedical data. As a consequence of this, it is anticipated that the platform will provide researchers with an integrated, scalable workflow development environment consisting of a suite of software tools to automate the computational process involved in carrying out scientific experiments and provide: 1) an easy-to-use environment; 2) interactive tools for executing workflows and visualizing real-time results through virtual reality; 3) the ability to share and reuse workflows; 4) the capacity to track workflow execution results and workflow usage; and 5) the ability to track workflow execution results. The selection of fundamental analysis data and significant features is based on research and comparative analyses, with the help of research specialists, for each targeted scientific area within the study spectrum. The data integration process relies heavily on data identification and data abstraction. Using a service-oriented architecture (SOA) based multi-agent technique for finding and integrating dispersed biological data aims to automate the data integration and permits quick administration of enormous quantities of heterogeneous data sets represented in different formats from multiple sources [11]. User-defined search parameters and simultaneous database access are both possible with this system. Multiple clients (mobile phones, web browsers, and desktop programs) can access the system over the Internet simultaneously, thanks to these services. For the sake of precision medicine, we develop a full-fledged service-oriented architecture (SOA)-based system that encompasses the whole data lifecycle (from discovery to integration to preprocessing to storage to analysis and visualization) [12]. In Fig. (**1**), we see the architecture of a system for analyzing large amounts of genomic data and deriving insights from a database of biological information. Through standardized interfaces, data sharing, and information interchange, the system facilitates application and data source compatibility. Each service operates autonomously, with its own data and business logic. The services are decentralized, linked to one another, and constitute an automated business logic. Accessing data from several sources, integrating that data, preparing massive data streams, analyzing and visualizing massive amounts of genetic data, and so on are all part of the answer. The suggested integrated system provides researchers with a straightforward, rapid, and adaptable method for processing data. Customers may pick and choose which services they want to run, draw from existing data sets in databases, or feed in their own information to be analyzed. The system's design is based on a processing pipeline for extracting insights from data; hence, it addresses the following: Fig. (**2**) shows a three-step procedure that includes collecting raw data, cleaning it, and selecting which data to analyze. Knowledge discovery and decision making are facilitated by a flexible software architecture that allows for

(1) a wide range of models and methodologies to be used, (2) extensive scaling, and (3) a polymorphic computational framework.

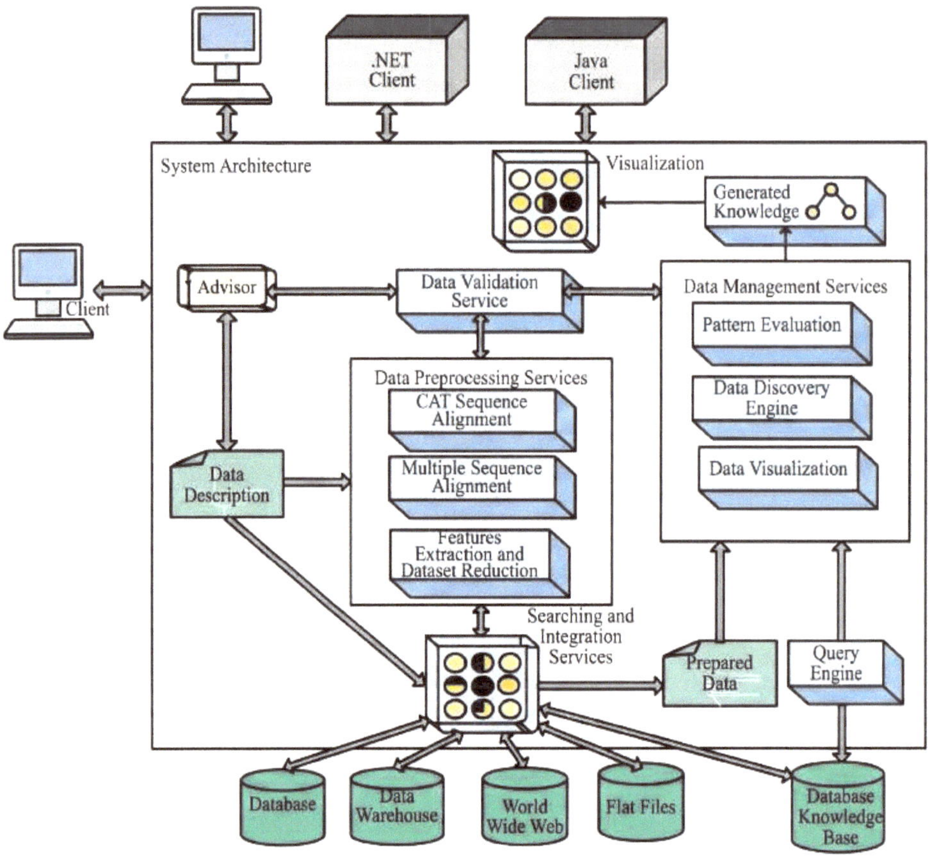

Fig. (1). Biomedical data analytics and knowledge discovery system.

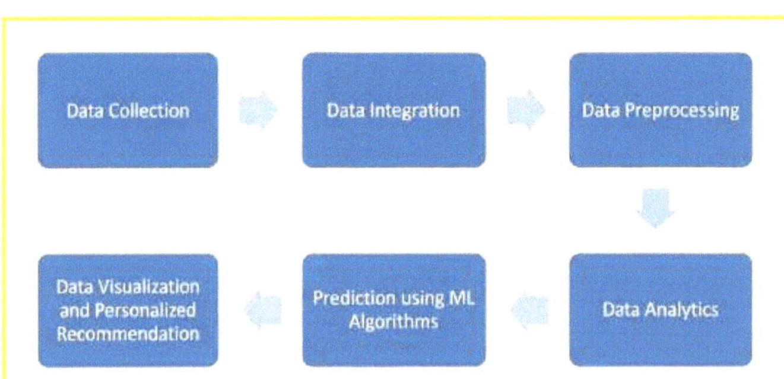

Fig. (2). Block Diagram of the Proposed Model.

It quickly manages big, heterogeneous data sets stored in a variety of relational, NoSQL, and flat file formats with the help of search and integration services. The Biomedical data analytics and knowledge discovery system is shown in Fig. (**1**). The integration system provides services for combining data from diverse sources and formats, and for translating standard requests into the language required by each local database. The block diagram of the proposed system is shown in Fig. (**2**). Massive, diverse, and complex data sets are available in public databases, underscoring the need for scalable data integration systems in modern biology. Software for sequence alignment, multiple sequence alignment, feature extraction, and dataset reduction are part of what we call "data preprocessing services." Software for analyzing patterns, a data discovery engine, and other methods of data visualization are all part of the services offered by data management companies. Classification, clustering, genetic algorithms, and prediction are just some of the data processing activities that may be run using the data discovery engine's individual modules. By abstracting away from the complexity of significant data sources, the query engine enables the development of data services. Servers dedicated to databases and data warehouses handle all data management tasks, are shown in Table **1**. All produced patterns may be found in the knowledge repository. When a pattern is produced through the big data analytics procedure, it is submitted to the pattern repository for long-term storage. Knowledge discovery from data is greatly aided by the database, which may be used for demand forecasting and model evaluation. For the purpose of system testing and validation, a software program has been developed for in silico display of biological data. Protein and DNA sequence illustrations are used as a case study. You may use it to see how a protein or DNA strand is folded. The created model allows for the examination of interatomic and internucleotide distances and forces. Modeling the three-dimensional structures of DNA and proteins aids in understanding theoretical knowledge. Data format at input: A protein.xyz or dna.xyz file, created by some molecular simulation tools, is read by the application to obtain structural information about a protein or DNA. The file may be read by using a text editor, as it is in text format. The kind of molecule and the numeral N that represents it are both located on the first line of the file. The value is the total number of lines containing atomic coordinates. In the next N lines, you'll find: x is an integer representing the number of the atom; x is a word consisting of one to four symbols, with the first symbol indicating the element of the atom (C for carbon, H for hydrogen, O for oxygen, N for nitrogen, etc.); x is a set of three real numbers representing the x, y, and z coordinates of the atom; and x is a set of one to four integers representing the numbers of the atoms.

Table 1. Dataset.

Data set example:	-	-	-	-	-	-	-	-
627	PEPTIDE	-	-	-	-	-	-	-
1	C	-3.968115	16.659998	44.612565	2	3	4	-
2	O	-5.087643	16.398799	45.076265	1	-	-	-
3	O	-2.961345	16.769981	45.325642	1	-	-	-
4	C	-3.798170	16.962676	43.111525	1	7	10	328
5	N	12.504650	28.110116	31.129835	6	320	321	322
6	C	11.433018	27.541559	30.322495	5	8	9	326
7	C	-2.824202	16.120704	42.270861	4	323	324	325
8	C	11.407359	26.042407	30.475216	6	12	327	329
9	C	10.087818	28.194122	30.663228	6	15	16	-
10	N	-3.416214	18.357338	42.909708	4	11	330	-

RESULT AND DISCUSSION

The application was built with the help of the OpenGL graphical visualization library and the Microsoft Visual Studio IDE. As a complement to OpenGL, we have been utilizing GLUT (OpenGL Utility Toolkit). With GLUT, one can quickly and easily construct a rendering window, use the keyboard and mouse, and draw sophisticated shapes like spheres. Objects in 3D scenes are typically represented by sets of geometric primitives, such as polygons, points, and lines. It is crucial to select the finest choice for the assignment because rendering large structures takes a lot of time and effort. At program startup, the readAtoms () function reads the protein data from the input file. An array is used to hold the information. Each item in this array is a data structure that specifies each individual atom's type, coordinates, and connections to the other atoms in the molecule. Protein or DNA centers are likewise determined by the same function. A scenario that revolves around this point. The intricacy of the presented items is often high. In order to create a sphere with pleasing proportions and lighting, at least 64 polygons are required. In this scenario, 256 polygons are employed for enhanced clarity. Some proteins consist of over 10,000 atoms, which places stringent demands on computing power. If each sphere were rendered separately, scenes with up to around 200 atoms could be shown at a smooth framerate. This is unacceptable; hence, the so-called Display Lists must be employed. Because they integrate OpenGL instructions and may be called multiple times, they resemble basic functions. Because they need to display the same items repeatedly, they may make good use of the program's Display List feature, which generates a separate list for each atom type (C, H, O, N, by default). You may integrate many Display Lists onto a single page. Therefore, all proteins and DNA are also Display Lists consisting of many atoms, with the latter being drawn by invoking the former to obtain the necessary coordinates. This keeps us from having to send and tally up the coordinates of each preview polygon in each frame. Making the appropriate rotation and distance modifications to the protein, then calling its Display List, is sufficient. Because the instructions in a Display List are compiled only once during its generation, rather than for each frame of visualization, this technique is incredibly efficient. Calculations are decreased because the same final object may be presented several times by computing the geometric changes of its points during compilation. To further minimize data transmission and access time, the computed results are stored in the video card's memory rather than the computer's RAM. In a few situations, a recompile of the object is necessary. When bonds are displayed, the radius of all atoms is halved, and linkages between atoms are drawn deeper in the protein's Display List, requiring a full recompile. If you need to make a modification to an object in a nested Display List, all you have to do is recompile the list. This is true whether displaying polygon boundary lines or adjusting atom size. GLUT utilizes the following functions: x resize the window () x render the scene initially () x update the scene for each frame - processing time () x signal input (keyboard/mouse) - glutFunction Keyboard () The character pressed and two numbers for the current mouse coordinates are passed as inputs to the function glutKeyboardFunc (), which also gets the name of the function that processes the keystrokes (keyDown ()). The pressing and releasing of specialized buttons activate a pair of additional functions. The ActiveMotion () feature tracks the mouse's position when a button is depressed. Depending on whether one of the arrows is pushed and if the constant rotation of the scene is active, the screen drawing function show () recalculates the variables for rotation and distance of the protein. To start sketching the protein, we first do a single translation along the z-axis using the zoom variable's value. Then, the y-axis is twisted by the amount specified by the rotateAngle variable. The protein structure is drawn by invoking the protein's previously constructed Display List. There is just one source of light illuminating the scene in all its ambient, diffuse, and specular guises. Atomic materials have specific definitions for their ambient, diffuse, specular, and emission hues. The visualization of DNA structure is shown in Fig. (**3**). The cycle to update the display is initiated when the main function returns, at which point the glutMainLoop() function is invoked. The protein model may be rotated and zoomed in on in two ways: with the arrow keys or by holding down the left mouse button. The visualization of protein structure is shown in Fig. (**4**). Other features include turning off the 3D model's continuous rotation, resizing atoms, configuring how connections are drawn between atoms, making objects translucent, and viewing polygon contours.

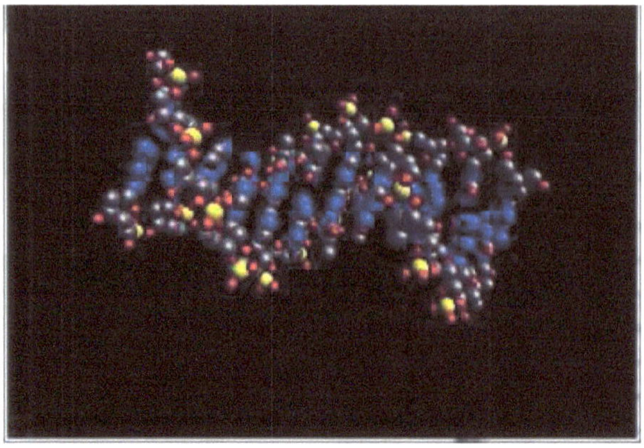

Fig. (3). Visualization of partial dna sequence.

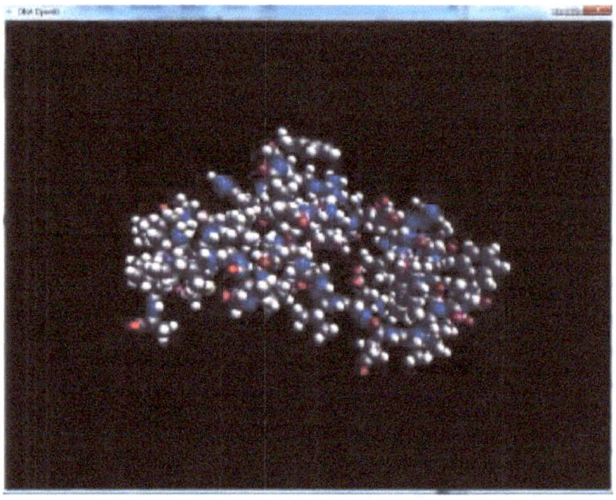

Fig. (4). Visualization of protein structure.

CONCLUSION

Biomedical data discovery, integration, storage, and analysis; knowledge discovery; and decision-making for medical needs can all benefit from a unified, open technology platform that employs cutting-edge methodologies, algorithms, and tools. Components for finding and integrating heterogeneous data from diverse data sources and in different formats; data preparation, cleansing, filtering, and selection; data processing and analyses; and knowledge representation and results display are all part of the system architecture that has been built. In order to test and validate the system, a software program has been built to visualize biological data. The suggested software allows users to view the three-dimensional structure of a protein or DNA sequence using OpenGL. When similar macromolecules are modeled in three dimensions, their atomic detail becomes clear. Using cutting-edge 3D modeling technology, scientists can now present even the most complex compounds.

REFERENCES

[1] S. Agrawal, and S. Gupta, "Data visualization for effective data analysis: A review", *J. Data Sci.,* vol. 20, no. 1, pp. 99-117, 2022.

[2] A. Bhatt, and N. Sharma, "Data visualization and exploratory data analysis: A systematic review", *International Journal of Advanced Intelligence Paradigms,* vol. 14, no. 1/2, pp. 3-17, 2021.

[3] N. Doshi, and S. Doshi, "Data visualization techniques for exploratory data analysis: A review", *J. Data Sci.,* vol. 19, no. 1, pp. 85-99, 2021.

[4] S. Kadam, and P. Mohite, "Data visualization for business analytics: A systematic review", *Int. J. Bus. Anal.,* vol. 8, no. 1, pp. 18-34, 2021.

[5] A. Khosla, and P. Singh, "Data visualization tools for exploratory data analysis: A comprehensive review", *J. Big Data,* vol. 8, no. 1, pp. 1-22, 2021.
[PMID: 33425651]

[6] T.M. Bohné, and A.T. Tredennick, "The potential of data visualization for exploratory data analysis", *Ecology,* vol. 103, no. 3, p. e03503, 2022.

[7] R.J. Crouser, and J.C. Lester, "Data visualization for data analysis", *Big Data Analytics,* vol. 6, no. 1, pp. 1-22, 2021.

[8] L. Danner, "Data visualization for exploratory data analysis: A review of tools and techniques", *Journal of Digital Information Management,* vol. 19, no. 2, pp. 55-64, 2021.

[9] K. Kafle, and R. Shrestha, "Data visualization techniques for exploratory data analysis: A review", *J. Big Data,* vol. 8, no. 1, pp. 1-24, 2021.
[PMID: 33425651]

[10] A. Kielar, "The potential of data visualization in exploratory data analysis", *Annals of Data Science,* vol. 8, no. 1, pp. 1-26, 2021.
[PMID: 38624463]

[11] J. Kim, and Y. Kwon, "Data visualization techniques for exploratory data analysis: A review", *J. Open Innov.,* vol. 7, no. 3, pp. 1-23, 2021.

[12] S. Li, J. Li, and C. Li, "Data visualization and exploratory data analysis: A comprehensive review", *J. Comput. Sci. Technol.,* vol. 36, no. 6, pp. 1055-1074, 2021.

[13] C. Liu, and Y. Zhao, "Data visualization techniques for exploratory data analysis: A review", *J. Data Sci.,* vol. 19, no. 2, pp. 238-259, 2021.

[14] M. Tavana, and M. Mohammadi, "Data visualization for exploratory data analysis: A review", *Int. J. Inf. Manage.,* vol. 57, p. 102387, 2021.

[15] Y. Wang, and J. Li, "The potential of data visualization in exploratory data analysis: A systematic review", *Inf. Process. Manage.,* vol. 58, no. 3, p. 102568, 2021.

CHAPTER 18

Exploring the Potential of Recommender Systems for Semantic Analysis

Vineet Saxena[1,*] and **Gaurav Londhe**[2]

[1] *College of Computing Science and Information Technology, Teerthanker Mahaveer University, Moradabad, Uttar Pradesh, India*

[2] *Department of Computer Science and Engineering, JAIN (Deemed-to-be University), Bangalore, Karnataka, India*

Abstract: Tourism destinations and their online and social media information have made choosing and visiting them difficult. Tourists find tourism suggestion systems attractive, but designers must be able to deliver personalised services. This study proposes a personalised tourist recommendation system that extracts user preferences. For this, tourist social network user reviews are a rich resource of preferences. To identify visitor preferences, remarks are preprocessed, semantically grouped, and sentimentally analysed. The characteristics of attractions are extracted from all user evaluations. Finally, the proposed suggestion system semantically matches user preferences with attraction attributes to suggest the most relevant attractions. The technology also filters undesirable goods and improves recommendations based on time, location, and weather. The Python-based recommendation algorithm is tested using TripAdvisor data. The suggested system improves the f-measure.

Keywords: Sentiment analysis, recommendation systems, big data, tourism.

INTRODUCTION

Lifelong educational platforms like MOOCs use AI to make online learning intuitive. AI-powered learning analytics and

Adaptive learning toolkits help the university 4.0 assess learning needs. Open learning platforms and learner-specific customization are essential to their success.

Thus, recommender systems enhance learning and facilitate MOOC search across platforms. A recommendation system predicts a user's opinion by comparing their profile to reference data [1]. Distance learners differ in background, history,

* **Corresponding author Vineet Saxena:** College of Computing Science and Information Technology, Teerthanker Mahaveer University, Moradabad, Uttar Pradesh, India; E-mail: tmmit_cool@yahoo.co.in

S. Kannadhasan, R. Nagarajan, & Kaushik Pal (Eds.)

competence, learning style, and academic activity [2]. "Recommending materials for learning to a specific learner" is tougher [3]. It is challenging to predict students' interests given the scope and variety of MOOCs. Employing information structures such as ontologies to personalize student profiles to meet their needs and attributes might simplify the selection of learning resources [4].

Tourism websites and social media generate massive amounts of data and comments. This data and visitor reviews help travelers choose places and attractions. Tourists struggle to analyse massive data sets manually. Personalized recommendation systems for tourism have been proposed. They extract user preferences and provide more personalized suggestions. Some recommendation algorithms group users by similarity in previously visited areas and provide them with the same suggestions. Users' visits to tourism attractions are not enough, thus their reviews are crucial. Another set of recommendation algorithms analyses comments to determine consumer tastes. User evaluations are matched to information regarding attractions to find the best matches [5].

This form of tourist recommendation algorithm exploits standard terms in comments, independent of user mood. Thus, negative terms emphasized in user input may be misinterpreted as desires. Tourism sentiment analysis is often neglected. Tourism recommendation systems should incorporate the following: determine preferences by looking for ideas rather than keywords, use sentiment analysis of user comments to identify positive and negative preferences, and provide background-aware recommendations. According to the authors, no tourist recommendation system has all of the following criteria. This research presents a sentiment-based tourist recommendation system. This system extracts user preferences using word processing and sentiment analysis. The preference extraction component extends the first study by extracting and preprocessing user ratings regarding attractions. Semantic clustering and sentiment analysis extract preferences. This study proposes a personalized recommendation system based on aggregated user evaluations of attractions [6 - 10].

The algorithm also takes into account the user's location (to find nearby attractions), the time available (to see whether those attractions are open), and the weather (to make suggestions suitable for the current climate). Python is used to create the suggested system. To test the effectiveness of the suggested approach, an experiment is carried out on TripAdvisor1, a popular travel website. To that end, have collected data from 2018, including the comments and visits of 100 individuals. Precision, recall, and f-measure all point to the suggested recommendation system's superior performance in the assessment [11 - 15].

RELATED WORKS

It is stated [4] that recommender systems may be categorized in accordance with the information learned about their users, the relationships between those users, the things to recommend, and, lastly, the classifications of objects that their users might determine. Most studies on recommenders in e-learning "focus on these traditional recommendation techniques" [3, emphasis added]; hence, we were able to categorize three different RS types for the filtering processes used in distant learning: content-based, collaborative-based, and hybrid-based. However, a recommendation strategy that gives weight to semantic links between ideas, is sensitive to learner preferences, and is regularly updated, is essential in the e-learning setting. When making recommendations, knowledge-based systems take into account the user's wants and requirements as well as the information they already possess. Knowing how to "reason about the connection between a need & a possible recommendation" [5] is the ultimate objective of any knowledge-based RS. Furthermore, it encourages information exchange and reuse, which is fundamental to the concept of online education.

Knowledge-based (KB) recommenders, first and foremost, establish a harmony between user requirements and product characteristics. Therefore, it recommends products based on deductions about the user's tastes and requirements [6, 7]. The system's acquired domain knowledge is then compared with the user's needs to determine which items are most appropriate and helpful for that user [1, 8]. "Knowledge-based systems depend on the concept 'Tell me whatever fits my needs'" [8]. Therefore, "this information will occasionally include explicit operational knowledge about how specific item features meet user needs" [7], such as when a platform for e-commerce asks its consumers to pick certain characteristics of offered items. KB recommenders depend heavily on a repository of data containing user, object, and inference rules that determine which items are most likely to appeal to which users. Unlike other recommendation systems that rely on users' evaluations of products, they incorporate a semantic component into the suggestion process and thus require knowledge engineering approaches [3] for their creation.

In addition to "the most used concept in the field of computer science research: Ontology is a formal, explicit description of a shared conceptualization...", ontologies provide the semantic web technologies and serve as a knowledge-based foundation for recommendations [9]. Indeed, by leveraging semantic and interoperability concepts across numerous platforms, it enables the integration of an inference framework for individualized suggestions. Therefore, it allows for "reusing as well as sharing information across a broad spectrum of systems" [10]. Collectively, "ontology to represent understanding of the items and users in a suggestion process" [3] is the backbone of Ontology-based (OB) recommenders, which are knowledge-based recommender systems. It is true that "the semantic relations among ontology concepts make possible inference on this foundation of information as well as preference extensions that help decrease the effect of simplicity and cold-start problems." [11].

The majority of travel advice engines use geotags. To promote tourist locations, for instance, tags on photographs published on Flickr1 are used to identify and cluster individuals who follow similar itineraries (Majid *et al*., 2013). Many recommendation systems incorporate comment analysis because user opinions about locations are highly valuable. Additionally, an understanding of context is crucial to the success of tourist recommendation systems. This section first explores context-aware tourist recommendation systems and then reviews tourism recommender systems. Current tourist recommendation systems rely heavily on geospatial data, which provides a wealth of contextual information. In this context, GIS was used to extract patterns of visitor behavior in the protected regions of Australia's Ningaloo Marine Park. It has also been used to provide suggestions based on the user's present location [16 - 23].

The 100 most popular tourist destinations in Taiwan are the focus of a similar Chinese-language recommendation system (Yeh & Cheng, 2015). As people of various ages, ethnicities, and economic brackets tend to see the world in different ways, suggestions have been made that take these factors into account (Lu, Wu, Mao, Wang, & Zhang, 2015). TripAdvisor data is then used to predict individual users' tastes (Pantano, Priporas, Stylos, & Dennis, 2019). Each user in this system is required to choose three out of eighteen possible tourism-related themes (e.g. Eco-tourism, Nature lover, *etc*.). So, consumers with comparable needs and interests are given recommendations for a similar collection of products. User reviews of attractions are the foundation of most existing travel recommendation systems. The accuracy of these algorithms can be considerably enhanced by reading user comments, since words convey far more information than ratings alone (Xiaoyao Zheng, Luo, Sun, Zhang, & Chen, 2018). Researchers have therefore begun using text-mining methods to examine user feedback (Bao, Fang, & Zhang, 2014; Xiaolin Zheng, Ding, Lin, & Chen, 2016). To this end, Loh *et al.* developed a closed-door messaging platform that polls users with queries about an ontology to unearth relevant terminology. Then, ontology concepts are used to infer the user's preferred attraction type; last, suggestions are made based on this information (Loh, Lorenzi, Saldaa, & Licthnow, 2003).

Post-visit attraction loyalty is the goal of the bio-inspired recommender system POST-VIA360 (Colomo-Palacios, Garca-Pealvo, Stantchev, & Misra, 2017). Recommendations are generated using a tourism Ontology that considers the user's travel history, geographic location, and social preferences. The sights of Bangkok have been the subject of a knowledge graph built by Yochum and company (Yochum, Chang, Gu, Zhu, & Zhang, 2018). The words from user comments are used to create a graph in which each word represents a distinct notion. Finally, a concept vector displaying the commonalities between travelers and the places they visit is shown. Lastly, the tourist-attraction correlation is computed using cosine similarity. Titles are extracted from users and other visitors' opinions of local attractions in another research using topic modelling (Leal *et al.*, 2017). Next, we assess the attractions' similarity to the user's preferences using WordNet's semantic similarity, and we propose the ones most similar to the user's preferred attractions.

PROPOSED WORK

There are three phases to the planned travel recommendation system. In the first step, feedback and ratings are parsed for user preferences. Similarly, the second phase involves gleaning features of attractions from travellers' experiences with them. In the last phase, relevant suggestions are provided based on the user's preferences and the features of the tourist sites they are most likely to be attracted to. The strategy takes advantage of environmental, temporal, geographical, and individual preferences. Algorithm 1 outlines the suggested recommender system's pseudocode. Here, we'll go through the specifics.

Algorithm 1: The proposed recommendation algorithm.

Inputs:
PoI Data: A = (PoI α, Location l, Reviews Tall tourists)
User Data: U = (Location l, Reviews Tuser)
Context Data: C = (Location l, Weather w, Time t)

Output:
Ordered list of recommended PoIs per user:
PoI_u = (PoI_α1, ..., PoI_αn)

Step 1:
Extract user preferences

Step 2:
In weather w
For each nearby user PoI do: TOPPoI ← Five most repetitious concepts of reviews of all tourists
For each nearby user PoI do: similarity-PoI ← Compute Similarity(user

preferences, TOP_PoI)
Return PoIs sorted by similarity-PoI
If in l, t, (w=rainy OR w=stormy OR w=snowy):

Step 3:
Give priority to indoor places as sorted above Else return previous results

This phase consisting of four key steps: preprocessing, forming a semantic network, clustering, and extracting preferences, is shown in Fig. (**1**).

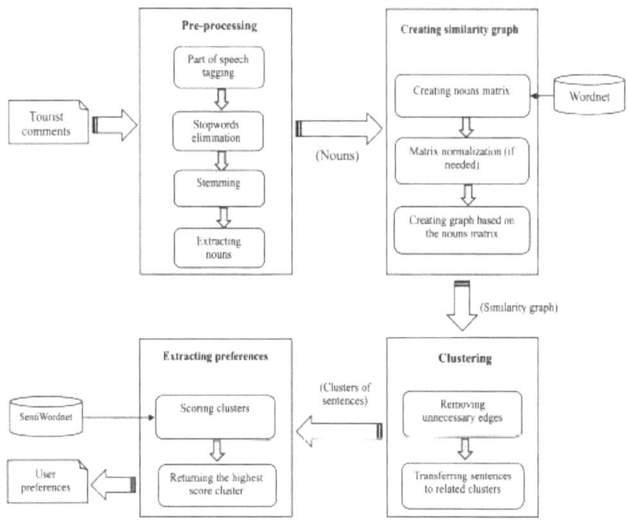

Fig. (1). Flow Chart of the Proposed Work.

The purpose of pre-processing is to transform an input document into a format more amenable to further processing, as shown in Fig. (**1**). The plan for this procedure is shown in Fig. (**2**). Details of the procedures are provided below. Preliminary Steps in the Processing Flowchart: Tags for different parts of speech (PoS) the noun, verb, *etc*., that make up the phrase are isolated and labelled at this step. This facilitates data mining of sentences. Eliminating Nonsensical Words: The meaningless words in a phrase are referred to as "stop words." Just the words contributing actual meaning will be left after this process.

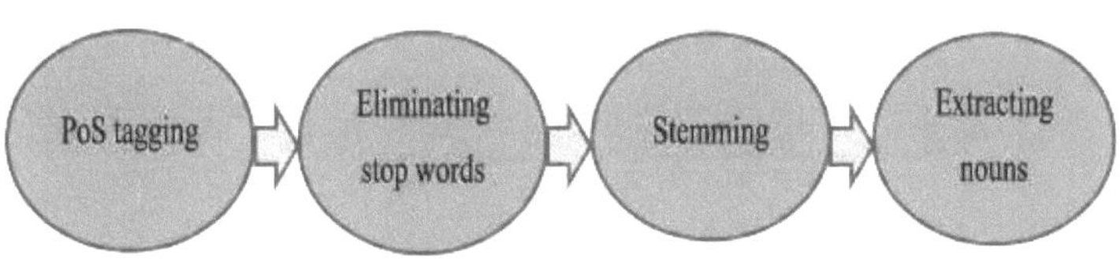

Fig. (2). Procedure of the Proposed Work.

Stemming is the reduction of a term to its component parts, or roots. Cats, catlike, and similar words are reduced to their ancestor word, cat, in this phase. Wordnet, which stores all words in their original stem form, is utilised for this purpose. Noun extraction: Nouns are the most informative parts of a sentence. As compared to using all of the words in a text, the clustering efficiency improves when just nouns are used (Fodeh, Punch, & Tan, 2011). So, at this step, only noun-tagged words are retrieved for further processing. The noun cosine similarity is built after some preliminary processing. It is a symmetric matrix where the rows represent the extracted nouns and the columns represent their antonyms (as shown in Fig. (**3**)). Each cell in the matrix represents the level of semantic similarity between two items. The matrix is built using a hybrid semantic similarity metric developed by Wei, Lu, Chang, Zhou, and Bao (2015). To improve the precision of its similarity calculations, this metric considers both direct and indirect connections between ideas in WordNet. It fixes the issues with the Extended glosses overlap (Banerjee & Pederson, 2003) and the Wu-Palmer similarity measures (Wu & Palmer, 1994) (Dearth of direct linkages between concepts). The approach is then tested using several metrics for measuring semantic similarity by normalising the matrix's members. To do this, we divide the sum of all matrix element values by the largest element. The preprocessed nouns are used as vertices in the matrix's network, while the edges' weights reflect the semantic similarity between the nouns they share (nouns). A pair of vertices is not related if they have no semantic similarities.

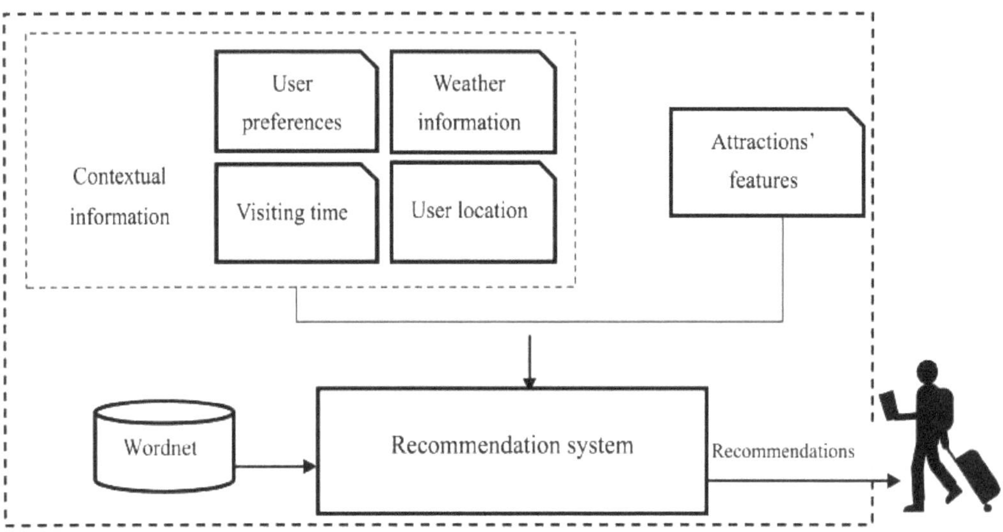

Fig. (3). Recommendation Systems.

The edges with a weight below the cutoff value are then removed. The graph may then be decomposed into a set of related subgraphs. While analysing the semantic similarity of nouns, each subgraph is treated as a cluster. At last, each phrase is distributed to the groups that house any of its individual words. So, depending on the nouns used, the statement might potentially fit into more than one category. If the nouns in cluster X are all letters A through D and the nouns in cluster Y are all letters E and F, then the "abg" sentence belongs to cluster X while the "afh" phrase belongs to both clusters. Noun frequency and sentiment analysis results are used to assign a score to each cluster in a continuous manner. Semantic Sentiment Analysis using the Sentiwordnet is used in this study (Baccianella, Esuli, & Sebastiani, 2010). Since a word's meaning and emotional weight might change depending on context, we take the mean of the beneficial and detrimental loads across its synsets to represent the word's beneficial and detrimental loads, respectively. Each sentence's score is calculated by subtracting its negative rating from its positive rating. The emotional weight of emojis is also considered. Each statement is assigned a score of 1 for positive emoticons and -1 for negative ones (Neidhardt *et al.*, 2017). The sentiment classification score for a cluster is the mean of the scores for the phrases inside it, as shown in equation (1).

$$ScoreSentimentAnalys(clusteri\ ) = \sum Scoreofeachsentenceof\ (clusteri\ ) \quad Totalnumberofsentencesin\,(clusteri\,) \tag{1}$$

In general, the more often a word appears in a text, with the exception of stop words, the greater its importance (Binwahlan, Salim, & Suanmali, 2010). As a result, clusters are rated based on the frequency of the words included inside them. The ith cluster score formula is presented in Equation (2).

$$Scoreclusteri = TFclusteri \times ScoreSentimentAnalys(clusteri) \tag{2}$$

Where the term frequency (TF) clusteri is equivalent to the total of all noun occurrences inside cluster i. The value of TFclusteri is 15, for instance, for a cluster I consisting of nouns with frequencies of 2, 5, and 6. The cluster with the highest total score is ultimately chosen. Other candidates for selection include clusters that are fewer than 10 points apart in the score from the chosen cluster. The words grouped together here stand in for the user's own tastes.

Feature Extraction for Attractions

Next, the characteristics of tourist destinations should be extracted, following the extraction of consumers' preferences. Tourist attractions rated less than 3 stars are not considered when evaluating suggestion quality. In addition, the qualities of tourist sites vary with the weather. The Alps, for instance, are recognised for their snowy terrain and freezing temperatures in winter, but for their lush landscape and mild weather in summer. So, for each tourist destination, we gather and preprocess evaluations from past visitors in five distinct climatic scenarios: snowy, rainy, sunny, stormy, and partly overcast. The top five most frequent terms of each attraction are then retrieved across all five climate conditions and interpreted as the attraction's highlights. Fig. (**3**) depicts the suggested procedure.

Lastly, indoor settings will be preferred over outdoor ones if snow, rain, or bad weather is expected. Nevertheless, the original result will be shown if good weather is forecast. In Fig. (**3**), we can see the overarching structure of the suggestion.

RESULT AND DISCUSSION

The suggested recommender system was built with the help of the Python programming language and the Anaconda1 infrastructure. As TripAdvisor is the most popular travel site, data from it has been collected to test the effectiveness of the proposed recommender system (Pantano, Priporas, & Stylos, 2017). The bulk of the data set (training data) consists of 100 travellers' six-month-long assessments of various tourist sites from a wide range of backgrounds and ages (January-June 2018). Users' first trip following this time frame (starting in July 2018) and all attractions visited during that trip are used for the experiment. Sentiment analysis using Sentiwordnet 3.0 has been completed (Baccianella et al., 2010). The suggested technique for sentiment analysis is initially tested against two well-known alternatives: those that utilize Support Vector Machines (SVM) & Bayesian network (Rana & Singh, 2016). Tourist feedback is divided into good and negative groups for this purpose. In addition, user ratings are taken into account throughout this sorting process. A positive evaluation would be provided if the user rated it 4 or 5 bubbles (very good or exceptional), and a negative evaluation would be given if the rating was 1 or 2 bubbles (awful or bad) (Valdivia, Luzón, & Herrera, 2017). The sentimental analysis method is shown in Fig. (**4**). Next, we plot each method's calculated proportions of beneficial and adverse feedback in Fig. (**6**). Results show that the recommended method yields the most consistent results with user ratings.

The next step is to assess the performance of the used hybrid semantic measure of similarity, which is based on both the Wu-Palmer (Wu & Palmer, 1994) & Extended Glossy Overlaps (Banerjee & Pedersen, 2003) criteria. The nouns in user comments are clustered and then compared to these two approaches. Cosine, Jaccard, and hybrid semantic similarity metrics (Wei *et al.*, 2015) are studied to determine how well user preferences align with attributes of tourist destinations

(Liu, Hu, Mian, Tian, & Zhu, 2014). If the user's current city has a radius of km, then 4, 2, and are all valid maximum distances from which a proposal may be made. Also, three distinct assessment approaches are taken into account, including recommending either one (Top1), three (3), or five (5) options. Precision, recall, and f-measure are measured and compared across all of these cases. Accuracy predicts how many of a user's recommended sites they actually visit. For top3 and top5, it is considered a success if the user enters one of the suggested attractions. The recall metric similarly shows the proportion of visited attractions that were truly suggested. The ratings for top1 are shown in Fig. (7). Measures of semantic similarity used for grouping user comment nouns and measures for similarity estimate of choices with feature attractions are represented by the values on the horizontal axis (A-B). In reality, A is the metric for noun clustering, while B is the metric for determining how much users' tastes align with the attributes of attractions. Precision recommendation is shown in Fig. (5).

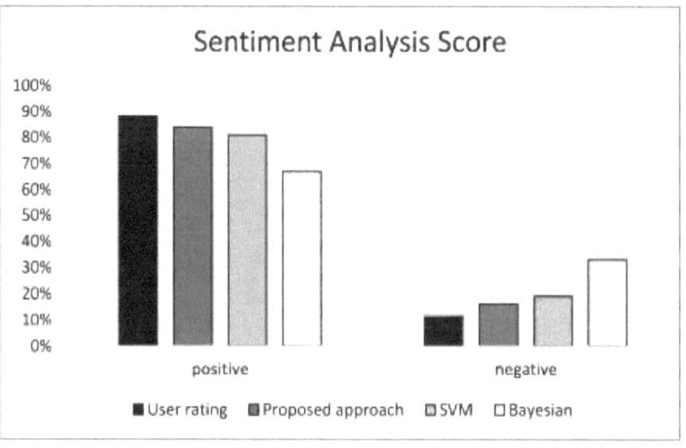

Fig. (4). Validating the proposed sentiment analysis method.

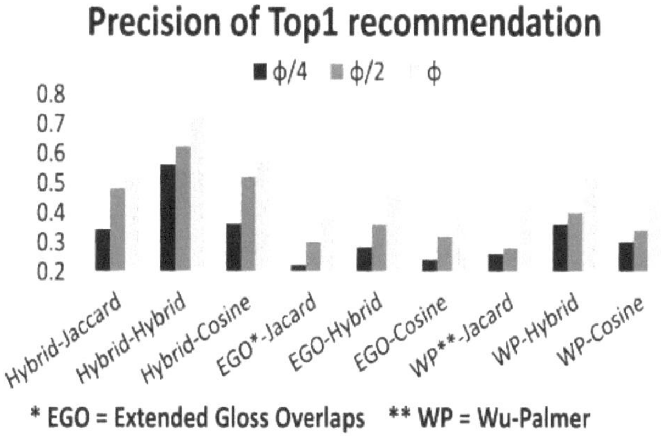

Fig. (5). Precision Recommendation.

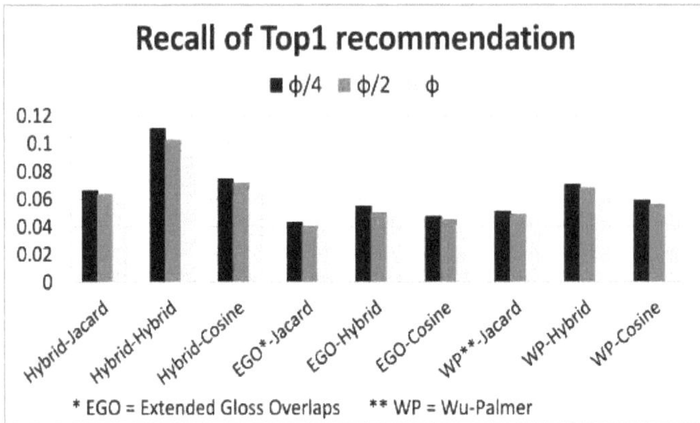

Fig. (6). Recall of the Proposed Work.

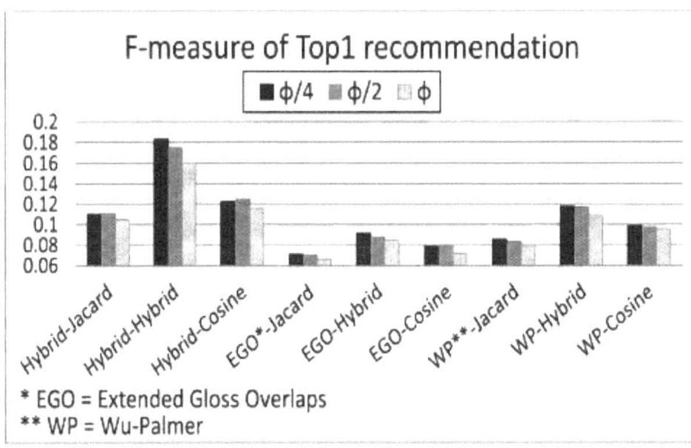

Fig. (7). F Measure of the Proposed Work.

The results highlight the advantages of the hybrid criterion over competing similarity measures for the top. The recall is shown in Fig. (**6**). In reality, for a variety of radii, hybrid approaches provide the highest values of accuracy, recall, and f-measure. The F measure is shown in Fig. (**7**). Lastly, a comparison is made between the proposed system and two existing systems: one by Leal *et al.* (2017) and one developed by Loh *et al.* (2003). Studies having a foundational premise similar to ours have been utilised to assess the viability of the suggested approach. In a private discussion, Loh *et al.* (described in the related study section) utilise the keywords of a user's reviews to infer the user's preferences and provide recommendations accordingly. Leal proposes an approach in which topic modelling is used to extract user preferences and aspects of tourist destinations, and recommendations are then made based on the similarities between the two.

CONCLUSION

This research introduces a context-aware tourist recommendation system that infers a user's tastes from their feedback and ratings using semantic clustering and sentiment analysis. The characteristics of a tourist attraction are also gleaned through customer feedback. Then, the user's preferences and the present environment are used to rank the attractions in the immediate vicinity. Ultimately, one hundred customer reviews from the TripAdvisor website were collected for an experiment. The system has indeed been trained on the first six months of each user's data, and tested on the first trip after this period, including all of the user's visits to attractions. The suggested system achieved better f-measure performance than competing systems in the evaluation.

REFERENCES

[1] Rahman, K.U., Ma, H., Arshad, A., & Baheer, A.K. (2022). Movie Recommender System Based On Heterogeneous Graph Neural Networks. 2022 8th International Conference on Systems and Informatics (ICSAI), 1-7.

[2] E. E. Milios and C. Domeniconi, "Semantic analysis of documents workshop (SemADoc): Extended abstract", In: *Proceedings of the ACM Symposium on Document Engineering (DocEng)* ACM, 2014, pp. 239-240.
[http://dx.doi.org/10.1145/2644866.2656329]

[3] Fioravera, M., Marchisio, M., Di Caro, L., & Rabellino, S. (2018). Alignment of content, prerequisites and educational objectives: Towards automated mapping of digital learning resources. 14th International Conference eLearning and Software for Education.

[4] Ankammarao, B., & Padma, M. (2017). International Journal of Scientific Research in Computer Science, Engineering and Information Technology.

[5] Wu, H., & Wang, M. (2016). Multi-view non-negative tensor factorization as relation learning in healthcare data. 2016 38th Annual International Conference of the IEEE Engineering in Medicine and Biology Society (EMBC), 3325-3328.

[6] W. Luo, Y. Wang, X. Liu, and S. Gao, *Cities as Spatial and Social Networks: Towards a Spatio-Socio-Semantic Analysis Framework.* Cities as Spatial and Social Networks, 2018.

[7] R.J. Filho, J. Wehrmann, and R.C. Barros, "Leveraging deep visual features for content-based movie recommender systems", *2017 International Joint Conference on Neural Networks (IJCNN),* pp. 604-611, 2017.
[http://dx.doi.org/10.1109/IJCNN.2017.7965908]

[8] B. Ramzan, I.S. Bajwa, N. Jamil, R.U. Amin, S. Ramzan, F. Mirza, and N. Sarwar, *An Intelligent Data Analysis for Recommendation Systems Using Machine Learning.,* 2019.
[http://dx.doi.org/10.1155/2019/5941096]

[9] S. Sridhar, and S. Sanagavarapu, "Twitter Social Networking Graph using Hypernym based Semantic Similarity Detection", *2020 International Conference on Smart Electronics and Communication (ICOSEC),* pp. 28-35, 2020.
[http://dx.doi.org/10.1109/ICOSEC49089.2020.9215279]

[10] M. Nourbakhsh, K. Degn, A. Saksager, M. Tiberti, and E. Papaleo. Prediction of cancer driver genes and mutations: the potential of integrative computational frameworks. Brief Bioinform, vol. 25, no. 2, bbad519, 2024.

[11] A.L. Mamuye, T.M. Yilma, A. Abdulwahab, S.C. Broomhead, P. Zondo, M. Kyeng', J.M. Maeda, M.

Abdulaziz, T. Wuhib, and B.C. Tilahun, Health information exchange policy and standards for digital health systems in africa: A systematic review. PLOS Digit Health, vol. 1, no. 10, e0000118, 2022. [http://dx.doi.org/10.1371/journal.pdig.0000118]

[12] Y. Xu, J. Hao, R.Y. Lau, J. Ma, W. Xu, and D. Zhao, "A Personalized Researcher Recommendation Approach in Academic Contexts", *Combining Social Networks and Semantic Concepts Analysis. Pacific Asia Conference on Information Systems,* 2010.

[13] T. Kupfer, S. Geier, U. Heber, R.H. Østensen, B.N. Barlow, P.F.L. Maxted, C. Heuser, V. Schaffenroth, and B.T. Gänsicke, "Hot subdwarf binaries from the MUCHFUSS project", *Astron. Astrophys.,* vol. 576, p. A44, 2015. [http://dx.doi.org/10.1051/0004-6361/201425213]

[14] J.D. Garcia, E. Kiesling, S. Kirrane, J. Neuschmid, N. Mizerski, A. Polleres, M. Sabou, T.W. Thurner, and P. Wetz, *Propelling the Potential of Enterprise Linked Data in Austria.,* 2016.

[15] R.S. Kulkarni, and V.D. Jadhav, *Friendbook: A Semantic-Based Friend Recommendation System for Social Networks.,* 2016.

[16] L. Ehrlinger, and W. Wöß, "Towards a definition of knowledge graphs", *Proceedings of the Posters and Demos Track of 12th International Conference on Semantic Systems,* 2016.Leipzig, Germany

[17] I. Tiddi, and S. Schlobach, "Knowledge graphs as tools for explainable machine learning: A survey", *Artif. Intell.,* vol. 302, p. 103627, 2022. [http://dx.doi.org/10.1016/j.artint.2021.103627]

[18] X. Wang, D. Wang, C. Xu, X. He, Y. Cao, and T. Chua, "Explainable reasoning over knowledge graphs for recommendation", *Proceedings of the AAAI Conference on Artificial Intelligence,* vol. Volume 33, pp. 5329-5336, .Honolulu, HI, USA. [http://dx.doi.org/10.1609/aaai.v33i01.33015329]

[19] F. Zhang, N.J. Yuan, D. Lian, X. Xie, and W. Ma, "Collaborative knowledge base embedding for recommender systems", *Proceedings of the 22nd ACM SIGKDD International Conference on Knowledge Discovery and Data Mining,* pp. 353-362, 2016.San Francisco, CA, USA. [http://dx.doi.org/10.1145/2939672.2939673]

[20] J. Huang, W.X. Zhao, H. Dou, J. Wen, and E.Y. Chang, "Improving sequential recommendation with knowledge-enhanced memory networks", *SIGIR '18: 41st International ACM SIGIR Conference on Research & Development in Information Retrieval,* pp. 505-514, 2018.Ann Arbor, MI, USA. [http://dx.doi.org/10.1145/3209978.3210017]

[21] Q. Guo, F. Zhuang, C. Qin, H. Zhu, X. Xie, H. Xiong, and Q. He, "A survey on knowledge graph-based recommender systems", *IEEE Trans. Knowl. Data Eng.,* vol. 34, no. 8, pp. 3549-3568, 2022. [http://dx.doi.org/10.1109/TKDE.2020.3028705]

[22] H. Wang, M. Zhao, X. Xie, W. Li, and M. Guo, "Knowledge graph convolutional networks for recommender systems", *Proceedings of the WWW'19: The World Wide Web Conference,* Association for Computing Machinery: New York, NY, USA, pp. 3307-3313, 2019.San Francisco CA USA. [http://dx.doi.org/10.1145/3308558.3313417]

[23] S.M. Choi, S.K. Ko, and Y.S. Han, "A movie recommendation algorithm based on genre correlations", *Expert Syst. Appl.,* vol. 39, no. 9, pp. 8079-8085, 2012. [http://dx.doi.org/10.1016/j.eswa.2012.01.132]

CHAPTER 19

Text Mining for Intelligent Information Analysis for Opportunities and Challenges

Saira Banu Atham[1,*] and **A. Alli**[2]

[1] *Department of Computer Science and Engineering, Presidency University, Bangalore, Karnataka, India*

[2] *Department of Computer Applications, Presidency College, Bangalore, Karnataka, India*

Abstract: One noticeable development of the expanding internet age is text mining. Accurate exploration of its potential will enable various real-time applications to leverage text mining's unique characteristics. Conversely, social media platforms like Facebook and Twitter provide vast amounts of data that must be processed to derive actionable insights. Therefore, the purpose of this work is to explore the feasibility of using text-mining algorithms to analyze Twitter data. We want to use this knowledge to improve disaster management by applying the suggested technique to datasets pertaining to natural disasters. The three steps that make up the suggested approach are as follows. The subject of the database is first determined using a Latent Dirichlet Allocation (LDA) model. An SA is then suggested as a second step. The themes found in the sample are categorized into three feelings using this SA, which is applied to the LDA findings. We suggested using an ANN model for sentiment analysis. The third step is to apply data-mining algorithms to the themes in each sentiment using textual analysis (TA). At last, we find out how the supplied tweet feels. Anybody looking to enhance business intelligence analysis (BIA) procedures across industries may benefit from the suggested methodology's significant improvements in data text mining, including correctness, reliability, and the discovery of new insights.

Keywords: Data Mining, Text Mining, Automated Information Analysis, and Latent Dirichlet Allocation (LDA).

INTRODUCTION

Because of the large amount of data and the highly dimensional structure of text, it is difficult to summarize data succinctly; hence, robust representation of complex data is crucial for efficient natural language processing for event categorization. Machine learning technologies derive insights from textual linkages; visualization helps clarify these patterns, especially in event extraction

* **Corresponding author Saira Banu Atham:** Department of Computer Science and Engineering, Presidency University, Bangalore, Karnataka, India; E-mail sairabanuatham@presidencyuniversity.in

S. Kannadhasan, R. Nagarajan, & Kaushik Pal (Eds.)

tasks [1]. Industry, education, and research all rely heavily on visualization systems for the insights they provide and for how they improve decision-making. These technologies enable the graphical depiction of information and complex procedures in an intelligible way, thereby improving comprehension, analysis, and data transmission [2].

The global electrical system might be affected by solar protons and other high-energy charged particles, as well as by phenomena such as Forbush reductions. In good weather places, these impacts have been examined by looking at disruptions to a chance gradient in ground-based measurements. The potential gradient nocturnal curve is examined in this work as it deviates from the average values observed in good weather situations between solar proton events as well as Forbush reductions [3]. Essential components of woodland fire prevention include risk assessment, suppression strategies, and damage evaluation. When it comes to weather prediction, topomorphology, and socio-economics, the data that is involved is dispersed and diverse. It also has a spatiotemporal analysis component with many scales. All of these things highlight how important it is to improve at making choices using the right tools and techniques [4]. Students will learn how to analyze data to identify potential policy problems that state legislatures face through this case study that uses IRS SOI data on migration. Learn how to use Alteryx for the extraction, transformation, and loading (ETL) process, as well as Tableau to create data visualizations; these are data skills that entry-level accountants will need in any area. First, to improve students' ETL abilities; second, to help them become better data visualizers; third, to help them become better critical thinkers; and fourth, to help them become better communicators both verbally and in writing. According to open-ended responses and pre- and post-learning assessments, the case accomplishes these educational objectives [5]. Adenomatous polyps can be detected and removed before they progress to colorectal cancer (CRC), thereby greatly improving patient outcomes. During a white-light colonoscopy, polyps are usually found and removed. Regrettably, there is still a substantial proportion of interim tumors that develop between CRC screening sessions. This is associated with inadequate polyp removal as well as poor screen visibility of polyps [6]. Adenomatous polyps may be detected and removed before they advance to colorectal cancer (CRC), which greatly improves patient outcomes. During white-light colonoscopies, tumours are typically identified and removed. Due to issues with polyp visibility as well as partial removal, the time frame for cancer rate among CRC screening appointments is still somewhat high [7].

RELATED WORKS

Using natural language processing (NLP), we show how visualization may help at every step of our example, which aims to find news stories that might trigger state-led mass executions [8]. This includes exploratory data analysis, neural network training evaluation, and post-inference validation.

Graphs were used to represent network traffic data, with nodes representing devices and edges representing interaction instances. Afterwards, we trained our artificial intelligence algorithms using these graph properties. Our results show that the evaluated machine learning models—including logistic regression, support vector regression, and K-means clustering—perform somewhat better when graph theory is applied to network data. These findings highlight the importance of graph-theoretic representations for improving machine learning algorithms' discriminative performance on network data [9].

Afterwards, we trained our artificial intelligence algorithms using these graph properties. Our results show that the evaluated machine learning models—including logistic regression, support vector machines, and K-means clustering—perform somewhat better when graph theory is applied to network data. These findings highlight the importance of graph-theoretic representations for improving machine learning algorithms' discriminative performance on network data [10].

A knowledge-based maintenance system (PMS) backed by RAM assessment is developed in this work. By analyzing data, the system can determine current RAM levels and forecast future trends, allowing for adjustments to the maintenance schedule. Decisions are supported at both the practical and managerial levels by monitoring the depicted information. Periodic data from the main engine on a cargo ship are used to demonstrate the suggested method. Fuel injection valves are the primary objects in the data display. The findings demonstrate that the improved PMS system enables the efficient, timely scheduling of both regular and unexpected ship repairs. The RAM study offers valuable insights to technical management and ship engine room personnel regarding the current and future possibilities of PMS systems aboard. To digitalize the process and enhance compliance with the requirements of ISM Code 10 Clause and TMSA 4A.4, the additional research focuses on developing an upkeep plan app [11].

This research aims to fill that void by analyzing scientific papers in the Scopus database through a bibliometric lens. The examined data spans the years 1980–2022, and its primary goal is to trace the origins, development, and rise of space programs through reference, events, cooperation, and grouping. The UAE ranks first in publishing activity, with Saudi Arabia and Egypt following closely behind. Based on the data, most articles pertain to optical devices used in space missions and remote sensing. Findings from this study shed light on recent technical developments in the Arab aerospace sector and point the way for further investigation in this important area [12].

For this, we had already suggested a way to forecast potential Hoops Pass recipients, which could be used in an interactive 3D tool to recreate games. We provide three approaches for possible pass receivers, all building on the prior forecasting technique. One use case for this approach is to show prospective pass receivers sample pass routes. As for the second, it is used to see how well prospective wide receivers score. Thirdly, data about defensive players may be quantified. Users may have a better grasp of assault patterns and plays using the visualization tool, aided by the findings generated by these three methods. Also, actual datasets from women's basketball were used to verify these approaches. Consequently, the efficacy of the suggested approaches was shown [13].

Augmented reality (AR) visualisation technologies that improve multimodal vision and interaction for complex decision-making are investigated in this research. The suggested solution integrates augmented reality's immersive and interactive features with the tangible, natural qualities of the actual environment. Users may engage in straightforward, intuitive interaction by merging real and virtual elements across multiple senses. As an example of a multimodal interaction technique, the system enhances the user experience by incorporating vision, touch, eye tracking, and sound. Because of its multimodal design, users can experience a more comprehensive and engaging interaction. The article includes an in-depth analysis of the proposed system's software and hardware engineering, architecture, and the outcomes of initial functional testing. In the end, the goal is to provide intriguing and immersive experiences for users across a range of use cases, and the results should help academics, practitioners, and architects of visualization systems accomplish just that [14].

To enhance live-watching for basketball fans, we conducted a user-centered study on creating interactive embedding graphics. We started with formative research that aimed to identify the actions and activities that basketball fans do while watching games. We provide a design methodology that accounts for different data-seeking scenarios to guide the creation of integrated infographics based on our results. We provide five unique embedded visualization designs that adhere to the design framework and aim to capture five fan-identified contexts: shooting, offensive, protection, player assessment, and club comparisons. Next, we created Omnioculars, a prototype device for watching basketball games online that incorporates the suggested integrated visuals for in-game analysis of data by fans.

With the help of virtual basketball supporters, we tested Omnioculars in a game simulation. Based on the findings, it seems that our design may provide individualized is-game analysis of data, which in turn improves player comprehension and involvement [15, 16].

PROPOSED WORK

One method for extracting useful information from massive datasets is textual analysis (TA), a subset of data mining text (DTM). These metrics and indications are referred to as KIs or insight in the MI setting. As a result, TA is a method for discovering attitudes as well as emotions used on a research sample that relies on indications like word weight and correctness.

As a DTM approach, TA's goal is to sift through mountains of information in search of useful insights. This data is a byproduct of looking for patterns and trends in the data set that share some statistical characteristic. These methods allow us to organize text inputs in a way that can be used to infer patterns from structured data, which will ultimately be used as outputs. Text classification, text indexing, as well as summary, entity, clustering, the extraction process, and learning relations among entities with names are some of the most common text mining methodologies.

Consequently, TA may be used to determine which insights carry the most weight in a given sample and to quantify the impact of those KIs on the data set being studied. When utilized for business intelligence (BI), DTM approaches may help uncover text-based interests as well as patterns that would otherwise go unnoticed by human programmers. Analysts may get exploratory findings from TAs and use them to make bold claims based on the data, pose questions for investigation, or develop hypotheses. The text mining technique of the proposed model is shown in Fig. (**1**).

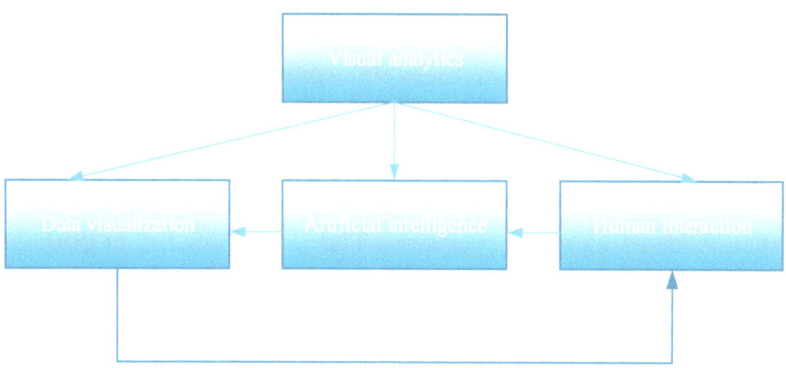

Fig. (1). Proposed model.

Fig. (**1**) shows that the first stage of text analysis is collecting data, which entails gathering or merging various types of information to form a dataset. To turn the acquired information into an organized form suitable for further analysis, the preprocessing stage involves applying filters and removing duplicate or repetitive data.

After that, in the text index phase, we hunt for patterns in the information and look into the readily identifiable KIs. On occasion, KIs are classified and organized into nodes or groups based on their attributes. The investigator should be able to draw conclusions from the information gathered in the following stage using text mining. Here, we use a variety of methods, including data analysis tools and algorithms, to draw conclusions from the collected information. Hence, whereas TA is qualitative in nature, it relies on sample statistics, such as the overall significance of the pattern that organizes the text's nodes or categories, or the frequency of repetition within each word grouping.

The last step is the analysis of texts, in which findings are examined, and exploratory judgments are made using qualitative or quantitative methodologies. To obtain well-structured, trustworthy KIs and insights, it is necessary to first identify and precisely describe the phases that follow and complete the process.

Data Sampling

The data collection procedure is crucial to the suggested methodological strategy because we aim to study user-generated content (UGC) and the interactions it may generate between businesses and online users to identify trustworthy knowledge indicators (KIs) and gain insight. Data may be retrieved from several digital networks' application programming interfaces (APIs), including but not limited to Twitter, TripAdvisor, Facebook, and Google Maps.

Furthermore, proper processing of the information filtering is critical. This is why it is critical to use the suggested procedure precisely and filter the user-generated information thoroughly. Here are some examples of what is considered appropriate: (i) eliminating any instances of duplicate material; (ii) limiting access to publicly available user-generated information; and (iii) gathering data that may be organized according to themes or topics, such as firms included in rankings, businesses with awards, #hashtags, and so on. A predetermined categorization of the data set will result from this process. The duration of data collection might range from one week to six years or more, depending upon the study's purpose and sample size.

Topic Identification Using Improved LDA

There are two distinct phases to an LDA approach, as mentioned before. The initial process involves identifying and categorizing words as well as their links across various sources. The second stage is to find out how words and phrases are distributed throughout various subjects. The next step is to sort the data set according to the most important themes. The process is shown by Equation (1), which highlights the significance of both the hidden and visible variables in the combined distribution.

Sentiment Analysis using ANN

In recent years, neural networks have become increasingly important as a classification technique. Over the last decade, neural network-based categorization has emerged as a viable substitute for several traditional classification approaches. Neural networks with the right architecture can handle the interdependence and connection among the input variables. Here are some theoretical advantages of neural networks. To start, neural networks do not need any operational or distributional model formulation, since they are data-driven and self-adaptive. Neural networks can approximate any function with arbitrary precision, making them universal function approximators. The ANN model is shown in Fig. (**2**). Accurately identifying this fundamental purpose is undoubtedly significant, since every categorization technique seeks a functional link between an object's group affiliation and its features.

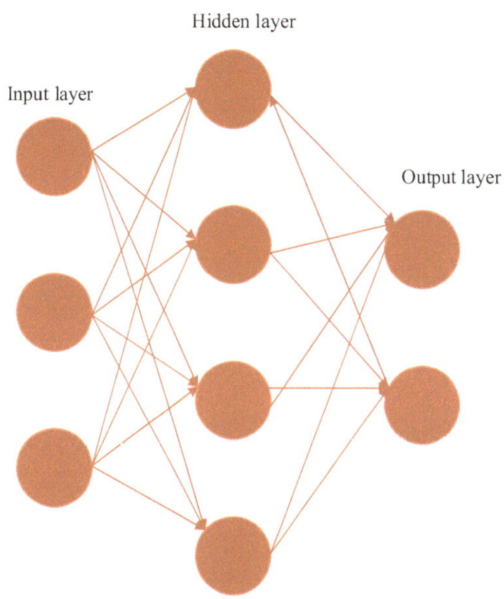

Fig. (2). ANN model.

An essential method for resolving categorization issues involves supervised learning. For the purpose of sentiment categorization in the suggested system, we have employed an Artificial Neural Network. The process consists of two stages: training and testing. Using the IMDB review dataset, the training step involves balancing the number of both favorable and adverse comments. Following that, during the training phase, give each remark a weight and use fuzzy logic to filter out negative words like never, not, *etc*. In terms of interdependencies as well as correlations, it aids in obtaining accuracy. In training, the primary goal is building a lexicon of words for good remarks. Training is necessary until the first favorable remark becomes a positive one. Review testing will follow. The trained vocabulary will serve as the foundation for the evaluations. To teach the system, an ANN activates neurons in the hidden layer, a process known as backpropagation. Here, BPN training using the training dataset begins.

There are two passes in the reverse propagation algorithm: one forward and one backward. Acquiring the activation number is the goal of the backward pass. When there is a discrepancy between the expected plus observed network outcomes, biases and weights may be adjusted using the backward pass. The network will converge after these two passes have gone through an iterative process. The following is a brief overview of the back-propagation method for training feed-forward networks. Presented in a random sequence, for every training pattern: Send the data to the network using the inputs. Find the output of each neuron starting from its input level and progressing *via* the hidden layer(s) to the output layer. Determine the result of the error. To calculate signals of error for the pre-output layers, utilize the output error. Calculate weight modifications using the error signals. Make the necessary changes to the weight. Check the network's efficiency on a regular basis. We determine whether or not the assessment is good or bad after the instruction.

RESULT AND DISCUSSION

We randomly divided every dataset into 30% for testing and 70% for training, and then executed the data splitting algorithm 30 times. We calculated the previously listed performance metrics on the test set for each run and reported the mean and standard deviation for each metric.

Compared to previous computations, this one is light-years ahead, although the outcomes are less than anticipated. While doing so, all characteristics are considered, leading to a greater effectiveness and precision of 98%. The importance of features in sentiment evaluation, as shown in this investigation, is shown in Table **1**.

Table 1. Result summarization.

Performance Measure	Random Forest	LightDL	Naïve Bayes	Fuzzy System
F-measure (%)	75%	94%	75%	76%
Precision (%)	75%	94%	71%	76%
Accuracy (%)	74%	97%	72%	79%
Recall (%)	71%	96%	73%	74%
Error Rate	0.8	0.3	0.85	0.75

The data are presented and compared in Table **1**. The results of the study demonstrate that the suggested lightDL approach is superior to the previous research.

CONCLUSION

The database topic is first determined using a Latent Dirichlet Allocation (LDA) model. To counter this, social networking platforms like Facebook and Twitter collect massive amounts of data that must be processed to derive actionable insights. Therefore, the purpose of this work is to explore the feasibility of using text-mining algorithms to analyze Twitter data. We want to use this knowledge to improve disaster preparedness by applying the suggested technique to datasets pertaining to catastrophic events. There are three steps to the suggested technique. After that, we suggest using sentiment evaluation (SA). After applying this SA on the LDA data, the sample themes are categorized into three feelings. Our intention was to use a machine learning model for sentiment analysis. The third step is to apply data text mining algorithms to the themes in each sentiment using textual analysis (TA). At last, we find out how the supplied tweet feels. Anybody looking to enhance business intelligence analysis (BIA) procedures across industries may benefit from the suggested methodology's significant improvements in information text mining, including correctness, reliability, and the discovery of new insights.

REFERENCES

[1] J. Tacza, A. Odzimek, E. Tueros Cuadros, J.P. Raulin, M. Kubicki, G. Fernandez, and A. Marun, "Investigating Effects of Solar Proton Events and Forbush Decreases on Ground-Level Potential Gradient Recorded at Middle and Low Latitudes and Different Altitudes", *Space Weather,* vol. 20, no. 3, p. e2021SW002944, 2022. [http://dx.doi.org/10.1029/2021SW002944]

[2] Huang, C., Lee, C., Chung, K., & Tsuei, Y. (2023). Feasibility and workflow analysis of IV-DS--based augmented reality-guided brain arteriovenous malformation resection in a hybrid operating room: i-Flow tailored method. Journal of neurointerventional surgery.

[3] P.K. Tyagi, A. Singh, P. Tyagi, and A.K. Singh, "Smart Tourism: Validation and Analysis of the Displacement of Tourists", *2022 International Conference on Innovations in Science and Technology*

for Sustainable Development (ICISTSD), pp. 173-178, 2022. [http://dx.doi.org/10.1109/ICISTSD55159.2022.10010672]

[4] A. Haghshenas, A. Hasan, O. Osen, and E.T. Mikalsen, "Predictive digital twin for offshore wind farms", *Energy Inform.,* vol. 6, no. 1, pp. 1-26, 2023. [http://dx.doi.org/10.1186/s42162-023-00257-4]

[5] C.T. Pérez, S. Salling, and S. Wandahl, "Location-Based Work Sampling: Field Testing and Utility Evaluation", *Proceedings of the 31st Annual Conference of the International Group for Lean Construction (IGLC31),* 2023. [http://dx.doi.org/10.24928/2023/0131]

[6] A. Belaroussi, K. Derbal, R. Benabdellah, and M. Belhadj-Aissa, "Towards a SOLAP Based Decision Support System for Forest Fire Management", *2023 International Conference on Earth Observation and Geo-Spatial Information (ICEOGI),* pp. 1-6, 2023. [http://dx.doi.org/10.1109/ICEOGI57454.2023.10292975]

[7] F. Jin, M. Zou, X. Peng, H. Lei, and Y. Ren, Deep Learning-Enhanced Internet of Things for Activity Recognition in Post-Stroke Rehabilitation. IEEE J Biomed Health Inform vol. 28, no. 7, pp. 3851-3859, 2024.

[8] S. Henn, A. Sticha, T. Burley, E. Verdeja, and P. Brenner, Visualization Techniques to Enhance Automated Event Extraction. arXiv:2106.06588, 2021.

[9] B. Alwasel, A. Aldribi, M. Alreshoodi, I.S. Alsukayti, and M. Alsuhaibani, "Leveraging Graph-Based Representations to Enhance Machine Learning Performance in IIoT Network Security and Attack Detection", *Appl. Sci. (Basel),* vol. 13, no. 13, p. 7774, 2023. [http://dx.doi.org/10.3390/app13137774]

[10] M. Alenazi and S. Mishra, "Cyberattack detection and classification in IIoT systems using XGBoost and Gaussian Naïve Bayes: A comparative study", *Engineering, Technology & Applied Science Research,* vol. 14, no. 4, pp. 15074-15082, 2024. [http://dx.doi.org/10.48084/etasr.7664]

[11] S. Bicen, and M. Celik, "A RAM extension to enhance ship planned maintenance system", *Aust. J. Marit. Ocean Aff.,* vol. 15, no. 3, pp. 357-376, 2023. [http://dx.doi.org/10.1080/18366503.2022.2075575]

[12] Brahimi, T. (2023). Data Mining and Visualization of Space Technology Research Trends in the Arab World. 2023 20th Learning and Technology Conference (L&T), 179-183.

[13] Y. Sano, and Y. Nakada, "Visualization for Potential Pass Courses and Quantification for Offensive and Defensive Players in Basketball", *2021 International Conference on Engineering and Emerging Technologies (ICEET),* pp. 1-6, 2021. [http://dx.doi.org/10.1109/ICEET53442.2021.9659701]

[14] L. Chen, H. Zhao, C. Shi, Y. Wu, X. Yu, W. Ren, Z. Zhang, and X. Shi, "Enhancing Multi-Modal Perception and Interaction: An Augmented Reality Visualization System for Complex Decision Making", *Systems (Basel),* vol. 12, no. 1, p. 7, 2023. [http://dx.doi.org/10.3390/systems12010007]

[15] T. Lin, C. Zhu-Tian, Y. Yang, D. Chiappalupi, J. Beyer, and H. Pfister, "The Quest for Omnioculars: Embedded Visualization for Augmenting Basketball Game Viewing Experiences", *IEEE Trans. Vis. Comput. Graph.,* vol. 29, no. 1, pp. 962-972, 2023. [http://dx.doi.org/10.1109/TVCG.2022.3209353] [PMID: 36155468]

[16] V. Gancheva, "Knowledge Discovery Based on Data Analytics and Visualization Supporting Precision Medicine", *2020 International Conference on Mathematics and Computers in Science and Engineering (MACISE),* pp. 102-105, 2020. [http://dx.doi.org/10.1109/MACISE49704.2020.00024]

CHAPTER 20

Bridging Logic and Data to Automated Reasoning for Big Data Analysis

Krishnan Batri[1,*] and **Ajay Chakravarty**[2]

[1] *School of Computer Science and Engineering, JAIN (Deemed-to-be University), Bangalore, Karnataka, India*

[2] *College of Computing Sciences & Information Technology, Teerthanker Mahaveer University, Moradaubad, Uttar Pradesh, India*

Abstract: The primary use of forecasting short-term loads is in control centres, where it is used to investigate shifting consumer load patterns and estimate the value of the load at a future time. It's a crucial piece of equipment for building a smart grid. Several dimensions of influence impact the load parameters. In this research, we present a Residual Neural Network (ResNet)/Long Short-Term Memory (LSTM) hybrid model for load forecasting, which can better take advantage of the time series properties of load data and lead to more reliable predictions. Before feeding the data into the ResNet network for the extraction of features, it is first rebuilt using numerous feature parameters. The second step in short-term load forecasting using LSTM is to feed the extractedfeaturevector into the network. Finally, the technique is compared to other models using a real example, demonstrating that the proposed combination method has better prediction accuracy and confirming the practicality and superiority of input featureextractionparameters. Additionally, this study conducts studies in weather prediction based on a variety of elements and characteristics

Keywords: Big Data Analysis, Automated Reasoning, LSTM, ResNet, smart grid.

INTRODUCTION

Big data analytics seeks to aid organizations in making better decisions by unearthing previously unseen trends, patterns, and insights within large datasets. Thanks to the rapid distribution of this data, businesses can maintain their competitive advantage more quickly and with greater agility.

Tools and systems such as business intelligence (BI) technology enable businesses to combine unstructured and structured data from many sources. In

* **Corresponding author Krishnan Batri:** School of Computer Science and Engineering, JAIN (Deemed-to-be University), Bangalore, Karnataka, India; E-mail krishnan.batri@jainuniversity.ac.in

S. Kannadhasan, R. Nagarajan, & Kaushik Pal (Eds.)

order to get insight into the inner workings and performance of a company, users (usually workers) submit queries to these tools. The four methods of data analysis are used in big data analytics to uncover useful information and arrive at workable conclusions. The practice of predicting the weather dates back to the eighteenth century [1, 2]. Weather forecasting is the study of atmospheric data such as temperature, irradiance, air pressure, wind speed and direction, humidity, and precipitation. Large amounts of information are needed for weather forecasting. Additionally, these records lack any kind of structure. Consequently, using meteorological data for weather forecasting is difficult due to the large number of variables involved. The often shifting weather conditions determine the range of these variables. It is important to take into account the unique properties of weather when proposing an algorithm for weather prediction, including its continuity, data intensity, multidimensionality, and chaotic behaviour [3, 4]. Originally performed by hand, weather forecasting is now a computer-based process that necessitates high-tech equipment [5, 6]. Many factors outside our control might influence our predictions. Season, location, quantity input information, weather classifications, lead time, and validity time are all factors that may affect the forecast accuracy [7, 8]. The term "big data" refers to large quantities of unstructured data in digital form [9]. Traditional methods of data management are neither practical nor easy for processing enormous data sets [10, 11]. To get meaningful insights from enormous data, we need an outstanding performance infrastructure and an applicable big data mining approach [9]. Exploring enormous data sets to uncover hidden patterns, new connections, and other useful information to aid decision-making is known as "big data analytics" [12]. The use of big data in weather forecasting has the potential to improve forecast quality [13]. Since precise predictions are essential, we may use big data analysis to improve our weather forecasts. Human forecasters were crucial to the process in the past. But in the modern age of information, we utilise data and technology to make predictions [14]. Atmospheric datasets include, but are not limited to, precipitation, humidity, air pressure, radiation, solar intensity, and data collection. We also need a large volume of data collected from many different sources (big data). To deal with this mountain of information, sophisticated hardware and software are needed [15, 16].

This investigation expands upon presentations made at the 9th International Symposium on Computation in the Cloud, Data Science, & Engineering (Confluence) [1], which laid the groundwork by applying Machine Learning Algorithms to Big Data Analytics. Predicting the weather is one of the most valuable applications of technology, allowing people to better prepare for everything from air travel and satellite launching to agricultural harvests and natural calamities. Four sorts of weather forecasts may be created, depending on how long they are expected to last: As Soon As Possible, a) Predictions are long-range forecasts often issued many days in advance. Long-term predictions go out months or even years, whereas short-term forecasts span only a few days or weeks [17 - 20]. In the beginning, forecasters compiled data from several weather stations and used statistical analysis to predict the weather. As ML methods gain in popularity and scope of application, faster processors become more widely available, and improved tools and methodology are introduced, researchers are starting to experiment with machine learning (ML) techniques in the field of meteorology, but it has stalled for a long time due to the descent of gradients problem and computer slowness. Technological advancements such as parallel processing, high-speed computer clusters, and graphics processors have enabled significant performance gains when applied to NNs. Recurrent neural networks (RNNs) are vulnerable to the Vanishing Gradient Problem due to their feedback connections. Gated RNNs, such as LSTM (Long Short-Term Memory neural networks, a term initially suggested by Schmidhuber and Hochreiter in 1997), produce gradients that neither grow nor shrink over time, therefore mitigating the aforementioned issue. They consist of one memory unit, a trio of gates (input, output, & forget), and a function that decides which data is saved, sent, and forgotten. Gradient-flowing paths may be built using forget-gate-controlled conditional weight self-loops in a long short-term memory network [2]. Its proficiency in learning causal relationships has made it a favourite in the text-sequencing industry [21 - 23].

RELATED WORKS

In this section, we review previous work on applying NN to the problem of weather prediction. Studies of the various Data Mining algorithms currently used for weather forecasting have identified potential pitfalls in applying more traditional data mining techniques [4]. Using a five-layer Deep NN and a four-layer Stacked Auto-Encoding mechanism to learn features from raw data, with SVR for prediction, the authors [5] examined 30 years of Hong Kong meteorological data. Several measures have been used in the review process, including Normalized Mean Squared Error (NMSE), R-squared, and Directional Symmetry (DS). Following the steps outlined in a study [6], we used a three-layer BPNN model to detect and analyze non-linear correlations in the normalized weather data that we obtained from www.weatherunderground.com. To develop a practical inference procedure, the authors studied IGRA data from 60 locations. The highest-quality validation results were achieved with two-layer RBMs containing either 50 or 150 hidden neurons. Using CNNs for the first time, the authors of [8] were able to better predict Australia's monthly rainfall than both the Bureau of Meteorology's model and an MLP on days with above-average annual rainfall. Researchers have also proposed using hybrid genetic algorithms (CFPS-HGA) based on climate factors and neural network parameters of choice to fine-tune these networks [9]. A team of researchers used RNNs, CRBMs, and Convolutional Networks [10] to examine meteorological data collected by BKMG (1973-2009) and ENSO data collected by NOAA. In a study [11], a recurrent NN called NARX NN (Nonlinear Auto Regression with exogenous variables) was utilised to surpass Case-Based Reasoning (CBR) in weather prediction over a wide range of factors. A novel layer called the Dynamic Convolutional layer was constructed by the researchers [12] to anticipate the succession of rain radar pictures. They used the Caffe framework and the Stochastic Gradient Descent optimizer. This layer not only reused the feature map from the prior one, but it also filtered the features. Deeper neural NN and shallow NN are evaluated in terms of their short-term prediction abilities in [13]. The results showed that NNs underperformed 3-layer stacked automated encoders when the parameters were reduced using a PMI (Partial Mutual Awareness)- oriented IVS technique. The authors of [14] proposed a Deep Multilayer Perceptron system trained using Cascade learning to use H1-B Visa application information and a cardiac dataset. The findings showed that the model was more accurate and took less time to train than the competitors. For meteorological data collected from the Underground website between 2007 and 2014, the authors of [15] developed a 2-layer stacked LSTM model (with a separate LSTM model for each location within each layer). The authors evaluated the ARIMA equation with LSTM (weather variables incorporated) using data from 2012-2016 from Weather Underground and found that LSTM performed better. In their demonstration of wind prediction using deep LSTMs, the authors present results from the Manchester Wind Farms for 2010 and 2011. They propose an approach that surpasses both BPNN and SVM. The model with three hidden layers, each with 300, 500, and 200 neurons, achieved top performance. In order to forecast the weather for the following two days and three weeks, a multi-stacked LSTM was used to examine fifteen years' worth of hourly data for nine Moroccan locations. Forward filling was utilised to replace missing data, and the RMSProp algorithm was used to find the best solution.

- Agriculture/Food With a growing population comes an obvious increase in the need for manufactured food. The quality of agricultural production might be enhanced by using weather forecasting & big data analysis in this area. Farmers may use weather forecasts to be ready for potential problems, including soil erosion, overwatering, and drought. Accurate precipitation projections allow farmers to make better decisions regarding their crops and the cost of food. Predicting the weather might help grocery stores better manage their inventory.

Going to a new place and staying there for a while is called "tourism" when one is not normally doing so for reasons such as leisure, business, education, socializing, or conferences. When deciding where to go on vacation, the weather is by far the most important factor. And therefore, climate change may have an impact on the location itself. Therefore, accurate weather forecasting is crucial for travellers' comfort and security, as well as for their intended destinations. Benefits to this sector may also be calculated using weather forecasting

An industry is a group of businesses that work together to produce a certain product or deliver a specific service. A firm or group's primary revenue stream will determine its industry classification.

All four elements heat, wind, humidity, and precipitation—can damage buildings. As a result, accurate weather predictions are crucial for safeguarding people, projects, and materials from the effects of bad weather. To rephrase, the sooner potential weather hazards are recognised, the earlier we can make preparations to deal with them. As a result, accurate weather predictions contribute to cost savings and worker safety.

Companies that rely on good weather hire weather forecasters because of the dangers posed by lightning to golfers and by wind that may drastically change the outcome of a sailing competition. If it looks like rain, you may plan when to cover the courts.

Shipping firms and their crews worldwide depend on weather forecasts to detect approaching storms and plan their voyages accordingly. It is also possible to prevent delays or cancellations of battle plans due to adverse weather by consulting predictions.

PROPOSED WORK

Residual Network

Accuracy suffers when shallow networks are layered directly on top of deep ones, since it is harder to fully leverage the deep systems' superior feature-extraction capabilities. ResNet was created as a solution to this problem. ResNet is a neural network that incorporates a residual block, fast training through the Batch Normalisation approach, and a super-deep network portion that exceeds 1000 layers. With these characteristics, we can handle the issues of a decreasing, vanishing, or rising gradient. When backpropagation reaches the vanishing gradient, which happens when the error gradients at each layer are less than 1, the gradient converges to 0. A phenomenon similar to the expanding gradient occurs when the angle of error in each layer exceeds 1; additionally, the gradient increases with increasing network depth.

Residual Block

To address the issue of deterioration, ResNet, a deep neural network design, uses the residual block. Cascaded convolution layers plus a shortcut connection (sometimes called residual mappings or identification mapping) make up the residual block. After all the block's inputs have been processed using the ReLU activation function, the block's output is the result. The input (X), weight layers (convolution procedures), residual mappings (F(x)), and output (H(x)) are graphically shown in Figure 1. As the translation relationship between all three variables in issue, H(x) = F(x) + X, may be shown. The connection between X and the final result of the residual network (1) is open. In this step, the network will stop trying to figure out the best mapping function on its own and instead focus on figuring out its residual, demonstrating equation (2): F (x) = H (x) X. (2) If the network is functioning correctly at the moment, there is no need to stop developing it. Theoretically, the network's efficacy should not decrease with increasing depth if the remainder mappings approach zero, which is the case when F(x) = 0. Therefore, H(x) == X under these conditions. The right mapping H(x) may be approximated by X if and only if F (x) = 0. This addresses the problem of gradient deterioration in multilayer networks. There are five different ResNet network architectures, each with its own set of layers: ResNet18, ResNet34, ResNet50, ResNet101, and ResNet152. Convolutional residual fragment variations include ResNet50, ResNet101, and ResNet152. Two-layer convolution employs ResNet18 and ResNet34. The implementation differences between the different scrap chunks will also be glossed over.

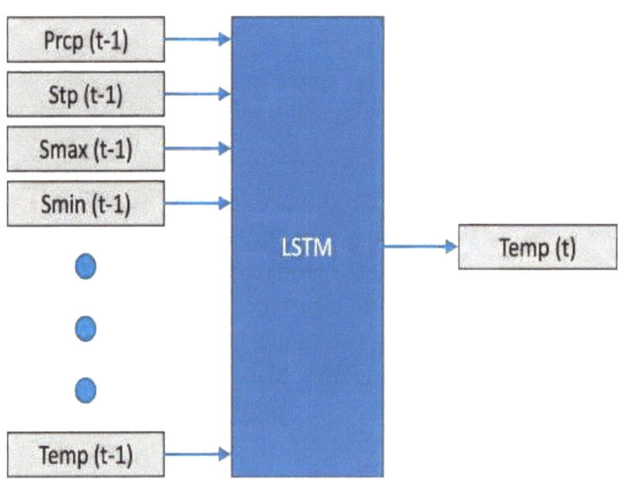

Fig. (1). Architecture of the LSTM network.

A PROCESS FOR GENERALLY NORMALISING INFORMATION: This method for batch standardized processing ensures that data inside a batch follows a standard distribution having a mean of zero and a variance of one. To speed up convergence and enhance accuracy, we conduct this operation between each conjunction as well as the excitation function to ensure that the input value passes through the sensitive region of the activation function. For a sample size of 2, the batch normalisation approach yields a mean of B and a variance of 2 B. A pair of feature matrix data, Feature 1 and Feature 2, is generated through convolving and pooling Images 1 and 2:

Where x (1) is all batch feature information from Channel 1. Similarly, all the features included in the Channel 2 data for the batch are represented by x(2). Two vectors are obtained by calculating equations (4) & (5) in terms of the average B variance 2 B of x (1) & x (2). Then, using equation (6) (in which is a minor parameter that stops the denominator from going zero), we can determine each channel's norm deviation. In addition, in a study (7), the mean and standard deviation of the data are both determined by two independent variables. The neural network learns these two parameters during back-propagation, enabling it to possibly select the optimal distribution while still in the training phase. While 1 is the default, 0 is the default.

LSTM NETWORK

The RNN was developed to address the inherent long-term dependencies in time-series problems. The architecture of LSTM is shown in Figure 1. RNN has been shown to work successfully in real-world settings, including this problem. Multiple experiments also show that the gradient disappears during standard RNN training and then increases thereafter. Hochreiter presented LSTM, an enhanced RNN, as a solution to this issue. LSTM employs a long-term memory component to preserve data transmission. Omission barriers, input barriers, & output gates make up the LSTM's fundamental structure. Coupling the input xt with the state memory unit's C(t1) as well as the intermediate output's h(t1) determines the forgetting section of the store memory modules all at once. This function is used in the gates for the input to the state memory module to compute the reserve vector, along with the Gaussian and tanh functions. Using the revised values for Ct and ot, a new intermediate result, ht, may be determined.

The ResNet-LSTM Framework. Based on the ResNet from before, we combined the LSTM time-series data feature-learning unit to present the ResNet-LSTM model. The model employs the Resnet18 network, which is broken down into the five nodes: Conv1, Conv2_x, Conv3_x, Conv4_x, & Conv5_x. Conv1 both convolves and max-pools the input. Only two of the original four blocks are still standing. Each residual block in the model is a convolution network with a few layers, and the model utilises the advantages of the Resnet18 network. The residual block is divided into two halves, and their combined feature matrices are subjected to the activation rule. The ResNet was given data in the form (None, 56, 1), where 56 is the total number of features, and 1 is the number of channels. Convolution kernels range in size from 32 to 256 in the various sections. The standard size of a kernel of convolution is 3. The concept is made easier to understand by using a bigger pool. The pool has two risers and three lanes. The retrieved features are then passed on to the neural network using LSTM via ResNet in the form of a three-dimensional (None, two-dimensional, 256-dimensional) vector. It is possible to immediately combine the main division and the short connecting sector (one line of residual structure) into the remaining block if the beginning characteristics matrix and the characteristics matrix of the final output are of the same shape. When a dotted residue wedge indicates that there is a difference between the characteristics of the inputs and the result matrices. The short-linked branch is subjected to a convolution phase that uses a stride of 2 before it is fused with the main branch. This is done to guarantee that the traits matrix regarding the short connected branch matches that of the primary branch. The incorporation of an LSTM network into the equation improved forecast accuracy, as shown by the experiments. In the final representation, the LSTM network is applied at two levels, resulting in 1,024,256 nodes. Dropout between layers may be used to prevent overfitting in LSTM networks. Finally, the predicted load quantity is produced twice using Dense. The first layer has 64 neurons, whereas the second has just 1.

RESULTS AND DISCUSSION

The Queensland, Australia, government made available, from January 1, 2006, to December 31, 2010, an online load data collection used in this study. This dataset has a massive 87649 rows of information, with a 30-minute sample period and 48 daily data points. Table 1 displays the five feature characteristics together with the load, clean-bulb temperatures (drybt), and dew point temperature (dewpt). Wetness, condensation, and the associated expenses. The initial four years of data are used for training, the first half of 2010's data for validation, and the most recent month for testing. The feature parameters are shown in Table 2. The proposed experiment uses a computer with 1 TB of storage, 16GB of RAM, & a 1.8 GHz processor. This dataset has 31 features and has 9.7 million (9,779,168) records. After importing everything into a Spark dataframe, we first exclude everything except 15 attributes (wsnm, wsid, elvt, lat, lon, inme, city, prov, mdct, date, yr, mo, da, hr, tmax, tmin).

Table 1. Parameter description of the proposed work.

Type	Name	Detailed description
Date	Data time	Sampling interval 30mins
Weather factors	Dry-bulb temperature °C	The true thermodynamic temperature of the measured air.
	Dew point temperature °C	The temperature at which water vapor and water reach equilibrium.
	Wet-bulb temperature °C	The thermodynamic adiabatic saturation temperature.
	Humidity °C	Indicates the degree of atmospheric dryness in the air
Economic factor	Price °C	Price of °C
Power load	Load(MW)	Power generation per unit time under rated conditions

Table 2. Attributes for weather prediction.

Attribute	Description
Prcp	Amount of precipitation in millimeters (last hour).
Stp	Air pressure for the hour in hPa to tenths (instant).
Smax	Maximum air pressure for the last hour in hPa to tenths.
Smin	Minimum air pressure for the last hour in hPa to Tenths.
Gbrd	Solar radiation KJ/m2
Temp	Instant Air Temperature (Celsius degrees)
Dewp	Instant Dew Point (Celsius degrees)
Dmax	Maximum Dew Point (Celsius degrees)
Dmin	Minimum Dew Point Temperature (Celsius degrees)
Hmdy	Relative Humidity of Air (%
Hmax	Maximum Relative Air Humidity (%)
Hmin	Minimum Relative Air Humidity (%)
Wdsp	Instant Wind Speed (meters per second)
Wdct	Wind direction in radius degrees (0-360)
Gust	Wind Gust Intensity (meters per second)

The inhabitants' work and leisure habits also contribute to the change. Because of this, we also use weekend and holiday data as features during training. There is a close relationship between the structure and frequency of time series and climatic conditions. Here, we examine and predict drybt and humidity. The hidden layer is shown in Table 3. Emotional data analysis. Due to communication errors or data loss, load information and meteorological conditions may have erroneous values. Eliminating inaccurate data from research and calculations is necessary to reduce the possibility of bias and improve the precision of predictions. Discrepancies in the data utilised in this study may be identified and addressed using a box diagram. Third, we will adjust the features' configurations. All data is transformed into time sequences using a variety of feature parameters to appropriately mine temporal features and couple each piece of data. Each reconstructed load value is linked to 56 characteristics such as location, price, vacation, holidays, sampling date, and load values from the prior 48 samples. The load vector has 8 + n items at each sample time, with a zero in the nth slot at t0 tn1. Starting at time t1, include the preceding sample point's load value into the feature vector. The weight at the tn sample point is affected by a wide variety of variables, such as the weather, pricing, holidays, weekdays, t, the demand at t0, the demand at t1, the demand at tn+2, etc. Similarly, by training a combination of ResNet-LSTM models on new data, one may forecast drybt, dewbt, wetbt, and humidity components. To reassemble the data, for example, we may examine the time-series characteristics of both the actual data and the projected variable, drybt.

Table 3. Hidden layer performance.

S. No	Number of hidden layers	Number of hidden units	Iterations	1 hour time lag		24 hour time lag	
				Runtime	MAE	Runtime	
1	1	10	100	0.015151	28041.47	0.041649	30256.38
2	1	20	100	0.015462	29292.39	0.041582	29889.34
3	1	30	100	0.015365	30854.15	0.042124	28289.06
4	2	10,10	100	0.015088	48892.43	0.040463	49878.65
5	2	20,20	100	0.015077	49898.42	0.040839	46737.57
6	2	30,30	100	0.015259	50805.43	0.040060	46829.74
7	2	10,20	100	0.015124	42302.25	0.040020	52487.23
8	3	10,10,10	100	0.015269	124915.8	0.040546	101543.68

The drybt input vectors (plus the nth point in the drybt series) have the same number of attributes as the load's input vector (dewbt, wetbt, humidity, load, expenditures, holiday, weekdays, and sample time). Zeros may be used to fill in any empty spaces in the vector. The value of n in this work is 48 as a decimal.

The sample points' feature vector may then be reconstructed in this fashion. Humidity, dryness, the dew point, and precipitation are the four main components of weather.

Since the Eigenvector is 0 from t0 to t47, this time period is disregarded. The fourth principle is the standardising of data. Features' parameters may span a broad spectrum, both qualitatively and quantitatively. The significance of the second and third-order data will not be diminished by standardised training. The experimental data set, denoted as x, undergoes a linear transformation utilising Min-Max Scales with a constraint range of [0, 1]. The normalised publish-value is found by using the formula x = x xmin xmax xmin (18), where x is the highest value in the sample data and xmin is the lowest.

B. Details of the Experiment Workstation hardware, including an Intel(R) Core(TM) i7-9750h CPU and an NVIDIA Quadro GPU running TensorFlow-GPU2.6.2, Keras as 2.6.0, CUDA11.6, and cuDNN8.3.2. The Keras framework, built on top of TensorFlow, is the heart of the software. Keras's consistent and easy-to-use API is only one of the many advantages of its modular architecture. The model error is shown in Table 4. It also allows for model flexibility, which aids in learning neural network structure and reduces the need for iterative human coding. The Adam optimizer is used to train the MSE loss function.

Table 4. Model error comparison for data on Dec.1, 2010.

Model	MAPE	RMSE	MAE
ML.R	0.645	67.980	50.862
LSTM	0.798	88.504	59.246
CNN	0.696	83.036	61.442
ResNet	0.692	70.137	58.416
CNN-LSTM	0.939	101.998	77.085
ResNet-LSTM	0.607	61.095	49.910

With LSTM serving as the reference model, the experimental parameters are optimized using the control variable technique. Multiple linear regressions (MLRs), convolutional neural networks (CNNs), long short-term memory (LSTM) networks, and recurrent neural networks (ResNets) are some of the models we compare to the proposed model for short-term load forecasting. The three models each provide forecasts for the first, second, and seventh of December 2010. As of December 1, 2010, the evaluation indicators for all models are shown in Table 4. When contrasted to other models, ResNet-LSTM scores the lowest on all three evaluation measures. The overall MAPE decline was 38%, followed by decreases of 30%, 13%, 12%, and 35%. The RMSE decreased by 10.13 percentage points, 30.97%, 26.42%, 12.89%, and 40.10%. The results of the models' forecasts for the first and second of December, 2010, are shown in Table 5. The MAPE changed by (-) 20.35, (-25.16), (-20.58), (-12.96), and (-) 36.7%. The RMSE was found to be decreased at the 25%, 34%, 31.69%, 28.56%, 15.38%, and 30.86% marks.

Table 5. Various model performance.

Model	MAPE	RMSE	MAE
MLR	0.708	78.431	60.426
LSTM	0.763	85.714	62.684
CNN	0.719	82.949	61.442
ResNet	0.656	69.198	55.997
CNN-LSTM	0.903	95.769	74.246
ResNet-LSTM	0.571	58.554	47.031

Table **6** displays the projection indicators used to evaluate each model from 1 to 7 December 2010. The MAPEV decline was as follows: 22.36%, 27.37%, 26.75%, 20.72%, and 28.07%. The RMSE was subsequently reduced by 25.35%, 29.61%, 27.24%, 20.99%, and 29.50%, respectively. The indicators for evaluating ResNet-LSTM models are consistent with the straightforward, well-designed MLR method. Because linear regression assumes that data change linearly, an MLR model's assessment index increases as more data are provided. ResNet-LSTM offers a lower assessment index than competing neural network models. Thus, its ResNet-LSTM frameworks outperform other methods. Table 6 displays the APE load on many models across all sample locations on December 1st, 2010. The APE in the area was reduced by 100 to make the data easier to read. Load forecasting for 48 sample locations on December 1, 2010, yielded average prediction errors (APEs) of 24.41, 27.56, 31.35, 28.04, 37, and 23.96, respectively. The load prediction diagram for each model for December 1, 2010, November 1-2, 2010, and December 1-7, 2010.

Table 6. Model performance of the proposed work.

Model	MAPE	RMSE	MAE
MLR	0.769	84.307	69.938
LSTM	0.822	89.396	65.982
CNN	0.815	86.494	67.747
ResNet	0.753	79.653	62.488

(Table 6) cont.....

Model	MAPE	RMSE	MAE
CNN-LSTM	0.830	89.264	69.501
ResNet-LSTM	0.597	62.933	49.301

Floating point operations (FLOPs) and the number of parameters are two common ways in which the complexity of models using deep learning is quantified. The ResNet-LSTM model uses a total of 19 convolution kernel parameters. k = K * 2 * Cin + 1.

Indicator = K 2 Cin the number of convolution layer variables is given by Cout + Cout (20). Here, H, W, and Cin denote the input map's attribute streams' length, height, and number of channels, respectively; K denotes the kernel's extent; and Cout denotes the output map's number of channels. Table 6 displays the final FLOPs and parameters for many neural network models. You can see how long each model took to complete in Table 6. Here you may find the first two days of December, in addition to the first two days and the seventh of December. Table 6 demonstrates that the ResNet-LSTM model can predict daily load in about 30 seconds, even though it has more training parameters and FLOPs than competing models. This study's ResNet-LSTM model is a powerful tool for accurate short-term load prediction.

CONCLUSION

This study proposes a ResNet-LSTM combination model to address the growing need for accurate short-term load forecasts in electric systems, leveraging ResNet's feature extraction ability to derive effective attributes and the LSTM network's processing of temporal relationships. The conclusion is as follows: 1) Using the characteristics of historical data and the time sequencing feature of load, the original data from Queensland, Australia, was reconstructed. Features include things like date variables, weather elements, economic variables, and load statistics from the last 48 sample instances. The ResNet-LSTM model reported in this research leverages ResNet's feature extraction advantages over other machine learning models. This technique not only better suits the time and the complex nonlinear connections, but also uncovers the probable temporal manifestations of authority load data. Compared to other methods for anticipating short-term loads, the model performs better in experiments. Finally, all meteorological variables exhibit time-series characteristics and periodicity. An experimental comparative study of dry-bulb temperatures and humidity demonstrates the efficiency of the ResNet-LSTM system for processing time series weather data. For researchers interested in learning more about how to enhance the accuracy of load forecasting across a wide range of smart grid applications, the present paper not only proposes a unified approach for swift load prediction with multifaceted input factors but also reinstates the data.

REFERENCES

[1] H.H. Guedea-Noriega, and F. García-Sánchez, "Semantic (Big) Data Analysis: an Extensive Literature Review", *Rev. IEEE Am. Lat.,* vol. 17, no. 5, pp. 796-806, 2019. [http://dx.doi.org/10.1109/TLA.2019.8891948]

[2] H. Sebei, M. A. H. Taieb, and M. Ben Aouicha, "SNOWL: Social networks unification-based semantic data integration", *Knowledge and Information Systems,* vol. 62, pp. 4297-4336, 2020. [http://dx.doi.org/10.1007/s10115-020-01486-3]

[3] E.P. Xing, "Toward personalized pan-omic association analysis under complex structures and big data", 2015 IEEE International Conference on Bioinformatics and Biomedicine (BIBM), Washington, DC, USA, 2015, pp. 4-4. [http://dx.doi.org/10.1109/BIBM.2015.7359647]

[4] J. Yang, L.T. Yang, Y. Gao, H. Liu, H. Wang, and X. Xie, "Tensor-Based Knowledge Fusion and Reasoning for Cyberphysical-Social Systems: Theory and Framework", *IEEE Syst. Man. Cybern. Mag.,* vol. 8, no. 2, pp. 31-38, 2022. [http://dx.doi.org/10.1109/MSMC.2021.3114538]

[5] K. Sasai, R. Fukutani, G. Kitagata, and T. Kinoshita, "Multiagent-Based Data Presentation Mechanism for Multifaceted Analysis in Network Management Tasks", *Sensors (Basel),* vol. 22, no. 22, p. 8841, 2022. [http://dx.doi.org/10.3390/s22228841] [PMID: 36433437]

[6] B. Li, "Design of early warning system for mental health problems based on data mining and database", *Rev. Bras. Med. Esporte,* vol. 29, p. e2022_0153, 2023. [http://dx.doi.org/10.1590/1517-8692202329012022_0153]

[7] S. R. Mounce, A. Fargus, M. Weeks, J. Young, D. Ejimbe, E. Goya, M. Holburn, T. Jackson, & J. B. Boxall, "An online advanced uncertain reasoning architecture with a binomial event discriminator for novelty detection in smart water networks", *Environmental Modelling & Software,* vol. 91, pp. 1-11, 2017. [http://dx.doi.org/10.1016/j.envsoft.2017.01.015]

[8] A. Suominen, and H. Toivanen, "Map of science with topic modeling: Comparison of unsupervised learning and human-assigned subject classification", *J. Assoc. Inf. Sci. Technol.,* vol. 67, no. 10, pp. 2464-2476, 2016. [http://dx.doi.org/10.1002/asi.23596]

[9] R. Benjamins, M. d'Aquin, and A. S. Gordon, Proceedings of the 7th International Conference on Knowledge Capture (K-CAP 2013). New York, NY, USA: Association for Computing Machinery (ACM), 2013. [http://dx.doi.org/10.1145/2479832]

[10] M.G. Vos, W.R. Hage, J. Wielemaker, and G. Schreiber, "Knowledge representation in scientific models and theirpublications: a case study", *Proceedings of the seventh international conference on Knowledge capture,* 2013. [http://dx.doi.org/10.1145/2479832.2479850]

[11] J. Yu, X. Luan, and Y. Sun, *An Automated Analytics Engine for College Program Selection using Machine Learning and Big Data Analysis.* Advances in Machine Learning, Data Mining and Computing, 2021. [http://dx.doi.org/10.5121/csit.2021.111417]

[12] S. Chen and S. Yang, "A web services, ontology and big data analysis technology-based cloud case-based reasoning agent for energy conservation of sustainability science", *Applied Sciences,* vol. 10, no.

21, p. 7729, 2020.
[http://dx.doi.org/10.3390/app10217729]

[13] P.R. Kumar, *Analysis of Big Data and Cloud Services with Experimental of Manually and Automated Testing.,* 2022.

[14] D. Zhang, "High-speed Train Control System Big Data Analysis Based on the Fuzzy RDF model and Uncertain Reasoning", *Int. J. Comput. Commun. Control,* vol. 12, no. 4, pp. 577-591, 2017.
[http://dx.doi.org/10.15837/ijccc.2017.4.2914]

[15] J.E. Smith, and N. Pinter-Wollman, "Observing the unwatchable: Integrating automated sensing, naturalistic observations, and animal social network analysis in the age of big data", *J. Anim. Ecol.,* 2020.
[PMID: 33020914]

[16] M. Koot, M.R.K. Mes, and M.E. Iacob, "A systematic literature review of supply chain decision making supported by the Internet of Things and Big Data Analytics", *Comput. Ind. Eng.,* vol. 154, p. 107076, 2021.
[http://dx.doi.org/10.1016/j.cie.2020.107076]

[17] L. He, M. Xue, and B. Gu, "Internet-of-things enabled supply chain planning and coordination with big data services: Certain theoretic implications", *Journal of Management Science and Engineering,* vol. 5, no. 1, pp. 1-22, 2020.
[http://dx.doi.org/10.1016/j.jmse.2020.03.002]

[18] L. Wang, and Y. Wang, "Supply chain financial service management system based on block chain IoT data sharing and edge computing", *Alex. Eng. J.,* vol. 61, no. 1, pp. 147-158, 2022.
[http://dx.doi.org/10.1016/j.aej.2021.04.079]

[19] Y. Kazancoglu, M. Ozbiltekin-Pala, M.D. Sezer, A. Kumar, and S. Luthra, "Circular dairy supply chain management through Internet of Things-enabled technologies", *Environ. Sci. Pollut. Res. Int.,* vol. •••, pp. 1-13, 2022.
[http://dx.doi.org/10.1007/s11356-021-17697-8] [PMID: 34988786]

[20] A. Sharma, J. Kaur, and I. Singh, "Internet of Things (IoT) in pharmaceutical manufacturing, warehousing, and supply chain management", *SN Computer Science,* vol. 1, no. 4, p. 232, 2020.
[http://dx.doi.org/10.1007/s42979-020-00248-2]

[21] A.K. Jha, M.A.N. Agi, and E.W.T. Ngai, "A note on big data analytics capability development in supply chain", *Decis. Support Syst.,* vol. 138, p. 113382, 2020.
[http://dx.doi.org/10.1016/j.dss.2020.113382]

[22] J.L. Hung, W. He, and J. Shen, "Big data analytics for supply chain relationship in banking", *Ind. Mark. Manage.,* vol. 86, pp. 144-153, 2020.
[http://dx.doi.org/10.1016/j.indmarman.2019.11.001]

[23] W. Yu, C.Y. Wong, R. Chavez, and M.A. Jacobs, "Integrating big data analytics into supply chain finance: The roles of information processing and data-driven culture", *Int. J. Prod. Econ.,* vol. 236, p. 108135, 2021.
[http://dx.doi.org/10.1016/j.ijpe.2021.108135]

CHAPTER 21

Investigating the Benefits of Text Mining for Information Analysis

S. Senthilkumar[1,*] and **M. Veera Nagaiah**[2]

[1] *Department of Computer Science and Engineering, Presidency University, Bangalore, Karnataka, India*

[2] *Department of Computer Applications, Presidency College, Bangalore, Karnataka, India*

Abstract: Thanks to advancements in educational technology, new approaches to controlling and understanding the teaching-learning processes have arisen, such as instructional analytics (TA). Instructional analytics is a new yet exciting approach to learning that has the potential to dramatically improve teaching quality and student outcomes by helping educational institutions better use the massive volumes of information generated from student data. This study offered a framework for educational process data mining with artificial intelligence (EPDM+ML) that uses student evaluation of teaching (SET) data to contextually evaluate teachers' performances and provide recommendations. The EPDM+ML model was created and implemented using a mix of text mining and artificial intelligence (AI) technology. It is based on descriptive decision theory, which examines why learners tend to make choices through quantitative analysis of textual data. To this end, the study considers instructors' gender while analyzing the pedagogical elements that influence students' suggestions for their professors and the effect of students' subjective experiences on their assessments of instructors. Predicting a student's potential recommendation for a teacher is conceivable with SET data such as students' gender, average mood, and emotional valence. In actuality, we mined text for the different sentiments and emotions (comment intensities) that students conveyed in the SET. Then, we used a Kruskal-Wallis test to determine which elements were the most important by analyzing the covariance using the quantitative data (average emotions and emotional valence). Furthermore, we examined the gender conceptions to see whether there were any differences in the suggestions students made for instructors. Taking into account both the mood and the sentiments expressed in the comments, we find that most (n=85,378) were positive in tone, while a sizeable portion was neutral. Female students were more likely than male students to propose that teachers take into account students' emotions in statements with an emotional valence (11.8%) and opinions (23.6% positive and negative) (p=.000). Men, on the other hand, exhibit borderline behavior in terms of sentiment (p=.077) and emotions (p=.056). The EPDM+ML model was also validated using the k-fold cross-validation method, with 63.6% of the optimal k-values observed, and it proved to be an efficient and effective predictor of students' recommendation scores for teachers, with high and acceptable values of precision (1.00), recall (1.00),

[*] **Corresponding author S. Senthilkumar:** Department of Computer Science and Engineering, Presidency University, Bangalore, Karnataka, India; E-mail: senthilkumars@presidencyuniversity.in

S. Kannadhasan, R. Nagarajan, & Kaushik Pal (Eds.)

specifcity (1.00), accuracy (1.00), F1-score (1.00), and zero error-rate (0.00). Theoretically, we find that the suggested approach (EPDM+ML) is helpful for effective examination of SET and its consequences in the field of education. There is a growing need to improve teaching and learning processes and students' learning experiences in an ever-evolving educational ecosystem. However, this can be done by identifying the most important factors that students use to evaluate and recommend teachers.

Keywords: Text mining, information analysis, teaching analytics, students' evaluation.

INTRODUCTION

Methods based on artificial intelligence (AI) have recently emerged as potent instruments for revolutionizing healthcare. Despite the impressive effectiveness of neural network classifiers (MLCs) in image-based diagnosis, analyzing vast amounts of EHR data is still a challenge [1]. Algorithmic law is a relatively new field of law that focuses on the automation of legal reasoning. New approaches based on artificial intelligence (AI) have the potential to revolutionize healthcare. Analysis of varied as well as enormous EHR data is still difficult, even if neural network classifiers have been effective in image-based diagnosis [2]. The study and documentation of computational legal argumentation is a relatively new area of study within the larger field of law.

An important aspect of creating Machine Learning algorithms is the input pipeline, which typically takes in information and processes it in some way. Thoughts on synchronicity, heterogeneity in fine-grained profiling data, and parallelism make effective input pipeline implementation difficult [3]. With applications such as reasoning monitors, decision summarizers, contention recommendations, and semantic viewers, mining trends in reasoning from evidence-intensive legal decisions can enhance the efficiency of legal services and broaden public access to justice. Automating the classification of phrases stating whether the prerequisites of relevant law have been met in a given legal case is a significant task for these use cases [4]. Text analysis, particularly in the malware realm, is a difficult task. Even when using a natural language processing technique to extract malware-related entities from unstructured information, such as text, there are limitations due to the lack of a specific Named Entity recognizer. We must automate the extraction of data from text, including Ransomware entities. This data could then be used for knowledge reasoning purposes, such as profiling Ransomware behavior using publicly accessible online information. The data analysis and extraction procedures are not without their difficulties when dealing with informal, unstructured content, such as that found in online forums [5]. Creating systems of control for autonomous manufacturing operations that can handle data integration, semantic interoperability, monitoring, and decision-making is a major challenge for the development of Industry 4.0 applications [6]. Automatic language analysis has recently shown promise as a tool for the diagnosis of moderate cognitive impairment (MCI). The majority of research on MCI prediction using a combination of linguistic processing and artificial intelligence has examined only one language task [7].

RELATED WORKS

For technological forensic systems that involve collaborative criminal analysis and prediction, we have developed an Automatic Learning Framework ontology. Execution of Automated Machine Learning (AutoML) is also performed based on the minimal viable ontology. This implementation will be evaluated both quantitatively and qualitatively to assess its effectiveness in helping investigative agencies represent, reason, and extract useful information from the diverse and extensive datasets they collect. By comparing our proposed generic Smart Forensic Framework with existing systems using qualitative and quantitative metrics, we can determine its performance in Digital Forensics applications. To encourage forensic intelligence organizations to utilize the features and capabilities of the AutoML Smart Forensic Framework, we will present insights along with performance indicators gathered in our study [8].

Here, we examine how using one's own memories can enhance facial behavior analysis. Automated facial recognition and two forms of contextual information are combined in a set of multisensory neural network trials we run to make emotional predictions about video viewers: Start counting using Arabic symbols. List the audiovisual content of a video and the reported free-text description of memories that are generated by it. Our findings show that, in addition to face analysis, both types of background offer a model for understanding the variability in viewers' emotional reactions [9].

Using a methodology known as computational grounded theory, we rigorously assessed students' written claims on the likelihood of opposing chemical reactions in this research. Our goal when applying an unsupervised clustering approach was to thoroughly assess the logic patterns as well as the granularity levels used by students in their written reports by evaluating their argumentation patterns. We combined data-driven clustering with a theory-driven architecture to automate the analysis of observed argument patterns, and a comprehensive 20-category rubric was developed based on this research. The use of state-of-the-art deep learning methods to assess the complexity of students' arguments was supported by almost perfect agreement between machine and human scores and by easily interpretable findings from pre-trained big language models coupled with deep neural networks. The results show how to locate textual arguments by integrating human as well as electronic analysis [10].

We found that a large percentage of model training operations could benefit from faster input data pipelines after analyzing over 2 million ML workloads in Google data centers. Also, the majority of operations do not overwhelm the host hardware; the bottlenecks are likely software-related, according to our investigation. In light of these results, we provide the plumber, an instrument for locating ML input pipeline bottlenecks. Plumber automatically tunes parallelism, prefetching, and caching within host resource constraints using an extendable, comprehensible operational analytical model. Plumber achieves speedups of up to 47x for misconfigured pipelines across five sample ML pipelines. Plumber achieves end-to-end speedups of more than 50% compared to cutting-edge tuners [11] through automated caching.

We contrast these findings with the efficiency of conventional ML algorithms trained and evaluated on a larger dataset (about 5,800 labelled phrases), although this dataset is still considered tiny compared to what is typical in ML. It seems that several access-to-justice use cases may be satisfactorily covered at a far lower cost than previously thought, according to this technique and these test findings. The datasets, scripts, ML programs, and conventions needed to determine sentence categories will all be made freely accessible. ACM Vern R. Walker, Krishnan Pillaipakkamnatt, Alex M. Davidson, Marysa Linares, and Domenick J. Pesce are the authors of the reference format. The year was 2019. An Analysis of Rules-based Scripts and Machine Learning for Automatic Rhetorical Role Identification in Phrases. Montreal, QC, Canada, 10 pages, in ASAIL 2019: Third Workshop on Automatic Semantic Evaluation of Knowledge in Legal Text [12].

This research compares the performance of several supervised learning methods for training models to extract Malware items from unstructured text, including CRF, Naive Bayes, and Support Vector Machines [13].

This study presents a new taxonomy for categorizing process-induced flaws identified in previous research on the production of metal additives. We include state-of-the-art ontologies in our understanding base, along with official explanations of the defining characteristics and fault causes. With the addition of more diagnostic, inference, and defect analysis terms, the knowledge we have aims to improve the modeling capabilities of additive manufacturing ontologies [14].

Determining the likelihood of Roman colonies within the research region is the primary purpose of the current study. First, we created a probability map showing the likelihood of locating a Roman site at various locations; second, we ranked the geo-environmental factors that affect the presence of archaeological sites. Both for confirming the data's dependability and for inspiring specialists in many ways, the results included in our findings are of utmost relevance. These findings also aid in assessing the pros and cons of employing such novel approaches and, in the long run, provide insight into how well machine-learning-based algorithms handle archeological data [15].

PROPOSED WORK

An overview of the EPDM+ML algorithm's primary components for implementing the approach is given in this article. There are two stages to the description of the design and execution of the EPDM+ML architecture. To begin, we used the primary features of the EPDM models to examine the student's SET remarks (written data) and infer and measure the overall feelings and sentiment ratings for each remark. In preparation for text mining and model deployment, the dataset was cleaned and filtered. To understand the extent to which students' comments, or the degree to which the sentiment/emotions they conveyed, were impacted, text analysis or written information quantification was carried out using suitable data mining tools, packages, and libraries. To be more technical, we analyzed the data using the R statistical programming language, an IDE that supports data mining techniques and methodologies such as sentiment analysis, sentiment evaluation, pander, *etc*. Consequently, we accounted for the impact and significant differences in students' recommendations of teachers by gender, and we used quantifiable results (*i.e*., average sentiment and emotional valence) to contrast them with the quantitative indicators and data provided by the SET instrument.

RESULT AND DISCUSSION

One motivation for using KG is to address sparsity, which often limits the flexibility of recommendation systems. Building optimal representations for passive consumers with little interaction is difficult. In this article, we investigate whether using connection information can help resolve this issue. To do this, we conduct experiments on user groups that are sparse in different ways. We aim to keep the median number of interactions across all groups constant and split the set of tests into four groups based on the median number of contacts per user. Generally speaking, DKG outperforms the competition, especially in the two user communities with the lowest membership, Amazon-Book and Yelp2018. Using high-order connectivity modelling, which 1) incorporates the lower-order connectivity used in baselines and recursive embedding propagation to enhance the depiction of idle users, we can verify the importance of the latter, as shown in Fig. (**1**).

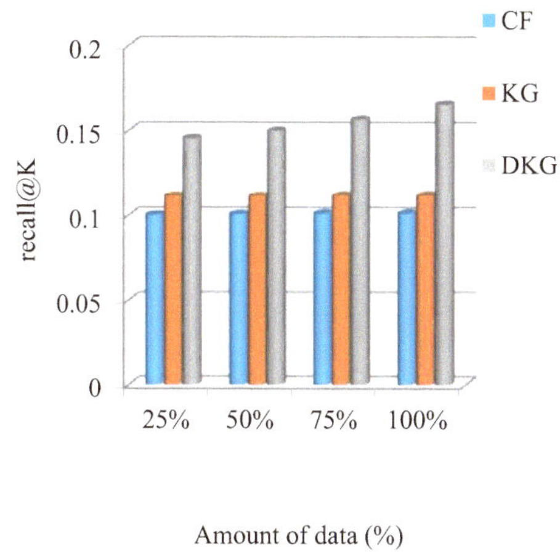

Fig. (1). NDCG@K on amazon dataset.

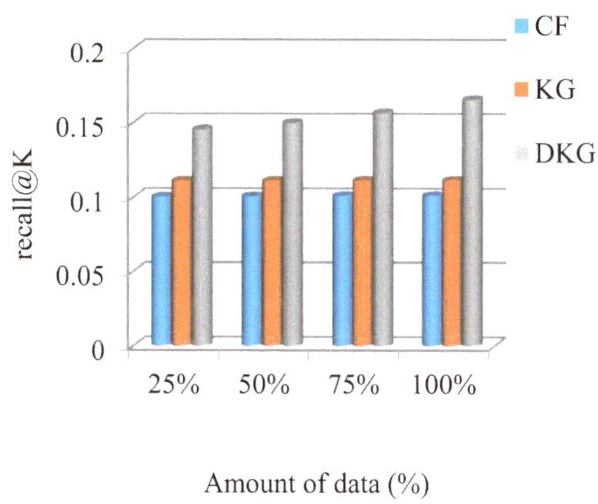

Fig. (2). NDCG@K on Last FM dataset.

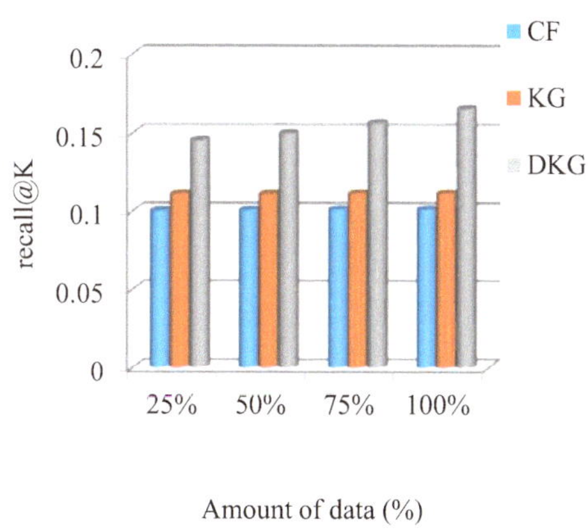

Fig. (3). NDCG@K on Yelp dataset.

Please take notice that, among the most densely populated user groups, DKG far surpasses more traditional baseline values, as shown in Fig. (**2**). An explanation is that customers who engage in too many transactions have too generalized tastes to be reliably captured, as shown in Fig. (**3**). A potential drawback of high-order connectivity is the additional interference it introduces to the user's decision-making process.

It is worth noting that the proposed DKG method achieves high recall and NDCG for top-K results. The results show that the proposed DKG method achieves accurate top-K results.

CONCLUSION

The research has shown the use of the various functional features or elements of the suggested approach by applying the EPDM+ML model to SET data collected in an academic environment. According to the study's practical assumptions, educationalists should also be responsible for using the EPDM+ML model to understand the many activities that underpin the educational procedures, methods of instruction, and performance assessments in their respective contexts. Not only will this ensure or justify an effective method for comprehending the experiences of instructors and students, but it could also demonstrate how to improve upon them. Additionally, educators could have ensured the implementation of a strong, effective analytical method for teaching that would have been beneficial for managing and innovating educational procedures. Applying the suggested model, data mining, and machine learning strategies from this study to future research on how students learn across contexts is a viable option. Additional research may examine recreating or enhancing the EPDM+ML architecture to include characteristics and elements not covered in this work.

REFERENCES

[1] W. Wang, D.M. Arya, N. Novielli, J. Cheng, and J.L. Guo, ArguLens: Anatomy of Community Opinions On Usability Issues Using Argumentation Models. In Proceedings of the 2020 CHI Conference on Human Factors in Computing Systems (CHI '20). Association for Computing Machinery, New York, NY, USA, 1–14. [http://dx.doi.org/10.1145/3313831.3376218]

[2] W. Lee, H. Yu, X. Rival, and H. Yang, "Towards verified stochastic variational inference for probabilistic programs", *Proceedings of the ACM on Programming Languages,* vol. 4, no. POPL, pp. 1-33, 2020. [http://dx.doi.org/10.1145/3371084]

[3] S.S. Bahadur, "Latest Advances of Natural Language Processing and their Applications in Everyday life", *International Journal for Modern Trends in Science and Technology,* vol. 6, no. 10, pp. 31-35, 20202020.

[4] I.R. Braun, C.F. Yanarella, and C.J. Lawrence-Dill, "Computing on Phenotypic Descriptions for Candidate Gene Discovery and Crop Improvement", *Plant Phenomics,* vol. 2020, p. 1963251, 2020. [http://dx.doi.org/10.34133/2020/1963251] [PMID: 33313544]

[5] Bratt, S.E., & Rieh, S.Y. (2022). Artificial Intelligence (AI) in Data Curation: How Curators Re-Imagine Legacy Database Systems to Advance Equitable AI in Libraries, Archives and Museums (LAMs) SIG AI WORKSHOP @ ASIS&T 2022.

[6] Pai U., Y., & K, K. (2021). Open Source Intelligence and its Applications in Next Generation Cyber Security - A Literature Review. International Journal of Applied Engineering and Management Letters.

[7] M. Rincón Zamorano, R. Martínez Tomás, and J.M. Ferrández Vicente, "IWINAC '2019: Intelligent systems for cognitive training and assessment", *Expert Syst.,* vol. 39, no. 4, p. e12965, 2022. [http://dx.doi.org/10.1111/exsy.12965]

[8] S.A. Johnson, and S. Ananthakumaran, "Smart Digital Forensic Framework for Crime Analysis and Prediction using AutoML", *Int. J. Adv. Comput. Sci. Appl.,* vol. 12, no. 3, p. 12, 2021. [http://dx.doi.org/10.14569/IJACSA.2021.0120349]

[9] B. Dudzik, J. Broekens, M.A. Neerincx, and H. Hung, "Exploring Personal Memories and Video Content as Context for Facial Behavior in Predictions of Video-Induced Emotions", In Proceedings of the 2020 International Conference on Multimodal Interaction (ICMI '20). Association for Computing Machinery, New York, NY, USA, 153–162. [http://dx.doi.org/10.1145/3382507.3418814]

[10] P.P. Martin, D. Kranz, P. Wulff, and N. Graulich, "Exploring new depths: Applying machine learning for the analysis of student argumentation in chemistry", *J. Res. Sci. Teach.*. vol. 61, no. 8, pp. 1757-1792, 2020.

[11] Kuchnik, M., Klimovic, A., Simsa, J., Amvrosiadis, G., & Smith, V. (2021). Plumber: Diagnosing and Removing Performance Bottlenecks in Machine Learning Data Pipelines. ArXiv, abs/2111.04131.

[12] [12]. Walker, V.R., Pillaipakkamnatt, K., Davidson, A.M., Linares, M., & Pesce, D.J. (2019). Automatic Classification of Rhetorical Roles for Sentences: Comparing Rule-Based Scripts with Machine Learning. ASAIL@ICAIL.

[13] Ariffini, N., Zainal, A.B., Maarof, M.A., & Kassim, M.N. Ransomware Entities Classification with Supervised Learning for Informal Text. 2019 International Conference on Cybersecurity (ICoCSec), 86-90, 2019.

[14] M. Carraturo, and A. Mazzullo, *An Ontology for Defect Detection in Metal Additive Manufacturing.* arXiv:2210.04772, 2020.

[15] Castiello, M.E., & Tonini, M. An Explorative Application of Random Forest Algorithm for Archaeological Predictive Modeling. A Swiss Case Study. Journal of Computer Applications in Archaeology, vol. 4, no. 1, pp. 110-125, 2021. [http://dx.doi.org/10.5334/jcaa.71]

CHAPTER 22

Data-driven Strategies for Resource Optimization Using Data Mining

Bhawna Wadhwa[1,*]

[1] *Department of Computer Science and Engineering, Noida Institute of Engineering & Technology, Greater Noida, Uttar Pradesh, India*

Abstract: Data mining has become an increasingly significant method for conducting data analysis as a result of the rapid increase in databases used by a large number of contemporary businesses. The community of people who study operations research has made major contributions to this discipline, particularly by formulating and solving a large number of data mining problems as optimization problems. Additionally, data mining techniques may be used to address a number of applications in operations research. The purpose of this study is to offer an overview of the relationship between operations research and data mining. The basic objectives of the study are to highlight the spectrum of interactions between the two areas, present specific instances of significant research effort, and provide extensive references to additional significant work in the area. The purpose of this study is to examine not only the many optimization techniques that may be used for data mining, but also the process of data mining itself, as well as the ways in which operations research techniques can be utilized at almost every stage of this process. The report also identifies many potentially fruitful avenues for further investigation throughout its body. In the last part of the study, many applications connected to the administration of electronic services, including customer relationship management and customization, are investigated.

Keywords: Data mining, resource optimization, goods, services, optimization, customization.

INTRODUCTION

Human resource management is the theoretical basis for and practical application of the HRM system. Data gathering and analysis are used to compile all HR-related material, including modules for hiring, approving employees, calculating salaries, and more [1].

Human resource managers will find this helpful in their day-to-day operations. The adoption of the human resources system is driven primarily by businesses'

* **Corresponding author Bhawna Wadhwa:** Department of Computer Science and Engineering, Noida Institute of Engineering & Technology, Greater Noida, Uttar Pradesh, India; E-mail: bhawna.wadhwa@niet.co.in

S. Kannadhasan, R. Nagarajan, & Kaushik Pal (Eds.)

desire to achieve the greatest possible financial returns from their investment in human capital. Human capital, a term coined in response to the rise of the information economy, is increasingly seen as on par with, or even more crucial than, physical assets like buildings and machinery. Furthermore, individuals are the repository of information [1]. The full potential of human resources can only be realised through careful human resource management, which is essential for making the most of one's expertise.

From its inception to the present, the HRM system has gone through three distinct phases:

1. The origins of the modern human resource management system may be traced back to the late 1960s, coinciding closely with the emergence of computing itself [2]. Nonetheless, the HRM system in its early stages can only realize extremely rudimentary computing capabilities owing to the embryonic development of computer technology.
2. Since the advent of the personal computer in the 1970s, significant progress has been achieved in the areas of database and application [3]; this includes the creation of effective tools for human resource management. Third-generation HRM is known as "Information Human Resource (Electronic Human Resource, E-HR)," in contrast to the second-generation system, which was developed primarily by computer scientists but failed to achieve both technical and practical improvement. It makes extensive use of computer and network technologies and takes into account the real requirements of human resource managers [4]. Unfortunately, the majority of HRM tools that companies use today are still in the early stages of data collection, storage, and querying. What's more, the data analysis operations that do exist can only extract superficial data [5], which makes it impossible to delve deeply into dynamic data, such as the company's changing development capabilities or workforce quality. It is challenging to provide scientific support for sustained business growth if the HRM system's central data value is not fully exploited [6].

As Internet technology has become more widely used, the amount of data available online has increased massively [7]. People are increasingly interested in learning how to use technology to unlock the hidden value in large data sets. Under these conditions, data mining technology has emerged at a massive scale. Data mining has a significant effect in numerous areas, including sports, transportation, and scientific research, in recent years [8]. Organizations need to leverage HR's resources to grow sustainably. The concept of human capital [9] proposes that a company's personnel are its most significant asset because they enable it to endure and thrive in the face of market competition. Accurate and comprehensive HR planning has to be the number one objective for any enterprise that strives to achieve sustained, long-term success as well as formulate a more permanent growth path in light of the present situation of increasing human resource expenditures [2]. The only way to bring down employee costs is to adopt a more effective way of distributing spending [3]. Suppose HR cost planning is thorough and accurate in advance. The best workers in a certain job should not be used as a benchmark for staffing [4], even if their labor productivity is much better than that of average or mediocre workers in the same position. We can only identify the most appropriate individuals for the role by carefully broadcasting the position and measuring the talents, knowledge, and level of various workers, as well as the demands of the position [5, 6].

It is important to remember, however, that the HR portion is not a straightforward selection procedure, but rather one that exclusively uses scientific methodologies. HR computing intelligence enables businesses to access all HR-related materials [10]. To make appropriate management decisions, businesses may rely on data and information that are both applicable in practice and easy to understand in terms of the enterprise's growth. Human resource management uses data mining technologies, and the results may be broken down into three broad classes of information: The first kind is time-sensitive information. Information of this sort is primarily reflected in people's rosters, both at the individual and organizational levels [14]. The former includes details such as headcount, job titles, years of experience, educational attainment, certifications, and even employees' family information. [11].

RELATED WORKS

Most people mean by "computational intelligence" the laborious task of discovering fresh, potentially valuable, and legitimate connections in data [12].

Data mining has been used in a variety of contexts and disciplines during the last few years. One such context is business management, which includes well-established specializations like customer management, manufacturing management, and finance management.

Human resource management (HRM) seems to have recently joined these corporate application fields [15 - 20]. More and more studies have been conducted over the past few decades to pave the way for broader deployments of HRM data mining. Human resource management (HRM) includes a wide range of tasks, from recruiting and hiring new employees to tracking turnover rates, planning training and development programs, and assessing performance. A cursory literature review reveals a rapidly expanding subfield of data mining study tailored to HR needs and, thus, of great practical use to HR practices.

However, it is difficult to provide a snapshot of the current state of research due to numerous important contributions and divergent outcomes. Therefore, the purpose of this thesis is to provide a practical framework for human resource management that can be successfully used in talent recruitment situations in human resource services [13].

PROPSOED WORK

The HR needs of a car manufacturer, for instance, may be analysed using this approach and the resulting predictions can be put to the test. The total value of production, total profit, sales condition, and model number are the primary variables used to foretell the need for human resources, and they are chosen after careful consideration of the association between them.

Preprocessing of Data

When the numerical scale variances among the main variables are large enough to significantly affect the sequential difference gap for each factor, and when factors with a large variance can immediately impact regression outcomes when used, the requirement to preprocess every record arises. We can get a z-score for each dataset by plugging the following values into the equation: x for the whole dataset, y for the predicted value, and the factor's variance. It was possible to obtain approximate numerical values for all key components after preprocessing.

Variable-Weight SVR HR Predictions

Here is how a Gaussian function is used to fill the kernel function:

To better depict the high-dimensional linearity of the data, we perform a rigorous analysis of the experimental results, effectively integrate the collected expertise over the years, and set the kernel width to. Avoiding the penalty factor, which causes performance degradation and data generalization when C = 100, is possible. When the relaxed parameter's base is set to 0.01, the model may be extended more effectively. This happens when the training model's accuracy is maximized, and the total number of backing flags is kept to a minimum. By including data from 2015 to 2019 in the training set, the approach constructed an adequate regression model, thereby improving the system's prediction accuracy. The forecasting method was successful, as the company's actual HR circumstances in 2019 met all the requirements for plan implementation. It seems that the strategy is bearing fruit. Using a training set comprising 6 years' worth of data collected between 2015 and 2020, we were able to predict the company's HR needs for 2020 by feeding all relevant information into the SVR model. This led to a prediction that the company would need 5,963 HR professionals in 2020, leaving a gap of over 300.

Problem Definition

This article covers methods for automatically generating job requirements *via* programming. Here is a set of C papers outlining the qualifications required for a specific employment. The job tasks describe the duties of the i-th status, while the demands outline the specific set of abilities and knowledge required to perform the job well. Each job need is expressed as, where is the -th phrase describing a necessary ability for that position. Specifically, we assume that each job obligation contains words. For example, in Fig. (**1**), the different colors represent different neurons, among the five job need statements correlate to schooling, programming, AI, audio processing, and teamwork.

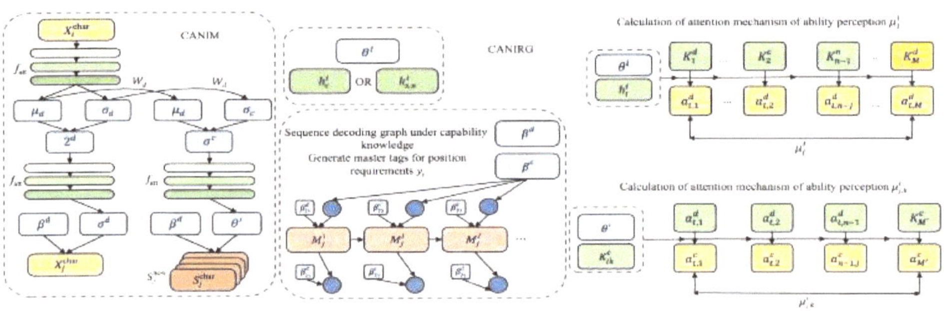

Fig. (1). Architecture without CAPGTA training.

You might also assume that they are all made up of words. Training neural networks to extract the skill words in each job demand allows us to analyze the granular competence needs of each position, using the notion of the article in this context. Annotating these terms allows us to produce a list of competence words for each. In light of this concept, the following challenge is defined: generating job descriptions.

To describe the problem, let us say we have some HR text blocks in C. Each specifies an expected task and a necessary skill for the position. Learning a model M that can produce smooth, acceptable job requirements whenever a new task is assigned is the ultimate aim of job requirements description generation.

Cajon employs CANTM, CANJRG, and CPGTA, a framework for autonomously generating job requirements based on skill prediction, as shown in Fig. (**1**).

CANTM

In this part, we propose a new approach. Following this, CANTM's generation process and inference procedure are broken down individually. To simulate the possible semantics of work duties and job needs, we assume two topic spaces, each with a potential topic count, and use this assumption in the CANTM creation process. Separate sections are provided for each subject.

Word distributions may be described using and, where with are topic-based parameters as well as similarly, with are word-based parameters; these associations will be picked up during training. The word count for "job responsibilities" is while "job requirements" is shown in Fig. (**2**). The job requirement section of CANTM receives only the list of competence terms as input, which helps eliminate extraneous information and enhances the system's ability to learn about possible competency subjects from the requirements.

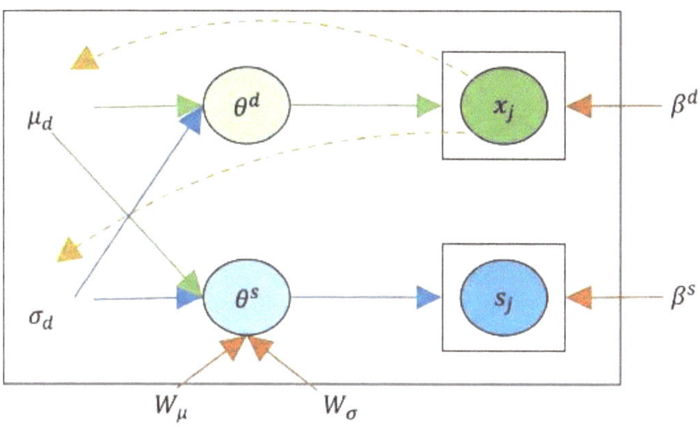

Fig. (2). CANTM for identifying prospective competency.

In this context, topic vectors are considered to exist for every job responsibility and for every list of competence terms in the job criteria, just as they do in the LAD topic paradigm. In this case, both are created using Gaussian softmax. More specifically, a post is created in the following ways:

Hidden-variable sampling:

This is where we find the L-th word in the sampled phrase, where a neuron is activated through a nonlinear function, and parameters are determined in advance.

The most important difference is that when creating competency word lists for work needs, just one competency problem is usually considered. The following describes the generating procedure based on this input:

Sampling Hidden Variables

Given a set of a priori variables and an ability word vector, we may calculate the likelihood that the word will appear in a phrase. To automate the creation of job specifications, this study proposes a neural job requirement-generation framework that accounts for competencies at every stage. This framework can also be used to anticipate the occurrence of skill terms inside job specifications. To improve the quality of the job requirement descriptions produced, a neural topic model, an encoder-decoder LSTM, and a proficiency-aware policy-differential-based training approach are developed. Compared with existing standards, the proposed structure and its modifications are both understandable and practical, as demonstrated by comprehensive testing on real-world HR datasets.

The remaining mapping link is investigated for a priori aspects of its potential themes to replicate the strong association between each task location and the competence term in the job criteria.

Here, we estimate using input based on the concept presented in the paper's introduction. Because of this, the CANTM model can investigate a variety of possible competence thematic representations based solely on responsibilities. In order to construct the aforementioned variance parameters, we establish an inferential network that relies on actual job responsibilities to do so

RESULT AND DISCUSSION

We used two legitimate HR data sets with technical (T) and product-related employment information. We collected data on 3,475 occupations and their tasks, and 2,351 job requirement texts, which were reviewed by 6 HR professionals for fluency and logic. Eighty percent of the dataset was utilised for training and testing purposes in the studies, while ten percent was used to fine-tune the parameters.

Training Parameters and Environment Setting

The competencies-aware neural topic system begins by converting the raw input of job tasks and competency words from the job description into a word bag vector. First, we enhanced the model by removing low-frequency words and inactive phrases. Then we removed out-of-date phrases and those with high or low frequency to improve the model's accuracy. Here, we used a total of 30 subjects for the T set and a total of 30 topics for the data set. To prevent the issue where KL divergence vanishes during training, we also used batch normalisation in computing.

Two embedding layers, one with 128 words and the other with 50 subjects, comprised the capability-aware post-requirement generation model. The 256-bit hidden layers of the bidirectional LSTM make up the sequence encoder. We employed two 256-hidden-layer unidirectional LSTMs to create a capability-aware sequence decoder. Moreover, in both the capacity-aware attention mechanism and the capacity-aware replication method, the size of all hidden-layer states was fixed at 256.

The Xavier method was used to first set the parameters of the whole Cajon framework during training.

Then, 200 CANTM pre-training cycles were completed. After that, we configured and trained Cajon's non-RL loss-function components, as shown in Table **1**. Finally, we used equation (12) to set and progressively increase the parameters to educate our model. Additionally, Adam was utilized in the optimizer, with an initial learning rate of 0.001. In addition, we also stabilised the training process by setting the gradient crop to 1.0. During the trial run of the generating process, we used the light beam Search method with a cluster size of 4. The performance of the proposed work is shown in Fig. (**3**).

Table 1. Experimental results of cajon and comparison methods.

Dataset	Method	BELU	ROUGE					Manual Evolution metrics
		BELU-1	ROUGE-1	ROUGE-2	ROUGE-L	BELU-4	Fluency	Validity
T	Seq2Seq	37.32	0.6389	0.4151	0.5996	16.22	3.66	3.58
	pGNet	38.14	0.6413	0.4246	0.6061	16.75	3.70	3.61
	UniLM	34.64	0.6167	0.3965	0.5863	12.29	3.52	3.41
	SAMA	39.30	0.6004	0.3277	0.5455	15.07	3.47	3.52
	Cajon	41.81	0.6531	0.4296	0.6077	19.41	3.73	3.81
P	Seq2seq	32.02	0.7236	0.5085	0.7138	7.28	3.63	3.34
	pGNet	32.72	0.7421	0.5410	0.7331	8.28	3.67	3.41
	UniLM	31.43	0.7542	0.5439	0.7452	6.42	3.46	3.28
	SAMA	34.76	0.7160	0.4788	0.7074	9.00	3.55	3.49
	Cajon	36.46	0.7522	0.5757	0.7531	10.84	3.78	3.74

Overall, a Linux server running RedHat 4.8.536 with a 2.40 GHz Intel Xeon Gold6148 CPU was used for the research, and TensorFlow was used as the basis for the resulting models.

In this case, the suggested model surpassed the best outcomes of all benchmarks by margins of 9.49%, 3.55%, and 6.73% for the technical data, and by margins of 20.62%, 5.29%, and 17.69% for the product data, as shown in Fig. (**4**). This provides strong evidence that the proposed framework's outputs better reflect the true nature of the position's required skills.

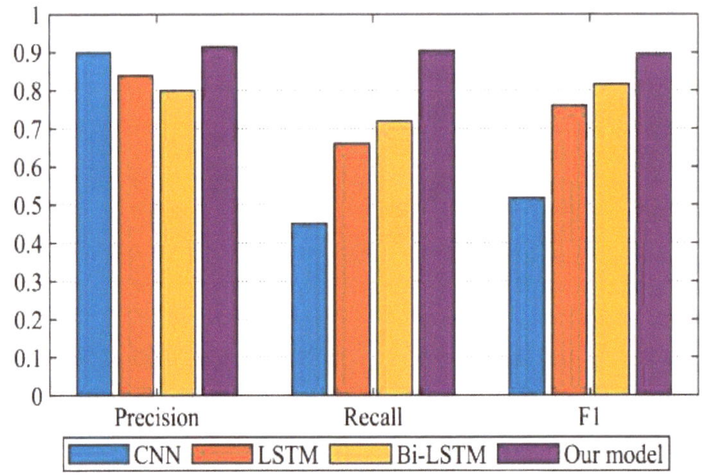

Fig. (3). Performance analysis of Precision, Recall, and F1.

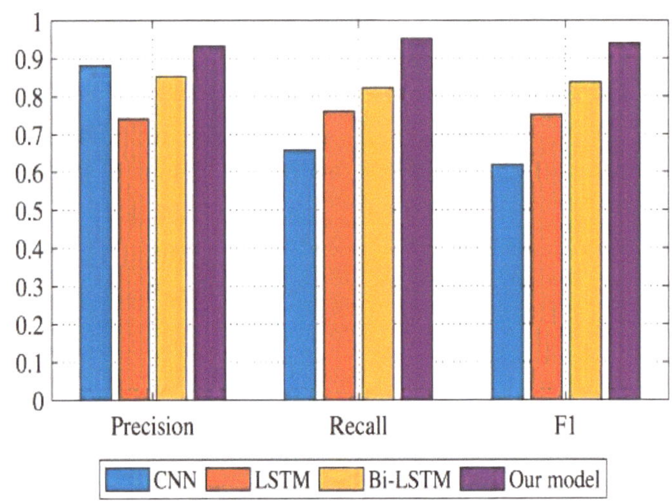

Fig. (4). Performance analysis of Precision, Recall, and F1.

CONCLUSION

To automate the process of creating job specifications, this study proposes a neural job requirement generating framework that takes into account competencies at every stage. This framework can also be used to anticipate the occurrence of skill terms inside job specifications. Lastly, a proficiency-aware policy gradation-based training strategy improves the logicality of job requirement descriptions generated by a sensor-decoder recurrent neural network. The efficacy and interpretability of the suggested structure and its modifications in contrast to state-of-the-art benchmarks are finally validated by comprehensive tests on real-world HR records.

REFERENCES

[1] B. Parbat, and R.K. Dhuware, "Study of Use of Classification Techniques in WSN Data Mining for Resource Optimization", *Int. J. Comput. Sci. Eng.,* vol. 6, no. 10, 2018.

[2] Z. Feng, X. Li, Q. Zhang, and W. Li, "Proactive Radio Resource Optimization With Margin Prediction: A Data Mining Approach", *IEEE Trans. Vehicular Technol.,* vol. 66, no. 10, pp. 9050-9060, 2017.
[http://dx.doi.org/10.1109/TVT.2017.2709622]

[3] D. Tang, "[Retracted] Optimization of Human Resource Management System Based on Data Mining Technology and Random Forest Algorithm", *Wirel. Commun. Mob. Comput.,* vol. 2022, no. 1, p. 9442369, 2022.
[http://dx.doi.org/10.1155/2022/9442369]

[4] C. Fan, *Research on the Structural Optimization of the Data Mining-Based Enterprise Human Resource Management.*. J. Inst. Eng. India Ser. C 103, pp. 931–938, 2022.
[http://dx.doi.org/10.1007/s40032-022-00838-4]

[5] J. Zhao, and Q. Zhu, "China's Energy Structure Optimization Based on Data Mining from the Perspective of Circular Economy: Take Qujing City as an Example", *Mob. Inf. Syst.,* vol. 2022, pp. 1-11, 2022.
[http://dx.doi.org/10.1155/2022/7905576]

[6] Yan, X. (2022). Application of Data Mining Technology in Optimal Configuration of Enterprise Resource. 2022 5th International Conference on Pattern Recognition and Artificial Intelligence (PRAI), 1287-1291.

[7] F. Zhang, and H. Lin, "Energy Economy and Energy Structure Optimization Countermeasures Based on Big Data Mining", *Wirel. Commun. Mob. Comput.,* vol. 2022, no. 1, p. 4711551, 2022.
[http://dx.doi.org/10.1155/2022/4711551]

[8] M. Xu, and C. Li, "Data Mining Method of Enterprise Human Resource Management Based on Simulated Annealing Algorithm", *Secur. Commun. Netw.,* vol. 2021, pp. 1-9, 2021.
[http://dx.doi.org/10.1155/2021/6342970]

[9] Z. Feng, "Rcsearch on Intelligent City Talent Information Fusion Management and Talent Training System Optimization Based on Data Mining", *Tob. Regul. Sci.,* vol. 7, no. 5, pp. 2045-2054, 2021.
[http://dx.doi.org/10.18001/TRS.7.5.124]

[10] G.E. Ye, *Research on Data Optimization of Communication Resource Management System Based on Data Mining.*. International Journal of Simulation- Systems, Science and Technology- IJSSST V16, 2020.
[http://dx.doi.org/10.5013/IJSSST.a.16.5B.25]

[11] Z. Fengli, and L. Xiaoli, *Resource Efficiency Optimization for Big Data Mining Algorithm with Multi-MapReduce Collaboration Scenario.*. In: Huang, DS., Huang, ZK., Hussain, A. (eds) Intelligent Computing Methodologies. ICIC 2019. Lecture Notes in Computer Science(), vol 11645. Springer, Cham.
[http://dx.doi.org/10.1007/978-3-030-26766-7_46]

[12] L. Liao, Y. Zeng, Y. Liang, and H. Zhang, Data Mining: A Novel Strategy for Production Forecast in Tight Hydrocarbon Resource in Canada by Random Forest Analysis." Paper presented at the International Petroleum Technology Conference, Dhahran, Kingdom of Saudi Arabia, January 2020.
[http://dx.doi.org/10.2523/IPTC-20344-MS]

[13] Y. Chen, "Research on Resource Allocation Optimization of Information Management System Based on Big data Association Mining", *J. Phys. Conf. Ser.,* vol. 1345, no. 2, p. 022073, 2019.
[http://dx.doi.org/10.1088/1742-6596/1345/2/022073]

[14] S. Qiu, X. Cui, Z. Ping, N. Shan, Z. Li, X. Bao, and X. Xu, "Deep Learning Techniques in Intelligent Fault Diagnosis and Prognosis for Industrial Systems: A Review", *Sensors (Basel),* vol. 23, no. 3, p. 1305, 2023.
[http://dx.doi.org/10.3390/s23031305] [PMID: 36772347]

[15] W. Zhang, D. Yang, and H. Wang, "Data-driven methods for Predictive maintenance of industrial equipment: A survey", *IEEE Syst. J.,* vol. 13, no. 3, pp. 2213-2227, 2019.
[http://dx.doi.org/10.1109/JSYST.2019.2905565]

[16] M. Pech, J. Vrchota, and J. Bednář, "Predictive maintenance and intelligent sensors in smart factory", *Sensors (Basel),* vol. 21, no. 4, p. 1470, 2021.
[http://dx.doi.org/10.3390/s21041470] [PMID: 33672479]

[17] T. Zonta, C.A. da Costa, R. da Rosa Righi, M.J. de Lima, E.S. da Trindade, and G.P. Li, "Predictive maintenance in the Industry 4.0: A systematic literature review", *Comput. Ind. Eng.,* vol. 150, p. 106889, 2020.
[http://dx.doi.org/10.1016/j.cie.2020.106889]

[18] Goyal, D.; Saini, A.; Dhami, S.S.; Pabla, B.S. Intelligent Predictive maintenance of dynamic systems using condition monitoring and signal processing techniques—A review. In Proceedings of the 2016 International Conference on Advances in Computing, Communication, & Automation (ICACCA) (Spring), Dehradun, India, 8–9 April 2016; IEEE Xplore: Piscataway, NJ, USA, 2016; pp. 1–6.

[19] Y. Ran, X. Zhou, P. Lin, Y. Wen, and R. Deng, "A survey of Predictive maintenance: Systems, purposes and approaches", arXiv:1912.07383, 2019.

[20] Z. Chen, F. Xiao, F. Guo, and J. Yan, "Interpretable machine learning for building energy management: A state-of-the-art review", *Adv. Appl. Energy,* vol. 9, p. 100123, 2023.
[http://dx.doi.org/10.1016/j.adapen.2023.100123]

CHAPTER 23

Investigating the Role of Data Mining in Enhancing Business Performance

Prabha Nair[1,*]

[1] *Department of IT and M.Tech Integrated, Noida Institute of Engineering & Technology, Greater Noida, Uttar Pradesh, India*

Abstract: While data mining finds extensive usage in the scientific and technical communities, it also finds beneficial uses in the financial and marketing spheres, where it helps address specific problems. By analyzing the actual situation, a data mining-based decision support system improves the organization's performance. Due to factors such as competition, costs, tax pressures, and other factors, every firm experiences economic volatility. A more competitive environment is dragged into the organization *via* privatization, globalization, and liberalization. To stay ahead of the competition and accomplish your goals, you need a well-planned and implemented marketing strategy. By using an effective data mining strategy, marketing decision support systems help organizations reduce the responsibilities associated with analysis and strategic planning. This study offered a data mining-based decision support system for estimating a company's marketing plans by combining decision trees and artificial neural networks: data mining, decision trees, artificial neural networks, and marketing decision support systems.

Keywords: Data mining, business performance, knowledge-driven decision support system, data-driven decision support system, communication-driven decision support system.

INTRODUCTION

The safety, efficiency, and integrity of building initiatives may be guaranteed by taking measures to prevent work-related crimes early on. With the use of sophisticated big data analytics and predictive models, crime prevention efforts can be taken to the next level. Construction projects begin with the following steps: bidding, acquiring land, demolishing, obtaining permission, and procurement. During the first phases of building projects, the most common types of work-related crimes are bribery, corruption, and dereliction of duty [1]. The

* **Corresponding author Prabha Nair:** Department of IT and M.Tech Integrated, Noida Institute of Engineering & Technology, Greater Noida, Uttar Pradesh, India; E-mail: prabha.snair@niet.co.in

S. Kannadhasan, R. Nagarajan, & Kaushik Pal (Eds.)

need for solutions to analyze large amounts of data is growing in tandem with the importance of information and communication technology (ICT) in facilitating and bolstering smart cities. A number of solutions based on AI, data mining, ML, and statistical analysis have been successfully implemented in areas such as climate research, energy management, transportation, air quality, and climate change analysis [2].

One of the most significant areas of application for big data analytics is predictive analysis, which uses a combination of complex analytical functions, primarily statistical analysis, along with other methods to forecast future events. The primary areas of use for large-scale data analytics technologies include corporate intelligence, public services, government decision-making, and related fields. To address the statistical analysis issues associated with time-series big data, one can use factor analysis, a method from classical statistics. However, factor analysis provides only information about the degree and variation of the data distribution around the median, and it does not account for how data object characteristics change over time [3]. Because of the exponential growth of AI and big data, which are grounded in the experiences of college students and made possible by cutting-edge technology, university curricula have also grown in many other ways. The design of electrical technology is based on a rational and scientific basis. Resulting from the optimization of derivative tools used in university courses as well as the use of digital information as a means of transport to enhance performance in other domains, including education and sports [4]. A Brief Overview: With the expected acceleration of global population growth in the coming decades, there will likely be a corresponding surge in demand for eggs and chicken meat. Pollution, land erosion, competition for limited resources, animal welfare, restrictions on growth promoters, antimicrobial agents, increasing dangers from animal infectious illnesses, and zoonoses are some of the many challenges that this expansion hides, despite the fact that it clearly represents an outstanding chance for the sector. Optimizing and increasing efficiency are the primary ways to boost chicken output. There is a once-in-a-lifetime chance to create tools that optimize farm profitability, reduce socio-environmental impacts, and increase human and animal health and welfare [5]. This opportunity is made possible by the growing capacity to generate massive amounts of data, also known as "big data," as well as by the availability of resources to organize, distribute, integrate, and interpret this data using effortless as well as flexible algorithms. If a company wants to improve its decision-making or reduce risks, it needs a data-driven strategy plan that uses analytics. In this case, company data is vital. This study presents a statistically informed strategy for LendingClub, a financial services provider, that includes investigating the feasibility of integrating a big data platform with sophisticated feature selection capabilities [6]. There are new possibilities and challenges for businesses in this age of unparalleled information accessibility. Consumer habits and market trends are both covered by the ever-increasing dataset. To make informed economic decisions, nevertheless, the issue of how to sift through such a mountain of data becomes paramount [7].

RELATED WORKS

In this post, we looked at how construction projects can leverage big data to improve planning and execution, making them safer for employees. The article began by examining the trends, patterns, and kinds of work-related offences that occur early in construction projects. Afterwards, we learned that big data technologies may help prevent such crimes. As a last step, we analyzed survey data and proposed using big data technologies to curb construction-related crimes at the preliminary phases of a project. Ten Chinese provinces rank first to 10th in the frequency of crimes committed on the job: Zhejiang, Beijing, China, Shandong, Guangzhou, Henan, Jiangsu, Hebei, Hubei, Fujian, and Liaoning. This study selected a number of construction projects across various locations using basic random sampling and quantitative research methods. The intended subjects of this study were workers in the construction sector, construction firms, key stakeholders, and associated professionals. To gather data, participants were asked to fill out an online questionnaire. The gathered data were examined using descriptive analysis methods in SPSS. This study's findings highlighted the value of big data technologies for preventing construction-related crimes at the project's first phases [8].

A comprehensive literature analysis of smart city big data analytics is presented in this work. For this research, we used a structured data mining process that included searching many sources for relevant materials using precise keywords. We have also reported the findings of a technical and thematic analysis of the selected literature, which included identifying different data mining and machine learning approaches. We also provide a categorization model that examines four facets of this field's research [9]. This includes models for data and computation, considerations for privacy and security, and the most important factors propelling the smart city industry. In addition, we highlight potential areas for further study and provide a gap analysis. We conducted a thematic analysis and identified the following themes: smart city governance, energy, transportation, economics, and environment. We lay out the most pressing issues in these areas, the most important data analytics studies that have attempted to address these problems, and the most promising avenues for further study [10].

Using an object-oriented programming approach, this research introduced a novel model that applies grey factor analysis to the large data analysis layer. At last, big data analytics uses this approach. Analyzing and comparing the findings yields a surprising and top-notch prognosis. Based on the results of the experiments, this method has advanced big data research and analysis of time series and is crucial for improving the value of large, complex datasets for predictive analytics and data mining. This, in turn, helps the government make better predictions based on the data [11].

The plan's primary goals are to increase the business's income and reduce the likelihood of loan defaults among the company's clientele. This research examines several theories proposed to address the company's issues. The findings show that the quantity of loans has a significant influence on the percentage of borrowers who pay off their debts. A key component of the planned strategy is the use of cutting-edge analytics tools, such as machine learning, to enable the organization to build more accurate, data-driven prediction models [12].

This paper will delve into the importance of data-driven economic forecasting and decision-making, highlighting particular algorithms in supervised and unsupervised learning. It will also center on upcoming breakthroughs and problems in this field [13].

The study's originality lies in its use of powerful scripting toolsets in sequence to provide a systematic categorization and comparative modeling of deep-sea trench geomorphic features. Utilizing a variety of tools, such as GIS, GMT, Python, AWK, and R, enables technological innovation. The paper in question really combines the following techniques, revealing its very interdisciplinary character: 4) study of geological literature; 5) modeling and modeling of cartographic features using GMT shell scripts as well as display in QGIS; 6) evaluation of statistical data using libraries of Python and R, AWK, and Octave/Matlab. If this study is to be repeated or applied to additional ocean trenches in future years, the complete technical scripts used for the advanced statistical assessment may be found in Appendix A of the manuscript [14].

This research article explores the use of machine learning methods and substantial data analysis to forecast the COVID-19 mortality rate. Multiple Linear Regression was used after a comparative study. The algorithm's exceptional performance proves its supremacy. The proposed method achieves a remarkable R-Squared score of 0.987 and an accuracy rate of 98.6% due to its exceptional adaptability across varied settings [15].

We theoretically examined the computational complexity and application of the statistical methods used for genetic assessment, and conducted a comprehensive analysis of their development history. The algorithms were then applied to diverse data situations [16 - 18]. Above all else, we introduced HIBLUP, a software package that is computationally efficient, functionally enhanced, multi-platform, and easy to use, with the goal of addressing the problems encountered when dealing with massive genomic data. With its cutting-edge algorithms, intricate design, and effective programming, HIBLUP outperforms other methods in terms of computational speed and memory usage [19 - 23]. What's more, its computational advantages increase as the number of genotyped persons increases. In addition, we proved that the suggested efficient 'HE + PCG' approach can only be executed by HIBLUP, and that no other tool can do the analysis for a dataset of UK Biobank size in under one hour. The HIBLUP project is expected to pave the way for more efficient genetic research involving humans, plants, and animals.

PROPSOED WORK

Using elements of both decision trees and artificial neural networks, the authors created the suggested hybrid model. The mathematical foundation for the suggested hybrid algorithm is laid forth in this section. A manufacturing business uses the suggested hybrid model to evaluate its marketing concepts in light of the company's and its marketing department's problems. Since choosing a retained firm results in a poor reputation among stakeholders and the environment, it is crucial to have a system that supports decision-making to develop marketing and production strategies that will increase the company's profits. To assess the actual situation, it is important to consider a number of pressures that enhance strategic benefits. A thorough set of guidelines is established and shared with the expert and marketing teams after much deliberation. To determine the suggested system's sub-criteria, we conduct further analysis of the marketing team's and experts' replies. Another time, the analysis is used to generate several lists, which are then disseminated to the whole team for feedback on the selected criteria. Finally, the sub-criteria used to improve the industry's manufacturing and marketing processes are used to determine the consensus. These stages include issue setting, model development, and action development.

The scope and the industry's inevitable difficulties are defined at the first problem formulation phase. To identify the source, a framework for manufacturing and goals is established, and the root-cause assessment and its link are crucial for the decision support system. At this tier, the fundamental marketing and production goals are further broken down to form a structure that connects upper-level management with frontline workers. These goal functions are constructed according to a hierarchical order. Formal models are part of the second step, which is model development. The current manufacturing and advertising elements might be reorganized using these models, which are based on the sub-objectives. Taking into account the matrix function that is provided, we get the normalizing, constituting, as well as tree of decision weight functions $D = [\ ]$ (1) *nxm* where each possible solution is represented by a column in the matrix and the triggered pressures by a row. Finally, the objective's enlarged matrix function is D1 . 1.... D1J .... . D1m. . . . D = Di1. .... Dij .... Dim. (2) | . . . . | . . . . Dn1.... Dnj .... Dnm. The Normalized decision matrix is given as Dn = [D'ij] (3) where D' =, 1,2,3 .... n, j = 1,2,3 ..... m. ij n k=1 D' Kj. Artificial neural network is used to refine the results of the decision tree model. The approach starts by using the three-level inputs in the decision tree system and converts them into nine separate intermediate levels, depending on the sub-objectives given for the suggested decision support system. The suggested system interacts with employees at all levels of a business, as shown by the interconnected processes. The ultimate marketing and production strategy is derived from the summation and classification of the sub-objectives.

RESULT AND DISCUSSION

Criteria, including internal pressure, objectives, and external pressures, are used to analyze the suggested hybrid model. In order to compare the suggested method to more traditional decision-support systems based on hidden Markov and support vector machines, and to assess each category independently. Here are the main objectives: A1 for internal pressure, B1 for outside influences, and C1 for target and production criteria. The subobjectives are as follows: SC1 for job fulfillment (a common practice for manufacturing and advertising employees), SC2 for cognitive skills, the SC3 for staff role in the business, SC4 for worker power, SC5 for one's own efforts, SC6 for promptly response, SC7 for accessible resource, SC8 for the culture of the organization, and SC9 for maturity towards company activities. The decision tree matrix is shown in Table **1**. As an output of the decision support system for the development of the organization, the classification results are grouped into C1, C2, and C3. The final classification results are then acquired.

Table 1. Decision tree matrix.

	SC1	SC2	SC3	SC4	SC5	SC6	SC7	SC8	SC9
A1	2	2	2	4	4	4	8	5	5
B1	5	5	4	5	5	5	6	3	7
C1	6	8	7	6	5	6	7	8	6

With regard to the primary and secondary goals, Table **2** shows the values of the clusters' decision tree matrices. There is a striking similarity between the three groups in terms of the external pressure. In fact, sub-objectives experience far higher levels of internal pressure. Compared with other traits, the level of individual effort is high, indicating that workers are eager to apply their expertise to help the company succeed.

Table 2. Clustering comparisoin for the cretreia.

SC1	SC2	SC3	SC4	SC5	SC6	SC7	SC8	SC9	Priority function values		
C1	SC1	1	1	2	3	4	2	4	1	1	0.1654
	SC2	1	1	2	3	4	2	3	1	1	0.1452
	SC3	1	2	3	1	4	2	2	1	2	0.0564
C2	SC4	½	½	1	3	3	2	¼	3	3	0.0562
	SC5	1/3	½	1	1	2	2	½	1/4	½	0.0445
	SC6	¼	1/4	1/3	1	2	2	1/4	1/2	¼	0.0812
C3	SC7	1	1	2	3	4	½	½	1	3	0.1256
	SC8	½	½	1	3	3	2	¼	3	3	0.1654
	SC9	1	2	3	1	4	2	4	1	1	0.0562

Using the answers to the goals and sub-objectives provided by managers and entry-level workers, Table **2** presents the details of the clustering comparison for the criteria. We get the value of the priority function by checking whether the clustering and threshold values are consistent. Values below 0.1 are deemed acceptable, whereas values beyond this threshold are deemed unacceptable. After surveying workers, shareholders, and upper management, we found that the suggested approach yielded superior priority values. As a result of their inadequate evaluation methods, the other models' priority ratings are lower.

CONCLUSION

This study proposes a decision assistance system that combines decision trees with artificial neural networks. To build this decision support system, we first had to identify problems with the current models. The goal is to help businesses with their marketing and production plans. The primary goal function is decomposed into sub-objective functions to conduct a top-down analysis of the company based on the options gathered from workers. Better categorization techniques are obtained by training an artificial neural network and analysing the provided answers using a decision tree. We compare the experimental results with those of a traditional hidden Markov model and a decision-support system based on support vectors. The suggested model outperforms competing models in classification accuracy, suggesting it may be helpful across a wide range of research applications. Integrating optimization models to boost assessment performance would be a significant next step for this study.

REFERENCES

[1] Farhangmehr, F. (2014). Statistical Approaches for Big Data Analytics and Machine Learning : Data-Driven Network Reconstruction and Predictive Modeling of Time Series Biological Systems. University of California, San Diego ProQuest Dissertations & Theses, 2014. 3673978.

[2] Y. Matsumoto, H. Hibino, M. Kimura, and Y. Mizukami, "Modeling and simulation of agriculture production system considering seasonal variable information using big data analysis", *J. Adv. Mech. Des. Syst. Manuf.,* vol. 13, no. 5, p. JAMDSM0097, 2019. [http://dx.doi.org/10.1299/jamdsm.2019jamdsm0097]

[3] H. Balti, A.B. Abbes, N. Mellouli, Y. Sang, I.R. Farah, M. Lamolle, and Y. Zhu, "Big data based architecture for drought forecasting using LSTM, ARIMA, and Prophet: Case study of the Jiangsu Province, China", *2021 International Congress of Advanced Technology and Engineering (ICOTEN),* pp. 1-8, 2021. [http://dx.doi.org/10.1109/ICOTEN52080.2021.9493513]

[4] R. Ren, J. Fang, J. Hu, X. Ma, and X. Li, "Risk Assessment Modeling of Urban Railway Investment and Financing Based on Improved SVM Model for Advanced Intelligent Systems", *Int. J. Semantic Web Inf. Syst.,* vol. 19, no. 1, pp. 1-19, 2023. [http://dx.doi.org/10.4018/IJSWIS.331596]

[5] A. Sharma, D. Shukla, T. Goel, and P.K. Mandal, "BHARAT: An Integrated Big Data Analytic Model for Early Diagnostic Biomarker of Alzheimer's Disease", *Front. Neurol.,* vol. 10, p. 9, 2019. [http://dx.doi.org/10.3389/fneur.2019.00009] [PMID: 30800093]

[6] K.H. Tan, "Relationship of Big Data Analytics Capability and Product Innovation Performance using SmartPLS 3.2.6: Hierarchical Component Modelling in PLS-SEM", *International Journal of Supply Chain Management,* vol. 7, pp. 51-64, 2018.

[7] B. Hoover, D. Zaengle, M. Mark-Moser, P.C. Wingo, A. Suhag, and K. Rose, Enhancing knowledge discovery from unstructured data using a deep learning approach to support subsurface modeling predictions. Front Big Data, vol. 6, 1227189, 2023. [http://dx.doi.org/10.3389/fdata.2023.1227189]

[8] L. Hao, K.T. Jing, Z. Ruirui, H.C. Yee, S. Yangle, and C. Siyao, Application of Big Data in the Prevention of Work-Related Crimes in Early-Stage Construction Engineering. Adv Res Appl Sci Eng Technol, vol. 32, no. 2, 2023. [http://dx.doi.org/10.37934/araset.32.2.457474]

[9] K. Soomro, M.N.M. Bhutta, Z. Khan, and M.A. Tahir, "Smart city big data analytics: An advanced review", *Wiley Interdiscip. Rev. Data Min. Knowl. Discov.,* vol. 9, no. 5, p. e1319, 2019. [http://dx.doi.org/10.1002/widm.1319]

[10] Jiang, C. (2022). Research and Application of Grey Factor Analysis in Big Data Analytics. 2022 2nd International Conference on Computer Science, Electronic Information Engineering and Intelligent Control Technology (CEI), 427-431.

[11] S. Sarraf, *Formulating A Strategic Plan Based On Statistical Analyses And Applications For Financial Companies Through A Real-World Use Case.*. arXiv:2307.04778, 2023.

[12] Z. Liu, *Review on the influence of machine learning methods and data science on the economics.* Applied and Computational Engineering. vol. 22, pp. 137-141, 2023. [http://dx.doi.org/10.54254/2755-2721/22/20231208]

[13] P. Lemenkova, "Deep-Sea Trenches of the Pacific Ocean: A Comparative Analysis of the Submarine Geomorphology Using Data Modeling by Gmt, Python and R", *SSRN,* 2021. [http://dx.doi.org/10.2139/ssrn.3858289]

[14] Laxmikant, K., G, A., & Usman, S.M. (2023). Predicting the Deaths rate of COVID-19 Using Big Data Analytics and Machine Learning. 2023 14th International Conference on Computing Communication and Networking Technologies (ICCCNT), 1-5.

[15] L. Yin, H. Zhang, Z. Tang, D. Yin, Y. Fu, X. Yuan, X. Li, X. Liu, and S. Zhao, "HIBLUP: an integration of statistical models on the BLUP framework for efficient genetic evaluation using big genomic data", *Nucleic Acids Res.,* vol. 51, no. 8, pp. 3501-3512, 2023. [http://dx.doi.org/10.1093/nar/gkad074] [PMID: 36809800]

[16] M. Zhou, X. Yao, Z. Zhu, and F. Hu, "Equilibrium Optimizer-Based Joint Time-Frequency Entropy Feature Selection Method for Electric Loads in Industrial Scenario", *Appl. Sci. (Basel),* vol. 13, no. 9, p. 5732, 2023. [http://dx.doi.org/10.3390/app13095732]

[17] R. Hou, X. Ye, H.B.O. Zaki, and N.A.B. Omar, "Marketing Decision Support System Based on Data Mining Technology", *Appl. Sci. (Basel),* vol. 13, no. 7, p. 4315, 2023. [http://dx.doi.org/10.3390/app13074315]

[18] A.A. Ali, A.M. Khedr, M. El-Bannany, and S. Kanakkayil, "A Powerful Predicting Model for Financial Statement Fraud Based on Optimized XGBoost Ensemble Learning Technique", *Appl. Sci. (Basel),* vol. 13, no. 4, p. 2272, 2023. [http://dx.doi.org/10.3390/app13042272]

[19] C. Li, and G. Qian, "Stock Price Prediction Using a Frequency Decomposition Based GRU Transformer Neural Network", *Appl. Sci. (Basel),* vol. 13, no. 1, p. 222, 2022. [http://dx.doi.org/10.3390/app13010222]

[20] A. Kołakowska, and M. Godlewska, "Analysis of Factors Influencing the Prices of Tourist Offers", *Appl. Sci. (Basel),* vol. 12, no. 24, p. 12938, 2022. [http://dx.doi.org/10.3390/app122412938]

[21] J.J. Cubillas, M.I. Ramos, and F.R. Feito, "Use of Data Mining to Predict the Influx of Patients to Primary Healthcare Centres and Construction of an Expert System", *Appl. Sci. (Basel),* vol. 12, no. 22, p. 11453, 2022. [http://dx.doi.org/10.3390/app122211453]

[22] F.E. Usman-Hamza, A.O. Balogun, L.F. Capretz, H.A. Mojeed, S. Mahamad, S.A. Salihu, A.G. Akintola, S. Basri, R.T. Amosa, and N.K. Salahdeen, "Intelligent Decision Forest Models for Customer Churn Prediction", *Appl. Sci. (Basel),* vol. 12, no. 16, p. 8270, 2022. [http://dx.doi.org/10.3390/app12168270]

[23] M. Mirkovic, T. Lolic, D. Stefanovic, A. Anderla, and D. Gracanin, "Customer Churn Prediction in B2B Non-Contractual Business Settings Using Invoice Data", *Appl. Sci. (Basel),* vol. 12, no. 10, p. 5001, 2022. [http://dx.doi.org/10.3390/app12105001]

CHAPTER 24

Learning Features and Preferences with Matrix Factorization Models for Recommendation Systems

C.R. Manjunath[1,*] and **Nitin Gaur**[2]

[1] *Department of Computer Science and Engineering, JAIN (Deemed-to-be University), Bangalore, Karnataka, India*

[2] *Department of Computer Science and Engineering, Galgotias University, Greater Noida, Uttar Pradesh, India*

Abstract: Over the last several years, research into recommender systems (RS) has grown to include a wide variety of artificial intelligence (AI) techniques, from more basic ones like Matrix Factorization (MF) to more complex ones such as Deep Neural Networks (DNN). Since they only examine a linear combination of consumer and item vectors, traditional CF recommendation algorithms like MF have little room for improvement in learning. Neuronal collaborative filtering (NCF) is a hybrid of deep neural networks (DNNs) and collaborative filtering (CF), enabling it to learn non-linear connections. But CF methods still have issues with cold beginnings and sparse data. This research presents a new hybrid RS, Neural Matrix Factorizing++ (NeuMF++), that can handle cold starts, boost recommendation accuracy, and address data sparsity. To improve NeuMF, we introduce NeuMF++, which uses Stacked Denoising Autoencoders (SDAEs) to better represent latent features. Merging GMF++ and MLP++ might yield NeuMF++. Mixed with Multilayer Perceptrons (MLP) and Generalized Matrix Factorization (GMF), NeuMF is a robust NCF architecture. By combining the linearity of GMF with the nonlinearity of MLP, NeuMF achieves state-of-the-art results. Simultaneously, the original GMF as well as MLP were enhanced with GMF++ and MLP++, respectively, by successfully including latent representations. Obtaining a latent representation from the SDAEs' hidden space significantly enhances NeuMF++'s learning power. This representation allows it to learn item and user attributes correctly. If feature extractions are shared across GMF++ and MLP++, however, NeuMF++'s performance could take a hit. As a result, its speed and flexibility are greatly enhanced when GMF++ and MLP++ are allowed to learn features separately. Using a real-world dataset, NeuMF++ achieved an experimental root-mean-square error of 0.8681, demonstrating its excellent performance. Additional data, such as text or photos, can be added to NeuMF++ in later development. NeuMF++ allows incorporating several neural network building blocks to create a more robust recommendation model.

[*] **Corresponding author C.R. Manjunath:** Department of Computer Science and Engineering, JAIN (Deemed-to-be University), Bangalore, Karnataka, India; E-mail cr.manjunath@jainuniversity.ac.in

S. Kannadhasan, R. Nagarajan, & Kaushik Pal (Eds.)

Keywords: Recommendation Systems, Matrix Factorization, Local Features, machine learning (ML), Generalized Matrix Factorization (GMF).

INTRODUCTION

In the last decade, machine learning (ML) has become increasingly popular due to advances in methodology enabled by the widespread availability of powerful computers and massive amounts of data. Recommender systems are one area where ML has been effectively used.

Recommender systems powered by machine learning are ubiquitous, influencing our choices across many domains, from entertainment to e-commerce. Companies increase revenue and customer loyalty while giving consumers a better, more individualized experience using recommender systems [1]. Despite the upsides, this achievement has spawned serious moral problems [2]. One of these is the rising number of privacy concerns arising from the proliferation of personal data collection for highly tailored suggestions. To train centralized models on the processors (servers or data processing organizations), conventional recommender ML approaches must collect sensitive user information, which might compromise their privacy. As consumers become more aware of the need to protect their personal information, they have higher expectations of the privacy protections offered by the services they use. For instance, while gathering and handling user data, systems of recommendations must comply with the GDPR (General Data Protection Regulation) of the European Union [3].

The information available to us today has grown at an exponential rate, making it more difficult than ever to sift through all of the available data and discover what we need. It's becoming increasingly esoteric to acquire the necessary info online. Therefore, word-of-mouth is quite important [4]. A recommender system is a type of knowledge filtering system that determines a user's preferences based on their past rating behavior [5] and the information at hand. News, movies, text mining, novels, *etc*., are only a few of the many applications of recommendation systems. Unfortunately, not every recommendation engine can deal with every conceivable scenario. There are two main approaches to designing a recommender system. In the first group, content-based filtering methods are used to define the characteristics of each individual or item. Think of a movie profile that details the film's genre, cast and crew, box-office performance, *etc*. Similarly, users' profiles may include numerical data or responses to an appropriate survey. The resulting profiles can be used in software to pair customers with items that meet their needs. A content-based recommendation system has the drawback of requiring external information, which can be difficult to obtain in practice. One alternative approach, and one of the most classic and eye-catching recommendation algorithms [6], is collaborative filtering (CF), which plays a significant role in producing tailored suggestions [7]. For the purpose of discovering novel user-item correlations, CF analyzes user-dependencies and product-relationships [8]. Based on user history alone—which might include item ratings or transactions—very few CF systems can deduce non-existent links between individuals and products. This is because very few CF systems can identify sets of items with comparable ratings or users with complementary ratings and buying habits. CF is domain-free and superior to the content-based approach [9] because it can handle confusing and challenging information types. However, the sparse user-rating matrix problem is a limitation of the CF approach, leading to subpar suggestion precision. When this happens, it is normal practice to use an average rating for that individual or item to fill in the blanks. The level of imprecision can only be reduced slightly with this method. The reliability of the final suggestions is significantly affected by the accuracy with which missing values are imputed [10]. The benefits of matrix factorization hidden factor models, such as preserving accuracy when scaling data, minimizing estimation cost, and mitigating issues arising from high sparsity levels, have recently brought them under investigation [11]. Among collaborative filtering methods, this one is the most popular for revealing the hidden factors that impact a user's preferences. The memory-efficient, more specialized Matrix factorization-based technology outperforms the similarity-based recommendation technique, which considers only similarities between individuals and products to provide recommendations [12]. Because of its usefulness in collaborative filtering, matrix factorization lends itself well to the use of SGD and ALS as learning algorithms. Matrix factorization is a technique developed and popularized by the winners of the Netflix award, in which a huge matrix is broken down into smaller matrices. This strategy improved upon the efficiency of previous, primarily neighborhood-based, approaches of creating recommendations. Finding hidden components and decreasing the dimensions are the goals of this type of decomposition [13]. Modern matrix factorization techniques are built with exact feedback data, making data analysis straightforward [14]. However, service providers must build feedback sites for consumer evaluations and ratings, a challenging, time-consuming process due to user engagement. Inferring user preferences from a larger volume of implicit data enables recommenders to provide indirect suggestions based on user behavior [15]. Some examples of implicit feedback data include a user's online purchase history, page views, search terms, and even their mouse movements.

RELATED WORKS

Many academics have devoted significant time and energy to recommendation systems in recent years. Hongmei H. Li *et al*. present a more effective, optimal recommendation framework based on an all-weighted strategy. Several prediction- and ranking-oriented evaluation metrics indicate that the proposed technique outperforms the alternative in experimental comparisons of two recommendation algorithms. To enable efficient calculations and an accurate time-varying implicit feedback MF recommendations system, C. Lin *et al.* presented a RI-SGD model that combines ALS with weight regularization during training and SGD during updates. According to the predicted results, RI-SGD may be able to retrain the whole model in around 0.02% of the time while still achieving the same recommendation accuracy. The discounting cumulative gain (DCG) approach is used to determine the worth of the advice. DCG, which is responsible for calculating a rating's worth. M. Li *et al.* created an improvised model called TimeMF that incorporates temporal information and is based on latent feedback; it is a critical solution for the overload of data in social e-commerce networks. By giving a unique learning rate for every feature in the latent features matrix, the improved model employs adaptive gradient descent to make periodic adjustments to the learning rate, ultimately improving accuracy. Compared to ranking-oriented evaluation standards, the model performs better in the experiments. Y. A. He *et al.* proposed a novel model, called Correlated Matrix Factorization (CMF), to better track user-object interactions. CMF merges Matrix Factorization (MF) with Canonical Correlation Analysis (CCA) to increase the accuracy of the model. Yelp, Flixster, MovieLens, and Ciao are used as data sources for the model. Extensive testing across four datasets demonstrates that CMF compares favorably to current state-of-the-art baselines. A novel prediction, estimation, and recommendation technique, dubbed the collaborative Kalman filter, was proposed by J. Z. Sun *et al.* The author of this study proposes an enhanced Gaussian PMF that accounts for user behavior trajectories. The method uses a state-space paradigm to enable probabilistic matrix factorization over longer periods. As a result, we have an iterative estimating process including item-level coupling between parallel Kalman filters and smoothers. The expectation-maximization approach is used to learn global parameters. This method has been shown to perform better on both synthetic and real-world movie recommendation datasets than existing techniques. Two measures used to evaluate performance are Collaborative Kalman Filtration (CKF) and Root-mea--square error (RMSE).

The goal of private ML is to develop models that do not reveal any of the underlying training data. This is a persistent problem in federated learning because user data is exposed across the many network connections between devices and the server [16 - 18]. Algorithms are developed to protect against threats such as membership inference attacks, inversion attacks, and the ability to recreate the training dataset. Homomorphic encryption models and differential privacy algorithms are two examples of recently developed techniques for achieving these aims. Matrix factorization using complete homomorphic encryption has been investigated both outside and within the federated learning environment, with the latter used to transmit data to the central server. In the federated collaborative filtering environment and beyond it, using count drawings as an approximation, differential privacy has been investigated as a means of providing security. To protect users' anonymity, some have recommended not storing any user data at all, and instead keeping only item matrices that are updated in real time online. While our work also aims to avoid storing data, unlike some other approaches, it does not require participants to share data points and does not store latent matrices that are updated in real time. In this paper, we investigate the confidentiality of this innovative approach. Most approaches in this area have the client send the server the gradients of their model's weights. The private learning data may be recovered from the shared gradients, as demonstrated. This approach uses the local model and its shared weights to optimize random inputs to the original data to generate the same gradients as the original model. As a result, several publications have investigated homomorphic encryption for gradient models [19 - 21]. The confidentiality of federated matrix factorization *via* gradient sharing has been studied previously in the context of federated collaborative filtering.

PROPOSED WORK

The GroupLens Research Project provided the real-world data collection. The University of Minnesota is home to the GroupLens Research Project, a research organization based in the Department of Computer Science and Engineering. Visit https://grouplens.org/datasets/movielens/1m/ to get the Movielens-1M dataset created by GroupLens Research.

To begin, we will introduce NeuMF++ as a high-level structure. Then, we will go into specifics about feature extraction, as well as neural collaborative filtering. Finally, we will detail how NeuMF++ is trained and improved. The most common notations are included in Table **1**.

NeuMF++: A Universal Structure. This section provides a high-level overview of the planned NeuMF++. NeuMF++ is a multi-SDAE-to-NeuMF hybrid model, as shown in Fig. (**1**). Feature extraction and neural collaborative filtering are the two main parts of NeuMF++. Each person and object feature is given a total of 2 SDAEs for feature extraction. As previously mentioned, using additional data can improve the efficiency and precision of your recommendations. To enable NeuMF++ to learn user-item characteristics, it is necessary to minimize the dissimilarities from the original. The bottleneck layer, often found in the middle of the stack, can then be used to extract compressed high-level features. Because of its superior performance, NeuMF was selected as our framework for neural collaborative filtering. As was previously noted, the results of the GMF and MLP interaction functions are combined to form the NeuMF. Like GMF++, NeuMF++ aggregates the results of the interaction functions of MLP++. As a first step, we may combine the user and item embeddings of GMF as well as MLP with the learnt user and item latent vector of features from the SDAEs to create latent vectors that reflect the object and the user itself. Next, the GMF++ and MLP++ interaction methods will receive the item as well as the user latent vectors. The last step in rating generation is to input the combined GMF++ and MLP++ outputs into the single-layer MLPNeuMF layer. NeuMF++: Extraction of Features An SDAE is created by piling up a number of DAEs. Subject qualities, such as users' ages and professions, or the shape and size of an object, are often what make up the supplementary data (features). Using a low-dimensional latent space, SDAEs in NeuMF++ encode user characteristics X and item features V before reconstructing Xb and Vb in the output space. Meanwhile, during training, sounds are deliberately inserted between layers. For instance, the SDAE can reduce the reconstruction error for a given feature set XRmp.

Table 1. Using 1 million MovieLens data points with a 70-30 train-test split, the RMSE of several models was compared.

Method	Testing RMSE	Training RMSE
MF	0.8958	0.8010
GMF	0.8928	0.7835
GMF++	0.8894	0.7738
MLP	0.8879	0.8696
MLP++	0.8864	0.8686
NeuMF	0.8725	0.8152
NeuMF++ (Ours)	0.8681	0.7964

NeuMF++: Neural collaborative filtering

If you take GMF++ and MLP++ and put them together, you get NeuMF++. When you see the notation "++," you know that the model has auxiliary data. The user and item embeddings are obtained using one-hot encoding of the respective identifiers. Then, the latent feature vectors for the user and the object are extracted and combined with their respective embeddings to generate the latent vectors pu and qi.

$$
\begin{aligned}
p_u &= \begin{bmatrix} P^{u} \\ X^{u}_{(L^X/2)} \end{bmatrix} \\
q_i &= \begin{bmatrix} Q^{i} \\ V^{i}_{(L^V/2)} \end{bmatrix}
\end{aligned}
\tag{4}
$$

$$
\begin{aligned}
p_u &= \begin{bmatrix} P^{u} \\ X^{u}_{(L^X/2)} \end{bmatrix} \\
q_i &= \begin{bmatrix} Q^{i} \\ V^{i}_{(L^V/2)} \end{bmatrix}
\end{aligned}
\tag{5}
$$

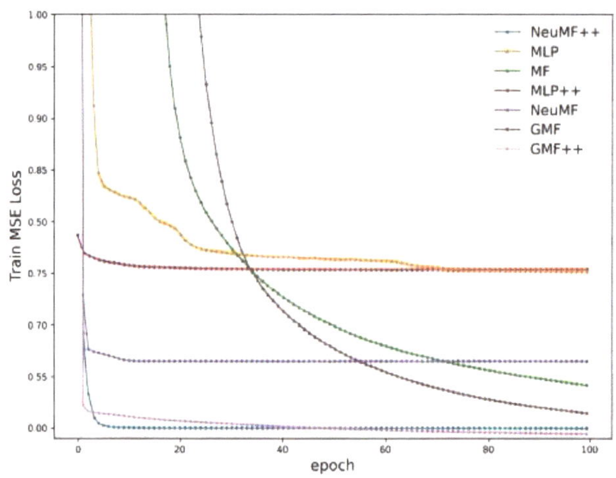

loss of compared models over 100 iterations/epochs.

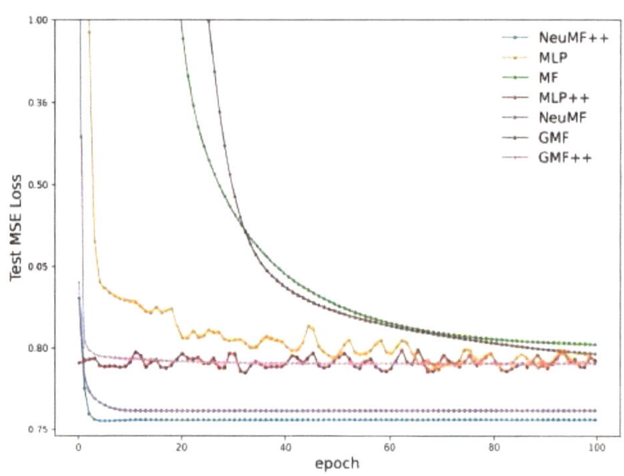

Fig. (1). Epochs Comparison Output.

In their interaction function, GMF++ and MLP++ employ distinct calculations and layers. According to Eq. (6), GMF++ carries out an element-wise product of pu and qi. MLP++, on the other hand, employs a normal MLP by piling on more hidden layers to an already-existing MLP, as shown in Eq. (7)

$$\phi^{(GMF++)} = p_u \odot q_i$$

$$\phi^{(MLP++)} = \sigma_L\left(\ldots\sigma_1\left(\begin{bmatrix} p_u \\ q_i \end{bmatrix} W_1 + b_1\right)\ldots\right) W_L + b_L \tag{6}$$

Introducing the NeuMF layer, a novel single-layer MLP that can combine the outputs of the GMF++ with MLP++ layers. The mathematical expression for NeuMF++, which is a single-layer MLP that combines GMF++ and MLP++, is Eq. (7).

$$\hat{r} = \sigma\left(\begin{bmatrix} p_u \odot q_i \\ \sigma_1\left(\begin{bmatrix} p_u \\ q_i \end{bmatrix} W_1 + b_1\right) \end{bmatrix} W + b\right) \tag{7}$$

The SDAEs for both users and items were used in both GMF++ and MLP++, as shown in Eq. (8). As a result, NeuMF++'s efficiency and learning capacity may be impaired. For instance, GMF++ and MLP++ may have distinct hyperparameters and latent vector sizes. Therefore, we allow both GMF++ and MLP++ to independently extract features for user items. The NeuMF++ gains in adaptability as a result. As a result, we can express the complete NeuMF++ method as

$$\phi^{(GMF++)} = p_u^{(GMF++)} \odot q_i^{(GMF++)}$$

$$\phi^{(MLP++)} = \sigma_L\left(\ldots\sigma_1\left(\begin{bmatrix} p_u^{(MLP++)} \\ q_i^{(MLP++)} \end{bmatrix} W_1 + b_1\right)\ldots\right) W_L + b_L \tag{8}$$

$$\hat{r} = \sigma\left(\begin{bmatrix} \phi^{(GMF++)} \\ \phi^{(MLP++)} \end{bmatrix} W + b\right)$$

NeuMF++: Learning and optimization

The goal function of NeuMF++ incorporates both neural collaborative filtering errors and feature-extraction prediction errors. The loss function for the user and item SDAEs can be seen in Eq. (9). If N is the maximum rating, the ratings forecasts by NeuMF++ range from 0 to 1, inclusive. Consequently, the following equation represents the loss function:

$$l_r = ||r_{ui} - \widehat{r_{ui}}||_F^2 + \lambda_\theta||\theta||_F^2$$

where θ denotes as the parameters of the models. λ_θ as the regularization term.

Therefore, the general loss function for optimizing NeuMF++ is formulated in Eq. (13). **(9)**

$$l = l_r + \alpha l_u^{(GMF++)} + \beta l_i^{(GMF++)} + \gamma l_u^{(MLP++)} + \delta l_i^{(MLP++)}$$

where α, β, γ, δ are trade-off parameter for each reconstruction loss.

RESULT AND DISCUSSION

Setting up the Lab

For this analysis, we make use of the MovieLens 1-M dataset, which is available to the public.11 With a sparsity of 95.8 percent, the dataset includes over 1 million ratings from 6040 distinct users covering 3,706 unique movies. At the same time, we make use of the dataset's supplemental data. The product data collection includes 18 distinct film categories, but the user data asks for gender, age, and employment. It is necessary to transform each feature into an integer array before encoding. We employed a root-mean-square error (RMSE) as our assessment index in this work; it is given by Equation (10). Our loss function has a one-to-one relationship with RMSE. The lower the RMSE, the more precise the recommendations.

$$RMSE = \sqrt{\sum_{u=1}^{m} \sum_{i=1} \left(\frac{(r_{ui} - \widehat{r_{ui}})}{N} \right)} \quad \textbf{(10)}$$

Our suggested NeuMF++ was compared with MF, GMF, MLP, NeuMF, GMF++, and MLP++.1-3 All experiments were written in Python and run using the PyTorch deep learning framework. To fine-tune our model, we used Adam optimization with a batch size of 1024, a regularization term of 0.001, and a learning rate of 0.001. At the same time, we divide the dataset into two halves, with each half used for either training or testing at 70% to 30%. Baseline models and their hyperparameter settings are documented in the literature. Previously, we discussed how we extracted features from user-provided items by adjusting hyperparameters in both GMF++ and MLP++. In GMF++ user-item SDAEs, 8 neurons were employed on a single hidden layer, while in MLP++ user-item SDAEs, 16 neurons were used over three hidden layers. Therefore, all SDAEs have the same 8-dimensional latent vector space. A little amount of Gaussian noise is also fed into each SDAE layer. The embedding vector dimension, d, selected for neural collaborative filtering is 8. As an activation function for

GMF++, we utilized ReLU, and for MLP++, we used SeLU. Simultaneously, MLP++'s interaction MLP layers are made out of 32,16,8 neurons. Finally, we decided on a value of 0.000001 for each of the four compromise parameters.

Experimental Result and Analysis

With a train RMSE of 0.7964 and a test RMSE of 0.8681, as shown in Table **1**, NeuMF++ clearly outperforms the other baseline models. NeuMF++ outperforms NeuMF by 1.37 percentage points and conventional MF by 2 percentage points. Therefore, NeuMF++ has proven that using DNN and ancillary data for rating prediction is successful. As can be seen in Fig. (**1**), with the exception of MF and GMF, most models converged quickly. This data clearly demonstrates that DNN-enabled models outperform those without in this dataset. MLP++ also has lower convergence rates than MLP. As a result, MLP is relatively unaffected by extraneous data. Table **1** shows the results of a comparison between three versions of NeuMF++, demonstrating the value of using independent feature extraction and pre-trained weights. NeuMF++, with its GMF++ and MLP++ layers kept completely distinct for training and feature extraction, performs admirably.

At the same time, when the feature extraction was split across the GMF and MLP layers, we observed that NeuMF++ overfitted in the first iterations, as shown in Fig. (**1**). At first, we found that NeuMF++ was less effective than NeuMF. So, we imported and froze pre-trained weights from GMF++ and MLP++ into NeuMF++, inspired by the notion of a pre-training approach from 2. As can be seen in Table **1**, this led to an increase of 8.11 percent. The NeuMF layer's weights are updated throughout this pre-training procedure, whereas the GMF++ and MLP++ layers' weights are not. This led to a significant improvement in performance between NeuMF++ with and without pre-trained weights. This proved the pre-training method's worth in setting up NeuMF++.

CONCLUSION

In this study, we developed an improved version of NeuMF, NeuMF++, a model for recommending HBs that effectively leverages latent representations of contextual information. Incorporating ancillary data into neural CF improved recommendation performance while addressing cold starts and data sparsity, as seen in our experiments. Additionally, NeuMF++ may be expanded to include data types beyond categories and numbers, such as text and even images. Using word2vec, ELMO, or BERT, which are pre-trained word embedding models, it is possible to transform textual data into input bags of words. By analyzing images for specific characteristics, CNNs can also be useful for neural collaborative filtering and feature extraction. Due to DL's adaptability, many components of neural networks may be combined. To further strengthen NeuMF++'s recommendation model and increase its suggestion precision, this idea may be applied to it as well.

REFERENCES

[1] Y. Zhang, "Deep matrix factorization models for personalized recommendation", *J. Comput. Sci. Technol.,* vol. 37, no. 1, pp. 180-196, 2022.

[2] Y. Li, "A scalable approach for high-dimensional matrix factorization in recommendation systems", *Neurocomputing,* vol. 495, pp. 389-398, 2022.

[3] Y. Li, "Multi-modal matrix factorization for personalized recommendation with implicit feedback", *Inf. Sci.,* vol. 598, pp. 22-38, 2022.

[4] X. Chen, "A matrix factorization model for cold start recommendation with implicit feedback", *J. Intell. Fuzzy Syst.,* vol. 41, no. 6, pp. 7789-7802, 2021.

[5] L. Duan, "Learning matrix factorization models for top-N recommendation with implicit feedback", *Knowl. Base. Syst.,* vol. 227, p. 107106, 2021.

[6] W. Yang, "Deep learning-based matrix factorization models for personalized recommendation with implicit feedback", *Neurocomputing,* vol. 434, pp. 69-79, 2021.

[7] X. Chen, "A matrix factorization model for recommendation with heterogeneous features", *J. Ambient Intell. Humaniz. Comput.,* vol. 12, no. 4, pp. 4373-4384, 2021.

[8] L. Peng, "Multi-objective matrix factorization for personalized recommendation with implicit feedback", *Knowl. Base. Syst.,* vol. 231, p. 107999, 2021.

[9] X. Song, "Matrix factorization models for cold start recommendation with heterogeneous features", *Inf. Sci.,* vol. 549, pp. 1-16, 2021.

[10] X. Wang, "A matrix factorization model for personalized recommendation with social information", *J. Ambient Intell. Humaniz. Comput.,* vol. 12, no. 8, pp. 7761-7772, 2021.

[11] K. Xu, "Deep matrix factorization models for recommendation with implicit feedback and item relationships", *Inf. Sci.,* vol. 568, pp. 389-402, 2021.

[12] Z. Zhang, "Learning matrix factorization models for collaborative filtering with item attributes", *Neurocomputing,* vol. 444, pp. 38-47, 2021.

[13] S. Zhou, "Matrix factorization with temporal dynamics for personalized recommendation with implicit feedback", *J. Intell. Fuzzy Syst.,* vol. 41, no. 3, pp. 4233-4245, 2021.

[14] Y. Cai, "A deep learning-based matrix factorization model for recommendation with implicit feedback", *Knowl. Base. Syst.,* vol. 212, p. 106661, 2021.

[15] Y. Xu, "An efficient matrix factorization model for recommendation with implicit feedback", *Inf. Sci.,* vol. 541, pp. 188-201, 2021.

[16] S. Naseem, "The Role of Tourism in Economic Growth: Empirical Evidence from Saudi Arabia", *Economies,* vol. 9, no. 3, p. 117, 2021. [http://dx.doi.org/10.3390/economies9030117]

[17] B.I.R. Fortune, *Saudi Arabia Food Service Market Size, Share and COVID-19 Impact Analysis.* Fortune Business Insights: Pune, Maharashtra, India, 2022.

[18] JLL Report. The Future of Food Service in Saudi Arabia: Current Market and Future Trend. Jones Lang LaSalle (JLL). MENA. 2020. Available online: https://argaamplus.s3.amazonaws.com/43ec514f-b182-4472-be10-74df48161f56.pdf (accessed on 27 May 2023).

[19] I. Elgammal, M.H. Baeshen, and G.T. Alhothali, "Entrepreneurs' Responses to COVID-19 Crisis: A Holistic Dynamic Capabilities Perspective in the Saudi Food and Beverage Sector", *Sustainability*

(Basel), vol. 14, no. 20, p. 13111, 2022.
[http://dx.doi.org/10.3390/su142013111]

[20] Z. Fayyaz, M. Ebrahimian, D. Nawara, A. Ibrahim, and R. Kashef, "Recommendation Systems: Algorithms, Challenges, Metrics, and Business Opportunities", *Appl. Sci. (Basel),* vol. 10, no. 21, p. 7748, 2020.
[http://dx.doi.org/10.3390/app10217748]

[21] R. Alabduljabbar, M. Alshareef, and N. Alshareef, "Time-Aware Recommender Systems: A Comprehensive Survey and Quantitative Assessment of Literature", *IEEE Access,* vol. 11, pp. 45586-45604, 2023.
[http://dx.doi.org/10.1109/ACCESS.2023.3274117]

CHAPTER 25

Leveraging Big Data to Enhance the Analysis and Use of Information

S. Gadug[1,*] and **Avadhesh Kumar**[2]

[1] *Department of Computer Science and Engineering, JAIN (Deemed-to-be University), Bangalore, Karnataka, India*

[2] *Department of Computer Science and Engineering, Galgotias University, Greater Noida, Uttar Pradesh, India*

Abstract: The goal of this research is to examine how e-commerce and web-based businesses might benefit from the use of Big Data Analytics in managerial decision-making. The data used in this analysis comes from a single e-commerce website's database. User interactions with the website, such as page views, product additions, and online purchases, would be recorded. Association Rule Mining Algorithm (APRIORI), K-Means Clustering, and Pearson's Correlation Coefficient are only a few of the algorithms that will be utilized to evaluate the dataset. The information will be analyzed and used to provide insights into users' interactions with the website, enabling the identification of patterns that may inform future actions. For instance, which product receives the most attention and sales, how many pages are viewed before a purchase is made, what percentage of customers buy the product again, and so on. This study would also determine whether the company's current Big Data implementation can be enhanced and whether doing so would be a clever use of resources.

Keywords: Big Data, Information Analysis, E-Commerce, ARM, Association Rule Mining Algorithm (APRIORI).

INTRODUCTION

Obtaining private space in the modern world is difficult. As more and more of our lives move online, so too does the risk of sensitive data leakage.

Data collection includes personal information from users of online services, including buying, trading, banking, and entertainment. While not all of these services are designed to abuse users' private information, some do. For instance, one method of Internet marketing is to use users' browser histories to provide

* **Corresponding author S. Gadug:** Department of Computer Science and Engineering, JAIN (Deemed-to-be University), Bangalore, Karnataka, India; E-mail: s.gadug@jainuniversity.ac.in

S. Kannadhasan, R. Nagarajan, & Kaushik Pal (Eds.)

specific suggestions based on their interests and preferences. The diagnostic process can benefit from the study of sensitive data, such as medical data. Such application situations have wide-ranging applicability. Data transformation technologies are used to preserve personal information while still enabling valuable analytics. Given the inherent tension between protecting individual privacy and doing thorough research, this is easier said than done. The sheer volume of big data makes this a very difficult task from several angles. The ability to strike a compromise between privacy, usefulness, and performance is essential for any privacy-protecting analytic system. Several strategies for protecting privacy in big data analytics have been presented. Specifically, they focus on the privacy algorithms k-anonymity [1, 2], and l-diversity [3]. Methods based on k-anonymity use data transformation techniques to render personal information useless. In k-anonymity-based methods, the choice of k is crucial, as it determines the level of anonymity. Better privacy can be achieved by optimizing k, but at the expense of some of the data's usefulness.

Another restriction of optimization methods is the performance overhead they impose. Anonymization allows a middle-ground approach, where one goal is prioritized over the others, and the application's context explains this. The mathematical groundwork offered by the privacy algorithm known as differential privacy [3] has lately attracted more attention. Differential privacy is the central method, and lenient variants have been proposed [4]. To keep their users' data secure, tech giants like Google and Apple have implemented algorithms that show only a sanitized version of their data. The fundamental idea behind the algorithm is to safeguard users' personal information, whether they actively participate in the data analysis or not. Even while this method has been endorsed for privacy protection [5], useful analytical findings require a learning mechanism at least as powerful.

Companies that can efficiently collect data, analyze it for insights, and turn that insight into strategic action are likely to succeed in the market. Not only information about the market as a whole or how tough the competition is, but also how consumers are responding to our offerings. Understanding how people feel, speak about, and respond to our product might help us decide what steps to take next. The company requires genuine, unprompted, and honest customer feedback to achieve this. When people are asked questions or given forms to fill out by hand, the answers they provide may not accurately reflect their true thoughts and feelings, as they may be motivated to give an answer that benefits them personally. The result would be the collection of useless information, which might lead to disastrous consequences for businesses. Therefore, the "unconscious" response is what we seek, and Big Data can help us get there [6].

RELATED WORKS

The 5Vs of big data are volume, velocity, variety, veracity, and variability; they will be discussed in more detail below [5]. One, the quantity of storage space needed is directly proportional to its volume. Second, velocity is a measure of how quickly and accurately data is transmitted and processed in real time. Data comes in many formats, including text, images, audio, and video, and this diversity is a reflection of the data's structure or lack thereof. Fourth, data trustworthiness is a function of data veracity. Five, variation shows how varied the data points are from one another. One of the most crucial factors in developing a website is the user's behavior. Abraham Maslow, a humanist psychologist, proposed a "hierarchy of needs" as a theory of what people need to achieve their "pinnacle" (the point at which they decide to engage) in terms of behavior. The CEO of WebFx, William Craig, lists the many factors that determine a person's ability to reach "self-actualization" and explains their relative weight. 1) Ease of access. Everyone has access to the website and may utilize it. 2) Dependability: the site's reliability and consistency are both high; 3) Practicality: the interface is intuitive and straightforward; 4) Dependability: there is no downtime in the website's availability; 5) Usefulness: site visitors can access useful information, resources, and services, 6) Capacity to adapt: the website changes to suit the preferences of its visitors. The model suggests that a website's primary purpose should be to drive sales; thus, it's crucial that the website cater to and prioritize its customers' needs [6].

The main goal of analytics is to help businesses make better decisions and fix issues. Thus, analytics is a repository of information that comprises mathematical and statistical tools, machine learning algorithms, data management procedures such as extraction, transformation, and loading (ETL), and computer technologies such as Hadoop, which together extract useful, actionable information from data. When discussing analytics and business intelligence solutions that rely heavily on statistical analysis and data mining, the term "analytics" is often used. Data warehouses (DW), online analytical processing (OLAP), ETL, and relational database management systems (DBMS) constitute the backbone of most of these approaches. "Data analytics" refers to the process of collecting and analyzing data to draw conclusions. With the use of data analytics, businesses may get valuable insights that can improve decision-making and lessen the likelihood of fraud, mistakes, abuse, and danger [7]. The list also includes data visualization, AI, natural language processing, analytical database capabilities such as MapReduce, in-memory database analysis, and columnar data warehouses. All of these case studies illustrate the use of sophisticated analytics [8], which are applications of specialized analytics methods and associated tools. It is possible to perform big data analytics on incomplete or inconsistent data. Actually, they make no assumptions about the best way to standardize data. Data analytics [9] can explore many forms of data, shedding light on models and ideas previously hidden. They use advanced techniques from statistics, deep learning, machine learning, artificial intelligence, feedback, and natural language processing to maximize data. Numerous technologies and platforms influence modern data analytics [10 - 12]. These include social media platforms like Facebook and Twitter, as well as information collected by the Internet of Things (such as barcodes, QR codes, GPS, NFC, and RFID chips). Data transportation is interconnected with many other industries, including finance, retail, media, manufacturing, and more.

Data analysis, as well as business analysis, which have an extensive history of application across all disciplines of study, particularly in businesses and companies, has rapidly expanded due to the demand for tools that assess information and support successful, effective decision-making [13]. Data analysis has become more complex in tandem with the exponential growth of data quantities. Intelligence tools have integrated data mining technologies such as text mining, web mining, and innovative analysis of social media data, which has relied on methods for assessing sentiment and opinion [14]. Many different programs and methods exist for doing data analysis. Data visualization, data mining, optimization, streaming media (audio, video, or photos), fuzzy logic, data searches and reports, and so on are all popular ways. Data analysis is the process of examining raw data and drawing conclusions from it. Organizations and businesses have embraced it due to its value in improving decision-making quality. When used in business intelligence, this term can mean different things depending on who developed the relevant software—many types of dashboards, OLAP, CRM, *etc* [15 - 21].

PROPSOED WORK

This study collected Big Data using a third-party data analytics platform that tracks user actions on the website. Users' interactions with the website were tracked and recorded by the Analytics tool, and the resulting data was then presented in attractive reports. Node.js was used to build a local web server that incorporated the analytics tools needed to process the data. In 2018, the input would be the website's usage data. After identifying the analysis's constituent parts, the analysis is carried out in stages, as depicted in the accompanying diagram.

The research starts by examining the pages users visit to understand how they interact with the website. The first step of the analysis is to search for the labeled actions “buy online” and “page visit” for every product URL. Each completed action is accompanied by a session ID (user ID), with distinct counts for session

IDs that view pages (but do not make an online purchase) and those that do both. Each quarterly report provides a summary, along with percentages for buy_online and visit. The proposed work is shown in Fig. (**1**). The formula for determining the "conversion rate for each product URL" is as follows. Online Sales Per Visitor = Conversion Rate. In the second part of our study, we calculate the website's overall conversion rate. This research considers all pages of the website, not just the Product Detail Page (PDP), to determine the overall conversion rate. User purchasing behavior is the focus of the research's third and final analysis. In particular, this analysis monitors the user's behavior just before purchase, determining whether the user is a "surf and buy" consumer (defined as opening more than 4 pages before purchase) or a "direct buyer" (defined as opening 4 pages or fewer before purchase). The program tracks how many times a given user views a product page before deciding to purchase. In the study's fourth analysis, we examine how many times each user made purchases. In essence, we tally how many times each individual user makes use of the online shopping cart. For this study, we use the session_id and buy_online action data fields. The analysis's "Repurchase Rate" output is the final product. The rate at which customers repurchase a product is a key performance indicator (KPI) in the online retail industry. Here is the formula for determining the repurchase rate.

RR=((PC1*O+PC2*O2+PC3*O3+□+PCn*On)/ Total Transaction)

PC= Purchase Count

O= Occurrence

The study produces a Repurchase rate, and we use this rate to compare XYZ with other e-commerce websites in order to gauge the success or failure of the firm. After analysis, recommendations may be made. The best pairing of the company's goods is the focus of the fifth and final examination here. We plan to examine the contents of each shopping cart shipped to a store to determine the most popular bundles of goods. One prevalent technique in Machine Learning is called Association Rule Mining, also known as the Apriori Algorithm. Here are the measures needed to reach the data sets:

Step 1: Gather all shopping carts that include multiple products

Step 2: The number of filter products purchased exceeds the Support Threshold

Step 3: Find a way to combine two goods using Apriori Array 1.

Step 4: Determine the frequency of each permutation that meets the support level specified in step 3.

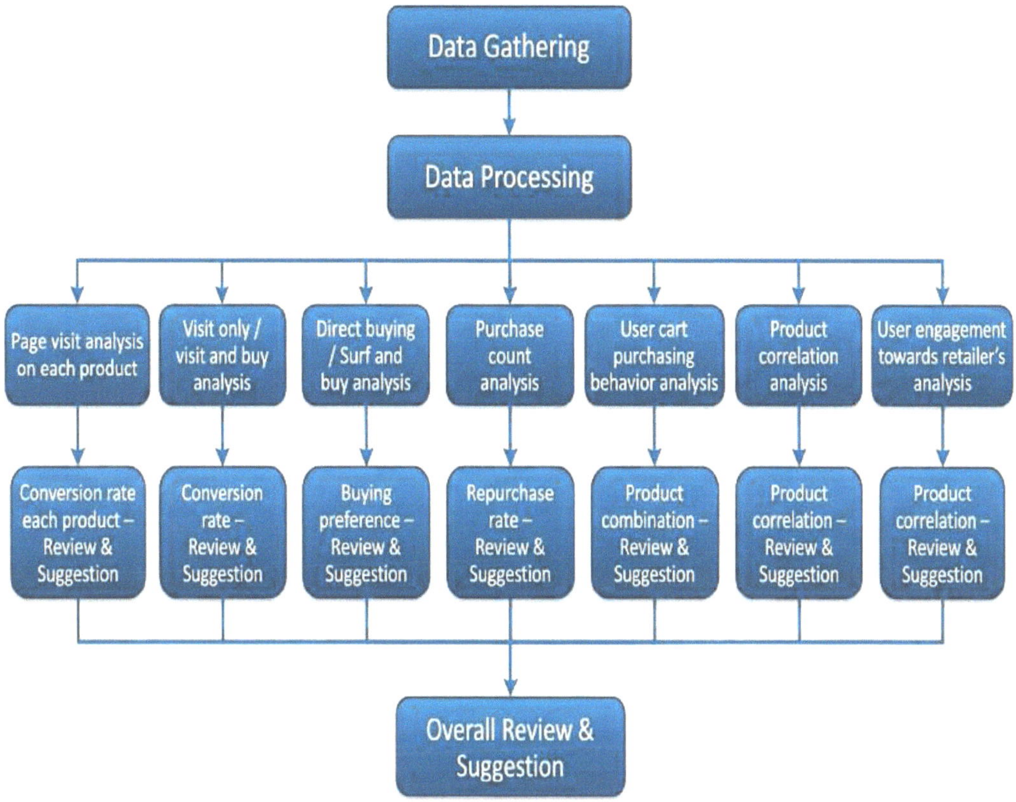

Fig. (1). Proposed Work Chart.

Discovering which goods have a substantial link with each other is the sixth evaluation in this investigation. This will be accomplished by using Pearson's Correlation.

Step 1: Get all the sales numbers.

Step 2: Locate every possible permutation of the five best items.

Step 3: Find the value of the correlation for each combination of products.

The seventh research focuses on the online performance of each shop. We review the effectiveness of each retailer to analyze user preferences and buying behaviors, because the XYZ website uses online retailers such as Walmart, Walgreens, and Amazon to provide customers with various retail channels. For this study, we keep track of all buy_online actions, the associated sales, and the online store visited. Once the data is analyzed, a sales report for each shop is prepared and assessed, and recommendations are made based on the report's findings.

RESULT AND DISCUSSION

Website page views provide initial insight into the dataset, as shown in Table **1**. The purpose of this research is to compare consumer interest levels across various products, specifically PDPs.

Table 1. Dataset features.

URL	Q1			Q2			Q3			Q4			total		
	visit	buy	percentage	visit	buy	percentage	visit	buy	percentage	visit	buy	percentage	visit	buy	percentage
Product 28	1005	21	2.09%	1235	57	4.62%	1195	45	3.77%	607	20	3.29%	4042	143	3.54%
Product 37	4263	91	2.13%	4950	102	2.06%	5009	173	2.93%	2415	101	4.18%	17537	467	2.66%
Product 36	19564	367	1.88%	18202	384	2.11%	25269	780	3.09%	12474	451	3.62%	75509	1982	2.62%
Product 11	3306	85	2.57%	4377	94	2.15%	4127	110	2.67%	1467	48	3.27%	13277	337	2.54%
Product 22	5695	108	1.90%	6520	143	2.19%	6302	161	2.55%	2710	125	4.61%	21227	537	2.53%
Product 49	4021	88	2.19%	4448	98	2.20%	4841	115	2.38%	2294	81	3.53%	15604	382	2.45%
Product 48	8510	130	1.53%	9002	146	1.62%	10965	238	2.17%	4391	176	4.01%	32868	690	2.10%
Product 46	3120	32	1.03%	3450	62	1.80%	5608	128	2.28%	2696	77	2.86%	14874	299	2.01%
Product 21	8908	140	1.57%	10040	186	1.85%	12343	245	1.98%	5713	148	2.59%	37004	719	1.94%
Product 3	364	6	1.65%	589	12	2.04%	703	13	1.85%	258	6	2.33%	1914	37	1.93%
...	...	...	...	...	...	...	...	+	...	...	...	...	...	-	...
Product 5	6203	5	0.08%	7271	13	0.18%	8613	14	0.16%	2172	6	0.28%	24259	38	0.16%
Total	402062	3725	48.06%	479445	4301	52.15%	494704	5743	61.56%	201758	3308	90.58%	1577969	17077	1,08%
Max Value	87901	818	2.57%	95982	769	4.62%	99573	980	3.77%	51343	471	4.61%	333799	3038	3.54%
Min Value	364	3	0.08%	589	8	0.17%	703	9	0.16%	258	4	0.18%	1914	26	0.16%

Pageview data reveals the most popular product URL throughout the measured time frame. Obviously, this reflects the product's effectiveness. On top of that, you can see the "conversion rate" (the ratio of visitors to purchases) for each product.

According to the data, the conversion rate ranges from 0.16% (product 5) to 3.54% (product 28). One possible solution to this discrepancy is to boost the product 5 conversion rate from 1 sale for every 28 visits to 1 sale for every 638 visitors. The second type of study is a quarterly recap of customer activity to see what fraction of visitors convert into buyers. The outcome is shown in Table **2** below.

Table 2. Performance analysis.

Quarter	Global	US	UK
Q4 2014	3.42%	3.60%	3.65%
Q1 2015	2.83%	2.91%	3.56%
Q2 2015	3.08%	3.18%	3.97%
Q3 2015	3.02%	3.09%	4.08%
Q4 2015	3.48%	3.62%	4.20%
Q1 2016	2.94%	2.89%	5.01%
Q2 2016	2.76%	2.72%	4.64%
Q3 2016	2.46%	2.44%	4.35%
Q4 2016	2.95%	3.00%	4.45%
Q1 2017	2.48%	2.46%	3.57%
Q2 2017	2.86%	2.62%	4.28%
Q3 2017	2.80%	2.56%	4.21%
Q4 2017	3.15%	2.96%	4.27%
Q1 2018	2.77%	2.60%	3.91%
Q2 2018	2.86%	2.63%	4.31%

From Q4 2014 to Q1 2018, the US conversion rate ranged from a low of 2.44% in Q3 2016 to a high of 3.62% in Q4 2015. In 2018, the approximate exchange rate was 2.60 percent. The information here serves as a standard against which XYZ Company's statistics may be measured. The third type of research examines how customers use a website by tracking how many pages they view before making a purchase. A surfer is someone who looks at more than 4 pages before making a purchase, whereas a direct buyer is someone who looks at 4 pages or less before making a purchase, since they already know everything they need to know about the product. Clustering was performed using the k-means analytics approach, and the results are shown below.

More than half of users (57.11%) only look at a maximum of four pages before making a purchase. One theory holds that consumers would rather skip the research phase and go straight to making a purchase. The preceding data shows a rather low conversion rate; therefore, it's reasonable to assume that when the path to purchase is lengthy, potential customers give up and go elsewhere. This data shows that the proof is rather pertinent. Analysis based on this presumption is carried out by examining the "road" buyers take to purchase the goods. Users favor in-person transactions. In light of this user behavior, we may modify the present XYZ website's 4 stages to complete a purchase of a product, by reducing the number of clicks required to buy a product, for instance. Add-to-basket buttons on category pages and direct links to product detail pages on the homepage are two ways to facilitate this. Adapting to users' preferences might also boost sales. In this fourth study, we look at how often individual users go on to make a purchase.

CONCLUSION

Big data analytics may provide invaluable insight into how successful the company's website is, according to the study's authors. Managers may gain valuable insight into the health of their e-commerce operations and the steps that need to be taken to improve them, thanks to the data that can be pulled from the dataset. The value of this study lies in demonstrating to the business world how Big Data Analytics can be used to enhance decision-making and ultimately provide a competitive edge.

REFERENCES

[1] Z. Cui, W. Li, and Z. Zhang, "A big data analysis framework for smart tourism services", *J. Ambient Intell. Humaniz. Comput.,* vol. 12, no. 10, pp. 11603-11621, 2021.

[2] Y. Yang, S. Wu, and H. Jin, "Big data analysis for credit risk assessment", *J. Intell. Fuzzy Syst.,* vol. 41, no. 5, pp. 6393-6403, 2021.

[3] C. Wang, X. Wang, and W. Xu, "Big data analysis for intelligent manufacturing systems", *J. Ambient Intell. Humaniz. Comput.,* vol. 12, no. 7, pp. 8291-8308, 2021.

[4] X. Li, Y. Li, and Q. Li, "Big data analysis for supply chain management optimization", *J. Intell. Fuzzy Syst.,* vol. 41, no. 5, pp. 6459-6469, 2021.

[5] Y. Wang, Y. Zhang, and L. Wang, "Big data analysis for urban traffic management", *J. Ambient Intell. Humaniz. Comput.,* vol. 12, no. 6, pp. 6987-7005, 2021.

[6] Y. Zhang, X. Wu, and K. Zhou, "Big data analysis for industrial internet of things", *J. Intell. Manuf.,* vol. 32, no. 5, pp. 1119-1136, 2021.

[7] Y. Xu, H. Zhang, and L. Zhou, "Big data analysis for smart grid operation and control", *J. Ambient Intell. Humaniz. Comput.,* vol. 12, no. 4, pp. 4577-4595, 2021.

[8] D. Wang, S. Zhou, and Y. Feng, "Big data analysis for healthcare management", *J. Ambient Intell. Humaniz. Comput.,* vol. 12, no. 3, pp. 3495-3506, 2021.

[9] Z. Tao, Q. Zhang, and X. Li, "A big data-driven framework for online user behavior analysis and recommendation", *J. Ambient Intell. Humaniz. Comput.,* vol. 13, no. 1, pp. 905-919, 2022.

[10] X. Li, H. Zhang, and X. Hu, "An intelligent big data-driven approach to decision-making", *J. Intell. Manuf.,* vol. 33, no. 1, pp. 61-76, 2022.

[11] J. Zheng, Y. He, J. Yan, and J. Tang, "A big data analysis framework for complex event processing in smart city", *J. Netw. Comput. Appl.,* vol. 196, p. 105186, 2022.

[12] J. Wang, S. Zhou, and Y. Feng, "Big data analysis for financial fraud detection", *J. Intell. Fuzzy Syst.,* vol. 41, no. 5, pp. 6511-6521, 2021.

[13] H. Zhang, X. Gao, and Y. Liu, "Research on the Application of Big Data Analysis in Higher Education Management", *Proceedings of the 2021 International Conference on Information Management, Innovation Management and Industrial Engineering,* pp. 529-532, 2021.

[14] Y. Song, J. Zhang, and K. Xu, "Big data analysis for disease prediction and prevention", *J. Ambient Intell. Humaniz. Comput.,* vol. 12, no. 12, pp. 14357-14373, 2021.

[15] T. Huang, L. Yu, and X. Sun, "Big data analysis for personalized recommendation", *J. Intell. Fuzzy Syst.,* vol. 41, no. 5, pp. 6575-6585, 2021.

[16] J. Tang, S.X. Zhang, and S. Lin, "To reopen or not to reopen? How entrepreneurial alertness influences small business reopening after the COVID-19 lockdown", *Journal of Business Venturing Insights,* vol. 16, p. e00275, 2021.
[http://dx.doi.org/10.1016/j.jbvi.2021.e00275]

[17] E. Nebolsina, "The impact of the Covid-19 pandemic on the business interruption insurance demand in the United States", *Heliyon,* vol. 7, no. 11, p. e08357, 2021.
[http://dx.doi.org/10.1016/j.heliyon.2021.e08357] [PMID: 34786513]

[18] S.A. Zarghami, "A reflection on the impact of the COVID-19 pandemic on Australian businesses: Toward a taxonomy of vulnerabilities", *Int. J. Disaster Risk Reduct.,* vol. 64, p. 102496, 2021.
[http://dx.doi.org/10.1016/j.ijdrr.2021.102496] [PMID: 36570387]

[19] W.J. Kettinger, S.Y. Ryoo, and D.A. Marchand, "We're engaged! Following the path to a successful information management capability", *J. Strateg. Inf. Syst.,* vol. 30, no. 3, p. 101681, 2021.
[http://dx.doi.org/10.1016/j.jsis.2021.101681]

[20] P.Y. Huang, B. Niu, and S.L. Pan, "Platform-based customer agility: An integrated framework of information management structure, capability, and culture", *Int. J. Inf. Manage.,* vol. 59, p. 102346, 2021.
[http://dx.doi.org/10.1016/j.ijinfomgt.2021.102346]

[21] R. Manandhar, and L.K. Siebeneck, "Information management and the return-entry process: Examining information needs, sources, and strategies after Superstorm Sandy", *Int. J. Disaster Risk Reduct.,* vol. 53, p. 102015, 2021.
[http://dx.doi.org/10.1016/j.ijdrr.2020.102015]

CHAPTER 26

Leveraging Text Mining Techniques for Automated Information Analysis

Vetrimani Elangovan[1,*] and **F. Rosita Kamala**[2]

[1] *Department of Computer Science and Engineering, Presidency University, Bangalore, Karnataka, India*

[2] *Department of Computer Applications, Presidency College, Bangalore, Karnataka, India*

Abstract: In recent years, the quantity of textual data carried *via* online digital files, e-mails, databases, and other formats has increased at an exponential rate due to the fast growth of Internet technology. Ontology and other contemporary models of knowledge representation rely heavily on attributes, which are formal descriptions of any real-world thing. Attributes may be either qualitative or quantitative. There is a wealth of literature attesting to the extensive research on mining non-qualitative attributes (such as part-of relations) from text and the web, but very little on mining qualitative attributes (such as size, color, taste, *etc.*). It became increasingly difficult for traditional intelligence data-processing technologies to meet the demands of these tasks. The accuracy of segmenting words in intelligence texts was significantly enhanced by our suggested intelligence dictionary-based word segmentation technique and the construction of an intelligence-specific dictionary.

Keywords: Text mining techniques, automated information analysis, ontology, word segmentation strategy, part-of relation.

INTRODUCTION

Cybercriminals target online social networks by creating fake identities and then using them to steal money, influence politics, or further their own agendas. OSNs often use machine learning (ML) abuse classifiers as a reaction. A practical and effective ML-based defense, however, requires the following: gathering sufficient ground-truth data with labels for model training; developing a scalable system to handle all current accounts on an OSN, which could number in the billions; and meticulously engineering features that are resistant to adversarial manipulation [1]. Finding social interactions is crucial for studying animal behavior, as it allows researchers to address several questions, such as how social hierarchies affect

* **Corresponding author Vetrimani Elangovan:** Department of Computer Science and Engineering, Presidency University, Bangalore, Karnataka, India; E-mail: vetrimani.elangovan@presidencyuniversity.in

S. Kannadhasan, R. Nagarajan, & Kaushik Pal (Eds.)

behavior and what causes agonistic behavioral disorders. The bulk of earlier research, however, relies on labor- and resource-intensive manual counting of social interaction kinds and numbers obtained from direct observation [2].

In practical contexts like computational finance, social networks, and recommender systems, graphs are an effective tool for depicting and evaluating intricate interactions. In complex systems, graph-based thinking is crucial for uncovering hidden trends and patterns and for forming conclusions about the interactions between elements. An understudied subject is reasoning about graphs using large language models (LLMs), despite the remarkable advances in automated reasoning from natural text [3]. In order to foster a more welcoming and courteous online environment, it is imperative to create automated systems that can recognize instances of sexism as well as other disrespectful and hateful actions. This is especially important given the growing importance of social media platforms. Still, given the variety of hatred categories and the author's goals to consider, these tasks are very difficult, particularly in the context of learning within a dispute regime [4]. To distribute spam and harmful content, violate users' privacy, or manipulate data to influence the stock market or electoral outcomes, social bots use social networks to create content and engage with network users, attempting to mimic or change user behavior. This can lead to numerous losses [5]. An automated method for identifying and making sense of the feelings expressed in text is known as sentiment analysis (SA). There has been a meteoric rise in SA's profile in the NLP community within the last decade. Social media analytics (SA) has grown in importance as a tool for businesses to gauge consumer sentiment and inform advertising campaigns, driven by the proliferation of online platforms. Furthermore, SA is used by academics to assess public opinion on many subjects [6]. Human values are qualities people hold in high regard, such as honesty, social responsibility, justice, privacy, and related concepts. There could be a wide range of negative consequences for people and society if software systems, particularly mobile app developers, disregard or violate such ideals. This mixed-methods research focuses on honesty as a crucial human value in software engineering, but previous studies have explored many other human values [7].

RELATED WORKS

The research referenced as [8] used a Real-Time Kinematic Global Navigation Satellite System (RTK-GNSS) localization device (RTK rover) affixed to the backs of sheep. The module was manufactured by u-blox of Thalwil, Switzerland. We tested the RTK rover's ability to continuously track the movement of seven sheep over four days, and the results showed an accuracy of around 20 cm. Using each sheep's geospatial data, we built social networks and tracked the first sheep to move during a grazing period (the movement of the leadership) in the one-hectare test field. Finding the optimal location update rate with a 20 cm or 30 cm threshold distance revealed that social networks could be detected just as accurately with location sampling at 1 sample every second for 1 minute, then no samples for 4 or 9 minutes, as with ongoing measurements at 1 sample every 5 seconds. While operating in an outdoor field setting, the RTK rover collected accurate data on the social networks of a single flock of sheep using sampling techniques developed to prolong battery life.

To identify abusive identities in OSNs that have eluded more conventional abuse-detection methods, the authors of [9] introduce Deep Entity Categorization (DEC), a machine-learning framework. We take advantage of the fact that accounts may be hard to categorize on their own, but attackers have a far harder time replicating or manipulating at scale the social graph, which contains information about the accounts' and others' networks, features, and actions. The technology we use: • Extracts "deep features" by aggregating characteristics and behavioral information from the accounts' immediate and indirect social network neighbors using a "multi-stage multi-task learning" (MS-MTL) paradigm. Using a combination of just a few high-precision human-labeled samples and a large number of lower-precision computational labels in consecutive phases, this method leverages imperfect ground truth information. This design can handle billions of users with ease by using several sampling and reclassification procedures to reduce system load, and it produces a single model that accurately classifies a wide range of abusive accounts. Since DEC's deployment, Facebook has been able to continually classify all users, reducing the number of abusive accounts by an estimated 27%, even when compared to accounts found by more conventional approaches.

Using the audio sensor capabilities of a generic, unmodified wristwatch, researchers provide a workable method for automatically recognizing in-person conversations [10]. It demonstrates the advantages of feature fusion and includes feature representations obtained from various neural network configurations in its suggested architecture. An audio model trained to the voice of the person wearing the wristwatch or others close by is not necessary for the framework to function. In a semi-naturalistic investigation with 39 people across 18 households and 4 persons in free living, we assess our framework with F1 scores of 83.2% and 83.3% for recognizing user talk with the watch, respectively. In addition, we describe several methods to make our framework more practical in real-world settings and assess its real-time performance by running an algorithm on an actual wristwatch. We also make available our annotated database of discussions to encourage further study in this field.

Use a network of CNNs to detect the location and orientation of pigs in a video and track their migratory routes using a Kalman filter (KF) technique, as shown in [11]. We can automatically detect social connections, such as head-to-head and head-tail contacts, using the tracking data. In addition, we built a social interaction network as an output by utilizing the individual animal IDs. We used two separate sets of tests for pig tracking and detection to measure how well our system worked. As a result, we achieved a MOTA of 94.4%, a sensitivity of 94.2%, and a precision of 95.4%. Our keypoint-based tracking-by-detection technique was shown to be useful in this investigation, and its results may be used to improve animal monitoring systems.

According to a study [12], this project aims to build a system that can automatically identify the people who are propagating anti-vaccine narratives in order to better comprehend anti-vaccine sentiment. In this article, we present a freely accessible Python tool that analyzes Twitter accounts and predicts the likelihood that they will express anti-vaccine attitudes. Using automated dataset creation, text embedding algorithms, and several million tweets for training, the software program is built. Up to a year before the tweet's use of an anti-vaccine hashtag or keyword, our technology correctly identifies people who are against vaccines. Additionally, we demonstrate how text analysis may provide light on anti-vaccine discourse by identifying emotional and moral distinctions between Twitter users who promote anti-vaccine sentiment and those who do not. Researchers and policymakers will find our findings useful in gaining a better understanding of the factors that lead Twitter users to express anti-vaccine sentiment. With this data, lawmakers may launch more precise efforts to dispel dangerous anti-vaccination falsehoods.

Instead of targeting specific social media identities or postings, the technique [13] aims to uncover coordinated efforts that deliberately aim to mislead. In this work, we analyze the Twitter activity of a Russian government-affiliated influence effort that spanned many years. We show that time correlations in the sequencing selection procedures across different social media accounts might expose coordinated inauthentic behavior by drawing on the impact model, a generative model that captures interactions among networked Markov chains.

To make graph-structured data usable by LLMs, the first thorough investigation of textual encoding was conducted [14]. Graph encoding technique, graph problem type, and, most intriguingly, graph structure are the three basic levels on which LLM effectiveness on graph reasoning assignments varies. These new findings shed light on how to encode graphs as text, which is quite helpful. Based on these findings, we show that task-specifically, properly selected encoders can improve LLM efficiency on graph reasoning assignments by 4.8% to 61.8%.

By training directly from dispute data without using any aggregated labels, the suggested method seeks to address the challenge of sexism detection and characterisation within the learning through disagreements paradigm [15]. But results are published that take both easy and hard assessments into account. The suggested system can detect and categorize instances of sexism in both English and Spanish by using ensemble techniques and big language models, such as mBERT and XLM-RoBERTa. Specifically, our system is designed with three distinct pipelines. Using both soft and hard label evaluations, the ensemble method achieved better results than the individual big language models. Taking a soft assessment into account, this work ranked first in Task 3 of EXIST and fourth overall in Task 2, with a maximum ICM-Soft of -2.32 and a standardized ICM-Soft of 0.79.

PROPOSED WORK

Centralized Database for Quality Context (QCKB) on the Web. An adjective may only be allocated to a quality group if there is at least one related context in both the adjective and the quality category, according to the suggested approach. Within the scope of this research, "contexts of QA" and "QV" refer to the many possible applications of the quality designation. Assigning the attribute "color" to the adjective "red" is as simple as looking it up in a catalog of possible color values. However, the credibility of the sources used to compile the list and its completeness will determine the correctness of the categorization. The framework eliminates this guesswork by categorizing adjectives abstractly based on meanings retrieved from the Web. We often use the Internet as a reference library to extract context information for different attributes, such as color, taste, texture, *etc*., as there is substantial and convincing evidence in the literature supporting the use of the Web as a learning corpus. An online dictionary called PyDictionary () has been used to address this objective. This module provides a dictionary with definitions, translations, synonyms, and antonyms for words in Python 2 and 3. The dictionary uses WordNet for definitions, Google Translate for translations, and Thesaurus.com for synonyms and antonyms. Some examples of web-based scenarios for QA "Colour" are as follows: What shade {{'Adjective': ['getting or being capable of producing colors']}},'verb': ['add color to', 'influence as in thought or feeling','modify or bias', 'decorate about colors', 'give a deceptive more information or excuse for', 'change hue, frequently in an undesired manner']}}, 'noun': ['a visual link of things that originates from the light they emit, transmit, or reflect', 'interest, variety and also intensity', 'the timbre of an instrument's sound', 'an outwards or tokens physical appearance or form which is deliberately deceptive', 'all substance utilized for its color', '(physics)', 'the appearance of things (or light sources)', 'or brightness 'The worth of red web-based contexts encompass: {'red': {u'Adjective': ['of a color at the bottom of the color spectrum (next to orange)', 'characterized by attack or bloodshed', '(especially of the face)', 'or crimson'], u'Noun': ['red color or pigments; the chromatic color that looked like the hue of the blood', 'a tributary of the river Mississippi that flows toward the east from Texas along the southern boundary of Oklahoma and through Louisiana', 'emotionally charged regards used to describe severe radicals and revolutionaries', 'the amount by which the expenditure of a business exceeds its revenue']}} The semantic representations of each QA are obtained and stored in a knowledgebase known as the Quality Context Information Basis (QCKB), as shown in Fig. (**2**). The knowledge base contains tuples that include names of QA and semantic descriptions of those names. Information about the QA context is retrieved from the web and stored in the knowledge base during the pre-processing step. An example would be: The "color" quality attribute's QCKB tuple looks like this: A wide range of definitions are attached to the word "color," including: "having or being capable of creating colors," "adding color to," "affect as in thought or feeling," "modify or bias, "decorate *via* colors," "change color, often in an undesired manner," "interest and variety as well as intensity," "physics," "the appearance of objects or light the sources," "or brightness," and many more.

Only five QA attributes in the QCKB used in this investigation have semantic explanations or contexts. Additional QAs may be simply added to the knowledge base by storing semantic descriptions. This study proposes a novel framework to address a research aim comparable to document classification, in contrast to previous publications that mostly rely on established syntactic patterns. Building a VSM entails producing a vector representation of words from the semantic explanations of each QA class, as well as each quality rating or adjective in the query, once descriptions have been obtained and saved in QCKB. Fig. (**1**) shows the system model.

RESULT AND DISCUSSION

For each dataset, we randomly split the interaction history for each user into 80% for training and 20% for testing. As a validation set for hyperparameter tuning, we randomly select 10% of the relationships from the training set. We employ negative sampling to pair each user-item interaction with a single negative item, treating each interaction as a positive occurrence. (Fig. **2**) represents the Proposed System Flow, and (Fig. **3**) shows the Performance Analysis.

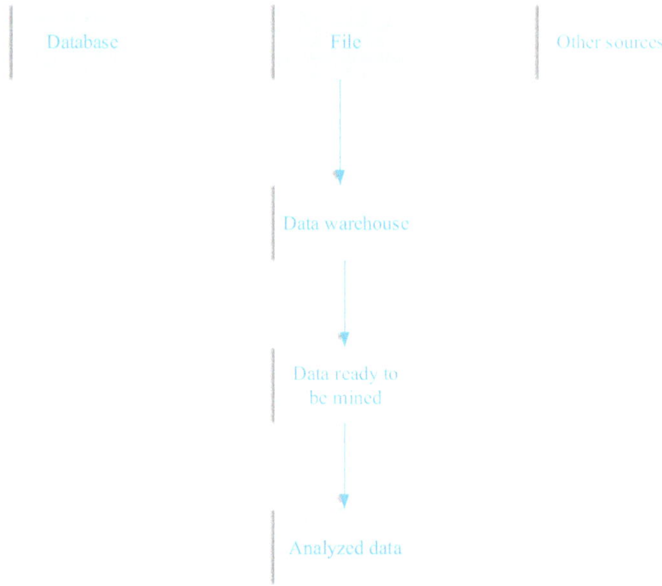

Fig. (1). System Model.

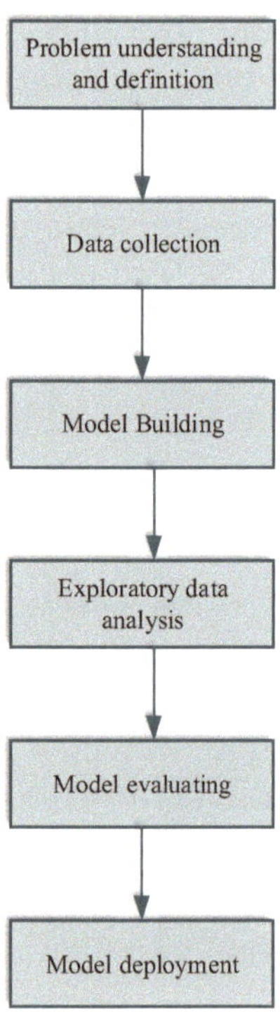

Fig. (2). Proposed System Flow.

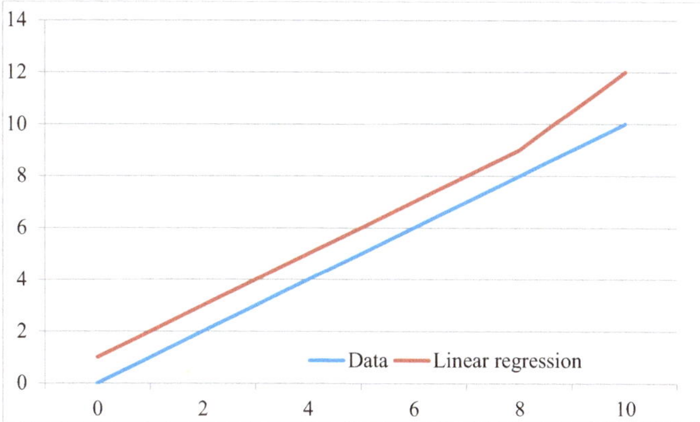

Fig. (3). Performance Analysis.

CONCLUSION

When discussing concepts such as "part relations," "semantic role labelling," and "attribute," scholars have employed a variety of approaches. This article presents a framework for the medicinal plant domain that may be used to extract and categorize qualitative features of ideas or entities. The suggested model enables differentiation between entities in two domains by defining real-world objects based on their fundamental traits or characteristics. We want to expand our approach so it may be used for ontology development or enrichment, but it can also be used for other applications that need to determine similarity measures between ideas. To keep things simple experimentally, this study analyses only a subset of the qualities linked to medicinal plant domain ideas. Our long-term goals include expanding the framework to include other qualities and studying the ambiguity between adjectives and nouns. We want to propose more resilient methods for managing complex phrase construction in the future, because attribute value acquisition is a system building block.

REFERENCES

[1] D. Gragnaniello, D. Cozzolino, F. Marra, G. Poggi, and L. Verdoliva, "Are GAN Generated Images Easy to Detect? A Critical Analysis of the State-Of-The-Art", *2021 IEEE International Conference on Multimedia and Expo (ICME),* pp. 1-6, 2021. [http://dx.doi.org/10.1109/ICME51207.2021.9428429]

[2] P.D. Angeli, and J.C. Reis, *Analyzing the Potential of Feature Groups for Misinformation Detection in WhatsApp..* Conference: Simpósio Brasileiro de Sistemas Multimídia e Web, 2022. [http://dx.doi.org/10.5753/webmedia_estendido.2022.227031]

[3] B. Cornwell, and J. Burchard, "Structural cohesion and embeddedness in two-mode networks", *J. Math. Sociol.,* vol. 43, no. 4, pp. 179-194, 2019. [http://dx.doi.org/10.1080/0022250X.2019.1606806]

[4] K. Li, S. Guan, and D. Lee, "Towards Understanding and Characterizing the Arbitrage Bot Scam In the Wild", *Proceedings of the ACM on Measurement and Analysis of Computing Systems,* pp. 1-29, 2023.

[http://dx.doi.org/10.1145/3626783]

[5] Lienkov, S.V., Juliy, V., Bernaz, A., Mulyar, I., & Pampukha, I. (2023). Method of forecasting information security vulnerabilities based on data analysis of thematic internet resources. Collection of scientific works of the Military Institute of Kyiv National Taras Shevchenko University.

[6] S. Tran, P. Rodrigues, B. Strauss, and E.M. Williams, *Accenture at CheckThat!-2023: Learning to Detect Factuality Levels of News Sources.* Conference and Labs of the Evaluation Forum, 2023.

[7] J. Li, F. Meng, Z. Lin, R. Liu, P. Fu, Y. Cao, W. Wang, and J. Zhou, "Neutral Utterances are Also Causes: Enhancing Conversational Causal Emotion Entailment with Social Commonsense Knowledge", *International Joint Conference on Artificial Intelligence,* 2022. [http://dx.doi.org/10.24963/ijcai.2022/584]

[8] H. Keshavarzi, C. Lee, M. Johnson, D. Abbott, W. Ni, and D.L.M. Campbell, "Validation of Real-Time Kinematic (RTK) Devices on Sheep to Detect Grazing Movement Leaders and Social Networks in Merino Ewes", *Sensors (Basel),* vol. 21, no. 3, p. 924, 2021. [http://dx.doi.org/10.3390/s21030924] [PMID: 33573163]

[9] T. Xu, G. Goossen, H.K. Cevahir, S. Khodeir, Y. Jin, F.H. Li, S. Shan, S. Patel, D.M. Freeman, and P. Pearce, "Deep Entity Classification: Abusive Account Detection for Online Social Networks", *USENIX Security Symposium,* 2021.

[10] D. Liang, A. Zhang, and E. Thomaz, "Automated Face-To-Face Conversation Detection on a Commodity Smartwatch with Acoustic Sensing", *Proc. ACM Interact. Mob. Wearable Ubiquitous Technol.,* vol. 7, no. 3, pp. 1-29, 2023. [http://dx.doi.org/10.1145/3610882]

[11] M. Wutke, F. Heinrich, P.P. Das, A. Lange, M. Gentz, I. Traulsen, F.K. Warns, A.O. Schmitt, and M. Gültas, "Detecting Animal Contacts—A Deep Learning-Based Pig Detection and Tracking Approach for the Quantification of Social Contacts", *Sensors (Basel),* vol. 21, no. 22, p. 7512, 2021. [http://dx.doi.org/10.3390/s21227512] [PMID: 34833588]

[12] M. Schmitz, G. Muri'c, and K.A. Burghardt, "Detecting Anti-vaccine Users on Twitter", *International Conference on Web and Social Media,* 2021.

[13] K. Erhardt, and D. Albassam, "Detecting the Hidden Dynamics of Networked Actors Using Temporal Correlations", In: Companion Proceedings of the ACM Web Conference 2023 (WWW '23 Companion). Association for Computing Machinery, New York, NY, USA, 1214–1217. [http://dx.doi.org/10.1145/3543873.3587672]

[14] Fatemi, B., Halcrow, J., & Perozzi, B. (2023). Talk like a Graph: Encoding Graphs for Large Language Models. ArXiv, abs/2310.04560.

[15] Paula, A.F., Rizzi, G., Fersini, E., & Spina, D. (2023). AI-UPV at EXIST 2023 - Sexism Characterization Using Large Language Models Under The Learning with Disagreement Regime. ArXiv, abs/2307.03385.

CHAPTER 27

Optimizing Recommendations in Real-Time with Hybrid Recommendation Systems

Ajay Rastogi[1,*] and **H.K. Shashikala**[2]

[1] *Department of College of Computing Sciences & I.T, Teerthanker Mahaveer University, Moradabad, Uttar Pradesh, India*

[2] *Department of Computer Science and Engineering, JAIN (Deemed-to-be University), Bangalore, Karnataka, India*

Abstract: Recently developed e-learning recommendation systems aid students and instructors. These conditions need specialist online learning for students and educators. Split-and-conquer clustering based on a strategy creates a clever recommender for learners' requirements, preferences, and abilities. An automatic self-learning recommender evaluates learners using a separate-and-conquer analysis. Cluster-based linear pattern mining may reveal learner functions. The application suggests properly utilising common pattern scores. This technique was evaluated across different learner groups and datasets to provide relevant learning tasks based on learning style, interest classification, and competence. The recommended cluster-based recommender improved trial recommendation performance, helping learners complete more courses than the no-recommender group. Students scored the suggestion tool over 65% in all areas. The recommender increased metric values for bigger learners in the simulation. Statistics showed huge disparities in student measures exceeding 1000. A computational framework using |L| (recommendation list size) and student qualities explained the disparities. The kids liked the recommender's speed and accuracy.

Keywords: Hybrid Recommendation Systems, Real-Time Optimization, Text Mining, separate-and-conquer analysis, e-learning recommendation systems.

INTRODUCTION

There is a wealth of data accessible in today's globally linked environment. Sometimes consumers feel overwhelmed by the sheer volume

of material available online. A recommendation system aids consumers in making sense of this deluge of data. Therefore, e-commerce sites like Amazon and Netflix, as well as video-on-demand services like Hulu, utilize recommendation

* **Corresponding author Ajay Rastogi:** Department of College of Computing Sciences & I.T, Teerthanker Mahaveer University, Moradabad, Uttar Pradesh, India; E-mail: ajayrahi@gmail.com

S. Kannadhasan, R. Nagarajan, & Kaushik Pal (Eds.)

systems. Both CBF and CF encounter difficulties when not enough people rate products, known as the cold-start problem [1 - 3] and the sparse rating problem [4]. As a result, there are two distinct varieties of cold-start issues: those associated with a brand-new user and those associated with a brand-new product. CBF, on the other hand, only has issues with new users for whom no prior preferences data exists. Also, determining nearest neighbors or nearby things might be difficult when user-item rating matrices are sparse [5]. Comments on many social media sites have been used to go around these restrictions [6]. The material has been evaluated based on the feelings expressed in the feedback. Most of this study has relied on analyzing social media comments about already released films to draw conclusions; however, there are still obstacles for forthcoming films. For upcoming movies, for instance, there is a dearth of metadata such as user reviews and ratings. It is difficult to build a recommendation system for a yet-to-be-released film due to limited data.

For the most part, traditional learning methods have been superseded by e-learning in recent years [7]. E-learning, which uses web innovations to provide students with access to learning online or offline at any time, is seen as more successful than traditional methods of education. Effective learning can occur anywhere, at any time, thanks to personalized e-learning [8]. Novel recommendation algorithms that should, in theory, exceed the state of the art have been the focus of e-learning research efforts as of late. Therefore, developing a better recommendation system is essential to raising the bar for student service. The suggested recommendation system relies heavily on the following subsystems: Learner, Domain, Application, Adaptation, and Session. This research provides a wealth of new strategies to enhance existing state-of-the-art recommendation systems. The proposed approach was used on a dataset including information on one thousand students. Based on our experiments, we found that students in the simulated cluster completed the course in less time and with fewer lessons than those in the no-recommender group. The suggested methodology was also shown to intelligently recommend learning materials based on learner profiles and preferences. The larger the gap between the performance measurements and the computational complexity required by well-known recommendation systems, the less accurate the recommendations will be. As a result, in order to address a wide range of practical concerns, it is necessary to create novel recommendation techniques that address the limitations of existing approaches.

RELATED WORKS

Some currently available e-learning systems were developed with a focus on certain aspects of instructional practices, data structures, and user profiles [9].

Some of the helpful tools and procedures that our team has developed include rules for content-based cooperative filtering and mining, a Bayesian model-based acquiring structure, a recommendation framework built around domain perspectives, a recommendation for mutual sorting for small files, an approach for filtering mutually *via* the estimated maximum likelihood, and a rules-based, tailored learning system through fuzzy theory. We presented ontology-based semantic recommendations and used artificial neural networks to construct an e-learning recommendation based on self-organized maps. To examine how students progress through courses, we built a machine learning and clustering-based recommendation model. Clustering algorithms and content filtering approaches were used to study and evaluate the various learning styles in the context of personalized object-based learning.

The following are some broad categories into which the newly developed recommender systems fall. Profile-Based Recommendation Methods: Recently, personalized recommendation systems have been created for use in a variety of contexts. Learner profiles may be examined using the User Profile-Oriented Diffusion (UPOD) technique. Based on the outcomes of the training phase, this system provides tailored suggestions. In the referral phase, suggestions are made based on characteristics of the student's profile. Systems for Suggesting Readable Material Content-based recommendations using convolutional neural networks (CNNs) were described. This technique is used to uncover the unseen aspects of various media uses. Textual data processing is used to suggest relevant materials in this approach. Mixed-Type Recommendation Frameworks: There have been some hybrid approaches to suggesting movie-based apps. Better movie suggestions were made using content-based filtering. The hybrid approach to personalized learning was created. The recommendation engine generates custom suggestions using data visualization. To address the ERP System and E-Agribusiness datasets, a feature-based recommendation system was also used. The processing speed, accuracy of suggestions, and average absolute error are just a few areas where reviewers have criticized prominent e-learning recommender systems. This paper proposes a recommender system that automatically adjusts to learners' needs, interests, and skill levels by fixing flaws in existing popular techniques. Students' tastes and habits may be automatically assessed and learned by the recommender. To accommodate these different learning styles, we use a split-and-conquer clustering strategy. The machine then makes insightful suggestions by considering the ratings of common patterns [9 - 12].

CF is a process that can hone in on what an individual user prefers by analyzing the preferences of people similar to that user. The inability to start up from cold is a major issue for people with CF. Yang *et al.* introduced a system that infers ratings based on user data. The greater the number of pages viewed by a user, the greater their apparent interest in the material contained therein. This approach is useful for overcoming the cold-start issue, but it is quite niche. The optimization issue in the recommendation system has several dimensions. As a result, several different optimization techniques have been presented. The list below includes a few examples. Using movie lens data, Katarya *et al.* constructed a recommender system based on fuzzy c-mean and grey wolf optimization to predict user ratings. For the purpose of creating a custom recommendation system for supplementary materials, Hsu *et al.* recommended using an optimization method inspired by artificial bee colonies. The recommendation service was enhanced by Bobadilla *et al.* using evolutionary algorithms. Particle swarm optimization and the genetic method were compared by Ujjin *et al.*. To enhance their collaborative movie selection approach, Katarya *et al.* combined a k-means clustering algorithm and an artificial bee colony (ABC km).

Cold starts are not an issue with their proposed method. It is possible to build a tailored movie recommendation system using a framework that sorts people according to their profile features. The work addresses the temporal complexity of CF. Using predicted ratings and implicit feedback, Lavanya *et al.* used CF. This method mitigates data sparsity. A CF framework was presented by Chen *et al.* that included creating user-specific lists of both preferred and disfavored films. One of the most studied types of recommendation systems is called content-based filtering (CBF). Systems that propose content based on metadata analysis are becoming increasingly popular. New strategies for enhancing item data with external knowledge sources are suggested by the emergence of linked open data (LOD). Uluyagmur *et al.* employed a content-based movie recommender, which suggested which users and movie features were used. A movie-centric dataset was employed for the suggested rating system. To construct a recommender system, content-based movie recommendation systems take into account a wide range of movie qualities. Using the Movie Lens dataset, Reddy *et al.* proposed a recommender system that considers consumers' favourite movie genres. The degree to which objects are alike is calculated by analyzing the correlations between their content and their qualities. When it comes to determining user preferences and calculating correlations, Son *et al.* advocated using a multi-attribute network. Network analysis is used to determine the degree of similarity between things that are either directly or indirectly connected. Based on the user's preferences, the hybrid method suggested by Ali *et al.* uses CBF and genomic markers from the movie to suggest similar films. Using principal component analysis (PCA) and Pearson correlation, Belarbi *et al.* provide a model that distributes low-variance data and minimizes duplicate tags, thereby reducing computational complexity. Elahi *et al.* used the categorization of characteristics into high-level and low-level. They created a hybrid recommendation system using film lighting, motion exceeds, and low-level feature colors. Deldjoo *et al.*

suggested a novel movie recommendation method. They created a video genome and provided audio and visual descriptions taken from videos. Breitfuss *et al.* used user ratings of previously released films to construct a knowledge graph. The knowledge graph served as the foundation for a subsequent recommendation system [13 - 15].

PROPSOED WORK

In this study, we construct a smart hybrid recommender that helps teachers and students make the most of available educational materials. When applied across all courses, the hybrid intelligent recommender helps students choose the most relevant study materials by considering their individual interests, learning styles, and other factors. Each of the following subsystems—Domain, Learner, Application, Adaptation, and Session—works in tandem to create the intelligent recommender proposed here. Each subsystem's functions are summarized. The general design of the recommendation system, including the components described earlier, is shown in Fig. (**1**).

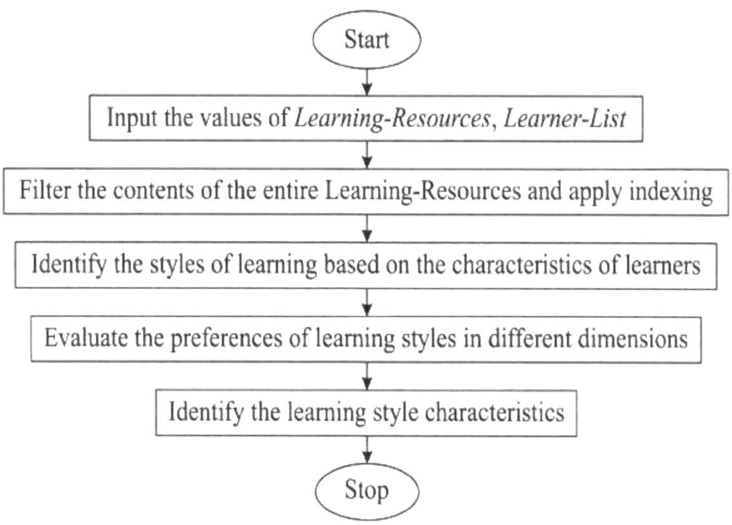

Fig. (1). System Flowchart.

The designed recommender employs the following methods:

- A cluster-based linear pattern-finding method;
- A split-and-conquer technique for partitioning datasets into clusters;

- Recommendations generated and updated inside each cluster;
- A linear pattern pruning approach to finding the maximal large sequences;
- Identifying the learning styles on the basis of learner characteristics;
- Taking a look at how different people learn best

The proposed recommender algorithm has the following advantages: Improved cluster-based recommendation generation; optimization of the recommendation process in terms of computing complexity; identification and analysis of learner-specific learning styles using the Index of Learning Styles approach; evaluation of differences in preferences based on modalities; enhanced precision in the creation of suggestion lists; reduced variation in performance evaluations when contrasted with established methodologies.

An intelligent hybrid recommendations model is suggested, which takes two inputs—Learning-Resources and Learner-List. The model's enhanced recommendation list is useful for students. Figure 1 depicts the entire flowchart of the recommended intelligent hybrid recommender. Algorithm 1 depicts the overall layout of the proposed model. This model takes as inputs a set of learning resources and a set of learners. The term "learning-resources" refers to the aforementioned content or materials, each of which is composed of discrete lessons. Topics covered in each class include the following: introduction, overview, applications, tutorials, tests, and exercises. The data for both teachers and students may be found in the "Learner-List." The instructor creates various instructional materials and opens the proper writing program. The needs, interests, and preferred approaches to studying individual students might vary widely. Learning preferences on several variables are used to define the features of individual learning styles.

Learners may take charge of their own education by deciding how to structure their learning. The methods used to generate new forms of education are up to the discretion of the students. The proposed intelligent system saves these scholarly endeavors. We can extract functional patterns from the learners using the suggested cluster-based linear patterns extraction approach. One may look at a student's full progress—from when they started working on a module and its lessons to when they finished (or didn't finish)—by looking for these patterns. The suggested approach is cluster-based linear pattern extraction. As seen in the suggested Algorithm 2, the students are fully grouped, and their functional patterns are evaluated. Beginning with the series of item sets (Item1, Item2... Itemn), the algorithm operates on the set Learning-Items. We find the strongest possible sequence by comparing all possible sequences of items and calculating their support, denoted as Support(s). After collecting the most significant and extreme sequences, we apply various transformations and operations to them, including sorting, finding the largest groups of items, linearizing the sequences, sequencing, and performing the maximal operation. Finally, the cluster's largest sequences are identified to extract learners' functional patterns.

Reviewing and eliminating duplicate data is key to achieving the biggest feasible sequences. To do this, we zero in on linear trends that are a subset of other linear designs. Method 3 is the linear patterns pruning method, and Figure 1 is a flow diagram showing the recommended linear pattern pruning approach. The suggested cluster-based evaluation assesses students' knowledge after they have completed the set of learning resources. Figure 6 depicts the assessment process using clusters. Algorithm 4 is a high-level diagram of the related algorithm. This program draws conclusions from the data based on the students' relative rates of correct responses. It also finds groups of students with many characteristics.

An improved recommendation list for students is obtained by first clustering the input resources using the divide-and-conquer technique, and then applying the suggested algorithms in conjunction with the updated recommendation and improved CF techniques.

According to the goal-oriented Index of Knowledge Styles, students' preferred learning methods are evaluated along four dimensions: processing speed, perception, reception, and understanding. The database was subjected to sequential pattern mining utilizing the following procedures: resource access time, learner ID, and transaction access path columns. The "Learner-Id" column served as the key for sorting the database. The study materials were ranked according to their availability time. A method of discovery was used to locate large sets of items. The sequencing process involves the algorithm applying a number of large item sets to generate the desired sequences over a certain number of iterations.

RESULT AND DISCUSSION

Here, we evaluate a simulated execution of this novel recommender on a few example datasets. The suggested procedure was written in Java. Mean Absolute Error, Accuracy (List, User), Recall (List, User), and Ranking Score (User) were among the measures used to evaluate how well the proposed approach performed. To evaluate the efficacy of the proposed intelligent recommender, simulations were conducted using educational datasets with 1,000 students. One of the following groups was randomly allocated to the students: a simulation group or a no-recommender group. The students in the no-recommender group were not directed to the available materials by the recommender. Students in the cluster that ran the simulation had to go through the proposed model. There were 900 students in the simulation cluster and 100 students in the no-recommender cluster. The results of the statistical t-test used to determine whether further group equalization was required showed that the data from both the simulated clusters with no recommender were normal. The objective of the study was to segment the simulation's learner population into smaller groups based on their unique learning styles and other characteristics. Sixteen separate groups were formed based on different student characteristics. To determine whether there were any notable differences between the no-recommender groups and the simulated cluster means, a statistical t-test was used. To find out where they stood academically, the students in each group completed the chapter's assignments and exams, then compared their results. We compared the average intellectual abilities of 900 learners in the simulation-based cluster (n1 = 900) and 100 students in the no-recommender clusters (n2 = 100) at the 5% significance level, with n1 + n2 degrees of freedom. The average intellectual skills in the simulation cluster group were 98.27, while in the no-recommender group, they were 93.73.

The actual T-test result of 1.57 is less than the expected theoretical result of 1.96. This indicates that there were no appreciable discrepancies between the clusters, and hence, no further balancing of the groupings was deemed necessary. Measures of Success: The effectiveness of the suggested approach was evaluated using a variety of metrics. Figure 8 compares MAEs between the proposed technique and the current CF method. The recommender's ability to foretell learners' evaluations improved as the MAE decreased. The suggested learning sequences met the accuracy requirements. According to the experimental findings, the suggested strategy significantly reduced the MAE measure compared to the baseline method across all clusters evaluated, as shown in Table **1**. Compared with the CF technique, a clear distinction was observed.

Table 1. Performance analysis.

Dataset	Embedding Scheme	F-measure	Accuracy	Precision	Recall
Learner Type 1	BERT	93.5	93.5	94.0	93.0
	FastText	90.9	91.0	90.0	91.8
	Glove	89,6	89.7	89,4	89.9
	Word2vec	88.7	88.7	89.0	88.4
Learner Type 2	BERT	94.7	94.7	95,0	94.5
	FastText	92.1	92.2	91.0	93.3
	Glove	90.4	90.5	90.0	90.9
	Word2vec	89.5	89.5	90,0	89.1

(Table 1) cont.....

Dataset	Embedding Scheme	F-measure	Accuracy	Precision	Recall
Learner Type 3	BERT	91.9	92.0	90.8	93.0
	FastText	90.0	90.0	89.5	90.4
	Glove	89.4	89.4	89.0	89.8
	Word2vec	88.8	88.9	88.5	89.1
Learner Type 4	BERT	94.7	94.7	95.0	94.5
	FastText	92.3	92.2	93.5	91.2
	Glove	91.8	91.7	92.5	91.1
	Word2vec	91.1	91.2	90.5	91.0
Learner Type 5	BERT	93.5	93.5	93.9	93.2
	Fast Text	91.9	91.9	91.8	92.1
	Glove	91.3	91.4	91.2	91.4
	Word2vec	90.9	90.9	91,2	90.8

We compare the performance of the proposed recommender to that of the current CF across a variety of parameters. The system provided superior resource suggestions for learning when the Recall (List, User) value was increased. As the Precision (List, User) values increased, the recommender system included more items in the proposal. A low Ranking Score (User) indicated that the sought-after item was readily accessible according to the recommender system.

How much time it takes for pupils to become proficient is determined by the efficiency measure. In comparison to the recommender built, the following methods were tested: Mass Diffusion Heat Spreading Resources (MDHS) and User Profile Oriented Diffusion (UPOD). |L| was set to a minimum before running the recommender. Results from the experiments demonstrated that students in the simulation cluster finished the course in less computational time and with a higher lesson completion rate than students in the no-recommender group. Learning resources might be intelligently offered based on learner attributes and preferences, as proposed. By examining the experimental outcomes of the metrics under investigation, we calculated the sample dataset's average and standard deviation. Tables **9** and **10** show the simulation results. We utilized the t-test to determine the relative efficacy of the approaches. All provided measurements indicate that the suggested algorithms outperform the state-of-the-art methods, as shown in the tables. When tested against both the current techniques and the dataset in question, the results showed a significant increase in Ranking Scores (User) and Recall (List, User). Even when pitted against state-of-the-art techniques, the suggested strategy performed well.

CONCLUSION

Improving performance in real-time e-learning environments calls for the use of intelligent recommender systems. This study developed a novel hybrid intelligent recommendation system that considers the individual preferences and characteristics of each student. After running several simulations, we compared the performance metrics of the proposed model with those of the current CF recommender. Compared with the current CF, the suggested algorithms for sequential pattern grouping, pruning, and recommender systems deliver superior results. Students in the simulated cluster outperformed those in the no-recommender cluster in course completion rates, suggesting that the suggested cluster-based recommender improved performance. For class sizes of, the suggested recommender's simulation revealed that, depending on $|L|$ and learner characteristics, we investigated important differences in the computational framework underlying the learning process. More than 65% of students considered all factors when evaluating the suggested recommender. Upper limits of 0.326 and 0.216 were reached for the Precision and Recall measures, respectively, while using the suggested technique on the training dataset. The students had similar positive reactions to the recommender's precision and quickness. Therefore, the offered solutions were successful in producing improved suggestions for students. The experimental findings demonstrated that the proposed strategy significantly reduced the MAE relative to the baseline method across all clusters studied. Compared with other approaches, the sample dataset's standard deviation and mean for the Recall (List, User) and Ranking Score (User) metrics were significantly different. The developed strategy outperformed the alternatives on all relevant parameters. The suggested methodology was also demonstrated to intelligently provide learning materials tailored to learner traits and preferences.

REFERENCES

[1] L. Liu, C. Zhang, X. Hu, and J.X. Yu, "Multi-Modal Social Network Analysis for Movie Recommendation", *Proceedings of the 2021 ACM SIGMOD International Conference on Management of Data,* pp. 2749-2751, 2021.

[2] S. Li, S. Li, X. Li, and X. Li, "An Improved Movie Recommendation Algorithm Based on Social Network Analysis", *Proceedings of the 2021 IEEE International Conference on Computer and Communications,* pp. 1253-1257, 2021.

[3] J. Dai, Y. Cui, H. Xiong, and W.Y. Ma, "Heterogeneous social network analysis for movie recommendation", *Knowl. Base. Syst.,* vol. 226, p. 107120, 2021.

[4] M. Zhang, M. Li, S. Li, and Y. Li, "Movie Recommendation Based on Collaborative Filtering and Social Network Analysis", *Proceedings of the 2021 IEEE International Conference on Computational Science and Engineering,* pp. 427-431, 2021.

[5] C. Lin, X. Li, X. Huang, and Z. Lu, "A Movie Recommendation System Based on Social Network Analysis and Deep Learning", *Proceedings of the 2021 IEEE International Conference on Artificial Intelligence and Big Data,* pp. 10-16, 2021.

[6] K. Singh, F. Siddiqui, D. Braga, M. Kamyab, C. Cheatham, and B. Harclerode, *ROP Optimization using a Hybrid Machine Learning and Physics-Based Multivariate Objective Function with Real-Time Vibration and Stick-Slip Filters.,* 2022. [http://dx.doi.org/10.2118/208751-MS]

[7] R.C. Nzeh, N.J. Ezeora, U. Izuchukwu, and U.B. Chimezie, *Optimization Of An Online Store Price Recommendation System Using Hybrid.,* 2021.

[8] K. Linnestad, S. Ollila, S.O. Wasbø, A. Bogdanoff, and T. Rotevatn, "Adaptive First Principles Model for the CAS-OB Process for Real-Time Applications", *Metals (Basel),* vol. 11, no. 10, p. 1554, 2021. [http://dx.doi.org/10.3390/met11101554]

[9] L. Ravi, V. Subramaniyaswamy, V. Vijayakumar, X. Gao, and G. Wang, "Hybrid bio-inspired user clustering for the generation of diversified recommendations", *Neural Comput. Appl.,* vol. 32, pp. 2487-2506, 2019.

[10] S.S. Prasad, R.C. Deo, N. Downs, D. Igoe, A.V. Parisi, and J. Soar, "Cloud Affected Solar UV Prediction With Three-Phase Wavelet Hybrid Convolutional Long Short-Term Memory Network Multi-Step Forecast System", *IEEE Access,* vol. 10, pp. 24704-24720, 2022. [http://dx.doi.org/10.1109/ACCESS.2022.3153475]

[11] F. Özcan, Y. Tian, and P. Tözün, "Hybrid Transactional/Analytical Processing: A Survey", *Proceedings of the 2017 ACM International Conference on Management of Data,* 2017. [http://dx.doi.org/10.1145/3035918.3054784]

[12] Y. Li, "The Role of Cognitive Science and Big Data Technology in the Design of Business Information Management Systems", *Adv. Multimedia,* vol. 2022, pp. 1-15, 2022. [http://dx.doi.org/10.1155/2022/2761661]

[13] C. Shahabi, F.B. Kashani, Y. Chen, and D. McLeod, Yoda: An Accurate and Scalable Web-based Recommendation System, In the Sixth International Conference on Cooperative Information Systems (CoopIS 2001), Trento, Italy , September 2001

[14] Y. Zhang, and K. Xie, "Incorporating intent propensities in personalized next best action recommendation", In Proceedings of the 13th ACM Conference on Recommender Systems (RecSys '19). Association for Computing Machinery, New York, NY, USA, 530. [http://dx.doi.org/10.1145/3298689.3346962]

[15] K.A. Aksvonov, and A. Antonova, "Development of a Hybrid Decision-Making Method Based on a Simulation-Genetic Algorithm in a Web-Oriented Metallurgical Enterprise Information System", *2018 Tenth International Conference on Ubiquitous and Future Networks (ICUFN),* pp. 197-202, 2018. [http://dx.doi.org/10.1109/ICUFN.2018.8436676]

CHAPTER 28

Proactive Automated Reasoning Systems for Spatial and Temporal Data Analysis

Amit Singh[1,*] and **Jagdish Chandra Patni**[2]

[1] *College of Computing Science and Information Technology, Teerthanker Mahaveer University, Moradabad, Uttar Pradesh, India*

[2] *Department of Computer Science and Engineering, JAIN (Deemed-to-be University), Bangalore, Karnataka, India*

Abstract: By analysing the geographical, chronological, and semantic components of geographic data, it is possible to reconstruct users' real route itineraries and get insights into their preferences and behavior. To analyse tourist traffic patterns at A-level scenic spots in Jiangsu and Zhejiang across time and space, this research collects and preprocesses Weibo check-in data for these locations. The author used a temporal perspective, examining how check-in data fluctuated between 2016 and 2018 and how it differed on weekends, holidays, and weekdays. The acquired data were subjected to a spatial kernel density analysis, which revealed the most active regions. Lastly, the vacation travel mode and characteristics were identified through an examination of spatial and locational flows and their orientations. The results of this study provide the groundwork for the growth of tourism.

Keywords: Spatial and Temporal Data Analysis , Automated Reasoning Systems, Textual Analysis , tourism, tourist traffic patterns.

INTRODUCTION

In today's big data world, more and more individuals expect to access and share information whenever and wherever they need it, and they have become accustomed to doing so *via* their mobile intelligent terminals.

When it comes to mobile apps for gathering and disseminating data, Location-Based Service (LBS) has quickly become a standard. The adoption of these applications has created massive amounts of social media data that includes location information (*i.e.*, geo-tagged social media big data), which is continually expanding. This new kind of enormous social media data has introduced both

* **Corresponding author Amit Singh:** College of Computing Science and Information Technology, Teerthanker Mahaveer University, Moradabad, Uttar Pradesh, India; E-mail: amit84376@gmail.com

S. Kannadhasan, R. Nagarajan, & Kaushik Pal (Eds.)

opportunities and challenges to many disciplines of study, piquing the interest of academics in these areas. Similar to "checking in" on Facebook, users of several local life information services (such as Dianping.com, Google NearYou, Jiepang.com, *etc.*) may rate and review various businesses, such as restaurants, hotels, and attractions. Geo-tagged photos, like those shared on platforms like Flickr and Instagram, include not only a descriptive caption but also a geographic coordinate. Users may document their travels in detail, take pictures at any time, and make notes as they go, using numerous applications (such as Baidu Tourism, Bread Trip, and others). The aforementioned social media data (geo-tagged photographs, check-in data) contains not only the typical metadata elements such as title, tags, and author, but also time data (the time the picture was shot or the check-in was performed) and geographical location information. Finding well-known landmarks is a common use case for geo-tagged data mining. Photos of tourist destinations are shared on social media so regularly that studies aimed at identifying the most popular destinations and selecting the best ones based on user interests have become prominent [1 - 5]. Tourists' geo-tagged picture albums or check-in data are interpreted as chronological sequences of places, from which information about hotspots and visitors' routes may be gleaned. Hence, proof and assistance for applications such as tourism planning, tourist attraction development, and intelligent travel suggestions may be obtained by analysing the activities of visitors from social networking geo-tagged big data.

Technology advancements in GIS, GPS, and map visualisation have contributed to the rise in the popularity of mobile positioning devices and location services in recent years. Location-based social networks (LBSNs) [6] have emerged as a result of the convergence of these technologies with established ones. Since the LBSN integrates positioning and social interaction [7], its users may save and broadcast their whereabouts at their convenience. Users and locations serve as the LBSN's fundamental building blocks. The SMG data consists of the two types of units taken from social media.

Each user's SMG data depicts that person's path through time, while collectively they provide information on the modes of transportation and residential neighborhoods frequented by the population as a whole. The LBSN is an improvement over conventional social networks since it allows members to broadcast their precise locations to others. By doing so, online communities may more closely mimic their real-world counterparts [8 - 12]. Twitter and Weibo, two of the most popular social media applications, play a significant role in fostering the fast growth of the LBSN. These applications herald the beginning of the "user-generated content" age (CGM). At any time and from any location, everyone can share their thoughts and emotions. Users of social media platforms may be thought of as a global network of sensors that report on breaking events in the physical world. As SMG matures, it will become more integrated with location services, generating massive amounts of SMG data. The popularity of reading travelogues online has increased as social media sites mature and web surfing becomes more mainstream. Researchers now have access to a wealth of information in the network environment, thanks to collected reputation data from visitors, allowing them to evaluate the image of tourist attractions and the spatial tourist pattern at individual locations. In particular, UGC from social platforms has become a trusted resource for travellers seeking information about potential destinations.

Furthermore, this data may include tourists' accidental thoughts and sentiments, allowing researchers to gather visitor evaluations and tourism destination images through opinion mining, as well as location data. The value of public opinion in networks has been established in several studies, with important implications for management. The study's goal is to shed light on critical challenges in tourism management by analysing the image and spatial pattern of popular tourist destinations through the lens of opinion mining.

RELATED WORKS

The first geographical information applications mainly catered to business requirements and specialised audiences. These services used one-on-one interviews to gauge consumer interest. Expert interviews alone are unlikely to be sufficient in this day and age, given the prevalence of location tracking and the growth in user numbers. The issue has been addressed by the introduction of network technology, which has enabled the development of effective solutions such as network observation [4] and network investigation [5]. The most up-t--date methods for gathering the locations of many users are summarised here. Harrower *et al.* [6] used the conventional assessment procedure to evaluate the knowledge, skills, and abilities of 16 geographers and lay users. Using an online poll, Huang *et al.* [7] gathered data on the accessibility of GIS applications from 385 legitimate respondents. Gareth *et al.* [8] used satellite imagery and Google Street View to determine camera tilt with latitude and longitude. Cao *et al.* [9] demonstrated the use of texture features as a visual component of images by retrieving them from GPS-tagged photos on photo-sharing websites and projecting land uses using supervised learning. Using GPS trajectories as a data source, Zheng *et al.* [10] retrieved user residence locations, produced the network structure by hierarchically clustering these sites, and used the Hyperlink-Induced Topic Search (HITS) method to identify interest points and hot scenic places. Interest points were extracted from GPS tracks by the authors Zhang *et al.* [11] and correlated with actions. As a first step in compensating for the dearth of location-activity labels, the activity-activity relationship was quantified using data scraped from publicly available websites. Then, low-dimensional characteristics were used in conjunction with the cooperative matrices decomposition to recreate the original matrix. Okazaki *et al.* [12] conducted a survey to determine user satisfaction with the current network map and participants' preferred features. Xiao *et al.* [13] investigated the factors that affect a mobile electronic map and developed a fuzzy comprehensive assessment model. Gerber *et al.* [14] used theme models to make crime predictions using Twitter analysis, demonstrating that tweet content may be used to make more accurate crime predictions in Chicago. Using data from the Chinese Disease Control & Prevention (CDC), Sun *et al.* [15] analysed the relationship between the prevalence of influenza-related terms on Weibo and attempted to predict the spread of the virus using this information.

Weibo postings' locations were inferred by the researchers by evaluating the posts' use of location-related vocabulary. Based on geographical data, places are sorted into categories including restaurants, shops, and more, and then the association between places is determined using user data from previous check-ins. The mean-shift technique is an example of a traditional spatial clustering approach used for locating tourist attractions. Crandal and Kurashima, for instance, clustered geographical coordinates and then extracted well-known tourism destinations using the mean-shift technique [7, 8]. Yin *et al.* [9] clustered the geo-tagged pictures and made position predictions using the mean-shift technique. Since the mean-shift approach only requires the width of the search area to be set in advance, rather than the number of classes, it can locate several clustering centres with little to no prior information [7, 10]. In addition, Kennedy *et al.* used the k-means technique to classify the geometric labels (*i.e.*, longitude & latitude) of the photos before collecting data on the sights [11]. For example, Kisilevich *et al.* [13] adapted the DBSCAN algorithm to produce P-DBSCAN, an adaptable density-based clustering algorithm that requires less field data and facilitates the detection of irregularly shaped clusters. In attraction mining, Yang adopted a spectrum-clustering strategy [14, 15]. This approach allows the number of clusters to be automatically adjusted, which is a significant time saver. Zheng and Yuan proposed a hierarchical approach to mining POIs and hotspots from GPS trajectory data. The algorithm initially processes the user's GPS trajectory data in order to determine their stopover locations. After this, a graph structure is built using hierarchical clustering of the locations of interest where people are staying. The more granular the clustering level, the greater the number of nodes in each cluster. Multiple levels of classification can filter last but not least, regions and locations to isolate tourist hotspots. Other researchers also showed how to use spatial clustering to lend meaning to the locations that attract tourists. Cao *et al.* investigated how to locate tourist destinations using geotagged images, then extracted sample images and associated text descriptions so users could search for these spots using either images or text. The semantics of the photographs were improved when Gao collected the user information from the preexisting trip advice website (Yahoo Travel). Extracted information from current travel sites may be used to determine whether a photograph's text label is relevant to a trip and to add the location's existing label to the image, thus expanding the photograph's semantics. Finding famous attractions using geo-tagged data is primarily a spatial clustering problem. Among the aforementioned clustering methods, DBSCAN stands out as an effective density-based clustering technique, making it a popular choice for usage in spatial clustering. Zhou's work on travel-destination prediction made use of the DBSCAN method. In Lee's work on attraction popularity analysis, he used the DBSCAN method. In addition, the DBSCAN spatial clustering approach has served as a foundation for other applications, including trip trajectory analysis, travel pattern analysis, and intelligent attraction suggestion, due to its widespread use in the tourism industry [16 - 20]. For instance, Cai used DBSCAN as a tourist attraction-discovery approach and then extracted its semantic trajectories from a geo-tagged dataset. After discovering attractions using geo-tagged photographs, Vu and Chen analysed travel behaviour and movement patterns. Using a geo-tagged dataset from Flickr, Memon and Lee investigated several methods for making tailored trip recommendations.

PROPSOED WORK

Data Pre-Processing

We scraped the Instagram public API for a total of 213,938 spatial photographs and associated metadata for Beijing, China, between 2005 and 2016. The sample size is 11,500 users from all across the globe. Next, we preprocess the Flickr dataset to get rid of the extraneous information. Here, it mostly pertains to removing duplicates; a user may take many images in quick succession at the same location, and all of them may end up on Flickr. In this case, it is important to get rid of the unnecessary detail. If a user takes many images in the same location within an hour of each other, they should be considered a single set. The total number of images is 185,531 after redundancy removal. After excluding duplicates, the geo-tagged points in Flickr. In addition, we use the historical Beijing weather data provided by the Underground website, which includes temperature and weather condition information, to evaluate the heat dispersion of tourist attractions at different times of day and under different weather conditions (*i.e.*, contexts): duplicated data, incorrect information, and missing data. The preprocessing in this study is split into two phases. Then, the retrieved data from the POIID field names were processed to get rid of any erroneous or duplicate POIID entries. Second, we eliminated all point-of-interest (POI) categories that had nothing to do with tourism (*e.g.*, hospitals and neighborhoods) and kept only those directly relevant to our study. The author acquired 1,360,087 entries in Jiangsu & 527,791 entries in Zhejiang after cleaning data from the two provinces for 2016 & 2018. After cleaning, the data was statistically compared to ensure its accuracy. Weibo users' check-in data is used to rank provinces from most frequent to least on a scale from most to least frequent visits. Canadian provinces with the highest rates of check-ins at Jiangsu rank first among Chinese provinces in terms of international visitors, followed by Shanghai, Beijing, Zhejiang, Anhui, Guangdong, Shandong, Henan, & Hubei, as reported by the Yearbook of China Tourism Statistics. The data acquired is sufficient for analyzing travelers' behavior while on vacation.

Spatial Clustering

To help people choose sights to see, a novel spatial grouping approach is applied. To begin, the cluster centers are retrieved adaptively using the CFSFDP (Clustering by Fast Search & Find of Density Peaks) concept introduced by Rodriguez and Liao. The leftover points are then assigned to the selected clusters to complete the first clustering. One method is to allocate the remaining points to the recovered cluster centers using recursion, with the particular approach being that an undeclared point I falls into the group where the density is higher than point I and the distance to point I is the shortest. Cluster centers are selected by maximizing the product of the granularity level and the spatial variation (*i.e.*, selecting the point with the largest product). The point density and relative index may be calculated using Equations (1) and (2).

$$\rho_i = \sum_{j=0}^{n} f(d_{ij} - r)$$

$$f(x) = \begin{cases} 1, & x < 0 \\ 0, & x \geq 0 \end{cases} \tag{1}$$

$$\delta_i = \min_{j:\rho_j > \rho_i}(d_{ij})$$

dij is the distance in the clustered zone from point I to the nearest site j, where I is the density of site I and j is the next location with a greater density than i.

Two assumptions are made without being stated. First, the cluster centre is relatively isolated from other high-density regions, and second, it has a high density while being accompanied by low-density regions. The limitation of the conventional DBSCAN method, which struggles to distinguish between nearby high-density regions, may be overcome by combining density and relative distance to select cluster centres. Moreover, we use the road network to split the categorization area into many zones, with the point density and spatial variations standardised across all zones to address the issue of large variations in the state density of the clustering region. As a result, our method is better equipped to adapt to clustering scenarios with significant changes in regional density, thanks to the zoning and standardisation processes. The outcome of Beijing's zoning by major highways is that there are 144 zones in total.

Class Combination Adjusting the threshold in the preceding clustering procedure allows one to control the granularity at which tourist attractions are discovered; lowering the threshold leads to a greater number of micro-scale clusters. Sometimes the same area is split into multiple distinct clusters due to factors such as the area's vastness or the scarcity of individual behaviour data. The following methods, together referred to as "class mergence," are employed to fix this problem: (1) As a standard text similarity metric, the TF-IDF (Maximum-Likelihood Temporary Files) method utilises the weight of the lexical tag for every initial cluster. The formula for determining mass is shown in Example (4). Where N is the total number of clusters and df(t) represents the fraction of clusters that include the current tag t. After that, we calculate the similarity measure between neighbouring clusters, build multivariate tag vectors for each cluster, and merge clusters that are exceedingly similar to one another. The formula is as follows: (5) where X as well as Y represents the clusters under consideration, X and Y represent the multimodal tag vector of X and Y, and X and Y represent the tag t TF-IDF values in cluster X and cluster Y. 3.4. Annotation Labels for Famous Sights: Each cluster's semantic labels are made up of the ten tags with the highest TF-IDF weight value. Points of Interest (POIs) are produced by feeding the cluster's point coordinates into Baidu's anti-geocoding API interface, and the name of the POI with the greatest occurrence count is given to the cluster. Main highways in Beijing provide a zoning effect.

$$sim(X,Y) = \cos\theta = \frac{\vec{x} \cdot \vec{y}}{\|x\| \cdot \|y\|} = \frac{\sum_{i=1}^{n} x_i \times y_i}{\sqrt{\sum_{i=1}^{n} (x_i)^2} \times \sqrt{\sum_{i=1}^{n} (y_i)^2}} \tag{2}$$

Annotation Labels for Famous Sights

Each cluster's semantic labels are made up of the ten tags with the highest TF-IDF weight value. The cluster's name is then determined by calling Baidu's anti-geocoding API with the cluster's point coordinates, which returns a collection of Points of Interest (POIs), and assigning the cluster the name of the POI that appears most often in the set. Lastly, the cluster is kept if the chosen POI type is a popular tourist destination; otherwise, it is discarded. Semantic information-rich tourism destinations are therefore produced. The Forbidden City and the Bird's

Nest are two examples of user-annotated Flickr picture tags and their accompanying TF-IDF weights used to construct word clouds. Each cluster's top 10 labels are used as its permanent label set. By analysing the labels, we may learn about tourists' perspectives and passions, which helps create a picture of the destination and assists tourism management in planning and resource development. 2017 ISPRS International Journal of Geo-Information 6(216):6-16. Last but not least, the cluster remains if the chosen POI category is a tourist spot, but disappears otherwise. This results in the emergence of attractions for semantic tourism. The Forbidden City and the Bird's Nest are two examples of user-annotated Flickr picture tags and their accompanying TF-IDF weights used to construct word clouds. Each cluster's top 10 labels are used as its permanent label set. Using the labels, we can learn about the demographics of the attractions' audiences, which helps create a profile of the destination and assists the tourism management office with planning and resource development decisions.

RESULT AND DISCUSSION

Explaining the Outcome: We built a Java-based tool for extracting tourism attractions using the aforementioned techniques. The input consists of geotagged photo data from Flickr taken in Beijing between 2005 and 2016. Geographical clustering in Step 1.2 generates 300 clusters; Class merger of Step 1.3 reduces that to 243; and semantic annotation of Step 1.4 narrows it down to 143, based on the kinds of tourist attractions they include, as shown in Table **1**.

Table 1. Performance analysis.

Data	Training Accuracy	Testing Accuracy	Validation Accuracy
Spatial Data (Kmeans)	77.5	79.0	74.0
Temporal Data (Kmeans)	73.8	70.0	77.0
Hybrid Data (Kmeans)	72.5	72.0	68.0
Spatial Data (K-means++)	82.3	76.1	83.9
Temporal Data (K-means++)	79.5	81.1	77.3
Hybrid Data (K-means++)	79.6	84.7	75.0
Spatial Data (DBSCAN)	82.9	83.0	82.7
Temporal Data (DBSCAN)	83.0	86.0	79.3
Hybrid Data (DBSCAN)	83.6a	87.1	79.3

The results of our attraction-discovery experiment demonstrate the adaptability of the proposed method to scenes with varying cluster densities. In the clustering zone, the extracted tourism destinations are more uniformly distributed across high- and low-population regions. This is a result of the measures taken to zone and standardise the area. Also, our method can reliably differentiate between neighbouring high-density regions. Tiananmen Square, in the heart of Beijing, has very precise original point coordinates. Using conventional spatial clustering techniques, distinguishing among multiple points of interest is challenging. Tiananmen Square, Tiananmen, and the People's Hero Memorial are easily distinguishable from one another.

In addition, we observe that the suggested method facilitates more efficient discovery of the tourist attraction despite its broad geographical area and atypical design. To do this, we apply the TF-DIF technique during the class-merger stage to combine neighbouring semantically similar clusters into larger ones. The triangle denotes the centre of one of two clusters, and the varying colours of the dots show which cluster they belong to. Tiananmen Square and neighbourhood hotspots are shown graphically. We also observe that the suggested method facilitates more efficient discovery of the tourist attraction despite its expansive size and non-rectilinear outline. The TF-DIF technique is used in the class-merger stage to combine neighbouring semantically related clusters into larger, more meaningful wholes. There are two groups here, each represented by a triangle in its centre; points belonging to each group are coloured differently. The two groups are then combined using a TF-IDF cosine similarity measure.

Comparative Results: We also use the popular machine learning bundle Scikit-learn to implement a DBSCAN-based programme to accomplish tourist attraction exploring from the Flickr spatial dataset. The density criterion minPts = 20, and the searching radius r = 15 metres are used as clustering parameters. The resulting total of tourist destinations is 100, and their distribution is shown in Table **1**. DBSCAN, a common density-based clustering technique, allows for the discovery of the cluster formed by a region of dense connection. The graphic demonstrates that the method can locate irregularly shaped clusters in the noisy data present in the feature space. It has several glaring flaws, however. To begin with, whereas the DBSCAN technique produces a higher concentration of results in the high-density area, our method's extracted tourist attractions are more uniformly distributed.

We utilise the popular machine learning tool Scikit-learn to construct a DBSCAN-based algorithm to find tourist attractions in the

Flickr geo-tagged dataset. The density criterion minPts = 20, and the searching radius r = 15 metres are used as clustering parameters. 2017;6(2):216 9 of 16 ISPRS International Journal of Geo-Information We utilise the popular machine learning tool Scikit-learn to construct a DBSCAN-based algorithm to find tourist attractions in the Flickr geo-tagged dataset. These values are used for the clustering parameters: the density criterion minPts = 20 and the search radius r = 15 metres.

Standard density-based clustering algorithms, like DBSCAN, allow the discovery of clusters with high connection density. The graphic demonstrates that the method can locate irregularly shaped clusters in the noisy data present in the feature space. It has several glaring flaws, however. Although the DBSCAN method's output is heavily weighted toward the high-density zone, our method's recovered tourist attractions are more uniformly distributed throughout the clustering region. The second problem is that DBSCAN can't distinguish between high-density areas that are close together (such as Tiananmen Square and its surrounding area). DBSCAN clustering groups together Tiananmen, Tiananmen Square, and the People's Heroes Monument.

Analyzing Fame in a Variety of Time Periods

Considering time constraints is essential when planning a trip. Researching visitors' patterns of site use over time might provide many travel guidelines. Attraction attractiveness is evaluated four times a year: quarterly, monthly, light/heavy, and weekend/weekday. The slow season runs from September 15 to March 15, while the high season runs from March 16 to November 14.

The statistics show that between April and August, the four tourism hotspots attract the most visitors each year. The heat map of the 4 attractions is broken down between the slow and busy seasons. The statistic shows that attendance at the four landmarks is much higher during the peak season than during the low season. Attractions see up to four times as many visitors during peak season as during off-peak season. A heat map of four tourist spots, broken down by weekdays and weekends. The results show that the four tourist hotspots experience a small increase in foot traffic on weekends compared to weekdays. There may not be a clear distinction between weekdays and weekends, since most Flickr users are not based in China, and international passengers' travel habits are not dictated solely by that distinction.

CONCLUSION

Human activity data on tourist destinations is gathered, paving the way for studies on the attractions' attractiveness and the extraction of tourists' spatiotemporal patterns and rules. In this study, we present a novel spatial clustering and text-mining technique that identifies hotspots, making it easier to find famous tourist destinations. Experiments in attraction discovery are conducted using geotagged photographs uploaded to Flickr in the Beijing metropolitan region between 2005 and 2016. Based on the identification of scenic hotspots, this article also analyzes the popularity distribution laws of China's new tourist destinations across multiple time and weather conditions. Geographic clustering, class merger, and label annotation are the three primary components of our suggested approach to discovering tourist attractions. Among the novel features of this method are: First, we apply the new grouping technique CFSFDP to the task of finding tourist attractions; second, we incorporate a zoning and standardisation step into the spatial clustering process to make our method more flexible in cases where there is a significant variation in population density between regions. So, in contrast to standard attraction-discovery techniques, such as the widely used DBSCAN clustering algorithm, our method takes a novel approach during the clustering phase. Using TF-IDF, we construct a tag vector for each original cluster, and then utilise vector similarity to combine semantically connected clusters, making it easier to explore the massive, asymmetrical tourist attraction. This is the benefit of a class-merger stage, which the prevailing methods of attraction discovery have not fully exploited. Overall, we present a novel strategy for finding well-known tourist spots that is substantially different from the standard DBSCAN-based approach. The experimental findings demonstrate that this unique strategy achieves much higher classification accuracy than the conventional DBSCAN method, can discriminate between neighbouring high-density regions, and offers superior flexibility in the presence of an unequal density distribution. Tourism planning and intelligent travel suggestions are only two examples of the kinds of applications that might benefit from analysing visitor behaviour gleaned from social media's geo-tagged big data. Research into optimising the discovery of new tourist attractions using a large geo-tagged dataset is planned for the future, as is an investigation into how best to propose destinations to visitors based on the laws and sights that already exist.

ACKNOWLEDGEMENTS

The State Key Laboratory of Resources and Environmental Information System and the Beijing Municipal Commission of Education's Scientific Research Key Program (KM201611417004) provided funding for this study. Other organisations that contributed include the Federal Natural Science Foundation of China (41501162, 41401449, and 41625003) and the Federal Key Research and Development Program of China (2017YFB0503602). Huang Z. contributed significantly to the writing by conceiving and designing the tests. The research and analysis were conducted by Peng X. The paper's authors are X. Peng and Z. Huang.

REFERENCES

[1] A.A. Cardenas, P.K. Manadhata, and S.P. Rajan, "Big data analytics for cybersecurity", *IEEE Conference on Communications and Network Security (CNS),* 2022. [http://dx.doi.org/10.1109/CNS56114.2022.10092919]

[2] Ö. Kafalı, and P. Yolum, "PISAGOR: a proactive software agent for monitoring interactions", *Knowl. Inf. Syst.,* vol. 47, no. 1, pp. 215-239, 2016. [http://dx.doi.org/10.1007/s10115-015-0848-1]

[3] A. Egyed, and R. Balzer, "Integrating COTS software into systems through instrumentation and reasoning", *Autom. Softw. Eng.,* vol. 13, no. 1, pp. 41-64, 2006. [http://dx.doi.org/10.1007/s10515-006-5466-4]

[4] J. William, M.M. Santos, M.D. Brito, J.F. Hübner, D.C. Vachtsevanou, and A. Gomez, "Increasing the intelligence of low-power sensors with autonomous agents", *Proceedings of the 20th ACM Conference on Embedded Networked Sensor Systems (SenSys),* 2022. [http://dx.doi.org/10.1145/3560905.3568301]

[5] M. Dennis, M. Fisher, and A. Lisitsa, "Proactive multi-agent explanation generation and evidence gathering in a service robot inhabited assisted living environment", *International Conference on Autonomous Agents and Multiagent Systems (AAMAS),* 2015.

[6] Ö. Kafalı, and P. Yolum, "PISAGOR: a proactive software agent for monitoring interactions", *Knowl. Inf. Syst.,* vol. 47, no. 1, pp. 215-239, 2016. [http://dx.doi.org/10.1007/s10115-015-0848-1]

[7] S.T. Iqbal, and B.P. Bailey, "MeWS-IT: A mental workload-based system for interruption timing", *Proceedings of the SIGCHI Conference on Human Factors in Computing Systems,* 2005.

[8] C.M. Kennedy, "Cognitive approaches to policy-based intrusion defence", *Proceedings of the IEEE Workshop on Information Assurance,* 2005.

[9] Y. Lirov, "Recycling troubleshooting experience with fuzzy logic", *IEEE Trans. Syst. Man Cybern.,* 2002.

[10] A. Biere, C. Tinelli, and C. Weidenbach, "Preface to the special issue on automated reasoning systems", *J. Autom. Reason.,* vol. 64, no. 3, pp. 361-362, 2020. [http://dx.doi.org/10.1007/s10817-019-09531-1]

[11] A. Steen, M. Wisniewski, H. Schurr, and C. Benzmüller, "Capability discovery for automated reasoning systems", *International Conference on Automated Reasoning,* 2017.

[12] O.G. Troyanskaya, P. Lió, and P. Zuliani, *Automated Reasoning for Systems Biology and Medicine.* Springer, 2019.

[13] T.N. Brooks, "Survey of automated vulnerability detection and exploit generation techniques in cyber reasoning systems", *ACM Comput. Surv.,* 2017.

[14] P. Cordero, M. Enciso, A. Mora, and V. Vychodil, "Parameterized simplification logic: Reasoning with implications in an automated way", *IEEE Trans. Fuzzy Syst.,* vol. 30, no. 12, pp. 5534-5543, 2022. [http://dx.doi.org/10.1109/TFUZZ.2022.3179847]

[15] W.L. Miller, R. Baker, M.J. Labrum, K. Petsche, Y. Liu, and A.Z. Wagner, "Automated detection of proactive remediation by teachers in reasoning mind classrooms", *Proceedings of the Fifth International Conference on Learning Analytics and Knowledge,* 2015. [http://dx.doi.org/10.1145/2723576.2723607]

[16] D. Shadrin, A. Menshchikov, A. Somov, G. Bornemann, J. Hauslage, and M. Fedorov, "Enabling precision agriculture through embedded sensing with artificial intelligence", *IEEE Trans. Instrum. Meas.,* vol. 69, no. 7, pp. 4103-4113, 2020. [http://dx.doi.org/10.1109/TIM.2019.2947125]

[17] D.I. Patrício, and R. Rieder, "Computer vision and artificial intelligence in precision agriculture for grain crops: A systematic review", *Comput. Electron. Agric.,* vol. 153, pp. 69-81, 2018. [http://dx.doi.org/10.1016/j.compag.2018.08.001]

[18] M. Trotter, and D. Lamb, *GPS tracking for monitoring animal, plant and soil interactions in livestock systems.* Precision Agriculture Journal, 2017.

[19] D.W. Bailey, M.G. Trotter, C.W. Knight, and M.G. Thomas, "Use of GPS tracking collars and accelerometers for rangeland livestock production research1", *Transl. Anim. Sci.,* vol. 2, no. 1, pp. 81-88, 2018. [http://dx.doi.org/10.1093/tas/txx006] [PMID: 32704691]

[20] H.A. Kumar, R. J., R. Shetty, S. Roy, and D. Sitaram, "Comparison of IoT architectures using a smart city benchmark", *Procedia Comput. Sci.,* vol. 171, pp. 1507-1516, 2020. [http://dx.doi.org/10.1016/j.procs.2020.04.161]

CHAPTER 29

Proving Knowledge Bases for Automated Reasoning for Information Analysis

G. Geetha[1,*] and **Abhilash Kumar Saxena**[2]

[1] *School of Computer Science and Engineering, JAIN (Deemed-to-be University), Bangalore, Karnataka, India*

[2] *College of Computing Sciences & Information Technology, Teerthanker Mahaveer University, Moradabad, Uttar Pradesh, India*

Abstract: New avenues for intelligence collection have been made possible by the advent and proliferation of the internet from the perspective of military intelligence activities, but the ever-increasing amount of information stored on it has put a strain on traditional methods of intelligence analysis. The current state of intelligence analysis must be corrected by expanding and improving military intelligence analysis practices. The control node to intelligence agency analysis must be abandoned if the military is to obtain the depth of intelligence knowledge it requires, if the technology of data mining is to be introduced into the analysis conducted by intelligence agencies, and if a data mining model is to be used to construct the network of military and intelligence analysis. The model's algorithm for intelligence analysis, which is based on semantic analysis rather than traditional types of association analysis, may improve the efficiency and accuracy of military intelligence gathering as a result.

Keywords: Knowledge bases, information analysis, automated reasoning, military intelligence, Fractional calculus.

INTRODUCTION

Integer calculus has been around just as long as its fractional counterpart. Fractional calculus is an important branch of mathematics, but its early development was modest over the last three centuries because it received little support from the foundations of physics and mechanics.

Several complex algorithms in the abnormal dynamics of nature have been shown to defy traditional integer-order calculus models as research has progressed. Its performance is easier to model using a fractional-order system. Because of its

* **Corresponding author G. Geetha:** School of Computer Science and Engineering, JAIN (Deemed-to-be University), Bangalore, Karnataka, India: E-mail: geetha.g@jainuniversity.ac.in

S. Kannadhasan, R. Nagarajan, & Kaushik Pal (Eds.)

non-locality and memory effects, a fractional calculus quasidifferential operator is ideal for modeling memory and inheritance systems as well as stochastic materials. Due to its lower performance, the second derivative is better suited to represent the historical dependence in the development of the system function than the integer derivative, which lacks localization. Fluid mechanics, electrochemistry, control theory, and viscoelasticity have all seen a rise in academic attention recently. The partial derivative operator method is gaining popularity and is being used more and more in many real-world contexts. Numerous sectors and organizations have embraced its tenets and methods, including engineering, economics, administration, the armed forces, and countless more. We may now build on the solid groundwork laid by these theoretical researches to address the theoretical challenges in systems engineering with greater knowledge and expertise.

What we call “Internet public information” is data that has been gathered and compiled from publicly available sources on the Internet. Timeliness, frugality, thoroughness, and a variety of credible sources define public information available online. On the other hand, the Internet makes knowledge accessible at any time and from anywhere, with great adaptability. The intelligence communities of many nations have come to recognise the significance of freely available public information online since the 1980s [1]. They have evolved into a crucial tool for spies to gather information. Because of its widespread use and ever-increasing bandwidth, the Internet is increasingly seen as a means of interaction with the wider world. The Internet has quickly become the “fourth medium,” alongside print, broadcast, and visual forms of communication [2]. The term “military intelligence” refers to the collection of intelligence for military purposes. Intelligence gathered by the military covers a wide range of topics, from the quantity and variety of equipment and weapons to their deployment and operational plans and the technological and economic status of the nation as a whole. The goal of military intelligence gathering is to provide decision-makers with a wealth of valuable information and to analyse recommendations for use in formulating military strategies. The term “open-source intelligence” describes the process of gathering data from open sources, processing it, and delivering it to targeted users in a timely manner to meet their intelligence requirements. Research shows that anywhere from 40-95% of Western industrialised nations’ national intelligence is gathered from open sources. There has been a plethora of research done in China on this topic in recent years. The growth of the Internet, and notably social media, has led to the network's progressive rise to prominence as people's primary information resource. The network has grown into the most significant open-source information resource, with vast databases covering commercial Industry, the military, consumer behaviour, and other related topics [3 - 5].

Now that data mining technology has advanced, users may extract meaningful insights from vast troves of network data that were previously inaccessible. In particular, research is now being conducted on the topic of "mining" social networks. Focus areas for studies include a wealth of information on military intelligence activities, such as weapons testing and the placement of weapons and equipment, among these networked resources. There is a vast amount of information available in the highly accessible online world, including news from all over the world, government regulations, research findings from academic institutions, and competitive economic intelligence, as well as ideas authored by individuals in the form of blogs, forums, and the like, and websites set up by terrorist organisations and anti-government groups for the purpose of promotion and liaision. Reportedly, the "Tibetan administration in exile" views the Internet as a "powerful instrument to recruit Tibetans opposing China," according to SIFY.COM. Study findings indicate that "Tibet independence" and the "Tibetan administration in exile" both maintain official websites [6]. Several Dalai Lama sites focus specifically on listing the online addresses of these "Tibet" groups.

Nowadays, all nations place a premium on gathering military intelligence online, with several having established whole departments devoted to the task. Although the proliferation of online data makes it easier to collect information, it also creates formidable challenges when analysing that data [7]. To some degree, military intelligence is affected by the fact that conventional methods of data analysis, although able to filter and anticipate data, are limited in their ability to perform complex statistical processing and analysis when data volumes are small [8 - 10]. Consequently, this paper's goal is to improve the efficiency of intelligence agency evaluation in a decentralized, open system that encompasses a plethora of established Chinese military intelligence analysis methods by introducing data mining methods into connectivity intelligence agency analysis and by building an intelligence agency conceptual framework based on data mining.

RELATED WORKS

Knowledge discovery *via* data mining is the process of uncovering hidden patterns and associations in large datasets. As of now, the technology has found widespread use across sectors such as banking, communications, retail, medicine, and even public security, intelligence, surveillance, and analysis. One way of looking at it is that its creation injects intelligence analysis into the realm of military action. Deeper intelligence agency analysis and so more effective intelligence decisions may be made with the use of modern data mining technologies, particularly in a network setting. The intelligence work of a data assimilation innovation goes even further by classifying the structures of smart analysis information and technology strategic planning in the field of natural language prepping, rather than simply considering how AI, IDP, stylistics, and other developments can be applied at the semantic level. Knowledge processing techniques, such as retrieval and visualisation, and research and innovation in command intelligent machines from a range of cognitive aspects to recognise intelligence incorporation and analysis, enhance the capability and level of intelligence required for the acquisition of large-scale intellect recognising [11]. To automatically analyse information and data stored separately on the Internet and extract potentially vital full espionage knowledge [12 - 13], data mining technologies are required for network intelligence analysis.

The field of data mining relies heavily on this technique. Classification aims for a one- or zero-valued output, whereas regression aims for a continuous one. Data mining technology allows for the classification and regression of network-based military intelligence, which not only improves the accuracy and precision of the classification result, but also, to some extent, the automation as well as intelligence level of classification, as well as the efficacy of military inquiry and analysis [14 - 15].

It is a looping procedure for organising things into categories. Particularly useful in text data mining, data mining technology enables tighter clustering of military records with the same or comparable semantics. Regular military intelligence analysis suffers from insufficient information grouping; however, this is remedied by the subject clustering approach. Another way to put it is that the group offers a more rational scientific strategy for enhancing military intelligence analytic methods.

Using correlation-based data mining, data can be processed and evaluated holistically, allowing intelligence professionals or organisations to view the data from multiple angles. Similarly, intelligence workers may benefit from correlation analysis when seeking information on potential adversaries or covert operations. This helps with early warning and better risk foresight.

PROPSOED WORK

Statistical modelling of topics, part 2. In terms of probabilistic topic models, the LDA model is the current gold standard. This Bayesian model has three distinct stages. For the PLSI model of relative probabilities in the latent semantic index, this is a full production probability model. Word, Topics, and Documentation are the LDA's three tiers. In the LDA, articles are represented as mixtures of many subjects, and topics are represented as multinomial distributions on a fixed vocabulary. Before introducing LDA, let's define some key terms and phrases. The smallest possible piece of textual data is a word. Words are represented by unit vectors, and because the vocabulary ranges from 1 to v, the vth word may have as many dimensions as there are digits in the integer v. When w is present, it denotes that wv=1 and all other elements of w were 0. Words in the text are represented by the notation w, where w = (w1, w2, w3,..., wN) and wn is the nth phrase in the series. D = w1, w2, w3,..., wN is the representation of an M-document set. The following is the generating procedure that LDA specifies for every document in the corpus:

1. The document's subject ratio, denoted by d, is drawn at random from the Dirichlet distribution Dir(), one document at a time.
2. Use the Dirichlet distribution Dir() to generate a random sample of T participants.
3. Take a random subject allocation z from topic scale d for every word w in the document d.
4. Create the matching word w based on the given topic z.
5. To create all of the text in the document, just repeat the steps above.

For a given subject, whose K-dimensional vectors serve as a prior distribution parameter, we may generate the following probability model of a message, N topics, and the probability of obtaining the N words of this document:

Training an LDA requires finding the parameters' sweet spot, where p (D |,) is maximized. Both the document's topic distribution and a prediction of the category to which each word belongs may be acquired using and, respectively.

$$p(\theta, z|w, \alpha, \beta) = \frac{p(\theta, z, w|\alpha, \beta)}{p(w|\alpha, \beta)} \quad (1)$$

Nevertheless, its analytical formulation for the integration in the numerator p(w|,) is not calculable, necessitating the use of a statistical estimate. To the extent that p(z| w) is estimated to its maximum, and provided that the parameter values are approximations, and to learn LDA models and draw conclusions from them, the parameters were estimated using the EM iterative technique. In contrast, the projected value was estimated using the variational inference sampling approach, as described in the original publication of LDA.

Crawling of Public Information Data

The real estate, education, and tourism industries are all booming, and this page compiles public classified listings for these sectors. The data is collected by searching the major microblogging search engines for the aforementioned three keywords, and then collecting the first fifty results for each trending subject. Both the original posts from each microblog as well as any forwarded posts are included in this archive. The batch acquisition programme locomotive collector was used to gather four different types of material across 200 pages due to the search results page's lack of support for Ajax asynchronous transfer of data.

Preprocessing of Public Intelligence Data

Vocabulary analysis and feature extraction might begin once a page has been denoised, or scrubbed of extraneous elements such as page tags. The primary tasks at this point are:

1. Preprocessing of Website Noise: The text is broken into individual words by analysing the case of the numerals, hyphens, punctuation, and letters. Young netizens use a wide variety of homophones, noises, and unusual symbols to represent their characteristics, whether for ease of usage or to stand out from the crowd. Even if it's possible to misplace information in a microblog, the Martian text was omitted from this post to keep the topic analysis unaltered. Defining a whitelist is how Mars handles text deletion; if a term is not on the whitelist, it will be removed from the text.
2. Analyzing syntax: Chinese does not employ spaces as participle markers, which is the most striking distinction here between Chinese and English vocabularies. In contrast, Chinese vocabulary lacks a distinct participle marker. Therefore, the Chinese phrase must be broken down into smaller vocabulary pieces before the text can be mechanically examined. Segmenting Chinese words is difficult. In this research, we employed the ICTCLAS word segmentation tool developed by the Chinese Academy of Sciences. Users can define their own words using ICTCLAS's user-friendly dictionary interface. The author offers appropriate user vocabulary for three types of text: domestic real, instructional, and tourist, in order to achieve satisfactory word segmentation accuracy.
3. Remove any filler words. Most of the keywords retrieved didn't cover what the user was seeking because they included high-frequency terms like “a” and “bar,” as well as other auxiliary phrases that appear in practically all documents but lack adequate document classification capacity in Chinese text. Articles, prepositions, conjunctions, and punctuation are all considered stop words in this research and are recorded in the file stopwords.txt file.
4. Extraction of Features: The term “feature extraction” might function as a search term. A threshold is defined in this study. The feature recovery process prioritizes words with greater frequencies and discards those with lower frequencies. Set a threshold of 10 for evaluating content related to hot subjects. In this experiment, we examine how feature-word extraction & LDA extraction

differ in their final results. It has been shown that LDA is a failed approach since it recovers feature words and the results are highly consistent. Fig. (1) is depicted in the System Model.

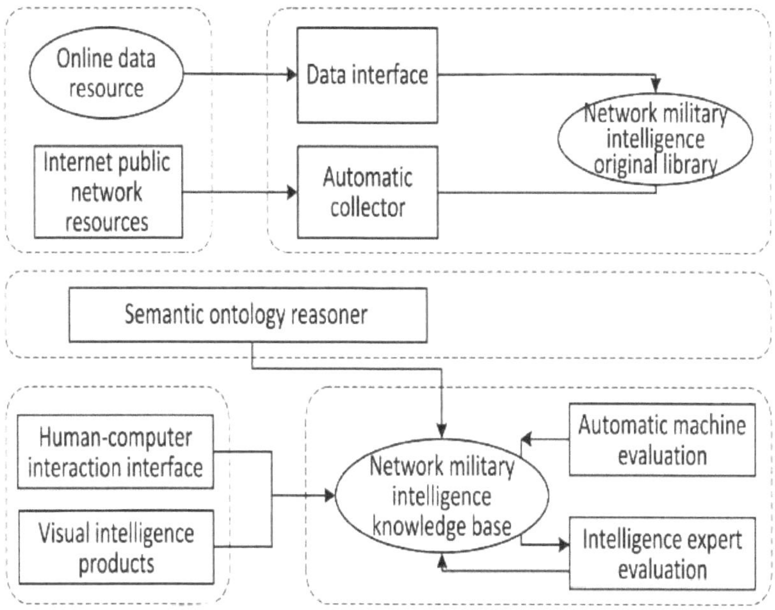

Fig. (1). System model.

In this study, the 50 most-visited search results for the microblog categories "Real Estate," "Education," and "Travel" are chosen. The raw text received after text preprocessing consists of a bunch of words separated by spaces, and is saved as three .txt files. After the original text is retrieved, it is examined from beginning to end to eliminate terms irrelevant to the theme-detection process, such as those in forwarded microblogs. Taking them out yields a dictionary with the word bag model—a compilation of all the words found in the document set—in a quasi-collective form. In practice, the MAP stores the dictionary and provides a reference for each term. The index value of a word is its position in the dictionary's numerical sequence. The next step is to build the vectorized file, which involves extracting the feature word and removing any words whose DF frequency is less than 10. It is made up of several terms, where term 1 is the dictionary index and count is the frequency with which that term occurs in a given text. The LDA technique may then be used to determine the vectored fle and extract the theme after the vectorization fle is acquired.

Network intelligence service mining and analytics of linguistic subject grouping and association analysis is made possible through the complete use of technology for data mining, as shown in the readily available analysis model of the network intelligence service. The investigation of algorithms for link analysis has proceeded to a higher level overseas. To demonstrate the practicality and utility of the text-mining method in intelligent mining through association analysis of networked open-source intelligence, José Palazzo examined real-world examples in 2004. Machine learning has been Juan Antonio Moya's primary tool ever since for sifting through mountains of network data in search of the insights he needs to lead his team to success.

RESULT AND DISCUSSION

To conduct this experiment, we use the following tools: the LDA package for topic modeling in microblogs, residential inference for predictive value estimation, and the EM algorithm for parameter estimation. For the sake of this article, we chose choose k=10 as our topic threshold and set it initially to 0.1. For each document category, we pulled out 10 subjects, and for each topic, chose ten keywords. During the time period of November 15, 2012, to November 20, 2012, the microblog hotspot data was selected for the source text. Words like "real estate," "tourism," and "education" appear frequently in the extracted data. This is due to the fact that Sina is being used by the popular microblog crawler. As these three terms are utilised as indices, they will appear in all of the obtained microblogs. The preceding results show that LDA effectively identifies trending themes.

Data Mining Method Results

Matching tuple sizes are used by the clustering method to group tuples together. As text length is variable, the text data is first represented as a fairly reasonable set of young-age attributes. A matrix of |D||V| is generated by TFIDF by calculating the TFIDF strength of every word in the feature dictionaries for every document. The document set comprises |D| documents, each of which is characterised by |V| characteristics. Each document may then be clustered as a set of tuples after the TFIDF matrix has been constructed. Clustering is performed using k-means, with cosine distance serving as the metric of separation between documents. Java is used for both the creation of the TFIDF matrix and the grouping of public intelligence data using K-means. Each of the three most common forms of microblog text may be clustered to get 10 central points. The meaning symbolised by TFIDF remains intact because the importance of TFIDF determines the importance of each centre point. In this analysis, we choose the 10 largest TFIDF weights for each cluster centre. The aforementioned is the trichotomous clustering results of the three most common forms of microblogs. The findings suggest that the presumption of TFIDF weights is associated with weak connections between topic terms. We also use this method for clustering several microblogs. The clustering result may be the result of combining information from many microblogs. The performance analysis of the proposed system is shown in Table **1**. Because some crucial data was lost during the fusion process, there have been discrepancies in how the issue has been interpreted. But it's clear that K-means produces fewer individual words; this is because K-content means' repetition rate is very high, leading to excessive document periodicity and, ultimately, a lower TFIDF score. This is why TFIDF takes into account the subtleties of each word.

Table 1. Performance results.

Classifiers	Accuracy%	Sensitivity%	Specificity%
RNN-LSTM	82.3	76.1	83.9
Random Forest	73.8	70.0	77.0
Naive Bayes	77.5	79.0	74.0
Decision Tree	72.5	72.0	68.0
RNN+LSTM+Word2Vec	83.0	86.0	79.3
NN (10 layers)	79.5	81.1	77.3
CNN Word2Vec	82.9	83.0	82.7
CNN	79.6	84.7	75.0
Hybrid Model	83.6a	87.1	79.3

The topic phrases are inconsistent and seem intermittent in TFIDF-based text clustering, but the LDA model reveals that the phrases provided by LDA are very significant and that the meaning of each topic can be grasped from the words. The LDA-derived data focuses heavily on real estate, education, and tourism; therefore, researchers should try to connect their study to the chosen source material by targeting keyword searches in the introduction of each topic. Since the LDA engine is responsible for the identification of similar public intelligence information, each of the fifty blog pages has a separate index of the relevant class. There is some redundancy; however, while certain terms are used more than once, the topics discussed are not the same. In contrast, when examining the TFIDF-based K-means clustering findings, it is clear that three index terms are never included. This is due to the presence of index terms inside each microblog, which causes an excessively high document frequency (DF).. As a result of the degradation of the TFIDF weights, the index phrases are no longer deemed to be distinct. In fact, if a word is more common in one kind of document but less common in another, it indicates that the term may better reflect the features of the first type of document in subject recognition in that type of document. Recognizing the microblog theme leads to the subject of extracting each document type, which is not suitable for TFIDF. For deleting single words and certain frequent terms, TFIDF is more effective than the LDA model. Yet, empirical experiments reveal that the initial centre point has a substantial impact on the K-means clustering outcomes based on TFIDF, leading to iterative clustering. The computations provide wildly different answers. The probabilistic model to which LDA belongs replicates the mental work involved in composing written works. Each article covers a variety of subjects. The word count for each section is shown below. LDA seeks the best distribution of both topics and words to form a single document. The odds of finding the article are the best. The experimental findings validate LDA's ability to effectively detect trending themes by modelling the thought processes of microblog writers. It works better for identifying trending topics on microblogging sites than K-means clustering does.

CONCLUSION

New opportunities for information collection have arisen with the emergence and widespread use of the network from a military intelligence perspective, but conventional intelligence analysis is becoming more difficult due to the ever-increasing volume of data in the network. There are gaps in the current system that must be addressed through enhanced military intelligence analytical procedures. If we want to acquire the kind of in-depth intellectual understanding that the military demands, integrate data mining into intelligence agency analysis, and establish network intelligence analysis on a data-mining model, we need to abandon the conventional wisdom about military intelligence assessment. We provide six new functional modules, analyze the paradigm for this sort of analysis, and incorporate data mining technologies into the investigation of network intelligence agencies. The development of an algorithm for analyzing military intelligence is now underway; it relies on semantic association analysis. Compared with more conventional forms of association analysis, this strategy offers several advantages that could lead to more accurate and efficient analysis of military information. The model's modules are not precisely defined by the tasks they perform. Semantic association-based intelligence analysis system in the military has room for improvement.

REFERENCES

[1] E.S. Litvinov, A.V. Daneev, D.A. Stepanenko, and A.S. Stepanenko, "Analysis of mechanisms of using the concept of probabilities to model plausible reasoning in technical diagnostics", *J. Phys. Conf. Ser.*, vol. 1661, no. 1, p. 012057, 2020. [http://dx.doi.org/10.1088/1742-6596/1661/1/012057]

[2] B. Kang, J.C. Suh, M. Wakakura, and E.S. Yoon, "Multimodeling approach for automated hazard

analysis of batch process plants", *J. Chem. Eng. of Jpn,* vol. 34, no. 6, pp. 802-809, 2001. [http://dx.doi.org/10.1252/jcej.34.802]

[3] J.W. Murdock, and C. Welty, "Obtaining formal knowledge from informal text", *Proceedings of the 15th International World Wide Web Conference (WWW),* 2006.

[4] J.H. Roodt, L. Leenen, J.J. van Vuuren, and Z.C. Khan, "Modelling of the complex societal problem of establishing a national energy sufficiency competence", *Proc. IEEE 23rd International Conference on Information Fusion (FUSION),* pp. 1-8, 2020. [http://dx.doi.org/10.23919/FUSION45008.2020.9190332]

[5] L. Soh, "ARKTOS: An intelligent system for satellite sea ice image analysis", *AI Applications,* vol. 16, no. 3, pp. 17-28, 2002.

[6] H.R. Myler, A.J. Gonzalez, and M. Towhidnejad, "Constraint mechanisms for knowledge acquisition from computer-aided design data", *Artif. Intell. Eng. Des. Anal. Manuf.,* vol. 7, no. 3, pp. 181-188, 1993. [http://dx.doi.org/10.1017/S0890060400000871]

[7] L. Soh, *ARKTOS: An intelligent system for satellite sea ice image analysis.* University of Nebraska Research Report, 2002.

[8] C. Zhang, and D. Lukose, *Multi-Agent Systems: Methodologies and Applications.* Springer: Berlin, Germany, 1997. [http://dx.doi.org/10.1007/BFb0030077]

[9] X. Ren, C.A. Knoblock, W.Y. Wang, and Y. Su, *Proceedings of the 11th ACM International Conference on Web Search and Data Mining (WSDM).,* ACM: New York, NY, USA, 2018.

[10] M. Kazaryan, "On the design of the automated monitoring system of waste disposal objects, industrial included, with the application of earth distance sensing technologies", *IOP Conf. Ser. Earth Environ. Sci.,* vol. •••, 2021. [http://dx.doi.org/10.1088/1755-1315/666/6/062090]

[11] T. Padmavathi, Ontological representation of knowledge for developing information services in food science and technology, 2012. [http://dx.doi.org/10.5771/9783956504402-145]

[12] A. Malhotra, M. Gündel, and M. Hofmann-Apitius, "ADO: A formal ontology for understanding structure of information and domain knowledge of Alzheimer's disease", *Proceedings of the International Conference on Biomedical Ontology,* 2012.

[13] B. Bouchon-Meunier, L. Foulloy, and R.R. Yager, *Intelligent Systems for Information Processing: From Representation to Applications.* Elsevier: Amsterdam, Netherlands, 2003.

[14] O.O. Varlamov, *Mivar Databases and Rules: A New Approach to Knowledge Representation and Processing.* Springer, 2021. [http://dx.doi.org/10.12737/1508665]

[15] Q. Wu, M. Lee, and C.W. de Silva, "Intelligent 3-D sensing in automated manufacturing processes", *Proceedings of the Joint 9th IFSA World Congress and 20th NAFIPS International Conference,* vol. vol. 1, pp. 334-339, 2001. [http://dx.doi.org/10.1109/NAFIPS.2001.944274]

CHAPTER 30

Social Network Analysis for Movie Recommendations and Information Extraction

Jayanthi Kannan[1,*] and **Anurag Singh**[2]

[1] *Department of Information Science and Engineering, JAIN (Deemed-to-be University), Bangalore, Karnataka, India*

[2] *Department of Computer Science and Engineering, Galgotias University, Greater Noida, Uttar Pradesh, India*

Abstract: Finding relevant information online has gotten increasingly difficult as the amount of data available on the internet has grown exponentially. In high-data-density, complex-domain settings, the recommendation system may be a big aid to users in making decisions. In the recommendation system, several approaches have been presented and collaborative filtering is a common practice. The cold-start problem is one of the remaining issues with collaborative filtering approaches. To address this issue, we offer a movie recommendation system that uses social network analysis and collaborative filtering. We use user preferences like age, gender, and profession to generate a connection matrix, and then that matrix is used to cluster people using community identification based on edge betweenness centrality. The suggested system then proposes movies to new members based on the preferences of the existing users in the group. Utilizing MAE, we demonstrate the superiority of the suggested technique.

Keywords: Sentiment analysis, movie recommendations, information extraction, social network analysis.

INTRODUCTION

The rate at which new knowledge is added to the world today far outstrips our capacity to absorb it. Online retailers frequently use the recommendation system. These recommendation systems emerged as a way to tailor content to individual consumers. Book, music, movie, news, CD, DVD, TV show, and product recommendation systems are all in use [1].

Providing a list of the best things, making recommendations based on demographics, and suggesting items based on users' past preferences are just a few of the numerous approaches to building a recommendation system [2].

* **Corresponding author Jayanthi Kannan:** Department of Information Science and Engineering, JAIN (Deemed-t--be University), Bangalore, Karnataka, India; E-mail: k.jayanthi@jainuniversity.ac.in

S. Kannadhasan, R. Nagarajan, & Kaushik Pal (Eds.)

Recommender systems are often classified into three groups based on the criteria they use to make recommendations: rule-based, content-based, and collaborative filtering (CF) [3]. The foundation of the CF algorithm is the assumption that a user's latent interests can be inferred from their shared experiences or preferences. Finding users or items that are similar to the expected person or object is its primary function. One of the benefits of a collaborative recommendation system is that users are more likely to find anything of interest in the product, and no prerequisites are needed to use the recommended materials. There are still flaws in the CF algorithm, such as the cold start problem [4].

The "community detection in huge networks", one of the techniques used to discover communities in social networks, has recently attracted the interest of researchers [5]. Researchers implemented this strategy in the movie recommendation system to improve the reliability of their recommendations. Many researchers focus on ranking measures, such as normalized discounted cumulative gain, which is a family of ranking measures widely used in practice and produces very efficient results alongside the method of community detection in social networks. The goal of this research is to provide a more effective approach than social network analysis. The proposed movie recommendation system uses social network analysis and the normalized discounted cumulative gain approach. The betweenness centrality approach was applied, which is important to social network research.

The cold-start problem occurs when the system has not had enough time to build up its user data to make any recommendations. An individual's tastes and interests must be included when creating a user profile for any recommender system. The user profile is created by considering how they interact with the system. The algorithm decides and offers recommendations based on the user's past history and actions [6]. The issue occurs when a new user or object is introduced into the system, for which there is insufficient data for the system to make a judgment. It can be challenging for the system to build a model from data for a new user who has not yet rated certain products or viewed some items. Because of this, similarity estimates between users may be off. There have been several attempts to find a solution to the issue. Embarak [7] proposed two methods to address the cold-start problem: node recommendation and batch recommendation. Then, he contrasted these two approaches with three others: the Triadic Aspect Technique, the Media Scout Stereotype Technique, and the Naive Filterbots Method. A new hybrid method was suggested by Basiri *et al.* [8] to address the cold start issue. With this method, you can get a sensible and useful recommendation.

RELATED WORKS

These days, you may find recommender systems employed everywhere from entertainment to information to product discovery [9]. Information about a user's interests can be automatically predicted or filtered using a technique called collaborative filtering (CF), which aggregates the preferences and tastes of multiple users. To better grasp what CF is, let us consider a common scenario: you want to see a movie right now, but you have no idea which one to watch. What do you do? In most cases, you ask your friends for recommendations. The CF approach centers on this principle [10].

Recently, recommender systems have gained much attention. It has found its way into literature, journalism, film, music, and even consumer goods. Additionally, there are expert recommenders [11], restaurant recommenders [12], collaborator recommenders [13], monetary service recommenders [14], romantic partner recommenders [15], and Twitter page recommenders. Users can shop for items that best suit their interests or needs with the help of these recommendation systems, which use filtering to predict ratings and customer satisfaction. Knowing the user's background can help predict how they'll respond in certain scenarios [15]. Because it may help users find things they might not otherwise, the recommender system is a valuable alternative to search algorithms. It is often done with a search engine that does not rely on conventional indexing methods. A recommender system is software that analyzes data, such as purchases or user preferences, to make educated guesses about what other people might like to buy. Some methods for building a recommender system are shown below [16 - 20].

Filtering based on content: Techniques for selecting content based on user input and object characteristics are constantly evolving. The information the user supplies is used by these techniques. Advice will be provided to users based on the information gleaned from their profiles. The accuracy of the engine improves as the user gives more information and follows the suggestions made by the engine. These formulas make an effort to suggest items that are quite similar to those previously enjoyed by the consumer. For instance, many of the goods that have been nominated are compared to things that the user has ranked in the past. Research into data retrieval and data filtering can build on this methodology.

Collaborative filtering, or CF, is a data-driven approach to user interest prediction and content filtering that relies on the aggregated preferences of many individuals. The CF approach is predicated on the idea that users who share each other's preferences are more likely to share their preferences on topics when those preferences differ from those of random users. Collaborative recommender systems get a list of products to recommend by looking at how similar users are and predicting how highly a user would rate an item based on how highly other users have rated it [21 - 23].

By gathering and analyzing large amounts of data on user actions, interests, or choices, the CF method can forecast which individuals are similar to others. A simple inquiry can help explain CF: what would someone do if they wanted to read a book but didn't know which ones were any good? Most individuals will poll their social circles for recommendations on good reads. Friends and individuals with similar tastes are always welcome to make recommendations to us. The CF approach centers on this central tenet. Two distinct categories of CF exist: user-based and item-based. The similarity between things in an item-based CF is determined by averaging people's ratings for those items. Users who enjoy Item 1 are more likely to prefer Item 2, and vice versa; hence, Item 1 and Item 2 are deemed comparable. Forecasting using user similarities is a key component of user-based CF. If Mr. James and Mr. Paul both saw the same movie and rated it similarly, then their similarities equal 1. However, if people rate it differently, there will be fewer similarities and more noticeable distinctions.

PROPSOED WORK

Social Network Analysis

To examine characteristics of social networks, the SNA can be employed. Nodes, or parts of a network, are the building blocks that define these architectures. In a network, vertices represent individual elements, whereas edges denote connections between those elements. Attributes can be applied to objects and connections. The system model is shown in Fig. (**1**). Information from the real world is used to build the networks. Data distillation, pre-processing, and the information structures used to transmit and maintain knowledge are just a few of the data fields that they imply could encounter some unexpected challenges.

A Movie Recommender System that Reduces the Cold-Start Issue by the Application of Social Network Analysis

Fig. (**1**) depicts the data-gathering and workflow operations required for the suggested system. To create a database for testing, the system must first collect data from users and movie listings. If you are a new user and wish to join the system, you'll need to log in. To update the database used for the test dataset, the system must gather fresh user data and movie listings. Adjacency matrices are created for each user based on their unique set of characteristics, such as age, gender, and profession. Here, we modify the user's evaluation group by computationally determining how similar the new user is to other users in every group using their personal data.

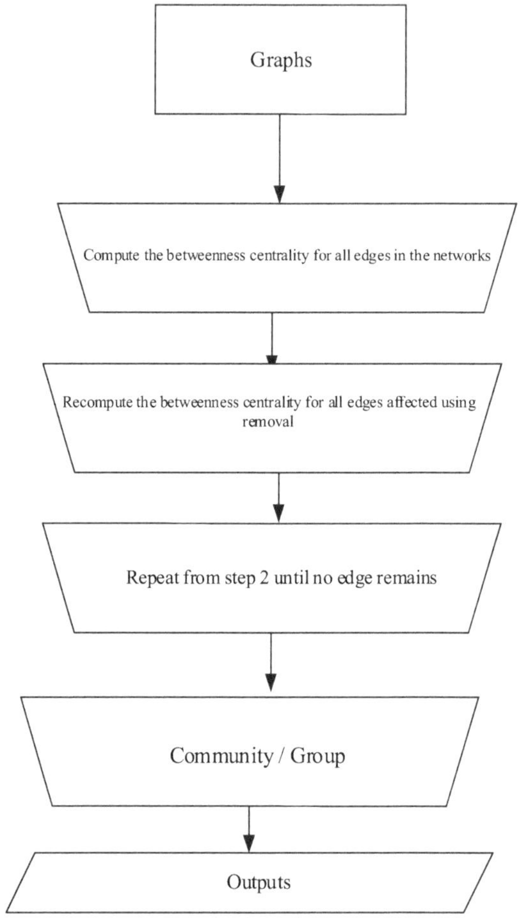

Fig. (1). System Model.

Cosine similarity between users is utilized in the computation. Then, in step 7, we determine which existing group is most similar to the new user, and add the new user to that group. The new user will get a ranked list of films based on how highly they were rated by users in their matched group. Here, the algorithm will select the five, ten, twenty, thirty, and forty most viewed films, then propose the ten most watched films from the group's collective viewing history to the new user.

To provide consumers with the most accurate movie recommendations, we must first collect basic information about them. Users who exhibit similar tendencies or behaviors may share a common preference for a certain product. In this study, we employ age, gender, and profession as personal predispositions for performance.

THE RELATIONSHIP BETWEEN USERS TABLE

We used the SNA centrality in our suggested approach. As a result, we need to compile a user connection table that includes demographic information such as age, gender, and profession. If two users have the same contact details, we infer that they are somehow connected to each other in some way. This table may be represented as a generalized graph in the formal language of classical mathematics.

The Use of Edge-Based Intersections for Community Detection

In this procedure, after retrieving the users' relationships table, we want to employ this information to cluster users into many categories. Clustering users into groups, or communities, is accomplished through the use of community detection based on edge betweenness. Since the shortest route from one module to the next must pass *via* these modules, the notion of discovering communities using edge betweenness is based on the possibility that edge connections among modules have the greatest betweenness value. The process of progressively deleting the edge with the greatest edge betweenness value produces hierarchical maps and rooted trees called dendrograms. Each node in a person's network is represented by a leaf, while the entire graph represents the root of the tree.

COSINE SIMILARITY AND COLLABORATIVE FILTERING

Common approaches to gauging user similarity focus solely on rating similarities. In actuality, users' affinity for one another is tied not just to their shared ratings of goods but also to their shared interest in the item categories themselves. Furthermore, two users are deemed extremely similar if they share a lot of personal data. Our study adjusted the cluster for the new member using the cosine similarity index. After users have been categorized into multiple groups using edge betweenness community detection, we can determine how similar a new user is to the individuals currently in each group by filtering on personal data such as age, gender, and job. An equation may be used to determine user similarity.

THE MATCHING GROUP FOR THE NEW USER

After tallying how similar new users were to existing users in each category, we compared their average similarity scores. For related users, the most comparable group was determined by calculating the degree of similarity between each pair of groups.

RANKING THE POPULARITY OF MOVIES

The popularity of movies, as measured by the average rating each film receives from users in a specific group, is taken into account when determining which group best fits a user's interests.

RESULTS AND DISCUSSION

The MovieLens dataset was donated by the GroupLens research group at the University of Minnesota, USA, and was utilized in the experimentation below. Measurements from three different levels are included. Each dataset includes information on users, their ratings, and the films themselves. One hundred thousand ratings, ranging from 1 to 5, were included in this dataset. There are a total of 943 individuals and 1,682 videos in this collection. Each user rates at least 20 films. User demographics like gender, age, and profession are also included in this dataset.

Two parts of the dataset, the training set as well as the testing set, are used to test our proposed technique. Importantly, you must utilize data that was not utilized when building the model to evaluate its performance. A total of ten datasets were randomly chosen from users who evaluated a minimum of twenty movies, fifty movies, one hundred movies, or two hundred movies, with the goal of improving the recommendation system's accuracy. This indicates that the procedure will need to be employed forty times in total.

Once a model has been developed, the training dataset can be used. Partitioning in this recommender system is carried out by randomly choosing people and ratings from the whole user base. The sample size of this data collection is 800 users. A model is constructed with the help of a training set. The model is put to the test by generating predictions using the testing dataset. This data collection includes 143 participants. Then, we pick some people and some ratings at random from among all users.

R is an open-source programming language and environment for statistical computing and graphics. It is free and available to everybody. With R's large library of built-in functions, you can easily do linear and non-linear modeling, as well as standard statistical approaches, classification, cluster analysis, and much more. It has maintained its popularity in academic environments because of its robust capabilities and the fact that its source code may be freely downloaded under the terms of the GNU General Public License from the Free Software Foundation. It may be compiled and run on UNIX, Linux, Windows, and Mac OS, among others. As a result, we can quickly locate the code's origin and observe its output. We don't have to wait for the vendor to make the necessary changes or additions. And we can always use it in tandem with other languages (C, C++). In addition, it allows us to communicate with fellow humans.The optimal number of movie suggestions was 5, which was the average across 10 random studies. As a consequence, we averaged four scenarios and found that when 5 films were suggested, the average score was 3.55. In all four instances when ten films were recommended, the average score was 3.79%. The average rating from the four scenarios was 4.34, while 20 films were proposed. In all four instances, the average score was 4.59 out of 30 movie suggestions. With 40 films to choose from, the average score across all four scenarios was 4.78. The MAE can't be higher than 10. So, it is safe to state that our solution to the cold-start issue works well. More than three out of five movies the algorithm suggested intrigued the user, as seen by these stats. Fig. (**2**) shows the F-score results.

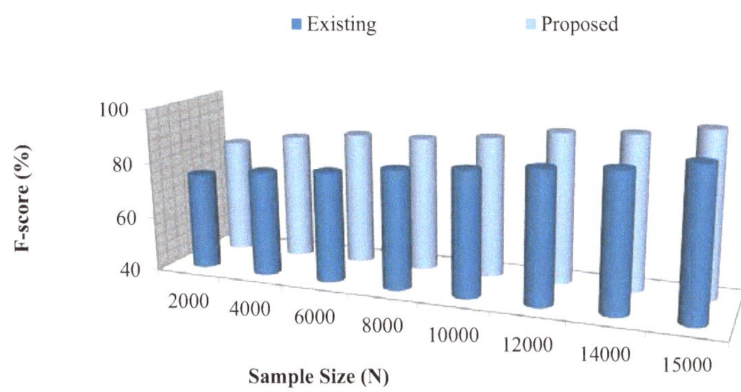

Fig. (2). F-score Results.

To ensure the methods presented in this research are effective, we have compared them with other methods, including the density-based clustering technique, the CF with k-NN technique, and the CF method alone. Fig. (**3**) displays accuracy results, Fig. (**4**) depicts precision results, and Fig. (**5**) illustrates recall results.

The k-NN and CF movie recommender system's average results across four tests averaged out to 3.60 when 5 films were suggested. Whenever 10 movies were suggested, the average score across all 4 cases was 3.96. When asked to rate a list of 20 movies, the average score across four cases was 4.35. When 30 movies were suggested, the average score from all 4 cases was 4.61. The average score after 40 films was suggested to be 4.85 across four situations. The MAE can't be higher than 10. As with other techniques, the optimal number of films to recommend was 5. Traditional CF algorithms have been used to assess untuned datasets. The user's neighbor with similar movie preferences was identified using the CF-based recommendation algorithm. The output of the CF-based movie recommender system is depicted. The recommendation for five films was 5.75. The average rating for a list of 10 suggested films was 5.84. A score of 6.06 was obtained when 20 films were suggested. The average rating for 30 suggested films was 6.29. The average recommendation for 40 films was 6.48. Like previous approaches, this one found that 5 was the optimal number of recommended films.

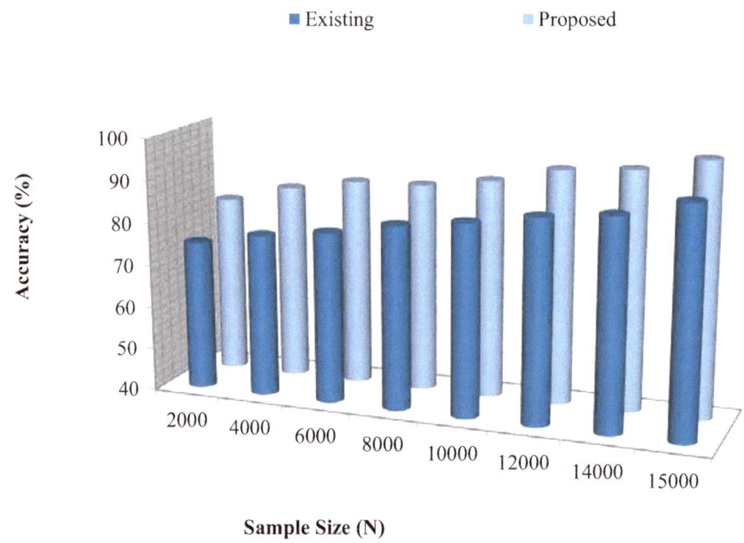

Fig. (3). Accuracy Results.

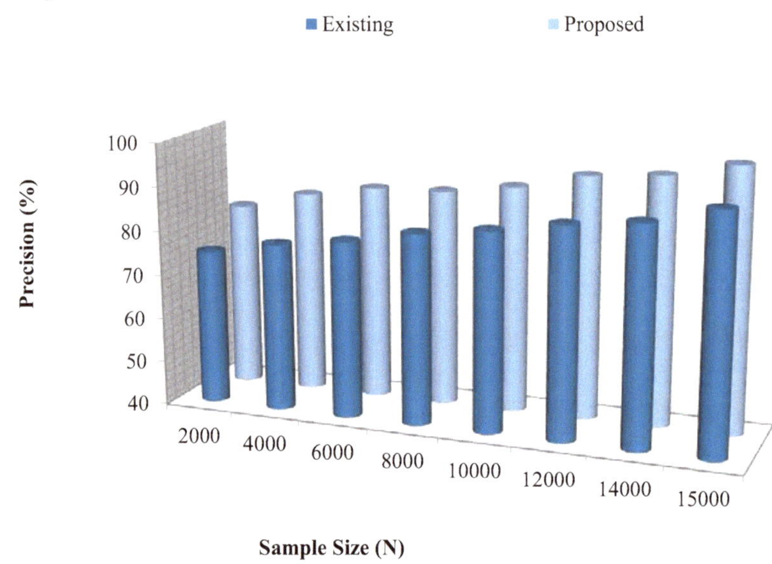

Fig. (4). Precision Results.

Then, we'll demonstrate the effectiveness of each approach by contrasting the combined MAE results of the four approaches. Compared with the suggested density-based clustering method, the overall average results of the k-NN and CF methods for movie recommendation exhibit superior performance. Similarly, the k-NN plus CF technique outperforms the suggested original CF method for movie recommendations. Our suggested solution, a movie recommendation system based on SNA and CF, outperforms the other three approaches on average. We must also defend the superior efficiency of our technique over the other three. Our strategy must also be defended on the grounds that it is the most effective of the three considered.

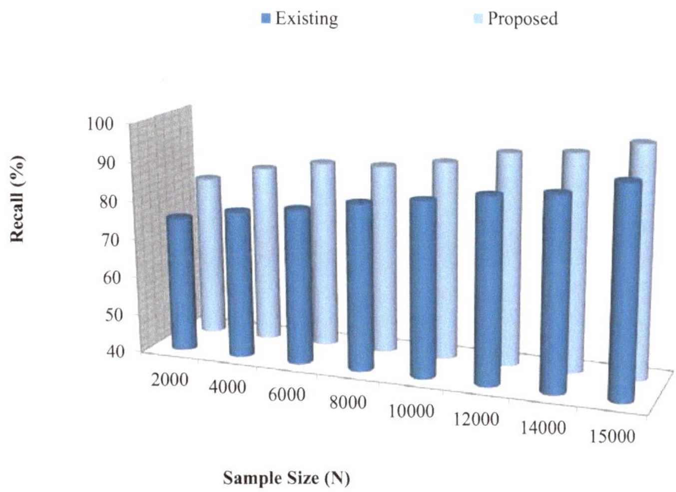

Fig. (5). Recall Results.

CONCLUSION

In order to resolve the CF problem, this study aims to include SNA in the recommender system. We use R programming, an open-source scripting programming language for data visualization and predictive analytics, for both the design and implementation phases. The recommendation system is a tool for facilitating quick and simple user information retrieval. In the recommender system, CF is among the most widely used and effective methods. But it has flaws, such as a cold start issue. In this research, we present a new method for a recommender system that leverages both SNA and CF to address this issue. Using edge betweenness centrality, we identified the user's most likely social circle. We found that our proposed strategy for recommending movies was highly accurate. According to the data, recommending 20 films is preferable to recommending 40, and the optimal amount is 5. Furthermore, the method shown in this study outperformed k-NN with CF and Density-based clustering with CF.

REFERENCES

[1] H. Chen, Y. Shen, S. Wu, and X. Liu, "Social network analysis for personalized movie recommendation", *Conf. on Communication Technology (ICCT),* pp. 321-325, 2021.

[2] W. Zhang, W. Chen, X. Chen, and J. Jiang, "Mining social network information for movie recommendation", *Proc. IEEE Int. Conf. on Data Mining Workshops (ICDMW),* pp. 197-204, 2021.

[3] X. Song, Y. Luo, Y. He, and M. Ye, "A social network analysis based recommender system for movies using user behavior data", *Proc. IEEE Int. Conf. on Systems, Man, and Cybernetics (SMC),* pp. 1039-1043, 2021.

[4] H. Oubanas, S. Aouat, and M. El Marraki, "A social network analysis-based approach for movie recommendation", *Proc. Int. Conf. on Wireless Networks and Mobile Communications,* pp. 147-152, 2021.

[5] H. Zhang, H. Wang, X. Hu, and H. Liu, "A social network analysis-based movie recommendation system using deep learning", *IEEE Access,* vol. 9, pp. 74749-74758, 2021. [http://dx.doi.org/10.1109/ACCESS.2021.3080203]

[6] L. Zeng, J. Tang, M. Zhang, and J. Li, "Exploring user's social influence for movie recommendation", *Proc. IEEE Int. Conf. on Big Data,* pp. 4502-4509, 2021.

[7] L. Liu, C. Zhang, X. Hu, and J.X. Yu, "Multi-modal social network analysis for movie recommendation", *Proc. ACM SIGMOD Int. Conf. on Management of Data,* pp. 2749-2751, 2021.

[8] S. Li, S. Li, X. Li, and X. Li, "An improved movie recommendation algorithm based on social network analysis", *Proc. IEEE Int. Conf. on Computer and Communications (ICCC),* pp. 1253-1257, 2021.

[9] J. Dai, Y. Cui, H. Xiong, and W.Y. Ma, "Heterogeneous social network analysis for movie recommendation", *Knowl. Base. Syst.,* vol. 226, p. 107120, 2021. [http://dx.doi.org/10.1016/j.knosys.2021.107120]

[10] M. Zhang, M. Li, S. Li, and Y. Li, "Movie recommendation based on collaborative filtering and social network analysis", *Proc. IEEE Int. Conf. on Computational Science and Engineering,* pp. 427-431, 2021.

[11] C. Lin, X. Li, X. Huang, and Z. Lu, "A movie recommendation system based on social network analysis and deep learning", *Proc. IEEE Int. Conf. on Artificial Intelligence and Big Data (ICAIBD),* pp. 10-16, 2021.

[12] Y. Xu, J. Shang, X. Wang, and X. Wang, "A social network analysis-based recommender system for movies", *IEEE Access,* vol. 10, pp. 2657-2668, 2022. [http://dx.doi.org/10.1109/ACCESS.2022.3140327]

[13] L. Chen, K. Chen, X. Hu, and H. Liu, "A novel personalized movie recommendation system based on social network analysis", *IEEE Access,* vol. 10, pp. 42967-42979, 2022. [http://dx.doi.org/10.1109/ACCESS.2022.3168714]

[14] Y. Li, Q. Li, J. Zhang, and X. Li, "Extracting user interest and movie themes from social media for personalized movie recommendation", *Proc. IEEE Int. Conf. on Artificial Intelligence and Knowledge Engineering (AIKE),* pp. 1-5, 2021.

[15] M.T. Yilmaz, and G.B. Erturkmen, "Social network analysis of movie recommendation platforms for developing movie recommender systems", *Appl. Soft Comput.,* vol. 108, p. 107450, 2021. [http://dx.doi.org/10.1016/j.asoc.2021.107450]

[16] A.C. Djedouboum, A.A. Abba Ari, A.M. Gueroui, A. Mohamadou, and Z. Aliouat, "Big data collection in large-scale wireless sensor networks", *Sensors (Basel),* vol. 18, no. 12, p. 4474, 2018. [http://dx.doi.org/10.3390/s18124474] [PMID: 30567331]

[17] B. Qolomany, A. Al-Fuqaha, A. Gupta, D. Benhaddou, S. Alwajidi, J. Qadir, and A.C. Fong, "Leveraging machine learning and big data for smart buildings: A comprehensive survey", *IEEE Access,* vol. 7, pp. 90316-90356, 2019.

[http://dx.doi.org/10.1109/ACCESS.2019.2926642]

[18] K. Guk, G. Han, J. Lim, K. Jeong, T. Kang, E.K. Lim, and J. Jung, "Evolution of wearable devices with real-time disease monitoring for personalized healthcare", *Nanomaterials (Basel),* vol. 9, no. 6, p. 813, 2019.
[http://dx.doi.org/10.3390/nano9060813] [PMID: 31146479]

[19] C. Lemonde, E. Arsenio, and R. Henriques, "Integrative analysis of multimodal traffic data: addressing open challenges using big data analytics in the city of Lisbon", *Eur. Trans. Res. Rev.,* vol. 13, no. 1, p. 64, 2021.
[http://dx.doi.org/10.1186/s12544-021-00520-3]

[20] S. Kirmani, A. Mazid, I.A. Khan, and M. Abid, "A survey on IoT-enabled smart grids: Technologies, architectures, applications, and challenges", *Sustainability (Basel),* vol. 15, no. 1, p. 717, 2022.
[http://dx.doi.org/10.3390/su15010717]

[21] Z. Fayyaz, M. Ebrahimian, D. Nawara, A. Ibrahim, and R. Kashef, "Recommendation systems: Algorithms, challenges, metrics, and business opportunities", *Appl. Sci. (Basel),* vol. 10, no. 21, p. 7748, 2020.
[http://dx.doi.org/10.3390/app10217748]

[22] L. Qin, X. Xu, and J. Li, "A real-time professional content recommendation system for healthcare providers' knowledge acquisition", *7th International Congress,* pp. 367-371, 2018.
[http://dx.doi.org/10.1007/978-3-319-94301-5_31]

[23] I. Rabiu, N. Salim, A. Da'u, and A. Osman, "Recommender system based on temporal models: A systematic review", *Appl. Sci. (Basel),* vol. 10, no. 7, p. 2204, 2020.
[http://dx.doi.org/10.3390/app10072204]

CHAPTER 31

Text Mining Approaches for Next-Level Information Analysis and Decision Support

R. Mahalakshmi[1,*] and **Veena S. Badiger**[2]

[1] *Department of Computer Science and Engineering, Presidency University, Bangalore, Karnataka, India*

[2] *Department of Computer Applications, Presidency College, Bangalore, Karnataka, India*

Abstract: A company's postmanagement entails assessing, selecting, and employing individuals who logically and scientifically match the post requirements as well as are a good fit for the company's growth into their appropriate positions. The data that most accurately portrays the market need for data analysis skills is the job recruiting information published on the employment website. Nevertheless, this work uses text mining to analyze the information in online recruiting materials. This research serves as a valuable resource for analyzing job search data, since most of the material is presented in textual form. Workplace matching is the focus of this research, which draws on text mining as well as multi-criteria decision-making. With 66.45% of the candidates coming from the Internet business, technical positions within text mining are mostly concentrated there. Technical data analysis is not as in demand in other sectors; in fact, demand is below 15% across the board. Education continues to dominate as a demand supplier, accounting for 30.53% of the market, despite the dispersed and expansive nature of the business data analysis industry. But at 24.28% and 22.34%, real estate and media are in close proximity. The service sector will have a greater need for business data analysts than technical ones, in addition to the aforementioned three sectors. During the data-gathering step, the recruiting website's data is analyzed to extract job details, including pay, qualifications, required work experience, and the total number of recruits. ¬The data gathering step is carried out by this paper, which crawls the recruiting website for job information. Along with further details about the post, such as the number of recruits, the position's remuneration, the qualifications required, and the required work experience, this study may aid in analyzing recruitment data published by the website and swiftly reflect data on the market need for data analysis abilities.

Keywords: Text mining, advanced information analysis, decision making, text mining, job recruitment information.

* **Corresponding author R. Mahalakshmi:** Department of Computer Science and Engineering, Presidency University, Bangalore, Karnataka, India; E-mail: mahalakshmi@presidencyuniversity.in

S. Kannadhasan, R. Nagarajan, & Kaushik Pal (Eds.)

INTRODUCTION

To boost performance, organizations should consider improving their data collection processes. Process improvement strategies are becoming more complicated due to the large amount of datasets and the diversity of their attributes. For processing large datasets, previous strategies have not been successful in improving performance. When applied to large process datasets, data mining may reveal useful hidden patterns, which in turn can help improve strategies [1].

By giving workers more agency, Customer relationship management (CRM) boosts customer satisfaction. The customer-firm connection is complex, and CRM data is rarely evaluated across different markets or customer categories; these factors contribute to CRM's challenges in B2B e-commerce. For this reason, the CRM paradigm makes it hard to make good judgments [2]. Discovering new processes and verifying their conformity are two common uses of process mining in big data analytics. However, finding issues, researching remedies, and implementing them are usually the last steps, even though event log analysis may also improve business performance [3]. The ever-increasing data volumes have impacted conceptual modelling as a discipline. In this setting, process mining refers to a set of methods for deriving a process architecture from an execution-related event stream. Preliminary findings from mining processes and analysis algorithms may be useful for weeding out extraneous data, but accurate interpretation of those results requires human judgment, creativity, subject expertise, visual examination, and automation algorithms. In addition, business users often end up with complex process models that are difficult to understand after conducting a process research on a log of events [4]. Research in business process management (BPM) has led to a range of methods, techniques, and resources for creating, deploying, overseeing, and evaluating effective business processes. Process mining (PM) is a relatively new field that aims to enhance business process model analysis by extracting useful information from large volumes of event records [5]. Data and event logs are the building blocks of process mining, a relatively young field of research. As it aids in improving data-based knowledge of business processes, it is widely used in business organizations. When a novel method for analyzing data is founded on an integrated business process with information technology. The integration of process mining with deep learning algorithms facilitates a robust connection between BPM and BI strategies [6]. To analyze trends and identify new ways to reengineer corporate processes, social media has become the most critical data source. There are many different ways to use the data made available by social media. One example is for an entrepreneur to research the industry they want to join and determine what their customers need before releasing new products [7].

RELATED WORKS

To convey the improvement ideas, the authors [8] developed a framework that uses data mining methods to identify important hidden patterns in high-volume process datasets. A genuine set of processes and their characteristics was collected to assess the suggested framework. Next, techniques for classification, clustering, and feature selection were used to identify interesting patterns in the process dataset, which included a large amount of data. The findings then suggested ways to improve after being evaluated. Findings demonstrate that recognized patterns may back up efforts to enhance processes by suggesting ways to do so.

A study presented a hybrid methodology for business-to-business customer relationship management (B2B CRM) that makes use of genetic algorithms as well as data mining methods to enhance decision making [9]. The approach divides consumers into two groups: those who shop often and those who just stop by. The decision tree method's rules were optimized using a genetic algorithm, and an altered Data Mining - C5.0 was employed for consumer categorization. According to the findings, the suggested strategy successfully distributes funds to the most lucrative clientele. Compared to other algorithms, such as the conversional C5.0, k-means, and the Support Vector Machine (SVM) method, the suggested model performs better and has higher accuracy [9].

The study suggests a method for helping company decision-makers narrow down their alternatives and improve performance by analyzing process logs and using process mining [10]. A technique is presented and then illustrated through a case study, after describing how event log evaluation may be used to run performance checks and thereby limit business opportunities. A logistic case study with three trials was used for evaluation; in this research, many business situations were explored, and the worst-performing ones were excluded after a certain time. The studies' results show that the suggested method for reducing business scenarios helps decision-makers identify the best scenario.

In our paper [11], we provide a method for displaying the results of event log analysis to identify business process bottlenecks. Using visual analytics in a process mining setting allows us to provide business process insights that are easy to understand and analyze, rather than presenting users with overly complicated process models. After applying the suggested method to a manufacturing company's process, the findings demonstrate that visual analytics within the framework of process mining may detect performance concerns and bottlenecks and present them to the company's users in a straightforward and unobtrusive manner.

This study aims to investigate process mining and business process management by reviewing the current methodologies and technologies used in these fields and showcasing the latest advancements [12]. The last section of this research delves into business process management (BPM) and project management (PM), in which PM facilitates the improvement of BPM by linking it with data science.

We will use the suggested framework as a starting point and put it through its paces for sentiment analysis [13]. A support vector machine trained using supervised machine learning uses a dataset for sentiment classification based on a vocabulary. The outcome shows great promise. There is a comparison of the precision and the amount of real feelings it can identify. This finding demonstrates the value of sentiment analysis and text mining on social media data, and it also gives operations and marketing teams a tool for forecasting sentiment direction using machine learning classifiers. Industries like telecom benefit from the abundance of data made available by today's digitally engaged society. With the help of text mining and sentiment analysis, these companies can stay ahead of the curve and build a stronger organization that can improve customer satisfaction and mitigate problems through creative business process reengineering techniques in the telecoms industry.

The authors of the study [14] provide a BP regulatory compliance model (BPCRM) that defines general controls for compliance. These controls may be used to specify specific requirements for BPs, which are then entered into process mining to analyze compliance breaches. As a cataloguing tool, this model compiles a collection of established compliance rules and patterns, making it easier for businesses to define and assess the compliance of their processes.

To help businesses improve their processes based on evidence, the authors of the study [15] propose a framework that combines data mining and process methodologies with process compliance, data quality, and appropriate technologies. By offering a unified framework to guide all operational phases, it aims to increase the capacity to analyze, evaluate, and improve organizational data and business processes while decreasing the effort required to identify and apply methodologies, tools, and techniques individually for each case.

PROPOSED WORK

These days, most internet content is delivered as web pages, and most of that content is written in text. Processing large amounts of textual data has proven challenging for conventional information retrieval methods. The goal of text mining is to effectively retrieve useful information from massive text databases. In practice, big data is often represented as unstructured text that overlaps at multiple levels, and is constantly evolving by merging a knowledge base and domain restrictions with massive amounts of unconstrained text data. The benefits of large-scale textual data can be fully leveraged to address the challenge of converting unstructured data into structured data. Give every phrase in the written space a numerical value to show how important it is for characterizing the document content. One way to think about the word weight di in a text is as its coordinates in the document's space. We may see document di as a point in document space and di as a vector that runs from the origin of document space to the point that determines di in this instance. After screening and summarizing, we may use the most often cited product qualities as categorization criteria, for instance. +is approach is universally extensible and applicable to different situations, but it requires human verification to see whether the standards are sensible. Its fundamental premise is to take a text at a time and evaluate how well it matches the current cluster—that is, how similar it is to the text in the cluster's core—based on the input text. If the current text is already part of a cluster, it will be added to that cluster; otherwise, a new cluster will be formed. As an illustration of the text-mining algorithm idea, consider the post-requirements clustering-mining algorithm shown in the following image. In Figure 1, we can see the flowchart of the text mining algorithm. Checking whether the model's output matches the original text's category is the primary goal of measuring the impact of the text mining algorithm. Since we don't know each text's category, we may assess its impact by either selecting texts based on their subject categories or manually labeling their categories. Manually segmenting the comment information into brief phrases based on punctuation is done before determining whether a statement clearly leans toward semantically-based criterion description. Finally, we use a number of criteria to divide the human population into subgroups, and then we label each subset with the corresponding criterion. This allows us to obtain the training set for the model of classification. After the results assessment index system is built, the next stages are to compute the assessment index weight, benchmark efficiency, as well as upper limit performance. After that, quantitative and qualitative performance calculations are performed. We can use this data to determine the efficiency classification interval, then plug it into the given formula to obtain the performance value of the evaluation object. Graphically shown in Figure 1 is the multi-criteria decision-analysis method. Following the normalization process, the resulting decision matrix is referred to as the normalized fuzzy choice matrix R(k).

After experiencing the project, people tend to express their happiness or discontent with a criterion using more emotive language, especially if they prioritize it above others when making a decision. In this case, users' expectations will vary significantly from the average standard set by other users because, when confronted with a higher-valued characteristic, individuals typically evaluate its suitability to their expectations using more stringent standards.

Incommensurability will result from dimensional and scale-related disparities across attribute indicators, including the most popular kinds of attributes, the effective benefit characteristic, and the cost attribute. A benefit characteristic is one where a higher value is considered better. As a general rule, a lesser number for a cost characteristic is preferable. As part of its operational procedures, the firm follows the principle of matching people to positions and uses a system of fair competition to select outstanding individuals for the company based on specific post needs. Inject new energy into the company's people team, harness employees' passion, make the most of their abilities, and contribute more effectively to the business's growth. A human resources supervisor requires to be able to do the following: recognize great talent, maximize that talent's potential in relation to their position and their own judgment, gather opinions from a variety of sources when choosing talent, weigh the pros and cons of potential candidates, put their knowledge to good use, choose talent that is a good fit for their position, maximize their potential, contribute to the company's growth, and so on. In most cases, businesses must have a thorough understanding of the responsibility requirements, text mining, and multicriteria decision-making before they can begin building them. Events alone will not allow them to create posts. To ensure a scientific match between people and posts, we should select talent in a systematic and reasonable manner once we have a thorough understanding of the post requirements. Enterprise and employee quality are not static. The post-demand will evolve in response to shifting social conditions. Adjustments to post-undermining of texts will also be made in response to changes in staff quality. To ensure the right people are working for the right company, it's crucial that they pay close attention to job matching and make timely adjustments to posting and personnel allocation. We will stifle business growth and staff engagement if we implement multi-criteria decision-making and the "one post for life" policy, which is why we need to put the individual in a loop where they are matched with jobs.

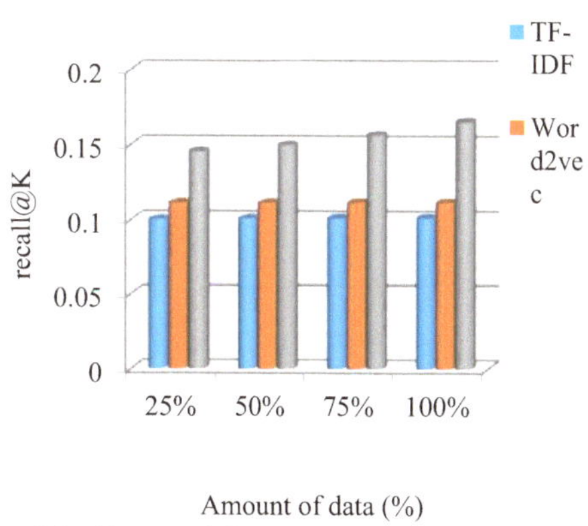

Fig. (1). Performance Analysis of the Proposed System.

RESULT AND DISCUSSION

This experiment explores the compatibility of people with certain job roles before making any changes, using the HR manager position at AS Industries as an example. Evaluating the effects of single-channel text clustering entails labeling each piece of data with a category via human annotation or another method, and then assessing the clustering's purity. For optimal picture clustering results, the K-means and visual clustering models are integrated. Before assigning weights to the job criteria, prioritize the most significant ones based on the job description. The combined weights of all the abilities equal 1. The next step is to assign numerical values between 0 and 100 to a wide variety of employee skills. As a general rule, the grades range from outstanding (90–100), good (75–90), fair (55–75), bad (40–55), and poor (0–40). Fill in the scoring section with the average score that someone achieved. Last but not least, multiply each skill's weight and score, then sum the results. Table **1** displays the information whether the workers' skills are a good fit for the company's job description and how well an employee performs in their role often depends on their own abilities. Possessing good organizational, communication, talent training, and flexibility skills is essential for this position. Pick out a few key aspects of workers' career aspirations and assign weights to them based on how significant they are. The combined weights of all the abilities equal 1. Afterwards, workers are asked to rate their job satisfaction on a scale from 0 to 100. The possible grades are outstanding (90 out of 100), good (75 out of 90), fair (55 out of 75), bad (40 out of 55), and poor (0 out of 40). Fill out the scoring section with the average score that other people have achieved. Lastly, the total is determined by multiplying each position's expectation by its weight. Using the same procedure, we can determine the degree to which certain jobs are a good fit for each individual. 1. Calculate the average for multiple posts; 2. A random survey is used to select 6 people from every workshop for examination and calculations because the number of specific worker positions—110—is too large for the 10 seminars of the manufacturing planning department. To assess the efficacy of single-pass text clustering, the literature suggests annotating each piece of data with a category label using various approaches, such as manual annotation, and then evaluating the clustering using purity. High levels of similarity inside clusters and low levels of similarity across clusters are the desired outcomes of the clustering goal function. Consider papers as an example. Similar documents are those in the same cluster, whereas dissimilar documents are those in other clusters. The internal metric for clustering quality is an example of an objective function. A high score for the internal criteria is no guarantee of success in real-world scenarios. As a percentage of the overall sample size, the purity is determined by the correlation component between the original category and the clustering algorithm's produced label set for that category. The grouping result is more accurate when the purity is close to 1. It is difficult to assess the model's success using this technique for one-time clustering of post requirements since we do not know in advance which types of data analysis posts are accessible. Therefore, it is hard to manually label them. For the best results when grouping images, combine K-means and visual clustering. Choosing the optimal word vector model is the first step. Then, run three trials to compare each model's output, input the data into K-means, and choose a cluster size (K) between 2 and 70. This experiment explores the compatibility of people with certain job roles before making any changes, using the HR manager position at AS Industries as an example. 2–70 clusters. This is in stark contrast to the models that use job requirements Word2Vec, Word Bag, and TF-IDF.

CONCLUSION

Recruiting for technical positions in text mining is concentrated in the Internet industry, accounting for 66.45% of total hiring. Technical data analysis is not as in demand in other sectors; in fact, demand is below 15% across the board. Though dispersed and vast, the business data analysis market is dominated by the education sector, which accounts for 30.53% of total demand. But at 24.28% and 22.34%, real estate and media are in close proximity. In addition to the aforementioned three sectors, the service sector will have a greater need for business data analysts than technical ones. During the data-gathering stage, the statistical analysis of the recruiting website crawls job-hiring information and other job details. This includes the number of recruits, work experience criteria, wage range, and job qualifications. Based on data from the recruiting website, this study crawls job recruitment information and completes the data collection step. In addition, the number of recruits, job qualifications, compensation, and the work experience required for the position are all factors to be considered. To examine the recruitment data and swiftly reflect the market need for data analysis skills, this paper's study may leverage data from the recruitment website.

REFERENCES

[1] J.T.N. Wibawa, R. Gunawan, M. Suhandi, and R. Setiawan, "Development of marketplace product data mining and analysis application as a reference in running a business", *ITandSociety,* vol. 8, no. 1, 2023.
[http://dx.doi.org/10.33021/itfs.v8i1.4724]

[2] Y. Rashnavadi, S. Behzadifard, R. Farzadnia, and S. Zamani, "Business process discovery from emails: Text classification and process mining—A case study of procurement process, Innovatus", *Digital Transformations in Business Information Systems,* vol. 5, no. 1, pp. 1-10, 2022.

[3] M. Siek, and R.M.G. Mukti, "Business process mining from e-commerce event web logs: Conformance checking and bottleneck identification", *IOP Conf. Ser. Earth Environ. Sci.,* vol. 729, no. 1, p. 012133, 2021.
[http://dx.doi.org/10.1088/1755-1315/729/1/012133]

[4] L. González, and A. Delgado, "Compliance requirements model for collaborative business process and evaluation with process mining", *Proc. XLVII Latin American Computing Conference (CLEI),* pp. 1-

10, 2021.
[http://dx.doi.org/10.1109/CLEI53233.2021.9640197]

[5] S.K. Chhajer, and R.B. Satpathy, *Adaptation of text mining as text data mining similar to text analytics for extracting high-quality information from text.* Technoarete Transactions on Intelligent Data Mining and Knowledge Discovery, 2022.
[http://dx.doi.org/10.36647/TTIDMKD/01.01.A001]

[6] I. Tlemsani, F. Marir, and M. Majdalawieh, "Screening of Murabaha business process through Quran and hadith: a text mining analysis", *J. Islamic Account. Bus. Res.,* vol. 11, no. 10, pp. 1889-1905, 2020.
[http://dx.doi.org/10.1108/JIABR-05-2020-0159]

[7] S. Decker, Data-Driven Business Process Improvement: An Illustrative Case Study About the Impacts and Success Factors of Business Process Mining, 2019.

[8] M. Khanbabaei, Framework of Using Data Mining for Business Process Improvement, 2019.

[9] A.S. Makinde, O.R. Vincent, A.T. Akinwale, A. Oguntuase, and I.D. Acheme, "An improved customer relationship management model for business-to-business e-commerce using genetic-based data mining process", *Proc. Int. Conf. on Mathematics, Computer Engineering and Computer Science (ICMCECS),* pp. 1-7, 2020.
[http://dx.doi.org/10.1109/ICMCECS47690.2020.240875]

[10] Y.V. Midden, J.J. Arachchige, and F.A. Bukhsh, "Optimal scenario mining for business strategy decision-making through process mining", *Proc. Int. Conf. on Frontiers of Information Technology (FIT),* pp. 311-316, 2021.
[http://dx.doi.org/10.1109/FIT53504.2021.00064]

[11] A. Kaouni, G. Theodoropoulou, A. Bousdekis, A. Voulodimos, and G. Miaoulis, "Visual analytics in process mining for supporting business process improvement", *International Conference on Novelties in Intelligent Digital Systems,* 2021.
[http://dx.doi.org/10.3233/FAIA210089]

[12] S. I. Abdelaal, *Business process management and process mining technologies: The progress of a discipline, .*
[http://dx.doi.org/10.54216/AJBOR.100105]

[13] H. Susanto, A. Sari, and F.Y. Leu, "Innovative business process reengineering adoption: Framework of big data sentiment improving customers' service level agreement", *Big Data and Cognitive Computing,* vol. 6, no. 4, p. 151, 2022.
[http://dx.doi.org/10.3390/bdcc6040151]

[14] L. González, A. Delgado, J. Canaparo, and F. Gambetta, "Evaluation of Compliance Requirements for collaborative business process with process mining and a model of generic compliance controls", *CLEI Electr. J.,* vol. 25, no. 2, 2022.
[http://dx.doi.org/10.19153/cleiej.25.2.7]

[15] A. Delgado, A. Marotta, L. González, L. Tansini, and D. Calegari, "Towards a data science framework integrating process and data mining for organizational improvement", *Proc. International Conference on Software and Data Technologies (ICSOFT),* pp. 492-500, 2020.
[http://dx.doi.org/10.5220/0009875004920500]

CHAPTER 32

Text Mining for Automated Data Analysis and Information Retrieval

Gopal K. Shyam[1,*] and **J. Vijay Fidelis**[2]

[1] *Department of Computer Science and Engineering, Presidency University, Bangalore, Karnataka, India*

[2] *Department of Computer Applications, Presidency College, Bangalore, Karnataka, India*

Abstract: One new piece of software that's making waves is the recommendation system, or RS. It uses knowledge-discovery methods to infer the user's goals and interests. It is becoming increasingly difficult to decipher the user's intent and activate the suggestion appropriately as data volume grows exponentially. This research proposes a new Deep Knowledge Grid (DKG) for RS construction and huge data analysis. The DKG uses a Deep Convolutional Neural Network (DCNN). This DKG explicitly models the KG's end-to-end high-order connectivities. Using an attention approach, it iteratively propagates embedded information from a node's neighbors—persons, objects, or characteristics—while determining the relative significance of those neighbors. From a conceptual standpoint, our DKG outperforms state-of-the-art KG-based recommendation methods that either use regularization to model high-order relations or extract paths to exploit them explicitly. Results on publicly available benchmarks show that KGAT outperforms state-of-the-art methods like RippleNet with Neural FM. The attention mechanism's benefits for interpretability and the efficacy of embedding propagation in high-order relation modeling have been demonstrated in subsequent studies.

Keywords: Text mining, automated data analysis, information retrieval, Deep Convolutional Neural Network (DCNN), Novel Deep Knowledge Graph (DKG).

INTRODUCTION

The goal of topic identification is to identify and monitor trending subjects on social media. When it comes to individuals voicing their opinions on various topics, Twitter is perhaps the most popular site. Among them, the COVID-19 pandemic stands out. Governments and healthcare organizations might benefit from topic detection and monitoring in dealing with these phenomena [1]. A plethora of information on trending subjects and popular sentiment may be found

* **Corresponding author Gopal K. Shyam:** Department of Computer Science and Engineering, Presidency University, Bangalore, Karnataka, India; E-mail: gopalkirshna.shyam@presidencyuniversity.in

S. Kannadhasan, R. Nagarajan, & Kaushik Pal (Eds.)

in the messages of microblogs, such as Twitter. A deeper understanding of data flowing in from social networks can be achieved through topic identification and monitoring. Research in this area often sticks to a consistent set of predetermined themes (clusters) while detecting.

When data is cumulative and subject to change, these methods become inefficient. Furthermore, brief texts are not well-suited for nonparametric evolutionary subject models owing to data shortage [2]. Since popular microblog posts reflect broader public sentiment, subject identification on these sites is crucial for tracking and controlling public opinion. Traditional clustering methods, however, struggle to handle the massive amounts of microblogging data, which span a wide range of themes and contain substantial noise [3]. Plagiarism is a contested issue in many industries, but particularly in the music industry, where commercially produced music is worth a small fortune. Music plagiarism detection is a challenging issue since there are no objective measurements to determine whether a song is plagiarized. As a result, choices are often dependent on subjective arguments. A useful tool is automated music analysis algorithms that can detect musical similarities [4]. Finding the subjects of published papers online is known as topic detection. Getting the subject terms right and making them easy to grasp are two of the most crucial things for topic identification [5]. Books on finance reflect current developments in the industry, which, in turn, affect market movements and investor choices. Subject identification technology is employed to easily and swiftly extract subject information from the vast financial textual corpus [6]. Topic models that rely on clustering to generate topics claim to be more effective than generative probabilistic topic models. These models group high-quality phrase embeddings using the appropriate word-selection method. Nevertheless, these methods have limitations, such as inadequate parameter selection and models that fail to account for the quantitative relationships between words and themes, as well as between texts and subjects [7].

RELATED WORKS

In a study [8], a new method is proposed for grouping 001 texts across languages based on two established techniques: aligned embedding and community identification in graphs. Using clustering, our technique aims to uncover fundamental top005 ics in a multilingual dataset. 006 A quantitative assessment using silhouette as well as V-measure metrics is presented, along with a qualitative evaluation for which a new systematic method is proposed. An analyst's empirical evaluation finds that our algorithm has strong overall performance. Our 014 novel algorithms were deployed and utilized on a 015 every day for a major 013 multidisciplinary public consultation, which is the backdrop of the work we discuss.

A new communicative clustering method, called ComStreamClust, was proposed [9] for grouping related sub-topics (such as COVID-19) within a larger subject. The two datasets used to assess the suggested method were the FA CUP and the COVID-19. Compared with current approaches such as LDA, the results obtained with ComStreamClust confirm its usefulness.

This paper presents a method for discovering new topics by combining BERT and seed LDA clustering [10]. Building a seed LDA (sLDA) model is the first step in optimizing the LDA model. First, the seed words that the LDA model uses were analysed. Second, by fusing sLDA and BERT, the B-sLDA paradigm was constructed. The process of topic generation is guided by the seed phrase set, which is used to generate phrases with a certain likelihood. The sLDA model was used to acquire topic characteristics, while the BERT model was used to obtain text features. The output of the feature fusion process was fed into the method of K-means clustering, which yielded topic groupings. As a last step in the topic identification process, we sent the first 10 words of every cluster through the TF-IDF framework. The official dataset, which included 20 newsgroups, and the real public opinion information for "Shanghai COVID-19" that was acquired using a crawler, were both used in the experiment that was conducted in this study. It is clear from the experiments that the seed term set guides the LDA model, as sLDA outperforms the initial LDA model in complexity and coherence. The Silhouette Coefficient and the Calinski-Harabasz metrics show a considerable improvement in the B-sLDA clustering approach.

An evolutionary clustering approach that automatically determines the number of clusters is proposed [11] by researchers using the Bayesian nonparametric Dirichlet process mixture model. To make the algorithm better at handling short social media communications, they combined text similarity in topic recognition and temporal information gathered from tweets and other social network characteristics in a weighted amalgamation. Data acquired from Twitter over a 2.5-month period was used to evaluate the model. The results show that the topic identification performance may be improved using information from social networks. When it comes to clustering performance and topic coherence, the suggested approach is superior to earlier research, resulting in superior clustering on brief texts.

The authors [12] proposed a hierarchical Bayesian stochastic framework based on clustering to detect and monitor themes in online news articles. This technique would enable the sharing of topics across various stories in the corpus. The hierarchical Pitman-Yor mixing model, whose component densities are the inverted Beta-Liouville (IBL) distribution, has shown greater efficacy in text data modeling compared to the typically used Gaussian distribution; we built our technique on this model. Also, we theoretically built an online learning system based on variational Bayes that can train the proposed TDT model from a continuous stream of news items. We show that our TDT approach is superior by comparing it with other well-specified clustering-based TDT techniques across different news datasets.

A text encoding model grounded in the algorithm for sentence embeddings and an evaluation of word closeness in texts, an innovative method for automatically determining the appropriate number of clusters was proposed [13]. Using Ward's method, it incorporates pre-processing of USE data, agglomerative hierarchical clustering, and the Markov stopping moment for optimal clustering. Finding the sweet spot for cluster size is done using the “e-2” hypothesis. Two real-world tagged information sets that we utilized in our experiment were News20 and BBC. We compared the suggested model to more conventional approaches to text representation, such as bag-of-words and word2vec, and found that it outperformed both the baseline DBSCAN as well as OPTICS models, which used different encoding techniques, in terms of output quality. It was observed that clustering quality remained constant with increasing cluster numbers using three quality criteria. As a result, text clustering with text classification is a good approach.

To solve this issue, the authors [14] suggest a hybrid algorithm with three layers. To efficiently group the microblog texts, they utilized the \inline-formula> \tex-math notation=”LaTeX”>K \/tex-math></inline-formula>-means algorithm in the first layer. In order to get cleaner clusters, they partitioned large clusters and removed text that is considered noise. To combine the smaller clusters that are related to the same subject, they used the agglomerative nesting (AGNES) method in the second layer. Subsequently, they minimized their influence on the <inline-formula> <tex-math notation=”LaTeX”> by removing the majority of noise. In the third layer, which fixes the incorrect merging in AGNES, K-means were placed. When tested on a real-world microblogging data set, this method fared better in topic identification and surpassed similar older techniques in clustering.

A text similarity-based approach and a clustering-based technique are the first two unique approaches proposed [15]. We next demonstrate how to merge them into a more effective hybrid approach. The end product is an innovative adaptive meta-heuristic for detecting instances of musical plagiarism. We conducted experiments on an extensive set of ascertained and non-plagiarism instances to evaluate the efficiency of the suggested approaches, both when examined separately and in the integrated meta-heuristic. According to the results, the meta-heuristic is more effective than the current approaches. Lastly, we integrated the meta-heuristic into a web-based application and conducted a study with 20 participants, half of whom had access to the tool, to evaluate its efficacy, use, and overall user acceptability. For this research, we asked participants to rate the degree to which they thought each song from a set of predetermined pairings constituted plagiarism. Our program helped the group identify all instances of plagiarism, and they completed all assignments without making a single mistake, according to the research. An automated method that gives a measure of music similarity was deemed beneficial by the whole sample.

PROPSOED WORK

First, we construct a user-item bipartite graph, which is graph 1 G1. A knowledge graph is a graph that has additional information along with the bipartite graph. The G1 can be formulated as,

$$G_1 \rightarrow \{U, I\}$$

Where U is the user and I itemset as depicted in Fig. (**1**).

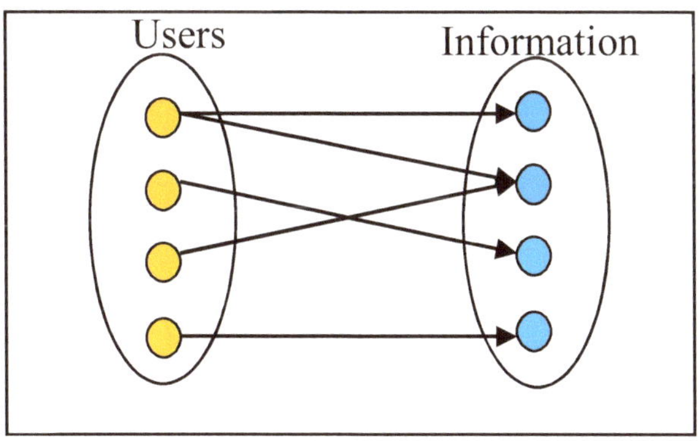

Fig. (1). Constructed Bipartite Graph Model.

In order to construct a knowledge graph, it is necessary to include additional information in theG1. The information added to the graph is further called a knowledge graph or G2. In addition, the relationship is also represented in the G2. Thus, it can be represented as follows,

$$G_2 \rightarrow \{U, I, R[h, r]\} \quad \textbf{(1)}$$

Where R is the relationship between information from head h to tail t of the information set. In Figure.2, the basic model of the knowledge graph is depicted.

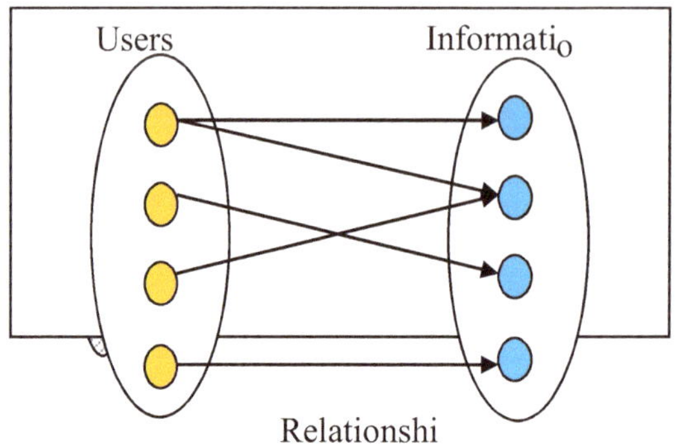

Fig. (2). Knowledge Graph Model.

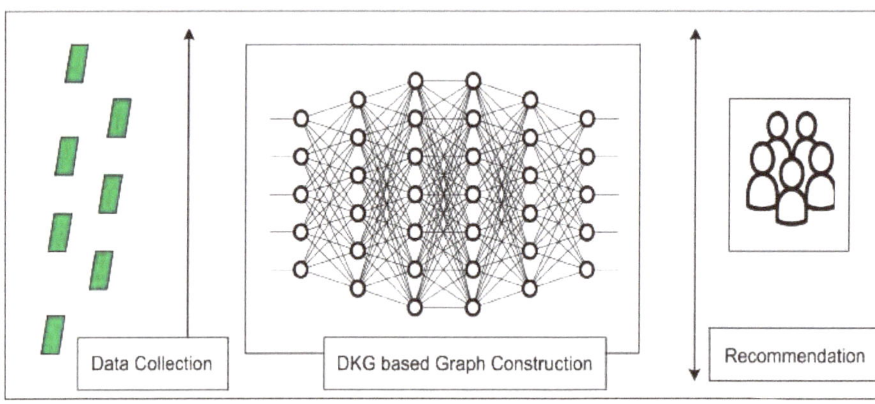

Fig. (3). Proposed DKG-RS architecture.

A. DCNN-based Knowledge Graph Model

The proposed DKG model has three major modules as shown in Figure.3. The three modules are,

- Data Collection Module
- DKG Construction Module
- Recommender Module

Data Collection Module

We have a stream of users U={u1,u2,…un}. All the user inputs are real-time and of high order. The data collection module is responsible for collecting data from all users at timeT. At every iteration, data collection is performed alongside data cleaning. The Knowledge Graph Model is shown in Fig. (**2**). This module first receives the data from user devices (like Internet of Things (IoT) devices). Then, it normalizes the data order in order to support high-order data. The DKG-RS architecture is shown in Fig. (**3**). Then it feeds the data into the DKG module, which constructs and updates the knowledge graph.

DKG Construction Module

This model is designed with DCNN, which is a deep learning approach.

Input Layer: At first, the system had L number of data points from n number of users. All data and users are initialized in the input layer. The input layer further computes the weight value for the data and constructsG2. For each new incoming data point, this layer updates the input data in the graph.

Hidden layers: We have m number of hidden layers, which compute the relationship between input data and the user. For relationship computation, we introduce an attention mechanism. To highlight the significance of this connectedness, we assign attentive weights to cascaded propagations. Here, we first outline a single layer, which is made up of three elements: information propagation, knowledge-aware attention, and information aggregation, and then we talk about how to apply it to several levels.

Information Propagation: It can be defined to represent a user who can be connected with more than one data source as u1→d1,u1→d2….

The neighbour connectivity is computed as follows,

$$NC = \sum_{H(r,t)} \pi R[h,t].\, e_t \tag{2}$$

Knowledge-aware Attention: The relational attention mechanism is formulated as,

$$\pi R[h,t] = \frac{e^{\pi R[h,t]}}{\sum e^{\pi R[h\prime,t\prime]}} \tag{3}$$

This value is considered an attention score, which gives the relationship between neighbouring nodes or users.

Output Layer: According to the attention score, the output layer constructs the graph and updates the graph for the recommending module.

Recommender Module

The recommender module operates on the knowledge graph constructed by the output layer. Based on the graph, a recommendation is generated and sent to the IoT device.

RESULT AND DISCUSSION

Three publicly available benchmark datasets, Amazon-book, Last-FM, and Yelp2018, with a range of domains, sizes, and sparsity, are used to assess the effectiveness of DKG.

- Amazon-book2: A popular dataset for product recommendations is Amazon-review. From this assortment, we choose Amazon Books. We employ the 10-core setting, which requires keeping people and things with at least 10 interactions, to ensure the dataset's quality.
- Yelp20184: This dataset was obtained from the 2018 Yelp challenge. Here, the items are neighbourhood establishments, such as pubs and restaurants. To ensure that each user and each object has at least 10 interactions, we also use the 10-core setting.
- The Last.fm music service was used to collect the Last. FM3 music listening dataset. When things are treated as tracks, we specifically use the portion of the dataset whose timestamps range from January 2015 to June 2015. We maintain data quality by employing the same 10-core configuration.

The three datasets are explicit feedback; therefore, we convert them into implicit feedback, sample an unwatched set for each user, and mark each entry with 1 to indicate that the user has positively assessed the item. For each dataset, we create a knowledge graph using Microsoft Satori7. From the entire KG, we first choose a subset of triples with a confidence level larger than 0.9. In light of the sub-KG, we gather Satori IDs for all legally produced films, books, and musicians by matching their names to the tails of triples (head, film, film name, tail), (head, book, book title, tail), or (head, type.object.name, tail). For ease of use, items with multiple matched entities or no matching entities are eliminated. The dataset details are summarized in Table.1

Table 1. Dataset description.

Data		Amazon-Book	Last-FM	Yelp2018
User-Item Interaction	Users	70670	23000	45000
	Items	24915	48000	45600
	Interactions	847133	303459	115768
Knowledge Graph	Entities	88000	58765	90763
	Relations	39	9	40

We randomly select 80% of each user's interaction history in each dataset as the training set, while the remaining 20% serves as the test set. We also randomly select 10% of the interactions from the training set as the validation set for hyper-parameter tuning. We treat each user-item interaction as a positive instance and use negative sampling to pair it with a negative item the user hasn't previously consumed.

A. Performance Evaluation

We consider two performance metrics, such as recall@K and ndcg@K to figure out the efficacy of retrieved top-K results. Both determine the accuracy of the top-K results recommended by the proposed system. For comparison, we considered the conventional CF method and the Knowledge Graph (KG) methods. The recall@K Amazon dataset is shown in Fig. (**4**).

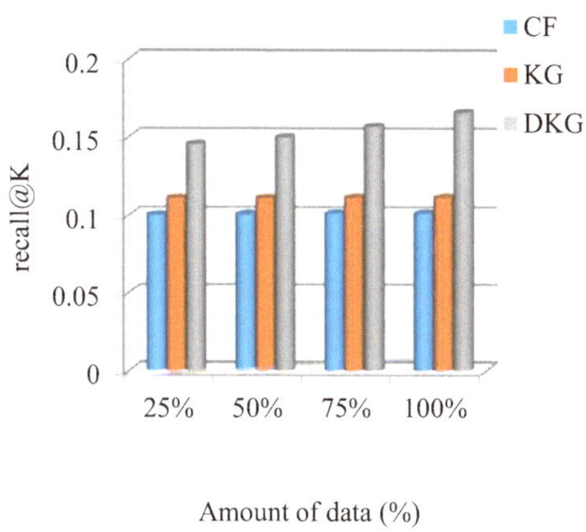

Fig. (4). Recall@K on the Amazon dataset.

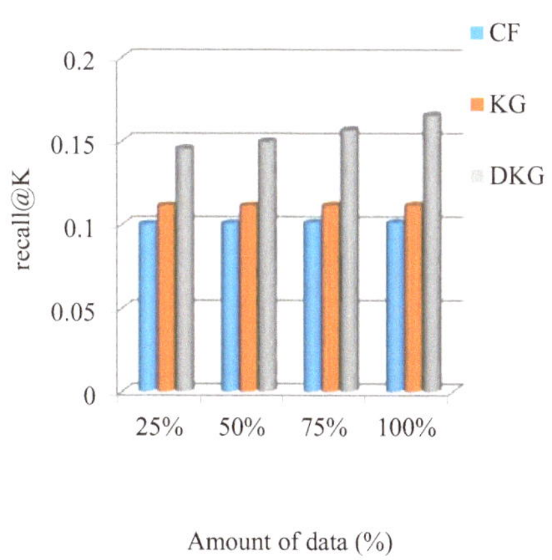

Fig. (5). Recall@K on Last FM dataset.

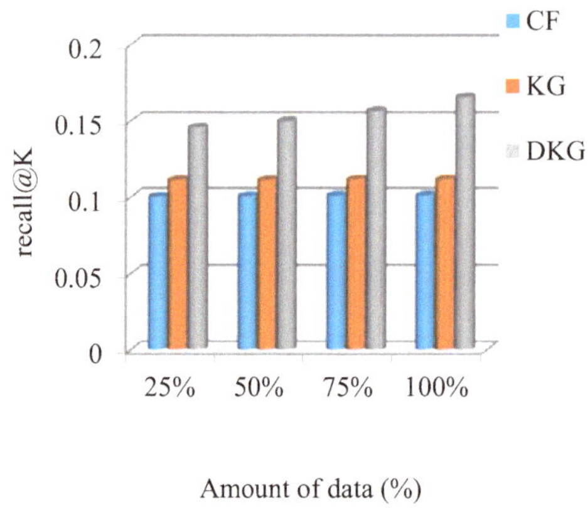

Fig. (6). Recall@K on Yelp dataset.

The sparsity problem, which typically limits the expressiveness of recommender systems, is one reason to utilise KGs. For inactive users with limited interactions, it is challenging to construct optimum representations. Here, we examine whether using connectivity data can help solve this problem. To do this, we run studies with user groups at varying levels of sparsity. We specifically divide the test set into four groups based on the average number of interactions per user, while maintaining an equal average across all groups. The recall@K Last FM Set dataset is shown in Fig. (**5**). In most situations, DKG beats the other models, particularly on the two user groups with the fewest members, Amazon-Book and Yelp2018. The recall@K YELP dataset is shown in Fig. (**6**). Recursive embedding propagation, which enriches the representations of inactive users, and high-order connectivity modelling, which 1) contains the lower-order connectivity utilised in baselines, are used to confirm the significance of the latter.

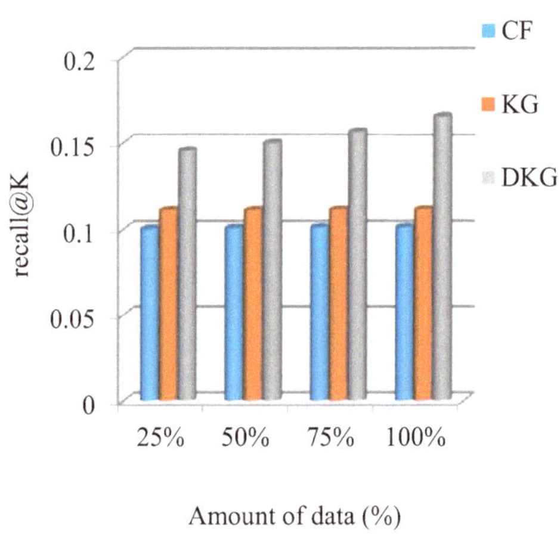

Fig. (7). Ndcg@K on amazon dataset.

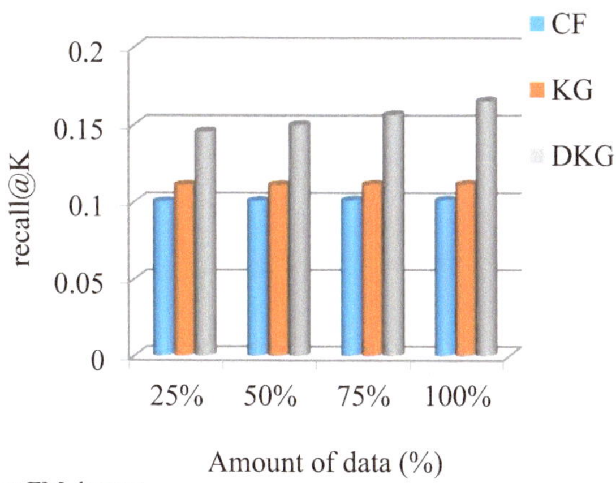

Fig. (8). Ndcg@K on Last FM dataset.

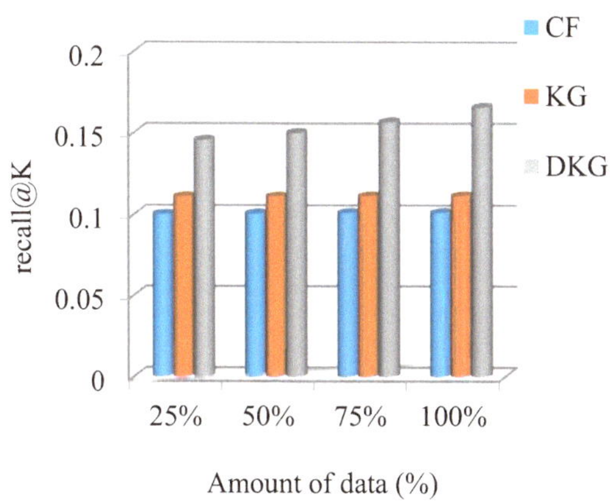

Fig. (9). Ndcg@K on Yelp dataset.

It is important to note that DKG significantly outperforms various baselines in the user group with the highest density (*e.g.*, the 2057 group in Yelp2018). The ndcg@K Amazon dataset is shown in Fig. (**7**). One cause could be that consumers with too many interactions have preferences that are too broad to be accurately recorded. The ndcg@K Last FM dataset is shown in Fig. (**8**). High-order connections could negatively impact user choices by introducing additional noise. The ndcg@K YELP dataset is shown in Fig. (**9**).

It is worth noticing that the proposed DKG method ensures high-level recall and NDCG for top-K results. The results show that the proposed DKG method achieves accurate top-K results.

CONCLUSION

In this paper, a novel Deep Knowledge Graph (DKG) approach is proposed for a recommendation system. The deep approach is built on a deep convolutional neural network (DCNN) that computes the interrelationships between users and data. The DKG first collects the stream of data, then computes the neighbouring connectivity values using an attention mechanism. The mechanism considers the link weight to construct the graph. Based on DKG, the recommendations are initialized for the users. In the future, we have planned to extend this work to large-scale IoT applications.

REFERENCES

[1] F. Kou, “Financial topic detection algorithm based on multi-feature fusion,” 2020.

[2] P. Cheng, J. Du, F. Kou, Z. Xue, and P. Chen, “Topic detection based on semantics, time and social relationship,” Lecture Notes in Electrical Engineering, Springer, 2019.

[3] L. Lin, G. He, and X. Liu, "Research on topic detection technology for information security texts", *Conf. on Computer and Communications (ICCC),* pp. 1621-1627, 2019. [http://dx.doi.org/10.1109/ICCC47050.2019.9064175]

[4] A. Ayorinde, J. Panneerselvam, L. Liu, and D. Miao, "Topic clustering using induced squared correlation thresholding with dimension reduction", *Proc. IEEE Int. Conf. on Parallel & Distributed Processing with Applications, Big Data & Cloud Computing, Sustainable Computing & Communications, Social Computing & Networking (ISPA/BDCloud/SocialCom/SustainCom),* pp. 948-957, 2020. [http://dx.doi.org/10.1109/ISPA-BDCloud-SocialCom-SustainCom51426.2020.00145]

[5] A. Najafi, A. Gholipour-Shilabin, R. Dehkharghani, A. Mohammadpur-Fard, and M. Asgari-Chenaghlu, "ComStreamClust: A communicative text clustering approach to topic detection in streaming data", *Expert Syst. Appl.,* 2020.

[6] “Graph-based approach for semantic text clustering: Topic detection in the context of a large multilingual public consultation,” European Commission Research Report, 2022.

[7] J. Wu, B. Li, and Q. Liu, "Topic detection based on BERT and seed LDA clustering model", *Proc. 7th Int. Conf. on Innovation in Artificial Intelligence,* 2023. [http://dx.doi.org/10.1145/3594409.3594418]

[8] H. Mashayekhi, E.S. Alavi, and B. Rezaie, "Microblog topic detection using evolutionary clustering and social network information", *Concurr. Comput.,* vol. 35, no. 27, p. e7847, 2023. [http://dx.doi.org/10.1002/cpe.7847]

[9] W. Fan, Z.H. Guo, N. Bouguila, and W. Hou, "Clustering-based online news topic detection and tracking through hierarchical Bayesian nonparametric models", *Proc. 44th Int. ACM SIGIR Conf. on Research and Development in Information Retrieval,* 2021. [http://dx.doi.org/10.1145/3404835.3462982]

[10] S.S. Bodrunova, A.V. Orekhov, I.S. Blekanov, N.S. Lyudkevich, and N.A. Tarasov, "Topic detection based on sentence embeddings and agglomerative clustering with Markov moment", *Future Internet,* vol. 12, no. 9, p. 144, 2020. [http://dx.doi.org/10.3390/fi12090144]

[11] X. Geng, Y. Zhang, Y. Jiao, and Y. Mei, "A novel hybrid clustering algorithm for topic detection on Chinese microblogging", *IEEE Trans. Comput. Soc. Syst.,* vol. 6, no. 2, pp. 289-300, 2019. [http://dx.doi.org/10.1109/TCSS.2019.2897641]

[12] D. Malandrino, R. De Prisco, M. Ianulardo, and R. Zaccagnino, "An adaptive meta-heuristic for music plagiarism detection based on text similarity and clustering", *Data Min. Knowl. Discov.,* vol. 36, no. 4, pp. 1301-1334, 2022.
[http://dx.doi.org/10.1007/s10618-022-00835-2]

CHAPTER 33

Text Mining for Effective Information Extraction and Analysis

Ramesh Sengodan[1,*] and **T. Harish Naik**[2]

[1] *Department of Computer Science and Engineering, Presidency University, Bangalore, Karnataka, India*

[2] *Department of Computer Applications, Presidency College, Bangalore, Karnataka, India*

Abstract: The study's overarching goal is to provide a methodology for employing domain ontologies to get health-related data from the Internet. The Internet has made patient-doctor dialogues commonplace. Solutions like HealthTap and AskTheDoctors make it possible for people to ask physicians questions about their health. The knowledge gap between experts and laypeople, as well as the language barrier, mean that most people seeking medical treatment online still struggle to ask effective questions. It is difficult to glean information from these non-expert accounts since they usually do not use technical language. The underlying applications, such as information retrieval, become less efficient as a result of this. In this paper, we provide an ontology-driven method for employing a meta-model to glean insights from such incomplete descriptions. When people seeking medical care don't share the same terminology as their doctors, a meta-model may help. To access the extensive medical vocabulary, the meta-model is mapped to SNOMED CT. To increase the coverage of layman's words during information extraction, it is mapped with WordNet. A data extraction prototype that relies on syntactical similarities is put into place in order to evaluate the approach's potential. Using the gold standard corpora established in Task 1 of ShARe CLEF 2013, the method demonstrated encouraging results in identifying medical ideas in actual medical papers, with an F-score of 0.79.

Keywords: Text mining, information extraction, ontology, WordNet, data-mining customer relationship management.

INTRODUCTION

With the growth of AI, data-mining customer relationship management systems may enhance Chinese businesses' management and decision-making capabilities while simultaneously boosting their bottom line [1]. Opportunities abound in big data analytics to support decision-making and expand our understanding of hospi-

* **Corresponding author Ramesh Sengodan:** Department of Computer Science and Engineering, Presidency University, Bangalore, Karnataka, India; E-mail: ramesh.sengodan@presidencyuniversity.in

S. Kannadhasan, R. Nagarajan, & Kaushik Pal (Eds.)

tality management. In marketing, consumer sentiment analysis, product and service enhancements, corporate valuation, and many other areas, hotel management stands to benefit greatly from user-generated content (UGC). What factors influence guests' happiness in the hotel industry has been the subject of much research [2]. CRM stands for customer relationship management and is a method for gathering information about customers, understanding their characteristics, and using that knowledge in targeted advertising. CRM has been around for a while. The truth is that CRM has always been around. But CRM has only lately become the center of interest. The following is some background: • Customers are now seen as a critical component of a company's competitive strength; • Businesses can better manage their customers thanks to data warehousing, mining data, and various other data technologies; and • E-Commerce has created a new platform for marketing and business, allowing us to convert online customer actions into data [3]. A large number of companies have made heavy use of data mining. The use of data mining is on the rise, if not already indispensable, in the healthcare industry. The healthcare industry as a whole stands to gain significantly from data mining technologies. Data mining has many applications in the healthcare industry, including fraud and abuse detection for insurers, decision-making for healthcare organizations on customer relationship management, treatment efficacy and best practices for clinicians, and improved, more cost-effective healthcare for patients [4]. If you want to make a smart choice about an RMS strategy that will increase efficiency and benefit, you need to know how service needs and RMS might interact. Mining efficiency is affected by the excessive number of candidate sets in classic association rule mining techniques, and the results are not straightforward for consumers to understand. In order to find service requests along with remanufacture services association rules, a mining approach based on the binary particles swarm optimization ant colony method is suggested [5]. Popular methods for discovering connections between things individuals buy in a database include market basket analysis (MBA). Mining association rules is a foundational data mining technique that extracts useful information from massive datasets. An ever-increasing amount of data is generated online as people use internet apps for activities such as online shopping and insurance. Large quantities are produced, and both people and society stand to gain substantially from efficient mining [6]. Numerical categorization has played a significant role in China's economic growth, driven by the country's rapidly expanding economy and society. The future of business is a customer-centric, complete operational service model. Improving the management strategy and the service quality procedure is the main concept. To manage the market in line with customers' genuine demand, the business economy takes appropriate steps to build a strong customer relationship, which involves understanding consumers' psychological consumption conditions [7].

RELATED WORKS

Classification of clients, cross-marketing, acquisition, and upkeep are the four data mining modalities discussed [8] under the framework of client relationship management (CRM). The data mining module's SPRINT method is used to classify customers. Utilizing FP-growth, an association rule technique without candidates, in cross-marketing further improves the system's practicability. Adopting the algorithm of the ideal customer retention plan within the context of digital intelligence technology helps businesses improve their operations and fine-tune their marketing tactics, while also compensating for the limitations of conventional CRM systems.

To find out what makes Greek hotel guests happy and what makes them unhappy [9], text analytics is used to dissect hotel reviews and identify how they correlated with guests' overall happiness. This study is helpful for hotel managers because it identifies the features and qualities of products and services that influence visitors' happiness or discontent, and it shows how the positioning and tactics of hotels influence customers' views about those features and qualities.

We set out to do two things with this essay: first, to define data analysis and its role in the sales and marketing domain; and second, to demonstrate the far-reaching implications of investigating and analyzing data in these areas. It also demonstrated that market operating companies are under pressure from the pervasive forces of competition to maximize profits for the benefit of shareholders by preserving and expanding their market share. The researcher conducted a critical literature assessment of relevant theoretical works in addition to the descriptive approach to accomplish the study's aims. All aspects of managing customer relationships rely on data analysis technologies, according to the report. The project can create a cohesive view of its customers from the mountains of data stored in its database by using data analysis tools [10]. Data mining methods are analytically powerful, which means they may help businesses transform their customers' data into valuable information for relationship management choices. The research also suggests that firms dealing with large volumes of data should adopt these approaches.

We demonstrate the use of web mining to automatically gather data from customers' websites for CRM systems in B2B settings in the case study [11]. In this case, we construct a data collection that satisfies the necessary high-quality requirements by extracting pertinent information using specialized local grammars. According to the examination, local grammars do a good job overall, though they may be too strict in some situations. To conclude, our case study shows that B2B CRM may benefit from web mining and local grammars, provided that the information need is well-defined and readily accessible online.

Understanding how satisfied Millennials would be with Shopee Indonesia was the primary reason for the study [12]. The Naive Bayes Algorithm is used for data mining in this research. The Naive Bayes method can estimate any possible outcome given enough data and combinations. It is a form of fundamental probability categorization. This study uses the following attributes: name, age, gender, cost, efficiency, dependability, control, security, adaptability, payment, contact, and a description of happiness worth. Findings from this study's categorization of happy and unhappy customers are based on a number of input qualities that form a causal link. With these findings, Shopee can improve customer happiness and grow its business. Experiment results show that the Naive Bayesian Network (NBA) achieves an accuracy rate of 89.65% when used in a classification procedure to determine the degree of Millennial satisfaction with Shopee Indonesia.

The article suggests that businesses can greatly increase their economic advantages by using DM for customer relationship management [13]. Formulate suitable considerations and preferential treatment in accordance with customers' diverse values; attract, retain, or upgrade actual customers; spend more to become senior customers; and develop marketing tactics and techniques for prospective customers in accordance with these values to turn them into actual customers. Boost your company's profit line by attracting genuine clients.

By examining the partner-to-customer relationship, innovative capabilities, and cost savings through the lens of [14], we can see how strategic partnerships increase customer loyalty and achieve a competitive advantage. Three hundred thirty-five employees from companies that have formed strategic agreements were surveyed. According to this research, the two most common outcomes of strategic partnerships are cost savings and innovative capabilities. Customer loyalty is enhanced through innovative capabilities enabled by strategic collaborations. Developing a client base in a strategic partner-to-customer connection cannot be achieved by cost reduction.

Data mining techniques are detailed in the article [15] with the intention of creating a prediction model that assigns data to a set of predetermined classes. In order to lay out the steps needed to create a CRISP-DM Framework data mining project that meets all of your requirements, data mining techniques such as multi-layer perception and logistic regression will be used in this project. Although cross-validation helps prevent overfitting in the model presented in this paper, it is still possible to overfit. With a 70% split, the Multi Layer Perceptron model offers the best average benefit.

PROPSOED WORK

Information Extraction

Information extraction makes use of textual relations. For this, it employs pattern matching. Data in an RDBMS, for instance, is accessible *via* tables. There is no easy way to extract information from data that is not structured (*i.e.*, lacks a fixed reference). Information extraction in IE begins by transforming a document from natural language to a structured format. Use pattern matching to extract tiny bits of content (people, location, time, date, address, *etc.*) from IE. Using this method on massive amounts of text yields remarkable results. While it is possible to build an IE system using machine learning, the results it produces will not be completely accurate. As a result, errors in the results of the automatically extracted database may be identified. Before employing mining to uncover knowledge that can be used to enhance the accuracy of IE, the authors of the DISCOTEX framework built a database using the learnt information extraction method. Several varieties of IE:-

i- Entity Extraction (associating nouns with entities)
ii- Concept Extraction (nouns and phrases)
iii- Token Extraction (characters without separator)
iv- Term Extraction (token with specific semantic purpose)
v- Atomic Fact Extraction (subject with actions)
vi- Complex Fact Extraction

It is not possible to mine the information contained in natural language text documents. Although vector models may be used to represent documents, which are essentially a "bag of words," this approach does not make use of them. Instead, they can be input into previously specified procedures like classification and clustering. Data mining methods may be used to extract information or interesting patterns from documents after they have been turned into structured databases. This process, known as information extraction, is shown in Fig. (**1**). Identification of entities, such as names of people, places, and businesses, is the job of IE. Pieces of information like "position" and "person name" that are needed have been located. The final product would be a structure that makes it easy to recognize all entities and their connections. The data is then placed in the database for use in data mining methods to uncover implicit information. Fig. (**1**) shows the steps involved in information extraction.

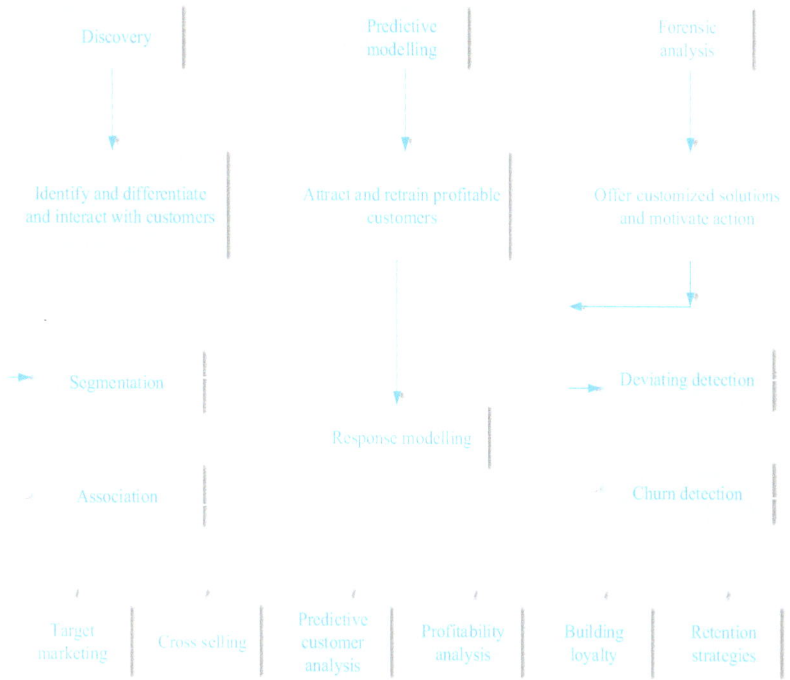

Fig. (1). Steps involved in information extraction.

RESULT AND DISCUSSION

The proposed system is compared in terms of performance metrics. In order to evaluate the performance we have used,

Accuracy – It is the fraction of the dataset that has been accurately classified out of all the information in the dataset. We have the result here:

$$Accuracy = \frac{TN+TP}{TN+TP+FN+FP} \quad (1)$$

$$Precision = \frac{TP}{TP+FP} \quad (2)$$

$$Recall = \frac{TP}{TP+FN} \quad (3)$$

$$F1\ Score = 2 * \frac{Precision*Recall}{Precision+Recall} \quad (4)$$

You get a final score based on all of the things mentioned before. "True negative," "false positive," "true negative," as well as "null," should all be abbreviated as appropriate. Existing SVM, Random Forest, and artificial neural network (ANN) methods are compared with the suggested TTL-FRNN approach.

We look at the correlation among iteration count and F1 score, recall, accuracy, and precision. The accuracy of the proposed work is shown in Fig. (**2**). An increase in iteration yields an increase in outcome (*i.e*., high accuracy) from a well-trained model. The precision of the proposed work is shown in Fig. (**3**). It can be seen that the proposed work achieves 98% accuracy, which is far better than that of the existing algorithms. The Recall of the proposed work is shown in Fig. (**4**). The F1 Score of the proposed work is shown in Fig. (**5**). From the detailed analysis, we can conclude that the proposed work performs better due to the inclusion of feature selection and deep classification. SVM and RF are the ML algorithms that lack in accuracy due to a slower learning rate. Similarly, an ANN is unable to learn the massive data deeply. For that, the proposed FRNN learns features that are optimally selected by the TTL algorithm. Thus, the proposed work is well-suited for credit card fraud detection in the financial sector.

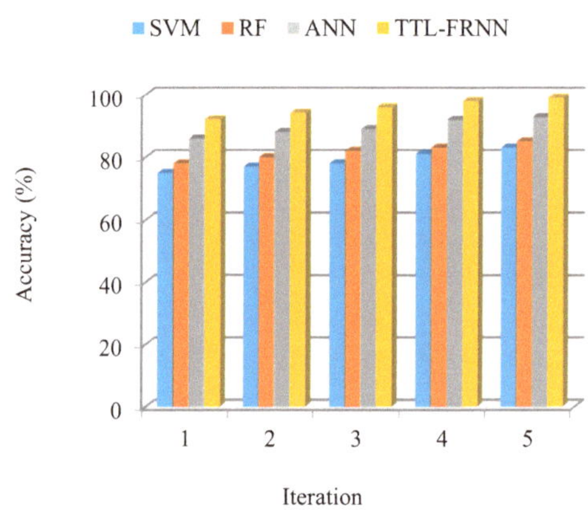

Fig. (2). Analysis on accuracy.

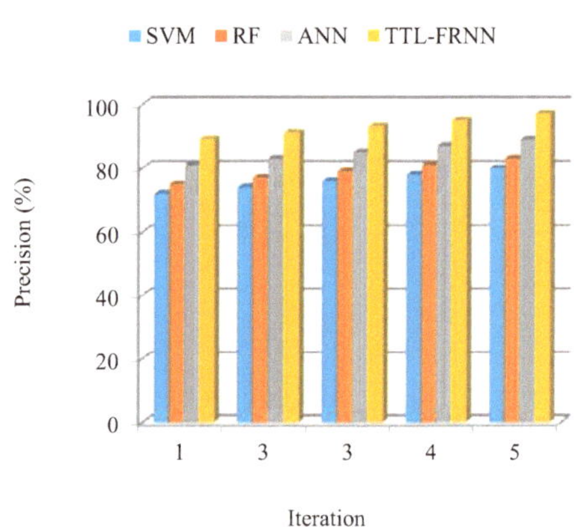

Fig. (3). Analysis on Precision.

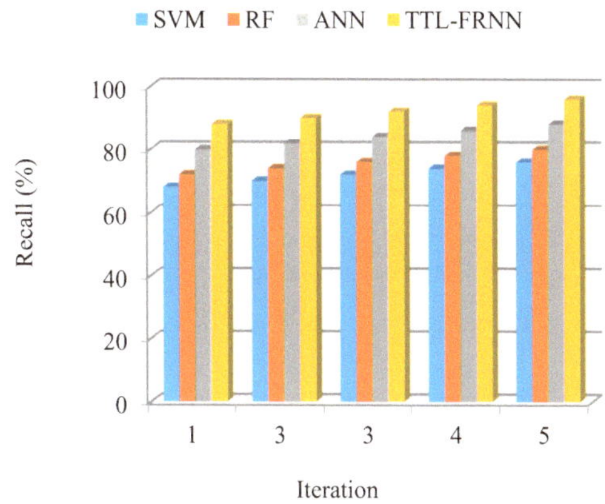

Fig. (4). Analysis on Recall.

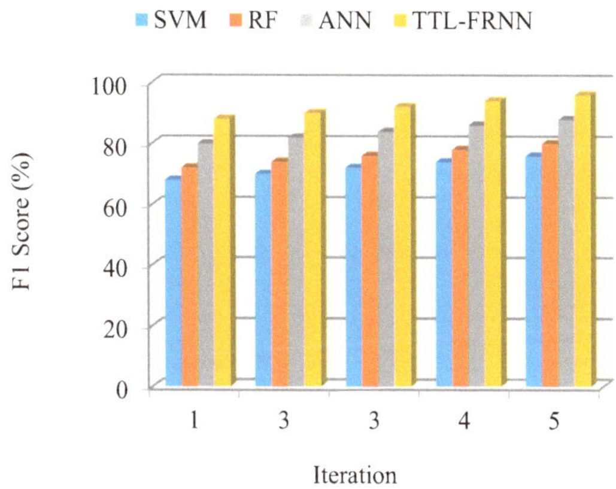

Fig. (5). Analysis F1 Score.

CONCLUSION

The article suggests a system for using domain ontologies to get health information from the internet. Online discussions between medical professionals and their patients have increased. Patients may ask doctors questions about their health *via* services such as HealthTap or AskTheDoctors. Yet, primarily due to the language and knowledge gap between experts and laypeople, the majority of internet health care customers still have trouble effectively expressing their questions. It might be difficult to glean information from these common explanations, as they often lack specialized vocabulary. The underlying programs, such as information retrieval, become less successful as a result. This article proposes an ontology-driven approach to using a meta-model to glean insights from such incomplete descriptions. To bridge the language gap between doctors' words and patients' experiences, a meta-model is developed. When extracting information, the meta-model uses WordNet to cover more common terms and SNOMEDCT to access the full medical vocabulary.

REFERENCES

[1] I. Berrada, F. Barramou, and O.B. Alami, "A review of artificial intelligence approach for credit risk assessment", *Proc. 2nd International Conference on Artificial Intelligence and Signal Processing (AISP),* pp. 1-5, 2022. [http://dx.doi.org/10.1109/AISP53593.2022.9760655]

[2] A. Woods, C.S. Meyer, B.C. Sauer, and D.O. Epidemiology, "Mining time-stamped electronic health records with referenced sequences", *J. Biomed. Inform.,* 2020.

[3] "Application of artificial intelligence for health and healthcare systems", *Health Care (Don Mills),* 2021.

[4] A.H. Patwary, M.T. Eshan, P. Debnath, and A. Sattar, "Market basket analysis approach to machine learning", *Proc. 12th International Conference on Computing Communication and Networking Technologies (ICCCNT),* pp. 1-9, 2021. [http://dx.doi.org/10.1109/ICCCNT51525.2021.9580175]

[5] D.B. Olazo, "Marketing competency, marketing innovation and sustainable competitive advantage of small and medium enterprises (SMEs): A mixed-method analysis", *Asia Pac. J. Mark. Log.,* 2022.

[6] D. Zhang, and F. Xia, "An interview with Dr. Shipeng Yu, winner of ACM SIGKDD 2021 service award", *SIGKDD Explor.,* 2021.

[7] P.K. Theodoridis, and D.C. Gkikas, *"How artificial intelligence affects digital marketing," in Strategic Innovative Marketing and Tourism.* Springer, 2019. [http://dx.doi.org/10.1007/978-3-030-12453-3_151]

[8] Y. Sun, and X. Tan, "Customer relationship management based on SPRINT classification algorithm under data mining technology", *Comput. Intell. Neurosci.,* vol. 2022, pp. 1-11, 2022. [http://dx.doi.org/10.1155/2022/6170335] [PMID: 35463233]

[9] F. Kitsios, M. Kamariotou, P. Karanikolas, and E. Grigoroudis, "Digital marketing platforms and customer satisfaction: Identifying eWOM using big data and text mining", *Appl. Sci. (Basel),* vol. 11, no. 17, p. 8032, 2021. [http://dx.doi.org/10.3390/app11178032]

[10] M.B.H. Al Atif, A. Shakir, A.K. Al Nussairi, J. Mohammed, and A.S. Almusawi, "Data mining with its role in marketing, sales support and customer identification data analysis", *International Journal of Artificial Intelligence and Informatics,* vol. 3, no. 2, 2022. [http://dx.doi.org/10.33292/ijarlit.v3i2.52]

[11] F.S. Bäumer, and B. Buff, "How to boost customer relationship management via web mining benefiting from the glass customer's openness", *Proc. International Conference on Data Technologies and Applications,* pp. 129-136, 2019. [http://dx.doi.org/10.5220/0007828301290136]

[12] M.I. Hant, and H. Hendry, *"Data mining technique using naïve Bayes algorithm to predict Shopee consumer satisfaction among millennial generation," Jurnal Teknik Informatika.* JUTIF, 2022.

[13] Y. Chang, "Research on marketing data mining model based on support vector machine algorithm", *Proc. International Conference on Artificial Intelligence and Autonomous Robot Systems (AIARS),* pp. 350-354, 2022. [http://dx.doi.org/10.1109/AIARS57204.2022.00085]

[14] S. Musa, "The roles of strategic alliances, innovation capability, and cost reduction towards customer loyalty and firm's competitive advantage", *Proc. 27th International Scientific Conference Strategic Management and Decision Support Systems in Strategic Management,* 2022. [http://dx.doi.org/10.46541/978-86-7233-406-7_230]

[15] T. Mauritsius, "Bank marketing data mining using CRISP-DM approach", *International Journal of Advanced Trends in Computer Science and Engineering,* vol. 8, no. 5, pp. 2322-2329, 2019. [http://dx.doi.org/10.30534/ijatcse/2019/71852019]

CHAPTER 34

Enhancing Information Processing and Analysis with Text Mining

C. Kalaiarasan[1,*] and **Philomine Roseline**[2]

[1] *Department of Computer Science and Engineering, Presidency University, Bangalore, Karnataka, India*

[2] *Department of Computer Applications, Presidency College, Bangalore, Karnataka, India*

Abstract: Many social media forums (blogs, Facebook discussions, *etc.*) have emerged as a result of the proliferation of the Internet, and users are able to access these sites from their mobile devices. These sites serve as venues for users to express and communicate their thoughts and experiences on current events and other global concerns. Before making a purchase, many customers check out review websites. In order to find useful product reviews and user experiences, people often explore popular websites. It is simple for us to gather massive volumes of product data, both structured and unstructured, and then analyze it to extract the specific product details you need. Researchers are increasingly turning to sentiment analysis—also called opinion exploration or opinion mining—to gather and assess customer sentiment and viewpoints. Emotional text mining is introduced in this paper, with a focus on reducing data dimensions *via* principal component analysis and singular value decomposition, and on improving accuracy and reducing implementation time through the use of an additional feature strategy. The research begins by proposing a method for preparing data to classify sentiment. Secondly, it leverages new features to improve emotion categorization precision. Singular value decomposition and principal component analysis are used to reduce data in the third step. Finally, it creates five modules with different features and analyzes their performance, both with and without stemming. When compared to the alternatives, the experimental results show that the proposed method is the most accurate and has the potential to drastically reduce implementation time.

Keywords: Text Mining, Intelligent Information Processing and Analysis, Principal Component Analysis, Data Dimension Reduction, Opinion Exploration (Opinion Mining).

[*] **Corresponding author C. Kalaiarasan:** Department of Computer Science and Engineering, Presidency University, Bangalore, Karnataka, India; E-mail: kalaiarasan@presidencyuniversity.in

S. Kannadhasan, R. Nagarajan, & Kaushik Pal (Eds.)

INTRODUCTION

In recent years, data cleansing, a sector of data mining, has seen tremendous growth. To provide the best service to consumers, it is crucial to ensure the reliability of data at every stage, from generation to reception. Data is complex, produced at tremendous velocity, and massive in volume, making the aforementioned job easier said than done. Data Cleaning has extensively used a wide range of approaches from several branches of computer science to achieve optimal performance [1]. Automatic fact-checking (AFC) evidence may take many forms, including text, tables, pictures, audio, and video. Although there is growing interest in using images for AFC, most prior research has focused on identifying altered or false images [2].

Recent advances in machine learning (ML) have enabled the training of high-accuracy predictive models even when dealing with complex multivariate relationships, such as interactions and heterogeneity. Knowledge exploration, accountability, and justice in domains such as healthcare require greater interpretability of ML models. Learning Classification Systems (LCSs) and other rule-based ML methods provide a happy medium between interpretability and prediction accuracy in complicated, noisy environments [3]. The capacity of transformer-based language models to reason in accordance with the logical principles stated in natural-language text has recently become the subject of study. Nevertheless, our current understanding of their thinking is limited because we cannot decipher the abstractions generated by the representations they use. Some argue that these models can't be applied to real-world scenarios because they rely too heavily on memorizing complex patterns in the data [4]. A novel context, unrelated to objects, as well as canonical concept patterns discovered in fact- or rule-based information sources, such as the UMLS ontology, may arise in complex querying scenarios, especially in the setting of EBM (evidence-based medicine) using biomedical literature. In addition, different lexical forms within the collection could conceal relationships between candidate ideas that are relevant to the present context, rather than in a single document [5]. Virtual reality (VR) provides a dynamic and immersive learning environment for construction workers to enhance their safety awareness. With the right VR peripherals, such as data-gloves and trackers that record events, users may experience a wide range of sophisticated interactions and realistic settings. Serious mishaps on construction sites may occur, for instance, when operators fail to properly interpret workers' hand signals [6]. The concept of the “smart home” is moving from the realm of fantasy to that of a practical, workable solution for assisted living, thanks to the proliferation and improvement of the Internet of Things. Recognizing activities is a crucial first step in providing prompt, correct help and service. Due to the prevalence of noise, similar activities, and missing data in everyday life, there are several problems with inferring complex events using knowledge-driven reasoning algorithms. These include issues with scalability, computational complexity, generalization, and real-time segmentation of raw sensor data [7].

RELATED WORKS

To ensure data reliability, the authors [8] propose a rules-based data-cleaning system that leverages natural language processing. Using natural language processing (NLP), the mechanism outperformed comparable mechanisms that do not employ NLP in both effectiveness and efficiency. Although tested across a variety of healthcare datasets, the mechanism's applicability extends beyond healthcare and lends credence to the idea of generic data cleansing.

In a study [9], researchers propose a new activity they term chart-based fact-checking and present ChartBERT as the first attempt to compare AFC with chart evidence. To determine whether textual assertions are true, ChartBERT uses chart text, structure, and visual data. Our new dataset, ChartFC, has 15,886 charts, and we use it for assessment purposes. We demonstrate that ChartBERT achieves 63.8% accuracy, surpassing VL models, by methodically evaluating 75 distinct vision-language (VL) baselines. Based on our findings, this is a challenging but doable endeavor with several obstacles to overcome.

An automated process for interpreting LCS models for complex biological categorization is described [10] as LCS-DIVE, which stands for LCS Discovery and Visualization Environment. For biomedical data mining, LCS-DIVE employs a novel scikit-learn framework called ExSTraCS, an LCS designed to overcome scalability and noise issues. For each training set, it generates a model with human-readable IF-THEN rules and feature-tracking scores. The LCS-DIVE system combines feature-tracking ratings and rules to automatically define feature relevance and underlying additive, epileptic, or heterogeneous association tendencies in three ways: clustering, visualization creation, and cluster interrogation. To test LCS-DIVE's discriminatory power, we ran it through a battery of synthetic and benchmark datasets that encoded a wide range of complex multivariate relationships; thereafter, we used it to describe associations in a real-world pancreatic cancer investigation.

The authors [11] postulate that classifiers would be more reliable if given both factual and counterfactual explanations. To delve into the process of creating these kinds of explanations, we provide a novel approach to producing factual and counterfactual explanations for pretrained decision trees with fuzzy rule-based classifier scores. When it comes to understanding how classification algorithms work, experimental findings show that combining factual and counterfactual explanations within the framework of fuzzy inference systems works well.

In a study [12], you may find a hierarchical structure for numerical reasoning abilities. It has four levels: representation, comprehending numbers, abuse, and complicated reasoning, and more than 10 different forms of reasoning are dispersed among them. Identifying the unique reasoning challenges faced by state-of-the-art models is our primary objective in this thorough examination. From here on, we use a semi-automated method to create a wide variety of numerical probes. For example, we examine changes in model performance on the tabular Language Inference (TNLI) task. No model consistently outperforms all modes of numerical reasoning, according to our data. In terms of general numerical thinking skills, FlanT5 (few-/zero-shot) and GPT-3.5 (few-shot) outperform all other evaluated models. Models often use dataset artifacts to forecast the right labels, as shown by label-flipping probes.

Condition assessment, problem diagnosis, and early warning are the main uses of the study's large volumes of distinctive data [13]. Prior to conducting an equipment-centered position analysis, it constructs a knowledge-mapping library of crucial factors by statistically analyzing historical data. After that, it employs induction-based knowledge processing to estimate fault risk and fault probability by building intelligent warning libraries of equipment index information. Lastly, it uses both logic and rule-based knowledge reasoning to determine the equipment status rating. At last, it establishes a closed-loop system to assess the equipment's state. The examples show that the assessment approach is appropriate and does things such as early warning for mining equipment operational status supervision, anticipatory sensing of equipment operational status, and reduction of power grid operating risk.

In another study [14], the application of probabilistic logical principles to language models based on transformers is examined. In particular, we provide a novel method, PCT, that simulates probabilistic logical reasoning directly by training on the norms of reasoning imposed as constraints. In contrast to the only current applicable benchmark, we propose a novel QA metric for assessing probabilistic reasoning over ambiguous textual rules that generate rules tailored to individual instances. When addressing probabilistic logical reasoning questions, our method increases the accuracy and explainability of basic language models, according to experimental findings. We also demonstrate that the learnings of probabilistic reasoning may be applied to new contexts.

Researchers develop a novel sequence-to-set technique, including brain attention [15] to meaningfully tag a large number of papers. Term transfer all through the corpus may be influenced by this framework's ability to learn document representations. In two distinct supervised multi-label classification scenarios, we demonstrate the efficacy of our proposed method for text classification: one with human-annotated document labels and another without, where training is driven solely by term statistics derived from corpus data and no external knowledge resources. In addition, we demonstrate that large quantities of unlabeled data may be used for semi-supervised training *via* our design to improve performance on the text classification task in the presence of limited labeled data. In various tests, such as the unsupervised query development assignment on the TREC CDS 2016 challenges data set, as well as supervised and semi-supervised multi-label forecasting tasks on the del.icio.us and Ohsumed datasets, our method for creating document encodings using our sequence-to-set techniques for semantic tag inference appears to surpass the MLTM baseline (Soleimani *et al.*, 2016). When we release our code and data to the public, they will be accessible to everybody.

PROPSOED WORK

Documents, texts, or reviews may be classified into pre-existing categories (such as positive, negative, joyful, or sad) using sentiment classification. Improving the accuracy of results is the most difficult task in sentiment categorization. This is because many factors may affect the results of an analysis. A few examples of these elements include preprocessing methods, features, lexicons, machine learning approaches, and the level of sentiment classification (document *vs.* sentence). A large body of research shows that feature selection methods (TF-IDF, n-gram sequences, POS tagging, unigrams, bigrams, *etc.*) provide different outcomes. Ravi & Ravi showed that not every study used the same experimental design. In order to expedite text categorization, decrease dimensionality, and improve accuracy, this research expands upon Cheng's previous work by using the "first SVD, then PCA" approach. Additionally, it enhances the analysis by adding additional features. Furthermore, this research builds five test modules with diverse characteristics utilizing stemming. The objective is to determine their efficacy and the variables that influence the classifier's precision. Fig. (**1**) depicts the proposed method. To begin the sentiment categorization process, the gathered dataset must be applied. Furthermore, R statistical software is employed throughout the preprocessing stages of POS tagging, tokenization, and stop word removal. In Step 3, features must be defined and extracted, including document sentiment score, number of adverbs and adjectives, negative and positive frequency bands, and word frequency–inverse document frequency (TF-IDF). The fourth step involves training the classifier and making predictions using the data. The final stage is to evaluate the outcomes. Algorithm 1 presents the suggested procedure. The data illustrate the five key components of the program's computational approach, which helps clarify the suggested method.

Step 1: Data Collection. We started by gathering a widely used dataset, the Movie database, which contains documents that generate strong emotions. This is because movie review language is more challenging to categorize than other types of review text. The dataset contains an equal number of positive and negative evaluations. To convert the tagged emotion sheets to Excel format, we imported the text file using Microsoft Excel VBA software.

The second dataset came from Hersh *et al.*'s OHSUMED dataset, which contains 23 distinct types of cardiovascular diseases. Because of their connections to the peripheral nervous system blood vessels, the five categories C02, C10, C11, C14, and C20 were chosen for the experiment.

Step 2: Data Preparation. Data acquired directly from the source often contains noise, and several steps are required to filter the data before applying machine learning techniques. Tokenization, stemming, POS tagging, feature extraction, and representation are the five preprocessing steps. The removal of punctuation marks from text is the main goal of tokenization, as these marks do not affect classifier accuracy. Stop words such as "a," "the," and "an" are ignored because their inclusion does not improve results and may even degrade performance. Stemming converts words to their base form without considering POS. POS tagging identifies the parts of speech for words in the text. Feature extraction is used to retrieve meaningful information from noisy data. In this study, POS data was processed using two R packages: RTextTools and openNLP.

Step 3: Feature Selection and Enhancement. Feature selection is as crucial as feature extraction in determining the final analysis outcome. Features determined in this study include TF-IDF, counts of positive and negative phrases, adjectives, and adverbs. Each document was converted to a TF-IDF weighting matrix, and additional features based on positive and negative frequencies were added. We then added other features after counting the number of adverbs and adjectives using POS tagging. Algorithm 1 depicts the suggested feature extraction method, as represented in Fig. (**1**).

Reducing dimensions. It is challenging to examine the TF-IDF matrix due to its enormous, sparse matrix with several zero members. In order to reduce the matrix's dimensions, this stage used the "SVD then PCA" technique. The algorithm of the work is shown in Fig. (**1**). The SVD input was the preprocessed matrix, which was used after feature extraction. The TF-IDF matrix was decomposed using the SVD approach, which resulted in the transformation of all values around zero to zero. The overall dimensions of the reduced matrices were further decreased using the principal component analysis (PCA) approach. The final result is a 20002000 vector area, down from a 2000′46467 vector size after the video is processed. Step 5: Organized Data. Following Step 4, the processed data is trained to detect text using four classifiers: naïve Bayes, maximum entropy, support vector machine (SVM), and random forest. In order to ensure accuracy, this research used a ten-fold cross-validation and ten-times random sampling with all four classifier parameters set to their default levels.

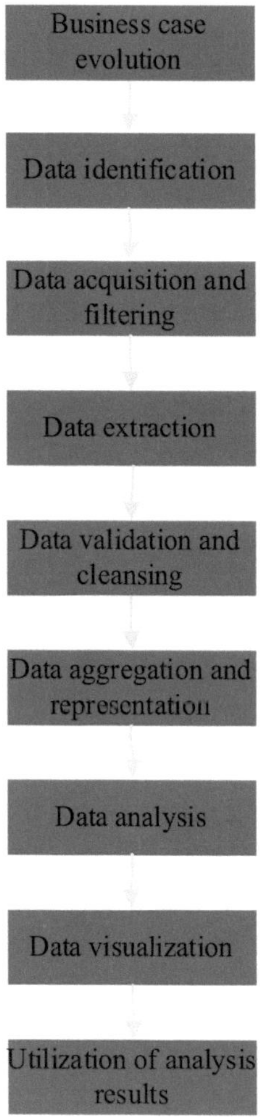

Fig. (1). Algorithm Flow.

RESULT AND DISCUSSION

The findings demonstrate that the extra qualities may achieve superior outcomes, particularly using the SVM-RBF approach, when they are merged into the feature set as shown in Fig. (**2**). In the Movie dataset, the suggested extra characteristics achieve greater accuracy. Hence, the "SVD then PCA" approaches and more characteristics may improve emotional classification performance.

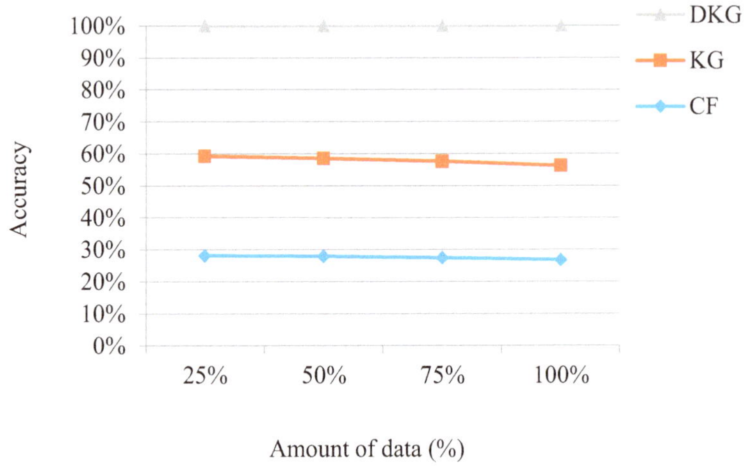

Fig. (2). Accuracy *vs.* Data.

For each dataset, we randomly split the interaction history for each user into 80% for training and 20% for test data, as shown in Fig. (**2**). As a validation set for hyper-parameter tuning, we randomly select 10% of the relationships from the training set. We employ negative sampling, pairing each user-item interaction with a single negative item, treating each interaction as a positive occurrence.

CONCLUSION

Findings from this study recommended an additional feature-based methodology, in addition to the "SVD then PCA" technique, for emotional text mining, which would increase accuracy and decrease implementation time. The adverb and adjective frequencies, both positive and negative, round out the characteristics. Two experiments show that the proposed approach is more accurate than competing techniques, and adding more features, especially to the SVM_RBF classifier, could further boost performance. The SVM and ME classifiers are shown to be the most effective for sentiment classification. Here are a few areas that might be explored further when this research is expanded upon: 1. The following topics may be covered in the feature selection method: (i) finding or filtering features using a domain-specific lexicon, (ii) improving accuracy by assigning various weights to features, and (iii) taking word-document correlations into account. 2. Expand the method's scope to include other domains, such as social mood detection and reputation monitoring.

REFERENCES

[1] Q. Li, H. Ning, T. Zhu, S. Cui, and L. Chen, "A hybrid approach to inferring the Internet of Things for complex activity recognition", *EURASIP J. Wirel. Commun. Netw.*, vol. 2019, no. 1, p. 251, 2019. [http://dx.doi.org/10.1186/s13638-019-1553-7]

[2] M.A. Ferrag, A.A. Battah, N. Tihanyi, M. Debbah, T. Lestable, and L.C. Cordeiro, "SecureFalcon: The next cyber reasoning system for cyber security", arXiv preprint arXiv:2307.06616, 2023.

[3] L. Westhofen, C. Neurohr, M. Butz, M. Scholtes, and M. Schuldes, "Using ontologies for the formalization and recognition of criticality for automated driving", *IEEE Open J. Intell. Transp. Syst.,* vol. 3, pp. 519-538, 2022.
[http://dx.doi.org/10.1109/OJITS.2022.3187247]

[4] D. Xiao, M. Dianati, W.G. Geiger, and R. Woodman, "Review of graph-based hazardous event detection methods for autonomous driving systems", *IEEE Trans. Intell. Transp. Syst.,* vol. 24, no. 5, pp. 4697-4715, 2023.
[http://dx.doi.org/10.1109/TITS.2023.3240104]

[5] L. Bellomarini, G. Gottlob, and E. Sallinger, "Datalog-based reasoning for knowledge graphs", *Proc. Alberto Mendelzon International Workshop on Foundations of Data Management,* 2019.

[6] F. Sovrano, M. Palmirani, B. Distefano, S. Sapienza, and F. Vitali, "A dataset for evaluating legal question answering on private international law", *Proc. 18th International Conference on Artificial Intelligence and Law (ICAIL),* 2021.
[http://dx.doi.org/10.1145/3462757.3466094]

[7] K. Mavrogiorgos, A. Mavrogiorgou, A. Kiourtis, N.E. Zafeiropoulos, S. Kleftakis, and D. Kyriazis, "Automated rule-based data cleaning using NLP", *Proc. 32nd Conference of Open Innovations Association (FRUCT),* pp. 162-168, 2022.

[8] M. Akhtar, O. Cocarascu, and E. Simperl, "“Reading and reasoning over chart images for evidence-based automated fact-checking,” in Findings of the Association for Computational Linguistics", *EACL,* vol. 2023, pp. 399-414, 2023.
[http://dx.doi.org/10.18653/v1/2023.findings-eacl.30]

[9] R.F. Zhang, R. Stolzenberg-Solomon, S.M. Lynch, and R.J. Urbanowicz, "LCS-DIVE: An automated rule-based machine learning visualization pipeline for characterizing complex associations in classification", arXiv preprint arXiv:2104.12844, 2021.

[10] I. Stepin, J.M. Alonso, A. Gatala, and M. Pereira-Fariña, "Generation and evaluation of factual and counterfactual explanations for decision trees and fuzzy rule-based classifiers", *Proc. IEEE International Conference on Fuzzy Systems (FUZZ-IEEE),* pp. 1-8, 2020.
[http://dx.doi.org/10.1109/FUZZ48607.2020.9177629]

[11] M. Akhtar, A. Shankarampeta, V. Gupta, A. Patil, O. Cocarascu, and E. Simperl, "“Exploring the numerical reasoning capabilities of language models: A comprehensive analysis on tabular data,” in Findings of the Association for Computational Linguistics", *EMNLP,* vol. 2023, pp. 15391-15405, 2023.
[http://dx.doi.org/10.18653/v1/2023.findings-emnlp.1028]

[12] X. Zhang, Y. Wang, R. Lin, Y. Zhang, X. Li, and J. Wang, "An electric equipment analysis method based on knowledge reasoning", *J. Phys. Conf. Ser.,* vol. 2132, no. 1, p. 012044, 2021.
[http://dx.doi.org/10.1088/1742-6596/2132/1/012044]

[13] A. Nafar, K. B. Venable, and P. Kordjamshidi, “Teaching probabilistic logical reasoning to transformers,” arXiv preprint, 2023.

[14] M. Das, J. Li, E. Fosler-Lussier, S.M. Lin, S. Moosavinasab, S. Rust, Y. Huang, and R. Ramnath, "Sequence-to-set semantic tagging: End-to-end multi-label prediction using neural attention for complex query reformulation and automated text categorization", arXiv preprint arXiv:1911.04427, 2019.

CHAPTER 35

Text Mining Approaches to Enhance Knowledge Discovery and Information Analysis

R. Pallavi[1,*] and **Sheetal**[2]

[1] *Department of Computer Science and Engineering, Presidency University, Bangalore, Karnataka, India*

[2] *Department of Computer Applications, Presidency College, Bangalore, Karnataka, India*

Abstract: A user's interests and goals can be deduced with the use of a Recommendation System (RS), a new form of technology that employs knowledge discovery methods. User intent analysis and corresponding suggestion triggering become increasingly challenging in the face of exponential data growth. This work proposes a unique Deep Knowledge Graph (DKG) to do the necessary data analysis and construct the RS. DKG employs a Deep Convolutional Neural Network (DCNN). Our proposed DKG explicitly models the KG's end-to-end high-order connectivities. It recursively propagates the embeddings from a node's neighbors, which can be people, things, or traits, using an attention mechanism to assess the relative significance of the neighbours. In terms of theory, our DKG outperforms existing KG-based recommendation methods since it does not rely on regularization or an explicit representation of high-order relations. Empirical results on public benchmarks show that KGAT outperforms state-of-the-art methods like RippleNet and Neural FM. The benefits of the attention mechanism for interpretability, as well as the efficacy of embedding propagation for high-order relation modeling, have been shown in subsequent studies.

Keywords: Text mining, knowledge discovery, information analysis, neural networks.

INTRODUCTION

With the rapid expansion of the internet came a corresponding explosion in data. Because there is so much data to choose from, users often feel overwhelmed and end up doing nothing.

Several applications of recommender systems aim to enhance the user experience. Some examples include music recommendations [1], movie suggestions [2], and

* **Corresponding author R. Pallavi:** Department of Computer Science and Engineering, Presidency University, Bangalore, Karnataka, India; E-mail: Id-pallavi.r@presidencyuniversity.in

S. Kannadhasan, R. Nagarajan, & Kaushik Pal (Eds.)

online purchasing [3]. The recommendation algorithm is the backbone of every recommender system. Recommender systems may be broken down into three distinct categories: those that rely on collaborative filtering (CF), those that rely on content, and hybrid systems that combine the two [4]. CF-based recommendations leverage similarities between people or items gleaned from interaction data to predict user preferences, whereas content-based recommendations leverage an item's content attributes. In recent years, it has been common practice to incorporate a knowledge graph (KG) into the recommendation engine. The supplementary data has aroused the curiosity of scholars. Nodes in a KG stand for entities, whereas edges show the relationships between them. It is possible to get insight into the relationships between items by mapping them and their attributes into the KG.

By including user and user-side data into the KG, it is possible to more accurately capture user preferences, object relationships, and user interactions [5]. Although KG has these benefits, it is not easy to use in RS because of its high dimensionality and unpredictability. The information graph embedding (KGE) technique is one way to preprocess the KG. It utilizes a vector of low-dimensional representations to map items and connections [6]. Classical KGE approaches, such as TransE and TransR, are better suited to in-graph applications, such as KG completion as well as link prediction, than to recommendation-making. These algorithms see semantic connections as head + relation = tail. Creating a chart is a process that comes more easily and intuitively.

As a rule, there are two main ways to represent RS systems [6],

- Path-based Methods - Path-based techniques provide predictive models with paths that include high-order information. To limit the routes, they have either constructed meta-path patterns or employed a route selection method to find relevant connections between the nodes. Such two-stage techniques have a considerable influence on overall performance; however, the first step of path selection is not optimal for the recommendation goal. It may be time-consuming to construct several meta-paths in a complicated KG with a wide range of interactions and entities, and this is because doing so effectively necessitates domain expertise.
- Finding new loss terms to replace the KG structure is one way regularization-based strategies help with recommender model learning. For instance, in order to train for both recommendation and KG completion, various studies make use of shared item embeddings. High-order relationships are only encoded indirectly in the recommendation-optimized model using these approaches. Lack of explicit modeling makes it impossible to reliably capture either high-order modeling

results or long-range connectivities.

- Modeling a novel RS for use in a number of contexts is important in light of the most pressing issues with existing approaches.
- In this study, we make the following contributions toward this goal:
- To simplify the suggested RS, we first collect data and do preliminary processing on that data.
- The Deep Knowledge Graph (DKG) is a knowledge graph constructed by a Deep Convolutional Neural Network (DCCN).
- The suggested DKG takes into account higher-order information when constructing DKG. In addition, the attention mechanism calculates the neighbour connectedness.
- Finally, the DKG-RS's performance is measured against the dataset.

RELATED WORKS

Yunkyoung Lee's System for Collective Filtering Suggestions

Collaborative filtering, one of the most well-known and thorough recommendation algorithms, considers the user's preferences while making product suggestions [7]. Because it is based on what people like, collaborative filtering-based recommendation systems may produce a reliable forecast when enough data is available. The recommendation system's user-based collaborative filtering has traditionally been its most critical component for predicting consumer behavior. Widespread usage, however, has exposed major issues, such as data sparsity and scalability, which are becoming more pressing as the population and diversity of commodities keep growing. Embedded representations, which may take up numerous terabytes of space in large-scale settings, are essential to machine intelligence in many applications, including recommendation systems. We take a look at mixed-dimension embeddings—a design for an embedding layer where the dimensionality of an embedded vector grows with the query frequency—as a potential remedy for this issue. Mixed dimensions has the potential to drastically decrease memory use without compromising or diminishing ML performance, according to our theoretical analysis and rigorous testing. Using the Criteo Kaggle dataset, our results demonstrate that the suggested mixed-dimensional layers may increase accuracy by 0.1 percent with half the amount of parameters and maintain accuracy with sixteen times fewer parameters.

In today's fast-paced world, recommendation algorithms are more useful than ever [8]. Because there are so many things that need to be done in a day, people are under continual pressure to get everything done. Since movie fans have limited mental capacity, movie recommendation systems are crucial for helping them find the greatest films. Using knowledge graphs with particle filtering, this research aims to provide a new method for making movie recommendations. While all existing methods for making movie recommendations make use of machine learning and clustering tools, this is not always the case. In order to provide the customer with the best possible movie suggestions, the article proposes a novel system that communicates *via* Knowledge Graphs, which operate effectively on the database.

To improve the accuracy of proposals, new research suggests that recommendation algorithms might use graphs containing knowledge (KGs) as supplementary material [9]. On the other hand, KGs cannot always avoid using external data that bad actors may alter. We designed a poisoning attack approach and used it on a recommendation system that relies on KG to assess the impact of malicious links. An attack is launched with the intention of raising awareness of a certain product. Most of the pertinent studies has focused on assaults on graph data, even if KG-based systems of recommendation have gained a lot of interest. We propose an attack model that takes these into account. By evaluating the effects of several attack decisions on the current suggested status and a particular item, the model determines the optimal attack combination. The assault combination pollutes the KG so that the trained recommendation model may provide the widest possible suggestions. We used a deep kind of reinforcement learning for the problem. By conducting trials using the film and financial data sets, we were able to investigate our poisoned-assault strategy in depth. Testing confirmed that the proposed method effectively increases an item's score within a set of suggestions.

There are millions of possible categories, including clicks and postings, and recommendation algorithms that use present-day deep learning sometimes use hundreds of thousands of categorization criteria [10]. Because categorical data may take many forms, embeddings provide distinct dense representations of each kind in their own space. The most memory-intensive component of inference and training is the embedding tables, since each feature can have millions of categories. We automatically generate a distinct embedding vector for each group using complementary partitions of the category set, eliminating the need for explicit descriptions. This article details a novel approach to eliminating unnecessary data at each stage of the embedding process. We can create a one-o--a-kind embedding for every division at a lower cost by keeping many smaller embedding tables, each complementing the embeddings of its division. To ensure that every group is represented uniquely, this technique might include employing a specified codebook. Experimental results show that our technique reduces embedding table sizes more accurately and with less model loss than the hashing method, while keeping the number of parameters reduced to a comparable degree.

We present a method for assessing and minimizing algorithmic bias in rating algorithms, which are widely used in massive-scale online search and recommendation systems [11]. To begin quantifying prejudice with regard to protected characteristics like gender and age, we provide supplementary measures. We then provide techniques for generating reranked results that are objective. If you offer our algorithms a search or recommendations assignment, they will try to come up with a variety of top results based on different protected characteristics. Adapting this structure to a specific distribution allows us to satisfy fairness standards such as demographic parity and equality of opportunity. By running simulations with varying values for critical parameters and looking at how Fairness-aware ranking impacts bias and usefulness measures, we assess the suggested algorithms. We next apply our theory to the practice of ranking LinkedIn members in their respective talent pools and give the results of our online A/B experiments, discussing the implications of our findings. All LinkedIn Recruiter users worldwide benefited from our solution, which increased fairness indicators (doubling the number of search queries with representative results) without affecting business KPIs. Our solution is the first of its kind to be extensively used, and it has the potential to improve the recruiting process for all 630 million LinkedIn users [12].

The role of knowledge graphs (KG) in recommending is growing in importance [13]. Graph neural networks (GNNs) are increasingly used in the development of comprehensive models. Both the identification of user-item relationships with fine-grained intents and the maintenance of the semantics of long-distance connections *via* the use of link dependencies remain unachieved by GNN-based models. Their relational modeling is hence coarse-grained. Investigating the reasons for user-item interactions, this research presents a novel model named the data Graph-based Intent Networks (KGIN) that makes use of additional item information. Separating intentions and modeling each one as a unique blend of KG relations allows for more model capacity along with interpretability, which is why we support this approach. Finally, we develop a novel GNN-based method for data aggregation that recursively accounts for relational pathways, or sequences of long-range connections. This method might be used to embed crucial information about user intent into product and user representations.

Users' product preferences can be mined using a recommendation system [14]. An explainable suggestion is one that is generated for the intended audience including an explanation of its rationale. Providing context for recommendations improves their clarity and increases the likelihood that customers will follow them [15]. Although the importance of explicable counsel is clear, it is insufficient to focus solely on this aspect. For recommendations to be more understandable without sacrificing precision or variety, an explainable recommendation framework must be developed [16 - 20]. We present a paradigm for multi-objective optimization based on knowledge graphs that can boost accuracy, variety, and transparency in suggestions all at once. The explanation is based on the route the recommended product takes to reach the intended user. Using the links between people and things in the knowledge graph, we may generate an explicable set of potential matches for the user. After the understandable candidate list has been optimized using a multi-objective optimization approach, the final suggestion list is generated [21 - 23]. The experimental findings show that the explainable recommendation architecture delivers detailed, diverse, and easily understandable suggestions.

PROPSOED WORK

Knowledge Graph Model

To begin, we create graph 1 (G_1), a user-item biparttitie graph. An example of a graph that includes extra information alongside the bipartite graph is a knowledge graph. One such formulation of the G_1 is,

$G\_1 \rightarrow \{U,I\}$

Where U is the user and I is the item set as depicted in Fig. (**1**).

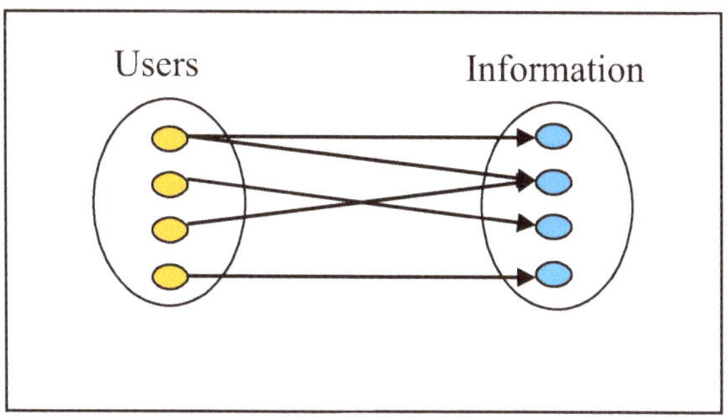

Fig. (1). Constructed Bipartite Graph Model.

A knowledge graph cannot be constructed until the additional data has been supplied to the G 1. Knowledge graph is an abbreviation for "information-added graph," which goes by G_2. Bipartite Graph Model is shown in Fig. (**1**). The G_2 also serves as a representation of the connection is shown in equation 1. This allows for the following representation:

$$G\_2 \rightarrow \{U,I,R[h,r]\} \quad (1)$$

Specifically, R denotes the connection between data points in the set that span from the beginning (h) to the end (t). Fig. (**2**) shows the knowledge graph concept at its most fundamental level.

DCNN based Knowledge Graph Model

There are three main components to the proposed DKG model, as seen in the Fig. (**2**). There are three modules:

- Data Collection Module
- DKG Construction Module
- Recommender Module

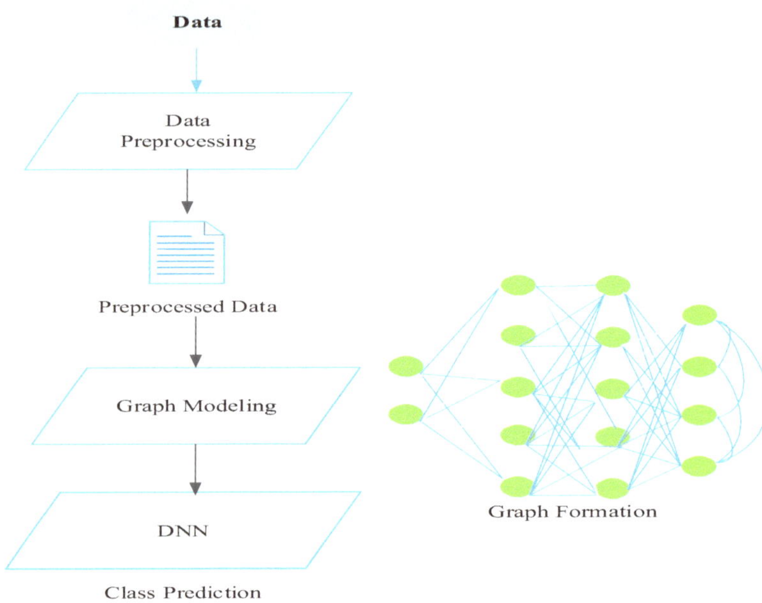

Fig. (2). Proposed DKG-RS architecture.

Data Gathering Subsystem

U is a sequence of users consisting of u_1, u_2,... u_n. The user inputs are all high-order and real-time. The data collection component's job at time T is to gather information from all users. Each cycle includes a new round of data collecting and cleansing. DKG-RS architecture is shown in Fig. (**2**). This component is responsible for receiving information from end-user devices, such as IoT devices. The data order is then normalized so that high-order data may be used. The information is then sent to the DKG component, which builds and refreshes the knowledge graph.

DKG Construction Module

The deep convolutional neural network (DCNN) technique was used to create this model. Input Layer: Initially, there were L pieces of data from n users in the system. Input layer initializes all users and data. Data weights are also calculated at the input layer, when G_2 is built. This layer is responsible for updating the graph's input data whenever new data is received. We have m hidden layers that calculate the user's connection to the input data. To benefit relational databases, we propose a novel attention technique. The caress of cascading propagations' weights highlights the significance of this inter-dependence. Information distribution, knowledge-aware attention, and data aggregation make up a single layer that we outline in this work (see equation 2). We then explain how to apply this to several layers.

A user may be represented *via* information propagation if they are linked to many datasets, as in $u_1 \rightarrow d_1$, $u_1 \rightarrow d_2 \ldots$

Here is the formula for calculating the neighbor connectivity:

$$NC=\sum_{(H(r,t))} [\![\pi R[h,t].e_t]\!] \quad \textbf{(2)}$$

Aware of their focus: the relational focus mechanism is described as,

$$\pi R[h,t]=e^{\pi R[h,t]} / \left(\sum e^{\pi R[h',t']}\right) \quad \textbf{(3)}$$

This number is used as a form of “attention score,” revealing the connections between nearby nodes or users is shown in equation 3.

The Attention Score is used by the Output Layer to build and update the Graph used by the Recommending Module..

Recommender Module

The output layer's knowledge graph serves as the foundation for the recommender module's operations. The IoT gadget receives the necessary suggestion directly from the graph.

RESULT AND DISCUSSION

Dataset Description

We use three publicly available benchmark datasets—Amazon-book, Last-FM, and Yelp2018—to test DKG. Domain, size, as well as sparsity are three ways in which these datasets vary.

One popular dataset for product recommendation is Amazon-book2: Amazon-review. We settled on a book by this group, available on Amazon. Our data is protected by a "10-core" arrangement that restricts access to all entities and persons with 10 or more interactions.

- Yelp20184: This data originated from the 2018 Yelp challenge. The local eateries and bars are the featured goods here. We also use the 10-core option to ensure 10 interactions between each user and each item.
- • The Last-FM3 music listening dataset was compiled with the use of the Last.fm online music services, where the entities are interpreted as songs. We focus on the data from the period of January 2015 to June 2015. Using the same 10-core setup, we have been able to maintain data quality.

For each user, we take an unwatched collection and give a score of 1 to each item to indicate a satisfactory assessment. We then alter the three datasets so they more closely resemble implicit feedback. Every dataset is built using a knowledge network using Microsoft Satori7. Finding triples in the KG with a confidence level higher than 0.9 is the first step. By matching the names and titles to the tails of triples like (head, book, books the title, tails), (head, film, film title, tail), as well (head, type.object.name, tail), we may get Satori IDs for all legally published works of literature, films, and musicians, as stated in the sub-3 KG. Things that have a large number of matching entities or none at all have been removed for your convenience. An overview table of the dataset's contents is shown in Table **1**.

Table 1. The description of the dataset.

Data		Amazon-Book	Last-FM	Yelp2018
User-Item Interaction	Users	70670	23000	45000
	Items	24915	48000	45600
	Interactions	847133	303459	115768
Knowledge Graph	Entities	88000	58765	90763
	Relations	39	9	40

For training, we use 80% of the user's historical interactions across all datasets, and for testing, we use the remaining 20%. Ten percent of the interactions from the original set are chosen at random to be used as a validation set for hyper-parameter tweaking. Utilizing the negative sampling strategy, for every excellent user-item interaction, there is a terrible item that the consumer has never tried before.

Performance Evaluation

To assess the quality of the top-K retrieved results, we employ two performance metrics: recall@K and ndcg@Ker. In other words, both demonstrate that the top K suggestions from the suggested method are reliable. Recall@K on amazon dataset is shown in Fig. (**3**). We compared the standard CF approach with Knowledge Graph (KG) approaches.

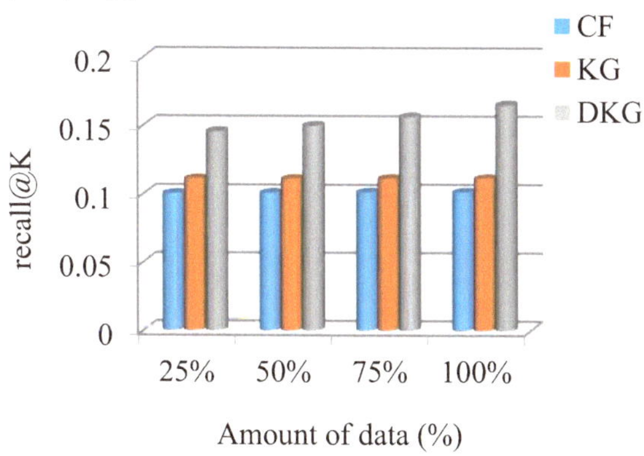

Fig. (3). Recall@K on amazon dataset.

On the Last FM dataset, recall@K displays the results (Fig. **4**). The sparsity issue restricts the expressiveness of recommendation systems; one reason to use KG is to circumvent this limitation. For those who do not move around much and do not engage with others, creating ideal representations is challenging. Whether using connection data could help fix this problem is something we look at in this post. Participants in the studies display different levels of sparsity. Using the mean number of transactions per user as a metric, we divided the test set into four subgroups to ensure that all groups had a consistent average. When compared to its competitors, DKG consistently performs better. This becomes especially clear when examining the two most diminutive user categories, Amazon-Book and Yelp 2018. In order to prove the latter's worth, we use high-order connections simulation, which 1) makes use of the lower-level connectivity seen in starting points, and 2) improves representation for inactive users by recursive embedding transmission. In Fig. (**5**), recall@K shows the Yelp dataset.

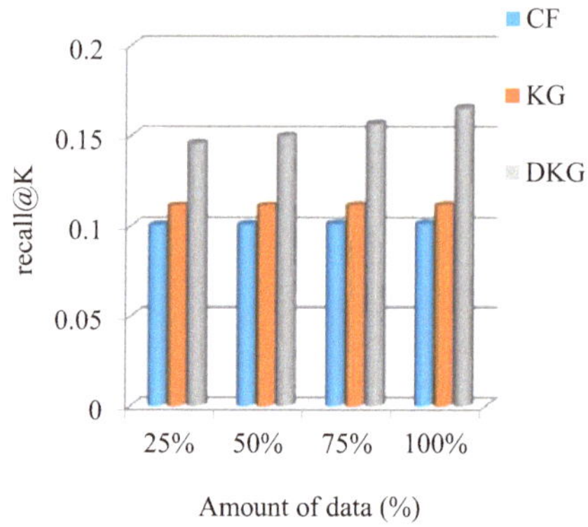

Fig. (4). Recall@K on Last FM dataset.

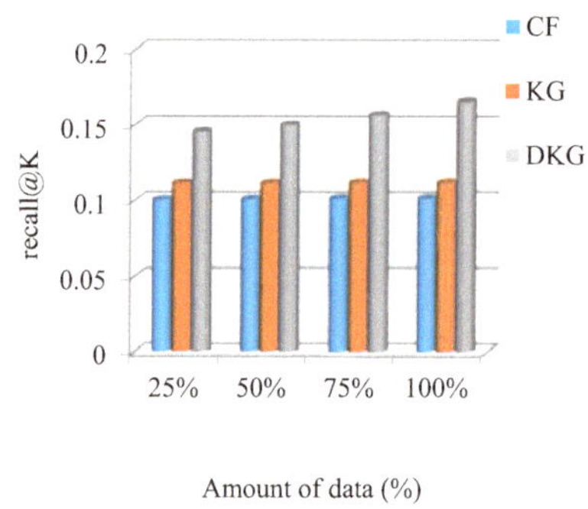

Fig. (5). Recall@K on Yelp dataset.

Several baselines, including the 2057 group from Yelp2018, are surpassed by DKG on the highest-density consumers group. Ndcg@K amazon dataset is shown in Fig. (**6**). One possible explanation is that customers who make too many purchases have preferences that are too general to track. Ndcg@K Last FM dataset is shown in Fig. (**7**). An additional level of uncertainty in the user's decisions may result from a high-order link.

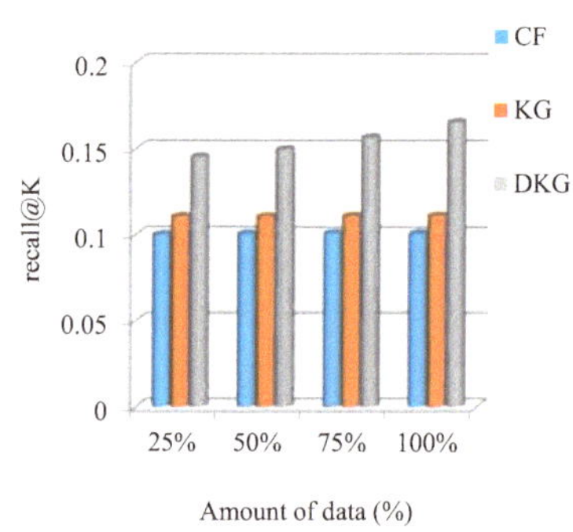

Fig. (6). Ndcg@K on amazon dataset.

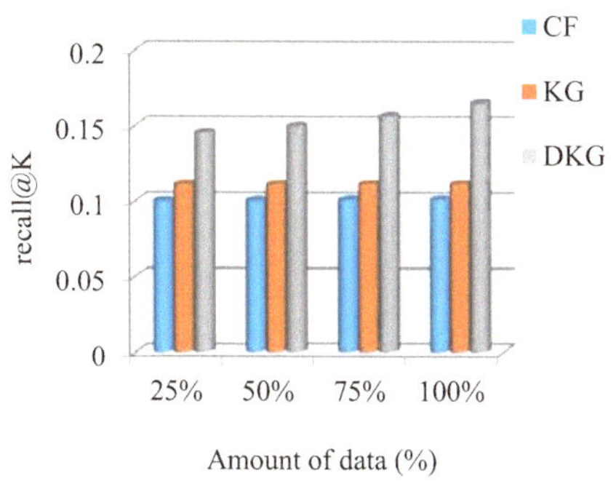

Fig. (7). Ndcg@K on Last FM dataset.

To emphasize, the suggested DKG approach guarantees high-level recall and ncdg for top-K outcomes. Ndcg@K Yelp dataset is shown in Fig. (**8**). The suggested DKG approach reliably achieves Top-K accuracy, as shown by the results.

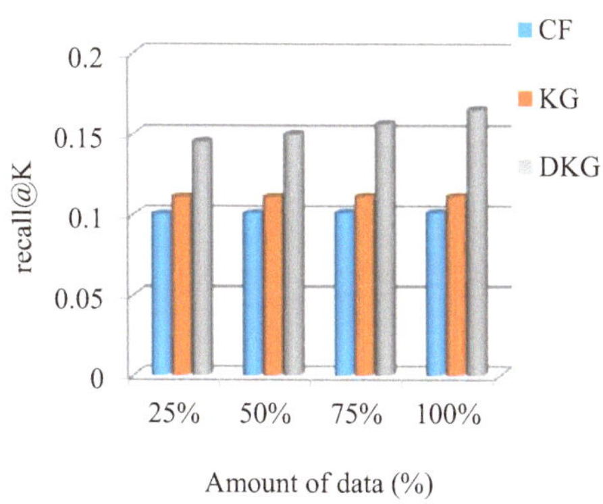

Fig. (8). Ndcg@K on Yelp dataset.

CONCLUSION

This study presents a new recommendation system that makes use of DKG. To construct the deep method, a convolutional neural network with deep learning (DCNN) analyses the data including user associations. The DKG begins by accumulating the data stream, after which it uses an attention mechanism to compute the values of the nearby connections. The process builds the graph, taking the connection weights into account. The suggestions are set up for the users initially based on DKG. We want to expand our work into more extensive Internet of Things applications in the future.

REFERENCES

[1] Y. Cui, "Intelligent recommendation system based on mathematical modeling in personalized data mining", *Math. Probl. Eng.*, vol. 2021, pp. 1-11, 2021. [http://dx.doi.org/10.1155/2021/6672036]

[2] Z. Cui, X. Xu, F. Xue, X. Cai, Y. Cao, W. Zhang, and J. Chen, "Personalized recommendation system based on collaborative filtering for IoT scenarios", *IEEE Trans. Serv. Comput.,* vol. 13, no. 4, pp. 685-695, 2020.
[http://dx.doi.org/10.1109/TSC.2020.2964552]

[3] K. Abbas, M. Afaq, T. Ahmed Khan, and W.C. Song, "A blockchain and machine learning-based drug supply chain management and recommendation system for smart pharmaceutical industry", *Electronics (Basel),* vol. 9, no. 5, p. 852, 2020.
[http://dx.doi.org/10.3390/electronics9050852]

[4] M. Kartheek, and G.P. Sajeev, "Building semantic based recommender system using knowledge graph embedding", *Proc. IEEE International Conference on Image Information Processing (ICIIP),* 2021.
[http://dx.doi.org/10.1109/ICIIP53038.2021.9702632]

[5] T.T. Ajith, "Enhanced movie recommendation using knowledge graph and particle filtering", *Proc. IEEE International Conference on Smart Electronics and Communication (ICOSEC),* 2021.
[http://dx.doi.org/10.1109/ICOSEC51865.2021.9591834]

[6] *Using knowledge graph for explainable recommendation of external content in electronic textbooks.* Springer, 2020.B. Rahdari, Lecture Notes in Computer Science

[7] Y. Wu, Q. Liu, R. Chen, C. Li, and Z. Peng, "A group recommendation system of network document resource based on knowledge graph and LSTM in edge computing", *Secur. Commun. Netw.,* vol. 2020, pp. 1-11, 2020.
[http://dx.doi.org/10.1155/2020/8843803]

[8] Y. Lee, "Recommendation system using collaborative filtering", *Int. J. Comput. Appl.,* 2015.

[9] A.A. Ginart, E.F. Xiang, E.K. Lee, and J.C. Niebles, "Mixed dimension embeddings with application to memory-efficient recommendation systems", *Proc. IEEE International Symposium on Information Theory (ISIT),* pp. 2786-2791, 2021.
[http://dx.doi.org/10.1109/ISIT45174.2021.9517710]

[10] Z.W. Wu, C.T. Chen, and S.H. Huang, "Poisoning attacks against knowledge graph-based recommendation systems using deep reinforcement learning", *Neural Comput. Appl.,* vol. 34, no. 4, pp. 3097-3115, 2022.
[http://dx.doi.org/10.1007/s00521-021-06573-8]

[11] H.J.M. Shi, J. Mao, Y. Liu, and M. Zhang, "Compositional embeddings using complementary partitions for memory-efficient recommendation systems", *Proc. 26th ACM SIGKDD International Conference on Knowledge Discovery and Data Mining,* 2020.
[http://dx.doi.org/10.1145/3394486.3403059]

[12] S.C. Geyik, S. Ambler, and K. Kenthapadi, "Fairness-aware ranking in search and recommendation systems with application to LinkedIn talent search", *Proc. 25th ACM SIGKDD International Conference on Knowledge Discovery and Data Mining,* 2019.
[http://dx.doi.org/10.1145/3292500.3330691]

[13] X. Wang, X. He, M. Wang, F. Feng, and T.S. Chua, "Learning intents behind interactions with knowledge graph for recommendation", *Proc. The Web Conference (WWW),* 2021.
[http://dx.doi.org/10.1145/3442381.3450133]

[14] L. Xie, Z. Hu, X. Cai, W. Zhang, and J. Chen, "Explainable recommendation based on knowledge graph and multi-objective optimization", *Complex & Intelligent Systems,* vol. 7, no. 3, pp. 1241-1252, 2021.
[http://dx.doi.org/10.1007/s40747-021-00315-y]

[15] S. Bhaskaran, R. Marappan, and B. Santhi, "Design and analysis of a cluster-based intelligent hybrid recommendation system for e-learning", *Appl. Math. Inf. Sci.,* 2021.

[16] B.D. Lund, and T. Wang, "Chatting about ChatGPT: how may AI and GPT impact academia and libraries?", *Libr. Hi Tech News,* vol. 40, no. 3, pp. 26-29, 2023.

[http://dx.doi.org/10.1108/LHTN-01-2023-0009]

[17] S. Zhang, Z.Q.G. Liau, K.L.M. Tan, and W.L. Chua, "Evaluating the accuracy and relevance of ChatGPT responses to frequently asked questions regarding total knee replacement", *Knee Surg. Relat. Res.,* vol. 36, no. 1, p. 15, 2024.
[http://dx.doi.org/10.1186/s43019-024-00218-5] [PMID: 38566254]

[18] “Top generative AI chatbots by market share,” FirstPageSage, 2024. [Online]. Available: https://www.firstpagesage.com

[19] M. Aljanabi, *ChatGPT: Future directions and open possibilities.* Mesopotamian Journal of CyberSecurity, 2023, pp. 16-17.
[http://dx.doi.org/10.58496/MJCS/2023/003]

[20] S.S. Gill, and R. Kaur, "ChatGPT: Vision and challenges", *Internet of Things and Cyber-Physical Systems,* vol. 3, pp. 262-271, 2023.
[http://dx.doi.org/10.1016/j.iotcps.2023.05.004]

[21] M. Javaid, A. Haleem, and R.P. Singh, "ChatGPT for healthcare services: An emerging stage for an innovative perspective", *BenchCouncil Transactions on Benchmarks, Standards and Evaluations,* vol. 3, no. 1, p. 100105, 2023.
[http://dx.doi.org/10.1016/j.tbench.2023.100105]

[22] A.S. George, and A.H. George, "A review of ChatGPT AI’s impact on several business sectors", *Partners Universal International Innovation Journal,* vol. 1, pp. 9-23, 2023.

CHAPTER 36

Advantages and Limitations of Big Data Analysis Tools

Dhruv Galgotia[1,*] and **S.H. Shruthishree**[2]

[1] *Department of Management, Galgotias University, Greater Noida, Uttar Pradesh, India*

[2] *Department of Computer Science and Engineering, JAIN (Deemed-to-be University), Bangalore, Karnataka, India*

Abstract: As the number and variety of data kept growing, conventional data processing technologies could not keep up with the demands of the big data setting. Because of this, new processing instruments tailored to specific needs have emerged. However, picking the ideal instrument could be difficult due to the abundance of options. To aid its mapping to different needs, this page provides a technical overview of the most common analytics tools, along with a literature review on the topic. Furthermore, we highlight the importance of choosing the correct tool for various uses, especially in smart city settings.

Keywords: Big Data, OpenSource Tools, Hadoop, MapReduce, Spark.

INTRODUCTION

From the first pictorial symbols to the most recent digital data, the evolution of data has been continuous and unfettered, expanding at an exponential pace. Properly structured and with a compact store design, a relational database may store little data. In contrast to large data sets, little data is built on a relational database design that allows for easy navigation across different subjects [1].

There is usually much familiarity with the little data stored in the data warehouse. In contrast, there is a deluge of complex, unstructured, non-relational data in our digital age that comes from all sorts of different fields. The major role of big data is to generate the ability to make sense of very small data sets; the term "Big Data" was not completely understood by science until after many others had done so. And materials, covering a wide range of fields such as academia, business, social media, and industry, Many fields have the potential to benefit greatly from

* **Corresponding author Dhruv Galgotia:** Department of Management, Galgotias University, Greater Noida, Uttar Pradesh, India; E-mail: ceo@galgotiasuniversity.edu.in

S. Kannadhasan, R. Nagarajan, & Kaushik Pal (Eds.)

the opportunities presented by big data. Despite big data's continued prominence as a hot issue, most people agree that big data methods, in particular, are best used in conjunction with more conventional data tools [2]. Big Data appears to be both the biggest challenge and the most promising field for future research as we adapt to the massive data transformation [3].

Big data is often described as "high-volume, high-velocity, as well as high-variety data assets requiring cost-effective, creative forms of data processing for enhanced insight as well as decision making," as stated by Gartner [4].

Following Gartner's three V's (Volume, Velocity, and Variety), IBM data scientists developed the fourth V, "Veracity" [5], to address ambiguity and incompleteness in data, which adds another layer of complexity to big data organizations [6]. Using the four Vs of big data volume, velocity, variety, and veracity to discover and evaluate previously overlooked but critical data might lead to the fifth V, "Value," which is the most desired prospect for most firms.

Each of the five dimensions of big data volume, velocity, diversity, and value is included under its purview. These five characteristics, sometimes referred to as the "5Vs," define modern big data:

- Terabytes, Exabytes, and Zettabytes are the units of measurement for the dataset's size.
- Data Velocity is a real-time metric that displays the pace of data input and output for a process. Due to the time-sensitive nature of data processing, data velocity is defined as the rate of data creation per unit of time.
- Uncertain or missing data is characterized by data veracity.
- Data Variety is the variety of data types generated from diverse areas and resources. It includes structured, semi-structured, and unstructured data.
- Exploring, finding, and analyzing the most essential data in the dataset is the goal of Data Value.

RELATED WORKS

Various sectors, including healthcare, sports, markets, businesses, network security, and educational systems, have adopted Hadoop-based applications, and the authors have devoted most of their attention to describing the concept in [4]. According to Bajaber *et al.* [5], we are now in the "big data 2.0" age, when many processing technologies have developed to improve processing capabilities (*e.g.*, MapReduce 2.0) and provide solutions tailored to businesses. For current distributed stream computing tools, there is a standard [6] that considers durability and fault recovery. Storm and Spark are pitted against one another in this article.

Open source real-time/near real-time processors have been studied by Liu *et al.* [7], who focused on their designs and platforms. In a research work [8], authors identified a few tools for real-time big data analysis and categorized the studies based on the tools used and the type of application for each. Their primary emphasis has been on applications in environmental protection, social media, healthcare, and surveillance.

The research paper [9] discusses big data analytics solutions. In addition, it has identified avenues for future study and open questions about platforms and techniques in this field. As a general, highly scalable Cloud-based solution, SMASH has been proposed by Gong *et al.* [10] for processing large-scale traffic data.

A different group of academics has already proposed a method for allocating resources in a shared cloud to handle streaming large data [11]. The goal is to maximize throughput utility with minimal variation across all topologies. It should be emphasized that Apache Spark is another appealing platform for large data processing, in addition to Hadoop. Although the two tools are frequently seen as rivals, it is well acknowledged that they are much more effective when used in tandem. Due to Apache Spark's growing profile as a premier big data analysis platform, many studies have focused on improving it.

BigDebug, a tool that provides dynamic, real-time debug primitives, was created by Gulzar *et al.* [12] for massive data processing in Spark. The spark long lineage issue may be solved with minimal impact on global performance using an automated checkpoint approach [13]. One may find an updated Spark framework, NetSpark [14]. Data serialization, network buffer management, and RDMA (hardware-supported Remote Direct Memory Access) improvements are part of this framework's plan to reduce Spark job execution times. To mitigate the effects of straggler machines, an approach known as Multiple Phases Time Estimation (MPTE) was proposed [15]. An improved task scheduler has also been designed, which allows for better scheduling of backup jobs. Additional research has developed spark-based frameworks to enhance the efficacy of big data analytics.

Actually, TR-Spark was developed by Yan *et al.* [16] to address the problems associated with transitory resources. This framework enables Spark-based apps to operate more efficiently by running as a secondary background activity on transitory resources. Two guiding ideas informed the development of this new framework: data size reduction, awareness scheduling, and resource stability. By combining these ideas, TR-Spark can adapt to the infrastructure's stability. A goal-oriented big data analytics paradigm is proposed by Park *et al.* [17] using Spark, with the aim of improving corporate decision-making. Decisions about shipments have been tested using this latter. Among the many potential uses for big data analytics techniques, smart cities have gained widespread attention. Building smart cities involves many diverse areas, including healthcare, education, travel, safety, governance, and resource management. Therefore, analyzing real-time data from numerous sources is crucial. Therefore, it is important to use the right tools to gain insights and, subsequently, improve everyday life. Because of this, incorporating data analysis into the concept of smart cities is gaining popularity. A business model for handling big data in smart cities was suggested, with the authors highlighting the importance of big data in this context.

On top of that, the writers have covered the history, definitions, problems, and areas of application of smart cities. The article compares and contrasts several smart city and big data definitions. The article continues by discussing the potential advantages, disadvantages, and prospects of integrating smart city big data applications. Various models' designs as well as implementations for developing smart cities utilizing the Hadoop ecosystem have been offered by researchers. A big data network model for a smart city project has also been developed. In the setting of smart cities, these four models have been suggested for data extraction, storage, and processing.

PROPOSED WORK

Ecosystem of Hadoop 3

Hadoop has become the de facto standard for processing massive amounts of data. The Apache Software Project first introduced the platform in 2007, and it is open source. Distributed systems, which consist of several interconnected units that exchange information and process, form their backbone. Hadoop really creates a cluster of networked computers by dividing calculations and storage across a set of grouped machines, or nodes. The second one is adjusted to scale from one node to hundreds of thousands, and then it is treated as a single unit. Section A explains Hadoop's store layer, whereas Section B details its processing layer. In Hadoop, a NameNode and a JobTracker comprise the master node, while many TaskTrakers and DataNodes make up the slave nodes. The Hadoop Framework is shown in Fig. (**1**). The cluster's high availability (HA) is guaranteed by the presence of a backup master. We describe the roles of each part here: Reconstructing files from blocks is controlled by the NameNode, which also manages the filesystem tree. On top of that, it manages and decides on the reproduction of blocks. When anything goes wrong, JobTracker restarts nodes, controls resources, and maintains tabs on tasks. As soon as a TaskTraker accepts the work, they must notify the

JobTracker of their progress. For fast data retrieval, DataNodes is used to store data in chunks. The NameNode is further notified of the blocks by them.

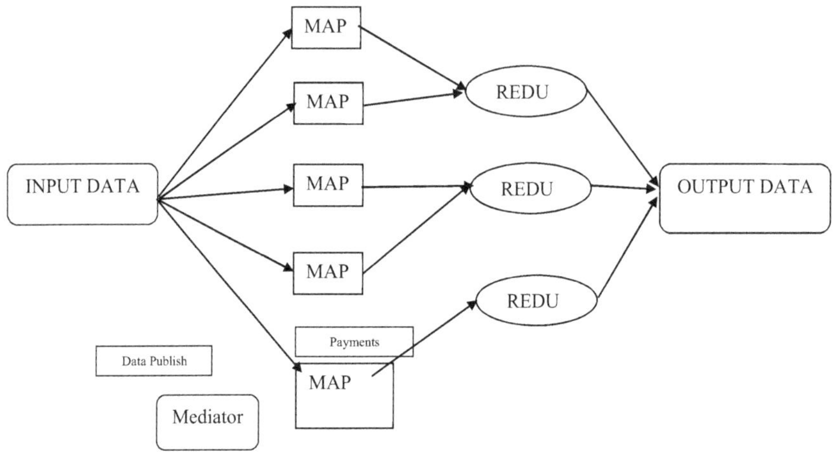

Fig. (1). Hadoop Framework.

Storage Layer

Using it, you can store enormous amounts of data across multiple devices and access your application data quickly. Blocks of 64 MB or greater often include files in HDFS, which may hold any kind of data. In addition, it comes with a predefined block replication mechanism that includes 3. The Hierarchical File System (HDFS) employs a mapping mechanism and a standardized naming system to maintain track of the locations of all files.

Processing Layer

What we call "big data" includes not just the data stored there but also the storage itself. Hadoop provides a processing layer for this purpose. Large volumes of unstructured data can be securely analyzed and distributed across clusters, where each node has its own storage. The MapReduce method is used to disseminate the data and gather the results. It was the MapReduce operations engine that Google first developed. It is a method for efficiently processing jobs involving massive amounts of data using parallel programming. Splitting the incoming data into separate blocks is the first step in a two-stage MapReduce task. The mapping step involves concurrent processing of data organized as key-value pairs, for the simple reason that the outcomes of processing tasks are unaffected by cluster size. These sorted outputs from this step reflect the inputs from the reduction phase. In the reduction phase, all of the intermediate results are merged into a single output. This means that MapReduce and the Hadoop framework make it easier to build analytics solutions. Although MapReduce is highly scalable and fault-tolerant, it has a few limitations, most notably in real-time processing and concurrent execution. The inclusion of YARN (Yet-Another-Resource-Negotiator) will help drive the evolution of massive data analysis. The Hadoop Distributed File System (HDFS) is enhanced with YARN, an operating system component, to support Big Data analytics applications. With this setup, data life cycle monitoring is improved, and many applications may operate at the same time. It also allows for the mixing of workloads in real time, interactively, and in batches. One other thing: YARN is always up to date with MapReduce's API. The core concept is to decouple the JobTracker's functionality into two separate "daemons": ResourceManager, responsible for equalizing resource allocation across all applications (MapReduce tasks), and ApplicationMaster, for requesting, launching, and managing apps. Because of this, MapReduce is only one of many applications that YARN supports.

Free Big Data Analytics Programmes

For the purpose of analysing and making available on local PCs, Hadoop employs simple tools and programming principles. To make sense of the data, however, better analytical methods are needed. Three categories best describe these instruments: Tools for Batch Processing. When the system's input is full, these techniques allow data processing to continue. Due to the progressive, continuous nature of the activities, the design may easily incorporate new data without requiring additional processing. To keep things consistent when dealing with this data, the results won't be shown until processing is complete. Popular technologies that facilitate batch processing include Apache Spark, Apache Flink, MapReduce in its Hadoop variant, and Apache Trident. Equipment for Microbatch Processing. You might think of this method as a hybrid of batch and stream processing. In order to process data in batches, it first divides streams into collections of short data segments. Because of this, data is processed in a flash.

Popular micro-batch processing technologies include Spark, along with Storm with Trident. The first Spark was created in Berkeley, California. It not only saves memory but also provides fault tolerance without replication. Spark MLlib, Spark R, Spark Streaming, and Spark SQL are some of the Spark libraries that facilitate processing and analysis of massive datasets. Also, by relying on in-memory computations, Spark is able to circumvent processing speed issues, as shown. Compared to native Hadoop solutions, it takes only 23 minutes to store up to 105 TB. Next, we will go over Trident, a Storm high-level abstraction layer that can help you achieve state persistence. Similar to Spark, Trident adds functionality by running on mini-batches. Toolbox for Stream Processing: Data streams, with a constant influx of new data records, are manageable with streaming technologies. This kind of data processing is most often used for: Storm is a real-time stream processor that uses tuples—data plus an identifier—to abstract stream data. Storm's real-time computation requires creating topologies and using directed acyclic graphs. Input nodes (spouts) and processing nodes (bolts) make up its topology, which serves as a data graph. The upstream backup-and-keep-track acknowledgment system in Storm ensures that rejected tuples can be reprocessed.

Flink is an ESP-based distributed framework. Instead of using pure streams, you may use micro-batches with Flink. Included in Flink's 592 I are all the positions. A directed network of jobs is used to sequence stream information, or DataStream, as a partially ordered set of records, according to El Alaoui *et al.* Distributed checkpoints, on which Flink is built, provide failure tolerance and preserve the current work state. Instead of using Spark, Hadoop MapReduce, or Storm, you may use Apache Flink.

Using YARN, Samza determines how to distribute resources between apps. Samza is particularly useful for data that Apache Kafka processes. The big data tools are shown in Table **1**. The second system is a decentralized publish-subscribe messaging system designed to collect and transmit large volumes of event data. There is sufficient data at the local scale to recalculate any relative outcomes; thus, the system will reissue them according to the calculation window after a late arrival.

Table 1. Comparison between big data tools.

Property	MapReduce	Samza	Storm	Spark	Flink
Streaming Model	Batch	Naïve Stream	Naïve Stream	Micro-batch	Naïve Stream
Latency	Low	Low	High	Medium	Low
Maturity	Low	Medium	High	High	Low
Fault Tolerance	Yes	Yes	Yes	Yes	Yes
In-Memory Processing	No	Yes	Yes	Yes	Yes
Enterprise Support	No	No	No	Yes	No

RESULT AND DISCUSSION

Applications and Frequently Used Tools

All publicly accessible health and sociodemographic data, whether collected internally or externally, is considered big data in the health sector. Predictions indicate that health data will increase by a factor of 50 by 2020, due to advancements in genetics, linked healthcare machinery, electronic medical records, and the widespread use of mobile health applications and sensors.

Possible applications for this data include identifying risk factors for illness, assisting with diagnosis, selecting treatments, and evaluating their efficacy. Giving patients their diagnoses and prognoses: For the purpose of diagnosing cardiorespiratory spells, the authors detail a method they developed. Experts have proposed a method that leverages users' health-related tweets. After that, it uses computing power to predict the user's current health status. An innovative approach that utilizes the k-Nearest Neighbours (KNN) method has been put forward to identify anomalies in massive amounts of healthcare data effectively. With this approach, processing effectiveness and precision were much enhanced compared to KNN and LoF. To evaluate the effect on public health, researchers used a spatial Durbin model with death rates from 116 cities across China. Additionally, they estimate the annual medical expenses and fatalities caused by air pollution. To handle massive data from health records in a cloud setting, the authors have proposed a NoSQL model. The sheer amount of data that this model can process is astounding. The model's efficiency was assessed by comparing it to a relational database architecture and by considering factors such as query time, data preparation, flexibility, and extensibility. Created by Al Rasyid *et al.*, the EepisCure application platform lets users input and view data acquired from unprocessed sensors. A network of these sensors, along with additional wearable computing equipment, makes up the Wireless Body Area Network, which monitors human vital signs. The architects behind developed what they dubbed "big health" in. By combining big data with the healthcare Internet of Things, the proposed method may extract valuable health insights from stored data. The construction of an alarm system requires authors to focus on establishing a connection between home air monitoring and a method for reporting individual health. The big data applications are shown in Fig. (**2**). The researchers discussed the impact of massive data sets on the insurance sector and their potential to transform healthcare in rural areas, aiming to reduce healthcare costs while improving population health. To improve service levels, we have reviewed e-health insurance patients' reports, symptoms, comments, and statistics. Consequently, the new patient may compare the costs of treatment for a given condition and choose the hospital that provides the best care.

Marketing and Commerce

Modern businesses are increasingly realising that big data analysis is an essential component in their quest to improve quality. A large body of research has shown that big data is a critical component for the sustained growth of the marketing and commercial sectors. Hadoop MapReduce is crucial for e-commerce businesses to implement a predictive prefetching solution.. In order to predict future financial market movements, this study employs high-frequency analysis of the Shanghai Composite Index. Another study suggests a method to examine how wind generation affects energy prices. Using the Alberta market as an example, the proposed technique shows that increasing wind power had a detrimental effect on the wholesale market. Researchers have also developed an advertising analytics solution that allows focused social networking posts by evaluating the impact of two variables: traffic and money. To address this problem, a big data mobile advertising analytics platform was developed to provide ads and suggestions based on many characteristics, such as user profile, navigation history, localization, and access behaviors.

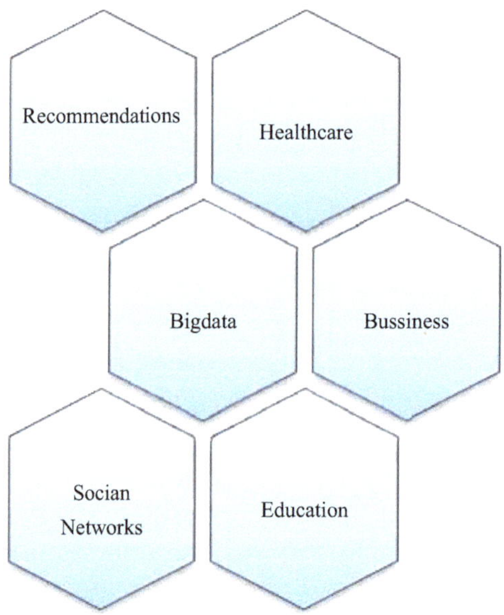

Fig. (2). Big Data Applications.

The marketing industry has released a new approach that uses telecom big data mining to predict who would buy expensive luxury cars. Additionally, this contribution demonstrates the model's efficacy *via* the use of social media, using data from Twitter to predict changes in the Dow Jones Industrial Average over time. A new algorithm that uses Facebook profiles to predict how buyers use e-commerce websites has been launched. A big data technique was released that proved the connection between social media sentiment analysis and stock performance.

Modern Urban Communities: We examined many real-world examples of big data applications that might enhance city residents' quality of life in several fields. This means these applications might serve as blueprints for future smart city initiatives. For example, previous applications in the health sector might play a significant role in smart city healthcare by improving residents' health or changing the way healthcare is delivered to people. Improving energy, transportation, governance, and public safety are among the many urban features that are often enhanced in a smart city, according to existing studies. This is why several national governments have actively encouraged the development of smart cities globally.

Frequently Employed Tools: This section organizes several investigations according to domains and subdomains and details the big data analytics techniques used. After reviewing the academic literature, we discovered that Hadoop, MapReduce, and Spark are the three most widely used frameworks for processing big data. Samza, Flink, and Storm are capable of real-time processing, but they have not been widely adopted. It was also noted that most authors did not provide justifications for their favored frameworks. We performed this comparison by examining the latency and fault tolerance of various frameworks. The technologies used to handle massive amounts of data are evolving all the time, with new tools being released on a daily basis. Their related tasks were also examined. Because of this, the tools used to build processing-based systems must be carefully selected.

CONCLUSION

In our work, we aim to emphasize the era of big data, along with all that it encompasses. Considering the importance of big data analytics and its ability to enhance many services we use every day, a significant portion of this contribution is devoted to analyzing and comparing the leading platforms and tools for processing big data. A review of large-scale data processing technologies and their applications across several industries, such as healthcare, business, and smart city planning, is presented in the section that follows. It should be noted that this contribution's main goal is to summarize various big data analytics technologies and the challenges they address. In future contributions, we will provide a comprehensive analysis of big data value chain components, including platforms for data collection, preprocessing, processing, visualization, as well as machine learning, and offer a practical evaluation of these technologies.

REFERENCES

[1] M. Bublyk, V. Vysotska, L. Chyrun, O. Slava, V. Panasyuk, and M. Shevchenko, "Features of big data analysis for apps sales via Google Play Store", *Proc. IEEE 18th International Conference on Computer Science and Information Technologies (CSIT),* pp. 1-6, 2023. [http://dx.doi.org/10.1109/CSIT61576.2023.10324075]

[2] L. Shu, and D. Zheng, *Exploring the application of big data visualization platform in urban traffic data analysis.* Boni Global Humanities and Social Sciences, 2023. [http://dx.doi.org/10.61360/BoniGHSS232014170805]

[3] J. Lukito, and M.L. Pruden, "Critical computation: mixed-methods approaches to big language data analysis", *Rev. Comm.,* vol. 23, no. 1, pp. 62-78, 2023. [http://dx.doi.org/10.1080/15358593.2022.2125821]

[4] L. Muradkhanli, and Z. Karimov, "Customer behavior analysis using big data analytics and machine learning," Problems of Information Society, 2023. [http://dx.doi.org/10.25045/jpis.v14.i2.08]

[5] N.P. Lyubushin, E.N. Letyagina, and V.I. Perova, "Neural network analysis of energy efficiency of the regional economy as a factor of Russia's sustainable development under conditions of big challenges", *Economic Analysis: Theory and Practice,* vol. 22, no. 2, pp. 206-234, 2023. [http://dx.doi.org/10.24891/ea.22.2.206]

[6] A. M. Abdelhalim, "How management accounting practices integrate with big data analytics and its impact on corporate sustainability," Journal of Accounting and Organizational Change, 2023.

[7] A.K. Samanta, and N. Chaki, "An enumerated analysis of NoSQL data models using statistical tools", *Innov. Syst. Softw. Eng.,* vol. 19, no. 1, pp. 5-14, 2023. [http://dx.doi.org/10.1007/s11334-022-00517-8]

[8] A.R. Wang, S.Z. Wu, S.Y. Liu, X.L. Xiu, J.Y. Zhou, Z.Y. Hu, and Y.F. Duan, "[Comparative study of medical common data models for FAIR data sharing]", *Zhonghua Liu Xing Bing Xue Za Zhi,* vol. 44, no. 5, pp. 828-836, 2023. [PMID: 37221075]

[9] Q. Zhang, Y. Zhou, J. He, B. Zhu, F. Han, and S. Long, "A review on global cooperation network in the interdisciplinary research of geochemistry combined with artificial intelligence", *Minerals (Basel),* vol. 13, no. 10, p. 1332, 2023. [http://dx.doi.org/10.3390/min13101332]

[10] A. Kozak, "Application of ICT in the co production of social services", *Journal of Economics and Management,* vol. 45, pp. 441-467, 2023. [http://dx.doi.org/10.22367/jem.2023.45.17]

[11] J. Nie, "Research on improving education quality and efficiency through artificial intelligence and big data analysis", *Educ. Inf. Technol.,* 2023.

[12] J.O. Environmental And Public Health, "Retracted: Higher education environment monitoring and quality assessment model using big data analysis and deep learning", *J. Environ. Public Health,* vol. 2023, 2023.9765368 [PMID: 37811451]

[13] S. Aldossari, U.A. Mokhtar, and A.T. Abdul Ghani, "Factors influencing the adoption of big data analytics: A systematic literature and experts review", *SAGE Open,* vol. 13, no. 4, 2023.21582440231217902 [http://dx.doi.org/10.1177/21582440231217902]

[14] X. Xiang, *Innovation, application, and trend analysis of digital health in the era of big data.* Theoretical and Natural Science, 2023. [http://dx.doi.org/10.54254/2753-8818/3/20220282]

[15] X. Sun, and Y. Song, "The impact of big data and AI on teacher performance reviews: A study of private higher vocational colleges", *J. Inf. Syst. Eng. Manag.,* vol. 8, no. 4, p. 23228, 2023. [http://dx.doi.org/10.55267/iadt.07.14050]

[16] J. Chen, Y. Mao, and X. Liu, "Big data: A survey", *Mob. Netw. Appl.,* vol. 29, pp. 1-16, 2024.

[17] M. Chen, S. Mao, and Y. Liu, "Big data: A survey on technologies, applications, and open research issues", *IEEE Access,* vol. 11, pp. 11524-11540, 2023.

CHAPTER 37

Utilizing Contextual Recommendation Systems for Advanced Comprehension of Information

Sahana Shetty[1,*] and **Ajay Shanker Singh**[2]

[1] *Department of Computer Science and Engineering, JAIN (Deemed-to-be University), Bangalore, Karnataka, India*

[2] *Department of Computer Science and Engineering, Galgotias University, Greater Noida, Uttar Pradesh, India*

Abstract: Creating a system to track the health of a machine is no easy feat. For this to work, a sufficiently large dataset of machine operation signals, operation-related background data, and diagnosis-related anecdotes is required. Nowadays, it is not difficult to address the two issues mentioned. Because it relies on non-numerical and imprecise information, the diagnostic experience is the most difficult to convey. However, in order to build a reliable monitoring system, the processing of the collected data is crucial. A system devoted to suggesting processing methods for condition monitoring is presented in this article's framework. A database and internal modules built using fuzzy logic are part of it. The technique proposes processing algorithms based on user-provided contextual information. The results of testing the suggested agent on two separate parallel gearboxes are also presented in this article. Processing algorithms using assigned model types are the outputs of the system. The findings demonstrate that the algorithms suggested by the system outperform those chosen at random. Accuracy gains ranging from 5% to 14.5% are achievable, according to the findings.

Keywords: Machine's condition monitoring system, user preferences, contextual recommendations systems, video recommendation system.

INTRODUCTION

Several practical uses of recommender systems include providing personalized product suggestions and aiding user decision-making. Since user preferences may vary depending on various circumstances (*e.g.*, time, place, and companion), it is possible to build context-aware recommender systems to tailor suggestions to different scenarios. Improved recommendation algorithms have recently benefited from deep learning and neural network approaches [1]. Online retail

* **Corresponding author Sahana Shetty:** Department of Computer Science and Engineering, JAIN (Deemed-to-be University), Bangalore, Karnataka, India; E-mail: s.sahana@jainuniversity.ac.in

S. Kannadhasan, R. Nagarajan, & Kaushik Pal (Eds.)

recommendation systems (like Amazon's) help consumers choose what to buy by suggesting related goods and services. For merchants to enhance revenue and maintain customer loyalty, it is essential to design a recommender system tailored to each client's needs. Having timestamps of user contact is crucial for learning sequential patterns from their interactions, understanding their short- and long-term preferences, and predicting what to propose next [2]. This is because users' hobbies and tastes change over time. Systems must be able to adapt to users' changing preferences across many online contexts in which they engage with end users. A user's preferences for an item can shift over time for a number of reasons, including changes in context or the nature of the work at hand, as well as external variables, both immediate and distant. To keep up with users' ever-changing interests, recommender systems must be able to record these changes in preferences [3]. Among the many applications of machine learning today, recommendation systems stand out. All parts of the contemporary user experience are affected by recommender systems, whether you're using Netflix to choose a new program to watch or Spotify to listen to an automated playlist. Matrix factorization is a popular technique for creating recommendation systems; it uses past ratings and user preferences to forecast how a user would rate a product [4]. One type of recommendation system is the video recommendation system found on e-learning platforms. This system uses algorithms to determine students' interests and preferences, then suggests instructional movies. Written evaluations and comments from students may give light on the instructional video's merits and shortcomings [5]. Combining recommendation algorithms with deep learning has become a research hotspot in the area of recommender systems, which are vital information technologies today. Numerous recommendation algorithms have been developed, each offering higher recommendation accuracy based on the LFM (Latent Factor Model) [6]. This model learns latent representations *via* matrix factorization with gradient descent to better match user preferences. In an effort to better match user ratings to specific items, recommendation systems inspired by cognitive science have gained significant interest in the last several years. Cognitive knowledge user-item evaluations are sparse and ambiguous, hindering the effectiveness of recommendation systems. Because of this, top-k recommendations are now among the most talked-about topics in the field. The purpose of top-k suggestions is to produce the best-ranked list of items based on user preferences [7].

RELATED WORKS

For context-aware suggestions, see reference [8] for an expanded, proposed generic framework for neural contextual matrix factorization, along with evaluation and comparison of a family of such models. Specifically, we consider two factors - the possible components into which contexts could be fused as well as the embedding technique used to express context situations-and analyze how these affect the effectiveness of recommendations that are aware of context.

New recommender systems for single-player role-playing games based on latent-component models are proposed [9]. More specifically, we offer a tensor factorization approach for decomposing sets of bipartite matrices that capture the time-dependent interests and actions of the participants. Our algorithm outperforms prior handmade or collaborative filtering methods in recommending more interesting missions and retaining more players, according to comprehensive online bucket-type testing conducted while a commercial game was running.

With an eye on e-commerce product recommendation, this article presents a taxonomy of sequential recommendation systems (SRecSys). It classifies SRecSys into three broad categories: (i) methods based on neural networks, such as advanced models and matrix factorization; (ii) methods based on factorization and latent representation, such as Markov models; and (iii) methods based on sequence similarity, pattern mining, and sequential pattern mining. Products could be better understood using this classification, based on the current SRecSys literature in the e-commerce application field; the classification also provides the current status of the solutions and future research directions [10]. In addition, the approaches and their limitations are outlined, followed by a categorization of the assessed systems based on eight critical aspects. Based on studies conducted on e-commerce datasets (Amazon and Online Retail), integrating sequential purchasing patterns into the recommendation process and modeling consumers' sequential behavior enhances suggestion quality.

To extract aspects, sentiment, and semantic characteristics from user and item evaluations, the aspect-based neural network rating prediction approach (ADLRP) is proposed [11]. After that, latent variables for both people and objects are generated using the deep learning approach. Items' ratings are predicted using the matrix factorization approach based on these three characteristics. The experimental findings demonstrate that the proposed approach outperforms standard artificial neural networks and traditional rating prediction methods. The suggested technique improves rating prediction accuracy by accurately and effectively extracting aspect-specific sentiments and semantics from review texts.

The fact that people's preferences evolve over time is included in our recommendation algorithm [12]. To identify change-points in a series of user interactions that indicate significant changes in preference, we propose a Hidden Markov Model (HMM)- oriented approach that accounts for the sequential actions of all users in the data. To provide recommendations, the proposed approach employs a sequence-aware non-negative matrix factorization model with the discovered change points. We provide empirical proof of the efficacy of the HMM-based change detection methodology and compare it to traditional baseline approaches. Furthermore, our performance study shows that the proposed recommendation technique beats the best state-of-the-art sequence-aware recommendation algorithms.

In order to identify missing values in a music recommendation system, some authors [13] compared several PMF-based algorithms. We created the constrained Kernelized PMF (cKPMF) models after observing that adding user network information does not perform as well as limiting the user feature vector *via* a latent constraint similarity matrix. We demonstrate that, among the models investigated in this study, cKPMF performs best for our current objective. Here, we reframe the issue of missing value estimation as one involving recommender systems.

An instructional video recommendation system based on student input, as described in [14]. Textual data was extracted from instructional videos using the LDA topic model to train language models. These models were then inputted into the supervised convolutional neural network (CNN) model. Also, a latent component algorithm was utilized to glean student preferences and traits from learners' past data, namely rating and evaluations of the instructional videos, which was generated by the CNN model. Our suggested method addresses the recommender system's sparsity and cold-start problems by combining user ratings and reviews. When making recommendations, our recommender considers user reviews. However, if a review is missing or the remark is ambiguous, we utilize the user rating instead. Coursera video content databases and large, varied learning courses were our real-world projects. The findings demonstrate that learners' evaluations can be used to provide fresh, high-quality suggestions for previously unseen films while simultaneously mitigating the impact of the cold start problem in sparsity-based systems.

With film recommendation as the subject of study, the article suggests a novel Latent Function Generator (LFG) network [15]. Without re-factoring or retraining, the LFG dynamically learns user latent factors using deep neural networks. In terms of suggestion accuracy, experimental findings show that the LFG recommendations model is superior to conventional matrix factorization methods, offering a viable alternative to the difficulties associated with LFM's real-time recommending capabilities [16 - 21].

PROPSOED WORK

Building a monitoring system for a specific machine requires background knowledge of the equipment's type, operating conditions, and measurement acquisition. In order to find the similarity measure, we first collect context information from survey respondents. Data from previous analyses of the same issue are used to determine the degree of similarity and then entered into the database. A color rectangle represents each machine that has been previously inspected on the diagram. A green hue indicates a strong connection to a specific prior issue, while a red hue denotes a poor match. We chose the many machines that have already been evaluated and found to have the greatest similarity value. As the processing algorithms were being developed, several solutions were presented for each challenge. An efficiency metric is used to compare these solutions. Different processing algorithms are ranked and selected based on their performance history and how closely they align with the issue under analysis. A number of algorithms are selected based on their performance in the comparison.

A machine condition assessment method is suggested for development using these approaches. The system model is shown in Fig. (**1**). Regarding the previously studied collection of structures, the following assumptions are necessary:

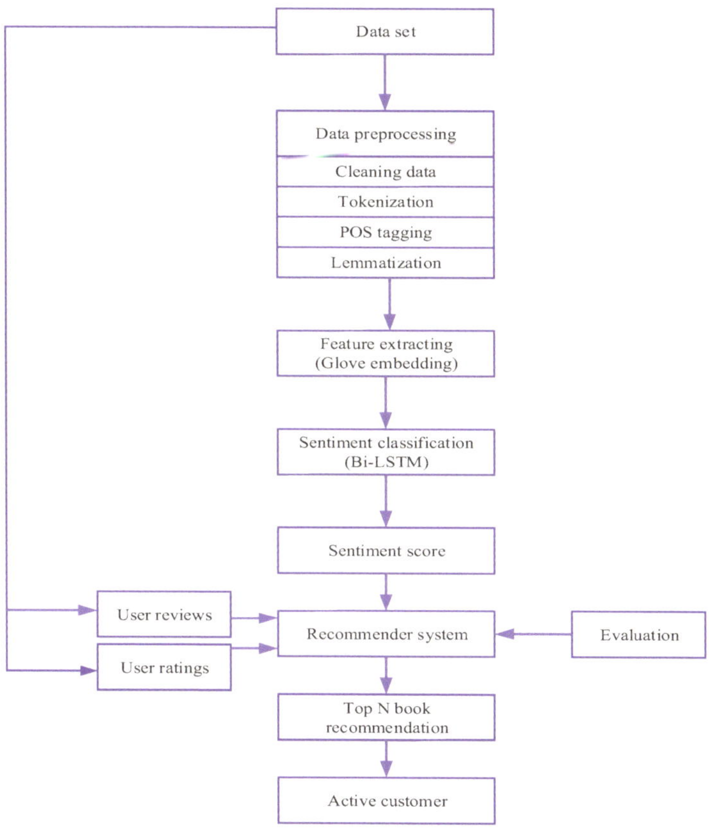

Fig. (1). System Model.

1. Many objects with varying degrees of resemblance to the current situation have their diagnostic results and prescriptions for signal processing stored in the database. Some of these degrees of similarity are really significant, and we have previously found solutions to issues that are extremely similar.
2. In the past, several signal processing and classification methods were used to keep an eye on these structures.
3. A brief overview of the buildings is available, including details on their construction and the environments in which they function.

One embedding value at a time is highlighted on the FLS structure selector's tree-like branches. This is the order of the branches, with "Variability" being the first. In the initial Sugeno-type FLS, data on load and speed fluctuations are combined to generate a hidden variable called difficulty. Taking the calculated hidden variable and adding it to the order of load and speed yields the embedding value, termed variability, in the following Mamdani FLS. The primary goal of the Sugeno subsystem is to create a continuous secret variable by combining the positions s, orientations, and types of sensors. The subsequent Mamdani subsystem generates an experimental embedding value using the retrieved hidden factor and the sensor bandwidth, along with speed data. Condition assessment, issue type, and monitored component are the focus of the final developed subsystem. Problem, problem_monitored, and problem_labels are the three inputs and three outputs of an identical Mamdani-type FLS. The number of membership-related duties and regulations can be found in the survey questions and types.

This subsystem is all about algorithms used in signal processing or for evaluating the structure's status. To determine the weight for each type of processing signal chain or model, this vector is supplied to the fuzzy system, which is then selected. Data acquired from structure selectors is filtered using those values. The utility value, derived from the weights, is then allocated to each algorithm. The geometric mean is a useful statistic for expressing an algorithm's usefulness, as shown in equation 1:

$$U_i = \left(\prod_{k=1}^{n} w_k\right)^{\frac{1}{n}} \tag{1}$$

RESULT AND DISCUSSION

The parallel gearbox system was developed using the framework. That required compiling a database of gears that had been previously tracked. The item that stood in for the virtual drivetrain was used as a structure to be monitored. It included a 22202EK rolling element bearing (REB), a one-stage gearbox, a slow shaft, and a driving shaft connected to the reference speed. The gearbox was used to decrease speed; the slowed shaft gear had 67 teeth, and the driving shaft gear had 23 teeth. By dividing 67 by 23, we get a total transmission ratio of 0.34328. Between 2400 and 6000 rpm, the virtual item runs at various nominal speeds, with a distinct speed variation between 3000 and 3000 rpm. The eight types of structural weaknesses that the simulated data represent are found in objects. The failure developmental function (FDF) represents each failure mode and dictates the specific evolution of the problem. Failure mode vibrational signals may be generated by the virtual item using three FDFs, corresponding to shaft, gearbox, and bearing faults, respectively. The features of each mode include a 25 kHz sample frequency, a 10-second time frame, and 150 separate vibratory signals. For half of the items, a phase-marking signal was also generated along with the vibration signals.

Processing Signals and Extracting Features

Indicators sensitive to the presence of damage were extracted from the prepared dataset. From the basic computation of raw-signal root-mean-squares (RMS) to more advanced spectral kurtosis, several signal processing and feature extraction techniques have been proposed over the years of vibrodiagnostic-related studies. In this one may get a comprehensive overview of several processing algorithms that are specifically designed for CM. In order to analyze the signals, we consulted the relevant literature and visually examined the signs.

Competent Models: A training set was created from the features and labels computed and saved in the database. The operation's end objective was to train several models to obtain a quantitative evaluation of the retrieved attributes. Algorithms varied in kind and in the operations pertaining to clustering, distances, trained weights, and training set division.

CONCLUSION

Here, we examine a preprocessed fuzzy-logic-based recommendation system for condition monitoring. Recommendations are made using contextual information, and the system is structured around knowledge. A database housing past structural analysis data is the backbone of the proposed system. Comparable items are selected based on the computed embedding values. Subsequent subsystems refine the acquired data for improved fit to the studied issue. This article shows how to put the framework into action and test the system provided by analyzing information for two different structures. To start with, there are digital items that act as a one-stage parallel gearbox signal simulator. A two-stage gearbox is the second. The algorithm took user preferences into account while recommending processing methods, which were compared to randomly chosen alternatives. In order to process data from test objects, all algorithms were used. The space of features and classifier accuracies is shown by the acquired findings. The findings show that the system's suggested processing algorithms, across all parameters, achieved an average improvement in the accuracy of 5 to 14.5 percent. Evidence like this suggests the recommender system architecture may help with condition assessment by providing useful processing suggestions.

REFERENCES

[1] P. Li, J. Cao, and Z. Guan, "Dual SVD++ recommendation model based on attention convolutional neural network", *Proc. IEEE 4th International Conference on Civil Aviation Safety and Information Technology (ICCASIT),* pp. 1053-1057, 2022. [http://dx.doi.org/10.1109/ICCASIT55263.2022.9986802]

[2] X. Yu, Q. Hu, H. Li, J. Du, J. Gao, and L. Sun, "Cross-domain recommendation based on latent factor alignment", *Neural Comput. Appl.,* vol. 34, no. 5, pp. 3421-3432, 2022. [http://dx.doi.org/10.1007/s00521-021-05737-w]

[3] D. S. Priya and T. A. Govindasamy, "Political optimizer based artificial neural network for intelligent movie recommendation system," Journal of Intelligent Systems, 2021.

[4] D.D. Le, and H.W. Lauw, "Stochastically robust personalized ranking for LSH recommendation retrieval", *Proc. AAAI Conference on Artificial Intelligence,* vol. 34, 2020. [http://dx.doi.org/10.1609/aaai.v34i04.5889]

[5] F. Liu, Z. Cheng, C. Sun, Y. Wang, L. Nie, and M. Kankanhalli, "User diverse preference modeling by multimodal attentive metric learning", *Proc. 27th ACM International Conference on Multimedia,* 2019. [http://dx.doi.org/10.1145/3343031.3350953]

[6] A. Ivanytska, L. Zubyk, Y. Zubyk, and D. Ivanov, "The advertising prediction model based on machine learning technologies", in Proc. IT&I Workshops, 2021.

[7] B. Xu, H. Lin, L. Yang, Y. Lin, and K. Xu, "Cognitive knowledge-aware social recommendation via group-enhanced ranking model", *Cognit. Comput.,* vol. 14, no. 3, pp. 1055-1067, 2022. [http://dx.doi.org/10.1007/s12559-022-10001-x]

[8] Y. Zheng, and G.F. Arias, "A family of neural contextual matrix factorization models for context-aware recommendations", *Proc. ACM Web Conference,* 2022. [http://dx.doi.org/10.1145/3511047.3536404]

[9] R. Sifa, R. Yawar, R. Ramamurthy, C. Bauckhage, and K. Kersting, *Matrix- and tensor factorization for game content recommendation.* vol. Vol. 34. KI – Künstliche Intelligenz, 2019, pp. 57-67.

[10] M. Nasir, and C.I. Ezeife, *A survey and taxonomy of sequential recommender systems for e-commerce product recommendation.* vol. Vol. 4. SN Computer Science, 2023.

[11] C.H. Lai, and K.C. Tseng, "Applying deep learning models to analyze users' aspects, sentiment, and semantic features for product recommendation", *Appl. Sci. (Basel),* vol. 12, no. 4, p. 2118, 2022. [http://dx.doi.org/10.3390/app12042118]

[12] F. Eskandanian, and B. Mobasher, "Modeling the dynamics of user preferences for sequence-aware recommendation using hidden Markov models", *Proc. ACM Conference on Recommender Systems,* 2019.

[13] U. Priyanka, and D. K. Kumar, "Recovery of missing data using enhanced probabilistic matrix factorization," International Journal of Data Science, 2020. [http://dx.doi.org/10.33564/IJEAST.2020.v05i02.045]

[14] M.J. Hazar, S. Zrigui, M. Maraoui, M. Zrigui, and H. Nicolas, "A recommendation system involving a hybrid approach of student review and rating for an educational video", *J. Braz. Comput. Soc.,* vol. 29, no. 1, pp. 73-85, 2023. [http://dx.doi.org/10.5753/jbcs.2023.3063]

[15] J. Liu, "LFG: A generative network for real-time recommendation", *Proc. ACM Conference on Recommender Systems,* 2023. [http://dx.doi.org/10.1145/3640872.3640881]

[16] A. Siddiqa, A. Karim, and V. Chang, "Modeling SmallClient indexing framework for big data analytics", *J. Supercomput.,* vol. 73, pp. 1-22, 2017.

[17] A. Siddiqa, A. Karim, and V. Chang, "SmallClient for big data: an indexing framework towards fast data retrieval", *Cluster Comput.,* vol. 20, no. 2, pp. 1193-1208, 2017. [http://dx.doi.org/10.1007/s10586-016-0712-4]

[18] V. Chang, M. Ramachandran, G. Wills, R.J. Walters, C.S. Li, and P. Watters, *"Editorial for FGCS special issue: Big data in the cloud," Future Generation Computer Systems.* Elsevier, 2016.

[19] V. Chang, "The big data analysis for measuring popularity in the mobile cloud", *Proc. International Workshop on Emerging Software as a Service and Analytics (ESaaSA),* 2014.Barcelona, Spain

[20] R. Alsufyani, K. Jama, Y. Yao, M. Ramachandran, and V. Chang, "Big data services security and security challenges in cloud environment", *Proc. International Conference on Internet of Things and Big Data,* 2016.Rome, Italy [http://dx.doi.org/10.5220/0005948904610468]

[21] M.V. Moreno, F. Terroso-Sáenz, A. González-Vidal, M. Valdés-Vela, A.F. Skarmeta, M.A. Zamora, and V. Chang, "Applicability of big data techniques to smart cities deployments", *IEEE Trans. Industr. Inform.,* vol. 13, no. 2, pp. 800-809, 2017. [http://dx.doi.org/10.1109/TII.2016.2605581]

SUBJECT INDEX

A

B

C

S. Kannadhasan, R. Nagarajan, & Kaushik Pal (Eds.)

D

F

G

H

I

N

O

P

Q

R

S

U

V

W

Y

Z

www.ingramcontent.com/pod-product-compliance
Lightning Source LLC
LaVergne TN
LVHW070943210926
848482LV00002B/83
* 9 7 9 8 8 9 8 8 1 5 3 3 2 *